Data-Centric Systems and Applications

T0135005

Milan Petković · Willem Jonker (Eds.)

Security, Privacy, and Trust in Modern Data Management

With 89 Figures and 13 Tables

 Springer

Editors

Milan Petković

Philips Research Europe
High Tech Campus 34
5656 AE Eindhoven
The Netherlands
milan.petkovic@philips.com

Willem Jonker

Philips Research / Twente University
Philips Research Europe
High Tech Campus 34
5656 AE Eindhoven
The Netherlands
willem.jonker@philips.com

ISBN 978-3-642-08926-8   e-ISBN 978-3-540-69861-6

ACM Computing Classification (1998): D.4.6, E.3, H.2.7, K.6.5

Springer is a part of Springer Science+Business Media
springer.com

© Springer-Verlag Berlin Heidelberg 2007
Softcover reprint of the hardcover 1st edition 2007

Cover Design: KünkelLopka, Heidelberg

Foreword

Advances in information and communication technologies continue to provide new means of conducting remote transactions. Services facilitated by these technologies are spreading increasingly into our commercial and private spheres. For many people, these services have changed the way they work, communicate, shop, arrange travel, etc. Remote transactions, however, may also open possibilities for fraud and other types of misuse. Hence, the requirement to authorize transactions may arise. Authorization may in turn call for some kind of user authentication. When users have to provide personal information to access services, they literally leave a part of their life on record. As the number of sites where such records are left increases, so does the danger of misuse. So-called identity theft has become a pervasive problem, and a general feeling of unease and lack of trust may dissuade people from using the services on offer.

This, in a nutshell, is one of the major challenges in security engineering today. How to provide services to individuals securely without making undue incursions into their privacy at the same time. Decisions on the limits of privacy intrusions – or privacy protection, for that matter – are ultimately political decisions. Research can define the design space in which service providers and regulators may try to find acceptable tradeoffs between security and privacy.

This book introduces the reader to the current state of privacy-enhancing technologies. In the main, it is a book about access control. An introduction to privacy legislation sets the scene for the technical contributions, which show how access control has evolved to address a variety of requirements that can be found in today's information technology (IT) landscape. The book concludes with an outlook on some of the security and privacy issues that arise in the context of ambient intelligence.

Given current developments in IT that aim to let users access the services they desire wherever they happen to be, or provide the means of monitoring people wherever they happen to be, such a book is timely indeed. It brings together in one place descriptions of specialized techniques that are beyond the scope of textbooks on security. For the security practitioner the book can serve as a general reference for advanced topics in access control and privacy-enhancing technologies. Last but not least, academics can use it as the basis for specialized courses on those very topics; the research results covered in this book will have a real impact only if they are appreciated by a wider audience. This book plays a valuable part in disseminating knowledge of these techniques.

Hamburg,   *Dieter Gollmann*
October 2006

Preface

Information and communication technologies are advancing fast. Processing speed is still increasing at a high rate, followed by advances in digital storage technology, which double storage capacity every year. In contrast, the size of computers and storage has been decreasing rapidly. Furthermore, communication technologies do not lag behind. The Internet has been widely used, as well as wireless technologies. With a few mouse clicks, people can communicate with each other around the world. All these advances have great potential to change the way people live, introducing new concepts like ubiquitous computing and ambient intelligence.

The vision of ubiquitous computing and ambient intelligence describes a world of technology which is present everywhere in the form of smart and sensible computing devices that are able to communicate with one another. The technology is nonintrusive, transparent and hidden in the background. In the ambient intelligence vision, the devices collect, process and share all kinds of information, including user behavior, in order to act in an intelligent and adaptive way.

Although cryptography and security techniques have been around for quite some time, emerging technologies such the ones described above place new requirements on security with respect to data management. As data is accessible anytime anywhere, according to these new concepts, it becomes much easier to get unauthorized data access. Furthermore, it becomes simpler to collect, store, and search personal information and endanger people's privacy.

In the context of these trends this book provides a comprehensive guide to data management technologies with respect to security, privacy, and trust. It addresses the fundamental concepts and techniques in this field, but also devotes attention to advanced technologies, providing a well-balanced overview between basic and cutting-edge technologies. The book brings together issues on security, privacy, and trust, discusses their influences and dependencies. It starts by taking a step back to regain some perspective on the privacy and security issues of the modern digital world. To achieve this, the book not only lists and discusses privacy and security issues, but gives the ethical and legislation background in the context of data storage and processing technologies, as well as technologies that support and implement fair information practices in order to prevent security and privacy violations.

The main goal of the book is, however, to clarify the state of the art and the potential of security, privacy and trust technologies. Therefore, the main part of the book is devoted to secure data management, trust management and privacy-enhancing technologies. In addition, the book aims at providing a comprehensive overview of digital asset protection techniques. The requirements for secure distribution of digital assets are discussed form both the content owner and consumer perspective. After that, the book gives an overview of technologies and standards that provide secure distribution and usage of information, namely digital rights management, copy protection, and watermarking.

Finally, as a viable route towards ambient intelligence and ubiquitous computing can only be achieved if security and confidentiality issues are properly dealt with, the book reviews these newly introduced issues as well as technological solutions to them.

Intended Audience

This book is directed towards several reader categories. First of all, it is intended for those interested in an in-depth overview of information security, privacy and trust technologies. We expect that practitioners will find this book a valuable reference when dealing with these technologies. System architects will find in it an overview of security and privacy issues, which will help them to build systems taking into account security and privacy requirements from the very beginning. System and software developers/engineers will find the theoretical grounds for the design and implementation of security protocols and privacy-enhancing technologies. In addition, the book includes more advanced security and privacy topics including the ones that arise with the concepts of ambient intelligence. As the book covers a balanced mixture of fundamental and advanced topics in security and privacy, it will be of interest to researchers, either those beginning research in this field or those already involved. Last but not least, we have made a considerable effort to make this book appropriate as a course book, primarily for undergraduate, but also for postgraduate students.

Acknowledgements

We would like to acknowledge all the people who have helped us in the completion of this book. It is a result of a concentrated and coordinated effort of 45 eminent authors who presented their knowledge and the ideas in the area of information security, privacy, and trust. Therefore, first of all, we would like to thank them for their work. Without them, this comprehensive overview of security, privacy and trust technologies in modern data management would have never seen the light of day. Next, we would like to mention Stefano Ceri and Mike Carey. Their comments were helpful in making this a better book. Ralf Gerstner from Springer was very supportive during the editing process. Finaly, special thanks also go to all the reviewers of the book, namely, Klaus Kursawe, Jorge Guajardo, Jordan Chong, and Anna Zych.

Eindhoven,   *Milan Petković*
October 2006   *Willem Jonker*

Contents

Part V Selected Topics on Privacy and Security in Ambient Intelligence

List of Contributors

Emile Aarts
Philips Research
High Tech Campus 34
Eindhoven, 5656AE
The Netherlands
emile.aarts@philips.com

Claudio A. Ardagna
Università degli Studi di Milano
Via Bramante 65
26013 Crema (CR) – Italia
ardagna@dti.unimi.it

Elisa Bertino
Purdue University
305 N. University Street
West Lafayette
IN 47907-2107, USA
bertino@cs.purdue.edu

Ljiljana Branković
The University of Newcastle
Callaghan, NSW 2308, Australia
ljiljana.brankovic@newcastle.
edu.au

Philip Brey
University of Twente
Postbox 217
7500AE Enschede
The Netherlands
p.a.e.brey@utwente.nl

Richard Brinkman
University of Twente
Postbus 217
7500AE Enschede
The Netherlands
brinkman@cs.utwente.nl

Ji-Won Byun
Purdue University
305 N. University Street
West Lafayette
IN 47907-2107, USA
byunj@cs.purdue.edu

Jan Camenisch
IBM Zurich Research Lab
Säumerstrasse 4,
CH-8803 Rüschlikon, Switzerland
jca@zurich.ibm.com

**Sabrina De Capitani di
Vimercati**
Università degli Studi di Milano
Via Bramante 65
26013 Crema (CR) – Italia
decapita@dti.unimi.it

Mehmet Celik
Philips Research Europe
HighTech Campus 34
5656AE Eindhoven
The Netherlands
mehmet.celik@philips.com

Claudine Conrado
Philips Research Europe
HighTech Campus 34
5656AE Eindhoven
The Netherlands
claudine.conrado@philips.com

Ernesto Damiani
Università degli Studi di Milano
Via Bramante 65
26013 Crema (CR) – Italia
damiani@dti.unimi.it

Marnix Dekker
TNO ICT
Postbus 5050
2600GB Delft, The Netherlands
marnix.dekker@tno.nl

Claudia Diaz
K.U.Leuven ESAT-COSIC
Kasteelpark Arenberg 10
B-3001 Leuven-Heverlee, Belgium
claudia.diaz@esat.kuleuven.be

Sandro Etalle
University of Twente
Postbus 217
7500AE Enschede
The Netherlands
sandro.etalle@utwente.nl

Sara Foresti
Università degli Studi di Milano
Via Bramante 65
26013 Crema (CR) – Italia
foresti@dti.unimi.it

Helen Giggins
The University of Newcastle
Callaghan, NSW 2308, Australia
helen.giggins@newcastle.edu.au

Jerry den Hartog
University of Twente
Postbus 217
7500AE Enschede
The Netherlands
jerry.denhartog@utwente.nl

Md. Zahidul Islam
The University of Newcastle
Callaghan
NSW 2308
Australia
zahid.islam@newcastle.edu.au

Willem Jonker
Philips Research Europe
HighTech Campus 34
5656AE Eindhoven
The Netherlands
willem.jonker@philips.com

Frank Kamperman
Philips Research Europe
HighTech Campus 34
5656AE Eindhoven
The Netherlands
frank.kamperman@philips.com

Ashish Kamra
Purdue University
305 N. University Street
West Lafayette
IN 47907-2107
USA
akamra@cs.purdue.edu

Stefan Katzenbeisser
Philips Research Europe
HighTech Campus 34
5656AE Eindhoven
The Netherlands
stefan.katzenbeisser@philips.com

Tom Kevenaar
Philips Research Europe
HighTech Campus 34
5656AE Eindhoven
The Netherlands
tom.kevenaar@philips.com

Paul Koster
Philips Research Europe
HighTech Campus 34
5656AE Eindhoven
The Netherlands
r.p.koster@philips.com

Klaus Kursawe
Philips Research Europe
HighTech Campus 34
5656AE Eindhoven
The Netherlands
klaus.kursawe@philips.com

Marc Langheinrich
Institute for Pervasive Computing
ETH Zurich
8092 Zurich, Switzerland
langhein@inf.ethz.ch

Aweke Lemma
Philips Research Europe
HighTech Campus 34
5656AE Eindhoven
The Netherlands
aweke.lemma@philips.com

Hong Li
Philips Research Europe
HighTech Campus 34
5656AE Eindhoven
The Netherlands
hong.r.li@philips.com

Panos Markopoulos
TU Eindhoven
P.O. Box 513
5600 MB Eindhoven
The Netherlands
p.markopoulos@tue.nl

Daniel Olmedilla
L3S Research Center and
University of Hannover
Expo Plaza 1, 30539
Hannover, Germany
olmedilla@L3S.de

Sylvia L. Osborn
The University of Western Ontario
London, ON, N6A 5B7
Canada
sylvia@csd.uwo.ca

Milan Petković
Philips Research Europe
HighTech Campus 34
5656AE Eindhoven
The Netherlands
milan.petkovic@philips.com

Birgit Pfitzmann
IBM Zurich Research Lab
Säumerstrasse 4
CH-8803 Rüschlikon, Switzerland
bpf@zurich.ibm.com

Bart Preneel
K.U.Leuven ESAT-COSIC
Kasteelpark Arenberg 10
B-3001 Leuven-Heverlee, Belgium
bart.preneel@esat.kuleuven.be

Boris de Ruyter
Philips Research Europe
HighTech Campus 34
5656AE Eindhoven
The Netherlands
boris.de.ruyter@philips.com

Pierangela Samarati
Università degli Studi di Milano
Via Bramante 65
26013 Crema (CR) – Italia
samarati@dti.unimi.it

Berry Schoenmakers
TU Eindhoven
P.O. Box 513
5600MB Eindhoven
The Netherlands
berry@win.tue.nl

Geert-Jan Schrijen
Philips Research Europe
HighTech Campus 34
5656AE Eindhoven
The Netherlands
geert.jan.schrijen@philips.com

Morton Swimmer
IBM Zurich Research Lab
Säumerstrasse 4
CH-8803 Rüschlikon, Switzerland
bpf@zurich.ibm.com

Boris Škorić
Philips Research Europe
HighTech Campus 34
5656AE Eindhoven
The Netherlands
boris.skoric@philips.com

Joop Talstra
Philips Research Europe
HighTech Campus 34
5656AE Eindhoven
The Netherlands
joop.talstra@philips.com

Jeroen Terstegge
Royal Philips
Groenewoudseweg 1
PO Box 218
5600MD Eindhoven
The Netherlands
jeroen.terstegge@philips.com

Pim Tuyls
Philips Research Europe
HighTech Campus 34
5656AE Eindhoven
The Netherlands
pim.tuyls@philips.com

Michiel van der Veen
Philips Research Europe
HighTech Campus 34
5656AE Eindhoven
The Netherlands
michiel.van.der.veen@philips.com

Part I

Introduction

1

Privacy and Security Issues in a Digital World

Milan Petković[1] and Willem Jonker[2]

[1] Philips Research, The Netherlands
[2] Twente University & Philips Research, The Netherlands

Summary. This chapter reviews the most important security and privacy issues of the modern digital world, emphasizing the issues brought by the concept of ambient intelligence. Furthermore, the chapter explains the organization of the book, describing which issues and related technologies are addressed by which chapters of the book.

1.1 Introduction

This book addresses security, privacy and trust issues in modern data management in a world where several aspects of ubiquitous computing and ambient intelligence visions are emerging. In the sequel, we give a short introduction to these issues and explain how the book is organized. The book consists of five parts. Following this introduction, the first part of the book contains two chapters on security and privacy legislation and ethics in this digital world.

Chapter 2 focuses on the common issues and developments in privacy law in relation to technology. This chapter explains the system of privacy protection in the law and surveys the internationally accepted privacy principles which form the basis of the law in most jurisdictions. Next to that, the most important interpretation rules by the courts are given and their applications to technology are discussed. Finally, the chapter gives an outlook on the future of the privacy law.

Chapter 3 reviews ethical aspects of information and system security and privacy. First it focuses on computer security, addressing topics such as the relation between computer security and national security, and then it concentrates on moral aspects of privacy and the impact of information technology on privacy.

The rest of the book is organized as follows. Part II covers security issues of modern data management. Privacy is addresses in Part III. Part IV deals with digital asset protection technologies while Part V provides a selection of more-specific issues brought about by the concepts of ambient intelligence and ubiquitous computing. The following sections introduce security, privacy and content protection issues, explaining in more detail each part of the book.

1.2 Security Issues

As already mentioned, information pervasiveness, along with all its benefits, brings concerns with respect to security issues. Data is no longer hidden behind the walls of a fortress. It does not reside only on mainframes physically isolated within an organization where all kind of physical security measures are taken to defend the data and the system. Systems are increasingly open and interconnected, which poses new challenges for security technologies. Instead of being a protection mechanism, as it is today, security will in the future serve as an enabler for new value-added services. The trends mentioned in the previous section influence every security mechanism. Therefore, Part II of this book covers fundamental security technologies and introduces advanced techniques.

Large and open distributed systems need flexible and scalable access control mechanisms where user authorization is based on their attributes (e.g. credentials). Consequently, languages and mechanisms for expressing and exchanging policies are indispensable. The basics of access control, including discretionary and mandatory access policies, administrative policies, as well as the aforementioned challenges, are described in Chap. 4.

The concept of role-based access control (RBAC) faces similar challenges. Chapter 5 introduces the basic components of RBAC and gives some guidelines with respect to emerging problems of designing role hierarchies in different environments.

Extensible markup language (XML) security provides an important opportunity to fulfill new requirements posed by the concepts of ubiquitous computing and ambient intelligence. It allows access privileges to be defined directly on the structure and content of the document. Chapter 6 describes the main characteristics of the key XML technologies such as XML signature, XML encryption, key management specification and policy languages.

The rising trend of openness also affects databases. An organization internal database of yesterday is today already open for access by users outside the organization. A number of attacks exists that exploits web applications to inject malicious SQL queries. Databases are facing insider threats as key individuals (often administrators) control all sensitive information and infrastructure. Chapter 7 provides most relevant concepts of database security, discusses their usage in prevalent database management systems, such as Oracle, DB2, and MySQL, and covers a number of challenges including the ones mentioned above.

As already mentioned, advanced security technologies should enable new services in the open environment of the future. Trust management is an important mechanism closely related to security that supports interoperation, exactly in this open environment. Therefore, trust management systems are becoming increasingly important and getting more and attention. In Chap. 8, state-of-the-art systems are described, as well as several research directions, such as trust negotiation strategies and reputation-based systems.

Consequently, the issue of trusting a computing platform to perform a task as expected is rising. There a new initiative on trusted computing plays an important role. It is expected that it will allow computer platforms to offer an increased level of security, making computers safer, less prone to viruses and malware and therefore more reliable. Trusted platform modules as well as the consequences for authentication, secure boot, protected execution, secure I/O and other related technologies are described in Chap. 9.

To further elaborate on the physical aspects of a trusted computing platform, this part of the book is completed with Chap. 10 on physical unclonable functions (PUFs). A PUF is a hardware system that realizes a function that is difficult to model and reproduce. This chapter describes their role in the security of modern data management systems and elaborates on the two main applications of PUFs, namely unclonable and cost-effective way of storing cryptographic key material and strong authentication of objects.

1.3 Privacy Issues

A number of privacy issues also arise with the proliferation of digital technologies. Personalized services, such as reward programs (supermarket cards, frequent flyer/buyer cards, etc.) require collection, (uncontrolled) processing, and often even distribution of personal data and sensitive information. With ubiquitous connectivity, people are increasingly using electronic technologies in business-to-consumer and business-to-business settings. Examples are financial transactions, credit card payments, business transactions, email, document exchange, and even management of personal health records. Furthermore, new technologies are being used for the purpose of monitoring and recording behaviors of individuals who may not even be aware of it. This data typically includes personal information and is essentially privacy sensitive. The flow of this information will almost certainly get out of the individuals' control, thus creating serious privacy concerns. Therefore, there is an obvious need for technologies that support these new services but ensure people's privacy. Part III of this book addresses these concerns and provides an overview of the most important privacy-enhancing technologies.

Thanks to the same trends described above, data mining technologies are becoming increasingly used. Organizations are creating large databases that record information about their customers. This information is analyzed to extract valuable nonobvious information for their businesses. However, these techniques are particularly vulnerable to misuse and revealing of individual data records. Chapter 11 deals with privacy-preserving data mining technologies that have been developed for this problem. It presents multiparty computation and data modification as the two main techniques currently used.

Chapter 12 continues on a similar topic, which is the protection of privacy-sensitive data used for statistical purposes. It presents the model and concepts of a statistical database and surveys two important techniques for privacy preservation: restriction and noise addition.

With increased connectivity data confidentiality becomes increasingly important. Although cryptographic techniques, which consequently gain more attention, solve basic problems, they also introduce new ones such as searching encrypted data. The basic problem is that it is difficult to search in an outsourced database in which the data is encrypted. Chapter 13 reviews and compares several search methods that support searching functionality without any loss of data confidentiality.

Chapter 14 extends on previous chapters and addresses a specific problem in multiparty computation of a server and a resource-limited client. It introduces a framework of secure computation based on threshold homomorphic cryptography and the necessary protocols needed for this specific setting. Then, the chapter describes two applications of this framework for private biometrics and secure electronic elections.

As already mentioned, people nowadays are involved in an increasing number of electronic transactions with a number of parties. These transactions usually include authentication and attribute exchange. To secure them and protect his privacy the user has to maintain a number of user names/passwords with these organizations. This is exactly the problem addressed by federated identity management technologies. Chapter 15 introduces two approaches to solve the aforementioned problems: browser-based federated identity management and private credentials.

The privacy-enhancing technologies presented in this part of the book often require anonymous communication channels and appropriate protocols. Furthermore, an important requirement in many systems is accountability, which is often conflicting with anonymity. Chapter 16 introduces the concept of controlled anonymous communications, presents the main building blocks of an anonymity infrastructure and shows how they can be used to build a large-scale accountable anonymity system.

1.4 Digital Asset Protection Issues

Digital content distribution is one of the fastest emerging activities nowadays. The trend towards digital content distribution gives great opportunities for commercial content providers and consumers, but also poses some threats, as digital content can be very easily illegally copied and distributed. Therefore, commercial content providers need technologies accompanied by legislation which can prevent illegal use of digital content. Digital rights management

(DRM) is a collection of technologies that provides content protection by enforcing the use of digital content according to granted rights. It enables content providers to protect their copyrights and maintain control over distribution of and access to content. Part IV of this book is devoted to these digital rights management technologies.

Chapter 17 gives an introduction to digital rights management. This chapter reviews the early approaches and explains the basic concepts of DRM using the Open Mobile Alliance DRM system as an example.

The fight against piracy started however with copy protection systems. The early methods dealt with audio and video tapes while copy protection is now an integral part of the distribution of all forms of digital content and software on mainly optical media. A historical overview of copy protection techniques is given in Chap. 18, which also describes popular copy protection techniques.

Chapter 19 elaborates on digital watermarking, which allows the addition of hidden verification messages (e.g. copyright) to digital data such as audio/video signals. As opposed to encryption-based DRM systems, watermarking-based systems leave the content in the clear, but insert information that allows usage control or usage tracking. This chapter describes the basic principles of digital watermarking and discuss its application to forensic tracking.

DRM systems are often accused of being against the consumers. In fact, initially, they are built to protect the interest of content owners. Chapter 20 looks at DRM systems from the consumer perspective and introduces two basic concepts relevant for them: authorized domains and person-based DRM. Finally it devotes special attention to the combination of the two, its architecture, user, license, and domain management.

Another big issue in DRM is interoperability. To achieve wide adoption of DRM technology, simple and seamless user experience is indispensable. Finally the dream of many people is that digital content will be available to anyone, anytime, anywhere, on any device. Therefore, DRM technology providers must find ways to make their products interoperable. This topic is addressed in Chap. 21. The chapter defines the interoperability problem and discusses it on three different layers: protected content, licenses, and trust and key management. Then, it describes state-of-the-art solutions to these problems on the level of platform and interfaces. Furthermore, business and user aspects in relation to DRM interoperability are discussed.

In parallel to the introduction of commercial multimedia download services, there is also a clear increase in the production of digital information such as digital photos and home videos by consumers. As a consequence, consumers have to deal with an ever-growing amount of personal digital data, alongside downloaded commercial content. Some of this personal content might be highly confidential and in need of protection. Consequently, the consumer wants to share it in a controlled way so that he can control the use of his content by persons with whom he shares it. Such a DRM system for controlled sharing of personal content is presented in Chap. 22. The chapter starts with scenarios and requirements and continues with the introduction of the DRM approach and the system architecture. Finally, the chapter presents practical solutions for protecting and sharing personal content as well as for ownership management and multiple-user issues.

Chapter 23 addresses privacy issues in DRM systems. The main challenge is how to allow a user to interact with the system in an anonymous/pseudonymous way, while preserving all the security requirements of usual DRM systems. To achieve this goal a set of protocols and methods for managing user identities and interactions with the system during the process of acquiring and consuming digital content is presented. Furthermore, a method that supports anonymous transfer of licenses is discussed. It allows a user to transfer a piece of content to another user without the content provider being able to link the two users.

1.5 Privacy and Security in an Ambient World

The vision of ambient intelligence (AmI) assumes that technology is present everywhere in the form of smart computing devices that respond and adapt to the presence of people. The devices communicate with each other, and are nonintrusive, transparent, and invisible. Moreover, as communication is expected to happen anytime, anywhere, most of the connections are done in a wireless and often ad hoc manner.

The concepts of ambient intelligence and ubiquitous computing that will have a major influence on security and privacy are:

- Ubiquity: smart digital devices will be everywhere and part of the living environment of people. They will be available, for instance, when driving a car or waiting for the train to arrive.
- Sensing: as already mentioned, the environment will be equipped with a large number of sensors. The sensors will gather information about general things like room temperature, but can also register who enters a room, analyze the movement of a person and even sense his/her emotional condition.
- Invisibility: the devices and sensors will not only be everywhere, but will also largely disappear from sight. People will not even be aware that sensors are monitoring them. Moreover, there is a big fear that control over personal information will get out of the hands of users.
- Memory amplification: the information gathered by the sensors will be stored and used for later behavior prediction, improving support of the ambient environment. No matter how sensitive the information is, there is a large chance that it will be stored and used for different purposes.
- Connectivity: smart sensors and devices will not only be everywhere but they will also be connected to each other. Connectivity also implies no control over dissemination of information. Once information has been collected it can end up anywhere.

- Personalization: in addition to connectivity, a chief concept to ambient intelligence is that of personalization. Personalization implies that information about the user must be collected and analyzed by the environment in order for adaptation to that user to happen. The environment will keep track of specific habits and preferences of a person. However, the concept of personalization is, in principle, contradictory to the privacy concepts of anonymity and pseudonymity.

As mentioned above, future ambient environments will integrate a huge amount of sensors (cameras, microphones, biometric detectors, and all kinds of sensors), which means that the ambient will be capable of capturing some of the user's biometrics (face, speech, fingerprints, etc.). Consequently, the ambient environment will be able of cross-referencing the user's profile, activities, location and behavior with his photo, for example. Furthermore, the concept of omnipresent connectivity may make it possible that biometric data could be cross-referenced with some public databases, which will result in the disclosure of the user identity.

It is obvious that security and privacy issues brought by the future ambient world go beyond the threats people are used to nowadays. On the other hand, people are increasingly aware and concerned about their privacy and security. Therefore, it is very important to investigate how the level of privacy and security which people currently have can be kept after the introduction of these new concepts. Furthermore, it is important to develop methods that will build trust in these new concepts.

Part V of this book addresses specific privacy and security topics of the ambient world. It starts with an introduction to ambient intelligence in Chap. 24. This chapter briefly revisits the foundations of ambient intelligence. Then, it introduces notions of compliance and ambient journaling to develop an understanding of the concept of ambient persuasion. Finally, the ethics of ambient intelligence is also addressed.

The following chapters address the privacy concerns mentioned above, beginning with privacy policies. Chapter 25 deals with different stages in the lifecycle of personal data processing, the collection stage, the internal processing stage and the external processing stage, which is typical for ambient intelligence scenarios. It reviews technologies that cover each of these stages, the platform for privacy preferences (P3P) for the collection stage, the platform for enterprise privacy practices (E-P3P) for the processing stage and audit logic for the external processing stage.

The semantic Web goes one step beyond the above mentioned exchange of information. It envisions a distributed environment in which information is machine-understandable and semantically self-describable. This in turn requires semantically enriched processes to automate access to sensitive information. Chapter 26 extends on the previous chapter, describing exchange and interaction of privacy policies on the semantic Web as well as the role of ontologies for conflict detection and validation of policies.

As already mentioned, in the future world of ambient intelligence it is expected that a user will be required to perform identification regularly whenever he changes environment (e.g., in a shop, public transportation, library, hospital). Biometric authentication may be used to make this process more transparent and user friendly. Consequently the reference information (user's biometrics) must be stored everywhere. However this information is about unique characteristics of human beings and is therefore highly privacy sensitive. Furthermore, widespread use of this information drastically increases chances for identity theft, while the quantity of this information is limited (people only have two eyes). In Chap. 27, a novel technology, called biometric template protection, that protects the biometric information stored in biometric systems is introduced.

Radio-frequency identification (RFID) is an automatic identification method that is expected to be prevalently used in the future concepts of ambient intelligence and ubiquitous computing. The number of potential applications is large. However, with its first deployment public fears about its security and privacy exploded. Chapter 28 is devoted to privacy of RFID tags. It introduces the RFID technology, provides an overview of RFID privacy challenges as well as an overview of proposed technical RFID privacy solutions. Furthermore, it considers the problem taking into account applications and policy to evaluate the feasibility of the proposed solutions.

Last but not least, in Chap. 29, the book devotes attention to malicious software and its evolution in the context of ubiquitous computing and ambient intelligence. This chapter brings the reader from current malicious software and defending methods to a projection of the problems of future systems, taking into account the aforementioned aspects of ambient intelligence.

2

Privacy in the Law

Jeroen Terstegge

Royal Philips Electronics
The Netherlands

Summary. This chapter addresses privacy and legislation. It explains common categories of legal protection in most jurisdictions and surveys the internationally accepted privacy principles which form the basis of the law in most countries. Next, the most important interpretation rules by the courts are given and their applications to technology are discussed. Finally, the chapter gives an outlook on the future of privacy law.

2.1 Introduction

All over the world, the right to privacy is considered a fundamental right, a constitutional right, a human right. It is found in international treaties such as the International Covenant on Civil and Political Rights, the European Convention on Human Rights, and the European Charter of Fundamental Rights. It can also be found in some form or another in the constitutions of many countries around the world, such as the Dutch constitution (art. 10: the right to privacy and data protection, art. 11: the right to integrity of body and mind, art. 12: the right to the privacy of the home, and art. 13: the right to confidentiality of correspondence and communications), the German constitution (art. 2: the right to self-determination), and the US constitution (amendment 14: protection against unwarranted searches and seizures).

From a historical point of view, these fundamental rights protect the citizens against intrusions into their private lives by the government. Already in the Middle Ages the law protected British citizens against the soldiers of the king entering their private homes. The right to privacy was defined for the first time by Warren and Brandeis in their article in the Harvard Law Review in 1890 as "the right to be let alone" [1]. The article was published after the list of invitees for the wedding of Samuel Warren's daughter appeared on the society pages of the Boston newspapers. He then consulted his good friend and future US Supreme Court justice Louis Brandeis to see what could be done against such unreasonable intrusion into the private life of his family. In the

1960s and 1970s, the public debate over privacy resurfaced again when governments started surveying their countries' population. Also, the first computers appeared, making the processing of these data simpler. Hence, the right to data protection was born.

Nowadays, the term "privacy" is applied to a wide variety of issues, ranging from the seclusion of the private home and garden, to the use of surveillance techniques by employers and law enforcement agencies, to the processing of personal data in large databases, and even to nuisance problems like spam and telemarketing. It also has close ties to issues like autonomy and self-determination and the right to family life.

2.2 Privacy Protection in the Law

The law protects privacy in many ways. The type of laws and the level of protection may differ between countries and jurisdictions. However, the following categories of legal protection can be identified in most jurisdictions:

- Constitutional laws and international treaties demonstrate the importance of the right to privacy. Legislators as well as the courts have to take these fundamental rights into account when drafting or interpreting the laws. In some countries, such as the United States and Germany, there are special courts to rule on potential conflicts between the law and the constitution. In other countries, such as The Netherlands, any court may invoke the fundamental right to privacy to annul a law when it is found contradictory to international obligations. In Europe, there is even a special European Court of Human Rights, based in Strasbourg, that may rule on privacy invasions as a violation of article 8 of the European Convention of Human Rights.
- Criminal laws define the minimum level of acceptable behavior by a society. All privacy-intrusive behavior below that threshold in punishable by society i.e. stalking, the use of hidden camera's, illegal wire-tapping of somebody else's telecommunications (such as spyware), hacking into a computer system, entering somebody's home without permission.
- Administrative laws, such as the Personal Data Protection Acts in Europe, laws on criminal procedure or laws on background checking, give rules and procedures for allowing certain types of privacy-intrusive behavior. Sometimes the obligation to cooperate with privacy-intrusive actions is written into the law. In such cases the law prescribes the circumstances under which the privacy invasion is permitted (i.e. the obligation to cooperate with a search when boarding an airplane). In most cases however, the intrusive behavior is only permitted when a certain protective procedure has been followed, such as judicial review for a search warrant to search somebody's home, the need for a permit to transfer personal data out of the European Union (EU), the need to ask parental consent for collecting

personal data from children, the need to ask a patient for his or her consent to disclose medical records to a third party, or giving the individual the possibility to object to a certain process or to opt out from it.

- Civil law and tort law provide obligations in the case of (unreasonable) invasions of privacy, such as paying damages or compensation, to undo harmful actions or to refrain from certain privacy-invasive behavior.

2.3 International Privacy Principles

Most of these laws use commonly recognized privacy principles as a basis. Probably the most influential principles have been developed by the Organization for Economic Cooperation and Development (OECD), in which 30 developed nations work together[1]. With the rise of the importance of computers in the western economies and global trade, the OECD issued its guidelines on the protection of privacy and transborder flows of personal data in 1980 [2]. This document has played a leading role in the development of privacy laws in the EU, Canada, Australia and other jurisdictions. Its main principles are: collection limitation, purpose specification, use limitation, data quality, security safeguards, openness, individual participation, and accountability.

Collection Limitation, Purpose Specification and Use Limitation

According to these principles, personal data should only be collected by lawful means and in a fair manner, including - where appropriate - with the knowledge or the consent of the individual. The fairness test is an important element of this principle, as it is the catch-all of all principles: even where the data collection is lawful, the manner in which it is done should be fair. Personal data can only be collected and used for predefined legitimate purposes. Collecting data without a predefined purpose is therefore illegal. Legitimate purposes for processing personal data include: the performance of a contract with the individual, complying with a legal obligation, protecting the vital interests of the individual, and legitimate business needs or legitimate public interest, which overrides the (privacy) interests of the individual[2]. Using data for other purposes (including disclosure of data to third parties) is in principle not allowed. However, so-called secondary use is sometimes allowed if the purpose for which the data have been collected and the purpose for which the data will be used are not incompatible[3]. For the secondary use of personal data for incompatible purposes, either the consent of the individual or a legal obligation is necessary.

---

[1] The OECD is comprised of the member states of the European Union, plus the United States of America, Canada, Mexico, Australia, New Zealand, Switzerland, Turkey, Japan, Korea, Iceland and Norway. The OECD is based in Paris.

[2] See also art. 7 of the European data protection directive 95/46/EC.

[3] Article 6(1)(b) of the European data protection directive 95/46/EC.

Data Quality

According to the data quality principle, personal data should be relevant for the purposes of processing, as well as accurate, complete and up to date. So, there should, for instance, be a data management process, which ensures that data are kept up to date and are deleted when the purposes are no longer there.

Security Safeguards

According to this principle personal data have to be protected against unauthorized access, use, destruction, modification or disclosure. Reasonable means should be used compared to the risks and the nature of the data.

Openness

The party which collects and uses the data has to inform the individual about: who he is, why he is collecting and using the data, and other information that is necessary to ensure fair processing, such as the right to object to the processing or to opt out from it, the fact that data will be disclosed or sold to third parties, or the fact that data are stored and used in another jurisdiction (with possibly different rules for privacy protection).

Individual Participation

The individual has the right to access the data stored about him, and has the right to ask for correction, updates or removal of the data. Note that access could be granted in many ways: either by allowing the individual to retrieve the data from the system himself (which requires extra security measures such as identity verification and authentication), or by providing the individual with a copy or summary overview of the data. The disclosed data cannot include data about other individuals. The individual also has the right to ask for an explanation about the meaning of the data or their origin.

Accountability

The party under whose authority the data are collected, processed and used, can be held accountable for complying with these principles. This accountability may include civil or criminal liability.

An interesting development is happening on the other side of the globe, where the organization for Asia–Pacific Economic Cooperation (APEC) is currently developing its own privacy principles. On the basis of the old OECD privacy principles, the APEC is trying to modernize them and make them better suited for application in today's day and age, as well as in their different (political) cultures. The leading principle in the APEC privacy principles is the obligation not to harm the individual when processing his data. Although this principle is very similar to the OECD's fairness principle, the APEC do-no-harm principle is much more aimed at the impact of the privacy intrusion on the individual. This leaves room for many different implementations of the principles, as long as the end result is the same and the interests of the individual are not harmed.

2.4 Reasonable Expectation of Privacy

As the laws are usually generic, so they can be applied to many cases with different circumstances, legal privacy protection is also shaped by court opinions and the opinions of supervisory authorities. For guidance on how the law should be applied supreme courts and international tribunals have developed tests according to which the particular circumstances of a case at hand can be measured. A very interesting and useful test for privacy protection that has been used by both the United States supreme court as well as by the European Court of Human Rights is the test of reasonable expectation of privacy. According to the courts, there is a certain level of privacy protection to be expected in any circumstance. The exact level of privacy is defined by the circumstances of the case. For instance, if somebody locks the door, he may expect that nobody enters the room, so there is a high level of privacy expectation and that individual's privacy is therefore better protected under the law and by the courts. On the other hand, private behavior in public places is less protected as people have to take into account that their behavior can be observed by others. However, unreasonable intrusion in public places such as stalking is usually still protected.

The circumstances that may be taken into account when defining the level of privacy expectation may be: legal obligations and rules to which the individual is subject; contracts and agreements to which the individual is a party (provided that the contract or agreement is legally valid); choices made by the individual to protect his privacy (i.e. using a password to protect content, opt-in or opt-out choices for receiving direct marketing communications); the amount and type of information about the privacy intrusion and its consequences provided to the individual, the way he has been informed, his understanding of such information, and his actions and decisions based on such information. Especially when using technology, the individual using it should be made aware of its risks and the ways to protect his privacy. However, the individual's failure to protect his privacy, informed or not, for instance because he forgot to install a password, to use a firewall, or just to close the curtains in the evening, does not give others implicit permission to invade his privacy. What is legally relevant is the complete set of circumstances.

2.5 Applying the Law to Technology

As privacy is a fundamental right valued by most people, privacy protection must be part of the design and use of a technology, even in the absence of a legal obligation or legal risks. Where privacy invasions are necessary as part of the use of the technology or the service, the individual must be informed and in many cases must give his (implied) consent. Think for instance of the collection of data about the use of the technology to enhance its performance (provided that such data is not completely anonymous[4]) or where data collection is necessary to protect the legitimate rights of the technology or service provider (i.e. protection of digital rights).

In most countries, legal privacy protection starts with just data security. The party collecting or processing the data bears the responsibility to secure the data. In many countries such as in the member states of the EU this is a legal obligation laid down in the data protection and privacy laws. It should be noted that in the EU even parties (so-called data processors) which process data as a service to the company which has the relationship with individual have security and confidentiality obligations of their own for which they can be held directly responsible by the individual. For all other privacy issues, the party which has the relationship with the individual (the so-called data controller) is responsible[5]. Other countries such as Russia have implemented special data security laws, but no specific privacy laws. Also, data security can be enforced via other type of laws. In the United States, for instance, the obligation to secure consumer data is implied in the trust relationship between the company and the consumer. The US Federal Trade Commission (FTC) enforces data security as a violation of the obligation to conduct fair trade via the Fair Trade Act. In a 2005 case the FTC found that the failure to protect financial data which were transmitted over a network after the consumer paid electronically was a violation of the Fair Trade Act, as the "consumers must have the confidence that companies that possess their confidential information will handle it with due care and appropriately provide for its security". Especially important for the FTC's decision were the fact that the data were not encrypted during transmission, the fact that the data were stored for a period longer than necessary, so unnecessary risks were created, the fact that the sensitive consumer data could be accessed using common default user IDs and passwords, the fact that the company did not use the available security measures for wireless transmissions, and the fact that the company did not have sufficient measures in place to detect unauthorized access. The FTC ordered the company to install a privacy and security program with inde-

---

[4] Note that anonymity is not only the removal of names from data, but the removal of all characteristics from which an individual can be directly or indirectly identified, such as Internet Protocol (IP) addresses.

[5] This stresses the fact that data security is only a part of privacy protection. In other words, there can be data security without data privacy, but no data privacy without data security.

pendent audits[6]. In another FTC case where lack of adequate data security had resulted in at least 800 cases of identity theft, the company had to pay additionally to the mandated privacy and security program an amount of 10 million dollars in civil penalties and another 5 million for consumer redress.

The fourth point in the FTC's opinion, which is similar to current legal opinion in the EU, shows that the legal responsibility for protecting privacy is directly connected to technological advancement. Privacy and security technologies that are available on the market for reasonable prices (compared to the risk) and can be implemented without unreasonable efforts have to be used. The trust relationship between the company and the consumer mandates this. Therefore, not investing in technological updates to protect privacy-sensitive data may result in legal liability when data are compromised as a result.

Intentional privacy invasions are illegal in many jurisdictions, and may lead to civil or even criminal prosecution. In one famous case in 1999, consumers filed a class action because a popular piece of music software transmitted all data about the use of the software, including data about the content which was played, back to the company without the knowledge or consent of the individuals. After the spyware function of the software was discovered, the company was slapped with a 500 million dollar lawsuit[7].

But also poor design of technology (malware) may lead to legal liabilities. This was again demonstrated in a recent case where DRM technology to prevent the copying of music on a consumer's computer unintentionally opened a backdoor in the computer, which could be used by hackers[8]. The resulting class action cost the music company millions of dollars.

2.6 The Future of Privacy Law

It is a public secret amongst lawyers that technology is always ahead of the law. Due to the lengthy process of law-making, by the time the risks of the technology have been identified by society and the legislators, the risks have been replaced by new ones and the laws that are put in place are out-dated by the time they are implemented. A good example is anti-spam laws. All over the world, anti-spam laws have recently been installed or are still being negotiated. The original anti-spam laws were targeted at the increasing mass of unsolicited marketing communications sent by companies to their (potential) customers via e-mail and fax because these means of communication were cheaper than other communication channels such as postal mail, broadcasting and general advertising. The solutions offered by the law to make the use of these communication channels lawful, such as the right to opt in and to

---

[6] See http://www.ftc.gov/privacy/index.html

[7] See http://www.wired.com/news/politics/0,1283,32459,00.html

[8] See http://www.wired.com/news/privacy/0,1848,69601,00.html

opt out, are aimed at legitimate advertising. However, spamming has rapidly changed into the mass mailing of garbage, criminal attacks such as *phishing* and denial-of-service attacks, and are an ideal means to spread viruses, trojans, and malware. The anti-spam laws that are put in place today are no match for these malicious attacks and therefore do not protect the consumers they way they are intended to. For example, the consumer's right to opt out of spam and the company's obligation to insert an opt-out address in a direct marketing e-mail is widely misused by spammers to collect confirmation of the validity of e-mail addresses, so consumers are discouraged from using the opt out functionality.

Furthermore, the way that the law protects privacy is by giving rights to people and imposing obligations on others in a such way that the people who have the rights are dependent on the others. They either need to be in direct contact with the other party, for instance by giving them consent to invade their privacy, or they have to call in the help of others such as data protection authorities, the police, lawyers and judges, when the counter-party is not listening and needs to be forced to change its behavior.

The result is that privacy laws as they are currently written are highly ineffective, and continue to be the more technologically advanced our world becomes, triggering more privacy invasions. OECD-type privacy laws are primarily aimed at institutional privacy invaders such as companies and governments. However, in the 21st century it is expected that the number and seriousness of consumer-to-consumer privacy issues will become increasing significantly as privacy invasions will become more invisible with new technologies such as sensors and wireless communication. Spying on your neighbor or even on somebody on the other side of the globe via remote means will be a popular way to kill some spare time for many people.

In the 21st century, the term personal data, which is the basis of OECD-type privacy protection, will have to be replaced by another term, for instance "electronic footprints". As mentioned before, by using the term personal data the protection of the law (insofar possible) only applies to data from which an individual can be identified. However, with sensor technologies and automatic identification[9] technologies on the rise, people's interests could be harmed even without their identity becoming known to others via their electronic footprints and the profiles that could be built from them. Such anonymous profiles currently lack adequate legal protection in most countries. Extending the scope of the term personal data to such anonymous profiles only because they belong to a person, as has been proposed by the French data protection authority (CNIL) in the debate over radio-frequency identification (RFID) technology and privacy, so it would be covered by the EU data protection directive is not a sensible thing to do, because that would bring all the for-

---

[9] The term "identification" in identification technologies does not necessarily refer to the identity of a person. It may also refer to IP addresses, IC numbers (as in RFID), product numbers, or other identities.

malities of the directive (notifications, prior checking, right of access, etc.) which cannot be easily applied to anonymous profiles. All one needs from the directive to protect privacy in ambient technologies are elements of material protection, not formal protection.

However, even the material privacy protection of the law will become problematic in the ambient world. With the increased use of sensor technologies, data collection becomes automatic. This means that the principles of collection limitation and purpose specification will become irrelevant in most instances. Also the openness and accountability principles will become increasingly problematic when data collection becomes increasingly invisible, as data collection devices shrink ("smart dust") and communication becomes more wireless and global in nature.

To counter these problems, it is in my view absolutely necessary that we come up with new privacy paradigms that can be used to protect privacy in the ambient world of the 21st century. We cannot and should not accept the famous statement of Scott McNeely, the former CEO of Sun Microsystems: "You have no privacy. Get over it!". In my view adequate privacy protection in the 21st century will mean a shift from proactive regulatory-focused privacy protection with procedural obligations to reactive sanction-based privacy protection where unreasonable privacy invasions are severely punished. In return, more focus should be put on privacy by design as a leading principle. This could be achieved in two ways: 1) building privacy-protective features into the technology, preferably by giving individuals the possibility to control their privacy themselves, or 2) building business cases with respect for privacy and following privacy-protective procedures. Both these principles however could be mandated by law in some form of another. Given the rapid technological and societal changes, we should start the discussion on the new privacy paradigms for the 21st century soon. For further reading on privacy in the law, the following books are recommended [3-9].

References

1. S.D. Warren and L.D. Brandeis. *The right to privacy, Harvard Law Review*, chapter IV(5), pages 193–220. 1890. Available from: http://www.lawrence.edu/fast/BOARDMAW/Privacy_brand_warr2.html.
2. OECD. Guidelines on the protection of privacy and transborder flows of personal data, 1980. Available from: http://www.oecd.org/document/18/0,2340,en_2649_34255_1815186_1_1_1_1,00%.html.
3. A. Büllesbach, Y. Poulet, and C. Prins. *Concise European IT Law*. Kluwer Law International, Alphen aan den Rijn, 2006.
4. A. Cavoukian and T.J. Hamilton. *The Privacy Pay-off*. McGraw-Hill, Toronto, 2002.
5. C. Kuner. *European Data Privacy Law and Online Business*. Oxford University Press, New York, 2003.

6. D. Lyon. *Surveillance as Social Sorting; Privacy, Risk and Digital Discrimination*. Routledge, London/New York, 2003.
7. C. Nicoll, J.E.J. Prins, and V. Dellen. *Digital Anonymity and the Law*. TCM Asser Press, The Hague, 2003.
8. R. O'Harrow. *No Place to Hide*. Free Press, New York, 2005.
9. J.E.J. Prins. *Trust in Electronic Commerce*. Kluwer Law International, The Hague, 2002.

3

Ethical Aspects of Information Security and Privacy

Philip Brey

University of Twente
The Netherlands

Summary. This chapter reviews ethical aspects of computer and information security and privacy. After an introduction to ethical approaches to information technology, the focus is first on ethical aspects of computer security. These include the moral importance of computer security, the relation between computer security and national security, the morality of hacking and computer crime, the nature of cyberterrorism and information warfare, and the moral responsibilities of information security professionals. Privacy is discussed next. After a discussion of the moral importance of privacy and the impact of information technology on privacy, privacy issues in various information-processing practices are reviewed. A concluding section ties the two topics together.

3.1 Introduction

This chapter will review ethical aspects of computer and information security and privacy. Computer security is discussed in the following two sections of this chapter, 3.2 and 3.3, and privacy follows in Sects. 3.4 and 3.5. A concluding section ties the two topics together.

Ethics is a field of study that is concerned with distinguishing right from wrong, and good from bad. It analyzes the morality of human behaviors, policies, laws and social structures. Ethicists attempt to justify their moral judgments by reference to ethical principles of theories that attempt to capture our moral intuitions about what is right and wrong. The two theoretical approaches that are most common in ethics are *consequentialism* and *deontology*. Consequentialist approaches assume that actions are wrong to the extent that they have bad consequences, whereas deontological approaches assume that people have moral duties that exist independently of any good or bad consequences that their actions may have. Ethical principles often inform legislation, but it is recognized in ethics that legislation cannot function as a substitute for morality. It is for this reason that individuals and corporations are always required to consider not only the legality but also the morality of their actions.

Ethical analysis of security and privacy issues in information technology primarily takes place in *computer ethics*, which emerged in the 1980s as a field [1, 2]. Computer ethics analyzes the moral responsibilities of computer professionals and computer users and ethical issues in public policy for information technology development and use. It asks such questions as: Is it wrong for corporations to read their employees' e-mail? Is it morally permissible for computer users to copy copyrighted software? Should people be free to put controversial or pornographic content online without censorship? Ethical issues and questions like these require *moral* or *ethical analysis*: analysis in which the moral dilemmas contained in these issues are clarified and solutions are proposed for them. Moral analysis aims to clarify the facts and values in such cases, and to find a balance between the various values, rights and interests that are at stake and to propose or evaluate policies and courses of action.

3.2 Computer Security and Ethics

We will now turn to ethical issues in computer and information security. In this section, the moral importance of computer security will be assessed, as well as the relation between computer security and national security. Section 3.3 will consider specific ethical issues in computer security.

3.2.1 The Moral Importance of Computer Security

Computer security is a field of computer science concerned with the application of security features to computer systems to provide protection against the unauthorized disclosure, manipulation, or deletion of information, and against denial of service. The condition resulting from these efforts is also called computer security. The aim of computer security professionals is to protect valuable information and system resources. A distinction can be made between the security of system resources and the security of information or data. The first may be called *system security*, and the second *information security* or *data security* [3]. System security is the protection of the hardware and software of a computer system against malicious programs that sabotage system resources. Information security is the protection of data that resides on disk drives on computer systems or is transmitted between systems. Information security is customarily defined as concerned with the protection of three aspects of data: their *confidentiality*, *integrity* and *availability*.

How does computer security pose ethical issues? As explained earlier, ethics is mostly concerned with rights, harm and interests. We may therefore answer this question by exploring the relation between computer security and rights, harms and interests. What morally important benefits can computer security bring? What morally important harm or violations of moral rights can result from a lack of computer security? Can computer security also cause harm or violate rights instead of preventing and protecting them?

A first and perhaps most obvious harm that can occur from breaches of computer security is economic harm. When system security is undermined, valuable hardware and software may be damaged or corrupted and service may become unavailable, resulting in losses of time, money and resources. Breaches of information security may come at an even higher economic cost. Valuable data that is worth much more than the hardware on which it is stored may be lost or corrupted, and this may cause severe economic losses. Stored data may also have personal, cultural or social value, as opposed to economic value, that can be lost when data is corrupted or lost. Any type of loss of system or data security is moreover likely to cause some amount of psychological or emotional harm.

Breaches of computer security may even cause grave harm such as injury and death. This may occur in so-called *safety-critical systems*, which are computer systems with a component or real-time control that can have a direct life-threatening impact. Examples are computer systems in nuclear-reactor control, aircraft and air-traffic control, missile systems and medical treatment systems. The corruption of certain other types of systems may also have life-threatening consequences in a more indirect way. These may include systems that are used for design, monitoring, diagnosis or decision-making, for instance systems used for bridge design or medical diagnosis.

Compromises of the *confidentiality* of information may cause additional harm and rights violations. Third parties may compromise the confidentiality of information by accessing, copying and disseminating it. Such actions may, first of all, violate *property rights*, including *intellectual property rights*, which are rights to own and use intellectual creations such as artistic or literary works and industrial designs [4]. The information may be exclusively owned by someone who has the right to determine who can access and use the information, and this right can be violated.

Second, compromises of confidentiality may violate *privacy rights*. This occurs when information that is accessed includes information about persons that is considered to be private. In addition to violations of property and privacy rights, breaches of confidentiality may also cause a variety of other harm resulting from the dissemination and use of confidential information. For instance, dissemination of internal memos of a firm damages its reputation, and compromises of the confidentiality of online credit-card transactions undermines trust in the security of online financial transactions and harms e-banking and e-commerce activity.

Compromises of the *availability* of information can, when they are prolonged or intentional, violate *freedom rights*, specifically rights to freedom of information and free speech. *Freedom of information* is the right to access and use public information. Jeroen van den Hoven has argued that access to information has become a moral right of citizens in the information age, because information has become a primary social good: a major resource necessary for people to be successful in society [5]. Shutting down vital information services could violate this right to information. In addition, computer networks have become important as a medium for speech. Websites, e-mail, bulletin boards, and other services are widely used to spread messages and communicate with others. When access to such services is blocked, for instance through denial-of-service attacks or hijackings of websites, such acts are properly classified as violations of *free speech*.

Computer security measures normally prevent harm and protect rights, but they can also cause harm and violate rights. Notably, security measures may be so protective of information and system resources that they discourage or prevent stakeholders from accessing information or using services. Security measures may also be discriminatory: they may wrongly exclude certain classes of users from using a system, or may wrongly privilege certain classes of users over others.

3.2.2 Computer Security and National Security

Developments in computer security have been greatly influenced by the September 11, 2001 terrorist attacks in the United States and their aftermath. In response to these attacks, national security has become a major policy concern of Western nations. *National security* is the maintenance of the integrity and survival of the nation state and its institutions by taking measures to defend it from threats, particularly threats from the outside. Many new laws, directives and programs protective of national security have come into place in Western nations after 9/11, including the creation in the US of an entire Department of Homeland Security. The major emphasis in these initiatives is the protection of state interests against terrorist attacks [6].

Information technology has acquired a dual role in this quest for national security. First of all, computer security has become a major priority, particularly the protection of critical information infrastructure from external threats. Government computers, but also other public and private infrastructure, including the Internet and telephone network, have been subjected to stepped-up security measures. Secondly, governments have attempted to gain more control over public and private information infrastructures. They have done this through wire-tapping and data interception, by requiring Internet providers and telephone companies to store phone and e-mail communications records and make them available to law enforcement officials, by attempting to outlaw certain forms of encryption, or even through attempts to require companies to reengineer the Internet so that eavesdropping by the government is made easier. Paradoxically, these efforts by governments to gain more control over information also weaken certain forms of security: they make computers less secure from access by government agencies.

The philosopher Helen Nissenbaum has argued that the current concern for national security has resulted in a new conception of computer security in addition to the classical one [7]. The classical or ordinary concept of computer security is the one used by the technical community and defines computer security in terms of systems security and integrity, availability and confidentiality of data (see Sect. 3.2.1). Nissenbaum calls this *technical computer security*. The other, which she calls *cybersecurity*, involves the protection of information infrastructure against threats to national interests. Such threats have come to be defined more broadly than terrorism, and have nowadays come to include all kinds of threats to public order, including internet crime, online child pornography, computer viruses, and racist and hate-inducing websites. At the heart of cybersecurity, however, are concerns for national security, and especially the state's vulnerability to terrorist attacks.

Nissenbaum emphasizes that technical computer security and cybersecurity have different conceptions of the aims of computer security and the measures that need to be taken. Technical computer security aims to protect the private interests of individuals and organizations, specifically owners and users of computer systems and data. Cybersecurity aims to protect the interests of the nation state and conceives of computer security as a component of national security. Technical computer security measures mostly protect computer systems from outside attacks. Cybersecurity initiatives include such protective measures as well, but in addition include measures to gain access to computer systems and control information. The two conceptions of security come into conflict when they recommend opposite measures. For instance, cybersecurity may require computer systems to be opened up to remote government inspection or may require government access to websites to shut them down, while technical computer security may prohibit such actions. The different interests of technical computer security and cybersecurity can in this way create moral dilemmas: should priority be given to state interests or to the interests and rights of private parties? This points to the larger dilemma of how to balance national security interests against civil rights after 9/11 [8].

3.3 Ethical Issues in Computer Security

In this section, ethical aspects of specific practices in relation to computer security will be analyzed. Sections 3.3.1 and 3.3.2 will focus on practices that undermine computer security: hacking, computer crime, cyberterrorism and information warfare. Section 3.3.3 will consider the moral responsibilities of information security professionals.

3.3.1 Hacking and Computer Crime

A large part of computer security is concerned with the protection of computer resources and data against unauthorized, intentional break-ins or disruptions. Such actions are often called *hacking*. Hacking, as defined in this chapter, is the use of computer skills to gain unauthorized access to computer resources. Hackers are highly skilled computer users that use their talents to gain such access, and often form communities or networks with other hackers to share knowledge and data. Hacking is often also defined, more negatively, as the gaining of such unauthorized access for malicious purposes: to steal information and software or to corrupt data or disrupt system operations. Self-identified hackers, however, make a distinction between non malicious break-ins, which they describe as hack-ing, and malicious and disruptive break-ins, which they call *cracking* [9].

Self-identified hackers often justify their hacking activities by arguing that they cause no real harm and instead have a positive impact. The positive impact of hacking, they argue, is that it frees data for the benefit of all, and improves systems and software by exposing security holes. These considerations are part of what has been called the *hacker ethic* or *hacker code of ethics* [10, 11], which is a set of (usually implicit) principles that guide the activity of many hackers. Such principles include convictions that information should be free, that access to computers should be unlimited and total, and that activities in cyberspace cannot do harm in the real world.

Tavani has argued that many principles of the hacker ethic cannot be sustained [1]. The belief that information should be free runs counter to the very notion of intellectual property, and would imply that creators of information would have no right to keep it to themselves and have no opportunity to make a profit from it. It would moreover fundamentally undermine privacy, and would undermine the integrity and accuracy of information, as information could be modified and changed at will by anyone who could access it. Tavani also argues that the helpfulness of hacking in pointing to security weaknesses may not outweigh the harm it does, and that activities in cyberspace can do harm in the real world.

Both hacking and cracking tend to be unlawful, and may therefore be classified as a form of computer crime, or cybercrime as it has also been called [12]. There are many varieties of computer crime, and not all of them compromise computer security. There are two major types of cybercrime that compromise computer security: *cybertrespass*, which is defined by Tavani ([1], p. 193) as the use of information technology to gain unauthorized access to computer systems or password-protected websites, and *cybervandalism*, which is the use of information technology to unleash programs that disrupt the operations of computer networks or corrupt data.

Tavani distinguishes a third type of cybercrime that sometimes includes breaches of computer security, *cyberpiracy*. Cyberpiracy, also called *software piracy*, is the use of information technology to reproduce copies of proprietary software or information or to distribute such data across a computer network. Cyberpiracy is much more widespread than cybervandalism or cybertrespass, because it does not require extensive computer skills and many computer users find it morally permissible to make copies of copyrighted software and data. Cyberpiracy involves breaches in computer security when it includes the cracking of copyright protections.

Another type of cybercrime that sometimes involves breaches of computer security is *computer fraud*, which is deception for personal gain in online business transactions by assuming a false online identity or by altering or misrepresenting data[1]. Computer fraud may depend on acts of cybertrespass to obtain passwords, digital identities, or other transaction or access codes, and acts of cybervandalism involving the modification of data. Other types of cybercrime, such as the online distribution of child pornography or online harassment and libel, usually do not involve breaches of computer security.

3.3.2 Cyberterrorism and Information Warfare

A recent concern in computer and national security has been the possibility of *cyberterrorism*, which is defined by Herman Tavani as the execution of "politically motivated hacking operations intended to cause grave harm, that is, resulting in either loss of life or severe economic loss, or both" ([1], p. 161). The possibility of major attacks on information infrastructure, intending to debilitate or compromise this infrastructure and harm economic, industrial or social structures dependent on it, has become a major concern since the 9/11 attacks. Such attacks could be both foreign and domestic.

Controversy exists on the proper scope of cyberterrorism. Where should the boundaries be drawn between cyberterrorism, cybercrime, and cybervandalism? Should a teenager who releases a dangerous virus that turns out to cause major harm to government computers be persecuted as a cyberterrorist? Are politically motivated hijackings of the homepages of major organizations acts of cyberterrorism? A distinction between cyberterrorism and other kinds of cyberattacks may be found in its political nature: cyberterrorism consists of politically motivated operations that aim to cause harm. Yet, Mark Mainon and Abby Goodrum [13] have argued that not all politically motivated cyberattacks should be called cyberterrorism. They distinguish cyberterrorism from *hacktivism*, which are hacking operations against an internet site or server with the intent to disrupt normal operations but without the intent to cause serious damage. Hacktivists may make use of e-mail bombs, low-grade viruses, and temporary home-page hijackings. They are politically motivated hackers who engage in a form of electronic political activism that should be distinguished from terrorism [14].

Information warfare is an extension of ordinary warfare in which combatants use information and attacks on information and information systems as tools of warfare [15, 16]. Information warfare may include the use of information media to spread propaganda, the disruption, jamming or hijacking of communication infrastructure or propaganda feeds of the enemy, and hacking into computer systems that control vital infrastructure (e.g., oil and gas pipelines, electric power grids, or railway infrastructure).

---

[1] When the identity used in computer fraud is "borrowed" from someone else, this is called identity theft.

3.3.3 Moral Responsibilities of Information Security Professionals

Information security (IS) professionals are individuals whose job it is to maintain system and information security. By the nature of their profession, they have a professional responsibility to assure the correctness, reliability, availability, safety and security of all aspects of information and information systems. The discussion in Section 3.2 makes clear that this responsibility has a moral dimension: professional activities in computer security may protect people from morally important harms but could also cause such harm, and may either protect or violate people's moral rights. In the case of safety-critical systems, the decisions of information security professionals may even be a matter of life or death.

That IS professionals have moral responsibilities as part of their profession is reflected in the codes of ethics used by various organizations for computer and information security. These codes of ethics rarely go into detail, however, on the moral responsibilities of IS professionals in specific situations. For instance, the code of ethics of the Information Systems Security Association (ISSA), an international organization of information security professionals and practitioners, only states that members should "[p]erform all professional activities and duties in accordance with all applicable laws and the highest ethical principles" but does not go on to specify what these ethical principles are or how they should be applied and balanced against each other in specific situations [17].

For IS professionals, as well as for other computer professionals who have a responsibility for computer security, a code of ethics is clearly not enough. To appreciate the moral dimension of their work, and to cope with moral dilemmas in it, they require training in information security ethics. Such training helps professionals to become clear about interests, rights, and moral values that are at stake in computer security, to recognize ethical questions and dilemmas in their work, and to balance different moral principles in resolving such ethical issues [18].

3.4 Information Privacy and Ethics

We will now turn to issues of privacy in modern data management. In this section, we will consider what privacy is, why it is important and how it is impacted by information technology. Section 3.5 will then consider major privacy issues in modern data management.

3.4.1 What is Privacy and Why is It Important?

In Western societies, a broad recognition exists of a right to personal privacy. The right to privacy was first defended by the American justices Samuel Warren and Louis Brandeis, who defined privacy as "the right to be let alone"

[19]. Privacy is a notion that is difficult to define, and many more-precise definitions have since been presented. Often, the right to privacy is defined as the right of individuals to control access or interference by others into their private affairs. The philosopher Ferdinand Schoeman has defined it thus: "A person has privacy to the extent that others have limited access to information about him, limited access to the intimacies of his life, or limited access to his thoughts or his body." ([20], p. 3). Schoeman's definition shows that the concept of privacy does not only apply to the processing of personal information. It also applies to the observation of and interference with human behaviors and relations, the human body, and one's home and personal belongings [21].

Privacy is held to be valuable for several reasons. Most often, it is held to be important because it is believed to protect individuals from all kinds of external threats, such as defamation, ridicule, harassment, manipulation, blackmail, theft, subordination, and exclusion. James Moor has summed this up by claiming that privacy is an articulation of the core value of *security*, meant to protect people from all kinds of harm done by others [22]. It has also been argued that privacy is a necessary condition for *autonomy*: without privacy, people could not experiment in life and develop their own personality and own thoughts, because they would constantly be subjected to the judgment of others. The right to privacy has also been claimed to protect other rights, such as abortion rights and the right to sexual expression. Privacy moreover has been claimed to have social value in addition to individual value. It has, for instance, been held to be essential for maintaining democracy [23].

The right to privacy is not normally held to be absolute: it must be balanced against other rights and interests, such as the maintenance of public order and national security. Privacy rights may also vary in different contexts. There is, for example, a lesser expectation of privacy in the workplace or in the public sphere than there is at home. An important principle used in privacy protection in Western nations is that of *informed consent*: it is often held that citizens should be informed about how organizations plan to store, use or exchange their personal data, and that they should be asked for their consent. People can then voluntarily give up their privacy if they choose.

3.4.2 Information Technology and Privacy

Privacy is a value in modern societies that corresponds with the ideal of the autonomous individual who is free to act and decide his own destiny. Yet, modern societies are also characterized by surveillance, a practice that tends to undermine privacy. *Surveillance* is the systematic observation of (groups of) people for specific purposes, usually with the aim of exerting some form of influence over them. The sociologist David Lyon has argued that surveillance has always been an important part of modern societies [24]. The state engages in surveillance to protect national security and to fight crime, and the modern corporation engages in surveillance in the workplace to retain control over the workforce.

Computerization from the 1960s onward has intensified surveillance by increasing its scale, ease and speed. Surveillance is partially delegated to computers that help in collecting, processing and exchanging data. Computers have not only changed the scale and speed of surveillance, they have also made a new kind of surveillance possible: *dataveillance*, which is the large-scale, computerized collection and processing of personal data in order to monitor people's actions and communications [25]. Increasingly, information technology is not just used to record and process static information about individuals, but to record and process their actions and communications. New detection technologies like smart closed-circuit television (CCTV), biometrics and intelligent user interfaces, and new data-processing techniques like data mining further exacerbate this trend. As Lyon has argued, the ease with which surveillance now takes place has made it a generalized activity that is routinely performed in all kinds of settings by different kinds of organizations. Corporations, for instance, have extended surveillance from the workplace to their customers (*consumer surveillance*). In addition, the 9/11 terrorist attacks have drastically expanded surveillance activities by the state.

Many privacy disputes in today's society result from tensions between people's right to privacy and state and corporate interests in surveillance. In the information society, privacy protection is realized through all kinds of information privacy laws, policies and directives, or *data protection* policies as they are often called in Europe. These policies regulate the harvesting, processing, usage, storage and exchange of personal data. They are often overtaken, however, by new developments in technology. However, privacy protection has also become a concern in the design and development of information technology.

Information privacy has also become a major topic of academic study. Studies of information privacy attempt to balance privacy rights against other rights and interests, and try to determine privacy rights in specific contexts and for specific practices. Specialized topics include workplace privacy [26], medical privacy [27], genetic privacy [28], Internet privacy (Sect. 3.5.1), and privacy in public (Sect. 3.5.3).

3.5 Privacy Issues in Modern Data Management

3.5.1 Internet Privacy

The Internet raises two kinds of privacy issues. First, the posting and aggregation of personal information on Internet websites sometimes violates privacy. Websites on the Internet contain all sorts of personal information that is made publicly available, often without the bearer's explicit consent. They may contain, for instance, one's phone number and address, archived bulletin board messages from years past, information about one's membership of organizations, online magazines and newspapers in which one is mentioned, online databases with public records, pictures and video clips featuring oneself, etc. Using search engines, this information can easily be located and be used to create elaborate composite records about persons (see Sect. 3.5.2). Should there be limits to this? When should someone's consent be asked when his personal information is posted on the web, or when such information is used for specific purposes? (See also Sect. 3.5.3).

A second type of privacy issue involves the online monitoring of internet users. Their connection to the internet may be used by third parties to collect information about them in a way that is often invisible to them. Online privacy risks include *cookies* (small data packets placed by servers on one's computer for user authentication, user tracking, and maintaining user-specific information), *profiling or tracking* (recording the browsing behavior of users), and *spyware* (computer programs that maliciously collect information from a user's computer system or about a user's browser behavior and send this information over the internet to a third party). In addition, private e-mail and data traffic may be intercepted at various points, for instance by employers, internet service providers, and government agencies. When do such actions violate privacy, and what should be done to protect internet privacy? [29].

3.5.2 Record Merging and Matching and Data Mining

It frequently happens that different databases with personal information are combined to produce new data structures. Such combinations may be made in two ways ([1], p. 127-131). First, the records in two databases may be *merged* to produce new composite records. For instance, a credit-card company may request information about its prospective customers from various databases (e.g., financial, medical, insurance), which are then combined into one large record. This combined record is clearly much more privacy-sensitive than the records that compose it, as the combined record may generate perceptions and suggest actions that would not have resulted from any of the individual records that make it up.

Second, records in databases may be *matched*. Computer matching is the cross-checking in two or more unrelated databases for information that fits a certain profile in order to produce matching records or "hits". Computer matching is often used by government agencies to detect possible instances of fraud or other crimes. For instance, ownership records of homes or motorized vehicles may be matched with records of welfare recipients to detect possible instances of welfare fraud. Computer matching has raised privacy concerns because it is normally done without the consent of the bearers of personal information that are involved. Moreover, matches rarely prove facts about persons but rather generate suspicions that require further investigation. In this way, record matching could promote stereo-typing and lead to intrusive investigations.

Data mining is a technique that is usually defined over a single database. It is the process of automatically searching large volumes of data for patterns, using techniques such as statistical analysis, machine learning and pattern recognition. When data mining takes place in databases containing personal information, the new information thus gained may be privacy-sensitive or confidential even when the old information is not. It may for instance uncover patterns of behavior of persons that were not previously visible. Data mining may also be used to stereotype whole categories of individuals. For instance, a credit-card company may use data mining on its customer database to discover that certain zip codes correlate strongly with loan defaults. It may then decide not to extend credit anymore to customers with these zip codes. In summary, data mining may violate individual privacy and may be used to stereotype whole categories of individuals. Ethical policies are needed to prevent this from happening [30].

3.5.3 Privacy in Public

It is sometimes believed that privacy is a right that people have when they are in private places such as homes, private clubs and restrooms, but that is minimized or forfeited as soon as they enter public space. When you walk in public streets or are on the road with your car, it is sometimes believed, you may retain the right not to be seized and searched without probable cause, but your appearance and behavior may be freely observed, surveilled and registered. Many privacy scholars, however, have argued that this position is not wholly tenable, and that people have privacy rights in public areas that are incompatible with certain registration and surveillance practices [31, 32].

The problem of privacy in public applies to the tracking, recording, and surveillance of public appearances, movements and behaviors of individuals and their vehicles. Techniques that are used for this include video surveillance (CCTV), including smart CCTV for facial recognition, infrared cameras, satellite surveillance, global positioning system (GPS) tracking, RFID tagging, electronic checkpoints, mobile-phone tracking, audio bugging, and ambient intelligence techniques. Does the use of these techniques violate privacy even when they are used in public places? The problem of privacy in public also applies to publicly available information on the Internet, as discussed in section 3.5.1. Does the fact that personal information is available on a public forum make it all right to harvest this information, aggregate it and use it for specific purposes?

Helen Nissenbaum has argued in an influential paper that surveillance in public places that involves the electronic collection, storage and analysis of information on a large scale often amounts to a violation of personal privacy [31]. She argues that people often experience such surveillance as an invasion of their privacy if they are properly informed about it, and that such electronic harvesting of information is very different from ordinary observation, because it shifts information from one context to another and frequently involves record merging and matching and data mining. She concludes that surveillance in public places violates privacy whenever it violates *contextual integrity*: the trust that people have that acquired information appropriate to one context will not be used in other contexts for which it was not intended.

3.5.4 Biometric Identification

Biometrics is the identification or verification of someone's identity on the basis of physiological or behavioral characteristics. Biometric technologies provide a reliable method of access control and personal identification for governments and organizations. However, biometrics has also raised privacy concerns [33]. Widespread use of biometrics would have the undesirable effect of eliminating anonymity and pseudonymity in most daily transactions, because people would leave unique traces everywhere they go. Moreover, the biometric monitoring of movements and actions gives the monitoring organization insight into a person's behaviors which may be used against that person's interests. In addition, many people find biometrics distasteful, because it involves the recording of unique and intimate aspects *of* (rather than *about*) a person, and because biometric identification procedures are sometimes invasive of bodily privacy. The challenge for biometrics is therefore to develop techniques and policies that are optimally protective of personal privacy.

3.5.5 Ubiquitous Computing and Ambient Intelligence

Ubiquitous computing is an approach in information technology that aims to move computers away from the single workstation and embed micro-processors into everyday working and living environments in an invisible and unobtrusive way. *Ambient intelligence* is an advanced form of ubiquitous computing that incorporates wireless communication and intelligent user interfaces, which are interfaces that use sensors and intelligent algorithms for profiling (recording and adapting to user behavior patterns) and context awareness (adapting to different situations) [34]. In ambient intelligence environments, people are surrounded with possibly hundreds of intelligent, networked computers that are aware of their presence, personality and needs, and perform actions or provide information based on their perceived needs.

Marc Langheinrich [35] has claimed that ubiquitous computing has four unique properties that are potentially threatening to privacy: (1) *ubiquity*; (2) *invisibility*; (3) *sensing*; (4) *memory amplification* (the continuous recording of people's actions to create searchable logs of their past). I have argued that ambient intelligence adds two properties to this list: (5) *user profiling*; and (6) *connectedness* (wireless communication between smart objects) [36].

These unique features of the two technologies make the protection of privacy in them a major challenge. As critics have argued, ubiquitous computing and ambient intelligence have the ability to create a Big Brother society in which every human activity is recorded and smart devices probe people's actions, intentions and thoughts. The distinction between the private and the public sphere may be obliterated as dozens of smart devices record activity in one's home or car and connect to corporate or government computers elsewhere. Major privacy safeguards will be needed to avoid such scenarios (see Part V of this book for a discussion of privacy protection in ambient intelligence).

3.6 Conclusion

Privacy is a moral right of individuals that is frequently and increasingly at issue when information systems are used. It was explained in this chapter why privacy is important and how it is impacted by information technology, and various ethical issues in information privacy were reviewed. Computer security is not itself a moral right or moral value, but it has been argued that maintaining computer security may be morally necessary to protect correlated rights and interests: privacy rights, property rights, freedom rights, human life and health, and national security. It was argued that computer security can also work to undermine rights.

Ethical analysis of privacy and security issues in computing can help computer professionals and users recognize and resolve moral dilemmas and can yield ethical policies and guidelines for the use of information technology. In addition, it has been recognized in computer ethics that not only the use of information systems requires moral reflection, but also their design, as system designs reflect moral values and involve moral choices [37, 38]. A system can for example be designed to protect privacy, but it can also be designed to give free access to personal information to third parties. This fact is taken up in *value-sensitive design*, an approach to the design of information systems that attempts to account for values in a principled fashion [39]. Ideally, ethical reflection on information technology should not wait until products hit the market, but should be built in from the beginning by making it part of the design process.

References

1. H. Tavani, Ethics and Technology: Ethical Issues in an Age of Information and Communication Technology, Wiley, 2004.
2. D. Johnson, Computer Ethics, 3rd edn, Upper Sadle River: Prentice Hall, 2000
3. R. Spinello, H. Tavani, "Security and Cyberspace", In: Readings in Cyberethics, 1st edn, ed by R. Spinello and H. Tavani, Jones and Bartlett, Sudbury MA, 2001 pp. 443-450
4. D. Halbert, Intellectual Property in the Information Age: The Politics of Expanding Ownership Rights, Quorum, Westport CT, 1999

5. J. Van den Hoven, "Equal Access and Social Justice: Information as a Primary Good" in: Proceedings of ETHICOMP95, vol. 1, DeMontfort University, Leicester UK, 1995
6. J. Bullock, et al, Introduction to Homeland Security, 1st edn, Butterworth-Heinemann, 2005
7. H. Nissenbaum, "Where Computer Security Meets National Security", Ethics and Information Technology 7, pp. 61-73, 2005
8. D. Davis, B. Silver, "Civil liberties vs. security: Public opinion in the context of the terrorist attacks on America", American Journal of Political Science 48(1), pp. 28-46, 2004
9. K. Himma, (ed.), Readings on Internet Security: Hacking, Counterhacking, and Other Moral Issues, Jones & Bartlett, forthcoming
10. S. Levy, Hackers: Heroes of the Computer Revolution, Doubleday, Garden City NY, 1984
11. P. Himanen, The Hacker Ethic: A Radical Approach to the Philosophy of Business, Random House, New York, 2001
12. S. McQuade, Understanding and Managing Cybercrime, Allyn & Bacon, 2005
13. D. Mainon, A. Goodrum, "Terrorism or Civil Disobedience: Toward a Hacktivist Ethic", Computers and Society, 30(2), pp. 14-19, 2000
14. D. Denning, "Activism, Hacktivism, and Cyberterrorism: the Internet as a Tool for Influencing Foreign Policy", In Networks and Netwars: The Future of Terror, Crime, and Militancy, ed. J. Arquilla, D. Ronfeldt, Rand Corporation, 2002. Available at http://www.rand.org/publications/MR/MR1382/
15. D. Denning, Information Warfare and Security, Addison-Wesley, Reading MA, 1999
16. G. Rattray, Strategic Warfare in Cyberspace, MIT Press, Cambridge MA, 2001
17. ISSA, "ISSA Code of Ethics", In Information Systems Security Association, Available at: http://www.issa.org/codeofethics.html 2005
18. T. Bynum, S. Rogerson (eds.), Computer Ethics and Professional Responsibility: Introductory Text and Readings, Blackwell, 2003
19. S. Warren, L. Brandeis, The Right to Privacy, Harvard Law Review 4, pp. 193-220, 1890
20. F. Schoeman, "Introduction", In Philosophical Dimensions of Privacy: An Anthology, ed. F. Schoeman, Cambridge University Press, Cambridge UK, 1984
21. P. Brey, "The Importance of Privacy in the Workplace", In The Ethics of Privacy in the Workplace, ed. S. O. Hansson, E. Palm, Peter Lang, Brussels, 2005 pp. 97-118
22. J. Moor, "Towards a Theory of Privacy for the Information Age", Computers and Society 27(3), pp. 27-32, 1997
23. A. Westin, Privacy and Freedom, Atheneum, New York, 1967
24. D. Lyon, Surveillance Society. Monitoring Everyday Life, Open University Press, Buckingham UK, 2001
25. R. Clarke, Information Technology and Dataveillance, Communications of the ACM 31(5), pp. 498-512, 1988
26. S. Hansson, E. Palm, (eds.), The Ethics of Privacy in the Workplace, Peter Lang, Brussels, 2005
27. M. Steward, "Electronic Medical Records - Privacy, Confidentiality, Liability", Journal of Legal Medicine 26(4), pp. 491-506, 2005
28. G. T. Laurie, Genetic Privacy: A Challenge to Medico-Legal Norms, Cambridge University Press, Cambridge UK, 2002

29. C. Bennett, "Cookies, Web Bugs, Webcams and Cue Cats: Patterns of Surveillance on the World Wide Web", Ethics and Information Technology 3(3), pp. 195-208, 2001

30. L. van Wel, L. Royakker, "Ethical Issues in Web Data Mining", Ethics and Information Technology 6, pp. 129-140, 2004

31. H. Nissenbaum, "Protecting Privacy in an Information Age: The Problem of Privacy in Public" Law and Philosophy 17: pp. 559-596, 1998

32. P. Brey, "Ethical Aspects of Face Recognition Systems in Public Places", In Readings in Cyberethics, 2nd edn, ed. by R. Spinello, H. Tavani, Jones and Bartlett, Sudbury, MA, 2004, pp. 585-600

33. R. Clarke, "Biometrics and Privacy", 2001, Available at: http://www.anu.edu.au/people/Roger.Clarke/DV/Biometrics.html

34. W. Weber, J. Rabaey, E. Aarts, (eds.): Ambient Intelligence, Springer, Berlin Heidelberg New York, 2005

35. M. Langheinrich, "Privacy by Design - Principles of Privacy-Aware Ubiquitous Systems", In Lecture Notes In Computer Science; Vol. 2201 Archive, Springer, Berlin Heidelberg New York, 2001, pp. 273 - 291

36. P. Brey, "Freedom and Privacy in Ambient Intelligence, Ethics and Information Technology 7, pp. 157-166, 2006

37. H. Nissenbaum, "Values in Technical Design", In Encyclopedia of Science, Technology and Society, ed. by C. Mitcham, MacMillan, New York, 2005, lxvi-lxx

38. P. Brey, "Disclosive Computer Ethics", Computers and Society 30(4), 10-16, 2000

39. B. Friedman, "Value Sensitive Design", Encyclopedia of Human-Computer Interaction, Great Barrington, MA: Berkshire, 2004, pp. 769-774

Part II

Data and System Security

4

Authorization and Access Control

Sabrina De Capitani di Vimercati, Sara Foresti, and Pierangela Samarati

Università degli Studi di Milano
Italia

Summary. Access control is the process of controlling every request to a system and determining, based on specified rules (*authorizations*), whether the request should be granted or denied. The definition of an access control system is typically based on three concepts: access control *policies*, access control *models*, and access control *mechanisms*. In this chapter, we focus on the traditional access control models and policies. In particular, we review two of the most important policies: the discretionary and mandatory access control policies. We therefore start the chapter with an overview of the basic concepts on which access control systems are based. We then illustrate different traditional discretionary and mandatory access control policies and models that have been proposed in the literature, also investigating their low-level implementation in terms of security mechanisms.

4.1 Introduction

An important requirement of any computer system is to protect its *data* and *resources* against unauthorized disclosure (*secrecy*) and unauthorized or improper modifications (*integrity*), while at the same time ensuring their availability to legitimate users (*no denials of service*) [1]. The problem of ensuring protection has existed since information has been managed. A fundamental component in enforcing protection is represented by the *access control* service whose task is to control every access to a system and its resources and ensure that all and only authorized accesses can take place. A system can implement access control in many places and at different levels. For instance, operating systems use access control to protect files and directories and database management systems (DBMSs) apply access control to regulate access to tables and views. In general, when considering an access control system, one considers three abstractions of control: access control *policies*, access control *models*, and access control *mechanisms*. A policy defines the (high-level) rules according to which access control must be regulated. In general, access control policies are dynamic in nature because they have to reflect evolving business factors, government regulations, and environmental conditions. A model provides a *formal* representation of the access control security policy and its working. The formalization allows the proof of properties of the security provided by the access control system being designed. A mechanism defines the low-level (software and hardware) functions that implement the controls imposed by the policy and that are formally stated in the model. Mechanisms can be designed for their adherence to the properties of the model. Therefore, by proving that the model is secure and that the mechanism *correctly implements* the model, we can argue that the system is secure (w.r.t. the definition of security considered). The implementation of a correct mechanism is far from being trivial and is complicated by the need to cope with possible security weaknesses due to the implementation itself and by the difficulty of mapping the access control primitives to a computer system. Access control models and mechanisms are often characterized in terms of their policy support. On one hand, an access control model may be rigid in its implementation of a single policy. On the other hand, a security model will allow for the expression and enforcement of a wide variety of policies and policy classes. Researchers have therefore tried to develop access control mechanisms and models that are largely independent of the policy for which they can be used [2].

Access control policies can be grouped into three main classes: *discretionary*, *mandatory*, and *role-based*. A discretionary access control policy (DAC) controls access based on users' identities and on a series of rules, called *authorizations*, explicitly stating which subjects can execute which actions on which resources. A mandatory access control policy (MAC) controls access based on mandated regulations determined by a central authority. A role-based access control policy (RBAC) controls access depending on the roles that users have within the system and on rules stating what accesses are allowed to users in given roles. Since role-based access control is the topic of Chap. 5, we here focus on discretionary and mandatory policies only. Discretionary policies are usually coupled with (or include) an administrative policy that defines who can specify authorizations/rules governing access control. It is also important to note that discretionary and mandatory policies are not mutually exclusive, but can be applied jointly. In this case, an access to be granted needs both (i) the existence of the necessary authorization for it, and (ii) the satisfaction of the mandatory policy. Intuitively, the discretionary policy operates *within the boundaries* of the mandatory policy: it can only restrict the set of accesses that would be allowed by MAC alone.

By discussing different approaches with their advantages and limitations, this chapter hopes to give an idea of the different issues to be tackled in the development of an access control system, and of good security principles that should be taken into account in the design.

The remainder of this chapter is organized as follows. Section 4.2 introduces discretionary access control policies and models. We first describe traditional discretionary policies and then illustrate how these policies have been extended. Section 4.3 introduces mandatory access control policies and mod-

	Invoice1	Invoice2	Order1	Order2	Program1
Ann	read, write		read		execute
Bob		read, write		read	execute
Carol			read, write	read, write	
David	read	read, write			read, execute

Fig. 4.1. An example of an access matrix

els. In particular, we focus on the secrecy-based and integrity mandatory policies. Section 4.4 describes the administrative policies, that is, the policies regulating who can define the authorizations in a system. Finally, Sect. 4.5 concludes the chapter.

4.2 Discretionary Access Control Policies

A discretionary access control policy is based on the definition of a set of rules, called *authorizations*, explicitly stating which user can perform which action on which resource. These rules can be represented as triples of the form (s, o, a) stating that user s can execute action a on object o. When a user makes an access request, the policy is enforced on the basis of the identity of the requester and on the rules involving herself. Different discretionary access control policies and models have been proposed in the literature. The first proposal is the *access matrix* model [3, 4, 5]. Let S, O, A be a set of subjects that can interact with the access control system, a set of objects belonging to the system that need to be protected, and a set of actions that can be executed over the objects, respectively. In the access matrix model, the state of the system, that is, the authorizations defined at a given time in the system, is represented as a matrix A with a row for each subject and a column for each object in the system. Each entry $A[s, o]$ contains the list of actions that subject s is allowed to execute over object o. For instance, suppose that there are four users, namely Alice, Bob, Carol, and David, five objects, namely Invoice1, Invoice2, Order1, Order2 and Program1, and the set of actions contains read, write and execute. Figure 4.1 illustrates an example of an access matrix. The state of the system can be changed by invoking commands that execute primitive operations. These primitive operations allow one to create and delete subjects and objects in the system and to modify the set of actions that a subject can execute over an object.

Although the access matrix model can be easily implemented through a two-dimensional array, this solution is expensive because in general the matrix will be sparse and therefore many cells will be empty. To avoid such a waste of memory, the access matrix can actually be implemented through the following three mechanisms.

- *Authorization table.* The non-empty entries of A are stored in a table with three attributes, namely subject, action, and object. This solution is

Table 4.1. Authorization table corresponding to the access matrix in Fig. 4.1

User	Action	Object
Ann	read	Invoice1
Ann	write	Invoice1
Ann	read	Order1
Ann	execute	Program1
Bob	read	Invoice2
Bob	write	Invoice2
Bob	read	Order2
Bob	execute	Program1
Carol	read	Order1
Carol	write	Order1
Carol	read	Order2
Carol	write	Order2
David	read	Invoice1
David	read	Invoice2
David	write	Invoice2
David	read	Program1
David	execute	Program1

adopted in the database context where authorizations are stored in the
catalog.

- *Access control list (ACL)*. The access matrix is stored by column, that
  is, each object is associated with a list of subjects together with a set of
  actions they can perform on the object.
- *Capability.* The access matrix is stored by row, that is, each subject is
  associated with a list of objects together with a set of actions the subject
  can perform on the objects.

For instance, with respect to the access matrix in Fig. 4.1, the corresponding authorization table is illustrated in Table 4.1, while the access control lists
and capabilities are represented in Figs. 4.2 and 4.3, respectively.

Access control lists and capabilities allow the efficient management of authorizations with respect to specific operations at the expense of others. More
precisely, access control lists allow direct access to authorizations on the basis
of the object they refer to; it is expensive to retrieve all the authorizations of
a subject because this operation requires the examination of the ACLs for all
the objects. Analogously, capabilities allow direct access to authorizations on
the basis of the subject they refer to; it is expensive to retrieve all the accesses
executable on an object because this operation requires the examination of
all the different capabilities.

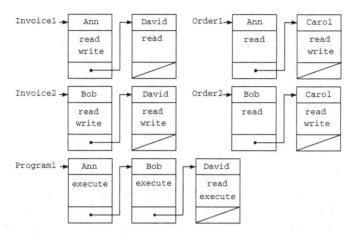

Fig. 4.2. Access control lists corresponding to the access matrix in Fig. 4.1

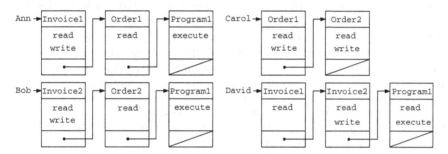

Fig. 4.3. Capability lists corresponding to the access matrix in Fig. 4.1

4.2.1 Enhanced Discretionary Policies

Although the access matrix still remains a framework for reasoning about accesses permitted by a discretionary policy, discretionary policies have been developed considerably since the access matrix was proposed. In particular, early approaches to authorization specifications allowed *conditions* [4] to be associated with authorizations to restrict their validity. Conditions can make the authorization validity dependent on the satisfaction of some system predicates, can make restrictions dependent on the content of objects on which the authorization is defined, or can make an access decision dependent on accesses previously executed. Another important feature supported by current discretionary policies is the definition of abstractions on users and objects. Both users and objects can therefore be hierarchically organized, thus introducing *user groups* and *classes of objects*.

Figure 4.4(a) illustrates an example of a user group hierarchy and Fig. 4.4(b) illustrates an example of an object hierarchy. The definition of groups of users (and resources) leads to the need for a technique to easily handle exceptions. For instance, suppose that all users belonging to a group

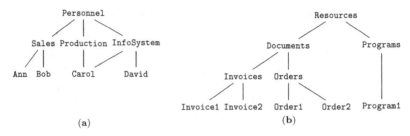

Fig. 4.4. An example of a user group hierarchy (a) and object hierarchy (b)

can access a specific resource but user u. In this case, it is necessary to associate explicitly an authorization with each user in the group but u. This observation has been applied to the combined support of both *positive* and *negative* authorizations. In this way, the previous exception can easily be supported by the definition of two authorizations: a positive authorization for the group and a negative authorization for user u. Hierarchies can also simplify the process of authorization definition because authorizations specified on an abstraction can be propagated to all its members. The propagation of authorizations over a hierarchy may follow different *propagation policies* [6]. We now briefly describe the most common propagation policies.

- *No propagation.* Authorizations are not propagated.
- *No overriding.* Authorizations associated with an element in the hierarchy are propagated to all its descendants.
- *Most specific overrides.* Authorizations associated with an element in the hierarchy are propagated to its descendants if not overridden. An authorization associated with an element n overrides a contradicting authorization (i.e., an authorization with the same subject and object but with a different sign) associated with an ancestor of n for all the descendants of n. For instance, consider the user group hierarchy in Fig. 4.4(a) and suppose that there is a positive authorization for the InfoSystem group to read Order1, and a negative authorization for reading the same resource associated with Personnel. In this case, Carol will be allowed to read Order1, as InfoSystem is a more specific element in the hierarchy than Personnel.
- *Path overrides.* Authorizations of an element in the hierarchy are propagated to its descendants if not overridden. An authorization associated with an element n overrides a contradicting authorization associated with an ancestor n' for all the descendants of n, only for the paths passing from n. The overriding has no effect on other paths. For instance, consider the user group hierarchy in Fig. 4.4(a) and suppose that there is a positive authorization for the InfoSystem group to read Order1, and a negative authorization for reading the same resource associated with Personnel. In this case, the negative authorization wins along the path

⟨Personnel, Production, Carol⟩; the positive authorization wins along the path ⟨Personnel, InfoSystem, Carol⟩. Consequently, there is still a conflict for managing Carol's access to Order1, as she inherits two contradicting privileges along the two paths reaching her.

The introduction of both positive and negative authorizations results in the following two problems: (i) *inconsistency*, which happens when conflicting authorizations are associated with the same element in a hierarchy; and (ii) *incompleteness*, which happens when some accesses are neither authorized nor denied (i.e., no authorization exists for them).

The inconsistency problem is solved by applying a *conflict resolution policy*. There are different conflict resolution policies and we now briefly illustrate some of them [6, 7].

- *No conflict.* The presence of a conflict is considered an error.
- *Denials take precedence.* Negative authorizations take precedence.
- *Permissions take precedence.* Positive authorizations take precedence.
- *Nothing takes precedence.* Neither positive nor negative authorizations take precedence and conflicts remain unsolved.

The incompleteness problem can be solved by adopting a *decision policy*. There are two main decision policies: (i) an *open policy* denies access if there exists a negative authorization for it, and allows it otherwise; (ii) a *closed policy* allows access if there exists a positive authorization for it, and denies it otherwise. The combination of a propagation policy, a conflict resolution policy, and a decision policy guarantees a complete and consistent policy for the system.

4.2.2 Drawbacks of Discretionary Policies

Although discretionary policies are in general expressive and powerful, they have some drawbacks mainly due to the fact that they do not distinguish between users and subjects. A *user* is a human entity whose identity is used by the access control module to identify her privileges on the system. A *subject* is instead a process generated by a user, which interacts with the system making requests on behalf of a user. Discretionary policies ignore this distinction and evaluate all requests submitted by a process running on behalf of some user against the authorizations of the user. This aspect makes discretionary policies vulnerable to processes executing malicious programs (e.g., *Trojan horses*) that exploit the authorizations of the user invoking them. In fact, discretionary access control policies leak control over the flow of information once data are acquired by a process.

For instance, consider the access matrix in Fig. 4.1 and suppose that David invokes an application hiding a Trojan horse. Since the application operates on behalf of David, it can read the content of Invoice2 and write it on a new file, say Invoice3. Suppose also that this new file can be read

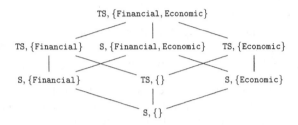

Fig. 4.5. An example of a security lattice

by **Ann** and **Carol**. In this way, information in **Invoice2** is made readable to **Ann** and **Carol**.

Moreover, the security of a system based on discretionary access control is not easy to evaluate, due to the so-called safety problem, which is undecidable.

4.3 Mandatory Access Control Policies

To solve the drawbacks of discretionary access control policies, mandatory access control policies make a distinction between users and subjects. Mandatory polices were introduced in the operating system context, where objects to be protected are essentially files containing the data. Later studies investigated the extension of mandatory policies to the database context [17, 18, 19, 20]. This topic will be treated in detail in a following chapter.

Mandatory policies are usually based on *classifications* associated with subjects and objects. The most common form of an access class is a pair of two elements: a *security level* and a set of *categories*. While security levels form a totally ordered set, a category is a member of an unordered set. Access classes form therefore a partially ordered set, where the partial order relation $\geq$, called *dominance*, is defined as follows: given two access classes c_1 and c_2, $c_1 \geq c_2$ (i.e., c_1 *dominates* c_2) iff the security level of c_1 is greater than or equal to the security level of c_2 and the set of categories of c_1 includes the set of categories of c_2. Access classes together with their partial order dominance relationship form a *lattice* [8]. Figure 4.5 illustrates an example of a lattice, where there are two security levels, namely **Top Secret** (TS) and **Secret** (S), with TS>S, and there are two categories, namely **Financial** and **Economic**.

4.3.1 Secrecy-Based Mandatory Policy

The main goal of a secrecy-based mandatory policy is to protect the confidentiality of information. In this case, the security level of the access class associated with an object reflects the sensitivity of the information it contains. The security level of the access class associated with a subject, called *clearance*, reflects the degree of trust placed in the subject not to disclose sensitive information to users not cleared to see it. The set of categories associated with both subjects and objects defines the area of competence of users and data. Categories reflect the *need-to-know* principle according to which a subject should only access the information she actually needs to know to perform her job. A user can then connect to the system using her clearance or any access class dominated by her clearance. For instance, with reference to the lattice in Fig. 4.5, a user cleared ⟨TS,{Financial}⟩ can connect to the system as a ⟨TS,{Financial}⟩, ⟨S,{Financial}⟩, ⟨TS,∅⟩, or ⟨S,∅⟩ subject. A user connecting to the system generates a process with the same access class associated with the corresponding user. The access requests submitted by a subject are then evaluated by applying the following two principles.

No-read-up. A subject *s* can read an object *o* if and only if the access class of the subject dominates the access class of the object.

No-write-down. A subject *s* can write an object *o* if and only if the access class of the object dominates the access class of the subject.

These two principles prevent information flowing from high-level subjects/objects to subjects/objects at lower (or incomparable) levels, thereby ensuring the satisfaction of the protection requirements. A subject can write only objects that are more sensitive than the objects she can read. Given the no-write-down principle, it is easy to see why users are allowed to connect to the system at different access classes, so that they are able to access information at different levels (provided that they are cleared for it).

Example 1. Suppose that resources Invoice1 and Invoice2 are classified ⟨TS, {Financial, Economic}⟩, resources Order1 and Order2 are classified ⟨S, {Economic}⟩, and the clearance of Ann is ⟨TS, {Financial, Economic}⟩. It is easy to see, that to modify objects Order1 and Order2, Ann has to connect to the system with, for example, access class ⟨S, {Economic}⟩. By contrast, independently from the access class with which Ann connects to the system, she can read objects Order1 and Order2.

Although the no-read-up and no-write-down principles prevent dangerous flows of information from highly sensitive objects to less sensitive objects, these principles may turn out to be too restrictive. For instance, in a real situation data may need to be downgraded (e.g., this may happen at the end of the embargo). To consider these situations as well, secrecy-based mandatory models should handle exceptions to processes that are *trusted* and ensure that information is *sanitized*.

The secrecy-based control principles just illustrated summarize the basic axioms of the security model proposed by David Bell and Leonard La-Padula [9, 10, 11, 12]. The first version of the Bell and LaPadula model is based on two criteria: the *simple property*, which formalizes the no-read-up principle, and the **-property*, which formalizes the no-write-down principle.

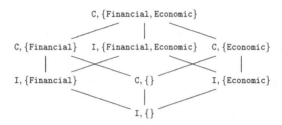

Fig. 4.6. An example of an integrity lattice

The first formulation of the model however presents a problem related to the fact that no restriction is put on transitions. This implies that the Bell and LaPadula notion of security is also satisfied by a system that, when a subject requests any type of access to an object o, downgrades to the lowest possible access class every subject and object, and the access is granted. Intuitively, this problem can be avoided if the security level of an object cannot be changed while it is in use.

This principle is captured by an informal principle, called the *tranquility* principle. Another property included in the Bell and LaPadula model is the *discretionary property*, stating that the set of current accesses is a subset of the access matrix $\mathcal{A}$. Intuitively, it enforces discretionary controls.

4.3.2 Integrity-Based Mandatory Policy

The mandatory policy described in the previous section only guarantees data confidentiality and does not protect data integrity. To avoid such a problem, Biba introduced an integrity model [13], which controls the flow of information and prevents subjects from *indirectly* modifying information they cannot write. Just as for the secrecy-based model, each subject and object is associated with an *integrity class*, composed of an *integrity level* and a *set of categories*. The integrity level of an integrity class associated with a user reflects the degree of trust placed in the subject to insert and modify sensitive information. The integrity level of an integrity class associated with an object indicates the degree of trust placed on the information stored in the object and the potential damage that could result from unauthorized modifications of the information. Figure 4.6 illustrates an example of an integrity lattice, where there are two integrity levels, namely Crucial (C) and Important (I), and two categories, namely Financial and Economic. Each access request of a subject on an object is evaluated with respect to the following two principles.

No-read-down. A subject s can read an object o if and only if the integrity class of the object dominates the integrity class of the subject.

No-write-up. A subject s can write an object o if and only if the integrity class of the subject dominates the integrity class of the object.

These two principles are the dual of the two principles defined by Bell and LaPadula. The integrity model prevents flows of information from low-level objects to higher-level objects.

Example 2. Suppose that the integrity class associated with `Invoice1` and `Invoice2` is ⟨C, {Financial, Economic}⟩, and the integrity class associated with `Order1` and `Order2` is ⟨I, {Economic}⟩. If user `Ann` invokes an application when she is connected to the system with integrity class ⟨C, {Economic}⟩, the corresponding subject will be allowed to read `Invoice1` and `Invoice2` and to write `Order1` and `Order2`.

Note that the secrecy-based and integrity-based policies are not mutually exclusive. This means that, if the main goal of a system is to protect both the confidentiality and the integrity of its resources, the system can apply these two policies at the same time. However, objects and subjects have to be assigned two access classes, one for secrecy control and one for integrity control.

Example 3. Consider Example 1 and Example 2 and suppose that the system applies both the secrecy-based policy and the integrity-based policy. In this case, `Ann` is only allowed to read `Invoice1` and `Invoice2`.

A major limitation of the Biba model is that it only captures integrity compromises due to improper information flows. However, integrity is a much broader concept and additional aspects should be taken into account [1].

4.3.3 Drawbacks of the MAC

Although the mandatory policy protects data better than the discretionary policy, it has some problems. The main problem is that the mandatory policy controls only flows of information in the system that happen through *overt* channels, that is, channels operating in a legitimate way. Mandatory policy is instead vulnerable with respect to *covert* channels, which are channels not intended for normal communication, but can still be exploited to infer information. For instance, if a low-level subject requests the use of a resource currently in use by a high-level process, it will receive a negative response. The system, by not allocating the resource because it is busy, can again be exploited to signal information at lower levels (high-level processes can modulate the signal by acquiring or releasing resources). Another important example of covert channels is represented by *timing channels* [14], used to infer information on the basis of the response time of the system: if the response time is longer than usual, a low-level subject can infer that there is another, more important, process using the same resource. Therefore, wherever there is a shared resource among different subjects or there exists a system property that can be measured, potentially there is also a covert channel [15]. It is important to note that these problems cannot be solved

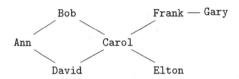

Fig. 4.7. An example of a privilege dependency graph

by giving higher priority to low-level processes as this policy may cause denials of service for high-level subjects. Covert channel analysis is usually carried out in the implementation phase, when it is possible to identify which system resources are shared among processes and which of them are measurable. There are also methods, called *interface models* [2, 15], that try to identify and eliminate covert channels in the advanced modeling phase. The most important principle on which interface models are based is the *noninterference* principle: high-level input should not interfere with low-level output [16]. Obviously, the correctness of the system is not absolute, but it is relative to the specific model used for individuating covert channels.

Another drawback of MAC is that subjects and objects have to be classified and this may not always be feasible. Moreover, access is evaluated only on the basis of this classification, consequently the system may be too rigid.

4.4 Administrative Policies

Both discretionary and mandatory policies assume the presence of an administrative policy, that is, a set of rules indicating who can modify the original access control policy, under which conditions. In the MAC case, the administrative policy is simple, since only the security administrator can change the subject and object access (or integrity) class. By contrast, discretionary access control policies can be coupled with different administrative policies. The most important policies are briefly described in the following.

- *Centralized.* There is a single security administrator, or a group thereof, allowed to grant and revoke authorizations.
- *Hierarchical.* The security administrators are hierarchically organized; a central security administrator assigns administrative tasks to the other administrators in the system.
- *Cooperative.* Specific authorizations can be defined only through the cooperation of several administrators.
- *Ownership.* Each object is associated with a user, called the owner, who is in charge of granting and revoking authorizations on it.
- *Decentralized.* Extending the above-mentioned approaches, the administrator of an object can delegate to other users the privilege of specifying authorizations, possibly with the ability of further delegation.

Clearly, a decentralized administration policy is very convenient, as it allows administrative task delegation. However, when an administrative authorization is revoked, the problem arises of dealing with the authorizations specified by the users from whom the administrative privilege is being revoked. For instance, suppose that Ann gives Bob and David the authorization to read Order1 and gives them the privilege of granting this authorization to others (in some systems, such a capability of delegation is called *grant option* [21]). Suppose then that Bob and David grant this privilege to Carol who in turn grants the authorization to Frank and Elton. Finally Frank, who has also received the privilege of granting the read authorization on Order1 to others, grants the authorization to Gary. Suppose that now Ann revokes the authorization from Bob. The problem here is that Bob has granted the received privilege to other users. To illustrate how revocation can work, it is useful to look at how revocation is treated in the database context. In the database context, grants are graphically represented by a *privilege dependency graph* [21], where there is a node for each user and a directed edge between two nodes u_1 and u_2 whenever user u_1 has granted a specific privilege to user u_2. For instance, Fig. 4.7 illustrates the privilege dependency graph corresponding to the grant operations described above. There are two different revocation strategies [22]: *cascade* [21] and *noncascade* [23] revocation. With the first strategy, not only is the identified privilege revoked, but also are all authorizations based on the revoked privilege. More precisely, cascading revocation recursively deletes authorizations if the revokee no longer holds the grant option for the access. However, if the revokee still holds the grant option for the access, the authorizations she granted are not deleted. For instance, if Carol revokes the authorization from Frank, the authorizations is taken away not only from Frank but also from Gary. The revocation by Bob of the authorization granted to Carol would only delete the authorization granted to Carol by Bob. Frank's authorization as well as Gary's authorization would still remain valid since Carol still holds the grant option of the access (because of the authorization from David).

With the noncascade strategy, all authorizations based on the revoked privilege are maintained. With respect to the previous example, if Carol revokes authorization Frank, the authorization of Gary is preserved.

4.5 Conclusions

In this chapter we introduced the most important concepts related to access control. We described two access control policies: discretionary and mandatory policies. Recent proposals in the area of access control models and languages are based on the consideration that often servers and clients do not know each other and a system may receive requests coming from subjects it does not know. For this main reason, it is no longer possible to base access control on users' identity. Therefore, a more appropriate approach would be that the access decision is based on properties (attributes) of the requester and of the resource. Basing authorization on attributes of the resource/service requester provides flexibility and scalability that is essential in the context of large distributed open systems, where subjects are identified by their characteristics. Therefore, new approaches based on *digital certificates* are becoming widespread, being much more suitable for an open communication infrastructure [24, 25] (see also Chap. 8). Another interesting aspect, which has been investigated in the past, is the definition of a language for expressing and exchanging policies based on a high-level formulation that, while powerful, can be easily interchangeable and both human and machine readable. Insights in this respect can be taken from recent proposals expressing access control policies as XML documents [26, 27] (see also Chap. 6).

4.6 Acknowledgements

This work was supported in part by the European Union within the PRIME Project in the FP6/IST Programme under contract IST-2002-507591 and by the Italian MIUR within the KIWI and MAPS projects.

References

1. P. Samarati, S. De Capitani di Vimercati (2001). Access control: Policies, models, and mechanisms. In: R. Focardi, R. Gorrieri (eds.), Foundations of Security Analysis and Design. Springer-Verlag, New York.
2. R. Focardi, R. Gorrieri (1997). The compositional security checker: A tool for the verification of information flow security properties. IEEE Transaction Software Engineering, 23(9):550–571.
3. G.S. Graham, P.J. Denning (1972). Protection-principles and practice. In AFIPS Proc. of the Spring Jt. Computer Conference, Montvale, NJ, USA.
4. H.H. Harrison, W.L. Ruzzo, J.D. Ullman (1976). Protection in operating systems. Communications of the SCM, 19(8):461–471.
5. B.W. Lampson (1974). Protection. ACM Operating Systems Review, 8(1):18–24.
6. S. Jajodia, P. Samarati, M.L. Sapin, V.S. Subrahmanian (2001). Flexible support for multiple access control policies. ACM Transaction on Database Systems, 26(2):214–260.
7. T.F. Lunt (1988). Access control policies: Some unanswered questions. In Proc. of IEEE Computer Security Foundations Workshop II, Franconia, New Hampshire.
8. R.S. Sandhu (1993). Lattice-based access control models. IEEE Computer, 26(11):9–19.
9. D. Bell and L. LaPadula (1973). Secure computer systems: A mathematical model. Technical Report MTR-2547, Vol. 2, MITRE Corp., Bedford, MA.

10. D. Bell and L. LaPadula (1973). Secure computer systems: Mathematical foundations. Technical Report MTR-2547, Vol. 1, MITRE Corp., Bedford, MA.

11. D. Bell and L. LaPadula (1974). Secure computer systems: A refinement of the mathematical model. Technical Report MTR-2547, Vol. 3, MITRE Corp., Bedford, MA.

12. Bell D and LaPadula L (1975). Secure computer systems: Unified exposition and multics interpretation. Technical Report MTR-2997, Vol. 4, MITRE Corp., Bedford, MA.

13. K.J. Biba (1977). Integrity considerations for secure computer systems. Technical Report MTR-3153, rev., MITRE Corp., Vol. 1, Bedford, MA.

14. J.C. Wray (1991). An analysis of covert timing channels. In Proc. of the IEEE Symposium on Security and Privacy, Oakland, CA, USA.

15. J. McLean (1994). Security models. In: Marciniak J (ed.), Encyclopedia of Software Engineering. John Wiley & Sons.

16. J.A. Goguen, J. Meseguer (1984). Unwinding and inference control. In IEEE Symposium on Security and Privacy, Los Angeles, CA, USA.

17. S. Jajodia, R. Sandhu (1991). Toward a multilevel secure relational data model. In Proc. of the ACM SIGMOD Conference on Management of Data, Denver, CO, USA.

18. T.F. Lunt (1991). Polyinstantiation: An inevitable part of a multilevel world. In Proc. of the IEEE Workshop on Computer Security Foundations, Franconia, New Hampshire.

19. T.F. Lunt, D.E. Denning, R.P. Schell, M. Heckman, W.R. Shockley (1990). The seaview security model. IEEE Transaction on Software Engineering, 16(6):593–607.

20. R.S. Sandhu, S. Jajodia (1992). Polyinstantiation for cover stories. In Proc. 2nd European Symposium on Research in Computer Security – ESORICS '92, Toulouse, France.

21. P.P. Griffiths, B.W. Wade (1976). An authorization mechanism for a relational database system. ACM Transactions on Database Systems, 1(3):242–255.

22. Database language SQL–part 2: Foundation (SQL/foundation) (1999). ISO International Standard, ISO/IEC 9075:1999.

23. E. Bertino, P. Samarati, S. Jajodia (1997). An extended authorization model for relational databases. IEEE-TKDE, 9(1):85–101.

24. P. Bonatti, S. De Capitani di Vimercati, P. Samarati (2002). An algebra for composing access control policies. ACM Transactions on Information and System Security, 5(1):1–35.

25. L. Wang, D. Wijesekera, S. Jajodia (2004). A logic-based framework for attribute based access control. In Proc. of the 2004 ACM Workshop on Formal Methods in Security Engineering, Washington DC, USA.

26. E. Damiani, S. De Capitani di Vimercati, S. Paraboschi, P. Samarati (2002). A fine-grained access control system for XML documents. ACM Transactions on Information and System Security, 5(2):169–202.

27. S. Godik, T. Moses (2003). eXtensible Access Control Markup Language (XACML) version 1.1. http://www.oasis-open.org/committees/xacml/repository/cs-xacml-specification-1.1.pdf.

Role-Based Access Control

Sylvia L. Osborn

The University of Western Ontario
Canada

Summary. Role-based access control (RBAC) models have been introduced by several groups of researchers. We first introduce the basic components of the American National Standards Institute (ANSI) RBAC model and the role graph model; then we contrast some of the details of these two models. Some design guidelines for successful role hierarchy design are given. Finally, we discuss some issues in designing a role-based system when mandatory access control constraints must be satisfied.

5.1 Introduction

Role-based access control (RBAC) models have been discussed since the mid 1990s [1, 2, 3, 4]. The traditional access control models are discretionary access control (DAC) and mandatory access control (MAC), which have been discussed in Chap. 4 of this book. These traditional models have shortcomings when dealing with complex, large systems, with possibly hundreds of users and thousands of data items. In DAC models, permissions are assigned to subjects directly. The disadvantage of such an approach is that, in a very large system, the granting of permissions to operate on individual data items to individual users is very time consuming and difficult to manage. It is also difficult to remember which permissions should be revoked from users when they leave the company or change jobs. MAC models, on the other hand, are very rigid, requiring that a lattice-based set of labels be applied to all objects and subjects and that constraints concerning reading and writing of objects must be satisfied [5]. MAC models are designed for applications where the keeping of secrets and the control of information flow are the primary requirements. It is very difficult to design a commercial security model which has such strict constraints on information flow.

The main goal of RBAC systems is to provide a model and tools to help manage access control in a complex environment with a very large number of users and an even larger number of data items. Since the introduction of RBAC models, many embellishments have been proposed, including administration, delegation and complex constraints. In this chapter, we will focus on the ANSI standard model [6] and the role graph model [7].

This chapter continues as follows. Section 5.2 describes the basic components of RBAC. This is followed by a discussion of the differences between the ANSI model and the role graph model in Sect. 5.3. In Sect. 5.4, some guidelines for successful role hierarchy design are given. Issues in designing role hierarchies for a MAC environment appear in Sect. 5.5.

5.2 Components of RBAC

All RBAC models involve users, permissions, and roles. As well as these three basic components, mappings among them further make up the model.

The first component of the model, users, are defined to be human beings in the ANSI standard [6]. This differs from classical access control models where the entity trying to access objects is called a *subject*, and is considered to be a process acting on behalf of a user.

The second component of RBAC is the set of permissions. The simplest form of permission relates a single object over which it is possible to exercise access control with an operation or access mode which is valid on this object. There may be different operations for different objects; for example, for a printer object, the operation USE is relevant, whereas for a file, READ, WRITE, CREATE and DELETE would be valid operations. A permission can also be defined to contain a single object with multiple operations, or multiple objects with multiple operations. An example of the latter would be the execution of a complex method which involves multiple accesses to multiple objects.

Roles are, of course, the main focus of RBAC models. A role should have a unique name. Usually, a role is designed to correspond to a job function in a company, e.g. clerk, manager, programmer, etc. It is also customary for roles to be arranged in a role hierarchy [4] or role graph [7]. In the ANSI standard, the model called Core RBAC does not include role hierarchies.

As well as the three main components just described, RBAC models also consist of a number of mappings. The *user assignment* (UA) mapping maps users to roles, and is many to many; it defines the roles a user can perform. The *permission assignment* (PA) mapping maps permissions to roles and is also many-to-many. Role hierarchies are many to many mappings between roles. Role hierarchies are not allowed to have cycles so that each role offers a unique set of permissions to users assigned to it. The remaining mappings deal with the concept of *sessions*. Sessions model the run-time activation of roles by users. Whereas the mapping between sessions and roles is many to many, only one user is mapped to a session. The components of hierarchical RBAC from the ANSI standard are shown in Fig. 5.1, adapted from [6].

The final components of the ANSI model deal with separation of duty (also known as conflict of interest). *Separation of duty* (SOD) constraints identify sets of roles which should not be assigned to the same user, because this

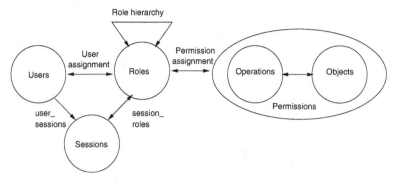

Fig. 5.1. Components of the ANSI hierarchical RBAC

would allow that user to perpetrate some fraud against the organization. *Static separation of duty* puts the constraint on the user-role assignment mapping. If the set of roles in the constraint has cardinality 2, the intent of a static SOD constraint is that no user should ever be assigned to these two roles, i.e. that the UA mapping should never contain the assignment of these two roles to the same user. *Dynamic SOD* constraints allow the roles to appear in the UA mapping, but prevent roles which are in conflict from being simultaneously activated in a session.

As well as these basic components, the role graph model has a user-group hierarchy (called the group graph) [8] and a permission hierarchy. A *group* is defined as a set of users. Users can be regarded as a group of cardinality 1, so that in the group graph, only one entity type exists. Groups can be used to focus on the appropriate collections of users, just as roles allow designers to focus on appropriate collections of permissions. For example, one can create groups based on user attributes, such as certain qualifications, or to model things like committees. Assigning the users to the committee is a different design activity from assigning permissions to the role that describes the allowed activities of the committee. The assignment of users to groups can be performed by a line manager or human resources department, whereas the role design would be performed by more security-minded systems personnel. Role design may be done before the system is deployed, whereas group memberships are more likely to change over time after the system is in use.

The hierarchy among permissions in the role graph model is used to model implications among permissions which arise because of object structure, or relationships among access modes. These ideas are based on some work for object-oriented databases [9, 10, 11]. When the object part of a permission is complex, like a deeply nested object or an XML document, implications based on the object structure can simplify the granting of permissions. For example, the permission to read an XML document can imply the permission to read all the subelements of that document, to an arbitrary number of levels. Having to specify the individual element-level permissions can be avoided if the system automatically deduces them from the document-level permission by implications based on object structure. The access modes may also have implications; for example, the ability to UPDATE an object may imply the ability to READ it. Clearly these implications vary from one application to the next. Having automatic implications based on the relationships among access modes can also simplify the design of the security model. The components of the role graph model are shown in Fig. 5.2.

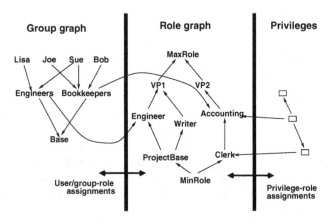

Fig. 5.2. Components of the role graph model

5.3 Contrasts Between the Role Graph and ANSI Models

The ANSI standard is given as a specification for RBAC implementations, but it is strongly based on the National Institute of Standards and Technology (NIST) model for which prototypes have been built [12, 13]. The role graph model was first discussed abstractly but with the support of a prototype [7, 14]. Both the role graph model and the ANSI model provide administrative commands or operations to create and alter a role hierarchy. The role hierarchy arranges the roles in a partial order, which can also be thought of as an acyclic graph. In this graph, an edge $r_i \rightarrow r_j$ indicates that role r_i *is junior* to r_j. In both the ANSI and role graph models, this relationship indicates inheritance: the permissions assigned to the junior role r_i are inherited by the senior role r_j. Another consequence of this role–role mapping is that all users assigned to the senior role are also implicitly assigned to the junior role (since the junior role's permissions are inherited, a user assigned to the senior role can perform all the operations of the junior role). Conversely, when considering all users assigned to a role, the users assigned to all seniors must be included.

Explicitly stated, the specification for the general role hierarchy in the ANSI model (rephrased to conform to the notation of this chapter) is:

$$r_i \to r_j \Rightarrow \text{authorized permissions}(r_i) \subseteq \text{authorized permissions}(r_j) \quad (5.1)$$

We focus here on operations that alter the role hierarchy, and omit user-role assignments and considerations concerning sessions. For the ANSI model, these commands are:

AddRole: checks for a unique role name, and adds the role with an empty user set and empty permission set.

DeleteRole: deletes a role from the system. Deletes all user-role assignments and permission-role assignments.

GrantPermission: adds a permission to a role.

RevokePermission: revokes a permission from a role.

AddInheritance: adds an inheritance relationship $r_i \to r_j$, after checking that this does not produce a cycle in the inheritance mapping.

DeleteInheritance: removes an inheritance relationship $r_i \to r_j$, and recomputes the transitive closure of the inheritance mapping. No alterations to roles' permission sets are given.

AddAscendant: adds a new role as the senior of an existing role. Calls Add-Role and AddInheritance; the new role has no direct permissions or users.

AddDescendant: adds a new role as the junior of an existing role. Calls Add-Role and AddInheritance; the new role has no direct permissions or users.

As well, there are review functions such as AssignedRoles, which returns all roles assigned to a user, RolePermissions, which for role hierarchies returns all permissions available in a role, etc. [6].

The role graph model presents operations on the role graph in terms of algorithms, which are guaranteed to restore role graph properties, or abort if the graph would have a cycle as a result of the proposed operation. *Direct permissions* of a role are those permissions assigned directly by the administrator and which are not available by inheritance. *Effective permissions* include the direct permissions and all permissions inherited from junior roles. Role graphs include a MaxRole and MinRole, which are the topmost and bottommost roles respectively. MaxRole has become important in consideration of administrative domains for decentralized administration of role graphs, which is beyond the scope of this chapter [15]. We can ignore MaxRole and MinRole in this discussion.

The role graph properties include:

$$\text{the role graph is acyclic} \quad (5.2)$$

and

$$\begin{gathered}\forall r_i, r_j, \text{authorized permissions}(r_i) \subset \text{authorized permissions}(r_j) \\ \Rightarrow \text{there must be a path from } r_i \text{ to } r_j\end{gathered} \quad (5.3)$$

Note that, in the case of property 5.3, the implication is actually $\Leftrightarrow$ since inheritance of permissions is also implied by the edges. In order to satisfy property 5.3, an edge $r_i \rightarrow r_j$ is added to the role graph by the algorithms whenever authorized permissions$(r_i) \subset$ authorized permissions(r_j). Before displaying the graphs, redundant edges are removed. Redundant edges are those edges $r_i \rightarrow r_j$ such that a path from r_i to r_j through another role also exists. This process is called reestablishing role graph properties (RRGP). Note that, because of property 5.2, it is never the case that for distinct r_i and r_j, authorized permissions$(r_i) \subset$ authorized permissions(r_j).

The algorithms concerning role graph manipulations, available in the role graph model are:

RoleAddition1: a role with its proposed juniors and seniors, and permission set is given. If no cycle would be created, the role is added. Direct and effective permissions of the new role and its seniors are adjusted. RRGP. After reestablishing role graph properties, some proposed immediate seniors (juniors) may not be immediate seniors (juniors), but will still be senior (junior).

RoleAddition2: a role with its proposed effective permissions is given. If no cycle would be created, the role is added. Juniors and seniors are determined by the algorithm. Direct and effective permissions of the new role and its seniors are adjusted. RRGP.

PermissionAddition: a new permission for a role is given. If no cycle would be created, the permission is added. Direct and effective permissions of this role and its seniors are adjusted. RRGP.

PermissionDeletion: a permission is deleted from a role, if no cycle would be created. Effective permissions of seniors are adjusted. RRGP[1].

RoleDeletion: the role and all incident edges are removed. The user is given a choice of whether to delete all direct permissions from the graph, or to transfer them to the immediate seniors. Direct and effective permissions of seniors are adjusted. RRGP.

EdgeInsertion: a new edge, $r_i \rightarrow r_j$, is added to the role graph, if it is not a redundant edge and if doing so does not create a cycle. RRGP.

EdgeDeletion: the edge is deleted from the role graph, if doing so does not create a cycle. RRGP.

To highlight the differences in these two approaches, let us consider an example. In Fig. 5.3 and subsequent examples, we see a role hierarchy in which directly assigned permissions are shown in bold, and inherited permissions are in italics. Let us call Step 1 the deletion of permission p3 from role R5. Figure 5.4(a) shows the ANSI role hierarchy, and Fig. 5.4(b) shows the role graph. For the ANSI diagram, the permissions shown are what was calculated by the

---

[1] Permission deletions and edge deletion may leave a role with an identical permission set to another role somewhere in the graph; so in the worst case, these operations could cause a cycle.

function RolePermissions before p3 was deleted from R5. This model does not distinguish between direct and inherited permissions, so they are all shown in bold. The shape of the graph for the role hierarchy defined by the ANSI model remains unchanged. The role graph, however, is altered as shown in Fig. 5.4(b). At first, edges R5 → R4, R5 → R2 and R5 → R1 are added, and then the latter two are removed as redundant edges. In the role graph algorithms, the direct permissions of role R4 will also be adjusted: since p1 is now inherited from R5, it is no longer a direct permission of R4. In the ANSI model, on the other hand, the RevokePermission operation has no rules to indicate that this deletion is propagated along the hierarchy.

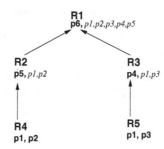

Fig. 5.3. Original role graph/hierarchy

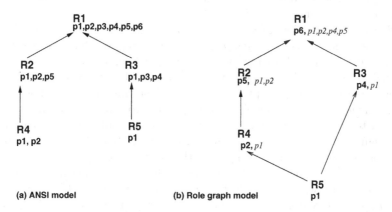

(a) ANSI model   (b) Role graph model

Fig. 5.4. After deleting p3 from role R5

Suppose after this permission deletion, as Step 2, permission p7 is added to role R5. This permission addition does not change the edge structure of the role graph. Permission additions never change the role hierarchy in the ANSI model. After adding p7 to R5, the permission set available to the senior roles in the two versions starts to diverge. Figure 5.5 gives the details.

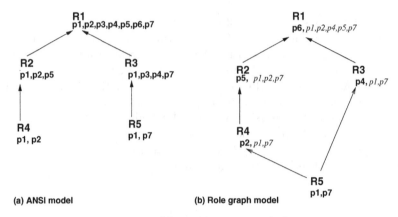

Fig. 5.5. After adding p7 to role R5

The examples above show roles whose permission sets are distinct. This is not required in the ANSI model. The ANSI AddRole command creates a new role with no users and no permissions assigned. If this is followed by AddInheritance, say from another role to the new role, the new role will inherit all the permissions of its junior and, having no directly assigned permissions, will thus have an identical permission set to this junior. In the role graph model, this would require edges in both directions, thus creating a cycle. No cycle is created in the ANSI model as edges are only added by AddInheritance, AddAscendant and AddDescendant, all of which check for cycles but do not check permission sets.

We can describe the ANSI model as *edges take precedence*, and the role graph model as *permissions take precedence*. Both approaches have merit. In the ANSI model, the role hierarchy can be designed before any permissions are assigned to the roles. The designer thus has a clear idea of how the inheritance of permissions should take place and can reflect this understanding in the design. In the role graph model, after Step 1, the role graph is altered to give feedback to the designer concerning the consequences of this modification of the design. By removing permission p3 from R5 in Step 1, R5's permission set becomes a proper subset of R4's, so the edge that is displayed in the role graph tells the designer that this role now offers a set of permissions which make it a junior role to R4. In effect, now, any user assigned to R4 can perform R5, since they have assigned to them all the permissions assigned to R5. The role hierarchy corresponding to this step for the ANSI model would not show this. After many alterations to the permission sets, the ANSI role hierarchy and the role graph can diverge a great deal; the beginning of this was shown above after Step 2.

In the ANSI model, then, only the explicit operations involving hierarchy relationships can alter the role hierarchy. In the role graph model, all operations can potentially alter the role graph. Another difference involves the uniqueness of permission sets. In the role graph model, roles always have distinct effective permission sets; if two roles which would be created have identical permission sets, the algorithms would be obliged to create a cycle, which is not allowed. In the ANSI model, it is possible for two roles to have identical permission sets (they will have distinct names); in the absence of a good user interface, the review functions can be used to list assigned permissions for the roles.

5.4 Guidelines for Role Hierarchy Design

In this section we will discuss some important advice to designers involved in producing an RBAC design. We will show how to follow these guidelines using either a system based on the ANSI model or on the role graph model.

The Role Hierarchy is not the Company Hierarchy

Many enterprises have a hierarchical administrative structure with a top manager or president, with several managers below this level, etc. It is important to remember when designing a role hierarchy that one is designing an *access control hierarchy*, not a reports-to hierarchy. To give an extreme example, the president of a company may have very few permissions; the bulk of the permissions may be correctly assigned to roles intended for users somewhere at a middle level in the management of the company. Consider the simple example in Fig. 5.6 (showing only direct permissions for each role). Suppose the company president should have the permissions {(computer, ACCESS), (ProductionArea, ACCESS), (forecast, READ), (WorkSchedule, READ)}. The dashed arrows show where the RoleAddition2 algorithm from the role graph model would place this role, as an immediate senior of Clerk and ProductionWorker, and with no junior or senior relationships to any of the other roles. This is where it belongs if the desired permission set is as stated just above. With the ANSI model, a designer would be tempted to start with a role hierarchy which mirrors the reports-to hierarchy. As we have just seen, this may not give the desired result.

Get Lots of Feedback

As we saw in Sect. 5.3, the side effects of the operations in both the ANSI model and the role graph are very subtle, and very different. Different researchers have made very different assumptions about how RBAC should be defined. There are many other tools available, or parts of bigger software packages such as relational database systems, which provide some RBAC functionality. It is imperative to do a review of the permissions available through a role, especially after alterations have been performed to an original design, to

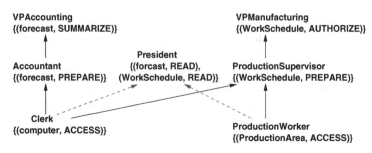

Fig. 5.6. Company role hierarchy showing direct permissions

make sure that the resulting roles have the desired sets of permissions. It is important to examine the permissions available to users, to make sure that no user has too much authority. In the ANSI model, these operations are given as review functions. In the role graph prototype, there are feedback windows available by clicking on roles and users. The overall design of RBAC in a large organization is very complex. Even though the two systems being highlighted in this chapter are very different, designers should be able to design their desired system using either paradigm, if they carefully examine the feedback.

Consider Abstract Roles

In object-oriented systems, there is the concept of an abstract class or interface, which contains a set of operations that form a handy unit for the purpose of inheritance. Roles can be created to contain a useful set of permissions which are then available for inheritance purposes. In Fig. 5.7(a), two abstract roles, BasicComputerAccess, which contains the permissions to access the company's computers, and BasicBuildingAccess, which allows access to relevant, controlled rooms that contain copying and printing machines, are shown. These can be inherited as necessary by other roles in the system, while not necessarily having users directly assigned. Without abstract roles in this example, we would have just AccountingClerk and PayrolClerk with their permissions as shown all being direct permissions, as in Fig. 5.7(b). Design with abstract roles conveys more information about the source of the permissions in the clerk roles. Having the abstract roles as units of permission assignment can be considered an extension of the classical divide-and-conquer problem-solving technique. Both the ANSI and role graph models would allow such roles, with or without direct user assignments.

Consider Groups

Finally, considering user groups can also enhance design. As discussed in Sect. 5.2, group design focuses on useful collections of users, whereas role design should focus on useful collections of permissions. Recall the example used

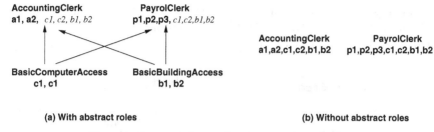

<table>
<tr><td>

AccountingClerk
a1, a2, *c1, c2, b1, b2*

PayrolClerk
p1,p2,p3, *c1,c2,b1,b2*

BasicComputerAccess
c1, c1

BasicBuildingAccess
b1, b2

</td><td>

AccountingClerk
a1,a2,c1,c2,b1,b2

PayrolClerk
p1,p2,p3,c1,c2,b1,b2

</td></tr>
</table>

(a) With abstract roles   (b) Without abstract roles

Fig. 5.7. Part role hierarchy showing abstract roles

above, of having a committee as simply a group of users, and having a role containing the permissions required by the committee. Group design differs from role design in several ways: assigning users to groups can be carried out by users who are not experts in access control. Once a system is deployed, group membership is more volatile than role-permission assignment.

The role graph model has, explicitly, a group graph where group design can take place. In the ANSI model, it is possible to have a Committee role which is senior to a CommitteePermissions role. The Committee role has user-role assignments but no permissions assigned except for the ones inherited from CommitteePermissions. So groups can be part of the design consideration in these two models. As noted above for abstract roles, separating group design from role design is another example of divide-and-conquer.

5.5 Comparing MAC and RBAC

In recent years, more emphasis has been placed on information security, and some security designers would like to consider MAC-like models in commercial environments. In this section, we will focus on issues of how to design an RBAC system in the presence of mandatory access control (MAC) requirements, and try to give some intuition about the consequences of satisfying MAC policies in an RBAC environment. In MAC, all subjects and objects have a security label, which comes from a set which is partially ordered and forms a lattice [5]. A lattice is a partial order in which every pair of entities has a unique least upper bound (LUB). The partial order shown in Fig. 5.7 is not a lattice as the two "Basic" roles have two least upper bounds. Two examples of security lattices are shown in Fig. 5.8.

The set of operations considered in MAC models is often just READ and WRITE. As well as the lattice, there are two properties which determine what objects the subjects are allowed to read and write. Let $\lambda(s)$ be the security label of a subject and $\lambda(o)$ the label of an object. The following are the *MAC properties*:

Simple security property: subject s can read object o only if $\lambda(s) \geq \lambda(o)$.
Liberal $\star$-property: subject s can write object o only if $\lambda(s) \leq \lambda(o)$.

The simple security property allows subjects to read at their own level or to read information with a lower security label. Writing to one's own level or to a higher level is allowed by the liberal ⋆-property.

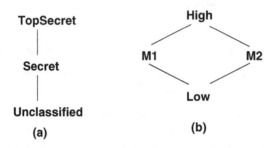

Fig. 5.8. Common MAC security lattices

A construction is given in [16] which shows how to take a security lattice like the one in Fig. 5.8(b) and produce the role hierarchy in Fig. 5.9. As well as the role hierarchy, the following constraints must also be enforced:

- (PA constraints:) For each object o with $\lambda(o) = l$, the permission (o, READ) is assigned to the reading role lRead.
  (o, READ) is assigned to lRead iff (o, WRITE) is assigned to lWrite.
- (UA constraint:) Each user is assigned to exactly two roles, lRead and lWrite, where $l = \lambda(s)$, and s represents the user.
- (Session constraint:) Each session has two roles, yRead and yWrite.

The only constraints supported by the ANSI RBAC model are static and dynamic SOD constraints, so any implementation supporting this MAC construction must also support these additional MAC constraints.

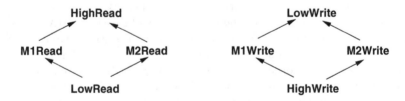

Fig. 5.9. RBAC hierarchy satisfying MAC properties

What we would like to discuss here is the implication on role design if the security designer has to deal with users and objects which are MAC labeled, where the MAC properties must be enforced, and where the security designer wants to have a role hierarchy other than the simple one given in Fig. 5.9. In such an environment, objects cannot be randomly assigned to roles. The essence of RBAC is that, when a role is assigned to a user and activated in a session, all of the permissions of the role are available; the units of permission activation are constrained by roles. The designer must, clearly, ensure that these units follow the MAC properties.

Let the *r-scope* (*w-scope*) of a role R be all objects o for which (o, READ) ((o, WRITE)) is in the permissions set of R. We can then define the *r-level* of a role R to be the least upper bound of the levels of the objects in r-scope of R. To satisfy the simple security property with a single user-role assignment, all users u assigned to a role R must have $\lambda(u) \geq$ r-level(R). Similarly, we can define the *w-level* of a role R to be the greatest lower bound (GLB) of the levels of the objects in w-scope, if the GLB exists. If the GLB does not exist, the w-level is undefined. To satisfy the liberal ⋆-property, for all users u assigned to a role R, w-level(R) must exist, and $\lambda(u) \leq$ w-level(R).

Simultaneously satisfying both the simple security and liberal ⋆-properties greatly constrains the levels of data which can appear together in a role. In Fig. 5.9, only Low data with READ can be in LowRead; direct permissions of M1Read include READ permissions of data classified at M1 plus any inherited permissions from LowRead, etc. Allowed combinations of labeled data which can appear in a role which is assignable, are shown in Fig. 5.10. The dashed horizontal lines indicate security levels which increase up the page, and correspond to a linear security lattice like the one in Fig. 5.8(a). The boxes containing either **r** or **w** indicate the security labels of the r-scope and w-scope of the roles, respectively. The arrows from u to a role indicate user levels which can be assigned to these roles. If a role has only reading permissions or only writing permissions, the appropriate conclusions can also be drawn from these examples; clearly the roles in Fig. 5.9 are assignable. From Fig. 5.10(a), we can conclude that a role R is assignable if and only if w-level(R) $\geq$ r-level(R) and $\{l \mid l \in$ r-scope(R) $\} \cap \{l \mid l \in$ w-scope(R) $\}$ is either a single level or empty.

The roles in Fig. 5.10(b) have permissions for reading and writing labeled objects for which no user label can simultaneously satisfy the simple security property and liberal ⋆-property.

Figure 5.10 shows what is allowed in terms of single roles. In a role hierarchy, these roles will also have inherited permissions, and with inheritance, the possibilities of having non-allowable combinations of permissions increases. Also, user-role assignment includes users assigned to senior roles, who are implicitly assigned to junior roles. To see how a role hierarchy can be constrained to only contain assignable roles, it is useful to consider a path in the role hierarchy, and keep in mind the characteristics for assignable roles mentioned above. In Fig. 5.11, we are assuming the security lattice from Fig. 5.8(a). In Fig. 5.11(a), in R2, we assume that additional read permissions involving unclassified objects have been added, and read permissions for some secret objects have been added to R1. Users classified at secret or higher can be assigned to R1, and these are valid users for R2 and R3. Similarly, users classified at unclassified or higher can be assigned to R3. In Fig. 5.11(b), R4 must have users assigned who are classified at secret or lower, and these are valid users for the junior roles R5 and R6. R6 can have top-secret users assigned.

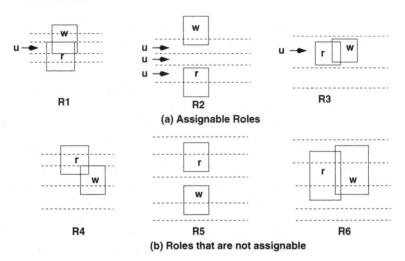

Fig. 5.10. Allowed combinations of levels in assignable roles [17]

In Fig. 5.11(c), users assigned to R7 and R8 must be classified ≤ secret and ≥ unclassified. R9 could be assigned to a user at unclassified or higher; i.e. R9 could have users assigned whose clearance is top secret.

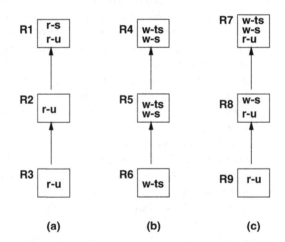

Fig. 5.11. Allowable roles and role hierarchies under MAC constraints

5.6 Conclusions

This chapter has described the essential features of RBAC models, and shown that the detailed properties of two RBAC models, namely the ANSI model and the role graph model, are subtly different. Some guidelines for role hierarchy design have been given. Finally the interactions between RBAC properties and the properties of mandatory access control were explored.

5.7 Acknowledgements

The financial support of the Natural Sciences and Engineering Council of Canada is gratefully acknowledged. Helpful ideas and comments were received from Cecilia Ionita, Xin Jin, He Wang, Noa Tuval, Ehud Gudes and the reviewers.

References

1. D. Ferraiolo and R. Kuhn. Role-based access control. In *Proceedings of the NIST-NSA National Computer Security Conference*, pages 554–563, 1992.
2. M.-Y. Hu, Steven A. Demurjian, and T. C. Ting. User-role based security profiles for an object-oriented design model. In B. M. Thuraisingham and C. E. Landwehr, editors, *Database Security VI, Status and Prospects*, Amsterdam, 1993. North-Holland.
3. M. Nyanchama and S. L. Osborn. Access rights administration in role-based security systems. In J. Biskup, M. Morgenstern, and C. E. Landwehr, editors, *Database Security, VIII, Status and Prospects*, pages 37–56. North-Holland, 1994.
4. R. Sandhu, E.J. Coyne, H.L. Feinstein, and C.E. Youman. Role-based access control models. *IEEE Computer*, 29:38–47, Feb. 1996.
5. R. Sandhu. Lattice-based access control models. *IEEE Computer*, 26:9–19, Nov. 1993.
6. American National Standards Institute, Inc. *Role-Based Access Control*. ANSI INCITS 359-2004. Approved Feb. 3, 2004.
7. M. Nyanchama and S. L. Osborn. The role graph model and conflict of interest. *ACM TISSEC*, 2(1):3–33, 1999.
8. S. Osborn and Y. Guo. Modeling users in role-based access control. In *Fifth ACM RBAC Workshop*, pages 31–38, Berlin, Germany, July 2000.
9. F. Rabitti, E. Bertino, W. Kim, and D. Woelk. A model of authorization for next-generation database systems. *ACM Trans Database Syst*, 16(1):88–131, 1991.
10. C. M. Ionita and S. L. Osborn. Privilege administration for the role graph model. In *Research Directions in Data and Applications Security*, pages 15–25. Kluwer Academic, 2003.
11. J. Wang and S.L. Osborn. A role-based approach to access control for XML databases. In *Proc. ACM SACMAT*, 2004.
12. D.F. Ferraiolo, R. Sandhu, S. Gavrila, D.R. Kuhn, and R. Chandramouli. Proposed NIST standard for role-based access control. *ACM TISSEC*, 4(3):224–275, 2001.

13. D. F. Ferraiolo, R. Chandramouli, G. Ahn, and S. I. Gavrila. The role control center: features and case studies. In *Proc. Eighth ACM SACMAT* , pages 12–20, New York, NY, USA, 2003. ACM Press.
14. S.L. Osborn, Y. Han, and J. Liu. A methodology for managing roles in legacy systems. In *Proc. 8th ACM SACMAT*, pages 33–40, 2003.
15. H. Wang and S.L. Osborn. An administrative model for role graphs. In I. Ray De Capitani di Vimercati, S. and I. Ray, editors, *Data and Applications Security XVII, Status and Prospects*, pages 302–315. Kluwer, 2004.
16. S.L. Osborn, R. Sandhu, and Q. Munawer. Configuring role-based access control to enforce mandatory and discretionary access control policies. *ACM Trans. Information and System Security*, 3(2):1–23, 2000.
17. S.L. Osborn. Mandatory access control and role-based access control revisited. In *Proceedings Second ACM RBAC Workshop*, pages 31–40, Nov. 1997.

6

XML Security

Claudio A. Ardagna, Ernesto Damiani, Sabrina De Capitani di Vimercati, and Pierangela Samarati

Università degli Studi di Milano
Italia

Summary. The extensible markup language (XML) is a markup language promoted by the World Wide Web consortium (W3C). XML overcomes the limitations of hypertext markup language (HTML) and represents an important opportunity to solve the problem of protecting information distributed on the Web, with the definition of access restrictions directly on the structure and content of the document. This chapter summarizes the key XML security technologies and provides an overview of how they fit together and with XML. It should serve as a roadmap for future research and basis for further exploration of relevant scientific literature and standard specifications.

6.1 Introduction

Accessing information on the global Internet has become an essential requirement of the modern economy. Recently, focus has shifted from access to traditional information stored in WWW sites to access to large *e-services* such as e-government services, remote banking, or airline reservation systems. Security has always been of paramount importance to ensure data protection and transactions integrity and to maintain information privacy and confidentiality. In today's web-based business environment, however, the means for providing that security have changed dramatically. One of the most challenging problems in managing large, distributed, and heterogeneous networked systems is specifying and enforcing security policies regulating interactions between parties and access to services and resources. Superimposing a single pervasive security infrastructure over the Internet turned out to be difficult, due to system heterogeneity and conflicting security requirements.

An essential requirement of new Internet-wide security standards is that they apply to content created using *extensible markup language* (XML) [1, 2]. XML has been adopted widely for a great variety of applications and types of content. Examples of XML-based markup languages are security assertion markup language (SAML) (see [3] for more details) used to exchange security credentials among different parties, geography markup language (GML), wireless markup language (WML), physical markup language (PML), and mathematical markup language (MathML) (`http://www.w3.org/Math/`), just to name a few. XML is also at the basis of interoperability protocols used to integrate applications across the Internet, such as Web services protocols: the Web service technology relies on different XML-based languages such as Simple Object Access Protocol (SOAP), Web Service Definition Language (WSDL), and Universal Description Discovery and Integration (UDDI) [4]. In this scenario, it is necessary to provide integrity, confidentiality and other security benefits to XML documents or portions of them, in a way that does not prevent further processing by standard XML tools.

Traditionally, XML security has developed along two distinct though related lines of research, corresponding to two facets of the XML security notion. The first facet defines XML security as a set of security techniques (access control [5], differential encryption [6], digital signature [7]) tightly coupled with XML to maintain the main features of the XML semi-structured data model while adding to it all necessary security capabilities. This is especially important in XML-based protocols, such as SOAP [8], which are explicitly designed to allow intermediary processing and modification of messages [9]. XML security relies on some legacy security algorithms and tools, but the actual formats used to implement security requirements are specifically aimed at XML applications, supporting common XML technical approaches for managing content, such as specifying content with uniform resource identifier strings (URIs) or using other XML standard definitions like XPath and XQuery for locating portions of XML content. A second important facet of XML security deals with models and languages specifying and exchanging access control policies to generic resources (see Chap. 4 for more details), which may or may not comply with the XML data model [10]. XML appears in fact a natural choice as the basis for the common security policy language, due to the ease with which its syntax and semantics can be extended and the widespread support that it enjoys from all the main platform and tool vendors. To this purpose, several proposals have been introduced for access control to distributed heterogeneous resources from multiple sources. One of the most important XML-based language is extensible access control markup language (XACML) [11, 12], a language for defining rules and policies for controlling access to information. Another security aspect that needs to be taken into consideration is the secure and selective dissemination of XML documents. Often, XML documents contain information with different level of sensitivity, which has to be shared by user communities and managed according to access control policies.

In this chapter, we illustrate recent proposals and ongoing work addressing XML security. The remainder of this chapter is organized as follows. Section 6.2 describes the main characteristics of XML signature and XML encryption. We also briefly review the XML key management specification.

Section 6.3 describes the XACML policy language and the WS-Policy language. Finally, Sect. 6.4 gives our conclusions.

6.2 XML Data Protection

Current security technologies are not sufficient for securing business transactions on the Net. XML represents an important opportunity to solve the problem of protecting information distributed on the Web, by ensuring authenticity, data integrity, and support for nonrepudiation. To this purpose, two important initiatives are *XML signature* [7, 13] and *XML encryption*. XML signature is a joint effort between the World Wide Web consortium (W3C) and the internet engineering task force (IETF), and XML encryption is a W3C effort. In the remainder of this section, we first describe the main characteristics of these two proposals and then briefly present the XML key management specification.

6.2.1 XML Signature

An XML signature is a digital signature obtained by applying a digital signature operation to arbitrary data. The concept of a digital signature is not new and several technologies have already been presented to the community (e.g., public key cryptography standards [14]). However, while the existing technologies allow us to sign only a whole XML document, XML signature provides a means to sign a portion of a document. This functionality is very important in a distributed multi party environment, where the necessity to sign only a portion of a document arises whenever changes and additions to the document are required. For instance, consider a patient record stored in a hospital repository. This record can contain several entries (diagnoses) coming from several doctors. Each doctor wants to take responsibility only over her diagnosis. In this case, every additional diagnosis added to the patient record must be singularly signed. This important feature is supported by XML signature. The extensible nature of XML also allows support for multiple signatures inside the same document. It is also important to highlight that the possibility of signing online a portion of a document and inserting the signature inside the document avoids the development of ad hoc methods to manage persistent signatures, and provides a flexible mechanism to sign and preserve part of the document.

The data to be signed are first digested (a digest is a fixed-length representation of a resource and is created using, for example, a hash function such as SHA-1) and the resulting value is placed in an element, called DigestValue, together with other information. This element is then digested and cryptographically signed. An XML signature is inserted in the signature element and it can be associated with the data objects in three different ways: (i) enveloping signature, where the signature element embedded the data

```
<patient>
  <patientId>123a45d</patientId>
  <diagnosis id="Diagnosis001">...</diagnosis>
  <Signature Id="Signature001" xmlns="http://www.w3.org/2000/09/xmldsig#">
    <SignedInfo>
      <CanonicalizationMethod Algorithm="http://www.w3.org/TR/2001/REC-xml-c14n-20010315"/>
      <SignatureMethod Algorithm="http://www.w3.org/2000/09/xmldsig#dsa-sha1"/>
      <Reference URI="#Diagnosis001">
        <Transforms>
          <Transform Algorithm="http://www.w3.org/TR/2001/REC-xml-c14n-20010315"/>
        </Transforms>
        <DigestMethod Algorithm="http://www.w3.org/2000/09/xmldsig#sha1"/>
        <DigestValue>dh5gf68fhgfjt7FHfdgS55FghG=</DigestValue>
      </Reference>
    </SignedInfo>
    <SignatureValue>MCOCFFrVLtRlk=...</SignatureValue>
    <KeyInfo>...</KeyInfo>
  </Signature>
</patient>
```

Fig. 6.1. An example of internal XML detached signature

to be signed; (ii) enveloped signature, where the **signature** is a child element of the data to be signed; (iii) detached signature, where the **signature** element and the signed data objects are separated. Figure 6.1 illustrates an example of internal detached signature, where a doctor's diagnosis (element **diagnosis**) is signed. As is visible from this example, the **signature** element is inserted within the XML document as a sibling of the signed element. The **signature** element contains three subelements: **SignedInfo**, **SignatureValue**, and **KeyInfo**.

The required **SignedInfo** element contains the information signed and has three subelements: the required **CanonicalizationMethod** element defines the algorithm used to canonicalize the **SignedInfo** element before it is signed or validated; the required **SignatureMethod** element specifies the digital signature algorithm used to generate the signature (DSA-SHA1, in our example); one or more **Reference** elements identify the data that is digested via a URI. The **Reference** element contains: an option **Transforms** element that in turn contains a list of one or more **Transform** elements describing a transformation algorithm used to transform the data before they are digested; the **DigestMethod** element specifies the method used to generate the digest value reported in the **DigestValue** element.

The **SignatureValue** element contains the signature value computed over the **SignedInfo** element.

Finally, the **KeyInfo** element indicates the key that must be used for signature validation.

6.2.2 XML Encryption

XML encryption [6] can be used to encrypt arbitrary data. As for XML signature, the main advantage given by XML encryption is that it supports the

```
<patient>
  <patientId>123a45d</patientId>
  <diagnosis id="Diagnosis001">
    <EncryptedData Type="http://www.w3.org/2001/04/xmlenc#Element"
      xmlns="http://www.w3.org/2001/04/xmlenc#">
      <EncryptionMethod Algorithm='http://www.w3.org/2001/04/xmlenc#tripledes-cbc'/>
      <ds:KeyInfo xmlns:ds="http://www.w3.org/2000/09/xmldsig#">
        ...
      </ds:KeyInfo>
      <CipherData>
        <CipherValue>H343HJS90F</CipherValue>
      </CipherData>
    </EncryptedData>
  </PaymentInfo>
  </diagnosis>
</patient>
```

Fig. 6.2. An example of XML encryption

encryption of specific portions of an XML document rather than the complete document. This feature is particularly important in a business scenario, where different remote parties cooperate to provide a service. A consequence of partial encryption is also support for multiple encryptions. For instance, in a health-care scenario, when a patient goes to a hospital for a visit, her record contains both doctor's diagnosis and information for billing payment. In this case payment information must not be seen by a doctor and diagnosis must not be seen by the billing administrator. This requirement can be obtained by encrypting the two types of information using a different encryption key. XML encryption supports encryption at different granularity levels: document, element, and element-content level. As an example, suppose that we need to encrypt the `diagnosis` specified within a patient record. Figure 6.2 illustrates the XML encryption, where the content of the `diagnosis` element has been replaced by the `EncryptedData` element with attribute `Type`, which specifies the type of the encrypted data (`Element` in the example). The `EncryptedData` element contains: the `EncryptionMethod` element, which keeps track of the algorithm used to encrypt the data object; the `KeyInfo` element, which carries information about the key used to encrypt the data; and the `CipherData` element, which in turn has a subelement, namely `CipherValue`, containing the encrypted value.

6.2.3 XML Key Management Specification (XKMS)

XML signature and XML encryption specifications provide mechanisms to sign and encrypt XML documents in critical e-services scenario and they involve the use of cryptographic keys. The need to integrate public key infrastructure (PKI) [14, 15] and digital certificates with XML-based applications arises and a W3C working group has been developing an open specification named XML key management specification (XKMS) [13, 16].

XKMS specifies a protocol for distributing and registering public keys, used together with XML Signature and XML Encryption. The main goal of

XKMS is to allow the development of XML-based trust services managing PKI-based cryptographic keys. XKMS is also aimed at reducing the complexity of PKI technology by simplifying the addition of security mechanisms in applications and relying on a trusted third party for all the activities related to PKI tasks.

In particular, XKMS specifies protocols for registering, distributing, and processing public keys that are fully integrable with XML signature and XML encryption. At a high level, the protocol defines a set of predefined services, a set of message formats, communication protocols bindings, processing rules, error models, and responsibilities. XKMS is composed of two major components described below.

XML Key Information Service Specification (X-KISS)

X-KISS defines a protocol that manages public key information providing two services, *locate* and *validate*, used to process and validate public keys, respectively. More precisely, X-KISS is the protocol that provides support for processing the ds:KeyInfo element used by both XML signature and XML encryption. Relying on the X-KISS service, the application is not involved in all the activities requiring an interaction with the public key infrastructure, which could require some knowledge about specific standards such as X.509, Simple PKI, and so forth. X-KISS allows the definition of the information that gives to the verifier suggestions on the public key to use. X-KISS is defined as a three-layer service: with the *tier-0* service the processing of element ds:KeyInfo is by the applications; with the *tier-1* service the processing of element ds:KeyInfo is delegated to a service; with the *tier-2* the processing of element ds:KeyInfo is delegated to a service that can also provide additional information on the data specified in the ds:KeyInfo element.

XML Key Registration Service Specification (X-KRSS)

X-KRSS defines a protocol that accepts the registration of public key information and is responsible for the entire key lifecycle management. In particular, X-KRSS supports the following four operations, involved in the management of public keys and provided by a registration service. The *registration* operation allows every entity to register a particular public key, binding it to some information. The generation of a public key could be performed by both a client or the registration server. The registration service can require the client to provide additional information to authenticate the request and if the client has generated the ⟨public, private⟩ key pair itself, the service could require the client to provide a proof of possession of the corresponding private key. The *revocation* operation allows every entity to revoke a previously issued key registration. The *recovering* operation allows every entity to recover the private key associated with a registered public key. Note that the recovering operation could require time and the Registration Service often performs a revoking operation after a recovering request. The *Reissue* operation allows a previously registered key binding to be reissued.

A registration service needs to guarantee the validity of all requests, their authenticity and integrity, and needs to manage proofs of possession of private keys. To this purpose, a registration service sets an authentication policy defining an authentication mechanism that establishes offline a secret with a client.

6.3 XML-Based Access Control Languages

Initially, XML-based access control languages were thought to be only for the protection of resources that were themselves XML files [17, 18, 19, 20]. Recent proposals instead use XML to define languages for expressing protection requirements for any kind of data/resources [3, 12, 21, 22]. Two relevant XML-based access control languages are the extensible access control markup language (XACML) [11, 12] and WS-Policy [22]. Based on WS-Security [23], WS-Policy provides a grammar for expressing Web service policies. XACML is the result of an Organization for the Advancement of Structured Information Standards (OASIS) standardization effort proposing an XML-based language to express and interchange access control policies. XACML is designed to express authorization policies in XML against objects that can themselves be identified in XML. While XACML and WS-Policy share some common characteristics, XACML has the advantage of enjoying an underlying policy model as a basis, resulting in a clean and unambiguous semantics of the language [21]. In the remainder of this section, we illustrate the main features of both XACML and WS-Policy.

6.3.1 XACML

The major functionalities offered by XACML can be summarized as follows.

- *Policy combination.* XACML provides a method for combining policies independently specified. Different entities can then define their policies on the same resource. When an access request on that resource is submitted, the system has to take into consideration all these policies.
- *Combining algorithms.* Since XACML supports the definition of policies independently specified, there is the need for a method for reconciling such a policies when their evaluation is contradictory. XACML supports different combining algorithms, each representing a way of combining multiple decisions into a single decision.
- *Attribute-based restrictions.* XACML supports the definition of policies based on properties (attributes) associated with subjects and resources other than their identities. This allows the definition of powerful policies based on generic properties associated with subjects (e.g., name, address,

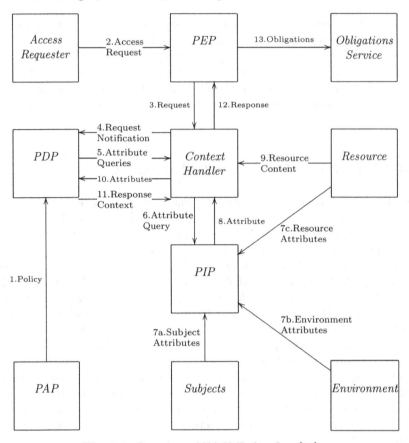

Fig. 6.3. Overview of XACML dataflow [11]

occupation) and resources. XACML includes some built-in operators for comparing attribute values and provides a method of adding nonstandard functions.

- *Multiple subjects.* XACML allows the definition of more than one subject relevant to a decision request.
- *Policy distribution.* Policies can be defined by different parties and enforced at different enforcement points. Also, XACML allows one policy to contain or refer to another.
- *Implementation independence.* XACML provides an abstraction layer that isolates the policy-writer from the implementation details. This means that different implementations should operate in a consistent way, regardless of the implementation itself.
- *Obligations.* XACML provides a method for specifying some actions, called *obligations*, that must be fulfilled in conjunction with the policy enforcement.

A typical scenario involving XACML is when someone wants to perform an action on a resource. For instance, suppose that a physician wants to access a patient's record for inquiry only. The physician would log on to the hospital information system, enter the patient identifier, and retrieve the corresponding record. Data flow through a XACML model can be summarized as follow (see the entities involved and the data flow in Fig. 6.3).

- The requester sends an access request to the *policy evaluation point* (PEP) module, which has to enforce the access decision that will be taken by the policy decision point.
- The PEP module sends the access request to the *context handler* that translates the original request into a canonical format, called *XACML request context*, by querying the *policy information point* (PIP) module. The PIP provides attribute values about the *subject, resource,* and *action.* To this purpose, PIP interacts with the *subjects, resource,* and *environment* modules. The *environment* module provides a set of attributes that are relevant to take an authorization decision and are independent of a particular *subject, resource,* and *action.*
- The context handler sends the XACML request to the *policy decision point* (PDP). The PDP identifies the applicable policies by means of the *policy administration point* (PAP) module and retrieves the required attributes and, possibly, the resource from the context handler.
- The PDP then evaluates the policies and returns the *XACML response context* to the Context Handler. The context handler translates the XACML response context to the native format of the PEP and returns it to the PEP together with an optional set of obligations.
- The PEP fulfils the obligations and, if the access is permitted, it performs the access. Otherwise, the PEP denies access.

As described above, XACML defines a canonical form of the request/response managed by the PDP, allowing policy definition and analysis without taking into account application environment details. Any implementation has to translate the attribute representations in the application environment (e.g., SAML, .NET, Corba [24]) into the XACML context. For instance, an application can provide a SAML [3] message that includes a set of attributes characterizing the subject making the access request. This message has to be converted to the XACML canonical form and, analogously, the XACML decision has then to be converted to the SAML format.

Policy Set, Policy and Rule

XACML relies on a model that provides a *formal* representation of the access control security policy and its working. This modeling phase is essential to ensure a clear and unambiguous language, which could otherwise be subject to different interpretations and uses. The main concepts of interest in the XACML policy language model are *rule, policy,* and *policy set.*

An XACML policy has, as root element, either `Policy` or `PolicySet`. A `PolicySet` is a collection of `Policy` or `PolicySet` elements. An XACML policy consists of a *target*, a set of *rules*, an optional set of *obligations*, and a *rule combining algorithm*. A `Target` basically consists of a simplified set of conditions for the *subject, resource*, and *action* that must be satisfied for a policy to be applicable to a given request. If all the conditions of a `Target` are satisfied, then its associated `Policy` (or `PolicySet`) applies to the request. If a policy applies to all entities of a given type, that is, all subjects, actions, or resources, an empty element, named `AnySubject`, `AnyAction`, `AnyResource`, respectively, is used. The components of a rule are a *target*, an *effect*, and a *condition*. The target defines the set of resources, subjects, and actions to which the rule is intended to apply. The effect of the rule can be `permit` or `deny`. The condition represents a boolean expression that may further refine the applicability of the rule. Note that the `target` element is an optional element: a rule with no target applies to all possible requests. An `Obligation` specifies an action that has to be performed in conjunction with the enforcement of an authorization decision. For instance, an obligation can state that all accesses to medical data have to be logged. Note that only policies that are evaluated and have returned a response of `permit` or `deny` can return obligations. This means that if a policy evaluates to `indeterminate` or `not applicable`, the associated obligations are not considered. Each `Policy` also defines a *rule combining algorithm* used for reconciling the decisions each rule makes. The final decision value, called *the authorization decision*, inserted in the XACML context by the PDP is the value of the policy as defined by the rule combining algorithm. XACML defines different combining algorithms. The *deny overrides* algorithm states that, if there exists a rule that evaluates to `deny` or if all rules evaluate to `not applicable`, the result is `deny`. If all rules evaluate to `permit`, the result is `permit`. If some rules evaluate to `permit` and some evaluate to `not applicable`, the result is `permit`. The *permit overrides* algorithm states that, if there exists a rule that evaluates to `permit`, the result is `permit`. If all rules evaluate to `not applicable`, the result is `deny`. If some rules evaluate to `deny` and some evaluate to `not applicable`, the result is `deny`. The *first applicable* algorithm states that each rule has to be evaluated in the order in which it appears in the `Policy`. For each rule, if the target matches and the conditions evaluate to true, the result is the effect (`permit` or `deny`) of such a rule. The *only-one-applicable* algorithm states that, if more than one rule applies, the result is `indeterminate`. If no rule applies, the result is `not applicable`. If only one policy applies, the result coincides with the result of evaluating that rule. According to the selected combining algorithm, the authorization decision returned to the PEP can be `permit`, `deny`, `not applicable` (when no applicable policies or rules could be found), or `indeterminate` (when some errors occurred during the access control process).

An important feature of XACML is that a rule is based on the definition of attributes corresponding to specific characteristics of a subject, resource, action, or environment. For instance, a physician at a hospital may have the attribute of being a researcher, a specialist in some field, or many other job roles. According to these attributes, the physician can be able to perform different functions within the hospital. Attributes are identified by the `SubjectAttributeDesignator`, `ResourceAttributeDesignator`, `ActionAttributeDesignator`, and `EnvironmentAttributeDesignator` elements. These elements use the `AttributeValue` element to define the requested value of a particular attribute. Alternatively, the `AttributeSelector` element can be used to specify where to retrieve a particular attribute. Note that both the attribute designator and `AttributeSelector` elements can return multiple values. For this reason, XACML provides an attribute type called *bag*, an unordered collection that can contain duplicates values for a particular attribute. In addition, XACML defines other standard value types such as string, boolean, integer, time, and so on. Together with these attribute types, XACML also defines operations to be performed on the different types such as equality operation, comparison operation, string manipulation, and so on.

As an example of XACML policy, suppose that a hospital defines a high-level policy stating that "any user with role `head physician` can read the `patient record` for which she is designated as head physician". Figure 6.4 illustrates the XACML policy corresponding to this high-level policy. The policy applies to requests on the `http://www.example.com/hospital/patient.xsd` resource. The policy has one rule with a target that requires a `read` action, a subject with role `head physician` and a condition that applies only if the subject is the head physician of the requested patient. For more details about roles and role-based access control (RBAC) see Chap. 5.

XACML Request and Response

XACML also defines a standard format for expressing requests and responses. The original request submitted by the PEP is then translated through the context handler in a canonical form, then forwarded to the PDP to be evaluated. Such a request contains attributes for the subject, resource, action, and, optionally, for the environment. Each request includes exactly one set of attributes for the resource and action and at most one set of environment attributes. There may be multiple sets of subject attributes each of which is identified by a category URI.

A response element contains one or more results corresponding to an evaluation. Each result contains three elements, namely `Decision`, `Status`, and `Obligations`. The `Decision` element specifies the authorization decision (i.e., `permit`, `deny`, `indeterminate`, `not applicable`), the `Status` element indicates if some error occurred during the evaluation process, and the optional `Obligations` element states the obligations that the PEP must fulfil. For instance, suppose that a user, belonging to role `head physician` and with ID 354850273 wants to read resource `www.example.com/hospital/patient.xsd`

```
<Policy PolicyId="Pol1"
  RuleCombiningAlgId="urn:oasis:names:tc:xacml:1.0:
  rule-combining-algorithm:permit-overrides">
  <Target>
    <Subjects> <AnySubject/> </Subjects>
    <Resources>
      <Resource>
        <ResourceMatch MatchId="urn:oasis:names:tc:xacml:1.0:function:stringmatch">
          <AttributeValue DataType="http://www.w3.org/2001/XMLSchema#string">
            http://www.example.com/hospital/patient.xsd
          </AttributeValue>
          <ResourceAttributeDesignator
            DataType="http://www.w3.org/2001/XMLSchema#string"
            AttributeId="urn:oasis:names:tc:xacml:1.0:resource:target-namespace"/>
        </ResourceMatch>
      </Resource>
    </Resources>
    <Actions> <AnyAction/> </Actions>
  </Target>
  <Rule RuleId="ReadRule" Effect="Permit">
    <Target>
      <Subjects>
        <Subject>
          <SubjectMatch MatchId="urn:oasis:names:tc:xacml:1.0:function:string-equal">
            <AttributeValue DataType="http://www.w3.org/2001/XMLSchema#string">
              head physician
            </AttributeValue>
            <SubjectAttributeDesignator
              AttributeId= "urn:oasis:names:tc:xacml:2.0:example:attribute:role"
              DataType="http://www.w3.org/2001/XMLSchema#string"/>
          </SubjectMatch>
        </Subject>
      </Subjects>
      <Resources> <AnyResource/> </Resources>
      <Actions>
        <Action>
          <ActionMatch MatchId="urn:oasis:names:tc:xacml:1.0:function:string-equal">
            <AttributeValue DataType="http://www.w3.org/2001/XMLSchema#string">
              read
            </AttributeValue>
            <ActionAttributeDesignator
              DataType="http://www.w3.org/2001/XMLSchema#string"
              AttributeId="urn:oasis:names:tc:xacml:1.0:action:action-id"/>
          </ActionMatch>
        </Action>
      </Actions>
    </Target>
    <Condition FunctionId="urn:oasis:names:tc:xacml:1.0:function:string-equal">
      <SubjectAttributeDesignator DataType="http://www.w3.org/2001/XMLSchema#string"
        AttributeId="urn:oasis:names:tc:xacml:1.0:subject:head-physicianID"/>
      <AttributeSelector RequestContextPath="/ctx:Request/ctx:Resource/ctx:
        ResourceContent/hospital:record/hospital:patient/hospital:
        patient-head-physicianID"
        DataType="http://www.w3.org/2001/XMLSchema#string"/ >
    </Condition>
  </Rule>
</Policy>
```

Fig. 6.4. An example XACML policy

with patient ID equal to 123a45d. This request is compared with the XACML policy in Fig. 6.4. The result of this evaluation is that the user is allowed (permit) to access the requested patient record.

6.3.2 WS-Policy

Web service policy framework (WS-Policy) provides a generic model and a flexible and extensible grammar for describing and communicating the policies of a Web service [22]. The WS-Policy includes a set of general messaging related assertions defined in WS-PolicyAssertions [25] and a set of security policy assertions related to supporting the WS-Security specification defined in WS-SecurityPolicy [26]. In addition, WS-PolicyAttachment [27] defines how to attach these policies to Web services or other subjects such as service locators. A WS-Policy is a collection of one or more *policy assertions* that represent an individual preference, requirement, capability, or other properties that have to be satisfied to access the *policy subject* associated with the assertion. The XML representation of a policy assertion is called *a policy expression*.[1] Element `wsp:Policy` is the container for a policy expression. Policy assertions are typed and can be *simple* or *complex*. A simple policy can be compared to other assertions of the same type without any special consideration about the semantics' assertion. A complex policy requires comparison by means of type-specific assertions. The assertion type can be defined in such a way that the assertion is parameterized. For instance, an assertion describing the maximum acceptable password size (number of characters) would likely accept an integer parameter indicating the maximum character count. In contrast, an assertion that simply indicates that a password is required does not need parameters; its presence is enough to convey the assertion. Every policy assertion could be defined `optional`. WS-Policy provides an element, called `wsp:PolicyReference`, that can be used for sharing policy expressions between different policies. Conceptually, when there is a reference, it is replaced by the content of the referenced policy expression. WS-Policy also provides two operators, namely `wsp:All` and `wsp:ExactlyOne`, that can be used for combining policy assertions. The first operator requires that all of its child elements be satisfied; the second operator requires that exactly one of its child elements be satisfied. In case no operator is specified, the `wsp:All` operator is taken as default.

Figure 6.5(a) illustrates a simple example of policy stating that the access is granted if exactly one security token among the following is provided: a Kerberos certificate and a UsernameToken with Username `Bob`; an X509 certificate and a UsernameToken with Username `Bob`; an X509 certificate and a UsernameToken with Username `Alice`. The third option corresponds to the referred policy, called `opts`, illustrated in Fig. 6.5(b).

---

[1] Note that using XML to represent policies facilitates interoperability between heterogeneous platforms and Web service infrastructures.

```
<wsp:Policy xmlns:wsp="..." xmlns:wsse="...">        <wsp:Policy xmlns:wsse="..."
 <wsp:ExactlyOne>                                     xmlns:ns="...">
  <wsp:All>                                            <wsp:All wsu:Id="opts">
   <wsse:SecurityToken>                                 <wsse:SecurityToken>
    <wsse:TokenType>wsse:Kerberosv5TGT</wsse:TokenType>  <wsse:TokenType>
   </wsse:SecurityToken>                                   wsse:X509v3
   <wsse:SecurityToken>                                 </wsse:TokenType>
    <wsse:TokenType>wsse:UsernameToken</wsse:TokenType> </wsse:SecurityToken>
    <wsse:Username>Bob</wsse:Username>                  <wsse:SecurityToken>
   </wsse:SecurityToken>                                 <wsse:TokenType>
  </wsp:All>                                              wsse:UsernameToken
  <wsp:All>                                             </wsse:TokenType>
   <wsse:SecurityToken>                                 <wsse:Username>
    <wsse:TokenType>wsse:X509v3</wsse:TokenType>          Alice
   </wsse:SecurityToken>                                 </wsse:Username>
   <wsse:SecurityToken>                                </wsse:SecurityToken>
    <wsse:TokenType>wsse:UsernameToken</wsse:TokenType> </wsp:All>
    <wsse:Username>Bob</wsse:Username>                </wsp:Policy>
   </wsse:SecurityToken>
  </wsp:All>
  <wsp:PolicyReference URI="#opts" />
 </wsp:ExactlyOne>
</wsp:Policy>
        (a)                                                            (b)
```

Fig. 6.5. A simple example of WS-Policy (a) and the corresponding referred WS-Policy (b)

6.4 Conclusions

In this chapter we introduced the most important XML security technologies. We described two important initiatives, namely XML signature and XML encryption, facing the problem of protecting information distributed on the Internet. We then briefly reviewed the XML key management specification, which provides facilities for the management of public keys used together with XML signature and XML encryption. We concluded the chapter with the description of two XML-based access control languages, namely XACML and WS-Policy, discussing their peculiarities and their principal features.

6.5 Acknowledgements

This work was supported in part by the European Union within the PRIME Project in the FP6/IST Programme under contract IST-2002-507591 and by the Italian MIUR within the KIWI and MAPS projects.

References

1. Apache XML Project. http://xml.apache.org/.
2. N. Bradley (2002). The XML Companion. Addison Wesley, 3rd edition.

3. OASIS Security Services TC. http://www.oasis-open.org/committees/tc_home.php?wg_abbrev=security.

4. E. Newcomer (2002). Understanding Web Services: XML, WSDL, SOAP, and UDDI. Addison Wesley.

5. P. Samarati, S. De Capitani di Vimercati (2001). Access control: Policies, models, and mechanisms. In Focardi R, Gorrieri R, editors, *Foundations of Security Analysis and Design*, LNCS 2171. Springer-Verlag.

6. XML Encryption Syntax and Processing, W3C Recommendation (2002). http://www.w3.org/TR/xmlenc-core/.

7. XML-Signature Syntax and Processing, W3C Recommendation (2002). http://www.w3.org/TR/xmldsig-core/.

8. D. Box et al. (2000). Simple Object Access Protocol (SOAP) version 1.1. http://www.w3.org/TR/SOAP.

9. E. Damiani, S. De Capitani di Vimercati, S. Paraboschi, P. Samarati (2002). Securing SOAP E-services. International Journal of Information Security (IJIS), 1(2):100–115.

10. E. Damiani, S. De Capitani di Vimercati, P. Samarati (2002). Towards securing XML web services. In Proc. of the 2002 ACM Workshop on XML Security, Washington, DC, USA.

11. OASIS eXtensible Access Control Markup Language TC. http://www.oasis-open.org/committees/tc_home.php?wg_abbrev=xacml.

12. T. Moses (2005). eXtensible Access Control Markup Language (XACML) version 2.0. http://docs.oasis-open.org/xacml/2.0/access_control-xacml-2.0-core-spec-os.pdf.

13. B. Galbraith, W. Hankinson, A. Hiotis, M. Janakiraman, D.V. Prasad, R. Trivedi, D. Whitney (2002). Professional Web Services Security. Wrox Press.

14. A. Arsenault, S. Turner (2002). Internet X.509 Public Key Infrastructure: Roadmap. Internet Draft, Internet Engineering Task Force.

15. A. Essiari, S. Mudumbai, M.R. Thompson (2003). Certificate-Based Authorization Policy in a PKI Environment. ACM Transactions on Information and System Security, 6(4):566–588.

16. W. Ford et al (2001). XML Key Management Specification (XKMS), W3C Note. http://www.w3.org/TR/xkms/.

17. E. Damiani, S. De Capitani di Vimercati, S. Paraboschi, P. Samarati (2000). Securing XML documents. In Proc. of the 2000 International Conference on Extending Database Technology (EDBT2000), Konstanz, Germany.

18. E. Damiani, S. De Capitani di Vimercati, S. Paraboschi, P. Samarati (2002). A fine-grained access control system for XML documents. ACM Transactions on Information and System Security (TISSEC), 5(2):169–202.

19. A. Gabillon (2004). An authorization model for XML databases. In Proc. of the ACM Workshop Secure Web Services, George Mason University, Fairfax, VA, USA.

20. A. Gabillon, E. Bruno (2001). Regulating access to XML documents. In Proc. of the Fifteenth Annual IFIP WG 11.3 Working Conference on Database Security, Niagara on the Lake, Ontario, Canada.

21. C.A. Ardagna, E. Damiani, S. De Capitani di Vimercati, P. Samarati (2004). XML-based access control languages. Information Security Technical Report.

22. S. Bajaj et al (2004). Web Services Policy Framework (WS-Policy). http://msdn.microsoft.com/library/default.asp?url=/library/en-us/dnglobspec/html/ws-policy.asp.

23. B. Atkinson, G. Della-Libera et all (2002). Web services security (WS-Security). http://msdn.microsoft.com/library/en-us/dnglobspec/html/ws-security.asp.
24. Object Management Group.   The CORBA Security Service Specification. ftp://ftp.omg.org/pub/docs/ptc.
25. D. Box et al. (2003). Web Services Policy Assertions Language (WS-PolicyAssertions)   version   1.1.   http://msdn.microsoft.com/library/en-us/dnglobspec/html/ws-policyassertions.asp.
26. G. Della-Libera et al (2005). Web Services Security Policy Language (WS-SecurityPolicy).   http://msdn.microsoft.com/library/en-us/dnglobspec/html/ws-securitypolicy.pdf.
27. S. Bajaj et al. (2006). Web Services Policy Attachment (WS-PolicyAttachment) version 1.2.   http://msdn.microsoft.com/library/en-us/dnglobspec/html/ws-policyattachment.asp.

7

Database Security

Elisa Bertino, Ji-Won Byun, Ashish Kamra

Purdue University
USA

Summary. As organizations increase their reliance on information systems for daily business, they become more vulnerable to security breaches. Though a number of techniques, such as encryption and electronic signatures, are currently available to protect data when transmitted across sites, a truly comprehensive approach for data protection must also include mechanisms for enforcing access control policies based on data contents, subject qualifications and characteristics, and other relevant contextual information, such as time. It is well understood today that the semantics of data must also be taken into account in order to specify effective access control policies. Also, techniques for data integrity and availability specifically tailored to database systems must be adopted. In this respect, over the years the database security community has developed a number of different techniques and approaches to assure data confidentiality, integrity, and availability. However, despite such advances, the database security area faces several new challenges. Factors such as the evolution of security concerns, the 'disintermediation' of access to data, new computing paradigms and applications, such as grid-based computing and on-demand business, have introduced both new security requirements and new contexts in which to apply and possibly extend current approaches. In this chapter, we first survey the most relevant concepts underlying the notion of database security and summarize the most well-known techniques. We then discuss current challenges for database security and some preliminary approaches that address some of these challenges.

7.1 Introduction

Today, many organizations rely on database systems as the key data management technology for various tasks, such as day-to-day operations and critical decision-making. This implies that security breaches to database systems not only affect a single user or application, but may also lead to catastrophic consequences for the entire organization. The increasing adoption of web-based applications and information systems has further increased the risk exposure of databases, and, thus, the demand for secure database systems today is stronger than ever.

Security breaches are typically categorized as *unauthorized data observation, incorrect data modification,* and *data unavailability.* Unauthorized data observation results in the disclosure of information to users not entitled to gain access to such information. All organizations, ranging from commercial organizations to social organizations, in a variety of domains such as health care and homeland protection, may suffer heavy losses from both financial and human points of view as a consequence of unauthorized data observation. Incorrect modifications of data, either intentional or unintentional, result in an incorrect database state. Any use of incorrect data may also result in heavy losses for the organization. When data is unavailable, information crucial for the proper functioning of the organization is not readily available when needed. Thus, a complete solution to data security must meet the following three requirements: 1) *secrecy* or *confidentiality* refers to the protection of data against unauthorized disclosure, 2) *integrity* refers to the prevention of unauthorized and improper data modification, and 3) *availability* refers to the prevention and recovery from hardware and software errors and from malicious data access denials making the database system unavailable. These three requirements arise in practically all application environments. Consider a database that stores health care information of a hospital. It is important that patient records not be released to unauthorized users, that records are modified only by the users that are properly authorized, and that patient history is available to the doctors at any time of the day.

The security of data is ensured collectively by various components of a database management system (DBMS). In particular, data confidentiality is ensured by an *access control mechanism* . Whenever a user tries to access a data object to perform a particular action, the access control mechanism checks whether or not the user has an authorization to perform the action on the object. Authorizations are granted to users according to the access control policies of the organization, usually by a security administrator. Data confidentiality is further enhanced by the use of encryption techniques, applied to data when being stored on secondary storage or transmitted on a network. Recently, the use of encryption techniques has gained a lot of interest in the context of outsourced data management; in such contexts, the main issue is how to perform operations, such as queries, on encrypted data [1]. Data integrity is jointly ensured by the access control mechanism and by semantic integrity constraints. Whenever a subject tries to modify some data, the access control mechanism verifies that the user has the right to modify the data, and the semantic integrity subsystem verifies that the updated data are semantically correct. Semantic correctness is verified by a set of conditions, or predicates, that must be verified against the database state. To detect tampering, data can be digitally signed. Finally, the recovery subsystem and the concurrency control mechanism ensure that data is available and correct despite hardware and software failures and accesses from concurrent application programs. Data availability, especially for data that are available on the Web, can be further strengthened by the use of techniques protecting against denial-of-service (DoS) attacks, such as the ones based on machine learning techniques [2].

In addition, it is important to note that data need to be protected not only from external threats, but also from *insider* threats. Insiders can be defined as trusted employees of an organization who are given authorizations to the organization's proprietary and sensitive information but may abuse such authorizations for their own benefits. Insider threats have long been recognized as a serious problem in security [3, 4]. Not only are insider attacks more pervasive, but they are also more destructive. Insiders usually have wider access to sensitive resources, deeper knowledge of internal systems, and greater opportunity to carry out their plans. One possible approach to prevent such attacks is to apply intrusion detection techniques to database queries. For instance, such techniques may detect unusual queries issued by employees and alert security officers to take necessary actions.

The remainder of this chapter is organized as follows. In Sect. 7.2, we discuss the evolution of various access control mechanisms for databases and their usage in popular relational database management products such as Oracle, DB2, and MySQL. We then present some of the emerging research trends in the area of database security in Sect. 7.3 and conclude in Sect. 7.4.

7.2 Access Control Mechanisms

Research efforts in the field of database security have been mainly centered around the confidentiality requirement, and access control models and techniques that provide high-assurance confidentiality. In this section, we will first review some of the basics concepts behind different access control models and authorization mechanisms related to DBMSs. Then we will present a brief survey of various access control models currently employed to protect data, and the ongoing research to extend them. Because, however, access control deals with controlling accesses to the data, the discussion is also relevant to the access control aspect of integrity, that is, enforcing that no unauthorized modifications to data occur. It is also important to note that an access control mechanism must rely for its proper functioning on some authentication mechanism. Such a mechanism identifies users and confirms their identities. Moreover, data may be encrypted when transmitted over a network in the case of distributed systems. Some databases like Oracle 10g also support an authentication system based on public key infrastructure [5]. Both authentication and encryption techniques are widely discussed in the current literature on computer network security and we refer the reader to [6] for details on such topics.

Early research in the area of access control models and confidentiality for DBMSs focussed on the development of two different classes of models, based on the *discretionary access control* policy and on the *mandatory access control* policy[1]. This early research was cast in the framework of relational database systems. The relational data model, being a declarative high-level model specifying the logical structure of data, made the development of simple declarative languages for the specification of access control policies possible. These earlier models and the discretionary models in particular, introduced some important principles [7] that set apart access control models for database systems from access control models adopted by operating systems and file systems. The first principle was that access control models for databases should be expressed in terms of the logical data model; thus authorizations for a relational database should be expressed in terms of relations, relation attributes, and tuples. The second principle is that for databases, in addition to name-based access control, where the protected objects are specified by giving their names, *content-based access control* has to be supported. Content-based access control allows the system to determine whether to give or deny access to a data item based on the contents of the data item. The development of content-based access control models, which are, in general, based on the specification of conditions against data contents, was made easy in relational databases by the availability of declarative query languages, such as SQL.

In the area of discretionary access control models for relational database systems, an important early contribution was the development of the System R access control model [8, 9], which strongly influenced access control models of current commercial relational DBMSs. Some key features of this model included the notion of decentralized authorization administration, dynamic grant and revoke of authorizations, and the use of views for supporting content-based authorizations. Also, the initial format of well-known commands for grant and revoke of authorizations, that are today part of the SQL standard, were developed as part of this model. Later research proposals have extended this basic model with a variety of features, such as negative authorization [10], role-based and task-based authorization [11, 12, 13], temporal authorization [14], and context-aware authorization [15].

Discretionary access control models have, however, a weakness in that they do not impose any control on how information is propagated and used once it has been accessed by subjects authorized to do so. This weakness makes discretionary access controls vulnerable to malicious attacks, such as Trojan horses embedded in application programs. A Trojan horse is a program with an apparent or actually useful function, which contains some hidden functions exploiting the legitimate authorizations of the invoking process. Sophisticated Trojan horses may leak information by means of covert channels, enabling illegal access to data. A covert channel is any component or feature of a system that is misused to encode or represent information for unauthorized transmission, without violating the stated access control policy. A large variety of components or features can be exploited to establish covert channels, includ-

---

[1] These models have been described in detail in Chap. 4 of this book; hence discussion will be limited to their applicability to DBMSs.

ing the system clock, operating system interprocess communication primitives, error messages, the existence of particular file names, the concurrency control mechanism, and so forth. The area of mandatory access control and multilevel database systems tried to address such problems through the development of access control models based on information classification, some of which were also incorporated in commercial products. Early mandatory access control models were mainly developed for military applications and were very rigid and suited, at best, for closed and controlled environments. There was considerable debate among security researchers concerning how to eliminate covert channels while maintaining the essential properties of the relational model. In particular, the concept of polyinstantiation, that is, the presence of multiple copies with different security levels of the same tuple in a relation, was developed and articulated in this period [16, 17]. Because of the lack of applications and commercial success, companies developing multilevel DBMSs discontinued their production several years ago. Covert channels were also widely investigated with considerable focus on the concurrency control mechanisms that, by synchronizing transactions running at different security levels, would introduce an obvious covert channel. However, solutions developed in the research arena to the covert channel problem were not incorporated into commercial products. Interestingly, however, today we are witnessing a multilevel security reprise [18], driven by the strong security requirements arising in a number of civilian applications. Companies have thus recently reintroduced such systems. This is the case, for example, of the Labeled Oracle, a multilevel relational DBMS marketed by Oracle, which has much more flexibility in comparison to earlier multilevel secure DBMSs. Early approaches to access control have since been extended in the context of advanced DBMSs, such as object-oriented DBMSs and object-relational DBMSs, and other advanced data management systems and applications, such as data made available through the Web and represented through XML, digital libraries and multimedia data, data warehousing systems, and workflow systems. Most of these systems are characterized by data models that are much richer than the relational model; typically, such extended models include semantic modelling notions such as inheritance hierarchies, aggregation, methods, and stored procedures. An important requirement arising from those applications is that it is not only the data that needs to be protected, but also the database schema may contain sensitive information and, thus, accesses to the schema need to be filtered according to some access control policies. Even though early relational DBMSs did not support authorizations with respect to schema information, today several products support such features. In such a context, access control policies may also need to be protected because they may reveal sensitive information. As such, one may need to define access control policies the objects of which are not user data, rather they are other access control policies. Another relevant characteristic of advanced applications is that they often deal with multimedia data, for which the automatic interpretation of contents is much more difficult, and they are in most cases accessed by a variety of users external to the system boundaries, such as through Web interfaces. As a consequence both discretionary and mandatory access control models developed for relational DBMSs had to be properly extended to deal with additional modelling concepts. Also, these models often need to rely on metadata information in order to support content-based access control for multimedia data and to support credential-based access control policies to deal with external users. Recent efforts in this direction include the development of comprehensive access control models for XML[2] [19, 20].

In the remainder of this section, we first discuss in detail content-based access control mechanisms as applicable to RDBMSs. After that, we briefly discuss access control models for object-based database systems. Lastly, we present a glimpse of some of the access control features present in popular RDBMS products like Oracle, DB2 and MySQL.

7.2.1 Content-Based and Fine-Grained Access Control

Content-based access control is an important requirement that any access control mechanism for use in a data management system should satisfy. Essentially, content-based access control requires that access control decisions be based on data contents. Support for this type of access control has been made possible by the fact that SQL is a language for which most operations for data management, such as queries, are based on declarative conditions against data contents. In particular, the most common mechanism, adopted by relational DBMSs to support content-based access control is based on the use of *views*. A view can be considered as a dynamic window able to select subsets of column and rows of a table. These subsets are specified by defining a query, referred to as a *view definition query*, which is associated with the name of the view. Whenever a query is issued against a view, the query is modified through an operation called *view composition* by replacing the view referenced in the query with its definition. There are several advantages to such an approach. First, content-based access control policies based on views can be expressed at a high level in a language consistent with the query language. Second, modifications to the data do not need modification to the access control policies; if new data are entered that satisfy a given policy, these data will be automatically included as part of the data returned by the corresponding view.

Recently, pushed by requirements for fine-grained mechanisms that are able to support access control at the tuple level, new approaches have been investigated. The reason is that conventional view mechanisms, like the ones sketched above, have a number of shortcomings. A naive solution to enforce fine-grained authorization would require the specification of a view for each tuple or part of a tuple that is to be protected. Moreover, because access control policies are often different for different users, the number of views would

---

[2] Refer to Chap. 6 of this book for details

further increase. Alternative approaches that address some of these issues have been proposed, based on the idea that queries are written against the base tables and, then, automatically rewritten by the system against the view available to the user. The Oracle virtual private database mechanism [15] and the Truman model [21] are examples of such approaches. These approaches, however, introduce other problems, such as inconsistencies between what the user expects to see and what the system returns; in some cases, they return incorrect results to queries rather than rejecting them as unauthorized. Thus, a lot more research effort is needed to address such problems.

7.2.2 Access Control Models for Object-Based Database Systems

Existing access control models, defined for relational DBMSs, are not suitable for an object-based database system because of the wide differences in data models. An access control system for object-based database systems should take into account all semantic modelling constructs commonly found in object-oriented data models, such as composite objects, versions, and inheritance hierarchies. We can summarize these two observations by saying that the increased complexity in the data model corresponds to an increased articulation in the types and granularity of protection objects. A key feature of both discretionary and mandatory access control models for object-based systems is that they take into account all modelling aspects related to objects. We refer the reader to [22] for a detailed discussion on a discretionary access control model for the Orion object-oriented DBMS.

The application of a typical MAC model to object-based systems in not straightforward, due to the semantic richness of object data models. To date the problem of MAC models for object-based database systems has been investigated only in the context of object-oriented databases [23]; no work has been reported dealing specifically with object-relational databases.

7.2.3 Access Control in Commercial DBMSs

In this section, we briefly describe some of the common access control mechanisms present in popular RDBMSs products; namely, Oracle [5], DB2 [24], and MySQL [25]. We note that the access control mechanisms presented in each of these DBMSs follow neither the standard RBAC nor the pure DAC models. Instead, the access control features in these systems incorporate a combination of the access control models that have been discussed so far.

Oracle 10g Database Server

The basic unit of authorization in a Oracle database is a *privilege*. A *privilege* is defined as a right to execute a particular type of SQL statement or to access another user's object. There are six major categories of privileges present, namely *system privileges, schema object privileges, table privileges, view privileges, procedure privileges, type privileges* [5]. Such privileges are granted to users in two different ways; either they can be granted explicitly or they can be granted to a role and then the role can be granted to users. There are two types of roles defined in Oracle: *user roles*, which are granted to a group of database users with common privilege requirements, and *application roles*, which contain all necessary privileges to run a database application. An application role can be granted to other roles or users who use that application. An application can also have several different roles, with each role assigned a different set of privileges that allow for more or less data access while using the application. Privileges can be granted to a role, and any role can be granted to any database user or to another role (but not to itself).

To provide selective availability of privileges, Oracle database allows applications and users to enable and disable roles. Each role granted to a user is, at any given time, either enabled or disabled. To keep track of all the privileges assigned to a user in a given session, Oracle introduces the concept of *security domains*. Each role and user has its own unique security domain. The security domain of a role includes the privileges granted to the role plus those privileges granted to any roles that are granted to the role. The security domain of a user includes privileges on all schema objects in the corresponding schema, the privileges granted to the user, and the privileges of roles granted to the user that are currently enabled. Note that a role can be simultaneously enabled for one user and disabled for another. Oracle supports role hierarchies (as a role can be granted to another role), but does not provide any support for separation of duty constraints presented in the standard RBAC model [26].

As previously discussed, support for fine-grained access control is provided by the Oracle virtual private database (VPD) mechanism [15]. The key idea underlying VPD is that a database object can be associated with VPD policies. Each VPD policy is expressed as a PL/SQL function and returns a predicate when the associated object is to be accessed by a query. The returned predicate is added to the conditions of the 'WHERE' clause with a conjunction (i.e., AND); thereby enforcing row-level access control. Although VPD feature provides a powerful and flexible access control, it also has some shortcomings. First, as VPD policies are not declarative, the formal analysis of VPD policies cannot be done. Moreover, without careful administration, VPD policies can cause many undesirable effects such as cyclic policy invocations.

IBM DB2 UDB 8.2

Authorization in DB2 is performed using DB2 facilities. DB2 tables and configuration files are used to record the permissions associated with each *authorization name*. The authorization name of an authenticated user, and those of groups (collection of users) to which the user belongs, are compared with the recorded permissions. Based on this comparison, DB2 decides whether to allow the requested access. A DB2 universal database (UDB) records two types of permissions for users: *privileges* and *authority levels*. A privilege defines a single permission for an authorization name, enabling a user to create or access database resources. Authority levels provide a method of grouping privileges and control over higher-level database manager maintenance and utility operations. *Database authorities* enable users to perform activities at the database level. Privileges, authority levels, and database authorities can be used together to control access to the database manager and its database objects. Users (or groups) can access only those objects for which they have the required privilege, authority level, or database authority, which DB2 determines when it performs an authorization check for an authenticated user. A user or group can be authorized for any combination of individual privileges or authorities.

Thus we see that DB2 essentially follows its own kind of access control model with minimal support for RBAC features like role hierarchies and separation of duty constraints.

MySQL 5.1

MySQL has a very simple access control mechanism compared to that of Oracle or DB2. Privileges to use databases resources are assigned to users and stored in system tables. For every action performed by the user, an in-memory copy of the privilege tables is checked to determine if the user possesses the privileges to perform that action. There is no concept of roles or even grouping of privileges (as in DB2). Thus, as compared to the access control models discussed in this chapter, MySQL has the most rudimentary access control system in place.

7.3 Emerging Research Trends

Besides the historical research that has been conducted in database security, several new areas are emerging as active research topics. A first relevant recent research direction is motivated by the trend of considering databases as a service that can be outsourced to external companies [1]. An important issue in this regard is the development of query-processing techniques for encrypted data. Several specialized encryption techniques have been proposed, such as the order-preserving encryption technique by Agrawal et al. [27]. A second research direction deals with privacy-preserving techniques for databases, an area recently investigated to a considerable extent. We leave discussion on this aspect of database security to the later chapters in this book.

In the remainder of this section, we present some of the challenges faced by the database security community for which satisfactory solutions are still far from sight. These include, but are not limited to, protecting databases from insider threats, ensuring high-integrity databases and securing Web-enabled databases.

7.3.1 Detecting Insider Threats

As organizations embrace more and more information technologies for their day-to-day operations, control has invariably shifted into the hands of some key individuals who manage and use this information technology infrastructure. For example, employees like database administrators, who manage an organization's database systems, control virtually all sensitive and proprietary information. This has been addressed for a long time in the research community as the problem of *insider threats*. The problem is a nontrivial problem to address because an organization must devise ways to secure its information systems from the very personnel it trusts to secure them. In this section, we present some of the work which is being carried out to address the problem of insider threats to databases.

It is important to understand that defining fine-grained access control policies or ensuring the principle of least privilege cannot completely address this problem. A database administrator (or someone with a similar role) by virtue of its role controls almost all resources of a database including its security policies. This leads to the classic catch-22 situation where a person is trying to define security policies for himself. This can obviously be easily subverted with even a little bit of determination. Moreover, apart from database administrators, even users who have limited privileges over the database can abuse them to gain access to sensitive information. As an example, suppose that a clerk in a hospital usually accesses the tables and corresponding attributes containing the addresses of specific patients to whom billing information need to be send. Suppose now, that suddenly this clerk issues a query accessing all attributes from the relevant tables and retrieving all patient addresses at once. This is a typical example of an employee exercising their privileges to access information which they would not have accessed normally.

One promising approach is based on the use of machine learning techniques for anomaly detection. Anomaly detection techniques have been studied extensively in the overall context of intrusion detection for networks and operating systems. The key idea is to create profiles of normal subject behavior and then raise alarms for activities deviating from the normal profiles of subjects [28]. Applying the same principle to databases, the idea is to create behaviorial profiles of external entities (i.e. users and applications) interacting with a database and then raise alarms for activities that deviate from these profiles. An approach along these lines has been developed by Bertino et al. [29]. In this paper, profiles based on database roles are formed by extracting table and column access information from the SQL queries submitted to the database. A naive Bayes classifier is then trained on this data. For every new query under observation, the classifier predicts the role based on the maximum aposteriori probability (MAP) rule. If the predicted role does not match the actual role of the query, an alarm is raised. The motivation for using roles as classes for classification is the observation that users with the same role in an organization tend to behave in a similar manner. Thus using roles reduces the number of classes to be discriminated against for the classifier in an effective manner. Their approach has, however, three main shortcomings. First, only the projection information is extracted from queries, information from selection clauses are not recorded. This makes it difficult to counter attacks such as SQL injection, which tend to modify the query predicate to gain unauthorized access to a database. Second, contextual information like IP address of login and temporal information like time of login, frequency of login and so forth has not been considered while building profiles. These features could be potentially useful when defining normal behavior for users or applications. Lastly, an important observation is that for many organizations, access to databases is mediated through application programs. Hence, it would be interesting to create profiles of not only database users but also of application programs themselves, that interact with the database on users' behalf.

7.3.2 High-Integrity Databases

Integrity is a fundamental requirement for security of computer systems, and for DBMS, integrity of data (or data integrity) is especially crucial. Without the assurance of data integrity, any information extracted from databases is not useful as it cannot be trusted with sufficient confidence. It is also important to observe that data integrity can be undermined not only by errors introduced by users and applications, but also by malicious subjects who may inject inaccurate data into a database with the goal of deceiving other subjects.

Despite the significance of the issue and ongoing research efforts theoretical/technical solutions available today for data integrity are still limited. A key difficulty comes from the fact that, unlike confidentiality and availability, the concept of integrity is difficult to grasp with a precise definition. In fact, integrity often means different things to different people [30]. The most widely accepted definition of integrity is perhaps *the prevention of unauthorized and improper data modification* [31, 32]. This definition also seems to coincide with the primary goal of Clark and Wilson's approach, "preventing fraud and error" in the commercial environment [33]. Another well-known interpretation of integrity concerns with the *quality or trustworthiness of data* [34], on which Biba's integrity model is based [35]. Inspection of mechanisms provided by database management systems (DBMS) suggests yet another view of integrity. Many commercial DBMSs today enable system administrator to express a variety of conditions, often referred to as integrity constraints, that data must satisfy [36]. Such constraints are used mainly for *data consistency and correctness*.

This multifaceted concept of integrity makes it challenging to adequately address integrity, as different definitions require different approaches. For instance, Clark and Wilson addressed the issue of improper data modification by enforcing "well-formed transaction" and "separation of duty" [33], whereas Biba's integrity model prevents possible data corruption by limiting information flow among data objects [35]. On the other hand, many current DBMSs ensure data consistency by enforcing various constraints, such as key, referential, domain, and entity constraints [36].

In order to provide a comprehensive approach to the problem of data integrity, we thus need a multi-faceted solution. Such a solution must mirror the generally accepted security approach according to which we need to provide tools and mechanisms for: preventing and controlling security breaches; monitoring and validating systems for detecting possible security incidents; and for recovering from security incidents, as no security mechanisms, or combination of them, can offer complete protection. We believe that we need to specialize such an approach to integrity. Also, viable solutions to integrity must take into account the fact that integrity requirements may vary depending on the organizations and on a large number of factors. Therefore, we do not need integrity systems with built-in policies; we need flexible systems supporting the specifications and enforcement of application-dependent integrity policies. A comprehensive solution to integrity must thus support:

- The specification and enforcement of *data acceptance policies*, stating which data can be entered in the database by which subjects (users or applications) under which circumstances. Acceptance policies represent an important form of prevention of integrity violations and attacks. Current access control mechanisms provide some support for enforcing such policies; however, they need to be provided with an extensive set of *metadata information* concerning both subjects and data objects.

- The specification and enforcement of *validation policies*, stating how often the data have to be controlled once they have been entered in the database. Although acceptance policies may do a good job in avoiding the introduction of low integrity data, one still has to deal with the possibility that integrity be degraded or compromised later on. Validation policies can be considered a form of auditing, according to which data can be periodically controlled with respect to integrity.

- The development of mechanism for recovering from integrity violations and attacks. Such a mechanism should enable the system to react, possibly in real-time, to integrity violations. For instance, it may stop the user or application program introducing the erroneous data, assess and repair the damage, and, perhaps most importantly, prevent the spread of errors.

We note that data integrity cannot be assured by access control alone, although it must play a primary role. Many other mechanisms, such as transaction manager and user authentication system, are also required. Moreover, a solution for integrity management must be supplemented with data validation process as data integrity is often dependant upon various external factors such as time or changes on external data. The management of integrity thus requires continuous control and monitor of data in their whole life cycle, from the moment they are introduced to the system to the moment they are deleted from the system. As such, a design for integrity management systems requires one to identify and combine necessary components so that they can together provide a comprehensive solution to integrity control and management.

7.3.3 Securing Web-Enabled Databases

With the recent advancement of Internet technologies and adoption of Web-based applications for e-commerce by organizations, more and more internal databases are now being accessed by users outside the organization. Though access is not direct and is usually mediated by application programs, the security risks associated with opening up internal databases to untrusted users in the public domain are still significant.

One of the most common ways to attack a database through a web application is *SQL injection*. SQL injection can be defined as an attack technique used to exploit Web applications that construct SQL statements from user-supplied input. Web applications traditionally use user-supplied input to create custom SQL statements for dynamic Web page requests. Problems occur, however, when an application fails to properly sanitize user-supplied input, which makes it possible for an attacker to alter the construction of back-end SQL statements. When an attacker is able to modify a SQL statement, the process runs with the same permissions as the component that executed the command (e.g. database server, Web application server, Web server, etc.). The impact of this attack can allow attackers to gain control of the database or even execute commands on the system.

To date, no satisfactory solutions have been proposed to mitigate or detect such attacks on databases. One reported approach is an automated universal server-level solution (AUSELSQI) proposed by Abdulkader et al. [37]. Their solution operates at the Web-server level by intercepting browser requests containing SQL queries. It then inspects the SQL query string for the presence of some known special characters that are indicative of a SQL injection attack. A SNORT-like signature-based scheme is described by Mookhey et al. [38]. However, as shown in the paper by Imperva [39], most of these signatures can be evaded by exploiting the richness of SQL that allows multiple ways to achieve the same result.

7.4 Conclusion

Data security and maintaining confidentiality of data in particular remain prime objectives of any data management system. In this chapter, we have discussed the applicability of various access control mechanisms to databases, which are needed for ensuring confidentiality of data. We then discussed some of the ongoing research in the field of database security. The area of database security involves several other relevant topics, such as inference control and statistical database security, for which we refer the readers to [40, 41, 42].

References

1. B. Iyer, S. Mehrotra, E. Mykletun, G. Tsudik, and Y. Wu. A framework for efficient storage security in rdbms. In *Proceedings of 9th International Conference on Extending Database Technology (EDBT)*, March 2004.
2. E. Bertino, D. Leggieri, and E. Terzi. Securing dbms: Characterizing and detecting query flood. In *Proceedings of 9th Information Security Conference (ISC)*, September 2004.
3. National Security Telecommunications and Information Systems Security Committee. The insider threat to U.S. government information systems, July 1999.
4. F. Schneider, editor. *Trust in Cyberspace*. National Academy Press, 1999.
5. Oracle Corporation. *Oracle Database Security Guide 10g Release 2*, June 2005. Available at www.oracle.com.
6. C. Kaufman, R. Perlman, and M. Speciner. *Network Security: Private Communication in a Public World*. Second Edition, Prentice Hall, 2002.
7. E.B. Fernandez, R.C. Summers, and T. Lang. *Database Security and Integrity*. Addison-Wesley, 1981.
8. P.G. Griffiths and B. Wade. An authorization mechanism for a relational database. *ACM Transactions on Database Systems*, 1(3):242–255, 1976.
9. R. Fagin. On an authorisation mechanism. *ACM Transactions on Database Systems*, 3(3):310–319, 1978.
10. E. Bertino, S. Jajodia, and P. Samarati. An extended authorization model. *IEEE Transactions on Knowledge and Data Engineering*, 9(1):85–101, 1997.
11. R. Sandhu, E.J. Coyne, H.L. Feinstein, and C.E. Youman. Role-based access control models. *Computer*, 29(2):38–47, 1996.
12. R. Thomas and R. Sandhu. Task-based authorization controls (TBAC) models for active and enterprise-oriented authorization management. *Database Security XI: Status and Prospects*, pages 262–275, 1998.
13. D. Ferraiolo, R. Sandhu, S. Gavrilaa, R. Kuhn, and R. Chandramouli. Proposed nist standard for role-based access control. *ACM Transactions on Information and System Security*, 4(3):224–274, 2001.
14. E. Bertino, C. Bettini, E. Ferrari, , and P. Samarati. An access control model supporting periodicity constraints and temporal reasoning. *ACM Transactions on Database Systems*, 23(3):231–285, 1998.
15. Oracle Corporation. *The Virtual Private Database in Oracle9iR2: An Oracle Technical White Paper*, January 2002. Available at http://www.oracle.com.
16. R. Sandhu and F. Chen. The multilevel relational data model. *ACM Transactions on Information and System Security*, 1(1):93–132, 1998.
17. S. Jajodia, R. Sandhu, and B. Blaustein. Solutions to the polyinstantiation problem. *Information Security: An Integrated Collection of Essays*, 1994.
18. O. SamySayadjari. Multilevel security: Reprise. *IEEE Security and Privacy*, 2004.
19. E. Bertino, S. Castano, and E. Ferrari. Securing xml documents with author-x. *IEEE Internet Computing*, 5(3):21–30, 2001.
20. OASIS Consortium. *eXtensible Access Control Markup Language (XACML) Committee Specification, Version 1.1*, 2000. Available at: http://www.oasis-open.org/committees/xacml/.
21. S. Rizvi, A. Mendelzon, S. Sudarshan, and P. Roy. Extending query rewriting techniques for fine-grained access control. In *Proceedings of ACM SIGMOD conference*, June 2004.

22. F. Rabitti, E. Bertino, W. Kim, and D. Woelk. A model of authorization for next-generation database systems. *ACM Transactions on Database Systems*, 16(1):88–131, 1991.
23. B. Thuraisingham. Mandatory security in object-oriented database systems. In *Proceedings of International Conference on Object-Oriented Programming Systems, Languages, and Applications (OOPSLA)*, 1989.
24. IBM. *DB2 Information Center*. Available at http://publib.boulder.ibm.com/infocenter/db2luw/v8//index.jsp.
25. MySQL. *MySQL 5.1 Reference Manual*, 2006. Available at http://dev.mysql.com/doc/refman/5.1/en.
26. ANSI. American national standard for information technology – role based access control. ANSI INCITS 359-2004, February 2004.
27. R. Agrawal, J. Kiernan, R. Srikant, and Y. Xu. Order-preserving encryption for numeric data. In *Proceedings of ACM SIGMOD Conference*, 2004.
28. S. Axelsson. Intrusion detection systems: A survey and taxonomy. Technical Report 99-15, Chalmers Univ., March 2000.
29. E. Bertino, A. Kamra, and E. Terzi. Intrusion detection in rbac-administered databases. In *Proceedings of Annual Computer Security Applications Conference (ACSAC)*, 2005.
30. R. Sandhu. On five definitions of data integrity. In *the IFIP WG11.3 Workshop on Database Security*, 1993.
31. E. Bertino and R. Sandhu. Database security - concepts, approaches, and challenges. *IEEE Transaction on dependable and secure computing*, 2005.
32. R. Sandhu and S. Jajodia. Integrity mechanisms in database management systems. In *NIST-NCSC National Computer Security Conference*, 1990.
33. D.D. Clark and D.R. Wilson. A comparison of commercial and military computer security policies. In *IEEE Symposium on Security and Privacy*, 1987.
34. M. Bishop. *Computer Security: Art and Science*. Addison-Wesley, 2003.
35. K.J. Biba. Integrity considerations for secure computer systems. Technical Report TR-3153, Mitre, 1977.
36. R. Ramakrishnan and J. Gehrke. *Database Management Systems*. McGraw-Hill, 2000.
37. A.A. Alfantookh. An automated universal server level solution for sql injection security flaw. In *Proceedings of International Conference on Electrical, Electronic and Computer Engineering (ICEEC)*, 2004.
38. K.K. Mookhey and N. Burghate. *Detection of SQL Injection and Cross-site Scripting Attacks*, 2003. Available at http://www.securityfocus.com/infocus/1768.
39. Imperva. Sql injection signatures evasion. Technical report, 2004.
40. B.M. Thuraisingham, W. Ford, M. Collins, and J. OKeeffe. Design and implementation of a database inference controller. *Data Knowledge Engineering*, 11(3):271–285, 1993.
41. D.E. Denning. Secure statistical databases with random sample queries. *ACM Transactions on Database Systems*, 5(3):291–315, 1980.
42. D.E. Denning and J. Schlo rer. A fast procedure for finding a tracker in a statistical database. *ACM Transactions on Database Systems*, 5(1):88–102, 1980.

8

Trust Management

Claudio A. Ardagna, Ernesto Damiani, Sabrina De Capitani di Vimercati,
Sara Foresti, and Pierangela Samarati

Università degli Studi di Milano
Italia

Summary. The amount of data available electronically to a multitude of users
has been increasing dramatically over the last few years. The size and dynamics
of the user community set requirements that cannot be easily solved by traditional
access control solutions. A promising approach for supporting access control in open
environments is *trust management.*

This chapter provides an overview of the most significant approaches for managing and negotiating trust between parties. We start by introducing the basic concepts
on which trust management systems are built, describing their relationships with
access control. We then illustrate credential-based access control languages together
with a description of different trust negotiation strategies. We conclude the chapter
with a brief overview of reputation-based systems.

8.1 Introduction

Accessing information over the Internet has become an essential requirement
in the modern economy, where unknown parties can interact for the purpose
of acquiring or offering services. The open and dynamic nature of such a scenario requires the development of new ways of enforcing access control, as
identity-based mechanisms are not able to manage these issues any more. In
fact, interacting parties may be unknown to each other, unless they have already had transactions before. Consequently, a mechanism that allows one to
decide which requesters are qualified to gain access to the resource and, on
the other hand, which server is trusted to provide the requested resource, on
the basis of certified statements provided by the interacting parties is needed.
Trust management has been developed for this specific purpose and has received considerable interest from the research community [25]. Early research
identified three main components of trust management: (i) *security policies*,
which are local trust assertions that the local system trusts unconditionally;
(ii) *security credentials*, which are signed trust assertions made by other parties; the signature must be verified before the credential may be used; (iii) *trust
relationships*, which are special cases of security policies. Early approaches to

trust management, such as PolicyMaker [5] and KeyNote [4], basically use credentials to describe specific delegation of trusts among keys and to bind public keys to authorizations. Although early trust management systems do provide an interesting framework for reasoning about trust between unknown parties, assigning authorizations to keys may be limiting and make authorization specifications difficult to manage. Moreover, the public key of a subject may eventually be considered as her pseudonym, reducing the main advantages of trust management.

A promising direction to overcome this disadvantage is *digital certificates*. A digital certificate is basically the online counterpart of paper credentials (e.g., driver licenses). Access control models exploiting digital certificates make access decisions on whether or not a party may execute an access on the basis properties that the requesting party may have. These properties can be proven by presenting one or more certificates [6, 13, 15, 18, 34]. The development and effective use of credential-based access control models require tackling several problems related to credential management and disclosure strategies, delegation and revocation of credentials, and the establishment of credential chains [10, 16, 23, 24, 28, 29, 31]. In other words, trust between two interacting parties is established based on the parties' properties, which are proven through the disclosure of digital certificates. First of all, parties must be able to state and enforce access rules based on credentials and communicate these rules to their counterpart to correctly establish a negotiation. The resolution of this problem requires the development of new access control (authorization) languages and systems.

The main advantages of trust management solutions can therefore be summarized as follows.

- Trust management allows unknown parties to access resources/services by showing appropriate credentials that prove their qualifications to get the resources/services.
- Trust management supports delegation and provides decentralization of control as it allows trust chains among parties to propagate access rights.
- Trust management is more expressive than classical access control mechanisms as it allows the addition of new restrictions and conditions without the need to rewrite the applications enforcing access control.
- The use of trust management systems for controlling security-critical services frees the application programmers from designing and implementing security mechanisms for specifying policies, interpreting credentials, and so on.
- Each party can define access control policies to regulate accesses to its resources/services.
- Trust management systems increase the expressiveness and scalability of access control systems.
- Trust establishment involves just two parties: the requester and the service provider.

The concept of *reputation* is closely linked to that of trustworthiness. Reputation is often considered as a collective measure of trustworthiness based on ratings from parties in a community and can be used to establish trust relationships between parties [9]. The basic idea behind reputation management is to let remote parties rate each other, for example, after the completion of a transaction, and use the aggregated ratings about a given party to derive a reputation score. Reputation can then be used by other parties when deciding whether or not to transact with that party in the future. Linking reputations to parties and/or to their attributes impacts on the trust framework inasmuch as it poses additional requirements on credentials production and management. A rapidly growing literature is becoming available around trust and reputation systems, but the relation between these notions needs further clarification.

The purpose of this chapter is to give an overview of existing and proposed approaches to trust management. The remainder of this chapter is organized as follows. Section 8.2 gives an overview of early approaches for trust management, namely PolicyMaker, KeyNote, and rule-controlled environment for evaluation of rules and everything else (REFEREE). Section 8.3 presents the main characteristics of credential-based access control systems and illustrates a credential-based access control language together with some trust negotiation strategies. Section 8.4 presents a brief overview of reputation-based systems. Finally, Sect. 8.5 gives our conclusions.

8.2 Early Approaches to Trust Management

With the growing popularity of the Internet, trust-based systems are becoming increasingly prevalent. In such a context, trust is an inherently dynamic measure. For instance, party A previously trusting party B but its public key authority may decide to stop trust if party B vouches for bad public key bindings. The level of trust may therefore increase or decrease depending on new knowledge and experiences learned from exercising the trust. In general, trust management systems may differ in the approach adopted to establish and evaluate trust relationships between parties. Early approaches to trust management used credential verification to establish a trust relationship with other parties. These systems start from the proposal of binding authorizations with keys rather than with users' identities.

We now give an overview of the early trust management approaches to authorization and access control, focusing on the *PolicyMaker, KeyNote,* and *REFEREE* systems.

8.2.1 PolicyMaker and KeyNote

PolicyMaker [5] and KeyNote [4] provide a comprehensive approach to trust management, defining a language used to specify *trusted actions* and relations. In the past, identity-based certificates were used to create an artificial layer of indirection, linking a user's public key to her identity (e.g., X509 certificates [7]), and the user's identity to the set of actions she is authorized to execute. PolicyMaker and KeyNote are, instead, systems that integrate the specification of policies with the binding of public keys to the actions they are trusted to perform. The ability to express security credentials and policies without requiring the application to manage a mapping between the user identity and authority is of paramount importance in systems where it is necessary to protect users' anonymity (e.g., electronic voting systems).

Both PolicyMaker and KeyNote are based on *credentials* and *policies*, which are correctly referred to as *assertions*. More precisely, signed assertions are credentials, while policies are unsigned assertions. Credentials are mainly used for *trust delegation* under some specific conditions. Consequently a trusted entity can issue a credential to a nontrusted entity that becomes trusted and, in turn, can issue a similar credential to another entity and so on, thus forming a delegation chain without any length restrictions. An entity can therefore obtain access to a certain resource through a delegation from an authorized entity. Delegation is an important feature of a trust management system since it guarantees system scalability. Authority delegations can be graphically represented as a graph, where each node corresponds to a key and an edge from node n_1 to node n_2 indicates that there is a credential delegating authority from n_1 to n_2.

While credential statements are signed with the issuer's private key, policies, on the contrary, are not signed and the issuer entity is a standard entity, represented by keyword Policy, meaning that the specific assertion is locally trusted. An access request is accepted if there exists a path from some trusted node (with label Policy) to the node corresponding to the requester's key in the delegation graph. Another common characteristic of PolicyMaker and KeyNote is *monotonicity*, meaning that if an assertion is deleted, the set of privileges does not increase.

KeyNote is a trust management system where policies and credentials are expressed in a language directly managed by the KeyNote *compliance checker*. The main difference between PolicyMaker and KeyNote is that the latter directly performs signature verification inside the trust management engine, while PolicyMaker leaves this task up to the calling application. Moreover, as mentioned above, KeyNote defines a specific language for credentials, designed for request and policy evaluation, while PolicyMaker supports credentials written in any programming language. Also, PolicyMaker returns to the calling application a True of False answer, while KeyNote allows the definition of an application-dependent set of answers. Obviously, the syntax of assertions and requests is different between the two methods.

It is important to note that PolicyMaker and KeyNote do not directly enforce access control policies, but simply provide an advice to the calling application. The advice is based on the list of credentials and policies defined at application side. The calling application then decides whether to follow the received advice or not.

8.2.2 REFEREE

Rule-controlled environment for evaluation of rules, and everything else (REF-EREE) [8] is a trust management system for Web applications. Like Policy-Maker, it supports full programmability of assertions (i.e., policies and credentials). The REFEREE system provides both a general policy-evaluation mechanism for Web clients and servers and a language used to define trust policies, putting all trust decisions under explicit policy control. More precisely, the REFEREE model imposes that every operation, including its policy evaluation and credential fetching mechanism, happens under the control of some policy. REFEREE is then a system for writing policies about policies, as well as policies about cryptographic keys, certification authorities, or trust delegation. A significant difference between REFEREE and Policy-Maker and KeyNote is that REFEREE supports non-monotonic assertions: policies and credentials may be used to express denial of specific actions. The three main primitive data types in REFEREE are *tri-values*, *statement lists*, and *programs*. The tri-values are true (accept), false (deny), and unknown (insufficient information). A statement list is a set of assertions expressed in two-element expressions. Both policies and credentials are programs that take a statement list and return a tri-value. An access request (query) to the REFEREE trust engine takes a policy name and additional arguments as input, including credentials or statement lists. REFEREE then downloads the relevant policies and executes them. The output is a tri-value and an optional statement list.

8.3 Credential-Based Trust Management Systems

While the approaches described in the previous section represent a significant step towards the support of access control in open environments, the assignment of authorizations to keys may result limiting, as the public key of a party can be seen as a pseudonym for the party. Therefore, an access control method granting or denying access to resources on the basis of requester's attributes would be advisable. In many situations, before an interaction can start, a certain level of trust is established through the exchange of information (credentials) between the interacting parties. However, the access control process should be able to operate without the requester's knowledge of the set of credentials she should have to access the resource. Consequently, the information about the needed credentials has to be communicated to the counterpart during the access control process itself. The access control decision is therefore obtained through a complex process and completing a service may require communicating information not related to the access itself, but related to additional restrictions on its execution, introducing possible forms of *trust negotiation*. Trust negotiation is an approach to *automated trust establishment*. Automated trust negotiation has gained much consideration in recent

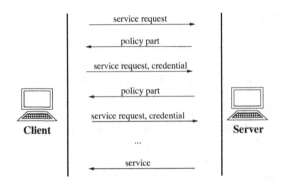

Fig. 8.1. Gradual trust establishment

years and various negotiation strategies have been proposed (see Sect. 8.3.2). In general, the interactions between a server and a client that need to establish a trust relationship can be summarized as follows.

- The client requests an access to a service.
- Upon receiving the request, the server checks if the client has provided the necessary credentials. In the case of a positive answer, the access to the service is granted; otherwise the server sends to the client the policies that she must fulfil to gain access.
- The client selects, if possible, the requested credentials and sends them to the server together with the service request.
- If the submitted credentials are appropriate, the user gains access to the service.

There are two major drawbacks to this protocol: a server has to disclose its, potentially sensitive policies to an unknown client, a client has to release all her relevant credentials in a single step without any possibility of negotiation.

A first improvement to reduce the release of irrelevant information during a trust establishment process consists in a *gradual trust establishment*. With a gradual trust establishment, upon receiving an access request, the server selects the policy that governs the access to the service and discloses only the information that it is willing to show to an unknown party. The client, according to her practices, decides if she is willing to disclose the requested credentials. Note that this incremental exchange of requests and credentials can be iteratively repeated as many times as necessary (see Fig. 8.1).

For the sake of simplicity, Fig. 8.1 shows a one-way protection schema, where the server controls access to some resources and communicates to the client the access control policies that the client should satisfy to gain the access. However, current approaches focus on a full negotiation process, where policies and credentials flow in both directions. In such a scenario, the server defines policies that protect its sensitive resources and the client defines policies that restrict the disclosure of her credentials: both client and server can then require credentials the counterpart to release their sensitive information.

8.3.1 An Approach for Regulating Service Access and Information Disclosure

To address the aforementioned issues, new credential-based access control languages, models, and mechanisms have been developed. One of the first solution providing a uniform framework for credential-based access control specification and enforcement was presented by Bonatti and Samarati [6]. The framework includes an access control model, a language for expressing access and release policies, and a policy-filtering mechanism to identify the relevant policies for a negotiation. Access regulations are specified by mean of logical rules, where some predicates are explicitly identified. The system is composed of two entities: the *client* that requests access, and the *server* that exposes a set of services. Abstractions can be defined on services, grouping them in sets, called *classes*. Server and client interact by mean of a *negotiation process*, defined as the set of messages exchanges between them. Clients and servers have a *portfolio*, that is a collection of credentials (certified statements) and declarations (unsigned statements). A declaration is a statement issued by the party, while a credential is a statement issued and signed (i.e., certified) by authorities trusted for making the statements [11]. Credentials are essentially digital certificates, and must be unforgeable and verifiable through the issuing certificate authority's public key. In this proposal, credentials are therefore modeled as *credential expressions* of the form *credential_name(attribute_list)*, where *credential_name* is the attribute credential name and *attribute_list* is a possibly empty list of elements of the form *attribute_name=value_term*, where *value_term* is either a ground value or a variable. The main advantage of this proposal is that it provides an infrastructure to exchange the minimal set of certificates, that is, a client communicates the minimal set of certificates to a server, and the server releases the minimal set of conditions required for granting access. For this purpose, the server defines a set of *service accessibility rules*, representing the necessary and sufficient conditions for granting access to a resource. More precisely, this proposal distinguishes two kinds of service accessibility rules: *prerequisites* and *requisites*. Prerequisites are conditions that must be satisfied for a service request to be taken into consideration (they do not guarantee that it will be granted); requisites are conditions that allow the service request to be successfully granted. The basic motivation for this separation is to avoid unnecessary disclosure of information from both parties, and can therefore be seen as twofold: (i) server's privacy, and (ii) client's privacy. Therefore, the server will not disclose a requisite rule until after the client satisfies a corresponding prerequisite rule. Also, both clients and servers can specify a set of *portfolio disclosure rules*, used to define the conditions that govern the release of credentials and declarations.

The rules both in the service accessibility and portfolio disclosure sets are defined through a logic language that includes a set of predicates (listed in the following) whose meaning is expressed on the basis of the current *state*. The state indicates the parties' characteristics and the status of the current negotiation process, that is, the certificates already exchanged, the requests made by the two parties, and so on. Predicates evaluate both information stored at the site (persistent state) and acquired during the negotiation (negotiation state). Information related to a specific negotiation is deleted when the negotiation terminates. In contrast, persistent state includes information that spans different negotiations, such as user profiles maintained at Web sites. The basic predicates of the language can be summarized as follows.

- `credential(c, K)` evaluates to true if the current state contains certificate c verifiable using key K.
- `declaration(d)` evaluates to true if the current state contains declaration d, where d is of the form *attribute_name=value_term*.
- `cert-authority(CA, K_CA)` evaluates to true if the party using it in her policy trusts certificates issued by certificate authority CA, whose public key is K_{CA}.
- A set of non-predefined predicates necessary for evaluating the current *state* values. These predicates can evaluate both persistent and negotiation states, and they are defined by each of the parties interacting.
- A set of non-predefined *abbreviation* predicates that are used to abbreviate requirements in the negotiation phase.
- A set of standard mathematical built-in predicates, such as $=$, $\neq$, and $\leq$.

The rules, both for service accessibility and portfolio disclosure, are composed of two elements: the *body*, containing a boolean expression composing, through boolean operators **and**, **or**, **not**, the aforementioned predicates; and the *head*, specifying the services accessible, or the certificates releasable, according to the rule. Figure 8.2 illustrates the following client/server interaction.

- the client sends a request for a service to the server;
- the server asks from the client a set of prerequisites, that is, a set of necessary conditions for granting access;
- the client sends back the required prerequisites;
- if the prerequisites are sufficient, than the server identifies the credentials and declarations needed to grant access to the resource;
- the client evaluates the requests against its portfolio release rules and makes, eventually, some counter-requests;
- the server sends back to the client the required certificates and declarations;
- the client fulfils the server's requests;
- the service is then granted to the client.

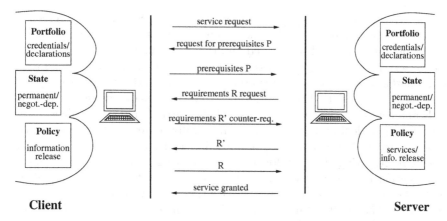

Fig. 8.2. Client server negotiation

Since there may exist different policy combinations that may bring the access request to satisfaction, the communication of credentials and/or declarations could be an expensive task. To overcome this issue, the *abbreviation* predicates are used to abbreviate requests. Besides the necessity of abbreviations, it is also necessary for the server, before releasing rules to the client, to evaluate state predicates that involve private information. For instance, the client is not expected to be asked many times the same information during the same session and if the server has to evaluate if the client is considered not trusted, it cannot communicate this request to the client itself.

Communication of requisites to be satisfied by the requester is then based on a filtering and renaming process applied on the server's policy, which exploits partial evaluation techniques in logic programs [6, 17]. Access is then granted whenever a user satisfies the requirements specified by the filtering rules calculated by means of the original policy and the already released information.

8.3.2 Negotiation Strategies

Besides solutions for uniform frameworks supporting credential-based access control policies [6], different automated trust negotiation proposals have been developed. Trust negotiation occurs whenever credentials themselves carry some sensitive information. In such a situation, a procedure needs to be applied to establish trust through negotiation. Trust is then established gradually by disclosing credentials and requests for credentials. It is however important to note that different parties may have different requirements for how such a negotiation process should be performed and each party can therefore rely on its *trust negotiation strategy*. We now provide a brief description of some negotiation strategies suitable for different scenarios.

In [31] the *prudent negotiation strategy* (PRUNES) has been presented. This strategy ensures that the client communicates her credentials to the server only if access will be granted and the set of certificates communicated to the server is the minimal necessary for granting it. Each party defines a set of *credential policies* that regulates how and under which conditions the party releases its credentials. The negotiation is then a series of requests for credentials and counter-requests on the basis of the parties' credential policies. The established credential policies can be graphically represented through a tree, called a *negotiation search tree*, composed of two kinds of nodes: *credential nodes*, representing the need for a specific credential, and *disjunctive nodes*, representing the logic operators connecting the conditions for credential release. The root of a tree node is a service (i.e., the resource the client wants to access). The negotiation can therefore be seen as a backtracking operation on the tree. The backtracking can be executed according to different strategies. For instance, a *brute-force* backtracking is complete and correct, but it is too expensive to be used in a real scenario. The authors therefore proposed the *PRUNES* method, which prunes the search tree without compromising completeness or correctness of the negotiation process. The basic idea is that if a credential C has just been evaluated and the state of the system is not changed too much, then it is useless to evaluate again the same credential, as the result will be exactly the same as the result previously computed.

In [22] different negotiation strategies are introduced together with the concepts of *safeness* and *completeness*. A strategy is *safe* if all possible negotiations conducted by the parties are safe and hence there exists a sequence of resource disclosures that culminates in the sensitive resource disclosure. A strategy is *complete* if, whenever there exists a safe sequence of disclosure, the original requested resource is released. Negotiation strategies can be divided between *eager* and *parsimonious* credential release strategies. Parties applying the first strategy turn over all their credentials if the disclosure is safe. The eager approach releases credentials as soon as possible, minimizing the time requested for negotiation but increasing the amount of released data. A *naive eager approach* requires the parties to send each other all the credentials for which an authorized path has been found, without the need to distinguish between credentials needed to take the decision and credentials not relevant for the negotiation. The major advantage of this strategy is that there is no need for policy disclosure. On the other side, a great amount of unmotivated disclosure of data is performed. According to a *parsimonious* strategy, the parties delay as much as possible data disclosure until the negotiation reaches a certain state. In addition, parties applying a parsimonious strategy only release credentials upon explicit request by the server (avoiding unnecessary releases).

In [33] a large set of negotiation strategies, called a *disclosure tree strategy* (DTS) family, has been defined. The authors show that, if two parties use different strategies from the DST family, they are able to negotiate trust. The

DTS family is a closed set, that is, if a negotiation strategy can interoperate with any DST strategy, it must also be a member of the DST family.

In [32] a *unified schema for resource protection* (UniPro) was proposed. This mechanism is used to protect the information specified within policies. UniPro gives (opaque) names to policies and allows any named policy P_1 to have its own policy P_2, meaning that the content of P_1 can only be disclosed to parties who have shown that they satisfy P_2.

Another solution for implementing access control based on credentials is the *adaptive trust negotiation and access control* (ATNAC) approach [21]. This method grants or denies access to a resource on the basis of a *suspicion level* associated with subjects. The suspicion level is not fixed but may vary on the basis of the probability that the user has malicious intent. In [26] the authors propose to apply the automated trust negotiation technology for enabling secure transactions between portable devices that have no pre-existing relationship.

8.4 Reputation-Based Trust Management Systems

Related to trust is the concept of *reputation*. Reputation is another popular mechanism that people employ to deal with unknown parties. Reputation-based solutions do not require any prior experience with the party for reputation to be used to infer trustworthiness. It is then suitable for establishing initial trust. Parties in such systems establish trust relationships with other parties and assign trust values to these relationships. Generally, a trust value assigned to a trust relationship is a function of the combination of the party's global reputation and the evaluating party's perception of that party. There is however a clear distinction between *trust* and *reputation*: a trust value T can be computed based on its reputation R, that is, $T = \phi(R, t)$, where t is the time elapsed since the reputation was last modified [2]. Traditionally, research approaches [3, 14] distinguish between two main types of reputation-based trust management systems, namely *centralized reputation systems* and *distributed reputation systems*. In centralized reputation systems, trust information is collected from members of the community in the form of *ratings* on resources. The central authority collects all the ratings and derives a score for each resource. In a distributed reputation system there is not a central location for submitting ratings and obtaining resources' reputation scores; instead, there are distributed stores where ratings can be submitted. Recently, reputation-based trust management systems have been applied in many different contexts such as peer-to-peer (P2P) networks, where the development of P2P systems largely depends on the availability of novel provisions for ensuring that peers obtain reliable information on the quality of the resources they are retrieving [19]. Reputation models allow the expression and reasoning about *trust* in a peer based on its past behavior [20] and interactions other peers have experienced with it. The proposed approaches use different techniques for combining and propagating the ratings [1, 9, 12, 27, 30]. Here we describe a few related examples. In [1] a trust model is proposed, where, after each transaction, and only in the case of malicious behaviour, peers may file a complaint. Before engaging in an interaction with others, peers can query the network about existing complaints on their counterparts. One limitation of this model is that it is based on a binary trust scale (i.e., an entity is either trustworthy or not). Hence, once there is a complaint filed against a peer p, p is considered untrustworthy even though it has been trustworthy for all previous transactions. In [27] a Bayesian network-based trust model is proposed, where peers are evaluated with respect to different capabilities (e.g., capability to provide music files or movies). Basically, peers develop a naive Bayesian network for each peer with which they have interacted and modify their corresponding Bayesian networks after each interaction. When a peer has no experience with another one, it can ask other peers to make recommendations for it. Such recommendations are partitioned into two groups, recommendations from trustworthy peers and recommendation from unknown peers, and are combined by taking a weighted sum. In [30] an adaptive reputation-based trust model for P2P electronic communities is presented. It is based on five trust parameters: feedbacks, number of transactions, credibility of feedbacks, a transaction context factor, and a community context factor. The trust value associated with a peer is then defined as a weighted sum of two parts. The first part is the average amount of credible satisfaction a peer receives for each transaction. The second part increase or decrease the trust value according to community-specific characteristics or situations (e.g., the number of files a peer shares can be seen as a type of community context factor that has to be taken into consideration when evaluating the trustworthiness of a peer).

P2PRep is an example of a reputation-based protocol, formalizing the way each peer stores and shares with the community the reputation of other peers [9]. P2PRep runs in a fully anonymous P2P environment, where peers are identified using self-assigned *opaque identifiers* (e.g., a digest of a public key for which only the peer itself knows the corresponding private key). For simplicity, reputation and trust are represented as fuzzy values in the interval $[0, 1]$. This approach can however be readily extended to more-complex array-based representations taking into account multiple features [2]. The P2PRep protocol consists of five phases. In phase 1, a requester r locates available resources sending a `Query` broadcast message. Other peers answer with a `QueryHit` message notifying r that they may provide the requested resource. Upon receiving a set of `QueryHit` messages, r selects an offerer o and, in phase 2, r polls the community for any available reputation information on o, sending a `Poll` message. `Poll` messages are broadcasted in the same way as `Query` messages. All peers maintain an *experience repository* of their previous experiences with other peers. When a peer receives a `Poll` message, it checks its local repository. If it has some information to offer and wants to express an opinion on the selected offerer o, it generates a vote based on its experiences, and returns a `PollReply` message to the initiator r. As a result of phase 2, r receives a set V of votes, some of which express a good opinion while others express a bad one. In Phase 3, r evaluates the votes to collapse any set of votes that may belong to a clique and explicitly selects a random set of votes for verifying their trustworthiness [9]. In phase 4 the set of reputations collected in phase 3 is synthesized into an aggregated community-wide reputation value. Based on this reputation value, the requester r can take a decision on whether to access the resource offered by o or not (phase 5). After accessing the resource, r can update its local trust on o (depending on whether the downloaded resource was satisfactory or not). While a naive implementation of P2PRep can be expensive in terms of storage capacity and bandwidth, this cost can be minimized by applying simple heuristics. The amount of storage capacity is proportional to the number of peers with which the initiator has interacted. With respect to the bandwidth, it is easy to see that P2PRep increases the traffic of the P2P network by requiring both direct exchanges and broadcast requests. It is, however, reasonable to assume that the major impact of the protocol on network performance is due to broadcast messages and their answers. To overcome this issue, several heuristics can be applied. For instance, *intelligent routing* techniques can be applied for enabling custom forwarding of poll packets to the right peers. Vote caching is another technique that can be applied to improve the effectiveness of P2PRep. Finally, P2PRep scalability depends on the technique used for vote aggregation.

8.5 Conclusions

We have presented an overview of existing and proposed approaches to trust management, clarifying the link between trust and reputation. We have analyzed the current trends and developments in this area, and described some recent approaches for trust management based on a more sophisticated notion of credential-based language and negotiation to establish trust between unknown parties.

8.6 Acknowledgements

This work was supported in part by the European Union within the PRIME project in the FP6/IST programme under contract IST-2002-507591 and by the Italian MIUR programme within the KIWI and MAPS projects.

References

1. K. Aberer, Z. Despotovic (2001). Managing trust in a peer-2-peer information system. In Proc. of the Tenth International Conference on Information and Knowledge Management (CIKM 2001), Atlanta, Georgia.

2. R. Aringhieri, E. Damiani, S. De Capitani di Vimercati, S. Paraboschi, P. Samarati (2006). Fuzzy techniques for trust and reputation management in anonymous peer-to-peer systems. Journal of the American Society for Information Science and Technology (JASIST), 57(4):528–537.

3. M. Blaze, J. Feigenbaum, J. Ioannidis, A.D. Keromytis (1999). The role of trust management in distributed systems security. Secure Internet Programming, pp. 79–97.

4. M. Blaze, J. Feigenbaum, J. Ioannidis, A.D. Keromytis (1999). The KeyNote Trust Management System (Version 2), Internet RFC 2704 edition.

5. M. Blaze, J. Feigenbaum, J. Lacy (1996). Decentralized trust management. In Proc. of the 17th Symposium on Security and Privacy, Oakland, California, USA.

6. P. Bonatti, P. Samarati (2002). A unified framework for regulating access and information release on the web. Journal of Computer Security, 10(3):241–272.

7. CCITT (Consultative Committee on International Telegraphy and Telephony) (1988). Recommendation X.509: The Directory—Authentication Framework.

8. Y. Chu, J. Feigenbaum, B. LaMacchia, P. Resnick, M. Strauss (1997). REFEREE: Trust management for web applications. The World Wide Web Journal, 2(3):127–139.

9. E. Damiani, S. De Capitani di Vimercati, S. Paraboschi, P. Samarati (2003). Managing and sharing servents' reputations in p2p systems. IEEE Transactions on Data and Knowledge Engineering, 15(4):840–854.

10. C.M. Ellison, B. Frantz, B. Lampson, R.L. Rivest, B.M. Thomas, T. Ylonen (1999). SPKI certificate theory. RFC 2693.

11. B. Gladman, C. Ellison, N. Bohm (1999). Digital signatures, certificates and electronic commerce. http://ya.com/bg/digsig.pdf.

12. M. Gupta, O. Judge, M. Ammar (2003). A reputation system for peer-to-peer networks. In Proc. of the ACM 13th International Workshop on Network and Operating Systems Support for Digital Audio and Video, Monterey, California, USA.

13. K. Irwin, T. Yu (2005). Preventing attribute information leakage in automated trust negotiation. In Proc. of the 12th ACM Conference on Computer and Communications Security, Alexandria, VA, USA.

14. A. Jøsang (1996). The right type of trust for distributed systems. In Proc. of the 1996 Workshop on New Security Paradigms, Lake Arrowhead, CA.

15. N. Li, J.C. Mitchell, W.H. Winsborough (2005). Beyond proof-of-compliance: Security analysis in trust management. Journal of the ACM, 52(3):474–514.

16. N. Li, W.H. Winsborough, J.C. Mitchell (2003). Distributed credential chain discovery in trust management. Journal of Computer Security, 11(1):35–86.

17. M. Minoux (1988). LTUR: A Simplified Linear-Time Unit Resolution Algorithm for Horn Formulae and Computer Implementation. Inf. Process. Lett., 29(1):1–12.

18. J. Ni, N. Li, W.H. Winsborough (2005). Automated trust negotiation using cryptographic credentials. In Proc. of the 12th ACM Conference on Computer and Communications Security, Alexandria, VA, USA.

19. A. Oram edt. (2001). Peer-to-Peer: Harnessing the Power of Disruptive Technologies. O'Reilly & Associates.

20. P. Resnick, R. Zeckhauser, E. Friedman, K. Kuwabara (2000). Reputation systems. Communications of the ACM, 43(12):45–48.

21. T. Ryutov, L. Zhou, C. Neuman, T. Leithead, K.E. Seamons (2005). Adaptive trust negotiation and access control. In Proc. of the 10th ACM Symposium on Access Control Models and Technologies, Stockholm, Sweden.
22. K. Seamons, M. Winslett, T. Yu (2001). Limiting the disclosure of access control policies during automated trust negotiation. In Proc. of the Network and Distributed System Security Symposium (NDSS 2001), San Diego, CA, USA.
23. K.E. Seamons, W. Winsborough, M. Winslett (1997). Internet credential acceptance policies. In Proc. of the Workshop on Logic Programming for Internet Applications, Leuven, Belgium.
24. K.E. Seamons, M. Winslett, T. Yu, B. Smith, E. Child, J. Jacobson, H. Mills, L. Yu (2002). Requirements for policy languages for trust negotiation. In Proc. of the 3rd International Workshop on Policies for Distributed Systems and Networks (POLICY 2002), Monterey, CA.
25. Security and trust management (2005). http://www.ercim.org/publication/Ercim_News/enw63/.
26. T.W. van der Horst, T. Sundelin, K.E. Seamons, C.D. Knutson (2004). Mobile trust negotiation: Authentication and authorization in dynamic mobile networks. In Proc. of the Eighth IFIP Conference on Communications and Multimedia Security, Lake Windermere, England.
27. Y. Wang, J. Vassileva (2003). Trust and reputation model in peer-to-peer networks. In Proc. of the Third International Conference on Peer-to-Peer Computing, Linköping, Sweden.
28. L. Wang, D. Wijesekera, S. Jajodia (2004). A logic-based framework for attribute based access control. In Proc. of the 2004 ACM Workshop on Formal Methods in Security Engineering, Washington DC, USA.
29. M. Winslett, N. Ching, V. Jones, I. Slepchin (1997). Assuring security and privacy for digital library transactions on the web: Client and server security policies. In Proc. of the ADL '97 – Forum on Research and Tech. Advances in Digital Libraries, Washington, DC.
30. L. Xiong, L. Liu (2003). A reputation-based trust model for peer-to-peer ecommerce communities. In Proc. of the IEEE International Conference on E-Commerce, Newport Beach, California.
31. T. Yu, X. Ma, M. Winslett (2000). An efficient complete strategy for automated trust negotiation over the internet. In Proc. of the 7th ACM Computer and Communication Security, Athens, Greece.
32. T. Yu, M. Winslett (2003). A unified scheme for resource protection in automated trust negotiation. In Proc. of the IEEE Symposium on Security and Privacy, Berkeley, California.
33. T. Yu, M. Winslett, K.E. Seamons (2001). Interoperable strategies in automated trust negotiation. In Proc. of the 8th ACM Conference on Computer and Communications Security, Philadelphia, Pennsylvania.
34. T. Yu, M. Winslett, K.E. Seamons (2003). Supporting structured credentials and sensitive policies trough interoperable strategies for automated trust. ACM Transactions on Information and System Security (TISSEC), 6(1):1–42.

Trusted Platforms

Klaus Kursawe

Philips Research
The Netherlands

Summary. This chapter describes some of the basic mechanism of building trusted platforms, i.e., platforms that behave in a way they are expected to. The main focus is the low-level implementation of such mechanism using secure hardware, including the trusted computing standard, security mechanisms inside the central processor unit (CPU) and external secure coprocessors. After describing the advantages and limits of these approaches, the chapter describes some basic services set up on such hardware, such as secure boot, remote attestation, and secure I/O interfaces. Finally, we briefly discuss secure operating systems, and point out some future trends in secure hardware and trusted platform.

9.1 Introduction

With the increasing importance of computing for commercial and personal as well as public welfare, the issue of trusting a computer to perform a task as expected is becoming increasingly important. Simultaneously, there seems to be less reason to actually put trust into a computer – platforms are becoming increasingly complex and networked, and remote systems may be maintained by organizations that may not necessarily share the same interests as the user. How can one trust one's own computer under those circumstances, let alone somebody else's? Currently, such problems mainly occur in PC-based systems. However, embedded systems – such as cellular phones, but also increasingly consumer devices – are running open, complex operating systems and connections to the outside world. The first viruses for the Symbian cellphone operating system have already been implemented, and it is only a matter of time until attacks on such devices become a frequent problem. The idea of a trusted platform is to reinstate some level of trust in the platform. This is usually done by adding extra hardware that withstands a certain amount of physical attack, and offers a protected environment for security-critical code and data. The exact functionality and protection of this hardware varies widely with the application – it can take the form of essentially adding a separate computer (like the IBM 4758 secure coprocessor), modifications to the processor core (like the ARM TrustZone), or some minimalistic functionality on a smartcard or trusted platform module.

9.2 Trust in Hardware

While it is not impossible to build a purely software-based trusted system, such a solution has some fundamental issues to overcome. For one, an attacker with physical access can easily circumvent pure software solutions. Cryptographic keys need to be stored somewhere on the platform, usually on a hard disk (where they can be found by an attacker), and code can be manipulated without a chance of detecting it. Furthermore, there is less possibility for defense in depth – once an attacker has found an exploitable weakness in the right part of the software, e.g., by means of a buffer overflow, all protection is gone.

Not surprisingly, using hardware as a root of trust has a long history, though the industry has only recently started providing cheap solutions that are applicable for the consumer domain. Various technologies have emerged since, aimed at different applications, security requirements and financial restrictions.

It is important to note that there are different definitions of trust, which also affects the functionality of trusted hardware. While the intuitive definition of trust is that a trusted device does something the user *wants* it to do, the trusted computing group (TCG) defines a trusted device as one whose behavior the user knows; it is then up to the user to act upon this knowledge in the interactions with the platform.

9.2.1 Secure Coprocessors

The most straightforward way to protect critical resources is to create a completely independent execution environment with its own memory, program ROM, and processing unit. This device is not accessible to an attacker other than through well-defined interfaces. Usually, the unit also offers some protection against hardware-based attacks such as sidechannel analysis (e.g., measuring power consumption or electromagnetic radiation) or fault injection (e.g., creating a memory error and observing how the platform behaves). For simple tasks, such a coprocessor can be a smartcard; for more-complex operations and high-security requirements, coprocessors like the IBM 4758 offer essentially a separate computer, and actively react to attempts to probe or otherwise manipulate the device. While a completely separate hardware unit can offer a very high degree of protection, they also have their limitations for many use cases. For one, building an entire secure execution environment in hardware can be comparatively expensive, considering the resources such a platform offers. If the secure coprocessor has to execute complex tasks, its cost may well exceed the price of the rest of the system to be protected – the more advanced devices can easily cost more than a 1000 dollars. Secondly, most secure coprocessors are designed to keep one application secure; once several, mutually distrusting applications need to be protected, the benefit of having a separated hardware environment largely goes away.

9.2.2 Secure Processor Mode

As an entirely separate processing unit is rather expensive, the idea of building a virtual secure coprocessor is appealing. In this case, the processor knows two modes, a secure mode and an insecure mode. The hardware guarantees that no process running in the insecure mode can access the resources of the secure mode, thus creating a protected environment in which critical processes can operate. The best-known example of such a technology is the ARM Trust-Zone, though similar technologies are now adapted in other processor cores. While generally cheaper than a separate hardware security module, this solution shares one of the problems; without significant software effort, it is only possible to have one protected application on the platform. An additional problem is that hardware-based attacks are much easier; while a separate security module has its own protected memory, the secure processor mode still needs to get code and data from an untrusted medium like the hard disk. Without additional hardware support, it is thus difficult to ensure that the secured code is not compromised.

9.2.3 Trusted Platform Modules

The idea of a *trusted platform module* (TPM) is to provide the minimal hardware needs to build a trusted platform in software. While usually implemented as a secure coprocessor, the functionality of a TPM is limited enough to allow for a relatively cheap implementation – at the price that the TPM itself does not solve any security problem, but rather offers a foundation to build upon. Thus, such a module can be added to an existing architecture rather cheaply, providing the lowest layer for a larger security architecture. The main driver behind this approach is the Trusted Computing Group (TCG), a large consortium of the main players in the IT industry, and the successor to the Trusted Computing Platform Alliance (TCPA) [1].

The trusted platform module is a passive subsystem that offers a number of security-related services to the platform. Examples of such services are secure storage, random-number generation, counters, and public key encryption. These services can be used directly by security applications. Various vendors offer hard-disk encryption with secure key storage in the TPM, and the upcoming Windows Vista operating system will integrate this approach for hard-disk encryption. While the TPM is certainly useful in such applications, its main strength is to serve as a building block for a secure operating system, which then can implement the functionality of larger hardware solutions such as a secure coprocessor by software means. The core root of trust for measurement (CRTM) is the active part of the concept that ensures that the TPM is informed about the boot process. It is usually implemented as a nonmodifiable part of the BIOS, and is executed before any other code that may have been manipulated by an attacker. Being optimized for price and flexibility, the TPM usually provides very limited bandwidth and internal nonvolatile memory. Thus, it relies on the host platform to store information. A TPM is, for example, explicitly not supposed to do any bulk encryption, but rather maintain keys for the software that does perform encryption on the host processor. Also, keys maintained by the TPM are not usually stored in the module itself, but encrypted under a master key (which is stored inside the TPM) and then stored on the host platform. While this allows unlimited storage for a small price, it also opens the TPM to denial-of-service attacks, as it cannot prevent its keys from being deleted.

9.2.4 Limits and Pitfalls

The goal of the hardware approach is to create a root of trust from which trust in the whole platform can be leveraged either by delegating all critical functions to the trusted hardware, or by using the trusted hardware to assist a software-based architecture. When deciding which hardware to choose, one has to be careful about the limits that come with each approach. Unfortunately, as all technologies offer a great deal of flexibility and can be used in many ways, the temptation exists to use them for purposes they where never designed for. The TCG approach, for example, initially did not consider advanced hardware attacks. Thus, in many platforms currently sold, the keys transported from the TPM to the main processor are transferred unencrypted over a very slow bus, where it is easy prey for an attacker with access to the hardware and some measurement equipment [2]. Secure coprocessors and secure processor modes may reach their limit once several mutually distrusting application need to run on the same platform – the benefit of a separate execution environment is lost in this case.

Furthermore, even secure hardware can be attacked by software means if integrated into the overall system incorrectly. One point of attack is the API, the interface through which the hardware communicates with the rest of the system. Such interfaces can be huge and complex – even an architecture initially designed for simplicity (such as a TPM) can quickly grow out of proportion as new requirements evolve. An example of an attack on the interface level is described in [3], where creative requests for legal commands to a hardware security module proved sufficient to extract a key that should never have left the module.

Special care is also required when changes to the platform that interact with the security implementation occur; recently, an attack has been published to abuse hyper-threading (a technology that allows very fast switching between different tasks) in a way that one process can monitor the memory access patterns of another one and thus obtain key information from an encryption process [4]. Thus, even if the hardware ensures that insecure processes can not interact with secure ones, technologies like this may be used to sidestep the separation completely.

Finally, the hardware itself is not immune to attacks, and various methods have been developed over the last decade to circumvent hardware-based security. Early pay-TV systems have been subject to increasingly advanced sidechannel attacks. Those attacks measure information that leaks from the device through alternative channels, such as power consumption or electromagnetic radiation from a smartcard. More recently, attackers have begun to insert faults into the execution of the trusted hardware, for example by manipulating the external clock or heating the device to its operational limit and observing the reaction of the device. While countermeasures have advanced significantly since the first attacks – most known sidechannels are largely under control, and modern hardware security modules feature sensors to detect tampering (and subsequently delete all keys) — one should keep in mind that no device can offer absolutely security. A device that costs 10 cents in production should not be expected to withstand a motivated attacker with a million dollars to spend. Some guidance can be obtained by standard certifications, such as FIPS 140-1 and common criteria, though these too can only be relied on to a certain extent, and – especially in the case of common criteria – may not certify security against a the required set of attacks.

9.3 Trusted and Secure Boot

Largely independent of the actual implementation of the secure hardware, it is usually only a small building block of the overall system. The first step to extend trust from the hardware security onto the whole platform is to ensure that the software running on the platform is indeed the software that is expected to run on there. This is reasonably easy if all critical software is stored and executed inside the security hardware. If trust needs to be leveraged from the security hardware onto an open, general-use platform, however, some form of boot protection is required. We have to distinguish between two different flavors of boot protection, one that does not allow an illegal configuration to be executed (which can be done with relatively little hardware support), and one that allows everything to run, but in some way restricts access rights for improper configurations and/or notifies the user of a possible corruption. In both cases, the system needs a trusted basic boot block i.e., the very first code that is executed when the platform is powered on; in the TCG standard, this is the core root of trust for measurement (CRTM); it is usually part of the BIOS ROM. This piece of code should never be modifiable, and does little more than verify the modifiable part of the boot-ROM and then hand over control. What happens then depends on what we want to achieve by securing the boot process.

In the *trusted or authenticated boot* scenario, the system does boot even if there is a corruption; however, it can be detected that the boot image was not what it was supposed to be. As a maliciously manipulated operating system may be in control after – or even during – boot, this approach requires a trusted component for two purposes, namely to

- Store information about the boot sequence in a way that cannot easily be modified afterwards,
- Act upon that information, e.g., block critical keys if the boot sequence was unsafe.

In the TCG concept, the role of that component is taken by the TPM. It contains a set of special registers, the platform configuration registers (PCRs). These registers cannot be directly written to, but only extended by means of a hash chain. If a new value is to be extended to the registers, it – and the value previously stored in there – are hashed together to form the value that actually is stored in the register. Thus, every value that has ever been written into the register has some influence on the value stored in it at any given time. When the platform starts up, all PC registers are reset to zero — this is the only time this is allowed to happen. Immediately afterwards, the CRTM, i.e., the first piece of the code (usually the BIOS) executed on the machine, generates a checksum of the main boot code and extends it to the first of the PC registers. By the design of the extend-mechanism it is now no longer possible to write a checksum belonging to another boot code into that register. Once booting is completed, the information stored in the PC registers can be destroyed, but not replaced by something meaningful. To act upon this information, the TPM allows keys to be bound to those register values (i.e., the keys are not revealed unless the right values are stored in the registers), or report them to an external entity that can then verify the correctness.

In the *secure boot scenario* [5], the system does not boot into an unsafe state. In the easiest implementation, this does not require secure storage; every component called in the boot sequence can verify a hash or a digital signature of its successor, and abort if an error is detected. As the potentially malicious code is never executed, there is no need for secure registers or key management. Nevertheless, secure storage may be useful. It can, for example, securely store the hash values the components are compared against, allowing a secure update of system components (which requires an update of the hashes). It can also provide a secure counter for version management, which can be used to prevent an attacker from rolling back to an old version of the software.

9.4 Remote Attestation

If a trusted platform is to be used in a networked environment, it is important that it can prove its status to an outside party. This requires two main functionalities:

- The trusted hardware needs to know what state the attested platform is in,
- The trusted hardware must be able to identify itself as such to an outside party.

If the trusted hardware only needs to attest itself, e.g., a smartcard with a banking application that executes largely independently of the host platform, the first functionality can be implemented rather easily by means of a certification from the producer. Otherwise, one usually uses some form of trusted boot – once the trusted hardware observes the boot sequence, it does know what state the platform is in. There are two largely unsolved problems though: Firstly, if the system becomes corrupted after startup, the trusted hardware usually does not notice such corruption, though research in the area of runtime observation is currently underway [6]. Secondly, if the configuration attested to is itself so complex that it cannot be trusted (as is the case with most modern operating systems), or if there are too many good configurations to keep track of (e.g., different kernel versions and patch levels), the value of such an attestation is limited. Mainly, it is reduced to recognizing known states, e.g., in a large organization to prescribe a standard configuration for user PCs.

The ability to identify the trusted hardware as such initially posed more of a political problem than a technical one. While hardware identities provide no problem in a military or commercial environment, using a unique platform identifier to attest platform properties to outside parties causes problems in the consumer area. The first attempt to this end, the processor serial number in the Pentium III, had to be revoked after massive consumer protests [7].

To prove it is genuinely secure hardware according to specification, a TPM needs some certificate. It is, however, required that such a certificate can be revoked, for example if an individual TPM is hacked and its keys are extracted. The TCG therefore originally decided to give each TPM its own identity, the endorsement key, (a public key encryption key), but to avoid exposure of this key to outside parties. Rather than using it directly to prove the genuineness of the TPM, an indirection is used. The user proposes a pseudonym (an attestation identity key) to a trusted third party (TTP), which verifies the TPM identity and then certifies the pseudonym. The certificate is then encrypted in a way that only the TPM with the original endorsement key can decrypt it again. Thus, only the TPM is able to use the attestation identity key. As long as the user trusts the TTP not to abuse the information it gathers, and verifiers of the platform trust the TTP to verify correctly, this provides users with a way to attest their platform status without giving up their anonymity.

Unfortunately, the concept of anonymizing the TPM by means of a trusted third party quickly reached its limits if applied on a large scale. It never became clear who would operate the trusted third parties under which conditions, and the mere existence of a platform identity was sufficient to create user outrage. Thus, the latest version of the TPM specification offers a zero-knowledge proof based attestation protocol, *direct anonymous attestation* (DAA) [8]. This is a highly advanced cryptographic protocol that allows a TPM to prove knowledge of a certificate, without the need to show the certificate itself. Revocation is still possible to a limited extend; if the verifier knows the TPM's secrets, e.g., because an illegal software emulation appears on the Internet that used that secrets, it can recognize (and thus invalidate) that TPM. Furthermore, TPMs are recognizable if they access the same verifier twice in a short time period – a TPM making 10 requests from five countries within an hour can thus be detected, though not identified. In addition to offering an anonymous authentication mechanism, users may now permanently delete the endorsement key and thus the only unique identity of the platform. This deletion does, however, take the TPM out of the TCG trust infrastructure. The TPM cannot prove anymore that it is real, unless some trusted party issues a new certificate.

In practice, attestation on arbitrary PC platforms still faces significant limits. It does work well to detect changes to a previously known platform, e.g., a computer in a large organization or an embedded system. If the concept is to be extended to remotely verify properties of generic PCs, however, the verifier has to take into account every plausible version of BIOS and operating system, including various patch levels. Furthermore, the amount of information transmitted creates a privacy problem, and opens the door for abuse. As the verifier receives all data from the platform and then locally decides if this platform configuration is good, it is possible to discriminate against platforms running, for example, a competitor's operating system – a possibility that caused massive criticism. One solution to both problems is property-based attestation [9,10]. In this model, the platform receives a certificate for properties a verifier might be interested in, and uses the security hardware to ensure that the certificates can only be accessed if the platform is actually in the configuration that was certified. The verifier then asks for a certificate for the property he is interested in, and receives exactly this information. Thus, the user does not need to tell the verifier everything about the platform, and the verifier needs to be open about the requirements; denying a service to a platform for questionable reasons immediately exposes the verifier.

9.5 Secure I/O and User Interfaces

Beside demonstrating to another platform that it is genuine, a trusted platform may need further secure ways to communicate with external parties. There are two main communication paths, with different properties:

- The trusted platform may want to build a secure channel to another (trusted) platform.
- The trusted platform wants to talk to the user.

While another computer can run the remote attestation protocol and thus establish a secure link to the trusted platform (though the details, especially the key management, are still a huge issue), a user obviously cannot perform the cryptographic operations necessary. In most cases, however, the trusted part of a system – be it a full-blown cryptographic coprocessor or a TPM – do not have their own user interface, but share it with other, untrusted applications. As pointed out in [11], even small manipulations to the user interface can have a large effect; if an attacker can change the font, for example, a user may think he is signing a contract over $1000, while in fact it is £1000. Sometimes the user may not even know what application he is currently talking to – as for example demonstrated by Web pages that disguise hyperlinks as system pop-up windows. Work is currently underway to both add I/O directly to the hardware and to build security-aware window managers, but with little commercial impact so far.

9.6 Protected Execution and Secure Operating Systems

The ability to boot securely and to reliably attest the status of a platform to a user or a third party is of limited use if the software booted on the platform is not trusted in the first place. For some applications, trust in the software can be achieved by only allowing authorized code to run on the platform in the first place. This is a plausible solution for many smartcard solutions or specialized hardware security modules. On more-general platforms, like a personal computer or a mobile phone, however, this approach is hardly possible. For one, commonly used operating systems feature a complexity that makes it practically impossible not to have security vulnerabilities in the operating system itself. With a kernel size of several million lines of source code, and (estimated) the order of one security-relevant bug for each 1000 lines of code, such systems are insecure by design. Furthermore, it is harder to impose restrictions on programs run on such a platform. On both user and business platforms, it is very common to have various applications on the same platform that may try to negatively interfere with each other. Therefore, the next important step towards a trusted platform is to build trust into the correctness of the software, and prevent it from being corrupted at runtime.

Most current operating systems show a great weakness in this area, which is due to the basic design principles. The kernel, i.e., the part of the operating system that has unlimited access rights, features millions of lines of code, and one corrupted application can quickly compromise the entire system. To make things worse, automated attack tools that use already compromised systems to scan the network for vulnerable platforms have drastically increased the probability of an attack on the running system; in some experiments, we saw the first attacks in less than a minute after connecting a computer to the Internet. Thus, currently the greatest challenge on the way towards trusted platforms is the design of operating systems in a way that allows the containment of an attacker and prevents security problems in a single application to compromise the whole system. The first step towards this goal is mandatory access control, as already implemented in some Linux versions [12]. This ensures that each program gets only the access rights it absolutely needs to perform its tasks. Thus, for example, a game has no access rights to the email program's address book. To achieve real security, however, a more fundamental change in the structure of the operating system is necessary:

- Different processes on the platform must be strongly separated from each other. Apart from a clearly defined and controlled API, two processes on the same machine should not even be able to send messages to each other, let alone tamper with each other's execution.
- The trusted computing base, i.e., the code that one has to trust to have no security-relevant bugs or back doors, must be as small as possible. Current security kernels have about 10,000 lines of source code, which makes a formal verification for correctness possible. This code should do not much more than resource management and message passing between the processes; all other functionality, ideally including the user interface and device drivers, should already be protected from each other.

While systems exist that implement these principles, most legacy operating systems have not been designed with process separation in mind; as applications for such systems need to be able to run on a secure operating system, this requires a major redesign of the operating system while keeping the system compatible with legacy applications. The first attempt towards this goal was to create a secure operating system in parallel with the legacy one by using a secure processor mode [13]. While the insecure mode would run legacy applications without change, a new, independent operating system in the secure mode would execute security-critical applications, protected from the original, insecure system by the hardware and from each other by a security kernel. While this approach worked for some systems, it met significant problems in many others, especially in the PC world. The design would have required many applications to be split in two parts, the (large) legacy part and the security-critical part. The problems of splitting applications in this way, and defining the proper APIs between the two components, caused this approach to be largely abandoned. The alternative approach is to run the legacy operating system on top of the secure system. On top of the security kernel, a virtualization layer is built that emulates one or several independent platforms. The legacy operating system – or even several instances of it – run in a virtual machine, protected from the other instances that run on the same platform, but in different virtual machines. A number of systems are already available that implement variations of this design, though only recently have security issues become a major focus, and received major funding [14,15,16,17]. For the time being, though, hardware support is insufficient; the virtualization layer requires either a modification of the legacy code, or imposes a high performance penalty on the system. Future processor architectures, such as AMD's Pacifica and Intel's Silvervale, will have integrated support for virtualization techniques.

A different approach has been taken by Microsoft's Singularity project and the JCOP JavaCard. Instead of building a virtual machine for generic code, the system only allows applications in a programming language that itself ensures isolation of different programs, as Java does due to the Java virtual machine. While this proved successful for small, largely legacy-free systems such as a smartcard, it remains to be seen if the approach can be scaled into a large platform.

9.7 Future Trends

Originally, trusted platforms were mostly needed in high security sectors such as banking and military applications. Over recent years, however, the trust requirements for normal users have increased substantially. Consumer-owned devices such as personal computers and cellular phones now store sensitive data, authorize financial transactions, and start to take decisions on behalf of their owners. In addition, third-party interests in such devices have emerged. Cell phones are sponsored by the network providers (who can subsequently do not allow the phone to be used on a competing network), digital content may involve restrictions on redistribution, and manufacturers want to securely distribute updates. Additionally, trusted platforms are required in various settings that require more constraints than the PC environment, for example in cars or cellular phones.

Even though the Trusted Computing Group always had platforms beyond PCs and servers in mind, many of the new constraints – such as a host platform with limited resources – are not addressed by the current specifications.

In the mobile computing world, the issues of trusted platforms are becoming increasingly important due to several factors. On one hand, mobile platforms such as cell phones are being used for increasingly critical tasks, such as for electronic payment, authentication, and location-based services. On the other hand, formerly closed platforms are becoming open to third-party services and different wireless communication protocols, significantly increasing the attack surface. One issue in adapting trusted computing technologies as discussed above is due to restricted resources. In a cell phone, there is no powerful main processor for computationally intensive tasks and no huge external storage for key data, and even battery power consumption has to be taken into account. Beside this, a mobile phone offers a different trust model. While a PC usually has a well-defined owner (which consequently has the main authority over the trusted hardware) cell phones tend to be subsidized by the network providers, which subsequently demand their own privileges, such as blocking other network providers or imposing their own user interface on the device. Thus, user management on such devices may pose a major challenge for future development. Thinking a step further, in the world of ubiquitous computing, the challenges of TPMs with restricted resources and a cap on the price tag will become extremely difficult. On one hand, some concept of *roots of trust* will be needed in such a setting – devices will have the need to authenticate themselves and securely communicate, and thus require at least some secure key storage. On the other hand, margins on those devices will not allow for anything close to existing TPMs; essentially, the root of trust has to be put into the existing platform, with very little room to add any extra hardware.

As another example, computing platforms in the automotive setting are getting new exposure. The amount of software in a car is steadily increasing, and manipulations to the firmware in order to boost the car's performance are already common. In the foreseeable future, cars may also get interconnected, for example to drive in a caravan mode, or receive software updates via wireless networks – both functions one would not want a third party to tamper with. Also, in this setting, reliability and lifecycle management become interesting issues. While a PC can – and under some circumstances even should – just shut down in response to an intrusion, a car system needs to maintain a number of safety properties. Also, the lifetime of a PC is rather limited, allowing relatively quick fading out of old hardware versions and replacing them with updated versions. However, a car may be around for 20 years or longer, and the failure of a critical component can prove fatal.

Another challenge for the way we perceive trusted platforms lies in the increasing amount of distributed functionality. In the past, trusted platforms have mostly been seen as isolated systems. They may need to be able to demonstrate their trustworthiness to the user or a remote system, but apart from that, they act largely on their own. In a modern environment, however, this is not necessarily the case anymore. A platform may have external storage (such as a networked file system), consist of several different processors, and interact in security-relevant ways with remote peripherals (such as printers, but also displays or input devices). Thus, a system that looks like one platform to the outside consists in fact of several largely independent components, forming a virtual platform. Apart from assuring the functionality of an individual platform, it is thus getting important to assure the functionality of an entire network. The trusted computing group has performed some first steps in this direction with the formation of a peripherals working group and the trusted network connect specification, which defines the interaction of clients with an overall cooperative network [1].

The final challenge comes with the introduction of trusted platforms beyond the scope of single organizations, especially in end-user devices and PCs. In many such platforms, the trust model is no longer well defined – the owner may want to trust the platform to perform an e-banking application correctly in spite of viruses, while a content provider may want to trust the platform to prohibit the distribution of the content in spite of the owner of the platform.

This mix of interest has led to a deep distrust towards trusted computing by consumer organizations [18].

References

1. Trusted Computing Group. https://www.trustedcomputinggroup.org/
2. K. Kursawe, D. Schellekens, B. Preneel (2005) Analyzing trusted platform communication. In ECRYPT Workshop, CRASH – CRyptographic Advances in Secure Hardware.
3. M. Bond (2001) Attacks on Cryptoprocessor Transaction Sets. In Proceedings of the CHES 2001 Workshop, pp. 220–234
4. D. Osvik, A. Shamir, E. Tromer (2006) Cache Attacks and Countermeasures: The Case of AES. In CT-RSA, pp. 1–20.
5. W. Arbaugh, D. Farber, J. Smith (1997) A Secure and Reliable Bootstrap Architecture. In Proc. IEEE Symposium on Security and Privacy, pp. 65–71.
6. J. Molina, W. Arbaugh (2002) Using Independent Auditors as Intrusion Detection Systems. In Proceedings of the Fourth International Conference on Information and Communications Security, pp. 291 – 302.
7. http://www.cdt.org/privacy/issues/pentium3
8. E. Brickell, J. Camenisch, L. Chen (2004) Direct anonymous attestation. In Proceedings of 11th ACM Conference on Computer and Communications Security, pp. 132 – 145.
9. A. Sadeghi, C. Stüble (2004) Property-based attestation for computing platforms: caring about properties, not mechanisms. In Proceedings of the 2004 Workshop on New Security Paradigms NSPW '04, pp. 67–77.
10. J. Poritz, M. Schunter, E. van Herreweghen, M. Waidner (2004) Property Attestation—Scalable and Privacy-friendly Security Assessment of Peer Computers. IBM Technical Report RZ3548, IBM Research, Zurich Laboratory.
11. B. Pfitzmann, J. Riordan, C. Stüble, M. Waidner, A. Weber (2001) The PERSEUS system architecture. Technical Report RZ 3335, IBM Research Division, Zurich Laboratory
12. http://www.nsa.gov/selinux/
13. M. Peinado, Y. Chen (2004), NGSCB: A Trusted Open System. In Proc. of 9th Australasian Conf. on Information Security and Privacy ACISP, pp. 13–15.
14. P. Barham, B. Dragovic, K. Fraser, S. Hand, T. Harris, A. Ho, R. Neugebauer, I. Pratt, A. Warfield (2003) Xen and the art of virtualization. In Proc. of the 19th ACM Symposium on Operating Systems Principles SOSP, pp. 164–177.
15. R. Sailer, T. Jaeger, E. Valdez, R. Caceres, R. Perez, S. Berger, J. Griffin, L. van Doorn (2005) Building a MAC-Based Security Architecture for the Xen Open-Source Hypervisor. In Proceedings of the 21st Annual Computer Security Applications Conference (ACSAC), pp. 276–285.
16. A. Sadeghi, C. Stüble, N. Pohlmann (2004) European Multilateral Secure Computing Base – Open Trusted Computing for You and Me. Datenschutz und Datensicherheit (DuD), 9/04, pp. 548–553.
17. http://www.opentc.net/
18. S. Schoen (2004) EFF comments on TCG design, implementation and usage principles. www.eff.org/Infrastructure/trusted_computing/20041004_eff_comments_tcg_principles.pdf.

Strong Authentication with Physical Unclonable Functions

Pim Tuyls and Boris Škorić

Philips Research
The Netherlands

Summary. Physical unclonable functions (PUFs) can be used as a cost-effective means to store cryptographic key material in an unclonable way. They can be employed for strong authentication of objects, e.g., tokens, and of persons possessing such tokens, but also for other purposes. We give a short overview of security applications where PUFs are useful, and discuss physical realisations, noisy measurements and information content of PUFs. Then we describe an integrated authentication token containing an optical PUF, a challenging mechanism and a detector. Finally, we discuss authentication protocols for controlled and uncontrolled PUFs.

10.1 General Introduction to PUFs

A physical unclonable function (PUF) is a function that is realized by a physical system, such that the function is easy to evaluate but the physical system is hard to characterize, model or reproduce.

Physical tokens were first used as identifiers in the 1980s in the context of strategic arms limitation treaty monitoring. The concept was later investigated for civilian purposes [1]. The studied tokens were hard to reproduce physically, but easy to read out, i.e., all the physical parameters necessary for successful identification are readily given up by the token. This makes these tokens suitable for systems where the verifier knows with certainty that an actual token is being probed and that the measuring device can be trusted. However, the tokens are not suitable for online identification protocols with a remote party. An imposter can copy the data from someone's token, and then enter that data through a keyboard. The verifier cannot tell if a token is actually present.

PUF-based tokens were introduced by Pappu [2, 3]. These tokens are so complex that it is infeasible to fully read out the data contained in a token or to make a computer model that predicts the outputs of a token [4]. This makes

PUFs suitable for online protocols as well as verification involving physical probing by untrusted devices.

A PUF is a physical system interacting in a complicated way with stimuli (*challenges*) and leads to unique but unpredictable *responses*. A challenge and the corresponding response are together called a *challenge-reponse pair* (CRP). A PUF behaves like a keyed hash function; the physical system, consisting of many 'random' components, is equivalent to the key. In order to be hard to characterize, the system should not allow efficient extraction (by measurements) of the relevant properties of its interacting components. Physical systems produced by an uncontrollable random process, e.g., mixing of substances, turn out to be good candidates for PUFs. Because of this lack of control, it is hard to produce a physical copy. Furthermore, if the physical function is based on many complex interactions, then mathematical modeling is also hard. These two properties together are referred to as *unclonability*.

10.2 Applications

From a security perspective the uniqueness of the responses and unclonability of PUFs are very useful properties. PUFs can be used as unique identifiers [1, 5, 6, 7], means of tamper detection and/or as a cost-effective source for key generation (common randomness) between two parties [8, 9]. The latter is useful for authenticating objects and persons. By embedding a PUF inseparably into a device, the device becomes uniquely identifiable and unclonable. Inseparable means that any attempt to remove the PUF, will with high probability, damage the PUF and destroy the key material it contains. A wide range of devices can be equipped with a PUF in this way, e.g., tokens, smartcards, credit cards, RFID tags, value paper (such as banknotes and passports), chips, security cameras.

We list a number of functions that the embedded PUF can have in such devices. We distinguish between uncontrolled or bare PUFs on one hand, which can be probed by attackers, and 'Controlled' PUFs (CPUFs) on the other, where the embedding severely restricts the attacker's ability to challenge the PUF and to read the unprocessed PUF output (see Sect. 10.2.2 for a more precise definition). As a rule, any goal that can be achieved with an uncontrolled PUF can always be achieved with a CPUF as well. We use the term integrated PUF to denote a miniaturized device containing a PUF, the challenging mechanism, the detector and optionally a processor as well. An integrated PUF is not necessarily a CPUF. In Sect. 10.6 we discuss in more detail how to use a PUF in an authentication token. We describe an integrated optical PUF containing the PUF, a challenging mechanism and a detector, and we give authentication protocols for controlled and uncontrolled PUFs.

10.2.1 Applications of Uncontrolled PUFs

Identification and Authentication

Several secure identification and authentication protocols based on CRPs were worked out in [8, 10, 11]. Typically there are two phases: enrolment and verification. In the enrolment phase, a number of challenges are chosen randomly, and the measured PUF responses are stored. In the verification phase the PUF is subjected to one or more of the enrolment challenges. The response is checked against the enrolled response data. The same CRP is never used twice. We distinguish between on the one hand identification, where a comparison is made between unprocessed PUF outputs, usually involving a correlation or distance measure, and on the other hand authentication, where a cryptographic key is derived from the PUF output for performing a cryptographic challenge-response protocol or for generating a message authentication code (MAC).

We consider an attack model in which an attacker can obtain a victim's embedded-PUF device for a short time without causing suspicion (e.g. a waiter taking a customer's credit card). He can measure self-chosen CRPs during this time. Afterwards, he tries to impersonate the PUF. However, we assume that the challenge space is so large and/or the PUF responses so slow that the attacker cannot cover a significant part of the challenge space [4]. Hence, after his attack he only has a very small probability of correctly guessing responses to future challenges.

Tamper Evidence, Tamper Detection and Tamper Resistance

A manufacturer attaches a PUF to a device in an inseparable way. He creates enrolment data by randomly choosing a number of challenges, measuring the responses and storing the CRPs. An invasive attack will inevitably damage the PUF. The manufacturer can see the evidence of this tampering by subjecting the PUF to the enrolled challenges and verifying if the responses are sufficiently close to the enrolled responses. Real-time tamper detection can be achieved if the PUF is an integrated PUF having access to the enrolment data. The PUF then performs regular self-checks and, as soon as a response does not match the enrolment data, it takes appropriate action, e.g., raises an alarm or shuts down. Tamper resistance is achieved by encrypting critical secrets with a key derived from a PUF response. When an attacker damages the PUF, the complete CRP behavior changes. Measurements no longer reveal the decryption key. Note that the key is permanently stored in the physical structure of the PUF and not in digital memory. A possible drawback of this method is that the critical secrets are destroyed. From a security perspective, however, such self-destruction is an advantage.

Anti-counterfeiting

In order to protect a product against counterfeiting, a detection mark is embedded into the product or its packaging by a trusted authority (TA). This mark consists of a physical part (e.g., a PUF) and a digital part. Any verifier is able to check the authenticity of the product by inspecting the mark. The physical part has unique responses to physical challenges. The digital part consists of certified data, signed by the TA, that describes how to challenge the physical part and how to check whether the responses are correct. Typically, the TA chooses a small random set of challenges for each PUF. He measures the responses and signs the set of CRPs with his private key. The signed data is stored on the product, e.g., in the form of a barcode. The verifier reads the barcode and verifies the signature using the TA's public key. If the signature is valid, he proceeds to measure the responses to the recorded challenges. If these responses match the recorded responses, the verifier is convinced that the product is authentic. Optionally, if he has limited time, he can choose to check a random subset of the enrolled CRPs. The attacker (counterfeiter) has access to all components of the detection mark: he can read it, remove it from the product and investigate it. Based on the information he obtains, he aims to produce a fake detection mark that has a non-negligible probability of passing as an authentic one. The dual character of the mark forces the counterfeiter to accomplish either of the following difficult tasks:

1. Copy the signature (easy); clone the physical part (extremely difficult).
2. Produce a new random PUF and enrol a random set of CRPs (easy); forge a TA digital signature under these data (extremely difficult).

Note that there is a limit to the number of CRPs that can be recorded on the product. There may also be a limit to the amount of time that the TA can spend on the enrolment procedure. The smaller the number of enrolled CRPs, the easier and cheaper it becomes to produce a physical clone of the PUF, since only the enrolled responses have to be reproduced by the clone.

Copy Protection

The application of PUFs for copy protection is similar to anti-counterfeiting. The underlying assumption for effective copy protection is that content is delivered in encrypted form bound to a data carrier (e.g., an optical disc), and that it can only be decrypted and rendered by compliant devices. The detection mark is embedded in the data carrier. Compliant devices always check the authenticity of the mark, and refuse to render the content if the check fails. Optionally, compliant devices derive the content decryption key from the PUF. The attack model is that a (professional) pirate aims to create clones of an original data carrier that are accepted by compliant devices. As in the anti-counterfeiting case, the pirate must either clone a PUF or forge a signature.

Brand Protection

A manufacturer wishes to verify if a product found in the field has been manufactured by him or by someone else. Brand protection using PUFs is almost the same as anti-counterfeiting, but faces slightly different requirements. Not everyone should necessarily be able to verify the authenticity. In many cases it is even preferable if only the manufacturer knows the authenticity marks. Furthermore, the manufacturer may use extensive resources for the verification (e.g., time, expensive equipment). The manufacturer embeds a PUF into each of his products. He stores the corresponding CRPs. In the verification phase, he looks up the CRP(s) for the specific PUF embedded in that product and verifies if the PUF behavior corresponds to the stored CRPs.

10.2.2 Applications of Controlled PUFs

A special class of applications becomes possible with so-called control [10]. A *controlled PUF* (CPUF) is a combination of a PUF and an integrated circuit (IC), bound together such that an attacker has no access to the communication between the PUF and the IC. Any attempt to force them apart will damage the PUF. The IC completely governs the PUF input and output, prohibiting frequent challenging and possibly forbidding certain classes of challenges. It can scramble incoming challenges. It hides the physical output of the PUF, revealing to the outside world only indirect information derived from the output, e.g., an encryption or hash. This is a very broad definition of a CPUF, encompassing more than implementation of the controlled challenge-response primitives described in [10]. The control layer substantially strengthens the security, since an attacker cannot probe the PUF at will and cannot interpret the responses. CPUFs allow for secure key storage and for new applications such as certified execution, e-proofs [8, 10] and certified measurement.

Secure Key Storage

Many hardware devices, such as DVD players and TPMs (see Chap. 9), need to have access to secret device keys that are stored inside the device. Often these keys are unique to each device. Hence, they have to be stored in digital memory in a separate process during or after manufacture. Special protective measures must be taken to ensure that attackers cannot read this memory, not even with invasive means such as a focused ion beam (FIB).

PUFs offer a powerful alternative. The secret is not stored in digital memory, but it is hidden inside a PUF. Only when the device needs the secret, it extracts it from the PUF by performing a measurement. After using the secret, the device immediately erases it from all digital memory. Hence attackers cannot steal the secret from nonvolatile digital memory, because it is stored elsewhere, and even the (static-)RAM memory only contains the secret when it is strictly needed. The presence of the control layer hides the response from attackers. Thus, the problem of protecting digital memory has been replaced by the (easier) problem of integrating the control layer and the PUF *insepara-bly* and in such a way that it is very hard to probe the PUF from the outside. Furthermore, the physical measurement process should not be vulnerable to side-channel attacks, i.e., measurements must be at least as silent as digital memory readout in their power consumption and electromagnetic radiation. They should also be at least equally resistant to fault-induction attacks.

Note that the same challenge is reused each time. In contrast to the applications listed above, the security here does not derive from a large challenge space but from the control. Hence the name PUF may be a misnomer, and the alternative name physically obscured key (POK) has been proposed [11].

Certified Execution and Certified Measurement

If the control layer contains a general-purpose processor integrated with the PUF, then the CPUF is a secure and identifiable processing environment. A user can send a program to this environment for execution and receive, together with the execution result, a proof of integrity and origin, i.e., a proof that the result was actually obtained by running the program on that specific CPUF and was not modified afterwards. This is called certified execution. The proof is CRP-based in one of the following ways: (i) the user possesses at least one certified CRP. Along with the program he sends the PUF challenge to the CPUF. The CPUF proves that it knows the response, e.g., by encrypting a hash of the program and the result with a key derived from the response. The proof can either be intended for verification by the user only, or for verification by arbitrary third parties (e-proof); (ii) The CPUF has a POK which it treats as a private key. The corresponding public key has been certified by a TTP and is available to the user. The CPUF proves knowledge of the POK, e.g., by signing the program and the result with it. The user (or any other verifier) checks the signature with the public key.

Instead of a processor, the CPUF could also contain an integrated sensor, such as a camera. In analogy with certified execution, the CPUF proves the integrity and origin of the sensor data.

10.3 Physical Realizations

Several physical systems on which PUFs can be based are known. The main types are optical PUFs [2, 3], coating PUFs [8], silicon PUFs [11, 12] and acoustic PUFs [8]. We briefly discuss coating PUFs and optical PUFs. The idea of using an active coating was proposed in [13] and further developed in the context of PUFs in [8]. Coating PUFs are integrated with an IC (see Fig. 10.1). The IC is covered with a protective coating doped with random dielectric particles. By random dielectric particles we mean several kinds of particles of random size and shape with a relative dielectric constant ε_r differing from the dielectric constant of the coating matrix. In order to challenge the coating PUF, an array of metal sensors (e.g., a comb structure of wires), is laid down directly beneath the passivation layer. Sufficient randomness is only obtained if the dielectric particles are approximately of the same size as the distance between the sensor parts, or smaller, and if the average dielectric constant is high enough to allow for significant deviations from the average. A challenge corresponds to a voltage of a certain frequency and amplitude applied to the sensors at a certain point of the sensor array. Because of the presence of the coating material with its random dielectric properties, the sensor plates with the material in between behave as a capacitor with a random capacitance value. The capacitance value is converted (see Sect. 10.4) into a bit string which can be used as an identifier or a key. Coating PUFs have the advantage of possessing a high degree of integration. The matrix containing the random particles can be part of a tamper-resistance coating. A coating PUF also has the advantage that it is easily turned into a controlled PUF (CPUF), as it is inseparably bound to the underlying device. The control electronics can simply be put underneath the coating.

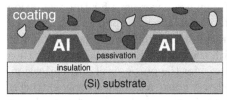

Fig. 10.1. Left: schematic cross section of a coating PUF. **Right:** scanning electron microscope image.

Optical PUFs consist of a transparent material (e.g., glass) containing randomly distributed light-scattering particles (e.g. air bubbles or plastic). They exploit the uniqueness of the speckle patterns that result from multiple scattering of laser light in a disordered optical medium. The response (output) is a speckle pattern. It is a function of the internal structure of the PUF, the wavelength of the laser, its angle of incidence, focal distance and other characteristics of the wave front. Optical probing of the PUF is difficult because light diffusion obscures the locations of the scatterers. At this moment the best physical techniques can probe diffusive materials up to a depth of approximately 10 scattering lengths [14]. Even if an attacker learns the positions of all the scatterers, this knowledge is of limited use to him. If he tries to make a physical copy of the PUF, he runs into the problem that precise positioning of a large number of scatterers is an arduous process. It would seem easier to make an electronic clone, i.e., a device that simply computes the correct responses to all challenges in real time or looks them up in electronic memory, without bothering with physical reproduction. However, even this turns out to be very hard. It requires accurate optical modelling of multiple coherent scattering. More precisely, the attacker has to solve the forward problem, which is a very complex task. Given the details of all the scatterers, the fastest known computation method of a speckle pattern is the transfer-matrix method [15].

It requires on the order of $(A/\lambda^2)^3 d/\lambda$ operations (where A is the illuminated area, λ is the wavelength, and d is the PUF thickness), which is larger than 10^{20} even if rather conservative values are chosen for A, λ and d.

10.4 Key Extraction from Noisy Measurements

For cryptographic protocols it is important to ensure that *exactly* the same key is derived from the enrolment and verification measurements. If measurement noise causes even one bit error in a cryptographic key, the protocol fails. In the case of uncontrolled PUFs, the noise level can sometimes be reduced by recalibrating the measurement setup (for optical PUFs, the calibration consists of setting a number of geometric parameters such as shifts and tilts of the laser, the PUF and the detector). A set of special nonsecret *calibration CRPs* [9] is reserved for this purpose. They are never used for the generation of secrets, but instead the verifier tests if the correct responses are obtained for these challenges. If his initial calibration is not too far off, he will be able to adjust it to get an optimal match with the calibration responses. Only then does he start measuring ordinary responses for the purposes of authentication.

To ensure robustness against the leftover noise, a so-called fuzzy extractor [16] is used. For instance, helper data [17] is generated during the enrolment phase. For each CRP, instructions are generated that describe how the PUF output should be processed, quantized, etc. to obtain a bit string. The helper data for each enrolled challenge is stored together with the challenge. In most applications only the keys need to be kept secret. Hence, the challenges and helper data can be stored anywhere (e.g., conveniently on the PUF), while the keys must either be stored in a safe place or in some encrypted or hashed form. In the verification phase the verifier selects an enrolled challenge with the corresponding helper data. The PUF is subjected to this challenge. Using the helper data he extracts a bit string from the PUF response. It is important to make sure that the helper data does not give away information about the secret extracted from the PUF response. Efficient masking methods have been developed for the discrete case [18] and for the analog case [17]. In general, they are based on error-correcting codes (ECCs). If the PUF output does not have a uniform probability distribution, then one must be extra careful because the redundancy present in the ECC, together with the non-uniformity, could reveal partial information on the secret. In that case an additional step is required called *privacy amplification* [16].

We list those applications from section 10.2 for which helper data is necessary: authentication, tamper resistance, copy protection (if the content key is derived from the PUF), key storage, certified execution and certified measurement. In the other applications helper data may be useful, depending on the implementation, but not strictly necessary.

10.5 Information Content of PUFs

An information-theoretic framework for the analysis of the security of uncontrolled PUFs was formulated in [4]. The central concept is the *entropy of a
measurement*, i.e., the amount of information about the PUF's structure that
is revealed by a measurement. One needs the notion of PUF space or configuration space, a discrete space where each point corresponds to a possible
PUF realization. A measurement is represented as a partitioning of the PUF
space. The measurement entropy is the entropy of this partitioning. The less
noisy the measurement, the more fine-grained the partitioning, and the higher
the measurement entropy. Using this formalism, a security parameter C is derived, the *number of independent CRPs* supported by the PUF. A set of CRPs
is called independent if knowledge of any part of the set gives zero information about the rest of the set. The parameter C is an information-theoretic
measure for the resistance of an uncontrolled PUF against an attacker who
has infinite resources. If an attacker has seen fewer than C CRPs, he does not
have enough information to predict other CRPs. If he has seen more than C
CRPs, he can predict new CRPs *in theory*. However, the practical difficulties
could be prohibitive. C also determines how much independent key material
a CPUF can extract from its PUF: the number of bits is given by C times the
entropy of a typical measurement. The analysis was applied to optical PUFs
in [4], where it was derived for a slab geometry that C lies in the interval

$$(\min \left\{ \frac{2\frac{d}{\lambda}(A_{\text{PUF}}/A_{\text{beam}})}{\pi \log(\frac{\pi e}{2}\frac{N_\varphi}{N_{\text{mod}}})}, \frac{\pi A_{\text{PUF}}}{\lambda^2} \right\}, \min \left\{ \frac{2\frac{d^2}{\lambda \ell}(A_{\text{PUF}}/A_{\text{beam}})}{3\pi \log(\frac{\pi e}{2}\frac{N_\varphi}{N_{\text{mod}}})}, \frac{\pi A_{\text{PUF}}}{\lambda^2} \right\})$$

with d the thickness of the PUF, λ the wavelength, ℓ the mean free path,
A_{PUF} the available area of the PUF, A_{beam} the area of the laser beam, N_φ
the number of photons used in the measurement and $N_{\text{mod}} = \pi A_{\text{beam}}/\lambda^2$ the
number of modes. In [19] the information content was computed for coating
PUFs with a 3D parallel-plate geometry, containing two types of particles.
The upper bound on the extractable entropy H is

$$H < \frac{1}{3}\sqrt{\frac{d}{s}p(1-p)} \left[\ln \frac{A^2}{2\pi p(1-p)ds^3} \right]^{3/2}$$

where d is the distance between the plates, s the size of the particles, A the
area of the plates, and p the fraction of particles of type 1.

10.6 PUF-Based Token

In this section we show how to make a *strong authentication token* based on
PUF CRPs. We first show how the whole measurement setup of an optical
PUF can be shrunk to a small integrated package that fits inside a token. Then
we present a backwards-secure authentication protocol for uncontrolled PUFs.
Finally we discuss more-advanced authentication methods using CPUFs.

10.6.1 Integrated Optical PUF

The token contains an optical PUF, a coherent light source, a challenge selection mechanism, a detector and electronics for processing and communication. In [2] a system with multiple lasers was proposed. Here we describe a more efficient integrated system containing only one laser (see Fig. 10.2). The complementary metal oxide semiconductor (CMOS) sensor has detector pixels as well as switchable display pixels. The display pixels are used to locally switch the liquid crystal (LC) layer between two phase rotation states, e.g., no rotation and 45° rotation. The configuration of the display pixels forms a challenge. The optical PUF is situated in the top layer. The laser light entering the PUF is scattered downward. There it may directly enter a detector pixel. Alternatively, it hits a display pixel, where it partly gets absorbed, and partly scatters with a phase rotation depending on the LC state. Part of the scattered light will eventually reach a detector pixel, possibly after a number of scatterings in the PUF or at other display pixels. At each detector pixel all contributions from the various scattering paths are added coherently. The configuration of the display pixels significantly influences the image recorded by the detector.

It is important to know the number of *independent* CRPs (see Sect. 10.5). Ordinarily, this number follows from the physical properties of the PUF. For the integrated PUF, however, the fixed measurement geometry puts constraints on the number of challenges that can be applied. We make an estimate based on the linearity of the Maxwell equations in a linear optical medium. We neglect scattering events where more than one display pixel is visited. This is a good approximation, since these events are far less likely than most paths containing zero or one display pixel visit. In this approximation, we can view the display pixels as (highly complicated) light sources in their own right which emit light in two states. Due to the linearity of the medium, the complex amplitude of the light hitting the camera is the sum of all the amplitudes generated by the light sources separately. We denote the number of display pixels as N_{pix}, the intensity at detector pixel j as I_j, and the amplitude at detector j originating from light source α in state s_α as $A_{j\alpha}(s_\alpha)$. The intensity registered by the camera is

$$I_j(\{s_\alpha\}) = \left| \sum_{\alpha=1}^{N_{\text{pix}}} A_{j\alpha}(s_\alpha) \right|^2 = \sum_{\alpha=1}^{N_{\text{pix}}} |A_{j\alpha}(s_\alpha)|^2 + 2 \sum_{\alpha>\beta} \text{Re} \, A_{j\alpha}(s_\alpha) A_{j\beta}^*(s_\beta).$$

(10.1)

Hence, if one knows all the speckle patterns generated by one or two light sources, then one can compute the response to an arbitrary challenge. If the PUF contains enough randomness and scatters strongly enough, then each term is independent of the other terms. The number of possible configurations of one or two sources follows from (10.1). The first summation has N_{pix} terms. Multiplying by 2 (for the possible state s_α of the source) gives the number of possible configurations of a single source. The second summation has

$\frac{1}{2}N_{\text{pix}}(N_{\text{pix}} - 1)$ terms. Multiplying by 4 (for the states s_α, s_β) gives the number of configurations of two sources. Added together, the number of possible one- or two-source configurations is $2N_{\text{pix}} + 4 \cdot \frac{1}{2}N_{\text{pix}}(N_{\text{pix}} - 1) = 2N_{\text{pix}}^2$. We conclude that, in a linear medium, the number of independent CRPs scales as N_{pix}^2. Hence, no matter how strong the PUF, a 1000-pixel configuration cannot yield more than $\mathcal{O}(10^6)$ independent challenges.

Of course, in a nonlinear medium the superposition rule does not apply, and the number of independent CRPs is expected to grow faster than N_{pix}^2.

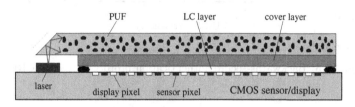

Fig. 10.2. Integrated system containing a laser, an optical PUF, switchable LC pixels for applying challenges, and a camera.

10.6.2 Authentication Protocol for an Uncontrolled PUF

We present a CRP-based protocol for authentication and session key establishment. The PUF is unprotected and fastened to a carrier such as a credit card. The carrier also has a small amount of rewritable nonvolatile memory. The holder of the PUF (the user) has to prove to the verifier (the bank) that he possesses the PUF. To this end he inserts the PUF in a reader e.g. automated telling machine (ATM) which communicates with the bank.

Attack Model

- The enrolment procedure and the bank's database are secure.
- The attacker cannot see the challenges and responses at the ATM side.
- The ATM↔bank channel is not secure. An attacker records all messages.
- The attacker gets hold of the user's PUF for a short time without being noticed. He has time to measure a limited number of CRPs. Using these CRPs he tries to impersonate the user or to decrypt past messages.

Enrolment

For a number of PUFs the bank performs the following procedure:

- Assign an identifier ID_{PUF} to the PUF.
- Generate a random string x.

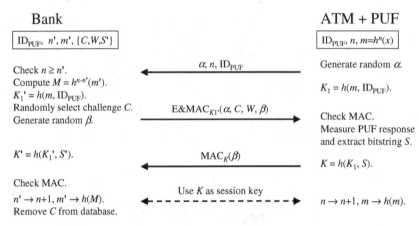

Fig. 10.3. Backwards-secure authentication protocol based on CRPs.

- Generate a set of random challenges C_i. For each challenge, choose a secret S'_i at random, and generate helper data W_i.
- Store ID_{PUF}, $n = 0$, and $m = x$ in the token memory.
- Coupled to ID_{PUF} store $n' = 0$, $m' = x$, and $\{C_i, W_i, S'_i\}$ in a database.

When a user account is opened, the user receives one of the enrolled PUF tokens, and the corresponding PUF identifier is coupled to his account.

Authentication

The user inserts his PUF token in an ATM and authenticates himself to the bank as follows.

- ATM: reads the token memory and generates a random nonce α. Sends α, ID_{PUF}, n to the bank.
- Bank: checks if $n \geq n'$. If not, it generates an error message and aborts. Computes $M = h^{n-n'}(m')$ and $K'_1 = h(M, \text{ID}_{\text{PUF}})$. Here h is a one-way function. Generates a random nonce β. Selects a random CRP j from the database, coupled to ID_{PUF}. Sends $E_1 = \text{E\&MAC}_{K'_1}(\alpha, C_j, W_j, \beta)$ to the ATM ($\text{E\&MAC}_\kappa$ denotes encryption and MAC with key κ).
- ATM: computes $K_1 = h(m, \text{ID}_{\text{PUF}})$. Decrypts E_1 with the key K_1 and checks the MAC. If the MAC is wrong or the decrypted α is wrong, the protocol is aborted with an error message. The ATM uses C_j to challenge the PUF. Converts the PUF response to a bitstring S_j using the helper data W_j. Computes $K = h(K_1, S_j)$. Sends $E_2 = \text{MAC}_K(\beta)$ to the bank.
- Bank: computes $K' = h(K'_1, S'_j)$. Checks the MAC E_2 using the key K'. If the check fails, it aborts with an error message.
- Bank and ATM: use $K = K'$ as a session key. Complete the transaction.
- ATM: modifies $n \to n + 1$ and $m \to h(m)$ in the token memory.

- Bank: modifies $n' \to n+1$ and $m' \to h(M)$ in the database. Removes the j'th CRP from the database.

Properties of the Protocol

- There are no public key operations. The most resource-intensive operations are hashing and symmetric encryptions/decryptions.
- The protocol is backwards-secure. Intuitively the argument goes as follows. Suppose an attacker records all communications, and then gets hold of a token long enough to read ID_{PUF}, n and $m_n = h^n(x)$ and to measure some CRPs. In order to reconstruct the previous session key K, he has to measure the response to the previous challenge C. To obtain C he has to reconstruct the key K_1. However, K_1 was derived from $h^{n-1}(x) = h^{-1}(m_n)$. Hence he is forced to invert the hash function.
- With each authentication session, the bank's list of usable CRPs shrinks. In order to prevent it from shrinking to zero, one can use a replenishment protocol [8]. Before the database gets empty, a successful authentication session can be used to let the bank query the PUF and store the responses.
- The security is broken if the attacker can see what happens inside the ATM, i.e., if he can hack it or replace it with his own fake ATM.

10.6.3 Authentication Token Based on a Controlled PUF

Much stronger authentication is achievable if the PUF in the token is a controlled one. In the simplest case, the protocol of Sect. 10.6.2 can be used. The CPUF computes all the hashes and encryptions/decryptions itself, and uses the ATM as a simple conduit for the messages. Hence, the ATM does not have to be trusted any more. A more sophisticated use of the POK(s) inside the CPUF is to employ asymmetric cryptography. As will be explained below, one advantage is that the bank no longer needs to maintain a CRP database for each PUF. Another advantage is that the authenticity of the CPUF can be verified by anyone, not just the bank. In [20] it was shown that the measurement processing for a coating PUF and the cryptography for a Schnorr zero-knowledge (ZK) protocol can be realized in surprisingly little hardware: 5 kilogates in total. This means that it can be implemented on an RFID tag. Hence, it is possible to make an unclonable RFID tag with strong ZK authentication.

Enrolment

The enroller (a TA) selects a random PUF challenge C for a CPUF with identifier i. The challenge is fed into the CPUF. The CPUF transforms the response into a bitstring, which it treats as an asymmetric private key S. Then the CPUF generates the corresponding public key P and outputs P. The TA creates a certificate, signed with his own private key, stating that the CPUF with identifier i has public key P associated with the challenge C. The certificate is stored in/on the CPUF.

Authentication

The verifier obtains the certificate from the CPUF. He checks the signature using the TA's public key. If the signature is invalid, the authentication fails. Then he sends C to the CPUF. Finally he runs the interactive ZK protocol with the CPUF [20], where the CPUF has to prove its knowledge of the PUF-based secret S associated with the challenge C and the public key P.

Remarks

In contrast to CPUF protocols based on symmetric cryptography, there is no bootstrapping mode [10]: the private key is never revealed to the outside world. Note that the computation of the public key inside the CPUF requires one exponentiation. Any CPUF capable of running a Schnorr ZK protocol is capable of performing this operation.

10.7 Conclusion

Physical unclonable functions can be used for a wide variety of security-related applications: Identification, authentication, tamper evidence, detection and resistance, anti-counterfeiting, copy protection, brand protection, key storage, certified execution and certified measurements. To prevent physical cloning, the production process should be uncontrolled, and uncontrollable in principle except at great expense. To prevent cloning by modelling, a response should be the result of complex physical interactions between the challenge and the disordered PUF structure. Furthermore, to prevent both forms of cloning the PUF must be hard to probe. Any PUF-based application needs a physical structure meeting these requirements, a device for applying challenges, a detector and a good cryptographic protocol. If a reproducible bitstring has to be derived, then helper data are needed as well. For several types of PUF (coating, silicon and optical), it is clear that all these components can be integrated in a small device. As the intrinsic cost of the PUF material itself is negligible, this means that PUF devices can have a low cost. The strength of an uncontrolled PUF can be expressed as the number of independent CRPs that it supports. The amount of POK key material that can be stored is roughly given by this number times the measurement entropy of a single measurement. The strength of a CPUF is based on the difficulty of disentangling the PUF and the control layer. In a switched-off device, a POK is protected much better than a digitally stored key. The cryptography involved in PUF applications requires modest resources. The authentication protocol described in Sect. 10.6.2, for instance, needs no public key operations, but only symmetric operations and a one-way hash function. Furthermore, in several scenarios involving asymmetric cryptography (e.g. anti-counterfeiting) the device containing the PUF is completely passive, while the hard work is done by the enroller and the verifier. Finally, even if the PUF device needs to do asymmetric cryptography, efficient (ZK) implementations exist that keep the hardware cost at a minimum, so that implementation is possible even on an RFID tag.

Acknowledgements

We thank Jan van Geloven, Hennie Kretschman, Wil Ophey, Geert-Jan Schrijen, Nynke Verhaegh and Rob Wolters for useful discussions.

References

1. D.W. Bauder, *An Anti-Counterfeiting Concept for Currency*, Systems Research Report PTK-11990, Sandia National Laboratories, 1983.
2. R. Pappu, *Physical One-Way Functions*, Ph.D. thesis, MIT 2001.
3. R. Pappu, B. Recht, J. Taylor, N. Gershenfeld, *Physical One-Way Functions*, Science Vol. 297, Sept 2002, p. 2026.
4. P. Tuyls, B. Škorić, S. Stallinga, A.H.M. Akkermans, W. Ophey, *Information-Theoretic Security Analysis of Physical Uncloneable Functions*, A.S. Patrick and M. Yung (eds.): Proc. 9th Conf. on Financial Cryptography and Data Security, March 2005, LNCS 3570, pp. 141–155.
5. Unicate BV's '3DAS' system, http://www.andreae.com/Unicate/Appendix%201.htm, 1999.
6. D. Kirovski, *A Point-Subset Compression Algorithm for Fiber-based Certificates of Authenticity*, IEEE Proc. ISIT 2004, p.173.
7. J.D.R Buchanan, R.P. Cowburn, A. Jausovec, D. Petit, P. Seem, G. Xiong, D. Atkinson, K. Fenton, D.A. Allwood, M.T. Bryan, *Forgery: 'Fingerprinting' documents and packaging* , Nature 436, p. 475 (28 Jul 2005), Brief Communications
8. P. Tuyls, B. Škorić, *Secret Key Generation from Classical Physics*, in 'Hardware Technology Drivers of Ambient Intelligence', S. Mukherjee et al (eds.), Philips Research Book Series Vol.5 Kluwer, 2005.
9. B. Škorić, P. Tuyls, W. Ophey, *Robust key extraction from Physical Uncloneable Functions*, Ioannidis, Keromytis, Yung (Eds.): Proc. ACNS 2005, LNCS 3531, pp.407–422.
10. B. Gassend, D. Clarke, M. van Dijk, S. Devadas, *Controlled Physical Random Functions*, Proc. 18th Annual Computer Security Applications Conf., Dec. 2002.
11. B. Gassend, *Physical Random Functions*, Master's thesis, MIT 2003.
12. B. Gassend, D. Clarke, M. van Dijk, S. Devadas, *Silicon Physical Random Functions*, Proc. 9th ACM Conf. on Computer and Communications Security, 2002.
13. R. Posch, *Protecting Devices by Active Coating*, Journal of Universal Computer Science, vol. 4, no. 7 (1998), pp. 652–668.
14. M. Magnor, P. Dorn, W. Rudolph, *Simulation of confocal microscopy through scattering media with and without time gating*, J.Opt.Soc.Am. B, vol. 19, no. 11 (2001), 1695–1700.
15. H. Furstenberg, *Noncommuting Random Matrices*, Trans. Am. Math. Soc. 108, 377, 1963.

16. Y. Dodis, L. Reyzin and A. Smith, *Fuzzy Extractors: How to Generate Strong Keys from Biometrics and Other Noisy Data*, Adv. in Cryptology – Eurocrypt 2004, LNCS 3027, pp. 523–540, 2004.

17. J.P. Linnartz and P. Tuyls, *New Shielding Functions to Enhance Privacy and Prevent Misuse of Biometric Templates*, Proc. 4th International Conference on Audio and Video Based Biometric Person Authentication, LNCS 2688, Springer-Verlag, pp. 238–250,2003.

18. A. Juels, M. Wattenberg, *A Fuzzy Commitment Scheme*, in G. Tsudik, ed., Sixth ACM Conference on Computer and Communications Security, 28–36, ACM Press. 1999.

19. B. Škorić, S. Maubach, T. Kevenaar, P. Tuyls, *Information-theoretic analysis of capacitive Physical Unclonable Functions*, J. Appl. Phys. 100, 024902 (2006).

20. P. Tuyls and L. Batina, *RFID-Tags for Anti-Counterfeiting*, in 'Topics in Cryptology' - CT-RSA 2006, The Cryptographers' Track at the RSA Conference, LNCS 3860, D. Pointcheval (ed.), Springer-Verlag, pp. 115–131, 2006.

Part III

Privacy Enhancing

Privacy-Preserving Data Mining

Ljiljana Brankovic, Md. Zahidul Islam, and Helen Giggins

The University of Newcastle
Australia

Summary. Despite enormous benefits and the extremely fast proliferation of data mining in recent years, data owners and researchers alike have acknowledged that data mining also revives old and introduces new threats to individual privacy. Many believe that data mining is, and will continue to be, one of the most significant privacy challenges in years to come.

We live in an information age where vast amounts of personal data are regularly collected in the process of bank transactions, credit-card payments, making phone calls, using reward cards, visiting doctors and renting videos and cars, to mention but a few examples. All these data are typically used for data mining and statistical analysis and are often sold to other companies and organizations.

A breach of privacy occurs when individuals are not aware that the data have been collected in the first place, have been passed onto other companies and organizations, or have been used for purposes other than the one for which they were originally collected. Even when individuals approve of use of their personal records for data mining and statistical analysis, for example in medical research, it is still assumed that only aggregate values will be made available to researchers and that no individual values will be disclosed.

Various techniques can be employed in order to ensure the confidentiality of individual records and other sensitive information. They include adding noise to the original data, so that disclosing perturbed data does not necessarily reveal the confidential individual values. Some techniques were developed specifically for mining vertically and/or horizontally partitioned data. In this scenario each partition belongs to a different party (e.g., a hospital), and no party is willing to share their data but they all have interest in mining the total data set comprising all of the partitions. There are other techniques that focus on protecting confidentiality of logic rules and patterns discovered from data.

In this chapter we introduce the main issues in privacy-preserving data mining, provide a classification of existing techniques and survey the most important results in this area.

11.1 Introduction

The problem of protecting privacy of individual data used for research is not new. It was originally investigated in the area of statistical database security [1]. An interested reader is referred to Chap. 12 for more details. However, *knowledge discovery and data mining* (KDDM) has brought this problem to an unprecedented level and has also introduced new threats to individual privacy. In 1998, The Ontario information and privacy commissioner Ann Cavoukian said in her report "Data Mining: Staking a Claim on Your Privacy" that data mining "may be the most fundamental challenge that privacy advocates will face in the next decade" [2]. As time goes by, this prophetic statement is coming to pass.

KDDM is an emerging area of data analysis that lies at the crossroads of statistics, machine intelligence, pattern recognition, databases, optimization, information visualization and high-performance computing. KDDM extracts valuable information and patterns from very large data sets. The ongoing expansion of computerization and networking has enabled massive data collection and processing, which have in turn created a huge demand for KDDM technologies. A classical example of KDDM applications is the so-called market basket analysis, which enables retail companies to 'guesstimate' shopping habits and preferences of their customers and pursue strategic initiatives such as direct marketing. Other major KDDM applications include fraud detection, as well as economic, medical and criminal research.

The primary tasks in KDDM include classification, clustering, mining association rules, estimation and prediction. *Classification* maps records into one of several predefined discrete classes. The tools for classification include *decision trees, neural networks, Bayesian classifiers* and *support vector machines*. *Clustering* groups similar records together into clusters and often involves identifying variables that best define the clusters. Unlike classification, clustering does not rely on predefined classes. *Estimation and prediction* refer to developing models to estimate and predict future values and trends of one or more variables. *Mining association rules* uncovers relationships among data. In a classical example, a market basket analysis uncovered that customers who buy diapers on Friday afternoons are typically males and they also buy beer; the store manager decided to place beer next to diapers on Friday afternoons, in order to increase sales of beer.

Together with the exciting promises of cutting-edge technologies, the computer age also created frightening prospects of routine monitoring and recording individuals' behavior, both in public and in the privacy of their own homes [3]. Privacy has now become a favorite topic of the media, a major issue for lawmakers and a source of anxiety and confusion for the general public. Data collectors and owners are now under pressure to ensure adequate protection of confidential information. If they fail to do so, they may face legal penalties and/or a loss of reputation through negative exposure in the media, which can in turn make the future collection of trustworthy data very difficult.

One of the early examples goes back to 1990, when the Lotus Development Corporation prepared for marketing the purchasing data about 120 million consumers. After this intention was made widely known through a letter from a concerned computer specialist, distributed via email, Lotus received around 30,000 protest letters from the public. They then decided to abandon the project because of unexpected costs involved in ensuring the privacy of the consumers [4].

Public opposition and ever-increasing legal and ethical obligations are not the only reason for growing data owners' interest in ensuring privacy [5]. It is now generally recognized that collected data are becoming more sensitive in nature. They now include criminal records, as well as health records. The latter could contain, for example, information about suffering from genetic or sexually transmitted diseases. Such information has a stigma attached to it and if disclosed would present an embarrassment to the individuals. Another reason for growing concern about privacy is the very existence of so many different databases and the possibility that the records could be cross-matched, which would then result in the larger-scale exposure of confidential information [5]. Finally, data owners are now moving from disseminating very crude statistical information into detailed, almost raw data that underwent very little or no processing prior to its release. Clearly, the latter kind is under much bigger risk of unauthorized disclosure [5].

It is our firm belief that a significant contributing factor to raised privacy awareness is the advent and escalation of KDDM techniques and methodologies. Although they have grown out of classical statistical methods, they pose more of a threat to privacy simply because they are concerned with discovering patterns in the underlying data. Unlike statistical parameters, some of the patterns may be considered very sensitive themselves. For example, disclosing the average salary of the population of town X belonging to a particular age group is surely much less sensitive than the pattern suggesting that 90% of the members of a particular race and age group in town X belong to a particular profession. The latter can lead to stereotyping and can even cross over to the very sensitive terrain of racial prejudices and potential discrimination [6].

Generally, we can assume that there are two kinds of users of large data sets containing personal information: an honest data miner, who is interested in patterns and information about groups of individuals, and a malicious data miner whose goal is to identify certain individuals and disclose confidential information about them. If it were possible to distinguish between these two kinds of users, then privacy-preserving data mining could be ensured by the usual security measures, such as access control and cryptography. Unfortunately, this is not possible, as a single user can actually assume both roles and can sometimes act as an honest data miner and other times as a malicious data miner [7]. A well-meaning researcher may try, consciously or subconsciously, to find a match between records in a data set and his/her own circle of acquaintances, especially for records with a rare combination of attribute values [5]. Just like in other areas of data security, it would be wrong to assume the innocence of the users and to base the security upon that assumption. A data set which is protected against a malicious, skillful and knowledgeable data miner will also be safe against other users [8]. In what follows we refer to a malicious data miner as an intruder.

In the next section we give a classification of the privacy-preserving techniques, as well as the evaluation criteria. In Sect. 11.3 we briefly examine secure multiparty computation techniques, and in Sect. 11.4 we take a closer look at data modification techniques. We give a comparative analysis and concluding remarks in Sect. 11.5.

11.2 Classification Scheme and Evaluation Criteria

In this section we propose a classification scheme and an evaluation criteria for existing privacy protection techniques, which build upon but do not strictly follow the classification and evaluation criteria proposed in [9].

For the purpose of our study, we assume that a data set is a two-dimensional table, where each row (record) corresponds to an individual (case) and each column (attribute) corresponds to a property that describes individuals. Some attributes are confidential and the others are assumed to be public knowledge and thus possibly known to an intruder. Certain attributes might uniquely, or almost uniquely, identify a record, for example a name or a social security number. We assume that such attributes are removed from the data set. However, this is usually insufficient to protect privacy of individuals, as a combination of nonconfidential attributes may also identify an individual.

The purpose of privacy-preserving data mining is to make the data set available for data mining tasks, such as classification, clustering and association rule mining, while at the same time prevent an intruder from re-identifying individual records and learning the values of confidential attributes. Moreover, very often the patterns that exist in the data set, for example association rules, are themselves considered sensitive and thus should also be protected from disclosure.

The data sets used for data mining can be either centralized or distributed; this does not refer to the physical location where data is stored, but rather to the availability/ownership of data. Centralized data is owned by a single party, and it is either available at the computation site or can be sent to it. Distributed data is shared between two or more parties, which do not necessarily trust each other and/or do not wish to share their private data. The data set can further be heterogeneous, or vertically partitioned, where each party owns the same set of records (rows in the two-dimensional table introduced above) but different subset of attributes (columns). Alternatively, the data set can be homogeneous, or horizontally partitioned, where each party owns the same set of attributes but different subsets of records.

There are two classes of privacy-preserving techniques that can be applied in the context of data mining. The first class of techniques encrypts the data set, while still allowing data mining tasks. Such techniques are typically based on cryptographic protocols and are applied to distributed data sets where data mining tasks are to be performed on the union of all data sets, but the data owners are not prepared to share their own data sets with each other or any third party. These techniques are commonly referred to as *secure multiparty computation* (SMC).

The second class of privacy-preserving techniques modifies the data set before releasing it to users. The data can be modified in such a way as to protect either the privacy of individual records or the privacy of sensitive underlying patterns, or both. *Data modification* techniques include data swapping, noise addition, aggregation and suppression. *Data swapping* interchanges the attribute values among different records. *Noise addition* perturbs the attribute values by adding noise. Note that in statistical database terminology, data swapping is often seen as a special case of noise addition [1]. *Aggregation* refers to both combining a few attribute values into one, and grouping a few records together and replacing them with a group representative. Finally, *suppression* means replacing an attribute value by a symbol denoting a missing value. Note that missing values naturally occur in data sets when values are either unapplicable or unknown.

In order to evaluate a privacy-preserving technique, the following properties should be considered.

1. *Versatility* refers to the ability of the technique to cater for various privacy requirements, types of data sets and data mining tasks. Versatility includes the following.
   - *Private: data versus patterns*
     Does the technique protect the privacy of data, underlying patterns, or both?
   - *Dataset: centralized or distributed (vertical or horizontal)*
     Is the technique suitable for centralized or distributed data sets, or both? If distributed, is it suitable for vertically or horizontally partitioned data?
   - *Attributes: numerical or categorical (boolean)*
     Is the technique suitable for numerical or categorical attributes (or Boolean, as a special case of categorical)?
   - *Data mining task*
     For which data mining tasks is the technique suitable? For example, is it suitable for classification by decision trees, clustering or mining association rules?

2. *Disclosure risk*
   Disclosure risk refers to the likelihood of sensitive information being inferred by a malicious data miner. It is inversely proportional to the level of security offered by the technique. Evaluating a disclosure risk is a very challenging task and is highly dependent on the nature of the technique. For example, in a technique that protects sensitive association rules, a dis-

closure risk may be measured by the percentage of the sensitive rules that can still be disclosed; in a technique that adds noise to protect individual records, a disclosure risk might be measured by the re-identification risk, a measure used in security of statistical databases (see Chap. 12, Sect. 12.5).

3. *Information loss*

   Modification of data by a privacy-preserving technique can lead to a loss of information. Information loss is highly dependent on the data mining task for which the data set is intended. For example, in mining association (classification) rules, information loss could be measured by the percentage of rules that have been destroyed/created by the technique, and/or by the reduction/increase in the support and confidence of all the rules; for clustering, information loss can be evaluated by the variance of the distances among the clustered items in the original database and the sanitized database [9].

4. *Cost*

   Cost refers to both the computational cost and the communication cost between the collaborating parties [9]. The higher the cost, the lower the efficiency of the technique. Computational cost encompasses both pre-processing cost (e.g., initial perturbation of the values) and running cost (e.g., processing overheads). Communication costs become relevant when a privacy-preserving technique is applied to a distributed data set.

In Sect. 11.5 we illustrate these criteria by presenting a comparative study of a few privacy-preserving techniques. The techniques have been carefully selected to exemplify a broad range of methods.

11.3 Secure Multiparty Computation

Secure multiparty computation (SMC) refers to a computation performed by two or more mutually untrusted parties [10, 11]. Each party owns some private data which it is not willing to share with other parties. However, all the parties are interested in performing a computation on the union of data belonging to individual parties. An example of such a situation may be a taxation office and a social security department which are both interested in mining their joint data but are legally precluded from sharing confidential individual information without the explicit consent of their clients.

The SMC problem was originally introduced in 1982 by Yao [11] and has been extensively studied since then. In addition to privacy-preserving data mining, the SMC problem has applications in other areas, including the security of statistical databases and private information retrieval (PIR).

In order to illustrate SMC in privacy-preserving data mining, we describe a computation of a secure sum, which is often used to illustrate the concepts of SMC, as well as to show how the system can be subverted if the parties collude [12]. In our example there are s parties (sites), where site i owns a value x_i which it is not willing to share with other parties. Suppose that the sum

$$x = \sum_{i=1}^{s} x_i$$

is in the range $[0 \ldots n]$. Then site 1 generates a random number R_1 in the range $[0 \ldots n]$, computes $R_2 = (R_1 + x_1) \bmod n$ and sends R_2 to site 2. Note that like R_1, R_2 is also uniformly distributed over the range $[0 \ldots n]$, and thus site 2 cannot learn anything about x_1. Site 2 then computes $R_3 = (R_2 + x_2) \bmod n$ and sends it to site 3. Finally, site s receives R_s, computes $R_{s+1} = (R_s + x_s) \bmod n$ and sends it back to site 1. Site 1 then calculates $x = (R_{s+1} - R_1) \bmod n$, and sends x to all the parties. Note that each party is assumed to have used their correct value x_i.

If there is no collusion, party i only learns the total sum x, and can also calculate $(x - x_i) \bmod n$, that is, the sum of values of all the other parties. However, if two or more parties collude, they can disclose more information. For example, if the two neighbors of party i (that is, parties $i - 1$ and $i + 1$) collude, they can learn $x_i = (R_{i+1} - R_i) \bmod n$. The protocol can be extended in such a way that each party divides its value into m shares, and the sum of each share is computed separately. The ordering of parties is different for each share, so that no party has the same neighbors twice. The bigger the number of shares, the more colluding parties are required to subvert the protocol, but the slower the computation. In general, collusion is considered to be a serious threat to SMC.

In the last few years a number of SMC algorithms for various data mining tasks have been proposed [13, 14, 15, 16, 17, 18, 19, 20, 21, 15, 22, 23, 24]. Most of these algorithms make use of similar primitive computations, including secure sum, secure set union, secure size of set intersection and secure scalar product. Clifton et al. have initiated building a toolkit of such basic computation techniques, in order to facilitate the development of more-complex, application-specific privacy-preserving techniques [12]. For the benefit of the interested reader, we next describe some of these application specific techniques, and where applicable we specify which primitive computation technique was used.

Secure multiparty computation for association rule mining has been studied in [13, 14, 15, 16]. The task here is to develop an SMC for finding the global support count of an item set. For data that is vertically partitioned among parties, and boolean attribute values, finding the frequency of an item set is equivalent to computing the secure scalar product [14]. For horizontally partitioned data the frequency of an item set reduces to the secure set union [15].

An algorithm for SMC of association rules that prevents a k-compromise is presented in [13], where k-compromise refers to the disclosure of a statistic based on fewer than k participants (for more details see Chap. 12, Sect. 12.2). However, this algorithm is not resistant to colluding participants.

Another technique for horizontally partitioned datasets [16] relies on the fact that a global frequent item set (GFI) has to be a frequent item set in at least one of the partitions [25]. GFIs are those itemsets having global support count greater than a user-defined threshold. In this technique, maximal frequent itemsets (MFI) of all partitions are locally computed by the parties. The union of all these local MFIs is then computed by a trusted third party. The support counts of all possible subsets of each of the MFIs belonging to the union are computed by the parties locally. Finally, the global summation of the support counts for each itemset is computed using the secure sum computation. GFIs can be used for various purposes, including the discovery of association rules and correlations.

Building a decision tree on horizontally partitioned data based on oblivious transfer was proposed in [21]. The protocol uses the well-known ID3 algorithm for building decision trees. Each party performs most of the computations independently on its own database. This increases the efficiency of the protocol. The results obtained from these independent computations are then combined using an efficient cryptographic protocol based on oblivious transfer and specifically tailored towards ID3.

A secure multiparty computation function for naive Bayesian classifier on horizontally partitioned data that relies on the secure sum was proposed in [15]. The same paper also provides an extension based on a secure algorithm for evaluating a logarithm [21] to enhance the security.

Secure protocols for classification on vertically partitioned data relying on secure scalar product were proposed in [17, 18]. The protocol proposed in [17] builds a classifier, but does not disclose it to any of the parties, due to legal and/or commercial issues. Rather, the parties collaborate to classify an instance. However, the classifier can be reverse-engineered from knowledge of a sufficient number of classified instances.

A solution for building a decision tree on vertically partitioned data was proposed in [19]. This method is based on a secure scalar product, and uses a semi-trusted third-party commodity server in order to increase performance.

A secure multiparty computation of clusters on vertically partitioned data was studied in [22]. Regression on vertically partitioned data was considered in [23, 20], while secure computing of outliers for horizontally and vertically partitioned data was studied in [24].

11.4 Data Modification

11.4.1 Data Swapping

Data swapping techniques were first devised in the context of secure statistical databases by Dalenius and Reiss for use on categorical databases [26]. Their method involves replacing the original database with another, whereby values within sensitive attributes are exchanged between records. This exchange is done in such a way as to preserve the t-order statistics of the original data, where a t-order statistic is a statistic that can be specified and computed from the values of exactly t attributes. The main appeal of this method is that all of the original values are kept in the database, while at the same time re-identification of the records is made more difficult. Unfortunately, most real databases do not have a data swap, and when they do, the task of finding one is a difficult problem (probably intractable) [1]. More recently, data swapping has been proposed in privacy-preserving data mining, where the requirement for preserving t-order statistics has been relaxed [27]. Instead, classification rules are to be preserved. The class values are randomly swapped among the records belonging to a same heterogeneous leaf of a decision tree. This technique appears to preserve most classification rules, even if they are obtained by another classification method [27].

11.4.2 Noise Addition

The basic idea of noise addition (NA) is to add noise to the original numerical attribute values. This noise is typically drawn at random from a probability distribution having zero *mean* and small *standard deviation*. Generally, noise is added to the confidential attributes of a microdata file before the data is released. However, adding noise to both confidential and nonconfidential attributes can improve the level of privacy by making re-identification of the records more challenging. NA techniques can be used both to protect confidential values and the privacy of confidential patterns, such as association rules [28, 29].

It is desirable for any NA method to be unbiased, that is, for there to be no difference between the unperturbed statistic and its perturbed estimate. Early NA techniques were relatively unsophisticated and only protected against bias in estimating the mean of an attribute. Gradually NA techniques have evolved and offered protection against bias in estimating variance and covariance between various attributes [30, 31]. A useful classification of bias types was presented by Mulalidhar et al. [32]. However, noise addition techniques that were originally designed for statistical databases did not take into account the bias requirements specific to data mining applications. In 2002, Wilson and Rosen [33] investigated a classifier built from a data set perturbed with an existing statistical noise addition technique, and found that for a testing data set the classifier suffered from a lack of prediction accuracy. This suggests the existence of another type of bias, *data mining bias*, which is related to the change of patterns discovered/used in KDDM. Patterns of a data set include *clusters, classification* and *association rule sets*, and *subpopulation correlations*.

One of the techniques specifically developed for privacy-preserving data mining controls the data mining bias by first building a decision tree from the original data set [34]. This is done in order to learn the existing patterns in the data set. The noise is then added in a controlled way so that the patterns of the data set remain unaffected. Finally, the perturbed data set is released to data miners, who now have full access to individual records and can build their own decision trees. It was experimentally shown that decision trees obtained from a perturbed data set are very similar to decision trees obtained from the original data set. Moreover, the prediction accuracy of the classifiers obtained from the original and perturbed data sets are comparable, thus this technique does not suffer from data mining bias. This technique has been extended to incorporate categorical attributes [35], and can also incorporate existing statistical database perturbation methods, such as GADP or EGADP, in order to preserve statistical parameters along with data mining patterns [34]. Additionally, the perturbed data set can also be used for other data mining tasks, such as clustering. This is possible due the low amount of noise that has been added to the data.

Another NA technique [36] adds a large amount of random noise and significantly changes the distribution of the original data values. In this technique it is in general no longer possible to precisely estimate the original values of individual records and a reconstruction procedure is used to regenerate the original distribution. A decision tree built on the reconstructed distributions has a very good prediction accuracy, even for higher levels of noise [36]. Another advantage of this technique is that it is also applicable to distributed data sets, as every party is free to add random noise to their own data set before sharing it with other parties. This technique suffers from information loss in the reconstructed distribution which can be minimized by a reconstruction algorithm called *expectation minimization* (EM) [37]. The EM algorithm works best for a data set having a large number of records.

Kargupta et al. questioned the usefulness of adding random noise for preserving privacy [38, 39]. They proposed a spectral filtering technique that is able to closely estimate the original from the perturbed data set when there exists a correlation between data samples. Consequently, Kargupta et al. explored random multiplicative and colored noise as an alternative to independent white additive noise.

One of the challenging problems in this area is adding noise to categorical attributes. Categorical values lack a natural inherent ordering, which makes it difficult to control the amount of noise added to them. One possible solution is to cluster them in order to learn about similarity between different values [40]. Various categorical clustering techniques are available, such as CACTUS, ROCK, COOLCAT, CORE and DETECTIVE [35]. DETECTIVE obtains attribute specific and mutually exclusive clusters of records. Values of an attribute are considered to be similar if they appear in records belonging to the same cluster. A possible way to perturb categorical values is to change them into other similar categories with a given, relatively high probability and change them into dissimilar values with a low probability.

11.4.3 Aggregation

In aggregation (also known as generalization or global recoding) a group of k records of a data set is replaced by a representative record. An attribute value of the representative record is generally the mean of the corresponding attribute values of the original k records. Generalization typically results in some information loss. Prior to generalization, the original records are often clustered (into mutually exclusive groups of k records) in order to reduce information loss. However, in the case of lower information loss, disclosure risk is higher because an intruder can usually make a better estimate of an attribute value. An appropriate balance of information loss and disclosure risk can be obtained by adjusting the cluster size, i.e., the number of records in each cluster [41].

Aggregation also refers to a transformation which makes an attribute value less informative. For example, an exact date of birth may be replaced by the year of birth, and an exact salary may be rounded to the nearest thousand. Excessive application of generalization may make the released data useless, for example, replacing the exact date of birth by the century of birth [42].

11.4.4 Suppression

Suppression deletes (suppresses) sensitive data values prior to the release of the microdata. An important issue in suppression is to minimize information loss by minimizing the number of suppressed attribute values. At the same time, suppression should be resistant to an intruder's attempt to predict the suppressed attribute value with reasonable accuracy. This can be done by building a classifier from the released microdata, where the attribute in question is considered to be the class [43]. For some applications, such as medical data, suppression is preferred over noise addition. Suppression has also been used for association and classification rule confusion [44, 45].

11.5 Comparative Study and Conclusion

In this chapter, we introduced privacy-preserving data mining and briefly presented two classes of techniques: secure multiparty computation and data modification.

Secure multiparty computation can be performed on vertically or horizontally partitioned data. Specific SMC techniques have been developed for association rule mining, Bayesian classifiers, building decision trees and clustering. On one hand, SMC techniques tend to incur a significantly higher running and communication cost. On the other hand, SMC techniques provide a much higher level of privacy than data modification techniques. Another advantage of SMC techniques is that they do not introduce any information loss to the data sets.

Table 11.1. Privacy-preserving techniques – comparative study

Technique	Versatility				Discl. risk	Info. loss	Cost
	Private data /rules	Data set: central /distributed (horizontal /vertical)	Attributes: categorical /numerical /boolean	Data mining task			
Outlier detection [17]	Data (both)	Distributed	Both	Outliers	Very low	None	High
Association rules [14]	Data	Distributed (vertical)	Boolean	Assoc. rules	Very low	None	Moderate
Randomized noise [36]	Data	Both	Numerical	Class	Low	Mod.	Low
Decision tree noise [34]	Data	Centralized	Both	Class	Mod.	Low	Low

Data modification techniques include data swapping, noise addition, aggregation and suppression. The main advantage of these techniques is simplicity and low cost. The main drawback is in balancing the competing requirements of disclosure risk and information loss. In particular, data swapping techniques appear to preserve data mining patterns well but disclosure risk is moderate. Depending on the nature of the data set, additive random noise may have low to moderate disclosure risk but the information loss is higher than for data swapping.

In Table 11.1, we compare two techniques from each of these two classes, against the evaluation criteria presented in Sect. 11.2. The first two techniques (outlier detection and association rules) belong to the secure multiparty computation category, while the other two (randomized noise and decision tree noise) are data modification techniques. It is clear from the table that SMC techniques are superior in terms of disclosure risk and information loss, while the main advantage of data modification techniques is low cost.

In conclusion, privacy has become a vital issue in data mining. Despite a constant effort by the academic and industry sector to invent new privacy-preserving techniques, so far most techniques are tied to particular data mining tasks. Future research will hopefully provide new universal techniques suitable for a variety of data mining tasks and data types.

References

1. D.E.R. Denning. *Cryptography and Data Security*. Addison-Wesley, 1982.
2. A. Cavoukian. Data mining: Staking a claim on your privacy. *Information and Privacy Commissioner Ontario*, pages 1–22, 1998.

3. O.H. Gandy Jr. and H.I. Schiller. Data mining and surveillance in the post-9.11 environment. In *Political Economy section, IAMCR*, pages 1–18, Barcelona, July, 2002.
4. M.J. Culnan. How did they get my name: An exploratory investigation of consumer attitudes towards secondary information use. *MIS Quarterly*, 17:341–361, 1993.
5. L. Willenborg and T. de Waal. *Statistical Disclosure Control in Practice*. Lecture Notes in Statistics. 1996. Springer.
6. L. Brankovic and V. Estivill-Castro. Privacy issues in knowledge discovery and data mining. In *Proc. of Australian Institute of Computer Ethics Conference (AICEC99)*, pages 89–99, Melbourne, Victoria, Australia, July 1999.
7. M. Trottini and S.E. Feinberg. Modelling user uncertainty for disclosure risk and data utility. *International Journal of Uncertainty, Fuzziness and Knowledge-Based Systems*, 10(5):511–527, 2002.
8. K. Muralidhar and R. Sarathy. Data access, data utility, and disclosure risk are not always mutually exclusive. In *NSF Workshop of Confidentiality*, Washington, DC, May 2003.
9. V.S. Verykios, E. Bertino, I. Nai Fovino, L. Parasiliti Provenza, Y. Saygin, and Y. Theodoridis. State-of-the-art in privacy preserving data mining. *SIGMOD Record*, 33(1):50–57, 2004.
10. W. Du and M.J. Atallah. Secure multiparty computation problems and their applications: A review and open problems. In *Proceedings of New Security Paradigms Workshop*, pages 11–20, Cloudcroft, New Mexico, USA, September 11-13 2001.
11. A.C. Yao. Protocols for secure computations. In *Proceedings of the 23rd Annual IEEE Symposium on Foundations of Computer Science*, 1982.
12. C. Clifton, M. Kantarcioglu, J. Vaidya, X. Lin, and M. Y. Zhu. Tools for privacy preserving data mining. *SIGKDD Explorations*, 4(2):28–34, 2002.
13. B. Gilburd, A. Schuster, and R. Wolff. Privacy-preserving data mining on data grids in the presence of malicious participants. In *Proceedings of 13th International Symposium on High-Performance Distributed Computing (HPDC-13 2004)*, pages 225–234, Honolulu, Hawaii, USA, June 2004.
14. J. Vaidya and C. Clifton. Privacy preserving association rule mining in vertically partitioned data. In *Proceedings of the Eighth ACM SIGKDD International Conference on Knowledge Discovery and Data Mining*, pages 639–644, Edmonton, Alberta, Canada, July 2002.
15. M. Kantarcioglu and J. Vaidya. Privacy preserving naive bayes classifier for horizontally partitioned data. In *Proceedings of IEEE ICDM Workshop on Privacy Preserving Data Mining*, pages 3–9, Melbourne, Florida, USA, November 2003.
16. A. Veloso, W. Meira Jr., S. Parthasarathy, and M. de Carvalho. Efficient, accurate and privacy-preserving data mining for frequent itemsets in distributed databases. In *Proceedings of XVIII Simpósio Brasileiro de Bancos de Dados (SBBD)*, pages 281–292, Manaus, Amazonas, Brasil, 2003.
17. J. Vaidya and C. Clifton. Privacy preserving naïve bayes classifier for vertically partitioned data. In *Proceedings of the Fourth SIAM International Conference on Data Mining*, Lake Buena Vista, Florida, USA, April 2004.
18. R.N. Wright and Z. Yang. Privacy-preserving bayesian network structure computation on distributed heterogeneous data. In *Proceedings of the Tenth ACM*

SIGKDD International Conference on Knowledge Discovery and Data Mining, pages 713–718, Seattle, Washington, USA, August 2004.

19. W. Du and Z. Zhan. Building decision tree classifier on private data. In *Workshop on Privacy, Security, and Data Mining at The 2002 IEEE International Conference on Data Mining (ICDM02)*, Maebashi City, Japan, December 9 2002.

20. W. Du, Y.S. Han, and S. Chen. Privacy-preserving multivariate statistical analysis: Linear regression and classification. In *Proceedings of the Fourth SIAM International Conference on Data Mining*, Lake Buena Vista, Florida, USA, April 22-24 2004.

21. Y. Lindell and B. Pinkas. Privacy preserving data mining. In *Proceedings of Advances in Cryptology - CRYPTO 2000, 20th Annual International Cryptology Conference*, pages 36–54, Santa Barbara, California, USA, 2000.

22. J. Vaidya and C. Clifton. Privacy-preserving k-means clustering over vertically partitioned data. In *Proceedings of the Ninth ACM SIGKDD International Conference on Knowledge Discovery and Data Mining*, pages 206–215, Washington, DC, USA, August 2003.

23. A.P. Sanil, A.F. Karr, X. Lin, and J.P. Reiter. Privacy preserving regression modelling via distributed computation. In *Proceedings of the Tenth ACM SIGKDD International Conference on Knowledge Discovery and Data Mining*, pages 677–682, Seattle, Washington, USA, August 2004.

24. J. Vaidya and C. Clifton. Privacy-preserving outlier detection. In *Proceedings of the 4th IEEE International Conference on Data Mining (ICDM 2004)*, pages 233–240, Brighton, UK, November 2004.

25. J.L. Lin and M.H. Dunham. Mining association rules: Anti-skew algorithms. In *Proc. of 1998 International Conference on Data Engineering*, pages 486 –493, 1998.

26. T. Dalenius and S.P. Reiss. Data-swapping: A technique for disclosure control. *Journal of Statistical Planning and Inference*, 6(1):73–85, 1982.

27. V. Estivill-Castro and L. Brankovic. Data swapping: Balancing privacy against precision in mining for logic rules. In *Proc. of Data Warehousing and Knowledge Discovery (DaWaK99)*, pages 389–398, 1999.

28. S.R.M. Oliveira and O.R. Zaïane. Algorithms for balancing privacy and knowledge discovery in association rule mining. In *Proc. of the 7th International Database Engineering and Applications Symposium (IDEAS03)*, page 5463, Hong Kong, China, July 2003.

29. V.S. Verykios, A.K. Elmagarmid, E. Bertino, Y. Saygin, and E. Dasseni. Association rule hiding. *IEEE Trans. Knowl. Data Eng.*, 16(4):434–447, 2004.

30. J.J. Kim. A method for limiting disclosure in microdata based on random noise and transformation. In *American Statistical Association, Proceedings of the Section on Survey Research Methods*, pages 303–308, 1986.

31. P. Tendick and N.S. Matloff. A modified random perturbation method for database security. *ACM Trans. Database Syst.*, 19(1):47–63, 1994.

32. K. Muralidhar, R. Parsa, and R. Sarathy. A general additive data perturbation method for database security. *Management Science*, 45(10):1399–1415, 1999.

33. R.L. Wilson and P.A. Rosen. The impact of data perturbation techniques on data mining accuracy. In *Proceedings of the 33rd Annual Meeting of the Decision Sciences Institute*, pages 181–185, 2002.

34. Md.Z. Islam and L. Brankovic. A framework for privacy preserving classification in data mining. In *Proceedings of Workshop on Data Mining and Web Intelligence (DMWI2004)*, pages 163–168, 2004.
35. Md.Z. Islam and L. Brankovic. Detective: A decision tree based categorical value clustering and perturbation technique in privacy preserving data mining. In *Proceedings of the 3rd International IEEE Conference on Industrial Informatics (INDIN 2005)*, Perth, Australia, 2005.
36. Rakesh Agrawal and Ramakrishnan Srikant. Privacy-preserving data mining. In *Proc. of the ACM SIGMOD Conference on Management of Data*, pages 439–450. ACM Press, May 2000.
37. D. Agrawal and C.C. Aggarwal. On the design and quantification of privacy preserving data mining algorithms. In *Proceedings of the Twentieth ACM SIGACT-SIGMOD-SIGART Symposium on Principles of Database Systems*, Santa Barbara, California, USA, May 2001.
38. H. Kargupta, S. Datta, Q. Wang, and K. Sivakumar. Random-data perturbation techniques and privacy-preserving data mining. *Knowledge and Information Systems*, 7:387–414, 2005.
39. K. Liu, H. Kargupta, and J. Ryan. Random projection-based multiplicative data perturbation for privacy preserving distributed data mining. *IEEE Transactions on Knowledge and Data Engineering*, 18(1):92–106, 2006.
40. H. Giggins and L. Brankovic. Protecting privacy in genetic databases. In R. L. May and W. F. Blyth, editors, *Proceedings of the Sixth Engineering Mathematics and Applications Conference*, pages 73–78, Sydney, Australia, 2003.
41. Y. Li, S. Zhu, L. Wang, and S. Jajodia. A privacy-enhanced microaggregation method. In *Proc. of 2nd International Symposium on Foundations of Information and Knowledge Systems*, pages 148–159, 2002.
42. S.V. Iyengar. Transforming data to satisy privacy constraints. In *Proc. of SIGKDD'02*, Edmonton, Alberta, Canada, 2002.
43. A.A. Hintoglu and Y. Saygin. Suppressing microdata to prevent probabilistic classification based inference. In *Proceedings of Secure Data Management, Second VLDB Workshop, SDM 2005*, pages 155–169, Trondheim, Norway, 2005.
44. S. Rizvi and J.R. Haritsa. Maintaining data privacy in association rule mining. In *Proceedings of the 28th VLDB Conference*, pages 682–693, Hong Kong, China, 2002.
45. Y. Saygin, V.S. Verykios, and A.K. Elmagarmid. Privacy preserving association rule mining. In *RIDE*, pages 151–158, 2002.

Statistical Database Security

Ljiljana Brankovic and Helen Giggins

The University of Newcastle
Australia

Summary. Statistical database security focuses on the protection of confidential individual values stored in so-called *statistical databases* and used for statistical purposes. Examples include patient records used by medical researchers, and detailed phone call records, statistically analyzed by phone companies in order to improve their services. This problem became apparent in the 1970s and has escalated in recent years due to massive data collection and growing social awareness of individual privacy.

The techniques used for preventing statistical database compromise fall into two categories: noise addition, where all data and/or statistics are available but are only approximate rather than exact, and restriction, where the system only provides those statistics and/or data that are considered safe. In either case, a technique is evaluated by measuring both the information loss and the achieved level of privacy. The goal of statistical data protection is to maximize the privacy while minimizing the information loss. In order to evaluate a particular technique it is important to establish a theoretical lower bound on the information loss necessary to achieve a given level of privacy. In this chapter, we present an overview of the problem and the most important results in the area.

12.1 Introduction

Statistical database security is concerned with protecting privacy of individuals whose confidential data is collected through surveys or other means and used to facilitate statistical research. In this context, *individuals* can refer to persons, households, companies or other entities.

The earliest example of statistical databases is undoubtedly census data whose collection, storage and analysis has undergone a great transformation in the last 6,000 years. The first recorded census was taken in the Babylonian empire in 3800 BC, for taxation purposes, and was then conducted regularly every six to seven years. In ancient Egypt census started around 2500 BC and was used to assist in planning the construction of the pyramids [1]. The first modern census in Great Britain was taken in 1801 and was initiated out of concern that food supplies might fail to satisfy the needs of the country's growing population [1]. The census asked only five questions of approximately 10 million people in two million households. In contrast, 200 years later, the UK census counted 60 million people in 24 million households and asked 40 questions.

Nowadays census is conducted regularly in virtually every corner of the world, and is used to facilitate planning by governments and various health and other authorities, for the benefit of the local population. In recent years, due to the rapidly growing storage and processing capabilities offered by modern computers, data has become one of the most valuable commodities in both public and private sectors of society, as it supports both day-to-day activities and strategic planning. In addition to census, national statistical offices (NSO) in various countries also collect many other kinds of data, typically through surveys, and then process and disseminate the data to numerous other organizations and bodies. Moreover, many other entities have started collecting their own data, including hospitals, retail companies, and a range of other service providers, either for their own research, strategic planning and/or marketing, or with the intention to sell it to other interested parties.

Not surprisingly, this massive collection and sharing of data has added to the already growing public concern about misuse and unauthorized disclosure of confidential individual information. In the context of this chapter, we refer to the person who collects and manages the data, as the *data owner*. Data owners are currently facing a very challenging task of obtaining and providing rich data and unrestricted statistical access to users while at the same time ensuring that dissemination is done in such a way as to make it impossible for the users to identify particular individuals. Unfortunately, these two requirements are typically mutually exclusive, and thus the most data owners can hope to achieve is preserving sufficiently high quality, while simultaneously making identification and disclosure as difficult as possible. This task is most commonly referred to as *statistical disclosure control* (SDC), or statistical database security.

There are various measures one can apply in order to implement SDC. They generally fall into three groups: legal, administrative and technical. It appears that a simultaneous application of all three kinds of measures is necessary in order to ensure a satisfactory level of protection and to win public trust [2]. In this chapter we focus our attention on technical measures to ensure privacy.

An important but still not fully explored issue refers to the information that an intruder has about the statistical database. This information is usually referred to as *supplementary knowledge* (SK). An intruder with extensive SK is in a position to disclose more confidential information from the database, and will need less effort to do so than a user without or with little SK. Thus, the so-called *intruder modelling* is an important step in designing an adequate SDC measure, but unfortunately more work is needed in this direction [3]. In the next section we shed more light on this important issue.

There are a few different methods for dissemination of statistical databases. Such methods have an impact on the level of security that can be achieved, and also dictate which SDC techniques can be applied. Traditionally, NSOs have been disseminating statistical databases in the form of summary tables, usually two dimensional. Summary tables contain aggregate data and thus are less exposed to the risk of statistical disclosure. However, the level of detail in summary tables does not allow for some of the more complex analysis of data that is now required. Consequently, NSOs have recently started releasing anonymized microdata files, which can be either public use or licensed files [2]. Both contain very detailed (raw) data but differ in the level of anonymization. Public use files are generally available without licensing and require a high level of anonymization, which makes identification of records more difficult. On the other hand, licensed files require the signing of a legal undertaking by all the users. Identification of individual records is in general easier in licensed than in public use files. Remote access facilities (RAF) and data laboratories (DL) provide users not with microdata files but rather with an access channel through which they can submit statistical queries and receive responses [2].

We conclude the introduction by considering briefly the two main groups of SDC techniques that can be deployed to protect confidentiality, namely *restriction* techniques and *noise addition* techniques. Restriction techniques restrict the information that is available to a user either directly or through responses to their queries. However, all the information that remains available is exact. On the other hand, noise addition techniques preserve the availability, but not the exactness of the data. In other words, all the data is available but it is only approximate as it went through a perturbation process before being released to users. Both groups of techniques have their advantages and disadvantages and it may be necessary to apply both simultaneously in order to provide a required level of privacy. In addition to these two classes of techniques, privacy can also be protected using *secure multiparty computations* (SMC), which is discussed in Chap. 11.

The organization of the remainder of the chapter is as follows. In the next section we introduce the abstract model of a statistical database and illustrate some important concepts. In Sect. 12.3 we discuss restriction and in Sect. 12.4 noise addition. Section 12.5 is devoted to studying information loss and disclosure risk. We give concluding remarks in Sect. 12.6.

12.2 A Closer Look

In this section we take a closer look at the abstract model of statistical databases, introduce some important concepts from statistical database theory and illustrate them using our working example.

Table 12.1 represents what could be part of a census database. This is, of course, just a toy example to help us exemplify some concepts. The real census in most countries typically contains millions of records and tens of variables.

Table 12.1. Census database for town x

	Address	HOH name	HOH gen	HOH income	HOH age	NoA	NoC	Total income	Dw_O	Dw_Rep
1	12 First St	Mary Smith	F	70	34	1	1	70	Y	No
2	37 Grey Ave	James White	M	99	39	2	2	99	Y	Major
3	100 Main St	Fran Brown	F	33	21	1	0	33	Y	No
4	4/18 Hunter Rd	Mike Doe	M	21	21	1	0	21	Y	Major
5	30 Second St	John Black	M	21	27	2	1	40	Y	Minor
6	15 Main St	Helen Jones	F	55	38	3	2	110	N	No
7	67 River Rd	Jane Smith	F	84	51	1	1	84	Y	Minor
8	92 Third Ave	Alice Chang	F	67	35	2	3	100	N	No
9	2 Kerry Ave	John Black	M	23	44	2	2	50	Y	Major
10	35 Smith St	Bob Ross	M	34	28	2	3	34	N	Major
11	200 King St	Ken James	M	45	47	2	1	45	N	No
12	7 Nice Rd	Jack Reed	M	12	60	1	0	12	Y	Minor
13	82 Michael St	Carol Doe	F	56	33	2	2	70	Y	Minor
14	26 William St	Mary Chen	F	23	31	2	3	45	Y	Major

In its abstract model a statistical database is a two-dimensional table where each row describes an individual, whether that is a person, business or some other entity. In our census database example, each row corresponds to an individual household. Each column describes one property of the individual. Following the database terminology, we refer to these properties as *attributes*. In the census database, *HOH* stands for head of the household, *NoA* (*NoC*) stands for number of adults (children), *Dw_O* for dwelling ownership and *Dw_Rep* for the need for dwelling repairs.

Each attribute has a domain associated with it, that is, a set of legal values that attribute can assume. For example, in our census database the domain of the attribute *NoC* is the set of nonnegative integers (possibly with a prescribed maximum value), while the domain of *Dw_Rep* is the set {No, Minor, Major}.

Attributes in a statistical database can be either confidential or nonconfidential, sometimes also referred to as identifiers and sensitive attributes, respectively. In the census database, arguably, nonconfidential attributes would be *Address*, *HOH name*, *HOH gen*, *NoA* and *NoC*. The remaining attributes are treated as confidential. Nonconfidential attributes are public knowledge and likely to be known to an intruder. These attributes may be used to identify individual records. Some attributes can identify records directly, and they are referred to as *direct identifiers*. In the census database, *Address* and *HOH name* act as direct identifiers. Others can only identify the records in combination with attributes, and are called *indirect identifiers*. A subset of indirect identifiers that can be used together to identify records is referred to as a *key*, also known as a *quasi-identifier*. Note that there is an important difference between a key in the database theory and our key here: in the database sense, a key is a combination of attributes that uniquely identifies every record in the database. In other words, there are no two records with the same values in all the attributes of the key. In our context, some values of a key may uniquely identify a record, while other values may not. For example, in the census database, (*HOH gen, NoA, NoC*) act together as a key. Record 13 is uniquely identified by the key value (F, 2, 2). However, the key value (M, 2, 2) matches both record 2 and record 9 and thus (*HOH gen, NoA, NoC*) would not qualify as a key in a database sense. The property of k-anonymity [4] arises from this concept of a key (quasi-identifier). We say that a database provides k-anonymity, if for every combination of values of the key in the k-anonymous database, there are at least k records that share those values.

The first logical step in protecting the confidentiality in a statistical database would be to remove all direct identifiers, which is typically done in practice before data is disseminated. However, it would be wrong to assume that this step alone is enough to truly anonymize the data. A large percentage of records, especially in smaller databases, are still identifiable using keys consisting of indirect identifiers. For example, about 25% of Australian households are uniquely identifiable based only on age, and the size and sex structure of the household [2].

Note that if the census database were released as a licensed anonymized microdata file, then it would probably be enough to remove direct identifiers, i.e., the attributes *Address* and *HOH name*. However, if the census database were to be released as a public use file, then removing direct identifiers would not suffice, as some records can be identified from keys containing only indirect identifiers. In that case, one of the techniques described in the next two sections should also be applied. If the data is not released in the form of a microdata file but rather accessed by users either through RAFs or DLs no identifiers need to be removed. However, a protection technique would have to be applied in order to ensure privacy. In addition to microdata files, RAFs and DLs, the census database can also be released in the form of summary tables. Table 12.2 is an example of such a two-dimensional table.

All users of a statistical database must have so-called *working knowledge*, which refers to the user's familiarity with attributes contained in the database and associated domains. If the data is released through RAFs and DLs, then the working knowledge is absolutely essential, otherwise the user would not be able for formulate a statistical query. The knowledge of attribute domains is also important in the case when data is released in the form of summary tables or anonymized microdata files.

In addition to working knowledge, a user of a statistical database may also have *supplementary knowledge* (SK). Miller [5] distinguishes between SK of

Table 12.2. *Total income* sum table of census database for *HOH gen* and *NoC*

		Number of children				
		0	1	2	3	Total
Head of	M	33	85	149	34	334
household	F	33	154	180	145	479
gender	Total	66	239	329	179	813

type I, II and III. SK I refers to knowledge of a value of a key, which consists either of a direct identifier or a combination of indirect identifiers. SK II refers to knowledge of a value of a confidential attribute, while SK III includes any SK that is not of SK I or SK II.

A user with SK I could be able to identify one or more records in the database. Statistical database compromise (disclosure) occurs if such a user can then disclose the values of confidential attributes for those particular records. This is also known as *exact compromise* or *1-compromise* to stress the fact that an exact single confidential value had been disclosed. However, if a user has SK II, preventing only exact compromise may not provide adequate privacy. If, for a given confidential attribute, a user learns the sum of values for k records, and as a part of their SK II they already know $k-1$ of them, they can easily deduce the remaining confidential value and compromise the database. We define a k-*compromise* to be a disclosure of a statistic based on k or less records.

It is often possible for a user to conclude that a particular record does not have a certain value in a confidential attribute. This is referred to as a *negative compromise*. *Approximate compromise* occurs when a user can learn that for a particular record the value of a confidential attribute lies in a range r with some probability p. This often happens when data is released in the form of summary tables and it is expressed as an *n-respondent, k%-dominance* rule, where n individuals contribute with $k\%$ or more to the value of a particular cell in the table. For example, if only one individual contributes 99% of the total value, than it is easy to estimate that particular value with an error of 0.5%. This rule has been traditionally used by NSOs. Finally, a *relative compromise* occurs when a user can learn the relative order of magnitude of two confidential values in the database [6]. For example, in the census database an intruder may be able to disclose that the total income of household 3 is greater than the total income of household 4.

12.3 Restriction

Techniques that restrict statistics can generally be divided into three broad categories: *global recoding, suppression* and *query restriction*. The purpose of global recoding and suppression is to eliminate rare combination of values in attributes of a key, that is, combinations that appear either in a single record or in a small number of records. Typically, global recoding is applied first to eliminate a majority of the rare combinations. Suppression is applied next, to eliminate the remaining cases. It is important to note that both techniques introduce some *information loss* to data. They can both be expressed as optimization problems where information loss needs to be minimized. For a very good overview of these two techniques an interested reader is referred to [7].

Global recoding (GR) transforms the domain of an attribute. If the attribute is categorical, GR implies collapsing a few categories into one. For numerical attributes, GR defines ranges of values and then replaces each single value with its corresponding range. For example, to eliminate rare combinations in values of indirect identifiers in the census database, we could replace the domains of the *NoA* and *NoC* by the ranges "0 or 1", and "2 or more".

GR can be combined with query restriction techniques in such a way as to (suboptimally) minimize the number of collapsed categories and maximize the percentage of queries that can be answered without compromise [8]. GR can also be applied to data released in the form of summary tables, in which case it is referred to as *table redesign* or *collapsing rows or columns* [9]. For example, in Table 12.2, the cell (1,4) describing the total income of all the households with three children and male head of the household is sensitive as it contains a single household (record 10). Similarly, the cell (2,1) is sensitive as it also contains a single household (record 3). In order to eliminate the sensitive cells, the table can be redesigned by collapsing *NoC* values 0 and 1 into a single category "0 or 1" and values 2 and 3 into a single category "2 or more". The new summary table is presented in Table 12.3.

Suppression replaces the value of an attribute in one or more records by a missing value. When applied to microdata, suppression is called *local suppression*, and when applied to summary tables it is called *cell suppression*. It is important to note that in the case of summary tables it is generally not sufficient to suppress sensitive cells. For example, if in Table 12.2 we suppress the two sensitive cells, (1,4) and (2,1), an intruder would still be able to deduce their values. They would only need to subtract the values of all the other cells in the corresponding row (column) from the marginal total for that row (column). Thus we need to suppress at least 2 cells in each row (column) that is affected by suppression. Table 12.4 shows an example with minimum number of suppressions that we need to perform - in this case four. These additional suppressions are referred to as *secondary suppressions*. When choosing cells for secondary suppression, the following three requirements should be satisfied [9]. Firstly, no empty cells should be suppressed. Table redesign can be applied first, in order to eliminate or minimize empty and sensitive cells. Secondly, in order to minimize the information loss, the total number of suppressed cells should be as small as possible. After the secondary suppression, an intruder will still be able to determine a feasibility range for each suppressed cell. For example, from Table 12.4 one can conclude that the value for cell (4,1) lies in the range [1,67]. The third requirement that secondary suppression needs to satisfy is that the feasibility ranges are not too narrow. Secondary cell

Table 12.3. Redesigned Table 12.2 after global recoding.

		Number of children		
		0 or 1	2 or more	Total
Head of	M	118	183	334
household	F	187	325	479
gender	Total	305	508	813

suppression is in general a challenging problem and can be formulated and (suboptimally) solved as a linear or mixed integer programming problem [7].

The third type of restriction techniques is the so-called *query restriction*, specifically tailored towards RAF and DL dissemination techniques, where users are not provided with microdata files but rather with a channel through which they can interactively ask queries. Since the user will never actually see the data, it is not necessary to remove direct and indirect identifiers. The user-posed queries are either answered exactly, or are rejected. The decision as to which queries to answer is made by using one of the following techniques [10].

The early techniques include *query set size, query set overlap* and *maximum order* control, which accept or reject queries based on their size, overlap with those previously answered or the total number of attributes involved in the query, respectively. All of these techniques were shown to be easily subvertible; additionally, maximum order unnecessarily restricts queries that do not lead to a compromise, and query set overlap is rather expensive as it requires storage and manipulation of all previously answered queries.

Partitioning groups records at the physical level into disjoint subgroups (*atomic populations*), each containing an even number of records [11]. A query is answered only if it involves whole atomic populations. Partitioning provides superior security but it tends to be overly restrictive.

Threat monitoring and *auditing* involve keeping logs of all the answered queries, either for each user separately, or collectively for all users [12]. A new query is only answered if together with all previously answered queries it does not lead to a compromise. The superiority of auditing lies in the fact that it is the only technique that can actually guarantee prevention of compromise without being overly restrictive. Recently there has been a renewed interest in this technique and many enhancements have been proposed [13, 14, 15, 16, 17, 18]. The main drawback of auditing is its excessive time and storage requirements [19]; however, for special types of queries such as additive queries, these requirements can be significantly reduced.

12.4 Noise Addition

The basic premise behind any noise addition (NA) technique is to mask the true values of the sensitive data by adding some level of error to it. This is done in a controlled way so as to best balance the competing needs of privacy

Table 12.4. Table 12.2 after secondary cell suppression.

		Number of children				
		0	1	2	3	Total
Head of household gender	M	X	85	149	X	334
	F	X	154	180	X	479
	Total	66	239	329	179	813

and information loss. The introduction of noise into the released statistics makes the task of ensuring the quality of statistical analyses a challenging one. Yet there are benefits for using NA methods, one being their relative ease of implementation and low running costs.

NA techniques can be categorized in several ways. One way is by the type of attribute they can be applied to. We say that an attribute is *numerical* if its values have a natural ordering, regardless of whether the values are actually numbers or not, and *categorical* otherwise. Techniques can also be classified according to how the noise is added. It can be added prior to release of the statistics, in which case the original database is generally replaced by a perturbed database on which the statistical queries are performed. This type of method is generally known as the *data perturbation* approach. For *output perturbation* techniques, the queries are evaluated on the original data and noise is added to the results of such queries. We now examine some of the classes of NA techniques for numerical data in more detail.

Additive noise methods were first introduced in the late 1980s and early 1990s by Kim [20] and Tendick [21], and subsequently in more detail [22, 23, 24]. The Kim and Tendick method, also known as *correlated-noise additive data perturbation* (CADP) [25] uses correlated noise to perturb a microdata file. The perturbed attribute X' is obtained by adding a noise term ε to the confidential attribute X, that is, $X' = X + \varepsilon$, where ε has a multivariate normal distribution with zero mean and a covariance matrix equal to the covariance matrix of the confidential attribute X, multiplied by the level of perturbation [25]. The interested reader is referred to [25] for a good summary of such early NA techniques, which can be seen as special cases of *general additive data perturbation* (GADP), described by the multivariate normal distribution. GADP perturbs both confidential and nonconfidential attributes, maintaining the correlations between them. For large data sets GADP performs well in both the information loss and disclosure prevention stakes, but like many methods does not perform well on small databases [26]. The so-called *enhanced general additive data perturbation* (EGADP) method can be effectively used on both large and small data sets [27].

Data distortion by probability distribution involves building an accurate statistical model M of the original data X. The perturbed data set X' is then created by randomly drawing records from the model [28]. The technique was first introduced by Liew et al. [29]. Burridge [30] uses such a model-based method of data perturbation for his information-preserving statistical obfuscation (IPSO). The attributes are grouped into two distinct sets, namely public data (Y) and specific survey data (Z). For a subset of records, a model for the conditional distribution $Y|Z$ is created. Then a sufficient statistic T is generated based on the information contained in Y. Then the perturbed dataset (Y', Z), generated from the conditional distribution of $Y|(T, Z)$, is released to the researcher. The advantage of this method is that it preserves the values of statistics in the sample for both large and small microdata files, unlike the GADP class of methods [30].

Duncan and Pearson showed that many perturbative methods are a specialization of *matrix masking*, which can be described as follows [31]. Given a microdata file X, the data user is given the masked version of the file $M = AXB + C$, where A is a record-transforming matrix, B is a variable transforming matrix, and C the noise or displacing mask [31]. *Random orthogonal matrix masking* (ROMM) [32] is a matrix masking technique whereby a random orthogonal matrix is drawn from a distribution G and applied to the original data to obtain the perturbed microdata. This microdata is then released along with the exact distribution G and the knowledge of how the microdata has been obtained [32]. The method preserves sample means and covariances and also controls the amount of perturbation.

One novel technique to arise from the area of data compression is *lossy compression*, based on the well-known JPEG algorithm [33, 34]. The basic premise behind the method is to convert the numerical data file to pixels, compress the resulting file, which is then regarded as a masked data file. Scaling of the original data will generally be required to achieve pixel grayscale values [33].

We defined a categorical attribute to be one that has no inherent ordering of the categories. This property makes it particularly difficult to sensibly add noise to such attributes. One of the earliest techniques specifically designed for categorical attributes is inspired by Warner's random sample method [35]. A promising disclosure protection method for categorical data, proposed by a group of researchers at Statistics Netherlands, is known as *post randomization method* (PRAM) [36]. PRAM can be applied to one or more attributes simultaneously. The method is similar to the randomized response technique, in that it misclassifies categories with known transition probabilities, allowing for unbiased estimates of certain underlying statistics to be obtained [37].

12.5 Information Loss and Disclosure Risk

A good SDC technique finds a balance between minimizing *information loss* on one hand and *disclosure risk* on the other. This is a challenging task and can be expressed as a *multiple-objective decision problem* [38].

In principle, for currently used noise addition techniques, a user can estimate the distribution of original data, which can sometimes lead to disclosure of individual values, especially when the number of attributes is large [39]. *Re-identification disclosure* occurs when a malicious user re-identifies a record and then learns the value of a sensitive attribute for that record; *prediction disclosure* occurs when a user estimates the value of a sensitive attribute without necessarily re-identifying the record [3]. *Re-identification risk* itself is very difficult to estimate and can be expressed as a risk per record or an overall risk [7]. One of the proposed measures for the re-identification risk is the probability that a unique match between a microdata record and a population unit is correct [40].

In the case of a noise addition technique, the information loss is measured by deterioration in data quality, in terms of *bias* (the difference between unperturbed statistics and the expected value of its perturbed estimate), *precision* (variance of an estimator) and *consistency* (absence of contradictions and paradoxes) [19]. More generally, entropy can be used to measure information loss for any technique that modifies the original data before releasing it to users. Other than noise addition, such techniques also include global recoding and suppression. For query restriction, percentage information loss is measured as $100\% - U$, where U is the usability, that is, the percentage of queries that are accepted under the given technique.

The idea behind the entropy-based measures is to evaluate the uncertainty that a user still has about the original data if they have been provided with the modified data. If the uncertainty is zero, there is no information loss. Formally, information loss can be expressed as $H(Original|Modified)$, which is the equivocation or the conditional entropy of the original data given the modified data. For example, in the case of local suppression $H(Original|Modified) = H(Original)$, which means that all the information has been lost.

The main drawbacks of using the entropy to evaluate the information loss are that it is a formal measure that is not always easy to calculate, and that it does not allow for the data owner's preferences regarding, for example, the importance of particular attributes. Other information loss measures include *subjective* measures that are based on weights indicating which attributes are more important than others and thus should be modified as little as possible [7]. Yet another measure evaluates how different the modified and the original data sets are, in terms of mean square and absolute error, and mean variation of the original and perturbed data sets and their covariance and correlation matrices [41].

In order to evaluate and compare different SDC techniques, it is important to determine the minimum information loss necessary to achieve a given privacy level. For example, it was shown that, for binary data protected by noise, a clever user who has access to perturbed subset sums can in fact reconstruct most if not all of the original values, unless the added noise is of the magnitude $O(\sqrt{n})$, where n is the number of records in the database [42]. If the data has been protected by a query restriction technique, we would like to determine the maximum usability for a given privacy level, that is, the maximum percentage of queries that be answered without database compromise. Determining maximum usability is a challenging problem, but some progress has been made for additive queries. For example, for a privacy level that requires prevention of exact compromise (or 1-compromise) in a database of n records where only additive queries are allowed, the maximum usability is of order $\Theta(n^{-\frac{1}{2}})$ [43]. This means that in a database with 100 records only 10% of the queries are answerable, and for $10,000$ records only 1% of queries are answerable. This is of course unacceptably low, which indicates that this level of privacy cannot be reasonably achieved by query restriction techniques alone. If the prevention of k-compromise is required, the maximum usability is $O(n^{-1-\frac{k}{2}})$ [44], and if a relative compromise is to be prevented then the maximum usability is $\Theta(n^{-\frac{3}{2}})$ [45, 44]. Thus in order to avoid a k-compromise, we can only answer a very small portion of additive queries. However, the situation is very different for *range* queries in multidimensional databases (OLAP cubes). For large m-dimensional databases that contain at least one record in each cell the maximum usability is at least $(2^m - 1)/2^m$ [46, 47]. Thus, most queries are answerable without causing a compromise. General OLAP cubes have been further studied in [48, 49, 50]. If the prevention of k-compromise is required then the maximum usability in a one-dimensional database is $\Theta(k^{-2})$ [51, 52].

12.6 Conclusion

In the past, most SDC techniques and software were produced by the NSOs for use within their own organizations. In 1995 Statistics Netherlands developed a prototype version of a software package, ARGUS, to protect microdata files against statistical disclosure. This prototype served as a starting point for the development of μ-ARGUS, a software package for the SDC of microdata. The project also saw the development of τ-ARGUS, software devoted to the protection of tabular data [53]. The SDC methods that can be used in μ-ARGUS include global recoding, local suppression, microaggregation and PRAM to name but a few. The sister package τ-ARGUS uses a combination of sensitive cell recognition and cell suppression to protect tabular data. The GHMITER hypercube heuristic software, developed by the Statistical office of Northrhine-Westphalia/Germany, has now also been incorporated into τ-ARGUS. Other commercially available software packages include the cell suppression packages ACS, which builds on an earlier software, CONFID, developed at Statistics Canada, and Datafly which was developed specifically for the anonymization of medical data [54].

Statistical database security has undergone a big transformation in the last few decades. What started off as disconnected efforts within NSOs and academia is now developing into a joint international venture. The importance of unifying policies as well as control and dissemination methods across national borders has been repeatedly stressed at conferences and other international gatherings of statisticians [2]. Such efforts, as well as undertakings to unify and standardize existing software should allow NSOs and academics to more easily combine their work and gain more widespread acceptance of SDC techniques.

References

1. Office for National Statistics. *200 Years of Census*. 2001.
2. D. Trewin. Managing statistical confidentiality and microdata access - draft principles and guidelines of good practice. In *UNECE/Eurostat Work Session on Statistical Data Confidentiality*, Geneva, Switzerland, 2005.

3. J. Domingo-Ferrer and J.M. Mateo-Sanz. Current directions in statistical data protection. *Research in Official Statistics*, 1(2):105–112, 1998.
4. P. Samarati and L. Sweeney. Protecting privacy when disclosing information: k-anonymity and its enforcement through generalization and suppression. In *Proceedings of the IEEE Symposium on Research in Security and Privacy*, Oakland, California, USA, 1998.
5. M. Miller. A model of statistical database compromise incorporating supplementary knowledge. In *Databases in the 1990s*, pages 258–267, 1991.
6. M. Miller and J. Seberry. Relative compromise of statistical databases. *The Australian Computer Journal*, 21(2):56–61, 1989.
7. L. Willenborg and T. de Waal. *Elements of Statistical Disclosure Control*. Lecture Notes in Statistics. 2001. Springer.
8. L. Brankovic and H. Fernau. Approximability of a 0,1-matrix problem. In *Proc. of the AWOCA2005*, pages 39–45, September 2005.
9. L. Willenborg and T. de Waal. *Statistical Disclosure Control in Practice*. Lecture Notes in Statistics. 1996. Springer.
10. D.E.R. Denning. *Cryptography and Data Security*. Addison-Wesley, 1982.
11. F.Y. Chin and G. Ozsoyoglu. Security in partitioned dynamic statistical databases. *Proc. of the IEEE COMPSAC Conference*, pages 594–601, 1979.
12. F.Y. Chin and G. Ozsoyoglu. Auditing and inference control in statistical databases. *IEEE Transactions on Software Engineering*, SE-8(6):574–582, 1982.
13. L. Brankovic, M. Miller, and J. Širáň. Towards a practical auditing method for the prevention of statistical database compromise. In *Proceeding of Australasian Database Conference, Australian Computer Science Communications*, volume 18, pages 177–184, 1996.
14. L. Brankovic. *Usability of Secure Statistical Databases*. PhD Thesis, The University of Newcastle, 1998.
15. F.M. Malvestuto and M. Mezzini. Auditing sum queries. In *Proceedings of 9th International Conference on Database Theory, ICDT 2003*, pages 126–142, Siena, Italy, 2003.
16. K. Kenthapadi, N. Mishra, and K. Nissim. Simulatable auditing. In *PODS '05: Proceedings of the twenty-fourth ACM SIGMOD-SIGACT-SIGART symposium on Principles of database systems*, pages 118–127, New York, NY, USA, 2005. ACM Press.
17. Y. Li, L. Wang, X. Sean Wang, and S. Jajodia. Auditing interval-based inference. In *Proceedings of 14th International Conference on Advanced Information Systems Engineering, CAiSE 2002*, pages 553–567, Toronto, Canada, 2002.
18. J. Kleinberg, C. Papadimitriou, and P. Raghavan. Auditing boolean attributes. *J. Comput. Syst. Sci.*, 66(1):244–253, 2003.
19. N.R. Adam and J.C. Wortmann. Security-control methods for statistical databases: a comparative study. *ACM Comput. Surv.*, 21(4):515–556, 1989.
20. J.J. Kim. A method for limiting disclosure in microdata based on random noise and transformation. In *American Statistical Association, Proceedings of the Section on Survey Research Methods*, pages 303–308, 1986.
21. P. Tendick. Optimal noise addition for preserving confidentiality in multivariate data. *Journal of Statisical Planning and Inference*, 27:341–353, 1991.
22. W.A. Fuller. Masking procedures for microdata disclosure limitation. *Journal of Official Statistics*, 9(2):383–406, 1993.

23. J.J. Kim and W.E. Winkler. Masking microdata files. In *American Statistical Association, Proceedings of the Section on Survey Research Methods*, pages 114–119, 1995.

24. W.E. Yancey, W.E. Winkler, and R.H. Creecy, editors. *Disclosure Risk Assessment in Perurbative Microdata Protection*. Lecture Notes in Computer Science: Inference Control in Statistical Databases. Springer, 2002.

25. K. Muralidhar, R. Parsa, and R. Sarathy. A general additive data perturbation method for database security. *Management Science*, 45(10):1399–1415, 1999.

26. K. Muralidhar, R. Sarathy, and R. Parsa. An improved security requirement for data perturbation with implications for e-commerce. *Decision Science*, 32(4):683–698, 2001.

27. K. Muralidhar and R. Sarathy. An enhanced data perturbation approach for small data sets. *Decision Sciences*, 36(3):513–529, 2005.

28. W.E. Winkler. Masking and re-identification methods for public-use microdata: Overview and research problems. In *Proceedings of Privacy in Statistical Databases: CASC Project International Workshop, PSD 2004*, pages 231–246, Barcelona, Spain, 2004.

29. C.K. Liew, U.J. Choi, and C.J. Liew. A data distortion by probability distribution. *ACM Transactions on Database Systems*, 10(3):395–411, 1985.

30. J. Burridge. Information preserving statistical obfuscation. *Statistics and Computing*, 13:321–327, 2003.

31. G.T. Duncan and R.W. Pearson. Enhancing access to microdata while protecting confidentiality: Prospects for the future. *Statistical Science*, 6(3):219–232, 1991.

32. D. Ting, S. Fienberg, and M. Trottini. Romm methodology for microdata release. In *UNECE/Eurostat Work Session on Statistical Data Confidentiality*, Geneva, Switzerland, 2005.

33. J. Domingo-Ferrer and V. Torra. Disclosure control methods and information loss for microdata. In P. Doyle, J. Lane, J. Theeuwes, and L. Zayatz, editors, *Confidentiality, Disclosure, and Data Access: Theory and Practical Applications for Statistical Agencies*, pages 93–112. Elsevier, 2002.

34. J.M. Mateo-Sanz, F. Sebé, and J. Domingo-Ferrer. Outlier protection in continuous microdata masking. In *Proceedings of Privacy in Statistical Databases: CASC Project International Workshop, PSD 2004*, pages 201–215, Barcelona, Spain.

35. S.S. Warner. Randomized response: A survey technique for eliminating evasive answer bias. *Journal of American Statistical Association*, 60(309):63–69, March 1965.

36. P.P de Wolf, J.M. Gouweleeuw, P. Kooiman, and L. Willenborg. Reflections on pram. In *SDP*, Amsterdam, 1998.

37. P.P. de Wolf and I. van Gelder. An empirical evaluation of pram. Discussion Paper 04012, Statistics Netherlands, Voorburg, September 2004.

38. M. Trottini. Assessing disclosure risk and data utility: A multiple objectives decision problem. In *Joint ECE/Eurostat Work Session on Statistical Confidentiality*, Luxembourg, 2003.

39. J. Domingo-Ferrer, F. Sebé, and J. Castellà-Roca. On the security of noise addition for privacy in statistical databases. In *Proceedings of Privacy in Statistical Databases: CASC Project International Workshop, PSD 2004*, pages 149–161, Barcelona, Spain, 2004.

40. C.J. Skinner and M.J. Elliot. A measure of disclosure risk for microdata. *Journal of the Royal Statistical Society*, 64:855–867, 2002.
41. J. Domingo-Ferrer, J.M. Mateo-Sanz, and V. Torra. Comparing SDC methods for microdata on the basis of information loss and disclosure risk. In *In Proceedings of NTTS and ETK*, 2001.
42. I. Dinur and K. Nissim. Revealing information while preserving privacy. In *PODS '03: Proceedings of the twenty-second ACM SIGMOD-SIGACT-SIGART symposium on Principles of database systems*, pages 202–210, New York, NY, USA, 2003. ACM Press.
43. M. Miller, I. Roberts, and J. Simpson. Application of symmetric chains to an optimization problem in the security of statistical databases. *Bulletin of the ICA*, 2:47–58, 1991.
44. J.R. Griggs. Concentrating subset sums at k points. *Bulletin Institute Combinatorics and Applications*, 20:65–74, 1997.
45. M. Miller, I. Roberts, and J. Simpson. Prevention of relative compromise in statistical databases using audit expert. *Bulletin of the ICA*, 10:51–62, 1994.
46. P. Horak, L. Brankovic, and M. Miller. A combinatorial problem in database security. *Discrete Applied Mathematics*, 91(1-3):119–126, 1999.
47. L. Brankovic, P. Horak, and M. Miller. An optimization problem in statistical databases. *SIAM Journal on Discrete Mathematics*, 13(2):346–353, 2000.
48. L. Wang, Y. Li, D. Wijesekera, and S. Jajodia. Precisely answering multi-dimensional range queries without privacy breaches. In *Proceedings of 8th European Symposium on Research in Computer Security, ESORICS 2003*, pages 100–115, Gjøvik, Norway, 2003.
49. L. Wang, D. Wijesekera, and S. Jajodia. Cardinality-based inference control in data cubes. *Journal of Computer Security*, 12(5):655–692, 2004.
50. L. Wang, S. Jajodia, and D. Wijesekera. Securing OLAP data cubes against privacy breaches. In *Proceedings of IEEE Symposium on Security and Privacy*, pages 161–, 2004.
51. L. Brankovic, M. Miller, and J. Širáň. Range query usability of statistical databases. *Int. J. Comp. Math.*, 79(12):1265–1271, 2002.
52. L. Brankovic and J. Širáň. 2-compromise usability in 1-dimensional statistical databases. In *Proc. 8th Int. Computing and Combinatorics Conference, COCOON2002*, pages 448–455, 2002.
53. L. Franconi and S. Polettini. Individual risk estimation in -argus: A review. In *Proceedings of Privacy in Statistical Databases: CASC Project International Workshop, PSD 2004*, pages 262–272, Barcelona, Spain, 2004.
54. L. Sweeney. Guaranteeing anonymity when sharing medical data, the datafly system. In *AMIA, Proceedings of Fall Symposium*, pages 51–55, Washington, DC, 1997.

Different Search Strategies on Encrypted Data Compared

Richard Brinkman

University of Twente
The Netherlands

Summary. When private information is stored in databases that are under the control of others, the only possible way to protect it is to encrypt it before storing it. In order to efficiently retrieve the data, a search mechanism that still works over the encrypted data is needed. In this chapter an overview of several search strategies is given. Some add meta-data to the database and do the searching only in the meta-data, others search in the data itself or use secret sharing to solve the problem. Each strategy has its own advantages and disadvantages.

13.1 Why Should We Search in Encrypted Data?

In a chapter about *searching in encrypted data* we should first ask ourselves the questions:

- Why should we want to protect our data using encryption?
- Why not use access control?
- Why should we want to search in encrypted data?
- Why not decrypt the data first and then search in it?

Access control is a perfect way to protect your data as long as you trust the access control enforcement. And exactly that condition often makes access control simply impossible.

Consider a database on your friend's computer. You store your data on his computer because he has bought a brand new large-capacity hard drive. Furthermore, he leaves his computer always on, so that you can access your data from everywhere with an Internet connection. You trust your friend to store your data and to make daily backups. However, your data may contain some information you do not want your friend to read (for instance, letters to your girlfriend). In this particular setting you cannot rely on the access control of your friend's database, because your friend has administrator privileges. He can always circumvent the access control or simply turn it off.

Fortunately, you read a book about cryptography a few years ago, and decide to encrypt all your sensitive information before storing it in the database.

Now you can use your friend's bandwidth and storage space without fearing that he is reading your private data.

Happy as you are, you keep on going storing more and more information. However, the retrieval of it gets harder and harder. In the situation before you encrypted your data you were used to send a precise query to the server and to retrieve only the information you needed. But in the current situation you cannot make the selection on the server. So, for each query you have to download the whole database and do the decryption and querying on your own computer. Since you have a slow Internet connection, you get tired of waiting for the download to finish. Of course, you can send your encryption key to your friend's database and ask it to do the decryption for you, but then you end up in almost the same situation as you started with. If the database can decrypt your data, your friend can read it.

Fortunately, there are mechanisms that solve the sketched problem. Some of the techniques will be explained in the remainder of this chapter.

13.2 Solutions

This section gives some solutions to the problem stated in the previous section. They all have one thing in common: the data are encrypted and stay encrypted for the time it resides on the server. The goal is to prevent the server (and everyone having access to it) from learning the data it is storing, the queries that are asked and the answers it gives back.

13.2.1 Index-Based Approach

Relational databases use tables to store the information. Rows of the table correspond to records and columns to fields. Often hidden fields or even complete tables are added to act as an index. This index does not add information; it is only used to speed up the search process. Hacıgümüş et al. [1, 2, 3] use the same idea to solve the problem of searching in encrypted data. To illustrate their approach we will use the example table shown in Table 13.1, which is stored on the server as shown in Table 13.2.

The first column of the encrypted table contains the encryptions of whole records. Thus $etuple = E(id, name, salary)$, where $E(\cdot)$ is the encryption

Table 13.1. Plain text *salary* table

id	name	salary
23	Tom	70000
860	Mary	60000
320	John	50000
875	Jerry	5600

Table 13.2. Encrypted *salary* table

etuple	id^S	$name^S$	$salary^S$
010101011...	4	28	10
000101101...	2	5	10
010111010...	8	7	2
110111101...	2	7	1

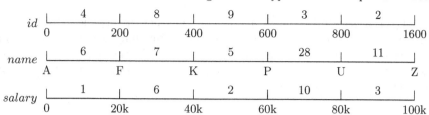

Fig. 13.1. Partitioning of the *id*, *name* and *salary* fields.

function. The extra columns are used as an index, enabling the server to prefilter records. The fields are named similar to the plain text labels, but are annotated with the superscript S which stands for server or secure. The values for these fields are calculated by using the partitioning functions drawn as intervals in Fig. 13.1. The labels of the intervals are chosen randomly. For example, consider John's salary. It lies in the interval $[40k, 60k)$. This interval is mapped to the value two which is stored as the $salary^S$ field of John's record. It is the client's responsibility to keep these partitioning functions secret.

Querying the data is performed in two steps. First, the server tries to give an answer as accurately as it can. Second, the client decrypts this answer and postprocesses it. For this two-stage approach it is essential that the client splits a query Q into a server part Q^S (working on the index only) and a client part Q^C (which postprocesses the answer retrieved from the server). Several splittings are possible. The goal is to reduce the workload of the client and the network traffic. In order to have a realistic query example, let us first add a second table containing addresses to the database. The plain *address* table is shown in Table 13.3. It is stored encrypted on the server as shown in Table 13.4.

Table 13.3. Plain text *address* table

id	street
23	4th avenue
860	Owl street 4
320	Downing street 10
875	Longstreet 100

Table 13.4. Encrypted *address* table

etuple	id^S	$street^S$
110111100...	4	5
110111110...	2	2
000111010...	8	6
001110110...	2	3

As an example we choose the following SQL query:

```
SELECT street
FROM address, salary
WHERE address.id=salary.id AND salary<55000
```

SQL is a descriptive query language. It does not dictate the database *how* the result should be calculated (like a programming language does) only *what* the result should be. The database has freedom in the sequence of operations e.g., selection (σ), projection (π), join ($\bowtie$), etc. In this case the optimal evaluation is the one drawn in Fig. 13.2.

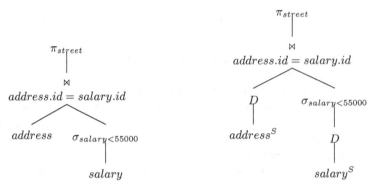

Fig. 13.2. Optimal query evaluation on uncrypted data

Fig. 13.3. Inefficient evaluation on encrypted data

The direct translation of the query tree to the encrypted domain is by simply decrypting the tables first (operation D) and then continuing with the standard evaluation (see Fig. 13.3). It clearly calculates the correct result but misses our goal of reducing network bandwidth and client computation. The operators should be pushed below the decryption operator D as much as possible. In Fig. 13.4 the selection on the salary is pushed below the decryption. Notice that the selection $\sigma^S_{salary^S \in \{1,6,2\}}$ also returns salaries between 55,000 and 60,000, so the client-side selection $\sigma_{salary<55000}$ cannot be left out. After the client selection is pulled above the join (not shown), the join can be pushed below the decryption as shown in figure 13.5.

The original strategy as described in [2] has two drawbacks: it cannot handle aggregate functions like SUM, COUNT, AVG, MIN and MAX very well and frequency analysis attacks are possible.

In a follow-up paper [4] the authors extend the method described in this section with privacy homomorphisms [5], allowing operations like addition and multiplication to work on encrypted data directly without the need to decrypt first.

The second drawback of the original method is dealt with by Damiani et al. [6]. Instead of using an encrypted invertable index, they use a hash function that is designed to have collisions. This way, an attacker has no certainty that two records are equal when they have the same index. This makes frequency analysis harder. As a down side, the efficiency drops when the security increases.

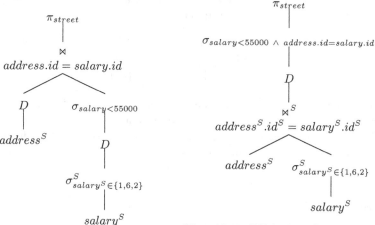

Fig. 13.4. Selection pushed down

Fig. 13.5. Efficient evaluation on encrypted data

13.2.2 Search *in* the Encrypted Data

In contrast to the approach of Hacıgümüş et al, Song, Wagner and Perrig [7] do not need extra meta-data. In their approach the search is done in the encrypted data itself. They use a protocol that uses several encryption steps, which will be explained in this section.

Using the protocols described below, a client (Alice) can store data on the untrusted server (of Bob) and search in it, without revealing the plain text of either the stored data, the query or the query result. The protocol consists of three parts: storage, search and retrieval.

Storage

Before Alice can store information on Bob's server she has to do some calculations. First of all she has to fragment the whole plain text W into several fixed-sized words W_i. Each W_i has a fixed-length n. She also generates encryption keys k' and k'' and a sequence of random numbers S_i using a pseudo random generator. Then she has, or calculates, the following for each block W_i:

W_i	plain-text block
k''	encryption key
$X_i = E_{k''}(W_i) = \langle L_i, R_i \rangle$	encrypted text block
k'	key for f
$k_i = f_{k'}(L_i)$	key for F
S_i	ith random number
$T_i = \langle S_i, F_{k_i}(S_i) \rangle$	tuple used by search
$C_i = X_i \oplus T_i$	value to be stored ($\oplus$ stands for xor)

where E is an encryption function, L_i and R_i are the left and right parts of X_i and f and F are keyed hash functions:

$$E : key \times \{0,1\}^n \rightarrow \{0,1\}^n$$
$$f : key \times \{0,1\}^{n-m} \rightarrow key$$
$$F : key \times \{0,1\}^{n-m} \rightarrow \{0,1\}^m$$

The encrypted word X_i has the same block length as W_i (i.e. n). L_i has length $n - m$ and R_i has length m. The parameters n and m may be chosen freely ($n > 0$, $0 < m \leq \frac{n}{2}$). The value C_i can be sent to Bob for storage. Alice may now forget the values W_i, X_i, L_i, R_i, k_i, T_i and C_i, but should still remember k', k'' and S_i (or the seed to regenerate S_i).

Search

After the encrypted data is stored by Bob in the previous phase, Alice can query Bob's server. Alice provides Bob with an encrypted version of a plain-text word W_j and asks him if and where W_j occurs in the original document. Note that Alice does not have to know the position j. If W_j was a block in the original data then $\langle j, C_j \rangle$ is returned. Alice has or calculates:

k''	encryption key
k'	key for f
W_j	plain-text block to search for
$X_j = E_{k''}(W_j) = \langle L_j, R_j \rangle$	encrypted block
$k_j = f_{k'}(L_j)$	key for F

Then Alice sends the value of X_j and k_j to Bob. Having X_j and k_j Bob is able to compute for each C_p:

$$T_p = C_p \oplus X_j = \langle S_p, S'_p \rangle$$
$$\text{IF } S'_p = F_{k_j}(S_p) \text{ THEN RETURN } \langle p, C_p \rangle$$

If $p = j$ then $S'_p = F_{k_j}(S_p)$, otherwise S'_p is garbage. Note that all locations with a correct T_p value are returned. However there is a small chance that T satisfies $T = \langle S_q, F_{k_j}(S_q) \rangle$ but where $S_q \neq S_p$. Therefore, Alice should check for each answer whether the correct random value is used or not.

Retrieval

Alice can also ask Bob for the cipher text C_p at any position p. Alice, knowing k', k'' and S_i (or the seed to generate it), can recalculate W_p by

$$p \qquad\qquad\qquad\qquad \text{desired location}$$
$$C_p = \langle C_{p,l}, C_{p,r} \rangle \qquad \text{stored block}$$
$$S_p \qquad\qquad\qquad\qquad \text{random value}$$
$$X_{p,l} = C_{p,l} \oplus S_p \qquad \text{left part of encrypted block}$$
$$k_p = f_{k'}(X_{p,l}) \qquad\quad \text{key for } F$$
$$T_p = \langle S_p, F_{k_p}(S_p) \rangle \qquad \text{check tuple}$$
$$X_p = C_p \oplus T_p \qquad\quad \text{encrypted block}$$
$$W_p = D_{k''}(X_p) \qquad\quad \text{plain text block}$$

where D is the decryption function $D : key \times \{0,1\}^n \rightarrow \{0,1\}^n$ such that $D_{k''}(E_{k''}(W_i)) = W_i$.

This is all Alice needs. She can store, find and read the text while Bob cannot read anything of the plain text. The only information Bob gets from Alice is C_i in the storage phase and X_j and k_j in the search phase. Since C_i and X_j are both encrypted with a key only known to Alice and k_j is only used to hash one particular random value, Bob does not learn anything about the plain text. The only information Bob learns from a search query is the location where an encrypted word is stored.

However, the protocol has two drawbacks:

- The splitting of the plain text into fixed-sized words is not natural, especially not for human languages.
- The search time complexity is linear in the length of the whole data. It does not scale up to large databases.

Both drawbacks are solved by Brinkman et al. [8]. They use XML as a data format and exploit its tree structure to get a logarithmic search complexity.

Waters et al. [9] use a similar technique, which is based on [7], to secure audit logs. Audit logs contain detailed and probably sensitive information about past execution. It should therefore be encrypted. Only when there is a need to find something in the encrypted audit log, a trusted party can generate a trapdoor for a specific keyword. Boneh et al. [10] use a different trapdoor strategy to achieve the same goal.

13.2.3 Using Secret Sharing

A third solution to our problem uses secret sharing [11, 12]. In this context, sharing a secret does not mean that several parties know the same secret. In cryptography secret sharing means that a secret is split over several parties such that no single party can retrieve the secret. The parties have to collaborate in order to retrieve the secret.

Secret sharing can be very simple. To share, for instance, the secret value 5 over 3 parties a possible split can be 12, 4 and 26. To find the value back all three parties should collaborate and sum their values modulo 37 ($5 \equiv 12 + 4 + 26 \pmod{37}$).

The database scheme described in this section uses the idea of secret sharing to accomplish the task of storing data such that you need both the server

and the client to collaborate in order to retrieve the data. Further requirements are:

- The server should not benefit from the collaboration. Its knowledge about
  the data should not increase (much) during the collaboration.
- The data split should be unbalanced, meaning that the server share is
  heavier (in terms of storage space) than the client share.

Encoding

A plain text XML document is being transformed into an encrypted database
by following the steps below. See Fig. 13.6 for the encoding of a concrete
example.

1. Define a function $map : node \rightarrow \mathbb{F}_p$, which maps the tag names of the
   nodes to values of the finite field $\mathbb{F}_p$, where p is a prime that is larger than
   the total number of different tag names (Fig. 6(b)).
2. Transform the tree of tag names (Fig. 6(a)) into a tree of polynomials (Fig. 6(d)) of the same structure where each $node$ is transformed to
   $f(node)$ where function $f : node \rightarrow \mathbb{F}_p[x]/(x^{p-1}-1)$ is defined recursively:

$$f(node) = \begin{cases} x - map(node) & \text{if } node \text{ is a leaf node} \\ (x - map(node)) \prod_{d \in child(node)} f(d) & \text{otherwise} \end{cases}$$

   Here $child(node)$ returns all children of a $node$.
3. Split the resulting tree into a client (Fig. 6(e)) and a server tree (Fig. 6(f)).
   Both trees have the same structure as the original one. The polynomials
   of the client tree are generated by a pseudo-random generator. The polynomials of the server tree are chosen such that the sum of a client node
   and the corresponding server node equals the original polynomial.
4. Since the client tree is generated by a pseudo-random generator it suffices
   to store the seed on the client. The client tree can be discarded. When
   necessary, it can be regenerated using the pseudo-random generator and
   the seed value.

Retrieval

It is simple to check whether a node n is stored somewhere in a subtree by
evaluating the polynomials of both the server and the client at $map(n)$. If
the sum of these evaluations equals zero, this means that n can be found
somewhere in the subtree n. To find out whether n is the root node of this
subtree, you have to divide the unshared polynomial by the product of all its
direct children. The result will be a monomial $(x - t)$ where t is the mapped
value of the node.

In a real query evaluation you start at the XML root node and walk
downwards until you encounter a dead branch. Whether you choose to traverse

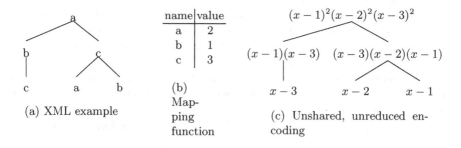

(a) XML example

name	value
a	2
b	1
c	3

(b) Mapping function

$(x-1)^2(x-2)^2(x-3)^2$

$(x-1)(x-3)$ $(x-3)(x-2)(x-1)$

$x-3$ $x-2$ $x-1$

(c) Unshared, unreduced encoding

$=$

$$f_1(x) = 2x^3 + 3x^2 + 2x + 3$$

$f_2(x) = x^2 + x + 3$ $f_4(x) = x^3 + 4x^2 + x + 4$

$f_3(x) = x + 2$ $f_5(x) = x + 3$ $f_6(x) = x + 4$

(d) Unshared, reduced encoding

$$c_1(x) = 2x^3 + x^2 + 1$$

$c_2(x) = x^3 + 2x^2 + 2$ $c_4(x) = 2x^3 + x + 2$

$c_3(x) = 3x^2 + 2x + 1$ $c_5(x) = 3x^3 + 2x^2 + x$ $c_6(x) = 2x^3 + x^2 + 3x + 1$

(e) Client encoding

$+$

$$s_1(x) = 2x^2 + 2x + 2$$

$s_2(x) = 4x^3 + 4x^2 + x + 1$ $s_4(x) = 4x^3 + 4x^2 + 2$

$s_3(x) = 2x^2 + 4x + 1$ $s_5(x) = 2x^3 + 3x^2 + 3$ $s_6(x) = 3x^3 + 4x^2 + 3x + 3$

(f) Server encoding

Fig. 13.6. The mapping function (b) maps each name of an input document (a) to an integer. The XML document is first encoded to a tree of polynomials (c) before it is reduced to the finite field $\mathbb{F}_5[x]/(x^4 - 1)$ (d) and split into a client (e) and a server (f) part.

the tree depth- or breadth-first, the strategy remains the same: try to find dead branches as early as you can. Fortunately, each node contains information about all the subnodes. Therefore, it is almost always the case that you find dead branches (where the unshared evaluation return a nonzero value) before reaching the leaves.

To illustrate the search process we will follow the execution run with the example query //c/a. This XPath query should be read as: start at the root node, go one or more steps down to all c nodes that have an a node as child. The roman numbers in Fig. 13.7 correspond to the following sequence of operations:

(i) We start the evaluation process at the root nodes of the server and the client. In parallel, they can substitute the values in the root polynomials. Both $s_1(map(c)) = s_1(3)$ and $s_1(map(a)) = s_1(2)$ should be evaluated, but it does not matter in which order (analogously for $c_1(\cdot)$). To mislead the server we choose to evaluate first the a nodes and then the c node, although the query suggests otherwise.

(ii) Each time the server has substituted a value for x in one of its polynomials, it sends the result to the client, which can add the server result to its own. In this example $f_1(2) = c_1(2) + s_1(2) = 1 + 4 = 0$, which means that either the original root node was a or the root node has a descendant a.

(iii) The next task is to check that the root node is or contains c.

(iv) $f_1(3) = 0$. Now we know that the root node contains both a and c, a prerequisite of our query. Thus, we proceed one step down in the tree.

(v) The left child is checked for a.

(vi) This time $f_2(2) = 4 \neq 0$. Thus the left subtree does not contain an a node. Apparently this is a dead branch. It is not even necessary to check for a c node; the query //c/a can never hold in this branch. We can stop evaluating it and backtrack to the right subtree.

(vii) In the right subtree we start checking for a c node.

$(viii)$ Since $f_4(2) = 0$, the right subtree seems promising.

(ix) Therefore we also check for an a node.

(x) The right tree still seems promising so we walk one level down.

(xi) Since the client knows the structure of the tree (if not, he can ask the server for it), he knows that we have reached a leaf node. Therefore, it is unnecessary to check for a c node.

(xii) Since this is a leaf node and $f_5(2) = 0$ we now know for sure that node 5 *is* an a node.

$(xiii)$ The rightmost leaf node is also checked for an a node.

(xiv) But it is not.

Until now, we have two possible matches:

1. node 1 matches c and node 4 matches a
2. node 4 matches c and node 5 matches a

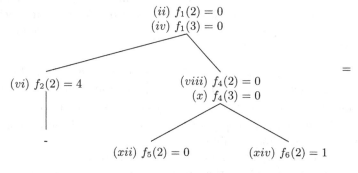

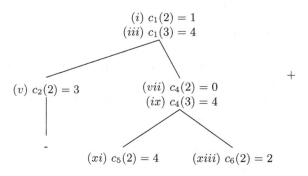

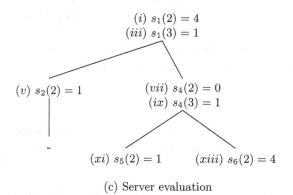

(a) Unshared evaluation

(b) Client evaluation

(c) Server evaluation

Fig. 13.7. Evaluation process of the query //c/a using the same mapping function and data encoding as in Fig. 13.6. The roman numbers indicate the sequence of operations.

It is sufficient to check the exact value of node 4 only. If this node *is* a c node then solution 1 holds, if this node *is* an a node solution 2 holds. If it is neither then there are no matches. The exact value of a node n can be found in two different ways:

- Ask the server for the polynomial $s_n(x)$ and the polynomials of all its children (let us name them $s_n^{(1)}(x), \ldots, s_n^{(k)}(x)$). In the mean time calculate $c_n(x)$ and its children $c_n^{(1)}(x), \ldots, c_n^{(k)}(x)$. The exact value can be calculated by dividing $f_n(x)$ by $\prod_{i=1}^{k} f_n^{(i)}(x)$. The result will be a monomial $x - t$ where t is the node's value.
- If $f_n(a) = 0$ for some value a and for all children i of n, $f_i(a) \neq 0$ then you know that node n *is* a. Note that for recursive document type definitions (such as our example) there is no guarantee that this method works.

13.3 Solutions Compared

Having seen three different ways to query encrypted data, one may ask which one is the best. This is not easy to answer, since each has its own advantages and disadvantages. It depends on the requirements which one is the most appropriate.

13.3.1 Index-Based Approach

Advantages

The index-based solutions uses a relational database as back-end. Since relational databases have been around for quite some time, there exists a huge theoretical background including all kinds of indexing mechanisms and even its own relational algebra. Hacıgümüş takes advantage of this to create an efficient solution, pushing as much of the workload to the server.

Disadvantages

This efficiency comes at a price, though. The storage cost doubles compared to the plain text case. Apart from the encrypted data the hash values for each searchable field are also stored. These hashes are almost as big as the original values.

Another disadvantage is the fact that the server can link records together without the cooperation of the client. Values that are equal in the plain text domain are also equal in the encrypted domain. Although the opposite does not hold, the server still learns which records are not the same. Therefore, it can estimate the number of different values or it can join tables fairly accurately.

A more practical disadvantage is that the user should choose the hash map in such a way that the intervals do not get too big or too small. The hash map strongly depends on the distribution of the plain text values. When the distribution changes drastically, the hash map should also be redesigned.

13.3.2 Search *in* the Encrypted Data

Advantages

The encryption method of Song et al. does not need a larger storage space than in the plain text case.

When a word occurs multiple times, the encryptions are different, which makes frequency analysis impossible.

Almost the whole workload is done at the server site. Only the encryption of the keyword and a single hash operation are performed at the client. This fact makes this strategy especially useful for lightweight devices like mobile phones.

Disadvantages

Song's strategy may be efficient when you only look at storage space, but it is not when looking at computation time. For each query all the data are searched linearly. Thus this strategy does not scale well. Brinkman et al. [8] reduce the computation time from linear to logarithmic by using more structured (trees) data input. Unfortunately, this also increases the communication from constant to logarithmic time. They also drop the requirement for fixed-sized keywords, which is another disadvantage of the original scheme.

13.3.3 Using Secret Sharing

Advantages

The main advantage of the secret sharing strategy is its security. Since all the data stored on the server are randomly generated, it is just worthless garbage for an attacker. Even the same nodes are encrypted differently.

Another advantage is the efficient storage. Although knowledge about the whole subtree is stored at each node, the storage remains similar in size to the plain text.

Disadvantages

A disadvantage, though, is the communication costs. Each node that is being traversed costs a round-trip communication (with very little data) between the client and the server. Also the workload on the client is similar to the workload on the server.

References

1. H. Hacıgümüş, Balakrishna R. Iyer, Chen Li, and Sharad Mehrotra. Executing SQL over encrypted data in the database service provider model. In *SIGMOD Conference*, 2002.

2. H. Hacıgümüş, B. Iyer, and S. Mehrotra. Efficient execution of aggregation queries over encrypted relational databases. In *Proc. of the 9th International Conference on Database Systems for Advanced Applications*, Jeju Island, Korea, March 2004.

3. H. Hacıgümüş, B. Iyer, C. Li, and S. Mehrotra. SSQL: Secure SQL in an insecure environment. *VLDB Journal*, 2006.

4. Hakan Hacıgümüş, Bala Iyer, and Sharad Mehrotra. Efficient execution of aggregation queries over encrypted relational databases. In Kyu-Young Whang Doheon Lee YoonJoon Lee, Jianzhong Li, editor, *Database Systems for Advanced Applications: 9th International Conference, DASFAA 2004*, volume LNCS 2973, pages 125–136, Jeju Island, Korea, March 2003. Springer Verlag.

5. Josep Domingo-Ferrer and Jordi Herrera-Joancomartí. A privacy homomorphism allowing field operations on encrypted data. *Jornades de Metemàtica Discreta i Algorísmica*, 1998.

6. E. Damiani, S. De Capitani di Vimercati, S. Jajodia, S. Paraboschi, and P. Samarati. Balancing confidentiality and efficiency in untrusted relational dbmss. In *Proc. of the 10th ACM Conference on Computer and Communications Security*, pages 93–102, Washington, DC, USA, October 2003. ACM Press New York, NY, USA. http://seclab.dti.unimi.it/Papers/ccs03.pdf.

7. Dawn Xiaodong Song, David Wagner, and Adrian Perrig. Practical techniques for searches on encrypted data. In *IEEE Symposium on Security and Privacy*, pages 44–55, 2000. http://citeseer.nj.nec.com/song00practical.html.

8. R. Brinkman, L. Feng, J. M. Doumen, P. H. Hartel, and W. Jonker. Efficient tree search in encrypted data. *Information Systems Security Journal*, 13(3):14–21, July 2004. http://www.ub.utwente.nl/webdocs/ctit/1/000000f3.pdf.

9. B. Waters, D. Balfanz, G. Durfee, , and D. K. Smetters. Building an encrypted and searchable audit log. In *Network and Distributed Security Symposium (NDSS) '04*, San Diego, California, 2004.

10. D. Boneh, G. Di Crescenzo, R. Ostrovsky, and G. Persiano. Public key encryption with keyword search. In *Proceedings of Eurocrypt*, pages 506–522, 2004. http://crypto.stanford.edu/~dabo/abstracts/encsearch.html.

11. R. Brinkman, J. M. Doumen, P. H. Hartel, and W. Jonker. Using secret sharing for searching in encrypted data. In W. Jonker and M. Petković, editors, *Secure Data Management VLDB 2004 workshop*, volume LNCS 3178, pages 18–27, Toronto, Canada, August 2004. Springer-Verlag, Berlin. http://www.ub.utwente.nl/webdocs/ctit/1/00000106.pdf.

12. R. Brinkman, B. Schoenmakers, J. M. Doumen, and W. Jonker. Experiments with queries over encrypted data using secret sharing. In W. Jonker and M. Petković, editors, *Secure Data Management VLDB 2005 workshop*, volume LNCS 3674, pages 33–46, Trondheim, Norway, Sep 2005. Springer-Verlag, Berlin.

Client-Server Trade-Offs in Secure Computation

Berry Schoenmakers[1] and Pim Tuyls[2]

[1] Technical University Eindhoven, The Netherlands
[2] Philips Research, The Netherlands

Summary. In the framework of secure computation based on threshold homomorphic cryptosystems, we consider scenarios in which a lightweight client device provides encrypted input to a secure computation to be performed on the server side. The computational power at the server side is assumed to be much higher than on the client side. We show how to trade-off work for the client against work for the server such that the total amount of work increases moderately. These client-server trade-offs are considered in detail for two applications: private biometrics and electronic voting.

14.1 Introduction

We consider the framework of secure computation based on threshold homomorphic cryptosystems (THCs), where the inputs and outputs as well as all intermediate values are available in encrypted form only (output values may be recovered in the clear by means of threshold decryption).

In this framework, we consider scenarios in which the main part of a secure computation requires the data to be represented in a specific way. A typical example is a computation that is inherently bitwise, which means that the input values as well as all intermediate values are represented as encrypted bits and all computation steps operate on encrypted bits. In other words, the computation is based on a Boolean circuit (operating on bits) rather than on an arithmetic circuit (operating on integer numbers). However, if the inputs have to be provided by a lightweight (computationally constrained) client device, it may be impracticable to let the client device encrypt all the input bits individually. Instead, we will let the client device just produce the minimum number of encryptions to contain the input values. For example, rather than encrypting each of a few hundred bits separately, it may be sufficient to encrypt a single integer representing all of these bits. The task at the server side is to convert the encrypted integer into encryptions of the bits, which are used in the ensuing secure computation.

We will illustrate this type of trade-off by means of two examples. The first example applies to privacy-preserving biometric authentication, where a biometric sensor (client) needs to encrypt biometric data obtained from a measurement for further processing (e.g., secure and private matching) at the server side. In this case, the data size may vary from a few hundred bits to a few hundred bytes (e.g., a 512-byte IrisCode®). The second example applies to secure electronic voting, where a voter using a client device such as a mobile phone or a personal digital assistant (PDA), casts a vote for one out of a few hundred candidates. For efficient and verifiable tallying of the votes, however, the votes are required to be encrypted in a specific way. The problem is that the computation of these specific encryptions is rather costly and impracticable for the client device. Therefore, we present a trade-off that allows the voter to perform just one, simple encryption, which is converted at the server side before tallying. We show how to limit the effort for the voter's client device to a minimum, while increasing the work at the server side moderately.

The remainder of this chapter is organized as follows. In Sect. 14.2, the basics on THCs are reviewed. Section 14.3 gives a brief description of the framework of secure computation based on THCs, followed by an overview of the basic gates and circuits (sub-protocols) that we need for our trade-offs in Sect. 14.4. Finally, Sect. 14.5 presents the client-server trade-offs for two applications, namely private biometrics and secure electronic elections, and we conclude in Sect. 14.6.

14.2 Threshold Homomorphic Cryptosystems

A threshold homomorphic cryptosystem (THC) is a specific type of public key cryptosystem, combining the properties of threshold cryptosystems and homomorphic cryptosystems, which we will briefly introduce below. At the end of this section, some details are given on a Paillier THC, but these may be skipped on first a reading. See also the next section for more background on THCs.

Assume that n parties $P_1, \ldots, P_n$ are involved. A (t, n)-threshold cryptosystem, $1 \leq t \leq n$, is a cryptographic scheme consisting of the following three components:

Distributed key generation. A protocol between $P_1, \ldots, P_n$ for generating a public key pk such that each party P_i obtains a private share sk_i (of the private key sk corresponding to pk) and a public verification key vk_i, $1 \leq i \leq n$. The protocol depends on the threshold t.

Encryption. An algorithm that, on input of a message m and a public key pk, outputs an encryption c of m under public key pk.

Threshold decryption. A protocol between any set of t parties $P_{i_1}, \ldots, P_{i_t}$ that on input of a cipher text c, private shares $sk_{i_1}, \ldots, sk_{i_t}$, and verification keys $vk_{i_1}, \ldots, vk_{i_t}$, outputs a message m.

In a typical threshold decryption protocol, party P_i will compute a share of the message m from the cipher text c using its private share sk_i; such a share may then be verified against the verification key vk_i. In addition to the standard requirements for public key cryptosystems, a main requirement for a (t, n)-threshold cryptosystem is that collusions of $t - 1$ or fewer parties are not able to find any information on the plain text for a given cipher text.

To introduce homomorphic cryptosystems, we assume that the plain text space forms an additive group, and the cipher-text space forms a multiplicative group. Using $[\![m]\!]$ to denote a (probabilistic) encryption of a message m, the homomorphic property can then be expressed informally as:

$$[\![m_1]\!][\![m_2]\!] = [\![m_1 + m_2]\!].$$

We note that no strict equality between cipher texts is meant here but rather an equality between sets of cipher texts ($[\![m]\!]$ can also be read as the set of all cipher texts corresponding to the plain text m, where each cipher text is equally likely).

A THC combines threshold decryption and homomorphic encryption. Two important examples of THCs are based on the ElGamal cryptosystem [1] and the Paillier cryptosystem [2]. We refer to [3] for a brief comparison between the merits of these THCs in the context of secure computation. For our purposes, we need to use a Paillier THC, which is more powerful than an ElGamal THC, at the price of being more costly to implement.

A summary of a Paillier THC is as follows. The Paillier cryptosystem [2] is a probabilistic, additively homomorphic encryption scheme, known to be semantically secure under the *decisional composite residuosity assumption*. The public key consists of an RSA modulus $N = pq$ of bit length k (security parameter), where p, q are safe primes, $p = 2p' + 1$ and $q = 2q' + 1$ for primes p', q'. The set of plain texts is given by the additive group $\mathbb{Z}_N$, and an encryption of a message $m \in \mathbb{Z}_N$ takes the form $[\![m]\!] = (N + 1)^m r^N \bmod N^2$ for a random $r \in \mathbb{Z}_{N^2}^*$.

Let $\tau = p'q'$. Following [4], the private key is given by the unique value $d \in \mathbb{Z}_{\tau N}$ satisfying $d = 0 \bmod \tau$ and $d = 1 \bmod N$. Given a cipher text $c = [\![m]\!] = (N + 1)^m r^N \bmod N^2$, the basic idea behind decryption is to compute $c^{2ud} \bmod N^2$, where u is an appropriate positive integer, which we do not specify here. Since $d = 0 \bmod \tau$, one sees that $r^{N2d} = 1 \bmod N^2$, and since $d = 1 \bmod N$, one sees that $(N + 1)^{m2ud} = 1 + 2um \bmod N^2$; hence the message m can easily be recovered from $c^{2ud} \bmod N^2$.

For a (t, n)-threshold decryption protocol requiring the cooperation of t or more parties, the private key d is assumed to be shared in a threshold fashion using polynomial shares d_i for $i = 1, \ldots, n$. Given a cipher text $c = [\![m]\!]$, these shares are used to jointly compute the value of $c^{2ud} \bmod N^2$, from which the message m can be recovered, as explained above. Distributed key-generation protocols ensuring that each party P_i gets such a share d_i (and that any group of $t - 1$ parties or less is not able to reconstruct the private key d, hence in particular, does not know the factors p, q of the RSA modulus N)

are complicated though and beyond the scope of this book; we refer again to [3], which points to [5, 6] as recent relevant work on this, which both build on the work of [7].

The Paillier cryptosystem is additively homomorphic over $\mathbb{Z}_N$: given $[\![m_1]\!]$ and $[\![m_2]\!]$ with $m_1, m_2 \in \mathbb{Z}_N$ we have $[\![m_1 + m_2]\!] = [\![m_1]\!][\![m_2]\!]$, where multiplication of cipher texts is done modulo N^2. Note that this implies that, for any $a \in \mathbb{Z}_N$, $[\![am]\!] = [\![m]\!]^a \bmod N^2$.

14.3 THC-Based Secure Computation

Soon after the introduction of public key cryptosystems, the idea of computing with encrypted data surfaced. In fact, as early as 1977, work by Rivest, Adleman and Dertouzos [8] suggested the notion of privacy homomorphisms which can be used to compute with encrypted data. This is a natural thought since many number-theoretic one-way functions and trapdoor one-way permutations possess algebraic properties, such as being additively or multiplicatively homomorphic. For secure digital signature schemes or public key cryptosystems, these algebraic properties actually cause problems which need to be resolved somehow. For instance, the RSA trapdoor one-way permutation, given by $g : x \mapsto x^e \bmod N$, for public exponent e and RSA modulus N, is homomorphic, as $g(x_1 x_2) = g(x_1)g(x_2) \bmod N$, and so is its inverse $g^{-1} : y \mapsto y^d \bmod N$, for private exponent d, $de = 1 \bmod \phi(N)$. To get a secure signature scheme one needs to combine the one-way function with a cryptographic hash function $\mathcal{H} : \{0,1\}^* \to \mathbb{Z}_N^*$, say, and define a signature s on a message m as $s = g^{-1}(\mathcal{H}(m))$. The cryptographic hash function is supposed to destroy all algebraic properties of the number-theoretic functions used. This way one constructs cryptographic schemes that withstand active attacks.

Leaving the algebraic properties intact, however, can also be very useful. This then results in cryptographic schemes that can only withstand passive attacks; e.g., a cryptosystem secure against passive attacks is only secure against eavesdropping. More precisely, a public key cryptosystem is said to be *semantically* secure (or, chosen-plain-text secure) if it is computationally infeasible to deduce any information on the plain text for a given cipher text: for any pair of messages $m_0 \neq m_1$, which may be optimally selected by the attacker, it should be computationally infeasible to guess the bit b with success probability nonnegligibly better than 50% when given an encryption of m_b, for uniformly random $b \in \{0,1\}$ [9]. A necessary requirement for semantic security is that the encryption algorithm is probabilistic.

The use of homomorphic properties in privacy-protecting cryptographic protocols is widespread. The particular idea of using homomorphic cryptosystems in the context of general secure computation was introduced in [10], mentioning even the use of THCs to make the protocols robust. The results of [10] cover the case of a passive (or, semi-honest, or, honest-but-curious) adversary, and this was extended in the later papers [11, 12, 13, 3] to the case of an active (or, malicious) adversary.

The basic idea of achieving general secure n-party computation based on THCs is as follows. Assume that a group of parties has completed a run of the distributed key-generation protocol of a THC, so they hold a public key and a corresponding private key shared among the group (see Sect. 14.2). A secure computation for a given n-ary function f is basically a protocol which on input $[\![x_1]\!],\ldots,[\![x_n]\!]$ produces $[\![f(x_1,\ldots,x_n)]\!]$ as output. An actual protocol is usually obtained by first representing f as an *arithmetic* circuit C consisting of elementary gates, and then replacing each elementary gate of C by a corresponding (sub)protocol.

The elementary gates operate in the same fashion, transforming encrypted inputs into encrypted outputs. Thus, the wires of the entire circuit C are all encrypted under the public key of the THC. It is customary to distinguish addition gates and multiplication gates. Addition gates can be evaluated without having to decrypt any value, taking full advantage of the homomorphic property of the cryptosystem. Multiplication gates, however, require at least one threshold decryption (of a suitably blinded cipher text) to succeed even for a passive adversary. To deal with an active adversary, multiplication gates additionally require the use of zero-knowledge proofs.

A major advantage of this type of protocols for secure n-party computation is that the communication complexity, which is the dominating complexity measure, is asymptotically a factor of $\Theta(n)$ smaller than for approaches based on verifiable secret sharing (see [14, 15, 16] and later papers). Also, the property of universal verifiability is achieved easily when using THCs, meaning that anyone can verify that the outputs are computed correctly. The price to be paid is that when using THCs one is stuck with the cryptographic setting (where the security depends on computational assumptions), whereas the use of VSS allows for solutions in the unconditional setting (without computational assumptions, but requiring private channels). Another possible disadvantage is that the hidden constants for the communication complexity can be large, which means that these hidden constants potentially outweigh the savings of a factor of $\Theta(n)$: in the unconditional setting one can work in a finite field $\mathbb{F}_p$, where the size of the prime p does not influence the security of the protocol; in a cryptographic setting using the Paillier cryptosystem, say, one is forced to work in $\mathbb{Z}_N$ or $\mathbb{Z}_N^*$, where N is a large RSA modulus (of bit length at least 1024 by today's standards).

14.4 Basic Gates and Circuits

Below we summarize the basic protocols on which our results of the next section depend. We view these basic protocols either as gates or as circuits: a protocol is a circuit if it can be entirely specified by connecting other gates and circuits; otherwise, it is viewed as an (atomic) gate, and it often involves one or more threshold decryption steps. We specify the protocols for the passive (semi-honest) case only.

For concreteness, a Paillier THC is assumed throughout. As explained above, we write $[\![m]\!]$ for a (probabilistic) encryption of a message $m \in \mathbb{Z}_N$, where N is an RSA modulus.

14.4.1 Arithmetic Gates

The most basic arithmetic gates are the additive gates, which comprise the addition gate and the negation (additive inverse) gate. Both of these gates can be implemented essentially for free due to the additive homomorphic property of the THC.

The more interesting arithmetic gates are the multiplicative gates, which comprise the multiplication gate and the inversion (multiplicative inverse) gate. Efficient n-party protocols for these gates, requiring a constant number of rounds only, have been developed in [12, 13]. The multiplication gate takes as input encryptions $[\![x]\!]$ and $[\![y]\!]$, with $x, y \in \mathbb{Z}_N$, and produces an encryption $[\![xy]\!]$ as output. The inversion gate takes as input an encryption $[\![x]\!]$, with $x \in \mathbb{Z}_N^*$, and produces $[\![1/x]\!]$ as output.

Multiplication gate. On input $[\![x]\!], [\![y]\!]$:

1. Each party P_i broadcasts encryptions $[\![r_i]\!]$ and $[\![x]\!]^{r_i} = [\![r_i x]\!]$, where $r_i \in \mathbb{Z}_N$ is chosen uniformly at random.
2. Write $r = \sum_{i=1}^n r_i$. The encryptions $[\![y + r]\!]$ and $[\![rx]\!]$ are publicly computed, using the homomorphic property.
3. The encryption $[\![y + r]\!]$ is jointly decrypted, revealing $z = y + r \bmod N$.
4. The encryption $[\![x]\!]^z / [\![rx]\!] = [\![xy]\!]$ is output.

Inversion gate. On input $[\![x]\!]$:

1. Each party P_i broadcasts encryptions $[\![r_i]\!]$ and $[\![x]\!]^{r_i} = [\![r_i x]\!]$, where $r_i \in \mathbb{Z}_N$ is chosen uniformly at random.
2. Write $r = \sum_{i=1}^n r_i$. The encryptions $[\![r]\!]$ and $[\![rx]\!]$ are publicly computed, using the homomorphic property.
3. The encryption $[\![rx]\!]$ is jointly decrypted, revealing $z = rx \bmod N$.
4. The encryption $[\![r]\!]^{1/z} = [\![1/x]\!]$ is output.

Note that if an input is private to one of the parties, say party P_i, simplified multiplication and inversion protocols can be used, which require no interaction at all. For multiplication, if party P_i knows x, it computes $[\![xy]\!]$ directly from $[\![y]\!]$ using the homomorphic property $[\![xy]\!] = [\![y]\!]^x$. We will refer to this gate as a *private-multiplier gate*. (Similarly, for inversion, party P_i simply outputs $[\![1/x]\!]$, if it knows x.)

14.4.2 Randomness Gates

Randomness gates generate encrypted output values according to some probability distribution. Two basic types of randomness gates can be distinguished. The first one generates an encryption of a jointly random element of $\mathbb{Z}_N$, which is done simply by letting each P_i produce an encryption $[\![r_i]\!]$, where $r_i \in \mathbb{Z}_N$ is chosen uniformly at random, and then taking $[\![r]\!] = [\![\sum_{i=1}^{n} r_i]\!]$ as output for the gate. As a result r is uniformly random in $\mathbb{Z}_N$, and consequently r is uniformly random in $\mathbb{Z}_N^*$ as well, as the statistical distance between these distributions is negligible for an RSA modulus N.

The second basic type of randomness gate generates encryptions of jointly random bits, We list three protocols for doing so. Each protocol starts the same. For $i = 1, \ldots, n$, party P_i generates encryption $[\![b_i]\!]$ for a uniformly random bit $b_i \in \{0, 1\}$. To combine bits $[\![b_i]\!]$ into a joint random bit $[\![b]\!]$, with $b = \oplus_{i=1}^{n} b_i$, we mention three options:

- use an unbounded fan-in multiplication gate to compute $[\![b]\!]$ in a constant number of rounds, see [12];
- use $O(n)$ multiplication gates to compute $[\![b]\!]$ in $O(\log n)$ rounds;
- use $O(n)$ private-multiplier gates to compute $[\![b]\!]$ in $O(n)$ rounds.

14.4.3 Addition and Subtraction Circuits

Given encrypted bit representations $[\![x_0]\!], \ldots, [\![x_{m-1}]\!]$ and $[\![y_0]\!], \ldots, [\![y_{m-1}]\!]$ of two numbers x, y, an addition circuit essentially computes the bits of $x + y$, given by $[\![z_0]\!], \ldots, [\![z_{m-1}]\!], [\![c_{m-1}]\!]$ as follows:

$$z_i = x_i + y_i + c_{i-1} - 2c_i$$
$$c_{-1} = 0, \quad c_i = x_i y_i + x_i c_{i-1} + y_i c_{i-1} - 2x_i y_i c_{i-1}.$$

A similar circuit can be used for subtraction.

14.4.4 Equality and Comparison Circuits

For a Boolean formula C, let $[C]$ denote the Iverson bracket defined by $[C] = 1$ if $C \Leftrightarrow$ true and $[C] = 0$ otherwise. Given encrypted bit representations $[\![x_0]\!], \ldots, [\![x_{m-1}]\!]$ and $[\![y_0]\!], \ldots, [\![y_{m-1}]\!]$ of two numbers x, y, equality and comparison circuits compute $[\![[x = y]]\!]$ or $[\![[x < y]]\!]$, respectively.

14.4.5 Matching Circuits

We need a specific matching circuit that determines whether the Hamming distance between two strings of encrypted bits exceeds a given threshold or not. A straightforward way to do so is to first xor the two given strings of encrypted bits (using multiplication gates), then compute the sum of these values (using an addition circuit), and finally compare this sum with a given threshold (using a comparison circuit).

14.4.6 Binary Conversion Gates

The three binary conversion gates of [17] are now presented, with each taking an encryption $[\![x]\!]$ as input and producing encryptions of (one or more) bits of x as output. The LSBs gate (of which the LSB gate is a special case) outputs a specified number of least significant bits of x, provided the length of x is sufficiently far below the length of the RSA modulus N. The BITREP gate outputs all of the bits of x, for any value $x \in \mathbb{Z}_N$.

LSB Gate

On input $[\![x]\!]$, an LSB gate outputs an encryption $[\![x_0]\!]$. For a particularly efficient solution, it is assumed that x is a bounded value, that is, $0 \le x < 2^m$ where the value of m is restricted as a function of N, the number of parties n, and a security parameter κ. The parameter κ is chosen such that $2^{-\kappa}$ is negligible. The restriction on m is that $m+\kappa+\log_2 n < \log_2 N$. In practice this is not a severe restriction. For example, if N is a 1024-bit modulus, $\kappa = 100$, and $n = 16$, then m is bounded above by 920.

The protocol for the LSB gate runs as follows:

1. The parties jointly generate a random bit $[\![r_0]\!]$, using a random-bit gate. In parallel, each party P_i chooses $r_{*,i} \in_R \{0, \ldots, 2^{m+\kappa-1} - 1\}$ and broadcasts $[\![r_{*,i}]\!]$. The encryption $[\![r_*]\!]$ with $r_* = \sum_{i=1}^{n} r_{*,i}$ is publicly computed.
2. The encryption $[\![x]\!][\![r_0]\!][\![r_*]\!]^2$ is formed and jointly decrypted to reveal the value $y = x + r$, where $r = r_0 + 2r_*$.
3. The output is $[\![r_0 \oplus y_0]\!]$, which can be computed publicly from $[\![r_0]\!]$ and y_0, as $r_0 \oplus y_0 = r_0 + y_0 - 2r_0 y_0$.

We note that, once x_0 is computed, the next bit of x can be computed by applying the protocol to $[\![x_*]\!]$, with $x_* = (x - x_0)/2$. Indeed, the homomorphic property implies $[\![x_*]\!] = ([\![x]\!]/[\![x_0]\!])^{1/2}$, where $1/2 = (N+1)/2$ is the inverse of 2 modulo N. This way all of the bits of x can be recovered.

LSBs Gate

The protocol for the LSB gate can be improved to output any number of least significant bits of x in one go. Let $m+\kappa+\log_2 n < \log_2 N$, as before. On input $[\![x]\!]$, where $0 \le x < 2^m$, the following protocol computes $[\![x_0]\!], \ldots, [\![x_{m-1}]\!]$ securely. The idea is to jointly generate a random value $[\![r]\!]$ and to decrypt $[\![x + r]\!]$ such that: (i) $y = x + r$ is statistically indistinguishable from random, and (ii) $[\![x_0]\!], \ldots, [\![x_{m-1}]\!]$ can be recovered from $y_0, \ldots, y_{m-1}$ and $[\![r_0]\!], \ldots, [\![r_{m-1}]\!]$. For technical reasons, we will actually compute $y = x - r$ in (i) and use an addition circuit to perform step (ii):

1. The parties jointly generate random bits $[\![r_0]\!], \ldots, [\![r_{m-1}]\!]$, using m random-bit gates. In parallel, each party P_i chooses $r_{*,i} \in_R \{0, \ldots, 2^{m+\kappa-1} - 1\}$ and broadcasts $[\![r_{*,i}]\!]$. The encryption $[\![r_*]\!]$ with $r_* = \sum_{i=1}^{n} r_{*,i}$ is publicly computed.

2. The encryption $[\![x-r]\!]$ is formed and jointly decrypted to reveal the signed value $y = x - r \in (-n/2, n/2)$, where $r = \sum_{j=0}^{m-1} r_j 2^j + r_* 2^m$. The signed value y is computed such that $y \equiv x - r \pmod{n}$.
3. Let $y_0, \ldots, y_{m-1}$ denote the binary representation of $y \bmod 2^m$. An addition circuit for inputs $y_0, \ldots, y_{m-1}$ (public) and $[\![r_0]\!], \ldots, [\![r_{m-1}]\!]$ is used to produce an output of m encrypted bits (ignoring the final carry bit, hence computing modulo 2^m).

For the client-server trade-off presented in Sect. 14.5.2, we need to analyze what happens if the LSBs gate is applied to a ciphertext $[\![x]\!]$, where x is out of range (i.e., $2^m \le x < N$). For our purposes, it suffices to note that in this case, the above protocol will still run to completion without leaking information on x but, obviously, producing an incorrect output. Whether or not x was in range can be determined by testing $[\![x]\!]$ and $[\![x']\!] = \prod_{i=0}^{m-1} [\![x_i]\!]^{2^i}$ for equality of x and x'.

BITREP Gate

For the LSB and LSBs gates, the value of x is restricted by requiring that $0 \le x < 2^m$ and $m + \kappa + \log_2 n < \log_2 N$. The BITREP gate is designed to work for any value x in the range $[0, N)$, where N is the Paillier modulus.

The protocol for generating a random value $r \in_R [0, N)$ uses the basic protocol for jointly generating m random bits between parties $P_1, \ldots, P_n$. We then test whether the integer represented by these m bits is in the range $[0, N)$:

1. The parties jointly generate random bits $[\![r_0]\!], \ldots, [\![r_{m-1}]\!]$, using m random-bit gates.
2. A comparison circuit for encrypted inputs $[\![r_0]\!], \ldots, [\![r_{m-1}]\!]$ and public inputs $N_0, \ldots, N_{m-1}$, denoting the bits of N, is used to compute $[\![[r < N]]\!]$, where $r = \sum_{j=0}^{m-1} r_j 2^j$.
3. The value $[\![[r < N]]\!]$ is decrypted to see if r is in range; if not, go back to the first step.

The average number of iterations is bounded above by 2.

The protocol for converting $[\![x]\!]$ into $[\![x_0]\!], \ldots, [\![x_{m-1}]\!]$, where $0 \le x < N$, runs as follows:

1. The parties generate encrypted bits $[\![r_0]\!], \ldots, [\![r_{m-1}]\!]$ of a random number $0 \le r < N$.
2. The parties compute $[\![x]\!] \prod_{j=0}^{m-1} [\![r_j]\!]^{2^j}$ and perform a threshold decryption to obtain $y = x + r \bmod N$, $0 \le y < N$.
3. Using a subtraction circuit with $y_0, \ldots, y_{m-1}$ and $[\![r_0]\!], \ldots, [\![r_{m-1}]\!]$ as inputs, the parties determine the bit representation $[\![z_0]\!], \ldots, [\![z_m]\!]$ of the value $z = x$ or $z = x - N$, where z_m is a sign bit.

4. The parties reduce the value of z modulo N, by adding Nz_m to z using an addition circuit with inputs $[\![(Nz_m)_0]\!], \ldots, [\![(Nz_m)_{m-1}]\!]$ and $[\![z_0]\!], \ldots, [\![z_{m-1}]\!]$.

The equality $y = x + r$ holds in $\mathbb{Z}_N$ but not necessarily in $\mathbb{Z}$. But if $y \neq x + r$ over the integers, then it follows that $y = x + r - N$ must hold over the integers, since $0 \leq x < N$ and $0 \leq r < N$. In step 3, the case $z = x$ occurs exactly when $y = x + r$ over the integers, and the case $z = x - N$ occurs when $y = x + r - N$.

14.5 Applications and Client-Server Trade-Offs

14.5.1 Private Biometrics

The goal of private biometric authentication is to identify people based on their physical characteristics without revealing any information on these characteristics to a, possibly malicious, verifier. This can be achieved in a cryptographic setting as follows.

During *enrolment* which is performed at a trusted authority, the biometric $\bar{x} = (x_1, \ldots, x_l)$ with $x_i \in \{0,1\}$ is measured, encrypted into $[\![\bar{x}]\!] = ([\![x_1]\!], \ldots, [\![x_l]\!])$ and stored in a reference database. During authentication (at a secure sensor) the biometric $\bar{y} = (y_1, \ldots, y_l)$ of a person is measured. The measurement $\bar{y}$ is slightly different from the corresponding enrolment measurement $\bar{x}$ due to noise. The sensor then forms the number $y = \sum_{i=1}^{l} y_i 2^i$ encrypts it and sends the value $[\![y]\!]$ to the verifier. The verifier retrieves the reference information $[\![\bar{x}]\!]$ of the claimed identity from the database and sends it together with the received value $[\![y]\!]$ to a set of secure servers to which the secure similarity computation is outsourced. Upon reception of $[\![\bar{x}]\!]$ and $[\![y]\!]$, the servers first run an LSBs or BITREPgate on $[\![y]\!]$ to obtain $[\![\bar{y}]\!]$. Then, they compute securely the similarity, e.g., the Hamming distance between the bit strings $(x_1, \ldots, x_l)$ and $(y_1, \ldots, y_l)$. Finally, they check securely whether the similarity is sufficiently high. The output of this protocol is then sent to the verifier who, based on this output, decides whether identification was successful or not.

The above approach strictly limits the exposure of the biometrics in the system to the sensors at the time of a measurement. Even the biometric template $\bar{x}$ is never exposed after it has been captured by a sensor during enrolment. In particular, it is avoided that the biometric template $\bar{x}$ is sent to the sensor, which could then match it with $\bar{y}$ itself: a compromised sensor may then be used to read out the entire reference database of biometric templates without any of the users being present.

The computational advantage that is gained by arranging biometric authentication in this way stems from the following facts. Consider the situation where the iris is used as a biometric. As already pointed out in Sect. 14.1, the size of a measured biometric (template) y is 4096 bits in this case (for a 512-byte IrisCode®). Without the availability of an LSBs or BITREPgate and some servers to outsource the computations to, the sensor would have to encrypt every bit of y individually and send those encryptions to the verifier. This means that 4096 Paillier encryptions, which each consist of at least 2048 bits (for a 1024-bit RSA modulus), need to be handled by the client device. Performing such an amount of work within a few seconds is probably too much for a computationally constrained sensor. The scheme presented above reduces the workload of the sensor to a few Paillier encryptions. Hence, the whole biometric measurement y can be securely sent to the verifier using only two or three Paillier encryptions, which yields a gain of about a factor of 1000 both in computational complexity and in communication complexity. Thus, the major part of the workload is shifted to the servers.

14.5.2 Secure Electronic Elections

Background

Since a secure electronic election is a special instance of a secure computation, THCs can also be used to construct secure election schemes, as first shown in [18], which in turn follows the approach for universally (or, publicly) verifiable elections as put forth by Benaloh et al. [19, 20, 21, 22]. Below, we first review the use of THCs in binary elections (yes-no votes only), and then consider an extension to multiway elections. The goal is to limit the work for the voter as much as possible.

A binary election runs as follows. First, an initialization phase is run to set up a THC for which the private key is shared among a set of *talliers*, who are responsible for counting the votes.

During the voting phase, each eligible voter will cast a single vote $v \in \{0, 1\}$ by publishing an encryption $[\![v]\!]$, where $v = 0$ represents a no vote and $v = 1$ represents a yes vote, say. The encryption $[\![v]\!]$ needs to be authenticated somehow by the voter, which can be done simply by means of a digital signature, or any other type of authentication deemed appropriate. Of course, only one vote will be accepted for each eligible voter.

Next, during the tallying phase, the votes are accumulated by forming the product $\prod_{i=1}^{m} [\![v_i]\!]$, where v_i is the vote cast by voter V_i, $1 \leq i \leq m$. Due to the homomorphic property, this product is equal to $[\![\sum_{i=1}^{m} v_i]\!]$. Hence, the final tally, which is the sum of the votes v_i, can be recovered by decrypting the product of all encrypted votes.

There is one caveat here: voters must be prevented from submitting encryptions $[\![v]\!]$ with $v \notin \{0, 1\}$. This can be done by requiring a noninteractive zero-knowledge proof from the voter, that shows that indeed $[\![v]\!]$ contains a value $v \in \{0, 1\}$, without revealing any information on the actual value of v. As shown in [18], an encryption $[\![v]\!]$ plus a noninteractive zero-knowledge proof can be rendered efficiently using homomorphic ElGamal encryption and assuming the random oracle model.

More-general types of elections than binary ones can be handled by extending the basic approach in several ways. As an illustrative example, we will consider the case of multiway elections, where each voter is supposed to pick one candidate from a (potentially long) list of candidates. We focus on the problem of *minimizing* the effort required of the voter in casting an encrypted ballot (e.g., when the voter's client software needs to run on a simple mobile phone). This problem has already been considered in [23], where incidentally Paillier encryption is used as well as the underlying THC.

Minimizing the Work for the Voter

A rather direct extension of the solution from the binary case to the multiway case would take the following form. Let K denote the number of candidates running for election. Further, let M denote an upper bound on the number of voters taking part in the election[3]. A vote for candidate x, $0 \leq x < K$, will be represented by the integer M^x. Adding these integers will thus yield the election result in radix M representation[4]. The voter would also be required to provide a proof that its vote is valid, i.e., the vote is in the set $\{1, M, M^2, \ldots, M^{K-1}\}$.

To minimize the voter's effort, however, we will simply require the voter to release an encryption $[\![x]\!]$. As will be explained below, the voter must also provide a noninteractive zero-knowledge proof of knowledge of x (a proof of plain-text knowledge). Assuming the random oracle model, such a noninteractive proof can be rendered efficiently for Paillier encryptions. By doing so, we deviate from [23], where the voter is required to prove that $[\![x]\!]$ contains a valid vote, meaning that $x \in \{0, 1, \ldots, K-1\}$, rather than just a proof of plain-text knowledge. Asymptotically the size of such a non-interactive validity proof is the same as the size of a non-interactive proof of plain-text knowledge, but the hidden constants are considerably higher though. For instance, [24] mentions a size of about 1700 bytes for a proof of $x \in \{0, 1, \ldots, K-1\}$, while a proof of plain-text knowledge will be one order of magnitude smaller, say about 170 bytes in size; the time to generate and verify these proofs will vary accordingly.

In our case, the check for validity of $[\![x]\!]$ is also done by the talliers, in a publicly verifiable way. We will perform this check by first computing the bits of x (in encrypted form) using the LSBs gate. For valid $[\![x]\!]$, the encrypted bits of x are then also used to compute an encryption of the form $[\![M^x]\!]$, which enables efficient tallying. The details are as follows.

Let $[\![x]\!]$ be an encrypted vote, which is supposed to satisfy $x \in \{0, \ldots, K-1\}$. Let m denote the bit length of $K-1$, hence $2^{m-1} \leq K-1 < 2^m$. Then

---

[3] Or, rather, M could be the maximum number of voters for which an aggregate result needs to be computed without disclosing partial results, e.g., M could be the maximum size of a precinct, or of a county.

[4] As an optimization, one may use $\lfloor M^{x-1} \rfloor$ instead, taking advantage of the fact that the total number of votes is publicly known.

$0 \leq x < 2^m$, so x can be viewed as an m-bit integer, and we may apply the LSBs gate to convert $[\![x]\!]$ into the encrypted bits of $[\![x_0]\!], \ldots, [\![x_{m-1}]\!]$.

To check that x is a valid vote, we proceed as follows. To begin with we check that the encrypted bits of x have been computed correctly by checking that $[\![x]\!] = \prod_{i=0}^{m-1} [\![x_i]\!]^{2^i}$, using a plain-text equality test with public output. This check will be successful if and only if $0 \leq x < 2^m$ holds. In addition, to test that $0 \leq x \leq K - 1$, we use a comparison circuit for comparing the encrypted bits of x and the (public) bits of $K - 1$. (Note that revealing information about invalid votes should not be a problem because of the proof of plain-text knowledge. Actually, one could publicly decrypt invalid votes, hence exposing all the information in this case. Ballot secrecy is only guaranteed if one submits valid votes.)

The proof of plain-text knowledge prevents that a voter duplicates someone else's vote, or computes thier encrypted vote as a function of other votes in some way (without knowing these other votes). The privacy problem is that the check for validity performed by the talliers can be abused to find out some information on encrypted votes. For instance, to see whether a voter voted for candidate $x = 0$, the attacker may submit (on behalf of another (corrupted) voter) $[\![x']\!] = [\![x]\!][\![2^m - 1]\!]$ as encrypted vote. Assuming that $0 \leq x < K$, we see that x' can only be in the range $\{0, \ldots, 2^m - 1\}$ if $x = 0$.

Finally, from $[\![x_0]\!], \ldots, [\![x_{m-1}]\!]$ we need to compute $[\![M^x]\!]$. Noting that $M^{x_0} = 1 + x_0(M - 1)$, $M^{x_1} = 1 + x_1(M - 1)$ and so on, it is easily seen that $[\![M^x]\!]$ can be computed securely, using $m - 1$ multiplication gates.

14.6 Conclusion

In this chapter we have presented two examples of secure multiparty computations based on THCs, focusing on a scenario in which the inputs to the computation are provided by lightweight clients and the actual computation is performed by a set of powerful servers. We have shown that the work for the clients can be reduced to the bare minimum, meaning that they only need to encrypt their input using the public key of the THC, and possibly provide a noninteractive proof of plain-text knowledge as well. Thus, the work for the clients is reduced to a few public key operations, which can be performed quickly on any crypto-capable smart card. The work for the servers increases though: e.g., in the case of private biometrics, the client is basically saving one Paillier encryption per bit, while the servers need to do extra work to reconstruct these bits from the encrypted data sent by the client. Clearly, it depends on the relative power of client and server whether our trade-off is advantageous or not.

References

1. T. ElGamal. A public-key cryptosystem and a signature scheme based on discrete logarithms. *IEEE Transactions on Information Theory*, IT-31(4):469–472, 1985.
2. P. Paillier. Public-key cryptosystems based on composite degree residuosity classes. In *Advances in Cryptology—EUROCRYPT '99*, volume 1592 of *Lecture Notes in Computer Science*, pages 223–238, Berlin, 1999. Springer-Verlag.
3. B. Schoenmakers and P. Tuyls. Practical two-party computation based on the conditional gate. In *Advances in Cryptology—ASIACRYPT '04*, volume 3329 of *Lecture Notes in Computer Science*, pages 119–136, Berlin, 2004. Springer-Verlag.
4. I. Damgård and M. Jurik. A generalisation, a simplification and some applications of Paillier's probabilistic public-key system. In *Public Key Cryptography—PKC '01*, volume 1992 of *Lecture Notes in Computer Science*, pages 119–136, Berlin, 2001. Springer-Verlag.
5. N. Gilboa. Two party RSA key generation. In *Advances in Cryptology—CRYPTO '99*, volume 1666 of *Lecture Notes in Computer Science*, pages 116–129, Berlin, 1999. Springer-Verlag.
6. J. Algesheimer, J. Camenisch, and V. Shoup. Efficient computation modulo a shared secret with application to the generation of shared safe-prime products. In *Advances in Cryptology—CRYPTO '02*, volume 2442 of *Lecture Notes in Computer Science*, pages 417–432, Berlin, 2002. Springer-Verlag.
7. D. Boneh and M. Franklin. Efficient generation of shared RSA keys. *Journal of the ACM*, 48(4):702–722, 2001.
8. R. Rivest, L. Adleman, and M. Dertouzos. On data banks and privacy homomorphisms. In *Foundations of Secure Computation*, pages 169–177. Academic Press, 1978.
9. S. Goldwasser and S. Micali. Probabilistic encryption. *Journal of Computer and System Sciences*, 28(2):270–299, 1984.
10. M. Franklin and S. Haber. Joint encryption and message-efficient secure computation. *Journal of Cryptology*, 9(4):217–232, 1996.
11. A. Juels and M. Jakobsson. Mix and match: Secure function evaluation via ciphertexts. In *Advances in Cryptology—ASIACRYPT '00*, volume 1976 of *Lecture Notes in Computer Science*, pages 162–177, Berlin, 2000. Springer-Verlag.
12. R. Cramer, I. Damgård, and J.B. Nielsen. Multiparty computation from threshold homomorphic encryption. In *Advances in Cryptology—EUROCRYPT '01*, volume 2045 of *Lecture Notes in Computer Science*, pages 280–300, Berlin, 2001. Springer-Verlag. Full version `eprint.iacr.org/2000/055`, October 27, 2000.
13. I. Damgård and J.B. Nielsen. Universally composable efficient multiparty computation from threshold homomorphic encryption. In *Advances in Cryptology—CRYPTO '03*, volume 2729 of *Lecture Notes in Computer Science*, pages 247–264, Berlin, 2003. Springer-Verlag.
14. O. Goldreich, S. Micali, and A. Wigderson. How to play any mental game - or - a completeness theorem for protocols with honest majority. In *Proc. 19th Symposium on Theory of Computing (STOC '87)*, pages 218–229, New York, 1987. A.C.M.
15. M. Ben-Or, S. Goldwasser, and A. Wigderson. Completeness theorems for non-cryptographic fault-tolerant distributed computation. In *Proc. 20th Symposium on Theory of Computing (STOC '88)*, pages 1–10, New York, 1988. A.C.M.

16. D. Chaum, C. Crépeau, and I. Damgård. Multiparty unconditionally secure protocols. In *Proc. 20th Symposium on Theory of Computing (STOC '88)*, pages 11–19, New York, 1988. A.C.M.
17. B. Schoenmakers and P. Tuyls. Efficient binary conversion for Paillier encryptions. In *Advances in Cryptology—EUROCRYPT '06*, volume 4004 of *Lecture Notes in Computer Science*, pages 522–537, Berlin, 2006. Springer-Verlag.
18. R. Cramer, R. Gennaro, and B. Schoenmakers. A secure and optimally efficient multi-authority election scheme. In *Advances in Cryptology—EUROCRYPT '97*, volume 1233 of *Lecture Notes in Computer Science*, pages 103–118, Berlin, 1997. Springer-Verlag.
19. J. Cohen and M. Fischer. A robust and verifiable cryptographically secure election scheme. In *Proc. 26th IEEE Symposium on Foundations of Computer Science (FOCS '85)*, pages 372–382. IEEE Computer Society, 1985.
20. J. Benaloh and M. Yung. Distributing the power of a government to enhance the privacy of voters. In *Proc. 5th ACM Symposium on Principles of Distributed Computing (PODC '86)*, pages 52–62, New York, 1986. A.C.M.
21. J. Benaloh. Secret sharing homomorphisms: Keeping shares of a secret secret. In *Advances in Cryptology—CRYPTO '86*, volume 263 of *Lecture Notes in Computer Science*, pages 251–260, Berlin, 1987. Springer-Verlag.
22. J. Benaloh. *Verifiable Secret-Ballot Elections*. PhD thesis, Yale University, Department of Computer Science Department, New Haven, CT, September 1987.
23. I. Damgård and M. Jurik. Client/server tradeoffs for online elections. In *Public Key Cryptography—PKC '02*, volume 2274 of *Lecture Notes in Computer Science*, pages 125–140, Berlin, 2002. Springer-Verlag.
24. H. Lipmaa. On diophantine complexity and statistical zero-knowledge arguments. In *Advances in Cryptology—ASIACRYPT '03*, volume 2894 of *Lecture Notes in Computer Science*, pages 398–415, Berlin, 2003. Springer-Verlag.

15

Federated Identity Management

Jan Camenisch and Birgit Pfitzmann

IBM Zurich Research Laboratory
Switzerland

Summary. The more real business and interaction with public authorities is performed in digital form, the more important the handling of identities over open networks becomes. The rise in identity theft as a result of the misuse of global but unprotected identifiers like credit card numbers is one strong indicator of this. Setting up individual passwords between a person and every organization he or she interacts with also offers very limited security in practice. Federated identity management addresses this critical issue. Classic proposals like Kerberos and PKIs never gained wide acceptance because of two problems: actual deployment to end users and privacy. We describe modern approaches that solve these problems. The first approach is browser-based protocols, where the user only needs a standard browser without special settings. We discuss the specific protocol types and security challenges of this protocol class, as well as what level of privacy can and cannot be achieved within this class. The second approach, private credentials, solves the problems that none of the prior solutions could solve, but requires the user to install some local software. Private credentials allow the user to reveal only the minimum information necessary to conduct transactions. In particular, it enables unlinkable transactions even for certified attributes. We sketch the cryptographic solutions and describe how optional properties such as revocability can be achieved, in particular in the idemix system.

15.1 Introduction

In many areas of society, transactions of increasing importance and volume are performed digitally. This concerns business-to-consumer and business-to-business commerce as well as public administration and direct interactions between individuals. In most cases, the first challenge is identity management: how do the partners recognize each other if they want to interact with a specific partner (*authentication*)? And how do they obtain the information about each other that is needed to perform the desired transaction (*attribute exchange*)? These questions become even more critical when the goal of making the transactions digital goes beyond re-implementing the paper world, towards what is known as *on-demand business*. This means more-flexible business relationships where everyone can perform every transaction with whatever enterprise or organization performs them best at just that time. On-demand business increases the identity management problem from trying to bootstrap existing relationships from the paper world to the digital world to a much more dynamic case: where there is no prior direct relationship between two partners, all information that must be trusted requires third-party confirmation. Approaches to optimizing the exchange of identity-related information across several relationships are called *federated identity management* (FIM). Identity management in general also has an enterprise-internal aspect of how to manage identity information received from partners consistently, with quick updates and suitable privacy; this is a significant problem in practice. In this article, however, we concentrate on recent approaches to the exchange of identity-related information between different individuals and organizations.

With respect to end users, there are two major challenges in federated identity management: ease of use, in particular very easy start of usage, and privacy.

A market observation currently taken for granted by the major players is that a large segment of users will not install additional software or even hardware such as card readers for identity management or electronic commerce in general, neither for ease of use nor for security or privacy. Identity management protocols must accommodate this user segment, i.e., people using nothing but a commercial browser. We call such protocols *browser-based* and the feature *zero-footprint*. A similar precondition is *mobility* in the sense that a user should be able to use the protocols from varying browsers, such as several personal devices or even Internet kiosks. While we stress that authenticating via unknown browsers is dangerous for security, nobody is forced to do this (at least in developed countries). These functional requirements distinguish FIM proposals made over the last five years such as Microsoft Passport, the OASIS SAML standard, the Liberty Alliance specifications, and Web Services Federation from classical approaches such as Kerberos, PKIs, form fillers, and wallets (which we do not survey here). Very recently, however, proposals that concentrate on local clients are coming into favor again, in particular the PRIME project (`http://www.prime-project.eu`), Microsoft CardSpace (`http://www.microsoft.com/presspass/features/2006/feb06/02-14InfoCards.mspx`), and the Higgins project (`http://www.eclipse.org/higgins/`), but now at least the last two emphasize making flexible identity management a standard feature of basic client software.

Privacy surveys show consistently that 80–90% of all people are concerned about privacy, and that 25% are willing to pay a considerable price in money or inconvenience for it, see e.g., [27, 43]. These numbers are actually increasing, partially due to the special problems of identity theft based on the misuse of widely available, unprotected numbers as authentication secrets. It is also known that about half of all people at least occasionally give wrong data to web sites on purpose because of privacy concerns. The privacy problem increases with on-demand business because users will interact with more partners, have less apriori trust in most of them, and the third parties that may be needed to confirm information may need very complex privacy policies because they no longer only collect and use identity-related information for specific well-defined business purposes. Altogether it is well accepted today that unaddressed privacy concerns would be a major inhibitor for electronic commerce, as made visible by privacy and trust initiatives by major software providers such as IBM and Microsoft and the fact that privacy statements have become common on e-commerce sites.

An important distinction in actual FIM protocols is between the recognition of a previously known partner, and the transfer of certified and uncertified attributes about a partner. The former is typically called authentication; it can happen under a real identity or under a *pseudonym*. All modern proposals for identity management allow for pseudonyms. A *certified attribute* is one that is confirmed by a third party, while an *uncertified attribute* comes witout such a confirmation. Currently, almost all attributes in electronic commerce are uncertified: users simply input their names, addresses, credit card numbers, preferences etc. into web forms. Some attributes, such as preferences, cannot and need not be certified by nature. For other attributes it is usually contrary to the interest of the user to give wrong data, e.g., for delivery addresses. For yet other attributes, mechanisms outside identity management make certification unnecessary, e.g., the right to revoke unsigned credit-card transactions. However, in the future, certification of attributes will gain in importance. For instance, if a person in a business-to-business scenario claims to be an employee of a partner company, this should be certified by the partner company. Or if individuals take advice from an online medical service, they would be well advised to expect a credential of the quality of this service.

In the following, we first give an overview of browser-based FIM protocols, i.e., protocols designed to solve the first of the end-user identity-management challenges by allowing users to work entirely with standard browsers (Sects. 15.2– 15.5). We survey the basic techniques used in such protocols, emerging standards, security issues, and privacy options and limitations. In particular it turns out that privacy can be almost optimal for uncertified attributes, while it is limited for certified attributes.

This limitation is overcome by *private credentials*, presented in Sects. 15.6–15.8. These are cryptographic protocols that essentially allow a user to transform a certified attribute obtained under one pseudonym so that it can be shown under another pseudonym of the same user in a secure but *unlinkable* way, i.e., the credential issuer and the party to whom the credential was shown cannot find out that these two pseudonyms refer to the same person (assuming that at least two persons hold such a credential). The credential can be transformed and shown multiple times in unlinkable ways, unless specific options to exclude this are selected. We sketch the underlying cryptographic ideas, in particular of the efficient and flexible *idemix* system, discuss additional features such as anonymity revocation and attribute combination, and survey the major initiatives where private credentials may come into practice soon.

We will use car rental as a running example. Figure 15.1 shows a simple scenario where browser-based FIM is appropriate: a person, called *the user*, wants to rent a car for a business trip. The employer has a contract with a car-rental company that gives its employees favorable conditions and settles insurance issues. Hence the user must be certified as an employee of the com-

Fig. 15.1. Example scenario for browser-based FIM

pany at the time of rental. Furthermore, at least during the first rental, the car rental company may need several other attributes about the user that the employer already knows, such as name and address; these may be transferred by the FIM protocol for the convenience of the user. This is a scenario without many privacy requirements, except that the employer and the car rental company should not exchange unnecessary information about the user. We will later also consider scenarios where the user rents the car for a private trip; we then consider stronger privacy requirements.

15.2 Example of a Browser-Based FIM Protocol

The easiest way to introduce the techniques used in browser-based protocols is to look at one such protocol. Figure 15.2 shows the message flow of the WSFPI protocol when no error occurs; WSFPI is a strict instantiation of the WS-Federation Passive Requestor Interop scenario [26] based on [29]. Strict means that we regard discretionary security-relevant constraints as mandatory and prescribe the use of secure channels. While these measures are not necessary in certain scenarios, we include them to get a general-purpose protocol.

User U at browser B wants to sign-in at a party C called *identity consumer* with the help of an *identity supplier* S where U has registered earlier. In our car rental example, the employer is the identity supplier and the car rental company is the identity consumer. Steps 1 and 10 show that user U is assumed to browse at identity consumer C before the protocol (step 1), e.g., at a car

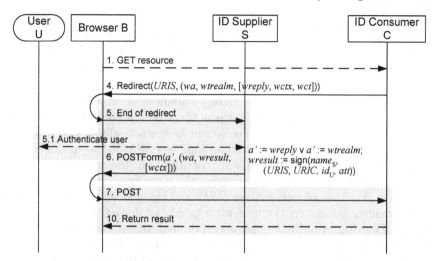

Fig. 15.2. WSFPI protocol with abstract parameters. Steps with uninterrupted lines are actually specified in the protocol. The gray boxes denote secure channels.

rental front page, and to get some application-level response after the protocol (step 10), e.g., a specific page that enables the rental under the favorable conditions agreed with the employer. To answer the request from step 1, the identity consumer C desires some authentication or attributes from the user. Thus in steps 4-5 the identity consumer redirects the browser to the identity supplier S. In step 5.1, the identity supplier authenticates the user, e.g., with a username and password exchanged in registration. In steps 6-7 the identity supplier S essentially redirects the user back to the identity consumer C with a so-called *token* denoted by *wresult* that contains the user identity id_U; in other terminologies it might be called a ticket or a credential.

The messages Redirect and POSTForm (steps 4 and 6) abstract from the syntax of browser redirects, i.e., HTTP 302 or 303 messages, and form posting, respectively. The first parameter in Figure 15.2 is the address and the second parameter the payload, here a list of protocol parameters. In a real redirect, these parameters are represented in the query string, i.e., the part of a URL behind a question mark. In a form POST, an HTML form, typically including a script, induces the user or the browser, respectively, to send the payload to the given address using an HTTP POST. The end of a redirect message (step 5) gets its parameters from the redirect message, and the POST message (step 7) from the POSTForm message. The gray boxes in the figure denote secure channels, i.e., HTTPS.

Figure 15.2 shows all the exchanged top-level parameters with their original names, as well as the most important elements of the token *wresult*. Square brackets include optional parameters. At the address *URIS*, the identity supplier S expects WSFPI redirects. The parameter *wa* is a constant denoting the so-called protocol action and version. The parameter *wtrealm* is the security realm of C under which it executes the WSFPI protocol; it should equal a fixed address *URIC* of C. With *wreply*, C may specify a URI to which S should redirect the browser in this specific protocol run; it must be within *wtrealm*. Furthermore, C may transport information through the WSFPI protocol using the opaque context parameter *wctx*, and add a timestamp *wct*. The identity supplier S selects the return address a' as *wreply* if present, else as *wtrealm*. The token *wresult* is syntactically a signed SAML assertion; the security assertion markup language (SAML) is an underlying standard for flexible statements about identities [34]. In our abstract representation *name*$_S$ is the name under which the identity supplier signs. In the assertion it includes its own address *URIS* and the address *URIC* of the intended identity consumer, the user identity id_U as derived in step 5.1, and additional attributes *att* about this user if desired. In our car-rental example, the user identity might be an employee number, the most important attribute is the fact that the user works for the employer, and the other attributes are the name and address.

15.3 Properties of Browsers and Protocol Variants

Scientifically, WSFPI is a three-party authentication protocol, but instead of a real protocol machine representing the user there is only a standard browser, and the user must even take one step in person. This distinguishes browser-based FIM protocols from all prior protocols.

The main capabilities that enable a browser to participate in a three-party protocol at all are redirects and form posting. (Cross-domain cookies, here for the identity supplier and identity consumer, are not considered because they are a too privacy-unfriendly concept.) Redirects can only carry a limited amount of information as URI lengths are limited in the network, while using form posting is not strictly zero-footprint because it typically relies on scripting; otherwise the user sees a rather strange form to submit. Hence protocols with both variants exist. To enable long tokens (e.g., digitally signed ones with credentials) while being strictly zero-footprint, some protocols first use a redirect to exchange a short one-time pseudonym of the user (instead of steps 6-7 of WSFPI) and then use a *backchannel*, i.e., a direct channel between S and C, to transport the actual token while referencing the one-time pseudonym, e.g., the SAML browser/artifact profile [34].

An advantage of browsers is that they can execute HTTPS and are pre-configured with trust roots for server credentials, i.e., scientifically they can set up secure channels with one-sided authentication. All browser-based FIM protocols make essential use of this capability.

Besides the functional restrictions, a problem with browsers is that they produce additional information flow of protocol variables, in contrast to the usual assumption that participants in security protocols carry out precisely the defined protocol and do nothing else. For instance, the browser divulges the previous URL it visited in the HTTP referrer tag if the new page is reached by the selection of a link on the previous page. Furthermore local storage such as the cache and the history may be exploited, e.g., by a later user in a kiosk scenario.

A core protocol like WSFPI will usually be augmented by an initial interaction between the identity consumer C and the user U to agree on a suitable identity provider, and by a detailed request by C within step 4 describing the desired attributes. For instance, SAML also defines request message formats. Furthermore, for privacy there may be constraints on how the identity supplier answers requests, e.g., whether it sends a real identity id_U, a previously used pseudonym, or a fresh pseudonym.

The first browser-based protocol was Microsoft Passport [33]; however, its details are not public. The SAML standardization produced protocols with form posting as well as with backchannels [34]. The Liberty Alliance project extended these protocols by further parameters and variants [31], which now seem to converge back into SAML 2 [35]. The Shibboleth project for university identity federation can be seen as a more complex SAML profile [14]. WS-Federation [28] is part of the IBM/Microsoft web services security roadmap. It links the web services world and the browser world by defining a joint identity-federation basis for both client types. Special aspects for browser-based FIM are defined as a passive requestor profile [29].

15.4 Security of Browser-Based FIM

The security of browser-based FIM has operational and protocol aspects.

Operationally, browser-based protocols belong to a rather risky class, but this is the price for the zero-footprint property, and one has to keep in mind that no other protocols for cross-enterprise three-party authentication or the exchange of certified attributes are widely deployed, except for the server authentication in secure server layer (SSL). The user has to trust his or her browser and operating system. If the user authentication (as in step 5.1 of WSFPI) is done by username and password, the security relies on the quality of this password and the user's resistance to phishing. Compared with using individual passwords with all services, a user of browser-based FIM needs fewer passwords and can thus choose them more carefully, remember them better, and be less likely to use the same password with partners of very different trustworthiness. On the other hand, the user may get used to being often redirected to his or her identity supplier S and get careless in using the browser capabilities to verify that he or she really has an HTTPS connection to S before inputting the password. A dangerous feature in Passport and the Liberty proposals is inline single sign-on, where the identity supplier uses a part of the identity consumer's window, because it disables these verification capabilities. Operational issues were first analyzed in detail in [30].

While all standards and standards proposals come with security considerations, several problems were later found (and then removed) [40, 22]. This
is not surprising as the design of cryptographic protocols is notoriously error-
prone, and browser-based FIM protocols are rather complex, e.g., because of
the modularity of the standards. One attack from [22] is particularly interesting as it exploits the HTTP referrer tag, i.e., information added automatically
by the browser that the protocol designers did not take into account. This
shows that one cannot analyze a browser-based FIM protocol by itself but
needs to consider it together with features of the browsers.

We have recently defined a detailed *browser model* that can be used as
a basis for security proofs of browser-based FIM protocols, and have proved
that WSFPI establishes authentic secure channels based on this model [24, 25]
(extending a more abstracted proof without a complete browser model [23]).
Very roughly, the security holds by the following chain of arguments. The
identity consumer C only accepts tokens signed by the identity supplier S. The
identity supplier S only signs messages of the token format, assuming it only
does so in WSFPI, if it has authenticated the corresponding user over a secure
channel. Then S sends the token in a form POST over the same secure channel.
The interesting part is now to show that the adversary cannot get the token.
Here first the details of the choice of the address a' play a role, and secondly
the use of *URIC* in the token to guarantee that one identity consumer, if
dishonest, cannot reuse a token to impersonate the user at another identity
consumer.

15.5 Privacy of Browser-Based FIM

Privacy, when broken down to a FIM protocol, essentially means that no
information about a user should be transferred between the identity supplier
and the identity consumer or stored there unless either the user has consented
to this, or another policy such as an employment contract or law-enforcement
issue permits it. We distinguish the privacy issues of the explicit attributes
such as *att* in WSFPI, and those of protocol-intrinsic information.

For the attributes, all general-purpose solutions must incorporate a *real-
time release* step, i.e., after receiving the request from an identity consumer C
and authenticating the user U, the identity supplier S asks the user whether it
is OK to release the desired attributes. In some business-to-business scenarios,
this step can be skipped. One may work towards enabling the user U to set
policies in scenarios where U acts as an individual; however, initially this is
not easy. For instance, even if the user wanted to permit S to release his or
her address to every airline, there is no general attribute credential structure
in place by which S would recognize all airlines. Furthermore, the user might
actually only desire the release when buying a ticket from an airline, not
when just looking at offers, but the identity supplier cannot distinguish this
reliably. Another issue, not yet really covered by standards proposals, is that

the release of attributes might depend on privacy promises from C or come with usage restrictions from S for C (such as "you may use this address for this transaction and your own marketing but not share it with further parties"). At the moment this must be fixed in apriori bilateral contracts between identity suppliers and identity consumers.

The main protocol-intrinsic parameters that may violate privacy are user identities such as id_U in WSFPI and URIs that might allow user tracking. As to identities it is easiest to put at most a one-time pseudonym into specific places in the protocols (such as in the redirect URI in protocols with backchannel) and to treat everything else as attributes that are put under policies. Indeed, no proposal after Microsoft Passport prescribed a global identity again; however, some have partner-specific long-term pseudonyms as a standard, which is not completely flexible. As to user tracking the main question is how much the identity supplier S learns about the browsing behavior of the user U. It seems unavoidable that S learns the identity of C in each execution of a browser-based protocol, both for the final redirect or form POST (steps 6-7 in WSFPI) and because the identity of C must be present in the token to prevent man-in-the-middle attacks (such as URI_C in $wresult$ in WSFPI). However, some standards or proposals recommend that one of the parameters in the request (corresponding to step 4 in WSFPI) is the entire URI of the resource that U requested; this seems an unjustified information release in general. Furthermore, services should have consent from U or another permission before even starting a browser-based FIM protocol because of the user tracking that it enables at S. For instance, our example user might not want her employer to be asked by the car rental company also when she is planning a private trip, and even less would she desire a mechanism that would cause her employer to be notified whenever she is doing some web shopping.

Another issue is that individuals may not want to share uncertified attributes, e.g., their taste in cars when on private trips, with any identity supplier (and even less with a fixed one, such as an employer). Hence if browser-based FIM becomes prevalent, it becomes important that the protocols can also be executed with *local wallets*. This means that users can store attributes locally instead of remotely if they choose. (These users no longer have the zero-footprint property, but it is their choice.) This seems easy in principle because one can build the local wallets as HTTP servers just like identity suppliers. However, it is not well supported in all standards and proposals for the case that the user acts under a pseudonym. One problem is requirements on the naming and credentials of the token (corresponding to $name_S$ in $wresult$ in WSFPI), although this could be the local wallet for uncertified attributes; another is specific address usage in backchannels – here the identity supplier should address the identity consumer so that an anonymous local wallet can play the identity-supplier role.

A detailed study of the consequences of privacy for browser-based FIM protocols can be found in [39], and specific considerations that show how complicated it can be to align a design with the promises made and the types of consent that the user is asked for in [37, 38].

If all these points are taken care of, the privacy of browser-based FIM can actually be very good. One limit, as already mentioned, is that the identity supplier learns the trail of identity consumers a user visits. Another is that, for certified attributes, even if the protocol allows local wallets and pseudonyms in principle, the identity supplier that certifies the attribute and the identity consumer can always link these two transactions, because the browser redirects or posts the token to the identity consumer exactly as the identity supplier sent it. This limit can only be overcome by private credentials as described in the following sections.

15.6 Private Credentials

In this section we are concerned with achieving optimum privacy for users in electronic transactions. That is, our goal is to enable the user to reveal as little information in transactions as possible. Of course, in most transactions, a user needs to reveal some information for it to take place. So our goal will be that the user need not reveal any further information than necessary to conduct a specific transaction. In particular, compared with the previous sections, we even desire that an identity supplier who certified certain attributes does not learn to which identity consumers the user shows these attributes, and that the two parties cannot link these transactions.

Let us illustrate this in the car rental example. Now we assume that the user wants to rent a car privately, and thus there is no other party (such as the employer above) that should naturally be informed of this rental. However, the user still has to show some certified attributes, such as a driver's license, and to pay for the rental (digital cash is just another form of a credential — one that can be used only once), see Fig. 15.3. Finally, the user is given a certificate from the rental agency that she can use as a key to the car, i.e., to show the car that she has the right to drive it for the rented period. Today, she would show her paper or plastic license and the car rental company would inspect it and learn her name, address, exact age, etc. However, it would be sufficient if they saw the user's picture, to verify that the license was issued to the individual renting the car, and possibly the expiration date, to verify that the license is still valid. (We will discuss anonymity revocation via a trustee in the case of problems later.) The agency that issued the license does not learn about the rental, and indeed this would seem unjustified with respect to privacy. However, the agency could learn this if it were corrupted and the car-rental company collaborated; we might want to prevent this. If we used a browser-based FIM protocol, we could make the driver's license agency the identity supplier and transfer only the necessary attributes; then, however, this agency would always learn about all rentals. It would also be conceivable to store the license as a fully signed credential in a local wallet, possibly in

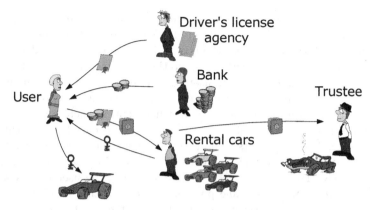

Fig. 15.3. Example scenario for private credentials

different versions that contain only pairs of attributes, but still the agency, if corrupted and collaborating with the car-rental company, could find out exactly which user rented which car (by matching the binary strings representing the credential). Regarding the payment, the bank and the car rental agency will need to communicate in order for the rental agency to receive the payment into its account. However, also here we want the user's privacy protected, i.e., the bank should not be able to learn (even when colluding with the rental agency – assuming that the rental agency is not privy to the user's identity with the bank) where a user spends her money.

With private credentials we can achieve all the properties that were mentioned as desirable above. Such credentials are very similar to a traditional public key infrastructure: a credential is basically a signature by the identity provider on a user's public key and on attributes of the user. The core differences to achieve privacy are that

1. the user uses a *different* public key (pseudonym) with each organization and,
2. instead of the credential (certificate) as obtained from the signer, the user sends the verifier a transformed credential. This transformation is either achieved by using a so-called *blind signature scheme* when issuing the credentials, or by applying so-called *zero-knowledge proofs* when producing credentials to the verifier.

However, for credentials or tokens such as in SAML, Kerberos or X.509 format signed with traditional signature schemes such as RSA or DSA, this would not be practical as we would need to employ general-purpose zero-knowledge proofs that are not efficient. Luckily, there exist special signature schemes that can be used for issuing credentials such that we can employ particular zero-knowledge proofs that are efficient [10, 11].

In the remainder of this chapter we will first explain the procedures of a private credential system, then describe the particular zero-knowledge proofs protocols and the special signature schemes and finally explain on a high level how one can actually build a private credential system with them.

Let us first, however, discuss the properties such a private credential system must provide. To this end, consider the following variation of our car rental scenario. Assume that our user wanted to rent a racing car and, as these are somewhat more dangerous than ordinary cars, the car rental agency require that the user be insured. Thus, when renting such a car, the user not only needs to show that she possesses a driver's license but also that she has insurance. The user wants to do this of course without revealing any further information using a private credential system. Now, if one implements a private credential system exactly as hinted above, the user proves with a zero-knowledge protocol that she possess a driver's license and an insurance policy. Such a solution, however, would not guarantee that the driver's license and the insurance policy were issued to the same person. Indeed, one person could prove possession of a driver's license and then a second person could prove possession of an insurance policy, which is most probably not what the car-rental agency had in mind. Thus a requirement to a private credential system is that it be consistent, i.e., that users cannot pool their credentials. In summary, a private credential system should enjoy the following properties [9].

Unforgeability. It must not be possible that a user can prove possession of a credential that was not issued to her.

Privacy. Different transactions by the same user with the same or different organizations must not be linkable (even if the user uses the same credential in some of these transactions), unless the user voluntarily uses the same public key (pseudonym) with these organizations or releases attribute information that by their uniqueness link transactions.

Consistency. Different users must not be able to team up and use each others' credentials.

Limited-use versus multi-use credentials. Unless otherwise specified, a user should be able to use a credential as many times as she wishes (without the respective transactions becoming linkable). However, she shall only be able to use so-called limited-use credentials as many times as specified. For instance an e-cash credential should be useable only once.

Apart from these basic properties, a credential system should allow for attributes to be included in credentials, e.g., name and address in a driver's license, and for selectively revealing these attributes. Indeed, in some cases the user might not want to reveal the attribute itself, but only certain properties about an attribute. For instance, to rent a car, a user might have to prove that she has had the driver's license for more than five years and that she is older than 25. Naturally, we want to enable the user to do that without revealing her age or the date she obtained the driver's license. Also, some scenarios might require conditional anonymity. Consider our car rental example where we assumed that the car rental agency gets not to know the user's name but need to see her picture only for verification purposes. However, if the user damages the car, the rental agency probably needs to know the user's name and address. That is, under some well-specified conditions (e.g., the user damaging the car) additional information about the user is required. Thus the system needs to allow for the specification of what (additional) information is available to whom under what circumstances. This might require the involvement of a third party, e.g., a trustee, who will make available this information upon checking the circumstances.

15.6.1 Historical Notes

As for many other privacy-enabling protocols, Chaum put forth the principles of anonymous (or private) credentials [15, 16, 17]. Later, Damgård gave the first proof of concept [19] of an anonymous credential where a credential was represented by a signature on an individual's name, obtained in a way that kept the name hidden from the issuer; while showing a credential was carried out via a general-purpose zero-knowledge proof of knowledge. Due to the practical inefficiency of these zero-knowledge proof, this first solution was of rather theoretical interest.

The first step towards efficient systems was Brands e-cash schemes [4] and protocols to issue a signature on a hidden message [4]. Brands later put these building blocks together to build a private credential system [5]. The first private credential system meeting the major properties as described above was introduced by Lysyanskaya et al. [32]. The first truly efficient and provably secure scheme was put forth by Camenisch and Lysyanskaya [9], whose construction was largely inspired by the Ateniese et al. group signature scheme construction. Their system allowed users for the first time to use a credential more than once. Their system was subsequently refined and extended [8, 11].

Today, probably the most prominent real application is the direct anonymous attestation protocol employed by the Trusted Computing group to authenticate a trustworthy computing platform while retaining the user's privacy [6]. Finally, the privacy and identity management for europe (PRIME) project www.prime-project.eu.org is currently building a holistic framework for privacy-enhancing digital transactions based on private credential systems.

15.6.2 Building Blocks

A private credential system is typically built with a number of cryptographic primitives. First, a public key signature scheme is used for signing credentials. That is, a credential is basically a signature on a message or a set of messages. A message might encode an attribute of the user or some parameter required for the system to work. Second, a public key encryption scheme with labels is required, e.g., [12]. Such an encryption scheme allows one to bind a public label to an encryption in such a way that decrypting a cipher text under any different label reveals no information about the original clear text. Third, a commitment scheme is required. Such a scheme allows a sender to compute a commitment to some value and then send this commitment to a party without revealing the value itself. Commitment schemes will come in handy when a user needs to prove to someone a property of an attribute without revealing the attribute itself. For instance, the user could send the car rental company a commitment to her birth date and then prove she is older than 21 if that is needed to rent a car, i.e., she proves the committed value encodes a date that lies more than 21 years in the past and that the committed value matches the birth date attribute in her driver's license. Finally, zero-knowledge proof protocols are required as sub-protocols to issue credentials, to show credentials, and to prove properties about committed values.

15.6.3 Procedures of a Private Credential System

We now describe how a private credential system works. We distinguish the roles of users, organizations (the identity consumers and identity suppliers from before), and trustees, who serve purposes such as anonymity revocation. A party might assume several roles. The private credential system consists of the algorithms Setup, OrgKeyGen, TruKeyGen, UserKeyGen, NymGen, IssCert, ShowCert, and RevealAttr.

The first algorithm, Setup, generates the system parameters such as the algebraic groups to be used by all the participants.

The algorithms OrgKeyGen and TruKeyGen take as input the system parameters and generate public and private keys for an organization and a trustee, respectively. In the idemix implementation we are going to describe later, the output of OrgKeyGen is essentially a key pair of a (suitable) signature scheme, and the output of TruKeyGen is a key pair of a (suitable) labelled encryption scheme.

The user has two key-generation algorithms: the algorithm UserKeyGen generates a secret key for the user, and the algorithm NymGen takes as input the user's secret key and generates a new pseudonym based on this secret key. If the user runs NymGen a second time with the *same* secret key, she gets a new pseudonym that is unlinkable to the first pseudonym.

The next algorithm, IssCert, is a protocol between the user and the organization from which the user would like a credential issued, i.e., the organization acts as an identity supplier. A prerequisite of this protocol is that the user has sent the organization one of her pseudonyms generated by NymGen. This could be a freshly generated pseudonym or one that the user has used with that organization (or even other organizations) before, e.g., under which she took driving lessons before getting the driver's license. The user and the organization also have to agree on the attributes that the credential shall contain. The typical case is that the attributes are input in clear text by both parties, e.g., the type of driver's license issued or the user's birthdate. However, there is also the option to input an attribute only via a commitment (about which the user has typically proved something in zero-knowledge) or a random attribute that will get known only to the user at the end of the protocol. These features are required when issuing credentials that should contain as attributes the same attributes as some credentials that the user has shown to the issuer and that should not be known to the issuer. For instance this allows one to bind a credential to a TPM [7]. Another example of the use of these features is the realization of an anonymous e-cash scheme from these basic protocols.

The algorithm ShowCert is a protocol between the user U and a verifying organization V (corresponding to an identity consumer in the earlier notation). The user holds a credential by some issuing organization I that contains a number of attributes, e.g., the driver's license. Prior to the protocol, U and V agree on which attributes shall be revealed to V, e.g., the driver's license type and the user's picture. They can also agree that U only proves properties about some of the attributes, e.g., that the age is greater than 21; then U additionally provides V with commitments to these attributes. Furthermore, they can agree that V obtains some attributes encrypted under the public key of one or more trustees, e.g., the actual name and address of the user. This is indicated by the locked box in Fig. 15.3. In that case, they also agree on a *decryption policy*, i.e., the conditions under which an encrypted attribute shall be retrieved by the trustee and what the trustee should do with it. For instance, the decryption policy for name and address in the car rental example could be that the user has had an accident or has disappeared with the car, and that if the car rental agency claimed the latter, the trustee after decryption first contacts the user and validates that she really did not return the car.

Finally, user U may provide V with a pseudonym in order to prove that the person holding the pseudonym is the same as the one to which the credential was issued. This feature is needed to ensure consistency. Let us expand on this. First, it is often required that the credential was issued to the very user who now shows possession of it; the driver's license is a clear example, while for a concert ticket this is not necessary. Second, if the user proves the possession of several credentials, then all these protocols should be run on input the same pseudonym to ensure that all the credentials were issued to the same person (although they might have been issued to different pseudonyms of this person).

After the two parties have agreed on all these options, they are ready to run the protocol. Their common input to the protocol is the public key of the credential's issuer and, depending on the agreed options, the public key of one or more trustees, commitments to attributes, and a pseudonym of the user. The user U's input additionally includes secret information, i.e., her secret key, the credential in question and all the attributes contained in it, and the secret values she used to construct the commitments. If the protocol finishes successfully, party V is convinced that the user possesses a credential by the issuer that contains the attributes that U revealed to him and also those to which he got commitments by U. Furthermore, if that option was chosen, V obtains encryptions of the specified attributes under the specified public keys of trustees with the agreed decryption policies attached as labels. The protocol can be carried out in two modes: a *signature* mode where V will obtain a transcript that will convince any other party that V indeed ran the protocol with a party possessing the respective credential(s) or a *zero-knowledge* mode, where V will not be able to later claim that V ran this protocol.

The last algorithm, RevealAttr, is the procedure for a trustee to reveal attributes that an organization obtained encrypted under this trustee's public key. The input to this algorithm is the trustee's secret key, an encryption, and a decryption policy as well as all the external information that the trustee needs to evaluate the decryption policy, e.g., a proof that the rental car had an accident while this user had rented it. If the external information fulfills the decryption policy, the trustee decrypts the cipher text with the decryption policy as a label and continues with the clear text as described in the decryption policy.

15.6.4 Example Use Case: Anonymous Offline E-Cash

Many applications providing privacy can be build on top of a private credential system as sketched above. In this paragraph we will discuss how to realize an anonymous offline e-cash scheme. The parties involved are a user, a merchant, and a bank with which both the user and the merchant have an account, i.e., have established a pseudonym with the bank.

An e-coin is basically a credential issued by the bank with special attributes. Thus, to retrieve an e-coin, the user identifies herself to the bank w.r.t. the pseudonym she holds with the bank. Then the two parties run the IssCert such that it will contain as attributes a unique identifier ID of the user (agreed upon jointly by the user and the bank) and a committed attribute s (that the user chose randomly beforehand) and a random attribute b. Recall that the bank does not learn s and b.

For a user to spend e-coins with a merchant, the two parties proceed as follows. First, the merchant chooses a random integer challenge c. Next, the user computes $u = ID \cdot c + b$ and sends the merchant the values u and s. Finally, the user and the merchant run the ShowCert protocol in signature mode and, in addition, the user also proves to the merchant that s is the second attribute contained in the credential and that the other attributes fulfill the property that u equals the first attribute times c plus the third attribute. If the merchant accepts the protocol, then the payment is carried out.

At some later point the merchant might want to deposit the obtained e-coin with the bank. To this end, the merchant sends the bank c, u, s and the transcripts of the ShowCert protocol and the other proof protocols he executed with the merchant. The bank first verifies the protocol transcript to see whether (c, s, u) correspond to a valid spending of an e-coin. Next the bank needs to check whether the merchant has already deposited this coin or if the user has spent the coin more than one. That is, the bank checks whether it has seen s before. If not, the bank accepts the coin and puts it in the merchant's account. Otherwise, the bank will have record (c', s, u') in its database. If $c = c'$, the bank rejects the coins as the merchant must have deposited the same coin already. If $c \neq c'$, the user must have double-spent the coins. In this case the bank also puts the coin in the merchant's account but additionally identifies the user by computing $ID = (u - u')/(c - c')$ and charges the user for the extra spending (plus possibly punishes the user in addition for having misused the system).

Note that, if the user does not double-spend then, by construction, the values u and s and the transcript do not reveal any identifying information about the user, i.e., the bank will not be able to figure out which user withdrew the coin. Also note that the system is secure for the bank, i.e., 1) no user or merchant can produce money, as for each coin one put into a merchant's account, is taken out of an account of a user, and 2) if the user is honest, then her money is taken out of her account only when she withdraws a coin. Finally, the merchant's security is obtained by the zero-knowledge proof protocols, i.e., if the merchant accepts the proof protocol, the bank will accept is as well and credit the merchant's account accordingly.

15.7 Concrete Building Blocks for a Private Credential System

Our goal in the remainder of this chapter it to convey that efficient private credential systems exist and explain how they work. Due to the large number of different option, a fully fledged private credential system can become quite involved. Therefore we are going to concentrate on a private credential system with a reduced set of features, that is, we are not considering (verifiable) encryption of attributes. In this section, we provide concrete instances of primitives to build such a basic private credential system and them put them together in the following section. As we do not consider (verifiable) encryption of attributes, the building blocks we need are an efficient signature scheme, a commitment scheme, and zero-knowledge protocols.

15.7.1 Protocols to Prove Knowledge of and Relations among Discrete Logarithms

In the following we will use various protocols to prove knowledge of and relations among discrete logarithms. To describe these protocols, we use the notation introduced by Camenisch and Stadler [13]. For instance,

$$PK\{(\alpha, \beta, \gamma) : y = g^\alpha h^\beta \ \wedge \ \tilde{y} = \tilde{g}^\alpha \tilde{h}^\gamma \ \wedge \ (v < \alpha < u)\}$$

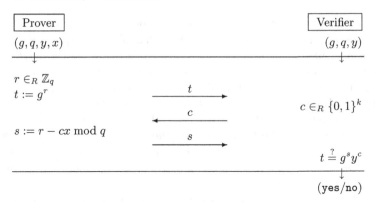

Fig. 15.4. The protocol denoted $PK\{(\alpha) : y = g^\alpha\}$. The verifier's input is (g, q, y) and the prover's input to the protocol is (g, q, y, x), where the quantity $x = \log_g y$ corresponds to α, knowledge of which the prover is proving. The prover has no output; the verifier's output is either **yes** or **no**, depending on whether or not he accepts the protocol, i.e., whether or not $t = g^s y^c$ holds.

denotes a zero-knowledge proof of knowledge of integers α, β, and γ such that $y = g^\alpha h^\beta$ and $\tilde{y} = \tilde{g}^\alpha \tilde{h}^\gamma$ holds, with $v < \alpha < u$, where $y, g, h, \tilde{y}, \tilde{g}$, and $\tilde{h}$ are elements of some groups $G = \langle g \rangle = \langle h \rangle$ and $\tilde{G} = \langle \tilde{g} \rangle = \langle \tilde{h} \rangle$. The notation $\langle g \rangle$ means the cyclic group generated by the element g, i.e., all the powers of g. The convention is that Greek letters denote the quantities whose knowledge is proved, while all the other parameters are known to the verifier. More precisely, the property of proof of knowledge means that there exists a *knowledge extraction* algorithm that can extract the Greek quantities from a successful prover if given rewinding and reset access to the prover. Thus, using this notation, a proof protocol can be described by just pointing out its aim while hiding the realization details. In the following we first explain how such protocols can be constructed.

15.7.2 Schnorr's Identification Scheme

The simplest case is the protocol denoted $PK\{(\alpha) : y = g^\alpha\}$, where $y \in G$ for a group $G = \langle g \rangle$ of prime order q. It is depicted in Fig. 15.4. This protocol is also known as Schnorr's identification protocol [42]. As the first step, the prover chooses a random integer r, computes the *protocol commitment* $t := g^r$ and sends it to the verifier. The verifier replies with a random *protocol challenge* c. Next, the prover computes the *protocol response* $s := r - cx \mod q$ and sends it to the verifier. Finally, the verifier accepts the protocol if the *verification equation* $t = g^s y^c$ holds.

This protocol is a proof of knowledge of the discrete logarithm $\log_g y$ with a cheating probability (knowledge error) of 2^{-k} (provided that $2^k < q$, which is typically the case in practice). The protocol is also zero-knowledge against an honest verifier.

To achieve zero-knowledge against an arbitrary verifier, one needs to choose k logarithmic in the security parameter and repeat the protocol sufficiently many times to make the knowledge error small enough, losing some efficiency by this repetition. Reasonable parameters seem to be $k = 10$ and repeating the protocol eight times to achieve an overall cheating probability of 2^{-80}. Luckily, one can alternatively use one of the many known constructions to achieve zero-knowledge that retain efficiency, e.g., [18]. This discussion holds for all the protocols considered in this chapter.

From the protocol just discussed, one can derive the Schnorr signature scheme denoted $SPK\{(\alpha) : y = g^\alpha\}(m)$, by using the Fiat–Shamir heuristic [20, 41]. Here the the verifier is replaced by a call to a hash function $\mathcal{H}$ and thus the challenge is computed as $c = \mathcal{H}(q\|g\|y\|t\|m)$, where $m \in \{0, 1\}^*$ is the message that is signed. The signature of m is the pair (s, c). Verifying a signature entails computing $\hat{t} := g^s y^c$ and then verifying whether $c = \mathcal{H}(g\|y\|\hat{t}\|m)$ holds. This signature scheme is secure in the so-called random oracle model [1].

15.7.3 Pedersen Commitments

One commitment scheme that is particularly suited for our purposes is the one by Pedersen [36]. Let $G = \langle g \rangle$ be a group of prime order q. Let h be a second generator of G such that $\log_g h$ is not known. To commit to a secret $x \in \mathbb{Z}_q^*$, one chooses a random value $r \in \mathbb{Z}_q^*$ and computes the commitment $C = g^x h^r$.

15.7.4 Signature Scheme

Camenisch and Lysyanskaya have proposed a number of signature schemes [10, 11] that allow one to efficiently prove possession of a signature with the class of protocols introduced in Sect. 15.7.1. They differ in the number of theoretic assumptions they rely on. In this section we present the one that is based on bilinear maps and relies on the hardness of computing discrete logarithms [11]. It is derived from the group signature scheme due to Boneh, Boyen, and Shacham [2]. It assumes a *bilinear map* setting, i.e., groups $G_1 = \langle g_1 \rangle$ and $G_t = \langle g_t \rangle$, both of prime order q, and an efficiently computable map $e : G_1 \times G_1 \to G_t$. The map e must be bilinear, i.e., it must fulfill

- $e(g^a, h^b) = e(g, h)^{ab}$ for all a, b and for any $g, h \in G_1$, and
- $e(g_1, g_1) \neq 1$.

Such bilinear maps exist for groups G_1 and G_t constructed from elliptic curves. We refer to [3, 21] and references therein for details.

The signer's secret key is a random element $x \in \mathbb{Z}_q$ and the public key consists of $y = g_1^x$ and a number of so-called bases $h_0, \ldots, h_\ell \in G_1$, where ℓ is a parameter.

A signature on messages $m_1, \ldots, m_\ell \in \mathbb{Z}_q$ is a pair (A, s), where $s \in \mathbb{Z}_q^*$ is a value chosen at random by the signer and $A = (g_1 h_1^{m_1} \cdots h_\ell^{m_\ell})^{1/(x+s)}$. A signature (A, s) can be verified by checking whether the single equation

$$e(A, g_1^s y) = e(g_1 h_0^{m_0} \cdots h_\ell^{m_\ell}, g_1)$$

holds.

15.7.5 Proving Knowledge of a Signature

Now assume that we have a signature (A, s) on messages $m_0 \ldots, m_\ell \in \mathbb{Z}_q$ and want to prove that we indeed possess such a signature. In other words, we need to prove possessions of values $m_1, \ldots, m_\ell, A$, and s such that the verification equation $e(A, yg_1^s) = e(g_1 h_0^{m_0} \cdots h_\ell^{m_\ell}, g_1)$ holds. To do this efficiently, we want to employ the zero-knowledge proof protocols described earlier in this section. So we need to be able to restate the verification equations such that we get a situation such as $y = g^\alpha h^\beta$, i.e., where on the left-hand side of the equations all values are known to the verifier and on the right-hand side all bases are known to the verifier but all exponents are the prover's secrets the knowledge of which is proved. First note, that we can rewrite the equation as follows $e(A, y)e(A, g_1)^s = e(g_1, g_1)e(h_0, g_1)^{m_0} \cdots e(h_\ell, g_1)^{m_\ell}$ and further as $e(g_1, g_1)/e(A, y) = e(A, g_1)^s e(h_0, g_1)^{-m_0} \cdots e(h_\ell, g_1)^{-m_\ell}$ with which we have almost achieved our goal, except that with A we have a base element that should not be revealed to the verifier. To overcome this, we blind A into $\tilde{A}$, which we can then reveal (basically, we ElGamal-encrypt A where noone knows the corresponding secret key). To do so, we need to augment the public key with the values $h_t \in G_t$ and $u_1, v_1, w_1 \in G_1$ such that $\log_{g_t} h_t$ and $\log_{g_1} u_1$ are not known to anyone (there are standard procedures for this). This leads to the following protocols.

1. Choose random values $r, r' \in \mathbb{Z}_q$ and compute $\tilde{A} = Au_1^{r+r'}$, $B = v_1^r$ and $C = w_1^{r'}$.
2. Compute the following proof:

$$PK\{(\alpha, \alpha', \sigma, \rho, \mu_0, \ldots, \mu_\ell) :$$
$$B = v_1^\rho \ \wedge \ C = w_1^{\rho'} \ \wedge \ 1 = B^\sigma v_1^{-\alpha} \ \wedge \ 1 = C^\sigma w_1^{-\alpha'} \ \wedge$$
$$\frac{e(g_1, g_1)}{e(\tilde{A}, y)} = e(\tilde{A}, g_1)^\sigma e(u_1, y)^{(\rho+\rho')} e(u_1, g_1)^{(\alpha+\alpha')} \prod_{i=1}^{\ell} e(h_i, g_1)^{-\mu_i}\} \ .$$

Let us explain this proof protocol. The first two statements prove that the prover knows values $\rho = \log_{v_1} B$ and $\rho' = \log_{w_1} C$. The next two statements assert that the prover knows values σ, α, and α' such that $\alpha = \rho\sigma$ and $\alpha' = \rho'\sigma$. The last line asserts the prover's knowledge of further values $\mu_1, \ldots, \mu_\ell$ such that

$$e(\tilde{A}, y)e(\tilde{A}, g_1)^{\sigma}e(u_1, y)^{(\rho+\rho')}e(u_1, g_1)^{\sigma(\rho+\rho')} = e(g_1, g_1)\prod_{i=1}^{\ell} e(h_i, g_1)^{\mu_i}$$

holds, where we have made use of the relations $\alpha = \rho\sigma$ and $\alpha' = \rho'\sigma$. Using the fact that $e(a, b)e(a, c) = e(a, bc)$ holds for any $a, b, c \in G_1$ (which follows from the bilinearity of the map e) we can reformulate this equation into the following one

$$e(\tilde{A}, yg_1^{\sigma})e(u_1, (yg^{\sigma})^{(\rho+\rho')}) = e(\tilde{A}, g_1^{x+\sigma})e(u_1, g_1^{(x+\sigma)(\rho+\rho')}) = e(g_1\prod_{i=1}^{\ell} h_i^{\mu_i}, g_1),$$

where $x = \log_{g_1} y$ is the secret key of the signer. Finally, using the property that $e(a^b, c) = e(a, c)^b = e(a^b, c)$ for any $a, c \in G_1$ and $b \in \mathbb{Z}_q^*$, which follows from the bilinearity of e, we have that

$$e(\tilde{A}u_1^{(\rho+\rho')}, g_1^{x+\sigma}) = e(\tilde{A}u_1^{(\rho+\rho')}, yg_1^{\sigma}) = e(g_1\prod_{i=1}^{\ell} h_i^{\mu_i}, g_1) \ .$$

Comparing this equation with the verification equations, we see that the pair $(\tilde{A}u_1^{(\rho+\rho')}), \sigma)$ must be a valid signature on the messages $\hat{m}_0, \ldots, \hat{m}_\ell$.

15.8 The idemix Credential System

This section describes how to construct the algorithms of a basic version our concrete private credential system, called idemix [8, 9, 10], from the signature scheme discussed in the previous paragraphs.

15.8.1 Setup – OrgKeyGen and UserKeyGen

We assume all parties agree on a number of parameters. These includes a cryptographic hash function $\mathcal{H}$ such as SHA-256 and on a bilinear map setting, i.e., on groups $G_1 = \langle g_1 \rangle$ and $G_t = \langle g_t \rangle$, and a bilinear map $e : G_1 \times G_1 \to G_t$. Furthermore, let the parties agree on a second generator h_t of G_t such that $log_{g_t} h_t$ is unknown (for instance h_t could be constructed from $\mathcal{H}(g_t)$).

The key-generation algorithms for the organizationas and the users are as follows. Each organization (at least if it wants to issue credentials) chooses a secret key x_I and publishes $y_I = g_1^{x_I}$. Each user chooses a random secret key $z \in \mathbb{Z}_q$.

15.8.2 Generating a Pseudonym – NyMGen

To generate a pseudonym, a user with secret key z chooses a random $r_i \in \mathbb{Z}_q$ and computes $P_i = g_t^z h_t^{r_i}$.

15.8.3 Issuing a Credential – **IssCred**

In order to get a credential (on a pseudonym P_i) with attributes $m_2, \ldots, m_\ell$, the user and the issuer perform the following steps.

1. The user chooses a random $r_i' \in \mathbb{Z}_q$, computes $P_i' = h_0^z h_1^{r_i'}$, and sends P_i' to the issuer.
2. The user engages with the issuer as verifier in the following proof:

$$PK\{(\zeta, \rho_i, \rho_i') : P_i = g_t^\zeta h_t^{\rho_i} \wedge P_i' = h_0^\zeta h_1^{\rho_i'}\}.$$

   This convinces the issuer that the pseudonyms P_i' and P_i encode the same secret key.
3. The issuer chooses a random $s_i \in \mathbb{Z}_q^*$, computes $A_i = (g_1 P_i' \prod_{i=2}^\ell h_i^{m_i})^{\frac{1}{x+s_i}}$, and sends (A_i, s_i) to the user.

After this protocol, the user possesses a signature on the tuple of messages $(z, m_1, m_2, \ldots, m_\ell)$, where z and m_1 are secret messages, i.e., known to the user only.

If the issuer follows the protocol, then it is ensured that the zeroth message signed corresponds to the user's secret key contained in the pseudonym P_i. Moreover, the protocol assures the issuer that the user that ran the protocol is indeed the holder of the pseudonym P_i as the proof in step 2 can be run successfully by the user only if she is privy to the secrets encoded in P_i.

15.8.4 Proving Possession of a Credential Containing a Given Attribute

Assume that the user with secret key z possesses a signature (credential) (A_i, s_i) with attributes $m_2, \ldots, m_\ell$ and wants to prove the possession of this to a verifier to whom she is known under pseudonym P_j. Also, she wants to convince the verifier that, say, the k-th attribute has a value a. To this end, they proceed as follows:

1. The user chooses random values $r, r' \in \mathbb{Z}_q$ and computes $\tilde{A}_i = A_i u_1^{r+r'}$, $B = v_1^r$ and $C = w_1^{r'}$.
2. The user and the verifier engage in the following proof:

$$PK\{(\alpha, \alpha', \sigma, \rho, \rho', \zeta, \mu_0, \ldots, \mu_\ell) :$$
$$P_j = g_t^\zeta w_1^{-\alpha'} \wedge B = v_1^\rho \wedge C = w_1^{\rho'} \wedge 1 = B^\sigma v_1^{-\alpha} \wedge 1 = C^\sigma w_1^{-\alpha'} \wedge$$
$$\frac{e(g_1, g_1)e(h_k, g_1)^a}{e(\tilde{A}_i, y)} = e(\tilde{A}_i, g_1)^\sigma e(u_1, y)^{-(\rho+\rho')} \cdot$$
$$\cdot e(u_1, g_1)^{-(\alpha+\alpha')} e(h_0, g_1)^{-\zeta} \prod_{i=1, i\neq k}^\ell e(h_i, g_1)^{-\mu_i}\}.$$

This is essentially the same proof as that in Sect. 15.7.5 for just showing the possession of a signature, but it additionally shows that the zeroth message signed is the secret key embedded in P_j and that the k-th message signed is a.

It is not hard to adapt the protocol just described to one where several attributes are revealed or where statements about the attributes are proved. An example of such a statement is the assertion that a signed message (e.g., encoding the user's age) is larger than 18.

15.9 Conclusion

Federated identity management (FIM) means authentication and attribute exchange for users across different interaction partners. The main challenges that have prevented the widespread deployment of earlier FIM proposals such as Kerberos or PKIs are ease of use, in particular ease of initial setup, and privacy. We have described two modern approaches that address these challenges: browser-based FIM, which primarily eases the setup and usage, and private credentials, which solve the privacy problem that no prior proposal could solve, the unlinkable transfer of certified attributes. Current initiatives at building FIM capabilities into standard clients may ultimately combine the best of both these approaches.

While we concentrated on the protocols, the quality of an overall solution also depends on other factors, in particular the user interface. This starts with the design of real-time release, i.e., forms for the user to consent to authentication and attribute transfer on the fly. The next steps are to enable the user to set meaningful privacy policies, partially at the same time as releasing information, and to keep track of which data were released to whom. For instance, if a user is using several pseudonyms with an ebook shop, he or she needs to keep them apart. Furthermore, to keep some of these pseudonyms really private, the user must not release too much additional information in relation to them. For the private credentials, another aspect that an overall solution must and can offer is the seamless integration with browsers and with simpler types of identity management.

Finally, we note that we only considered part of the information that a user reveals to a communication party. Indeed, the user reveals many other pieces of information about herself. This starts with the communication protocols typically revealing IP addresses and ends with application/service related information such as preferences, which pages of a newspaper a user accesses, etc. While some of this information can be withheld by using technologies such as anonymous communication networks as discussed in another chapter of this book, withholding other information requires that the way applications and services are provided be changed. For instance, service providers often fully identify the user even if they only need to know that she falls in some age group. Another example is the frequent (ab)use of the social security number as unique (local) identifier for the user. Thus, protecting the user's privacy in electronic transactions is a nontrivial task that involves many components, areas, and parties. We refer to the PRIME project `http://www.prime-project.eu` for a holistic approach to privacy-enhancing identity management.

15.10 Acknowledgments

This chapter would not have been possible without a lot of prior work with many coauthors, in particular Endre Bangerter, Thomas Groß, Susan Hohenberger, Anna Lysyanskaya, Dieter Sommer, and Michael Waidner. We thank all of them for the fruitful collaboration.

References

1. M. Bellare and P. Rogaway. Random oracles are practical: A paradigm for designing efficient protocols. In *First ACM Conference on Computer and Communication Security*, pages 62–73. Association for Computing Machinery, 1993.
2. D. Boneh, X. Boyen, and H. Shacham. Short group signatures. In Matthew K. Franklin, editor, *Advances in Cryptology — CRYPTO 2004*, volume 3152 of *LNCS*, pages 41–55. Springer Verlag, 2004.
3. D. Boneh, B. Lynn, and H. Shacham. Short signatures from the Weil pairing. In J. of Cryptology, vol. 17, no. 4, pp. 297-319, 2004.
4. S. Brands. Untraceable off-line cash in wallets with observers. In Douglas R. Stinson, editor, *Advances in Cryptology — CRYPTO '93*, volume 773 of *LNCS*, pages 302–318, 1993.
5. S. Brands. *Rethinking Public Key Infrastructure and Digital Certificates— Building in Privacy*. PhD thesis, Eindhoven Institute of Technology, Eindhoven, The Netherlands, 1999.
6. E. Brickell, J. Camenisch, and L. Chen. Direct anonymous attestation. In *Proc. 11th ACM Conference on Computer and Communications Security*, pages 225–234. ACM press, 2004.
7. J. Camenisch. *Cryptographic Protocols*, chapter Direct Anonymous Attestation Explained. Wenbo Mao and Markus Jakobsson (Editors). Addison-Wesley, 2006. to appear.
8. J. Camenisch and E. van Herreweghen. Design and implementation of the *idemix* anonymous credential system. In *Proc. 9th ACM Conference on Computer and Communications Security*. acm press, 2002.
9. J. Camenisch and A. Lysyanskaya. Efficient non-transferable anonymous multishow credential system with optional anonymity revocation. In Birgit Pfitzmann, editor, *Advances in Cryptology — EUROCRYPT 2001*, volume 2045 of *LNCS*, pages 93–118. Springer Verlag, 2001.
10. J. Camenisch and A. Lysyanskaya. A signature scheme with efficient protocols. In Stelvio Cimato, Clemente Galdi, and Giuseppe Persiano, editors, *Security in Communication Networks, Third International Conference, SCN 2002*, volume 2576 of *LNCS*, pages 268–289. Springer Verlag, 2003.

11. J. Camenisch and A. Lysyanskaya. Signature schemes and anonymous credentials from bilinear maps. In Matthew K. Franklin, editor, *Advances in Cryptology — CRYPTO 2004*, volume 3152 of *LNCS*, pages 56–72. Springer Verlag, 2004.

12. J. Camenisch and V. Shoup. Practical verifiable encryption and decryption of discrete logarithms. In Dan Boneh, editor, *Advances in Cryptology — CRYPTO 2003*, volume 2729 of *LNCS*, pages 126–144, 2003.

13. J. Camenisch and M. Stadler. Efficient group signature schemes for large groups. In Burt Kaliski, editor, *Advances in Cryptology — CRYPTO '97*, volume 1296 of *LNCS*, pages 410–424. Springer Verlag, 1997.

14. S. Cantor and M. Erdos. Shibboleth-architecture draft v05, May 2002. http://shibboleth.internet2.edu/docs/draft-internet2-shibboleth-arch-v05.pdf.

15. D. Chaum. Untraceable electronic mail, return addresses, and digital pseudonyms. *Communications of the ACM*, 24(2):84–88, February 1981.

16. D. Chaum. Security without identification: Transaction systems to make big brother obsolete. *Communications of the ACM*, 28(10):1030–1044, October 1985.

17. D. Chaum and J.H. Evertse. A secure and privacy-protecting protocol for transmitting personal information between organizations. In M. Odlyzko, editor, *Advances in Cryptology — CRYPTO '86*, volume 263 of *LNCS*, pages 118–167. Springer-Verlag, 1987.

18. I.B. Damgård. Efficient concurrent zero-knowledge in the auxiliary string model. In Bart Preneel, editor, *Advances in Cryptology — EUROCRYPT 2000*, volume 1807 of *LNCS*, pages 431–444. Springer Verlag, 2000.

19. I.B. Damgård. Payment systems and credential mechanism with provable security against abuse by individuals. In Shafi Goldwasser, editor, *Advances in Cryptology — CRYPTO '88*, volume 403 of *LNCS*, pages 328–335. Springer Verlag, 1990.

20. A. Fiat and A. Shamir. How to prove yourself: Practical solutions to identification and signature problems. In Andrew M. Odlyzko, editor, *Advances in Cryptology — CRYPTO '86*, volume 263 of *LNCS*, pages 186–194. Springer Verlag, 1987.

21. S. Galbraith. *Advances in elliptic curve cryptography*, chapter Pairings. Cambridge University Press, 2005.

22. T. Groß. Security analysis of the SAML Single Sign-on Browser/Artifact profile. In *Proc. 19th Annual Computer Security Applications Conference*. IEEE Computer Society, December 2003.

23. T. Groß and B. Pfitzmann. Proving a WS-Federation Passive Requestor profile. In *ACM Workshop on Secure Web Services (SWS)*. ACM Press, to appear, 2004.

24. T. Groß, B. Pfitzmann, and A.R. Sadeghi. Browser model for security analysis of browser-based protocols. In *Proc. 10th European Symposium on Research in Computer Security (ESORICS)*, volume 3679 of *LNCS*, pages 489–508. Springer, 2005.

25. T. Groß, B. Pfitzmann, and A.R. Sadeghi. Proving a WS-Federation Passive Requestor profile with a browser model. In *ACM Workshop on Secure Web Services (SWS)*, pages 54–64. ACM Press, 2005.

26. M. Hur, R.D. Johnson, A. Medvinsky, Y. Rouskov, J. Spellman, S. Weeden, and A. Nadalin. Passive Requestor Federation Interop Scenario, Version 0.4, February 2004. ftp://www6.software.ibm.com/software/developer/library/ws-fpscenario2.d%oc.

27. Harris Interactive.   First major post-9/11 privacy survey finds consumers demanding companies do more to protect privacy.   Rochester, http://www.harrisinteractive.com/news/allnewsbydate.asp?NewsID=429, February 2002.
28. C. Kaler and A. Nadalin (ed.).   Web Services Federation Language (WS-Federation), Version 1.0, July 2003. BEA and IBM and Microsoft and RSA Security and VeriSign, http://www-106.ibm.com/developerworks/webservices/library/ws-fed/.
29. C. Kaler and A. Nadalin (ed.).   WS-Federation: Passive Requestor Profile, Version 1.0, July 2003. BEA and IBM and Microsoft and RSA Security and VeriSign, http://www-106.ibm.com/developerworks/library/ws-fedpass/.
30. D.P. Kormann and A.D. Rubin. Risks of the Passport single signon protocol. *Computer Networks*, 33:51–58, 1994.
31. Liberty Alliance Project. Liberty Phase 2 final specifications, November 2003. http://www.projectliberty.org/.
32. A. Lysyanskaya, R. Rivest, A. Sahai, and S. Wolf. Pseudonym systems. In Howard Heys and Carlisle Adams, editors, *Selected Areas in Cryptography*, volume 1758 of *LNCS*. Springer Verlag, 1999.
33. Microsoft Corporation. .NET Passport documentation, in particular Technical Overview, and SDK 2.1 Documentation (started 1999), September 2001.
34. OASIS Standard. Security assertion markup language (SAML) V1.1, Nov 2002.
35. OASIS Standard. Security assertion markup language (SAML) V2.0, March 2005.
36. T.P. Pedersen. Non-interactive and information-theoretic secure verifiable secret sharing. In Joan Feigenbaum, editor, *Advances in Cryptology – CRYPTO '91*, volume 576 of *LNCS*, pages 129–140. Springer Verlag, 1992.
37. B. Pfitzmann. Privacy in enterprise identity federation – policies for Liberty single signon. In *Proc. 3rd International Workshop on Privacy Enhancing Technologies (PET)*, volume 2760 of *LNCS*, pages 189–204. Springer, 2003.
38. B. Pfitzmann. Privacy in enterprise identity federation - policies for Liberty 2 single signon. *Elsevier Information Security Technical Report (ISTR)*, 9(1):45–58, 2004. http://www.sciencedirect.com/science/journal/13634127.
39. B. Pfitzmann and M. Waidner. Privacy in browser-based attribute exchange. In *Proc. 1st ACM Workshop on Privacy in the Electronic Society (WPES)*, pages 52–62, 2002.
40. B. Pfitzmann and M. Waidner. Analysis of Liberty single-signon with enabled clients. *IEEE Internet Computing*, 7(6):38–44, 2003.
41. D. Pointcheval and J. Stern. Security proofs for signature schemes. In Ueli Maurer, editor, *Advances in Cryptology — EUROCRYPT '96*, volume 1070 of *LNCS*, pages 387–398. Springer Verlag, 1996.
42. C.P. Schnorr. Efficient signature generation for smart cards. *Journal of Cryptology*, 4(3):239–252, 1991.
43. A. Westin. Consumer privacy attitudes and actions: What the surveys find 2005-2006. Privacy Year in Review, Projections and Trends for 2006, Privacy & American Business, January 2006.

16

Accountable Anonymous Communication*

Claudia Diaz and Bart Preneel

K.U. Leuven ESAT-COSIC
Belgium

Summary. In this chapter we motivate the need for anonymity at the communication layer and describe the potential risks of having traceable communications. We then introduce the legal requirements on data retention and motivate the need for revocability of anonymity upon the request of law enforcement.

We describe the main building blocks for anonymous communication and for anonymity revocation. We explain how these building blocks can be combined in order to build a revocable anonymous communication infrastructure that fulfills both privacy and law enforcement requirements.

16.1 Introduction

Privacy is increasingly understood as an interdisciplinary subject. Legal, political and social considerations must be taken into account in the design of viable technical solutions that can be implemented on a large scale and accepted by the various players: citizens, governments, companies, etc. Anonymity and identity management technologies are powerful tools to protect privacy. Nevertheless, their potential for abuse is a factor that hinders the development and implementation of privacy-enhancing systems on a large scale.

This chapter discusses the requirements that a large-scale anonymity infrastructure should comply with in order to be acceptable for all parties. Anonymity infrastructures that protect the privacy of millions of individuals can only be possible if extreme care is taken in balancing the requirements of a multiplicity of interacting entities with sometimes conflicting interests. Otherwise, anonymity systems face the threat of remaining marginal in an environment in which privacy violations become ever more common.

The chapter is structured as follows: we first motivate the need for anonymity and for accountability. In Sect. 16.3 we present the requirements

---

* This work was supported by the IWT SBO project on advanced applications for electronic identity cards in Flanders (ADAPID).

for the system. Section 16.4 describes the building blocks that are used to construct our system. Section 16.5 describes the proposed model for an accountable anonymity infrastructure. Finally, Sect. 16.6 presents the conclusions of this work.

16.2 Anonymity and Accountability

16.2.1 Motivation for Communication Anonymity

Anonymity is defined by Pfitzmann and Hansen in [23] as *the state of being not identifiable within a set of subjects, the anonymity set.* This definition implies that, in order to achieve anonymity, we need a large population of users (*anonymity set*) performing actions in such a way that it is not possible to know which action was performed by which user. Users are more anonymous as the anonymity set and the indistinguishability increase (see [12, 26] for practical anonymity metrics).

According to Moore's Law, computer processing power doubles every 18 months. Storage capacity grows even faster, doubling every 13 months, according to Kryder's Law. If no anonymity infrastructure is put in place, all communication can (or will soon) be traced, registered, stored, mined, analyzed and aggregated. Furthermore, the collection of traffic data for law enforcement purposes has become a legal requirement. The 2006 approved EU directive on data retention [15] imposes that all communication providers keep traffic data for law enforcement purposes. It is unclear how stored communication data in communication providers' databases will be secured against abuse for other purposes.

As communication data often leaks information about the content being accessed by users (e.g., `http://www.teensforteens.net/homosexuality/` `aids_and_homosexuality.html`), this means that personal data can technically (either legally or illegally) be collected (without the consent or awareness of the data subject), in order to build profiles of potential customers, potential employees, potential terrorists, etc. Individuals lose control over their personal data, which implies that they become vulnerable to all kinds of commercial and political manipulation. It is also clear that the large amounts of information available on individuals could be exploited for criminal purposes such as identity theft or targeted crime (e.g., it would be useful for burglars to know who are the wealthiest home-owners in a given area and when they are going on holiday). Privacy should therefore not be considered as contradictory with security: the lack of privacy protection may lead to serious security problems. Moreover, privacy protection is only possible using secure systems.

In order to avoid these privacy violations, we need to hide the communication patterns of Internet users towards untrusted recipients (e.g., Web sites) and external observers (e.g., local eavesdroppers). An anonymous communication infrastructure should therefore be in place in order to protect users' privacy.

16.2.2 Motivation for Accountability

If a system is deployed for massive use, abuse is unavoidable; moreover, the sense of impunity generated by the impossibility of holding people accountable could further encourage abuse. Without *accountability* mechanisms in place, it is unlikely that an unaccountable system could gather support from public powers and even from many citizens, as security has to be traded with privacy (or, at least, that is a common perception).

Nevertheless, there are strong arguments against trading anonymity with accountability [1]. A similar debate over key escrow for confidentiality took place in the mid 1990s about the clipper chip [28]. One of the problems was that the escrow algorithm was secret (i.e., not verifiable) and its hardware implementation was not tamper-resistant. This is not the case with the system we propose here, which is based on public protocols and algorithms. The second argument against a key escrow system was that a voluntary system would not solve law enforcement problems. Indeed, criminals could easily create their own keys, use them to communicate, and not give the escrow information to law enforcement authorities, rendering the whole escrow system useless.

As we can derive from the definition of anonymity (Sect. 16.2.1), there is a fundamental difference between the nature of confidentiality and anonymity in communication networks. Confidentiality of content can be achieved by the communicating partners on their own: when establishing a shared secret, no third entity needs to participate. Even more, one could create a key for encrypting one's own data, without needing external entities. Anonymity is more complex. People act anonymously when their actions cannot be linked to their identities, or more precisely, when there is a set of subjects that could potentially be linked to the action, but there is not enough information to tell which of the subjects relates to the action. While confidentiality can be achieved by those who seek it alone, anonymity needs the cooperation of a group of people, the larger the better. Anonymity is therefore social (as it needs society to work together in order to be achieved), while confidentiality makes sense at the individual level.

While criminals would be able to bridge the key escrow systems using their own keys, they are not able to obtain anonymity on their own. If accountability mechanisms are built in the system, then the potential for abuse sharply decreases. Criminals may then choose not to use the system (exposing themselves to leave traces), or choose an unconditionally anonymous network. If this is the case, the people operating the network may find themselves in trouble, depending on the seriousness of the crime and on the legal framework in which they are operating.

It is still unclear how the EU directive on data retention will affect unconditionally anonymous communication networks. There have been cases in the past in which law enforcement has forced anonymous communication providers (e.g., `anon.penet.fi` or JAP [19]) to either shut down the service, or violate the principle of providing unconditional anonymity to their users by implementing tracing capabilities that were not in the original design. We propose a *checks and balances* model which involves different entities in the anonymity revocation process, in order to ensure that the revocation policy is well understood from the beginning, and only technically possible in specific conditions.

16.2.3 Related Work on Anonymous Communication

Some of the earliest real-time *anonymous communication* systems were based on trusted or semi-trusted relays (e.g., Anonymizer [2] and SafeWeb). In centralized trust systems, the anonymity depends critically both on the security level and on the integrity of the service provider and its staff.

Pfitzmann et al. proposed in 1991 ISDN Mixes [24], a system to anonymize ISDN telephone conversations. Their design, based on a cascade of relays (mixes), was later adapted for anonymous Web browsing and called Web Mixes [3]. A shortcoming of cascade topologies is that they require less effort for an attacker to monitor the entry and exit point of the anonymity system. Part of the design has been implemented as a Web anonymizing proxy, JAP. The use of multiple intermediate relays between the two ends of the communication improves the trust distribution over the use of a single relay, provided that, if some of the relays are honest, the anonymity of the user remains protected. On the other hand, the cascade topology does not have good scalability and availability properties. The JAP design did not consider mechanisms for anonymity revocation; however, upon a law enforcement request for identification of a particular user, an exception had to be made in order to comply wth the request.

Onion routing [16, 17, 25, 27] is a free route mix network topology for unconditionally anonymous communication. Free route mix networks are vulnerable to intersection attacks [4]. The users establish circuits through a number of onion routers of their choice, and distribute symmetric keys to those routers. Data traveling in an established circuit is encrypted in layers, using the symmetric keys distributed to the routers. TOR (*the onion router*) [14], an improved second generation of onion routing, was proposed and implemented in 2004 (available at http://tor.eff.org/). Two years after deployment, it counts hundreds of volunteer nodes and hundreds of thousands of users, making it a very successful anonymous communication network.

Claessens et al. propose in [10] a system for revocable anonymous communication based on blind signatures. They introduce the legal requirements relevant for (revocable) anonymous communication and present a proof-of-concept architecture. Von Ahn et al. [29] propose transformations to add selective traceability to anonymous systems based on threshold cryptography and group signatures. Kopsell et al. [21] proposed a revocable anonymity system based on threshold group signatures and threshold atomic proxy reencryption.

All practical low-latency anonymous communication systems are vulnerable to adversaries capable of monitoring the entry and exit points: high-speed and high-volume traffic patterns are too distinct in each connection, making it difficult to hide the correlation of the traffic going in and out [18]. End-to-end full padding solves this problem, but its deployment is very expensive. Whether intermediate solutions, using some cover traffic, can effectively hide the communication patterns, remains an open problem. Also, if all nodes in the anonymous communication path are corrupted by the adversary, then the communication is traceable.

16.3 Requirements

The system should comply with a basic set of requirements (see [13] for more details) which include:

- Application independence: it should provide a general-purpose low-latency bidirectional communication layer.
- Secure anonymity: untraceability of communication (i.e., the path connecting the communicating parties is hard to discover), unlinkability of sessions (i.e., from an adversary's point of view, it is hard to link two sessions as related to the same user), load-balancing mechanisms, secure implementation, usability and robustness against attacks.
- Availability: resistance against denial-of-service attacks and a sufficient number of entry and exit points.
- Scalability: the system must be able to provide service to a large numbers of users.

The second set of requirements are an attempt to balance the fundamental right to privacy and the accountability mechanisms needed to make the system acceptable for the public at large and usable at a large scale. Claessens et al. define a complementary set of requirements in [10], where the legal point of view on anonymity and accountability for communication networks is presented.

- *Default privacy protection.* The system must be designed to protect by default the privacy of the users by anonymizing the communication layer. A user remains anonymous unless a judge issues a warrant that demands his identification.
- *Accountability.* The communication system must implement mechanisms that allow for law enforcement, called *identification* and *investigation.* Two types of actions may be considered. First, mechanisms should exist to identify subjects involved in criminal activities acting through the anonymous system (*post factum*). Second, law enforcement agents should be able to conduct investigations of criminal networks (e.g., money laundering), that is, tracing of the communication of a user under criminal investigation.
- *Transparency.* Clear and public policies and contracts that define the rights, obligations and liabilities of all parties, as well as the activities that may lead to identification, discourage abuse in the first place.

- *Trust distribution* is one of the key aspects of the design of the system. In order to be accepted by all entities, the system must be trusted to provide anonymity for honest users, as well as transparent accountability mechanisms for those who abuse the system for criminal purposes. Trust should be distributed, in order to minimize the possibility of a collusion of entities illegally tracing or identifying a user.
- *Identity management at the user's side.* In order to empower the user in the management of his own identities, all the identity and profile information should be kept under the user's control. Users who wish to obtain personalized services may provide their preferences to their service provider without disclosing their identity (e.g., [11, 20]). Service providers may collect the anonymized data generated by the users' transactions, but they will not be able to link the behavioral data to an identifiable individual, nor to link the user's local pseudonym to other organizations' databases.

16.4 Building Blocks

Here we present various technologies that can be combined in order to implement the proposed anonymity infrastructure. These include: a mix network that provides the anonymous communication functionality; an anonymous credential system to support the identity management and optional revocation; key traitor tracing schemes to support the revocation process; exit policies to distinguish resources with different abuse potential; and secure hardware modules to perform the cryptographic operations.

16.4.1 Mix Network

A *mix* is a router that hides correspondence between inputs and outputs by performing cryptographic operations that provide bitwise unlinkability (semantic security); and by modifying the order of messages to hide timing correlations. A mix network is a network of interconnected mixes.

The core of the anonymity infrastructure is a mix network similar to Tor [14]. Users select a path of nodes in the network and create a circuit through them that later will carry the information of all applications using the anonymous communication infrastructure.

16.4.2 Anonymous Credentials with Optional Anonymity Revocation

Anonymous credential systems [6, 7, 8, 9, 22] allow anonymous yet authenticated and accountable transactions between users and service providers. The basic primitives provided by these systems allow for establishing pseudonyms and issuing, showing, verifying and deanonymizing credentials. All credentials and pseudonyms of a user are generated from a user master secret S_U. A full description of these protocols can be found in Chap. 15.

The anonymous credential infrastructure is a privacy-enhanced pseudonymous PKI which implements zero-knowledge protocols (see Chap. 15). A user U can establish a pseudonym N_I with an issuing organization O_I. U can also obtain a credential C signed by O_I certifying certain attributes. Later on, U may prove these attributes to a verifying organization O_V. In this system, the user may choose which attributes to prove to O_V (note that proving an attribute does not necessarily imply showing its value; for example, a user may prove he is older than 18 without actually showing his age). Multiple credential shows are unlinkable.

If a user is registered with several organizations, the pseudonyms established are not linkable. The anonymous credential system provides protocols that allow the user to prove ownership of multiple credentials.

These systems also implement optional revocation of anonymity for accountability purposes. In this case, the user must provide a verifiable encryption of his pseudonym or identity: he must encrypt the information with the public key of a trusted entity O_D and prove that it can be decrypted by O_D from the protocol transcript.

16.4.3 Key Traitor Tracing Schemes

Key traitor tracing schemes [5] are public key encryption systems in which there is one public encryption key, and many private decryption keys. They also provide the security feature that if a coalition of private key holders collude to create a new decryption key, then there is an efficient algorithm to trace the new key to its creators.

16.4.4 Exit Policies

Exit policies have been proposed in other systems [14] to provide flexibility for the nodes regarding the resources they want to give access to. In our model, we propose three categories of content, for which different rules apply:

- *Black list:* illegal content sites (e.g., child porn Web sites) should not be accessible from the mix network.
- *White list:* there are many services for which unconditional anonymity is desired (see Sect. 16.5.1 for some examples). Such locations must be included in a white-list, and access to white list resources should not require the user to provide deanonymization information (encrypted pseudonym). This communication is therefore unconditionally anonymous. Note that, in the case of abuse, the identity of misbehaving users cannot be recovered.
- *No list:* this refers to sites and applications which have a potential for criminal abuse and may require accountability mechanisms. Users are asked by the exit mix to provide a verifiable encryption of their pseudonym in order

to access unlisted content (once for the duration of the tunnel). Note that users should select (at least) two separate exit nodes for *white list* and *no list* requests. If they use the same exit node for both types of requests, their *white list* requests would be technically linkable to their pseudonym (due to the *no list* requests and the linkability of requests in the same tunnel).

Note that exit nodes are the visible initiator of the requests they route. If abuse is committed through them, they may face problems with law enforcement. It is therefore in their interest to require an encrypted identity to give access to resources with a potential for abuse (e.g., trade sites). Letting the mixes design their own white lists gives more flexibility to the system. On the other hand, agreeing on common exit policies helps keeping the system simpler. We leave the design of the white and black listing as an open question. One option would be self-regulation by the mixes, and another option would be to regulate the white and black listing by law.

16.4.5 Secure Hardware Modules

To prevent credentials from being stolen from a user, as well as users sharing their credentials (and thus undermining their value), it is helpful to execute the credential protocols in a secure subsystem that is protected from both other applications on the same platform and from the user. The trusted platform module (TPM), described in Chap. 9 of this book, provides this functionality. Other alternatives include smart cards and secure coprocessors.

16.5 Proposed Accountable Anonymity Infrastructure

In this section, we present the proposed model for building a large-scale accountable anonymity system. We first introduce the participating entities, and second we describe the protocols.

16.5.1 Entities

We introduce here the entities playing a role in the system. For each of these entities, we describe their role, what they are trusted for, the secrets they keep, the credentials or public keys they possess and the information they see and log.

Root Authority

The Root Authority (RA) is a credential issuer. Users registered with this authority with a pseudonym N_I may obtain a credential C_I on N_I signed by the RA. The RA is trusted to keep the civil identity of the user (i.e., an identifier with which the administration can uniquely identify the citizen, e.g., the passport number), together with N_I. Note that users may need to register in person with the RA.

The RA is required as part of the anonymous credential infrastructure that should be in place to support our system, but it is not part of the anonymity infrastructure itself. In order to provide better availability and robustness, the RA may be distributed across several entities.

Mixes

Mixes are the core of the anonymity service. They act as the registration authority for issuing credentials to users, and they anonymize the communication of registered users.

In order to obtain access to the anonymity network, users must first register with a node of their choice. The user establishes a pseudonym N_A with the node: (i) proving ownership of a credential C_I from a trusted RA, (ii) providing a verifiable encryption of his pseudonym with the RA, N_I, and (iii) paying the registration fee (one-show anonymous credentials can implement anonymous coins [6]). The node that registers the user logs N_A and the encrypted N_I. The user then requests from the node a credential C_A issued on N_A and signed by the mix.

In order to prevent abuse, nodes maintain a pseudonym revocation list which lists pseudonyms that should no longer be accepted at entry nodes. Users who abuse the system may have their pseudonym revoked.

Mixes have two public key pairs: one to receive encrypted information (PK_i), and another to digitally sign messages. Mixes also establish shared secret keys with their neighboring nodes for link encryption.

When a mix is the entry node of a tunnel, it must verify the validity of the credential C_A presented by the user, as well as the pseudonym of the user N_A; it should also verify that N_A has not been included in the pseudonym revocation list. C_A may have been issued by the mix itself, or by other mixes of the network. If C_A and N_A are valid, the user can continue to construct the tunnel.

The exit node of a tunnel must follow its exit policy. When the user is accessing white-list resources, the exit node does not need to log any information. If the user accesses unlisted resources (for which accountability measures may be needed), then the exit node must ask for a verifiable encryption of N_A, keep it for the time established in data retention laws, and log with it a timestamp and the unlisted resources requested by the user.

Nodes, besides being trusted for not logging information which is not strictly required for accountability measures, are trusted to:

- verify the validity of the encryption of N_I when registering a user;
- securely keep the encrypted N_I and N_A for registered users;
- verify the validity of C_A and N_A when acting as an entry node;

- verify the validity of the encryption of N_A when acting as an exit node and giving access to an unlisted resource;
- securely keep the encrypted N_A and the accesses to unlisted resources for the period of time specified in data retention laws, and delete it afterwards;
- collaborate with law enforcement when required by a judge.

User

The user is registered with an RA and with the anonymity infrastructure (he may choose the root authority and registration mix he trusts most), and routes anonymously his communication through the mix network. The user is trusted to store his master secret S_U securely (e.g., in a TPM or in a smart card). S_U is used to establish pseudonyms (N_I, N_A), to obtain credentials (C_I, C_A), and in the credential show protocols.

Resources

Resources are classified by the nodes of the anonymity network according to the three categories mentioned in Sect. 16.4.4: white list, black list and no list. Note that some of these services may also implement their own conditionally anonymous credentials at the application layer, or even require user authentication.

Judges

Judges are entities legally authorized to issue a warrant that demands identification of a user accused of criminal activities. They may also request mixes to collaborate in criminal investigations that require tracing of users.

A key traitor tracing scheme is implemented in order to make the identification procedure effective for law enforcement. In this scheme, there is a unique encryption public key PK_J of the judges, but every judge holds a unique private key for decryption. Users verifiably encrypt their pseudonyms N_I and N_A with PK_J when required to provide an encrypted identity as an accountability condition in certain protocols.

Judges are trusted to apply the law and protect their private keys against disclosure or abuse.

16.5.2 Protocols

We outline in this section the protocols for the proposed system. The protocols are based on the anonymous credential protocols described in [6, 7].

Registration with Root Authority

The user must be registered with an RA which is trusted by the anonymity network. The RA knows the user by a pseudonym N_I, and can link this pseudonym to the real identity of the user. If national electronic ID cards implement anonymous credentials, they could be used as root credentials. In this case, a local authority (e.g., in Belgium the city hall) would act as a trusted root authority.

Registration with Anonymity Infrastructure

The user U chooses one of the mixes, according to his trust preferences, to register for the system. With the registration request the user must:

- prove possession of a root credential C_I and knowledge of the secret S_U;
- provide a verifiable encryption of N_I, encrypted with PK_J;
- pay for the service (anonymous payments may be implemented with one-show anonymous credentials);
- establish a pseudonym N_A with the mix;
- request a credential C_A on N_A signed by the mix, which grants access to the network.

The mix must verify the correctness of the proofs, and issue a credential C_A on N_A for the user. This credential will have a certain validity period, and must be accepted by other nodes in the network. Once the user has established N_A with the mix, he may ask for new credentials once C_A has expired. Note that, during the registration process, the user should be informed of the terms of use of the network, and on the policies and conditions for identification.

Using the Anonymity Infrastructure

Once the user U has obtained C_A, he can start to use the service. U selects a path through the network for his tunnel, and connects to the entry node, M_1.

U has to prove to M_1 that he has a valid credential C_A issued by a mix of the network. He must also show N_A so the entry mix can check that his pseudonym has not been revoked.

If the verification of C_A and N_A is OK, the user may continue to establish the tunnel, contacting the other nodes in the path. The exit mix of a connection used to access unlisted resources asks a verifiable encryption of N_A, encrypted with PK_J. The exit mix logs the encrypted pseudonym and the IP addresses of the accessed unlisted resources, as well as a timestamp. The mix may keep this information for the time established in the legal framework in which the node is operating. After that period of time, the data must be deleted. The next item explains how the identification of the user is carried out if accountability measures need to be applied.

The user may want to use separate exit nodes (or tunnels) for different requests in very sensitive cases, e.g., he may want to use two exit nodes (or tunnels) to check information on a particular disease and to access the conditions of a life insurance.

Identification

If the user abuses the anonymous network for criminal purposes (e.g., dealing with child pornography, uploading a video which shows the murder of a hostage, or swindling people in eBay), then his identification may be required by a judge.

Note that identification can only be requested when the user has used an unlisted resource (accesses to white-list resources are unconditionally anonymous). If that was the case, U has provided to the exit node a verifiable encryption of N_A. As the address of the node is visible in the access to the resource, the judge may request the exit node to provide the encrypted pseudonym of the user who accessed a particular resource at a particular time. As N_A was encrypted with PK_J, the judge can extract the pseudonym N_A of the user in the network, and the name of the issuing mix.

The judge may contact the mix that registered the user, provide N_A and request the encrypted N_I that is kept in the mix. The judge may, again, decrypt this pseudonym and recover the root pseudonym, N_I. The root authority may now provide the judge with the identity of the subject.

In this system, four unrelated entities (the issuer node, the exit node, the root authority and the judge) need to collaborate in order to identify a user. This is done in order to distribute the trust and to minimize the possibility of collusion of entities for illegal identification.

Investigation

In some cases (e.g., money laundering, organized crime, terrorism, etc.) law enforcement needs to investigate individuals. In this model, a judge may sign a warrant asking the mixes for cooperation in an investigation on the user known by N_A. When the user contacts the entry node, he must show N_A. The mix can check if the N_A matches the name in the warrant issued by the judge, and if so, it forwards the warrant to the next mix in the path of the user, and logs the necessary information to allow tracing. The next mixes in the path also log the necessary information regarding that tunnel, and forward the warrant to the next node. The exit node receives the warrant and logs the required information. All mixes encrypt the logged information with the judges' public key, PK_J.

The judge may later request the information from the mixes regarding the N_A on the warrant and reconstruct the activities of the user. The entities that need to collaborate in this case are a judge, and all mixes in the tunnel. Note the judge needs to know N_A, which may not be obvious. If the user has been previously identified because of criminal abuse of the network, then N_A is already known to the judge. Otherwise, the judge could use the IP address of the user to ask entry nodes for the pseudonym. This protocol would however require some modifications (as entry nodes do not keep N_A in our model), and falls outside the scope of this chapter.

16.5.3 Deployment

In order to deploy such an accountable anonymity infrastructure, certain technical and political conditions should exist:

- We are assuming large computing power and high-speed links in order to implement the mix network. Today, these resources are still too expensive. The design of secure efficient anonymous communication networks remains a challenge.
- A trusted anonymous credential infrastructure (root authority) needs to be in place. The implementation of anonymous credentials in privacy-enhanced national electronic identity cards would provide a solid anonymous credential infrastructure.
- The institutional and legal framework is also important, as the system requires a well-coordinated judicial system.
- Finally, there should be social and political support for a large-scale infrastructure. If privacy protection becomes a political priority, or if the privacy awareness of the citizens significantly increases, the support could be gathered.

16.6 Conclusions

In this chapter, we have proposed an accountable anonymity communication infrastructure. We have motivated the need for implementing both anonymity and accountability mechanisms and argued the differences with the key escrow debate.

We have listed the requirements for a large-scale anonymous infrastructure, and proposed a model to comply with them. Our model is built by combining existing technologies and distributes trust among various entities.

The purpose of this work is to provide a solution that combines existing privacy-enhancing technologies, rather than presenting new contributions for the building blocks themselves. Here we summarize the main conclusions of this work:

- Both anonymity and accountability requirements should be satisfied in order to gain support for the deployment of large-scale anonymity infrastructures that provide privacy protection to the *masses*. Trust should be adequately distributed to minimize the risk of collusion.
- Existing cryptographic primitives and privacy-enhancing technologies can be combined in order to build an anonymous communication infrastructure that is both flexible and accountable.
- The implementation of such a system would allow for user-controlled identity management. Organizations may collect pseudonymous data from users, but they may not link the information to the identity of the user unless he willingly provides it.

- Unconditionally anonymous, pseudonymous and authenticated applications may communicate through this system. Anonymous credential and authentication protocols may be implemented at the application layer.
- The system must distribute the ability for revocation in order to be trustworthy for the users.
- The biggest shortcoming of the system is its cost. It needs a large amount of resources in terms of computing power, bandwidth and organizational and administrative overhead. Viable economic models need to be applied in order to deploy the system.
- The technical and political conditions for deployment of an infrastructure of these characteristics are not met today, but they may be met in the future if privacy protection becomes a real concern.

References

1. H. Abelson, R. Anderson, S. Bellovin, J. Benaloh, M. Blaze, W. Diffie, J. Gilmore, P. Neumann, R. Rivest, J. Schiller, B. Schneier (1997) The Risks of Key Recovery, Key Escrow, and Trusted Third Party Encryption. World Wide Web Journal 2(3):241-257.
2. Anonymizer, http://www.anonymizer.com/
3. O. Berthold, H. Federrath, S. Kopsell (2000) Web MIXes: A system for anonymous and unobservable Internet access. In: Federrath H (ed.) Designing Privacy Enhancing Technologies, LNCS 2009, pp. 115-129. Springer-Verlag.
4. O. Berthold, A. Pfitzmann, R. Standtke (2000) The disadvantages of free MIX routes and how to overcome them. In: Federrath H (ed.) Designing Privacy Enhancing Technologies, LNCS 2009, pp. 30-45. Springer-Verlag.
5. D. Boneh, M. Franklin (1999) An Efficient Public Key Traitor Tracing Scheme. In: Wiener M (ed.) Advances in Cryptology - CRYPTO'99, LNCS 1666, pp. 338-353. Springer-Verlag.
6. J. Camenisch, A. Lysyanskaya (2001) An Efficient System for Non-transferable Anonymous Credentials with Optional Anonymity Revocation. In: Pfitzmann B (ed.) Advances in Cryptology - EUROCRYPT'01, LNCS 2045, pp. 93-118. Springer-Verlag
7. J. Camenisch, E. van Herreweghen (2002) Design and Implementation of the idemix Anonymous Credential System. In: Atluri V (ed.) Proceedings of the 9th ACM conference on Computer and Communications Security, pp. 21-30. ACM Press.
8. D. Chaum (1985) Security without Identification: Transaction Systems to Make Big Brother Obsolete. Communications of the ACM 28(10):1030-1044.
9. D. Chaum, J. Evertse (1987) A Secure and Privacy-Protecting Protocol for Transmitting Personal Information Between Organizations. In: Odlyzko A (ed.) Advances in Cryptology - CRYPTO'86, LNCS 263, pp. 118-167. Springer-Verlag.
10. J. Claessens, C. Diaz, C. Goemans, B. Preneel, J. Vandewalle, J. Dumortier (2003) Revocable anonymous access to the Internet. Journal of Internet Research 13(4):242-258.

11. J. Claessens, C. Diaz, B. Preneel, J. Vandewalle (2002) A Privacy-Preserving Web Banner System for Targeted Advertising. Technical Report 9 p. Katholieke Universiteit Leuven.
12. C. Diaz, S. Seys, J. Claessens, B. Preneel (2002) Towards Measuring Anonymity. In: Dingledine R, Syverson P (eds.) Designing Privacy Enhancing Technologies, LNCS 2482, pp. 54-68. Springer-Verlag.
13. C. Diaz, V. Naessens, S. Nikova, B. de Decker, B. Preneel (2004) Tools for Technologies and Applications of Controlled Anonymity. Technical Report, 211 p. Project IWT STWW Anonymity and Privacy in Electronic Services.
14. R. Dingledine, N. Mathewson, P. Syverson (2004) Tor: The Second-Generation Onion Router. In 13th USENIX Security Symposium, pp. 303-320. USENIX.
15. Directive 2006/24/EC of the European Parliament and of the Council (13.4.2006) Official Journal of the European Union.
16. D. Goldschlag, M. Reed, P. Syverson (1996) Hiding Routing Information. In: R. Anderson (ed.) Information Hiding, LNCS 1174, pp. 137-150. Springer-Verlag.
17. D. Goldschlag, M. Reed, P. Syverson (1999) Onion Routing. In: Communications of the ACM 42(2):39-41.
18. A. Hintz (2002) Fingerprinting Websites Using Traffic Analysis. In: R. Dingledine, P. Syverson (ed.s) Designing Privacy Enhancing Technologies, LNCS 2482, pp. 171-178. Springer-Verlag.
19. JAP Anonymity & Privacy, http://anon.inf.tu-dresden.de/
20. A. Juels (2001) Targeted Advertising... and Privacy Too. In: D. Naccache (ed.) Topics in Cryptology - Proceedings of the Cryptographers' Track at RSA'2001, LNCS 2020, pp. 408-424. Springer-Verlag.
21. S. Kopsell, R. Wendolsky, H. Federrath (2006) Revocable Anonymity. In: G. Muller (ed.): Emerging Trends in Information and Communication Security - ETRICS, LNCS 3995, pp. 206-220. Springer-Verlag.
22. A. Lysyanskaya, R. Rivest, A. Sahai, S. Wolf (1999) Pseudonym Systems. In: H. Heys, C. Adams (eds.) Proceedings of the 6th Annual International Workshop on Selected Areas in Cryptography, LNCS 1758, pp. 184-199. Springer-Verlag.
23. A. Pfitzmann, M. Hansen (2000) Anonymity, Unobservability and Pseudonymity: A Proposal for Terminology. In: Federrath H (ed.) Designing Privacy Enhancing Technologies, LNCS 2009, pp. 1-9. Springer-Verlag.
24. A. Pfitzmann, B. Pfitzmann, M. Waidner (1991) ISDN-mixes: Untraceable communication with very small bandwidth overhead. In: W. Effelsberg, H. Meuer, G. Muller (eds.) GI/ITG Conference on Communication in Distributed Systems, Informatik-Fachberichte 267, pp. 451-463. Springer-Verlag.
25. M. Reed, P. Syverson, D. Goldschlag (1998) Anonymous Connections and Onion Routing. In: IEEE Journal on Selected Areas in Communications 16(4):482-494.
26. A. Serjantov, G. Danezis (2002) Towards an Information Theoretic Metric for Anonymity. In: Dingledine R, Syverson P (eds.) Designing Privacy Enhancing Technologies, LNCS 2482, pp. 41-53. Springer-Verlag.
27. P. Syverson, G. Tsudik, M. Reed, C. Landwehr (2000) Towards an Analysis of Onion Routing Security. In: Federrath H (ed.) Designing Privacy Enhancing Technologies, LNCS 2009, pp. 96-114. Springer-Verlag.
28. The Clipper Chip, http://www.epic.org/crypto/clipper/
29. L. von Ahn, A. Bortz, N. Hopper, K. O'Neill (2006) Selectively Traceable Anonymity. In: Danezis G, Golle P (eds.) Designing Privacy Enhancing Technologies, LNCS (pre-proceedings), pp. 199-213. Springer-Verlag.

Part IV

Digital Asset Protection

17

An Introduction to Digital Rights Management Systems

Willem Jonker

Philips Research / Twente University
The Netherlands

Summary. This chapter gives a concise introduction to digital rights management (DRM) systems by first presenting the basic ingredients of the architecture of DRM systems for (audio and/or video) content delivery, followed by an introduction to two open-standard DRM systems, one developed in the mobile world (Open Mobile Alliance DRM) and another one in the world of consumer electronics (Marlin).

17.1 Introduction

Digitization and new coding formats, together with the development of the Web, have led to a world where electronic distribution of audio and video to end users has become a reality. This reality however has at the same time led to increased concern about the protection of the rights of owners of the content that is distributed in electronic form. Digital right management (DRM) is the term for commercial, legal, and technical measures that can be taken to ensure that rights of owners of digital content are respected. So, DRM is more than technology, DRM can only function in a legal framework that includes legislation, conformance, enforcement, etc. In this chapter we will concentrate on the technical aspects of DRM systems. For a broader overview we refer to [1,2,3].

From the technical perspective there are two main approaches towards the application of DRM in the context of audio/video delivery; one is based on watermarking and the other is based on cryptography. Both approaches will be discussed in the following chapters. In this chapter we concentrate on systems that are based on cryptography.

Currently some proprietary DRM systems are out in the market, such as Apple FairPlay and Microsoft DRM, while other open-standard DRM systems, such as Open Mobile Alliance (OMA) DRM v2 and Marlin are under development.

17.2 DRM Systems: The Basics

The figure below shows the typical architecture of a DRM system for electronic delivery of audio. On the left are the components that normally reside on the server side, while on the right are the components that reside on the client side.

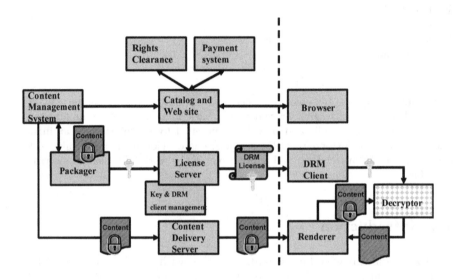

Fig. 17.1 A generic DRM Architecture for audio delivery

A typical usage scenario is one where the user uses the browser to select a specific audio item to be acquired. The browser connects to a catalogue Web site where the items are listed. When a specific item is purchased, a payment has to be handled, which is done by a payment system. At the same time the rights that the user wants to obtain need to be issued. Once this is done, the content management system is instructed to prepare the audio item for shipping. This includes encrypting the audio. This task is carried out by the packager, which sends the encryption key to the license server. The latter is responsible for creating the appropriate license[1]. Often the encryption key is part of the license. Once the content is properly packaged it is shipped to the delivery manager, which sends it to the client. At the same time the license manager sends the license to the client.

---

[1] Although often used intermixed, there is a difference between rights and licenses. Licenses are the actual carriers of the rights (in the form of rights expressions) and often contain additional information, most notably the content encryption keys.

At the client side the DRM client uses the license to decrypt the audio and controls usage. After decryption the audio is send to the renderer and played.

The following elements are the core ingredients of a DRM system:

1. The content to be protected. The content that needs to be protected can vary. DRM is currently most known from audio and video content delivery, but DRM is also applied to documents (e.g. Adobe) and can in principle be applied to any form of digital content.

2. The cryptographic protection scheme, including a key management scheme. Most DRM systems work with a combination of symmetric and asymmetric keys. Often content is encrypted in layers using a key hierarchy, where keys in the lower layers in the hierarchy are used to encrypt parts of the content.

3. The expression of the rights. In most systems rights expression languages are used to define the rights that are issued to the content users. Two well-known rights languages are ODRL[4] and XrML [5]. DRM rights languages are often expressed in XML. Since for digital assets in general there are a lot of possible situations, DRM rights languages tend to be complex.

4. License management. The license contains both the encryption key as well as the rights that have been entitled to the user. Without the presence of the license, content access is not possible. Since the license contains both the key and the rights it is important to protect the license as well. It should be impossible for an unauthorized user to get the key from the license or to change the rights expressions. Licenses should therefore be handled with care and either be encrypted or stored in a secure place in the client. Some systems support the explicit separation of content and licenses. This has the advantage that licenses and content can be send over different channels and at different times.

5. Compliance regulation. Compliance is a key issue in DRM systems. Only compliant devices can participate in content exchange. A compliant device is a device that respects the rules of the DRM system. This means that the device guarantees that the content is treated as described by the license rights and that the device also takes certain measures to prevent encryption keys from being obtained by unauthorized users. In the (open) PC environment compliance is often only supported in software by installing DRM client software. In the (closed) CE environment compliance is often supported by a combination of software and hardware. A way to deal with compliance is using certificates. For example a CE device may have a pre-installed certificate indicating that it is compliant with a specific DRM system. Upon request, this certificate can be send to a license server in order to verity compliance. A certificate authority that monitors compliance and acts in the case of violations issues such certificates. Certificates that have been issued to compliant de-

vices that nevertheless violate the rules can be revoked. Revoked systems will not be able to acquire content under the DRM scheme any longer.

6. Client-side enforcement. The enforcement of rights at the client side is the most challenging part of a DRM system. In principle the task is simple: at the client side specific DRM client software is installed that intercepts the access to the content and enforces the rights. However the challenging part is the prevention of attacks. The client side is not under the control of the DRM system and is therefore vulnerable to attacks. These attacks may be aimed at disclosing the encryption key or at circumventing the enforcements of the rights. In order to avoid such attacks the DRM client needs to be executed in a tamper-resistant environment with protected memory and isolated execution of the DRM client code. In the PC domain the trusted computing group [6] is working on tamper-resistant environments; this work has led for example to the specification of a TPM [7].

This concludes our discussion on the general basic aspects of DRM systems. In the remainder of the chapter we will focus on a number of concrete open-standard DRM systems.

17.3 OMA DRM

The Open Mobile Alliance (OMA) [8] is working on architectures to enable all kinds of value-added services over mobile networks. One class of services that is targeted is that of content download services. These services require content protection and for that reason OMA has developed a DRM specification, called OMA DRM. Actually there are two specifications out today: OMA version1 and OMA version2. We will briefly describe OMA version 1 and than concentrate on OMA version 2.

17.3.1 OMA DRM Version 1

OMA DRM v1 can hardly be called a DRM system, since it lacks almost all protection one would expect from a DRM system. The security of OMA DRM v1 depends completely on the security of the underlying mobile network. Over this network OMA v1 messages are sent in the clear and as a result OMA DRM v1 is very vulnerable to attacks.

OMA DRM v1 has three different content delivery schemes:

1. Forward lock
2. Combined delivery
3. Separate delivery

In the forward lock scheme, the content is downloaded by means of the download mechanism offered by the WAP protocol. The content is not encrypted but sent in the clear. Together with the content a wrapper is sent that indicates that the content may not be forwarded to other mobile devices. The OMA DRM v1 client implementation checks the wrapper and refuses to forward the content. As can easily be seen the system is vulnerable to several attacks. The content is not encrypted and thus can be read from the mobile device memory. Also the wrapper is not protected and thus can be easily changed. Finally, the DRM client is not protected and thus the intended operation can be easily circumvented.

The combined delivery scheme is to a large extent similar to the forward lock scheme. However, instead of sending the content with a wrapper, now the content is sent with a license that contains a simple rights description indicating what the user is allowed to do with the content. This scheme is vulnerable to the same attacks as the forward lock scheme.

Finally, in the separate delivery scheme the content and the license are downloaded to the client in separate messages. In this scheme the content is encrypted and downloaded using the download mechanism of the WAP protocol. The license now contains both the rights expression and the content key, which is used to encrypt the content. The license is sent to the client using an unconfirmed push mechanism from the WAP protocol. Although some security is added, the separate delivery scheme is still very vulnerable to attacks. The license can easily be intercepted due to the fact that the WAP push is not confirmed. Also the DRM client is still not protected.

17.3.2 OMA DRM Version 2

For more-serious content delivery services OMA DRM v2 has been developed. OMA DRM v2 follows very much the basic DRM architecture as described above. It distinguishes between a content issuer and a rights issuer as two separate entities. Rights are only issued to trusted DRM agents that reside in client devices (e.g., mobile phones).

Compliance in OMA DRM v2 is realized through the notion of trusted agents. The notion of a trusted agent is important and implemented by means of a public key infrastructure. This means that each trusted agent has a unique public/private key pair and a certificate belonging to it. Certificates play a role in the authentication protocol and are a means to revoke agents that exhibit noncompliant behaviour. Content is encrypted by means of symmetric keys, while licenses (or rights objects as they are called in OMA) are encrypted by asymmetric keys. The symmetric key belonging to some specific encrypted content is sent to a trusted DRM agent by means of a rights object. The rights object is encrypted with the public key of that specific trusted DRM agent. In this way only that specific trusted DRM agent can access the rights object by decrypting it with its corresponding private key. This is a way to bind content to a specific device and to prevent that content from being played on another device[2].

In order to allow some sharing of content OMA DRM v2 introduces the notion of domains. A domain is a group of devices defined by a rights issuer. Domains are optional and their use can differ among various content issuers and rights issuers. A rights issuer carries out domain management. In order to join a domain, a device has to register to that domain by making a request to the rights issuer. Once a group of devices has joined the domain, they can access the content that is issued to that domain. This means that devices can directly share rights objects for domain content amongst each other.

In addition to domains, OMA DRM v2 supports another mechanism for sharing content, namely super-distribution. Super-distribution can be used between any two trusted OMA DRM agents. It consists of sending the protected content from one agent to the other. For the other agent to gain access to the content, it has to contact the rights issuer in order to obtain a rights object for that specific content. The nice thing about super-distribution is that it allows direct exchange of the protected content and allows for the rights object to be acquired later. In a mobile environment this may be an advantage since rights objects will be much smaller than content objects. So a user may acquire the content through a fast direct connection with another mobile device, while obtaining the rights object via the mobile network. This is a direct result of the decision in OMA DRM v2 to separate content objects and rights objects.

The OMA DRM v2 rights expression language (REL) is a subset (or so-called mobile profile) of ODRL v1.1. The REL is an XML structure. It is beyond the scope of this chapter to give a detailed description of OMA DRM v2 REL.

As far as client-side enforcement is concerned, OMA requires the secure storage of the private device keys and the implementation of a secure clock in connected devices. In addition it is required that the execution of rights evaluation at playtime is secured and cannot be tampered with. The reason for requiring a secure clock is to support time-based usage rights (for example the right to use the content up to a certain date) and to prevent users from manipulating the clock in order to affect the impact of time-based rights.

---

[2] Binding content to devices is typical for so-called device-based DRM systems. Device-based DRM systems are limited in sharing content over various devices even when these are owned by the same end-user. In the section on Marlin we will see how so-called person-based DRM systems try to avoid this limitation.

17.4 Marlin

While OMA DRM originates from the mobile world, Marlin originates from the CE world. The core developers of Marlin [9] are InterTrust, Sony, MEI, Samsung, and Philips. Marlin is an open DRM standard targeting CE devices and supporting the controlled flow of audio and video content over collections of CE devices.

Marlin has a number of characteristics that differentiate it from other DRM systems. We will list them first and then elaborate on them below. Most important is that Marlin is user-based, rather than device-based, which means that licenses are bound to users rather than to devices. A second characteristic that differentiates Marlin is that it does not use a rights expression language, instead rights definition and enforcement in Marlin are taken care of by means of a control program. Such control programs are part of the generic DRM architecture called Octopus. A third characteristic of Marlin is that right from the start the notion of domain is designed in. The Marlin domain model builds on a graph of nodes and links that allow for very flexible rights sharing.

The overall Marlin architecture consists of four classes of actors: the Marlin client, the Marlin domain manager, the Marlin registration service, and the Marlin license service. The Marlin client has the same role as other DRM clients: control the access to the content based on the rights that have been issued to the user. The Marlin domain manager has the role of managing domains consisting of devices and users joining and leaving domains. The Marlin registration service is responsible for admitting users and devices to the Marlin system; it does so by means of issuing nodes and links. Finally, the Marlin license service issues licenses.

Nodes and links play a central role in Marlin. Nodes represent entities in a Marlin system. There are four kinds of nodes: device, domain, user, and subscription. In Marlin, links express an inclusion relationship.

The directed graphs play a central role in determining the access rights to content in a Marlin system. Roughly speaking content can be accessed when there is a path in the graph from the requester to the content. Note that this a pre-requisite, the actual access rights are expressed in the control program, the graph serves as a sharing mechanism that allows sharing of licenses between users and devices in a very flexible way.

17.4.1 Marlin: User-Centric

As stated before Marlin is user-based, which means that licenses are bound to users rather than to devices. Binding a license to a user in an actual Marlin implementation means that the content to which the license refers is encrypted with the *public* key belonging to that user. The *private* key of the user has to be stored somewhere in a secure place and processing of that key needs to be done in some secure environment. This can be on a token, on a device linked to the user, or somewhere in the network. When a user wants to play its content on a device, in some way a connection needs to be established between the device and the private key of the user, allowing for the decryption of the content on that device. As well as user-binding, graphs play a role in the sense that the license can contain additional requirements on the graph, for example that there is a path from the device to the user. The enforcement of such requirements is done by means of the control programme that is part of the license.

17.4.2 Marlin Domains

The domain concept in Marlin is very flexible and offers all kinds of ways to share content in a controlled way. Both users and devices can join a domain. By releasing content to a domain the content is made accessible to all devices that are part of that domain, and as such the content can be freely shared among the devices and (when authorized) users. Domains are very dynamic in various ways. New domains can be created, domains can be removed, devices can join and leave domains, and users can be (de)associated. In order to prevent the world as a whole from becoming one big domain in which everybody can freely exchange content, there are restrictions on the number of devices that can be members of a domain as well as restrictions on the number of domains a user can join. By separating the domain structure from the licenses Marlin has become very flexible. Once a service provider has installed a domain policy, changes of domains do not affect licences any more, which allows domain modifications (within the policy) without affecting licenses.

17.5 Concluding Remarks

In this chapter we have presented two open-standard approaches towards digital Rights Management. In addition to the open-standard approaches there are quite a number of commercial DRM solutions on the market of which Microsoft DRM and FairPlay from Apple are the best known. Especially this first generation of commercial DRM systems that is currently deployed still has a long way to go in terms of convenience to the end user. Important issues that need to be addressed are DRM interoperability, ubiquitous access to one's own content at any place at any time, sharing and gifting of content, as well as hiding the DRM complexity from the end-user. In the following chapters some of these issues will be addressed in more detail.

References

1. B. Rosenblatt, B. Trippe, S. Mooney, *Digital Rights Management*, Business and Technology, M&T, New York, 2002.
2. E. Becker, W. Buhse, D. Gunnewig, N. Rump, "Digital Rights Management: Technological, Economic, Legal and Political Aspects", LNCS 2770, Springer, Berlin-Heidelberg, 2003.
3. W. Jonker, J.P. Linnartz, "Digital Rights Management in Consumer Electronics Products", IEEE Signal Processing Magazine, Vol. 21, Issue 2, pp. 82-91, March 2004.
4. R. Iannella, Open Digital Rights Language (ODRL) Version 1.0, IPR System Ptd Ltd. November 2001. Available at: http://odrl.net/1.0/ODRL-10-HTML/ODRL-10.html
5. XrML - The Technology Standard for Trusted Systems in the eContentMarketplace. Available at: http://www.xrml.org/
6. www.trustedcomputinggroup.org
7. www.trustedcomputinggroup.org/specs/TPM
8. www.openmobilealliance.org
9. www.marlin-community.com

Copy Protection Systems

Joop Talstra

Philips Research
The Netherlands

Summary. The bulk of today's commercial audio and video content is distributed on (optical) media. As this business model is vulnerable to copying, the content is protected with some *copy protection system* (CPS) or other. In this chapter we look at the historic origins of Copy Protection and the basic technological ingredients of a CPS: media binding, broadcast encryption, and key hierarchies. Attention will also be devoted to auxiliary technologies such as watermarking and secure authenticated channels. We conclude with a review of new CPS components in upcoming protection systems.

18.1 Introduction

This chapter will discuss some of the major techniques used to prevent illicit copying of audio and video content by end users. There is no hard definition of exactly which subfield of digital rights management[1] copy protection systems cover. However, it seems generally accepted that a copy protection system protects those digital rights which would be violated if the end user could *copy* the content. Typically these rights are rather *static* and simple and are not bound to a particular time period or person, e.g.:

- *Copy never*: the content on this particular piece of media (disc, tape) may be played in any player (but may not be copied)
- *Copy one generation*: the content on this particular piece of media may be copied, but the resulting media may not be copied further; the right associated with the copied media is then called *copy no more*.

Note that the rights supported by CPSs actually cover the bulk of the commercial content enjoyed today, viz. distribution on optical media like CD and DVD. Despite the simple rights supported, Copy Protection Systems tend to be built from rather complex component technologies, because the devices in which these rights have to be enforced generally oper-

---

[1] See Chaps. 17, 20 and 21 for a discussion on modern DRM systems.

ate under rather harsh circumstances. For instance: they cannot depend on regular contact with a trusted server over a network. Also, the built-in CPS functionality has to be practically for free because the devices are produced for a massmarket with incredibly small margins.

The chapter will start out with a historical overview of the copy protection techniques employed in the analog era, mostly aimed at video cassette recorders (VCRs). We will then discuss how, with the advent of digital media in the 1990s, techniques like *encryption* and *media marks* were introduced to prevent copying. Also the role of auxiliary technologies like *revocation* (to prevent further content leakage from devices that have been hacked) and *watermarking* (to prevent content white-washing by copying it off an analog interface) will be taken into account.

After dealing with technologies aimed at media protection we will shift attention to protection of content on user-accessible digital interfaces, e.g., the interface between an optical drive and the host software in a PC. This involves additional techniques like *authentication* and *key exchange*.

We will also devote a section to the *legal framework* that accompanies any copy protection system to ensure that manufacturers in fact implement the system according to specification. Contrary to other standards, by deviating from the copy protection standard, the manufacturer may actually create a product which, from the perspective of the end user, is *more* attractive.

The chapter concludes with a review of recent developments in copy protection systems, with new technologies that are about to enter the copy protection domain.

As is evident from the topics mentioned above, this chapter will mostly deal with CPSs for optical media. Originally, *conditional access* (CA) systems for pay-TV featured usage rights which were very similar to those of content on media. However more recently, with smartcards, dedicated set top boxes, and return channels, CA systems have started to support more complicated rights, resembling the DRM systems from online downloads. Where appropriate we will indicate when CPS techniques for media also apply to CA systems.

18.2 Threat Model

Before going into the technical details of CPSs it makes sense to first agree on the *threat model*, that is, the type of attacks the CPS should be able to prevent. Obviously the CPS should be robust against attacks by casual hackers without special technical training. Almost all CPSs actually satisfy this requirement. So why are new CPSs introduced? The problem is that often a system is first hacked by a small group of *sophisticated hackers*, people with a strong technical background and access to (semi-)professional equipment, just because they see it as an interesting challenge, or in order to make some money off this hack. Given the economics and time-to-market pressure of the consumer electronics (CE) industry and the creativity of the sophisticated hackers, it is nearly impossible to stop this. In any case, the small group that can perform such hacks is not the real issue. The problem arises when the sophisticated hack is then propagated to the multitude of casual hackers by codifying it in a piece of software that is distributed via the Internet, or by selling it as a cheap tool over the web. Good CPSs are designed such that these attacks are still nearly impossible.

18.3 Early Copy Protection Systems

Up to about 1982, copy protection was simple: music was only available on analog records or tapes, and second- or third-generation copies on audio cassettes were of relatively low quality. Nevertheless, the problem was deemed big enough that (starting in Germany in 1965), levies[2] were instituted for tape-recording material. In the early 1980s, the story repeated itself with video tapes and recorders. To stop video copying, the American Macrovision Corporation introduced a type of VHS tape in 1987 that could be played by virtually any VHS recorder, but the quality of its copies are degraded and very unpleasant to watch. Although it was quickly found that the method could be hacked using equipment worth less than $10, this anti-copy method became very popular in Hollywood.

In essence the method relies on fooling the automatic gain circuitry (AGC) at the input of a VHS recorder [1] with a composite video TV signal which is not quite according to the NTSC, PAL or SECAM TV-standards. The AGC in the recorder serves to scale the luminance part of the input signal to a fixed level so as not to allow further processing steps (FM modulation and recording). The amplitude of the input signal is determined by measuring the video signal right after the synchronization pulse (see Fig. 18.1), which is normally corresponds to black. A Macrovision-modified signal presents, amongst others so-called AGC pulses where this level is increased above white which causes the AGC circuit to believe that the signal is much stronger than it really is, resulting in a strongly attenuated video recording. The AGC pulses are only present in a few video lines in the overscan area (outside the visible picture). TVs are not affected because they generally do not need such a video AGC circuit.

In later years, Macrovision and other companies found other ways to manipulate a standard video signal to achieve the same result, i.e., TVs display the original signal without problems, but recordings on a VHS tape suffer serious loss of quality.

---

[2] A tax on recording equipment or blank media to compensate rights owners.

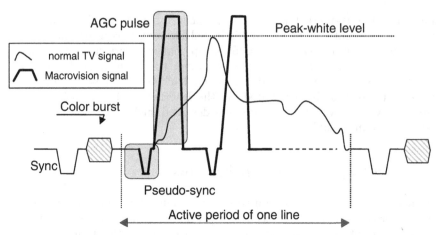

Fig. 18.1. How Macrovision changes a standard composite video signal

18.4 Digital Flags

The introduction of the CD in 1982 was very opportune to the music industry: it provided a chance to re-release their entire back catalogue. At the time, it was inconceivable that consumers would ever be able to digitally record CDs at home. This changed in 1990 with the advent of the first digital consumer recorder system, called digital audio tape (DAT). Methods like Macrovision to prevent digital copies are not easy to realize, and did not work for new digital interfaces. Then, the music and consumer electronics companies agreed on the serial copy management system (SCMS) to control copying. Essentially, SCMS is based on the use of two copy bits accompanying the content: copyrighted content on source media (e.g., CD Audio) would have these bits set to *copy once*; when feeding the content into a recorder, these bits would be changed to *copy prohibited* on the recorded media. Subsequent recorders would refuse to make second-generation copies by inspecting the SCMS bits on their digital inputs. In the United States, the SCMS system was even written into law: the Audio Home Recording Act (1992).

The SCMS system was also found to be easy to hack (a simple circuit would flip the SCMS bits to *copy once*), but the digital tapes were relatively expensive and SCMS held out. However, things got worse in the mid-1990s, when affordable CD burners (or CD writers) and ever-cheaper recordable CDs (CD-Rs) became available for PCs. Although special audio CD-Rs were introduced for use with SCMS — which carried an extra copy tax (of about €1) — PC software could be made to conveniently ignore SCMS bits, and PC writers could also use data CD-Rs (with lower levies) for making audio copies that were just as compatible.

For video content, a similar system has been introduced called the copy generation management system. Although technically weak, the SCMS and CGMS systems are widely in use today, and virtually every audio/video (A/V) transmission or media storage standard has defined a location in the stream for carrying SCMS/CGMS bits. We will have more to say about the legal mechanism behind SCSM/CGMS in the section about the legal framework of CPSs.

18.5 Copy-Protected Audio CDs

A few years after the introduction of the CD writer, a number of companies figured out ways to repeat for digital audio CDs what Macrovision's method had done for protecting analog VHS tapes. The idea was to create discs with slight violations of the CD standard chosen such that these CDs could not be read without errors in a PC (and therefore also not copied), but would play normally in regular audio CD players. Many such methods are based on manipulating *sessions*. The CD standard allows *multiple sessions* on one disc (e.g., an audio CD session which plays everywhere, followed by a data session with background information on the artist for use on the PC). Audio CD players only read the first session, but PC drives obviously try to read both. By cleverly manipulating the second session, many models of PC drives could be made to malfunction with such discs; e.g., the second session would have an illegal table of contents, or suggest yet a third session which did not exist (see, e.g., [2] for a review).

Music labels got very excited about this technology in the late 1990s but encountered a serious consumer backlash as it appeared that many non-PC consumer devices, such as DVD players or car stereos had playback problems because they tried to read these copy-protected discs in the same way as a PC. To add insult to injury, the firmware in PC drives improved over time to deal with "marginal discs" and nowadays many drives can read copy-protected discs effortlessly. Nevertheless today still quite a few new copy protected audio CDs titles are brought to the market.

18.6 Content Encryption and the Key Hierarchy

In 1996, the DVD was ready to be introduced, but the movie studios realized that, in committing movies to optical discs, they would be exposed to the same forms of copying as their music colleagues. Therefore they insisted that DVDs should be *encrypted*. Content encryption was already well known from the world of pay TV CA systems, where it had been used since the early 1990s to prevent people from watching channels they had not paid for. In its simplest form, the content would be encrypted by the content owner before transmitting it; the key used for encryption would also be present in the playback device or *set-top box* for decryption. The content in transmission would be unintelligible and therefore useless for the hacker. Similarly, content on a medium can also be encrypted, and the key only be made available to licensed devices (see Fig. 18.2). With the advent of encryption, control over the content was now in the *key management*.

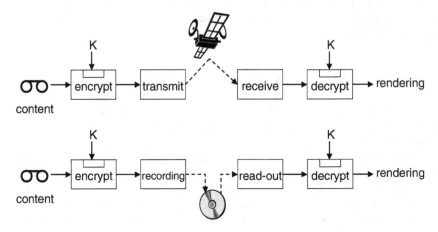

Fig. 18.2. Analogy between encryption for a Pay TV system and copy protection for media

Despite the fact that content encryption is useful for both pay TV systems and media copy-protection systems, the underlying use cases are quite different, so that as a result their key-management systems have evolved in very different directions. To understand these differences we need to study CA systems in a bit more detail [3,4]. Fig. 18.3 below describes CA systems compatible with DVB, but other CA systems work similarly. Pay TV systems are generally based on subscriptions: users only get access to the programs for which they have paid. This access is enforced by sending the set-top boxes of these users the keys for those programs only; such keys are often called *authorization keys*. The set-top box can use the authorization key to decrypt so called *control words* wrapped in encryption control messages (ECMs), which in turn decrypt the content. Control words are changed frequently (e.g., every 10 sec.) to prevent brute force attacks.

The distribution of authorization keys is also done via the broadcast channel to allow dynamic enabling/disabling of programs. To do this securely, these authorization keys are encrypted with the specific user key, which is embedded in the set-top box, or in a *smartcard* which is plugged into the set-top box. The encrypted authorization keys are transmitted in entitlement management messages (EMMs). Because there can be millions of subscribers, EMMs aimed at a specific set-top box are transmitted only rarely (e.g., once per month). The set-top box must monitor the broadcast channel continuously to receive its EMM. If a user stops paying, its EMMs are simply no longer broadcast. This is sometimes also called key revocation (the keys in the set-top box no longer work). Another reason to revoke a user key is when it is known to have been hacked out of a set-top box and distributed to others.

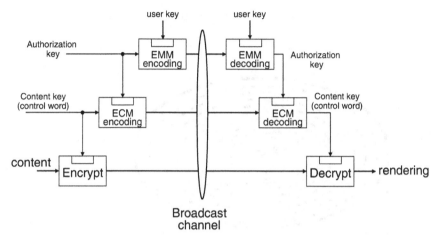

Fig. 18.3. Key management for a pay-TV CA system

A system like this does not work for content protection on physical media for at least three reasons:

1. Despite the fact that content is encrypted, the data on the media can still be copied, resulting in a copy which plays anywhere but has not been paid for. This is clearly not the intention of the content owners. To prevent such copying, the content should be *bound to the media*. In pay TV a broadcaster would generally not care if (encrypted) content were recorded and played back elsewhere. The receiving set-top box would only be able to decrypt the replayed content if it had a valid authorization key, i.e. its owner is also a subscriber[3].

2. There is no direct connection between the content distributor of physical media and the end users, so the equivalent of the EMMs has to be on the media. Because a particular disc or tape could potentially be read by hunderds of millions of players, a naive generalization of a CA system to protected media would require an inordinate amount of space on the media for key management.

3. If, as just stated, the space on physical media for enabling a new player or disabling hacked players is limited, it seems impossible for a distributor of physical media to revoke devices.

---

[3] In pay TV, the user pays for content through the playback equipment (set-top box and/or smartcard); in media distribution, the user pays through the carrier.

To solve these problems a number of techniques have been developed. Problem 1, *media-binding*, has been solved through so called *side-channels*. Problems 2 and 3 are dealt with elegantly through broadcast encryption. We will discuss them in turn in the following sections.

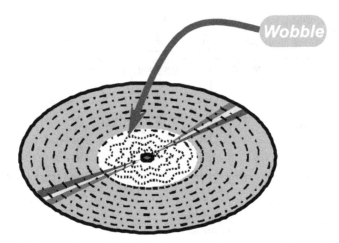

Fig. 18.4. A disc with a *wobble*. For illustrational purposes, the amplitude of the wobble has been greatly exaggerated

18.7 Media Binding

It is obvious that, to solve the problem of media binding, there needs to be some data on the media which is essential for the playback of the content, and which cannot be copied onto recordable media. From the world of PC games and games consoles there are many such examples. Essentially these methods rely on creating a physical mark on the media with professional equipment. Such a mark is sometimes also referred to as a *side-channel* as an alternative way to put data on the media. PC writers do not support writing side-channels, either because the writer is physically unable to, or because the firmware of the writer does not support it (the mark resides in an area where there is normally no user data or the mark represents a slight violation of the standard for this media type). Examples of the first category are:

- ROM wobble, see Fig. 18.4. On optical media the data (ones and zeros) are recorded in a spiral. Like an LP-record–the spiral can be recorded such that it undulates or *wobbles* a little bit. If the frequency of this wobble is in the order of a few kHz, the mechanics of the player will be too slow to follow it, but it will still show up in the error signal of the servo controlling the radial position of the read-out laser-beam. To record such a wobble, professional *laser-beam recorders* are required; PC writers cannot deflect the laser beam fast enough.

- BCA: for DVD-media the so called burst cutting area has been standardized. It is a bar-code like structure burnt into a disc with a high-power laser. The BCA is located on the very inside of the disc. It is easy to read out with the optics of a standard DVD player, but DVD burners do not have nearly enough power to burn such structures themselves. In the advanced access content system (AACS) CPS for HD-DVD [5] the BCA is used for storing a key.

Examples of the second type of side-channel include:

- Intentional errors (well-known from some game protection schemes): in a professional writer some sectors containing intentional errors are written (i.e., the error correction code (ECC) parities or an error detection code (EDC) are not consistent with the other sector data). It is easy to check on a normal player that a sector is corrupt, but normal writers do not support writing bad ECC or EDC.

- Data outside user data: besides the area for storing user data, most media also have space for storing management data to assist the player or writer. Examples are the *control* or *subcode* bytes on a CD [6,7] and the sector headers and the lead-in area on a DVD [8]. They contain data to, e.g., indicate where user data is written, how many layers are present, what the current sector address is, etc. Normal players can access these areas for read-out, but there is generally no reason for standard PC writers to give applications write access to these areas. The content scrambling system (CSS) [9] for DVD-video and content protection for prerecorded media (CPPM) [10] for DVD-audio and the video content protection system (VCPS) [11] for DVD+RW make use of this method to prevent bit-copies.

The second type of media marks are considered weaker: new writers have come to the market which do support writing such marks.

Both types of physical mark can be used in two ways in a CPS: (i) decision-based: the player only plays the content if the mark is present, and (ii) information-based: the player retrieves a payload or key from the physical mark, which is necessary for content decryption. In the case of decision-based marks, the security relies completely on the robustness of the implementation of the decisions. We will have more to say about this in the section on the legal framework.

18.8 Broadcast Encryption for Copy Protection Systems

The question that we want to address in this section is how we can enable players to decrypt content distributed via physical media. We also want to make sure that, on *new* media, hacked players are no longer able to get the decryption key. The general idea to solve this problem is as follows: there is a so-called key distribution center (KDC) which manages the distribution of keys. In the beginning, the KDC defines a (large) number of different groups of players and assigns a so-called group key to each group. Players are members of multiple groups. The group keys of all the groups of which a particular player is a member are then embedded into the player[4].

When media with new content are issued, the content is encrypted with a content key, and KDC selects N groups from the total set of predefined groups, such that:

1. the union of these N groups contains all the legitimate players; and
2. the union of these N groups does not contain any of the pirated players

A set of N *authorization records* is then stored on the media, each record containing a copy of the content key encrypted with the group key of one the different selected groups. Given the selection procedure of the groups, a legitimate player should always be able to find at least one record it can decrypt with one of the group keys that it has. This way of distributing a key is called *broadcast encryption* and the set of records is also called the *key block*. The essential problem of broadcast encryption is for the KDC to define all the groups such that, for any given set of pirated players, it is possible to satisfy the two requirements stated above, for minimum possible N.

As an example, let us consider the broadcast encryption scheme used in VCPS for DVD+R/RW discs. In VCPS, devices are represented by the leaves of a binary tree, see Fig. 18.5. The nodes of the tree have been labeled in the canonical way using numbers with binary digits. Randomly chosen keys are assigned to every node of the binary tree. Every device contains all keys on the path from its leaf to the root of the tree. In other words, in VCPS every node defines a group which contains all the devices assigned to the leaves of the full subtree rooted at that particular node.

In this example we consider a world of 16 devices. Now suppose that devices 0, 7, 8 and 9 have been revoked (their keys are exposed) and all other devices are still legitimate. New content key K can then be transmitted to the remaining devices by constructing the following key block:

$$\{ \text{E}[K_{0001}, K], \text{E}[K_{001}, K], \text{E}[K_{010}, K], \text{E}[K_{0110}, K], \text{E}[K_{101}, K], \text{E}[K_{11}, K] \}$$

---

[4] Misleadingly, these group keys are often referred to as device keys.

($E[K,M]$ denotes encryption of the plaintext message M with key K). In the picture $KA_x = E[K_x,K]$ represents an authorization record corresponding to group x. The general recipe for revoking devices [12] is to draw the paths from all the revoked devices (the dashed subtree in Fig. 18.5). The nodes directly hanging off this subtree define the set of selected groups (the doubly encircled nodes in Fig. 18.5). Within a VCPS key block, the description of the selected groups/nodes is referred to as the *tag part*, whereas the collection of authorization records is called the *key part*. There are also other choices for the authorization records, but the recipe above has minimal size[5].

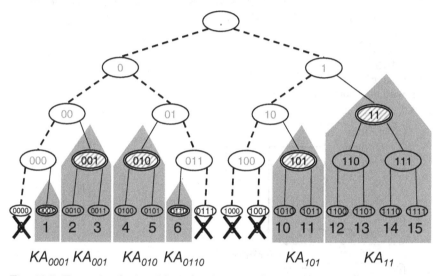

Fig. 18.5. Example of a key block for the case of 16 devices of which numbers 0, 7, 8,and 9 have been revoked

This particular flavor of broadcast encryption finds its origin in [14] and [15], and is sometimes referred to as the *complete subtree* method. In general, broadcast encryption schemes are characterized by the groups KDC can select from, i.e., which groups get keys assigned to. The selection of predefined groups represents a trade-off between the number of authorization records needed to transmit a content key securely (key block size) and the number of group keys that a device has to store: the more keys a device stores, the shorter the key block. For instance, in CSS, the CPS for DVD-video, there are only 408 groups, corresponding roughly to different manufacturers, and all players are member of only two groups [16]. In AACS [5] groups are defined on a binary tree, but they are characterized

---

[5] See [13] for an overview of how the size of the key block scales with revocation under more or less realistic assumptions.

by *two* nodes A and B, where B is a descendent of A. The group of devices consists of the leaves of the full subtree rooted at A minus the set of devices in the subtree rooted at B. This is why this system is also called the *subset-difference* method [12]. Interestingly in this scheme, the group keys are not chosen independently, but are derived from each other. In that sense this scheme goes back to the first example of broadcast encryption introduced in 1993 by Fiat and Naor [17].

Content protection for recordable media (CPRM) (CPS for DVD-RW/RAM) and aforementioned CPPM (CPS for DVD-Audio) [10], define N=16 different partitions, where every one of those partitions divides the total set of devices into M groups (M=4096 for CPRM, and M=65536 for CPPM). So in total there are $M{\times}N$ groups, and, barring some details, every player is a member of N of those.

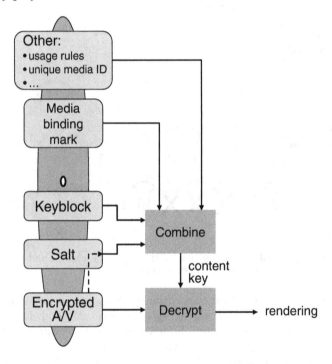

Fig. 18.6. Picture illustrating the key hierarchy for optical media

18.9 Key Hierarchy Revisited

Keys coming from ROM marks/media binding and a broadcast encryption key block are not used directly to decrypt content, but are first combined — possibly with other keys — to create the content decryption key, see Fig. 18.6. Examples of such other keys could be:

- *salt*: a random but known string, often drawn from the content itself which is introduced to prevent gigabytes of content being encrypted with the same key. The latter would facilitate certain attacks. Often this salt is changed with every sector of 2 kbytes.

- *unique media ID*: an alternative to the ROM-media binding mark on recordable discs. To enable making *protected* recordings bound to a particular piece of *recordable* media, such media is endowed with a *unique serial number*. If the content encryption key depends on this key bit copies to other recordable media are prevented.

- *usage rights*: some copy protection systems support not only usage rights as *copy never* but also *copy once* and others. To protect usage rights from being manipulated, e.g., on an open interface, these usage rights also contribute to the content encryrption key. If the usage rights are changed, the content cannot be decrypted.

18.10 Copying from Analog Outputs

Despite the substantial arsenal of methods to control copying A/V content, it is still nearly impossible to prevent leakage out of this protected domain. Given enough time and resources, determined hackers can reverse-engineer weak implementations of players to get content in plaintext, or simply point a camera/microphone at the screen/loudspeaker and post the result on the Internet and re-record on CD, DVD etc. Once content is released like this, the only thing one can do technically is to make sure that new compliant devices[6] will not play such content. The technical question is how such a device would know whether content came from a legitimate source like a home movie, or whether it was pirated. One way to achieve this is by *watermarking* all copyrighted content, i.e., invisibly hiding a signal in the content itself, in an unobtrusive but detectable way. See Chap. 19 for more details on this technology. Some of these watermarks methods are quite robust (e.g. surviving camcorder copying) and can also carry a (small) payload indicating the source of the content or the intended usage, e.g.: *copy never*, or *theatrical release*. Recording and playback devices equipped with watermark detectors can do *record control* (e.g., refusing to record a movie marked *copy never*), *or playback control* (e.g., refusing to play a movie marked *theatrical release* from a recordable disc).

A difficult problem with watermarking is enforcement, i.e., in what way to make sure that devices contain a watermark detector. Since they are not essential for content rendering, there is little incentive for manufacturers to

---

[6] A compliant devices is a device constructed such that it observes the compliance and robustness rules of a particular copy protection system, see the section on the Legal Framework.

install them in devices. Legal measures are required to get them deployed. See the section on the legal framework of CPSs.

18.11 Secure Authenticated Channels

Content should not only be prevented from being copied from one disc to the next, it should also be protected on digital connections. As with discs, this means that the content should be encrypted before crossing such a link. In addition, the source of the content should make sure that the key for decrypting this content (or essential components thereof) will not be handed to anyone but a licensed compliant receiver, i.e., the *source* should authenticate the *sink* before transferring the key. The process of authentication and exchanging keys between source and sink prior to sharing content is sometimes referred to as setting up a *secure authenticated channel* (SAC). Examples of connections requiring such measures and their SAC technologies are:

- the DVI or HDMI link between a player and a high-definition digital TV set. The protection system for this link is the high-bandwidth digital content protection system (HDCP) [18],
- the IEEE-1394 link between a set-top box and a digital recorder or between a DVD decrypter and an MPEG2 decoder in a modern car. This link can be protected with digital transmission content protection (DTCP) [19]. There is now also a version of this technology for protecting content on USB, MOST (an automotive interface), Bluetooth and IP connections (DTCP-IP),
- the ATAPI and SATA buses streaming content from the optical drive to host PC software application. All CPSs for A/V content on optical media (CSS, CPPM/CPRM, VCPS and AACS) have special protection for this link. This link is particularly dangerous because the attacker/sink does not have to be a separate hardware device but could be a software application (e.g., a driver). Note that the CPRM, VCPS and AACS systems also allow recording, so in addition they must also specify how the host application (source) can authenticate the drive (sink),
- the link in the PC between the microprocessor and the audio and graphics peripherals. To protect this link, Microsoft has introduced the Secure audio path [20] and certified output protection protocol (COPP) [21] for Windows XP, which will be succeeed by the protected media path-family of technologies in Windows Vista [22]. Note that COPP does not actually protect the content but only copy protection *metadata* such as CGMS flags and triggers for further downstream copy protection systems like HDCP.

The authentication phase is generally based on a challenge-response protocol: the source sends a randomly chosen number (challenge) to the sink, which is supposed to return a particular answer (response). Presumably only sinks with the correct key material can compute such a correct answer. In the case of CSS and CPPM/CPRM[7] this is a symmetric protocol based on a fixed shared secret. VCPS also uses symmetric cryptography, but rather than using a system secret stored in all devices, it uses a key block to share a key (see the section on broadcast encryption). Also symmetric cryptography-based HDCP avoids small system secrets by employing a variant of the Blom key distribution scheme [23-25]. Systems requiring more computational resources like AACS and DTCP[8] use public key cryptography, resisting stronger attacks.

Some of these standards include *mutual* authentication, i.e., additionally the sink also authenticates the source. This may help a legitimate sink to determine whether it is receiving content from a legitimate source. Another common step in authentication is *revocation*: although the challenge-response phase could be successfully completed, the authentication is stopped because one of the devices is known to be compromised. Obviously this is only possible in systems where device identification is part of the protocol. In a key-block-based system this is implicit (the compromised device cannot decode the key block), in others a revocation list is kept (e.g., HDCP, DTCP and AACS).

The symmetric cryptography-based systems use the random numbers exchanged as part of the challenge-response protocol to construct a *one-time* bus-key which will be used for protecting all further communication. The public-key-based systems generally use a form of the *Diffie-Hellman* key exchange protocol for establishing such a bus key. This bus key can be used to exchange a content key (DTCP, HDCP), or a component of the content key (the album identifier in CPPM, the media unique ID in CPRM, VCPS and AACS). Note that for the case where the bulk content moves from a disc to a host application, the CPSs do not need to encrypt this since the data is already stored on the media in encrypted form.

18.12 Legal Framework

As mentioned before, from the point of view of the manufacturer of media players or recorders, products with a lax implementation of the CPS will sell better. To create a level playing field, CPS implementations are subject to so-called *compliance rules* and *robustness rules*. These rules are enforced upon manufacturers through the CPS license contract (or *adopter agreement*). The manufacturer needs to sign such a contract to get access

---

[7] Note: we refer to the drive/host-SAC here; CPRM also defines a SAC between a playback/recording device and a *secure digital* (SD) memory card, but this is yet a different SAC technology which is also key block based.

[8] Strictly speaking, DTCP has two authentication modes: full and restricted. Only the full mode uses public key cryptography for authentication.

to necessary decryption keys and other trade secrets (watermark patterns), or to get a license for using patents, and copyrighted items like logos.

Compliance rules describe how the device can use the content protected by the CPS technology. Typically they list to which outputs the player can send the content, e.g., only to *standard definition* analog outputs with CGMS-A and Macrovision, or to digital outputs with an approved link protection technology like DTCP. Other rules could say that protected content may not be played from recordable media, or might also dictate that the player must search for a watermark in decrypted content and say how to respond to such a watermark (e.g., cease playback). For recorders they may also describe that, on input content has to be screened for CGMS bits and for a watermark.

Robustness rules describe how the copy protection technology is to be implemented. For example they prohibit decrypted compressed content to appear on *user-accessible buses* (e.g., PCI, or ATAPI). Also, they give an indication of how difficult it should be to break the integrity of the CPS components (change their functionality) and their confidentiality (steal keys). Robustness rules must still allow great flexibility in how these goals are achieved, and therefore, unfortunately the language of these rules is rather vague. A lot of CPS licenses classify attacker tools into three categories: widely available tools (screwdriver, soldering iron), specialized tools (EEPROM reader/writer, decompiler) and professional tools (in-circuit emulator, logic analyzer). Typically the CPS components should withstand all attacks with widely available and specialized tools, and should yield only with difficulty to professional tools.

Note that even if a CPS (like CSS) is broken — i.e., essential keys have been revealed, or a fatal flaw in the CPS design has been uncovered — it is still useful for enforcing correct behavior on the manufacturer side.

18.13 Recent Developments

In this section we summarize some of the developments of the last few years the field of copy protection.

18.13.1 Self-Protecting Digital Content

The fact that most copy protection systems have a weakest point somewhere and that it is just a matter of time for somebody to find this out, led researchers at Cryptography Research Inc. to the realization that the protection system should be *programmable*, i.e. every *title* should have its own protection system, not just every format [26]. If there is a weakness in a particular implementation, this could be accounted for in new titles. To make this system practical, every player consists of a virtual machine which runs dedicated code accompanying the content. This code computes a content decryption key based on device keys, and other cryptographic material present in the box. This system is marketed under the name Self-Protecting Digital Content, and a variant of this is being considered for the Blu-ray disc[9] protection system.

18.3.2 Digital Rights Protection on Media

Slowly new media copy protection systems are appearing which feature more advanced rights from the world of DRM, e.g., in the Philips/Sony protected data storage system [27] and AACS [5] it is possible to record content with usage rights, such as *move allowed*, *play 2×*, and *play until Wednesday*. But putting DRM-like rights on media creates a new challenge: the subset of so called *stateful rights* (e.g., play 2× and move allowed) are vulnerable to a *save-and-restore attack*. Before the right to play is consumed, the user makes a complete back-up of the disc. Then, after the rights are used up, the original image is restored. A way to prevent this rollback is to use a sort of media mark again. The idea is that (as in media marks for ROM) some part of the content decryption key is derived from a signal which is outside the main channel. This subchannel is intentionally modified by the writer when a right is consumed. The user may have an interface to restore a disc image, but not to revert to a previous value of the subchannel. Thus the restored rights do not work anymore.

18.3.3 Tracing Traitors

In a previous section we have discussed revocation. Of course revocation only works if we know which devices to revoke. That may not be so easy if the hackers publish the content key rather than their group keys. The authors of [28] propose a way to solve this problem going back to a method published in 2000 [29]: the idea is that some part of the content is stored on the media multiple times each time encrypted with a different key, and watermarked with a different mark. Players only have keys to decrypt one of the variants, so e.g., if a movie subjected to this scheme appeared on the Internet, the watermark in the redundantly recorded scenes would give away some information about the perpetrating device. With enough such scenes in a movie, or with multiple hacked movies, the key distribution center can determine the exact player with a high degree of certainty, and it can be revoked. A difficult problem with schemes of this kind is *collusion*: groups of hackers work together and mix part of their stolen content, in order to confuse the key distribution organization. The literature on how to encrypt the content *variants* such that the result is maximally resistant against collusion is an active research topic at the moment,

---

[9] Blu-ray disc is a successor to DVD featuring full high-definition video, interactivity with a Java virtual machine, network connections, and local storage, see http://www.bluraydisc.com

see, e.g., [30,31]. In general, greater collusion resistance requires more variants and more parts of the content which are recorded redundantly, i.e., a trade-off between security and space on the media.

References

1. http://www.repairfaq.org/filipg/LINK/F_MacroVision2.html
2. J.A. Halderman, Evaluating New Copy-Prevention Techniques for Audio CDs. In: Proc. of the 2002 ACM Workshop on Digital Rights Management, Lecture Notes in Computer Science; Vol. 2696. Springer, Berlin Heidelberg New York, pp. 101-117, and
http://www.cs.princeton.edu/~jhalderm/papers/drm2002.pdf
3. B. Macq, J.J. Quisquater (1995) Cryptology for Digital TV Broadcasting. Proc. of the IEEE 83:944-957
4. W. Jonker, J.P. Linnartz (2004) Digital Rights Management in Consumer Electronics Products. IEEE Signal Processing Magazine 21:84-91
5. http://www.aacsla.com
6. IEC 908 Compact disc digital audio system, 1987
7. ISO/IEC 10149IEC and ECMA-130: Data interchange on read-only 120 mm optical data disks (CD-ROM); see: http://www.ecma-international.org/publications/standards/Ecma-130.htm
8. ECMA-267: 120 mm DVD - Read-Only Disk, see
http://www.ecma-international.org/publications/standards/Ecma-267.htm
9. http://www.cs.cmu.edu/~dst/DeCSS
10. Copy Protection for Recordable Media and Copy Protection for Prerecorded Media, see http://www.4centity.com/tech/cprm/
11. Philips & HP, System Description Video Content Protection System, Version 1.32, see http://www.licensing.philips.com/vcps
12. D. Naor, M. Naor, J.B. Lotspiech (2001) Revocation and Tracing for Stateless Receivers. In: Proc. 21st Annual Int. Cryptology Conf. on Adv. in Cryptology, Lecture Notes In Computer Science; Vol. 2139. Springer, Berlin Heidelberg New York, pp. 41- 62
13. T. Staring, B. Skoric (2006) Revocation in the Video Content Protection System. In: 2006 Digest of Technical Papers, International Conference on Consumer Electronics, pp. 105-106
14. D.M. Wallner, E.J. Harder and R.C. Agee (1999) Key Management for Multicast: Issues and Architectures. Internet RFC 2627
15. C.K. WongK, M. Gouda and S. Lam (1998) Secure Group Communications Using Key Graphs. In: Proc. ACM SIGCOMM '98 conference. ACM Press, New York, pp. 68-79
16. http://www.eff.org/IP/Video/DVDCCA_case/20011128'bunner_sum_judg_motion.html section II A
17. A. Fiat, M. Naor (1993) Broadcast Encryption. In: Proc. 13th Annual Int. Cryptology Conf. on Adv. in Cryptology, Lecture Notes in Computer Science; Vol. 773. Springer, Berlin Heidelberg New York, pp. 480—491
18. http://www.digital-cp.com/home
19. http://www.dtcp.com/

20. http://msdn.microsoft.com/library/default.asp?url=/library/en-us/wmrm10/htm/understandingsecureaudiopathbyprotectingdigitalmed.asp
21. http://msdn.microsoft.com/library/default.asp?url=/library/en-us/dnwmt/html/using_certified_output_protection_protocol_copp_bwjn.asp
22. http://www.microsoft.com/whdc/device/stream/output_protect.mspx
23. R. Blom (1982) Non-public key distribution. In: Rivest et al. (eds.) Proc. CRYPTO 82. Plenum Press, New York, pp. 231–236
24. R. Blom (1984) An optimal class of symmetric key generation systems. In: Beth et al. (eds.) Advances in Cryptology: Proc. of EUROCRYPT 84, Lecture Notes in Computer Science; Vol. 209. Springer, Berlin Heidelberg New York, pp. 335-338
25. A cryptanalysis of the HDCP scheme has appeared in http://www.cs.berkeley.edu/~rtjohnso/papers/hdcp.ps
26. See also http://www.cryptography.com/technology/spdc/index.html
27. T. Staring et al. (2003), Protected data storage system for optical discs. In 2003 Digest of Technical Papers, International Conference on Consumer Electronics, pp. 332-333
28. H. Jin, J. Lotspiech, S. Nusser (2004), Traitor tracing for prerecorded and recordable media. In: proceedings of the 4th ACM workshop on Digital rights management. ACM Press, New York, pp. 83-90
29. J. Benaloh (2000), Key Compression and its Application to Digital Fingerprinting, Technical report, Microsoft Research. See also http://www.waea.org/tech/working_groups/dvd/1999/DVD99CFCR03-2_Microsoft.pdf
30. A. Barg et al. (2003) Digital fingerprinting codes: problem statements, constructions, identification of traitors. IEEE Trans. Information Theory 49:852-865
31. G. Tardos (2003) Optimal Probabilistic Fingerprint Codes. In: Proc. 35th annual ACM Symp. on Theory of Computing. ACM Press, New York, pp. 116-125

Forensic Watermarking in Digital Rights Management

Michiel van der Veen, Aweke Lemma, Mehmet Celik, and Stefan Katzenbeisser

Philips Research
The Netherlands

Summary. In this chapter, we give a brief introduction to digital watermarking and discuss its applications in DRM systems. Watermarks are particularly useful in DRM systems due to their ability to bridge the gap between analog and digital domains. In playback control applications, a watermark is embedded in the master copy of a content and encodes associated usage rules, which are enforced by compliant devices during playback. On the other hand, in forensic tracking applications, a unique watermark is embedded in each individual copy of the content; this watermark allows the authorities to identify the source of an illegal copy. After discussing the basic principles of spread spectrum watermarks, we outline the architecture of an online content distribution system that employs watermarks in order to enable forensic tracking.

19.1 From Playback Control Watermarks to Forensic Watermarks

Digital rights management (DRM) systems are designed to protect and enforce the rights associated with digital media content such as audio, video or still images. Much of this work was inspired by the introduction of optical discs (such as the CD or the DVD) and the utilization of digital distribution channels. Typically, a content owner sells content to a potentially untrusted consumer, who is not allowed to further distribute the content. DRM systems enforce this requirement by utilizing encryption and authentication procedures (such as link encryption, player authentication and the like). Even though encryption can secure digital content during transmission between digital devices, the content eventually needs to be presented to the consumer in decrypted format (in-the-clear) as an analog video or audio signal. These analog signals are vulnerable to copying and redistribution and may eventually re-enter a digital distribution chain through the use of recording devices.

In the late 1990s, digital watermarking technologies were proposed to enforce copyright rules of optical discs, even in the case of such analog copies

[19]. Watermarking allows one to embed an information signal in a host audio-visual signal by means of non-obtrusive modifications. Leaving the details for Sect. 19.2, watermark embedding and detection works in the manner as sketched in Fig. 19.1. A message m, which could represent copyright information, is embedded in the host signal x using a secret watermarking key k, to obtain the watermarked signal y. This watermarked signal is distributed and during its lifetime may undergo various intentional or unintentional signal processing operations, such as compression, digital-to-analog (DA) and analog-to-digital (AD) conversion, temporal modifications, or geometrical distortions. It is the challenge of the detector to recover, given the secret watermarking key k, an estimate m' of the originally embedded message from the distorted watermarked signal y'. A watermarking scheme is robust, if the detector succeeds in recovering m, i.e., if $m' = m$.

The ability to embed messages to survive even if the host signal is converted to analog makes them a suitable candidate for enforcing copyright rules beyond analog copying. The principle idea behind the proposal in [19] is the concept of *compliant* players, which detect the embedded watermarks and comply with the associated rules. In this context, all commercial content is embedded with a playback control watermark and encrypted before distribution. As a condition for accessing the associated decryption keys, all players are required to:

- encrypt all digital outputs,
- detect digital watermarks at all analog and unencrypted digital inputs, and prevent playback and further copying if a playback control watermark is found.

When commercial content is leaked through an analog output and gets redistributed, the embedded watermark prevents its playback on compliant players. This effectively limits the usability of analog copies and enforces the usage rules beyond the analog conversion. Note that noncommercial content created by the consumers, such as home videos, does not bear playback watermarks. Therefore, it can be played back and copied without restrictions.

Despite many standardization efforts like the secure digital music initiative (SDMI) [26] and the data-hiding sub-group (DHSG) and watermarking review panel (WaRP) video watermark selection committees, playback control watermarks have not been deployed on a large scale. Principal hurdles have been security issues of digital watermarking systems, standardization problems and low customer acceptance of compliant devices.

In contrast to playback watermarks, which eventually restrict the portability of content, digital watermarks—and the messages embedded thereby—can also be employed for forensic tracking purposes[1]. This usage model has been

---

[1] Note that in the literature forensic watermarks are also called fingerprints or active fingerprints. However, due to possible confusion with passive fingerprinting technologies, which can be used to identify objects based on their intrinsic properties, we prefer the term forensic watermark.

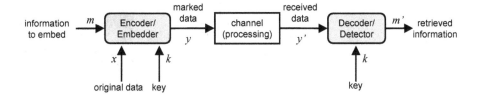

Fig. 19.1. Basic model for digital watermarking.

mainly motivated by consumers' desire to enjoy the content on a multitude of devices, including legacy devices, where enforcing compliance with playback watermarks is not feasible. Forensic tracking DRM models have been further bolstered by the tremendous increase in the popularity of online music distribution. Besides the early peer-to-peer systems like Napster, KaZaa, Gnutella and BitTorrent, today various legal commercial music download services (such as iTunes, Rhapsody, Emusic, Walmart, iMusic etc.) offer a wide selection of digital content for consumers. Soon, we will witness a similar trend in electronic video distribution as a result of further infrastructure improvements, higher broadband penetration, and better video compression algorithms.

DRM schemes for electronic content distribution, whether music or video, need to balance the interests of both the consumers and the content owners. While the consumers demand the right to freely control the media content they paid for, the content industry is wary of illegal distribution of their copyrighted material and demand strong assurances. One approach to balance these interests is to use a DRM model based on *forensic tracking* watermarks [7, 33]. The general concept of such a DRM system is presented in Fig. 19.2. Using the Internet, content is distributed from the content owner's database to that of the consumer. The content in this database can be freely used by the consumer on any of his playback devices. Prior to distribution, however, the content is marked with a unique watermark, which represents the identity of the user or a transaction code that can be linked to the user's identity. If the user distributes the content in violation of the usage rules agreed with the content owner, this watermark can be detected in the distributed copy. In that case, it allows the authorities to trace the violation back to its source, the consumer who illegally distributed the content. The most important advantage of forensic tracking watermarking is that it is completely transparent to honest users and offers great flexibility in terms of consumer actions. At the same time, it allows content owners to enforce their copyrights by tracing users who violate the distribution restrictions.

In the next section we give a brief outline of basic principles and concepts in digital watermarking. In the subsequent section, inspired by the work in [33], we will discuss how forensic tracking watermarks can be deployed effectively in client–server distribution models.

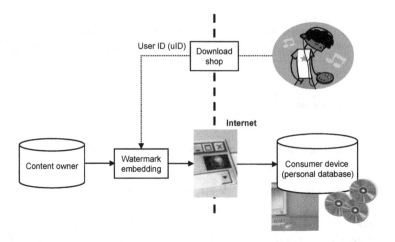

Fig. 19.2. Basic DRM model for electronic content distribution deploying forensic watermark technology.

19.2 Digital Watermarking: How Does it Work?

The purpose of watermarking is to establish a communication channel within a host signal (for example, digital content in a DRM system) such that the information transmitted therein is inseparable from the signal, which can be achieved through making small, unobtrusive modifications on the host signal. Furthermore, the embedded information should survive degradation of the content and at the same time should resist removal or access by unauthorized users.

19.2.1 Requirements

Practical watermarking schemes should fulfill four major requirements:

- **Transparency.** Unlike other communication channels where the transmission medium can be utilized liberally, the watermark channel is expected to be transparent. That is, the watermark should not degrade the quality or the usability of the host signal. In practical applications involving audio-visual signals, this requirement translates into perceptual transparency in subjective tests. When presented with the watermarked signal, a human observer should not be able to distinguish it from the non-watermarked (original) host signal. This requirement often brings along the use of perceptual models in watermark embedders. A good model of the human visual/auditory system enables optimum exploitation of human perception and maximizes the channel capacity subject to perceptual transparency constraints.

- **Robustness.** Digital watermarks' ability to withstand degradation of the host signal and resist unauthorized removal are the properties that make them useful, especially in DRM applications that involve hostile attackers. The set of signal processing operations that the host signal may undergo without destroying or disabling the embedded information depends on the application scenario. When watermarks are used for copyright protection systems, e.g., playback control or forensic tracking applications, the watermark should be detectable even after a considerable degradation in the quality of the host signal. Generally, whether malicious or not, any processing of the watermarked host signal should not damage or destroy the embedded information without rendering the host signal useless for consumption.[2]

  In many practical applications, robust audio watermarks are required to withstand multiple cycles of D/A-A/D conversion, graphic equalization, linear speed changes, band-pass filtering, different compression methods at various bit rates, noise addition, timescale modifications, down mixing, sample rate conversion or dynamic range reduction. Similarly, robust video watermarks may be required to be robust against D/A-A/D conversion, frame-rate changes, translation, scaling, partial cropping, rotation, and different compression algorithms.

- **Capacity.** In general, the robustness of watermarks against a wide range of attacks comes at the expense of the channel capacity, i.e., the amount of information that can be conveyed within the host signal. Depending on the severity of the attacks, the typical capacity for an audio watermark may be as low as 1-2 bits/sec [23]. On the other hand, if the robustness requirements are relaxed, the capacity may be several bits per second, e.g., 10-20 bits/sec [15, 10], or it may even be in the order of 100 kbits/sec [21], especially in the absence of hostile attackers. Similar trade-offs exists for video watermarks.

  In the playback control application mentioned in the previous section, the video watermark supports 8 bits per 10 seconds [19]. On the other hand, the payload requirement for digital cinema forensic tracking application is 35 bits per 5 minutes for both audio and video watermarks [9].

- **Complexity.** Digital watermarks are often utilized in consumer markets for the protection of commercial content which is distributed on a mass scale. When paired with the cost sensitivity of consumer electronics, this often implies severe complexity limitations for digital watermarks. Nonetheless, the complexity requirements may be asymmetric between the embedder and the detector, depending on the application.

---

[2] Digital watermarks may also be used for tamper detection, where the purpose of the watermark is to identify unauthorized manipulations on the content. In tamper detection applications, e.g., verifying integrity of police photographs when used as evidence, the watermarks are designed to be fragile to certain predefined data modifications such that the loss of the watermark indicates tampering.

In playback control watermarking, embedding is performed offline and only once during mastering on professional equipment which may tolerate high complexity. Contrarily, the detector is placed in every consumer device and has to perform detection during every playback with minimal complexity. For instance, the playback control watermark detector of [19] can be implemented in silicon with only 15k gates and is suitable for inclusion in DVD players.

In forensic tracking watermarking, the complexity requirements are reversed. Embedding is performed online for every copy of the content sold and is required to be simple. On the other, detection is performed offline, only when a pirated copy is found. Therefore, forensic tracking watermarks may involve more-elaborate detection schemes that counter an even wider range of malicious attacks.

- **Security** According to [14], watermark security refers to the inability of unauthorized users to: (i) remove, (ii) detect and estimate, (iii) write, or (iv) modify the original watermark message. It is important to note that, according to this definition, watermark security is not related to the semantics of the message, but only to its physical presence (as cryptographic tools may be deployed to protect the semantics of the message). Therefore, the general aim of a malicious attacker is to: (i) remove (ii) change or (iii) embed a watermark such that its effectiveness is undermined, its detectability is disabled, or its general application is discouraged. Adopting Kerkhoffs' principle [25] of cryptography, we assume that an attacker has knowledge of all the details of the embedding and detection algorithms. The security of the watermark should therefore rely only on the secrecy of the watermark keys.

19.2.2 Spread Spectrum Watermarking

In the literature [5, 28, 12, 31, 18], many different watermarking techniques are discussed. Among others, *spread spectrum* watermarks [4, 17, 19] are widely used. These are a class of watermarking schemes that add a predefined wideband noise pattern (controlled by the watermarking key) to audio-visual content such that the changes are unobtrusive. Information is transmitted by modulating the noise pattern with the information signal (payload). The basic principle of a spread spectrum watermark (WM) embedder is shown in Fig. 19.3.

In its simplest form, watermark embedding can be done by adding it to the content x. In this case, the watermark signal y is given by

$$y = x + \alpha w(pL), \tag{19.1}$$

where α is a global gain, preferably controlled by human visual or auditory models. This parameter controls the trade-off between the transparency and the robustness of the watermark. The watermark $w(pL)$ is a function of the

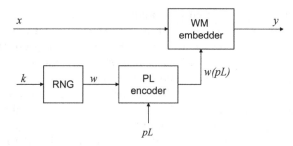

Fig. 19.3. Basic spread spectrum watermark embedder.

payload pL one wishes to embed in a digital signal. In a spread spectrum watermark system, one commonly used payload encoding method is the circular shifting technique. In this approach, given the reference watermark (spreading) pattern w, the payload is encoded by circular shifts of the pattern, where each possible shift corresponds to a different payload value. This technique can be used both for one-dimensional signals such as audio [18, 31] and for two-dimensional signals such as images and video [19]. In the latter case, the payload value is defined by the ordered pair of horizontal and vertical shift amounts $pL = (horz_{shift}, vert_{shift})$.

19.2.3 Spread Spectrum Watermark Detection

In principle, a spread spectrum watermarking system can be seen as a code division multiple-access (CDMA) communication system [24, 8, 29, 20], where the random sequence w corresponds to the spreading sequence and pL corresponds to the communicated signal. Furthermore, the host signal x corresponds to the channel noise that is much stronger than the information signal (the watermark). Similar to CDMA communication systems, matched filters can be used to detect the watermark and extract the information therefrom. A generic spread spectrum watermark detector is shown in Fig. 19.4. From the

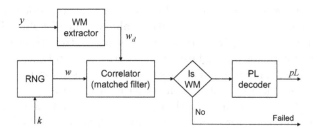

Fig. 19.4. Basic spread spectrum watermark detector.

potentially watermarked signal y a candidate watermark w_d is extracted. If the embedder works according to (19.1), then the watermark extraction block in Fig. 19.4 reduces to the identity operation. After this step, the extracted watermark w_d is correlated with circularly shifted versions of the reference watermark w. The shifting parameters that yield the highest correlation are considered to be an estimate of the watermark payload. Figure 19.5 illustrates this operation, showing a typical two-dimensional correlation function and the interpretation of payload; in this example $pL = (30, 40)$.

The height of the correlation peak is commonly referred to as the confidence level and is a measure of the reliability of the detection. The watermark is said to be detected if the correlation peak is larger than a certain threshold, which is fixed during system setup as a function of the desired failure rates as explained below. This process of detecting the presence of a watermark can

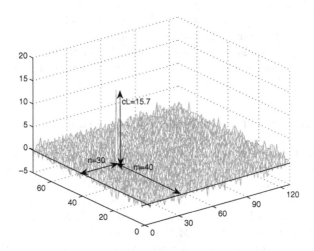

Fig. 19.5. Output of correlation.

be seen as a hypothesis test [30]. If the watermark is embedded in the shift considered (hypothesis H_1), the correlation value will be distributed around a certain mean, which is determined by the embedding strength, with a certain variance, which depends on the host signal distribution and the extent of processing the content undergoes. This distribution is illustrated by the curve on the right-hand side in Fig. 19.6. On the other hand, if no watermark has been embedded in the content (hypothesis H_0), then the correlation value will be distributed around zero (assuming a zero-mean signal or watermark spreading sequence) with a variance which depends on the host signal distribution. The corresponding distribution is illustrated on the left-hand side in Fig. 19.6.

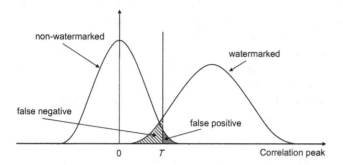

Fig. 19.6. Distribution of correlation values under H_0 and H_1. Area under the tails represent the false positive and false negative rates.

The shaded regions correspond to the probability of making wrong decisions. The crosshatched region is the probability of failing to detect a watermark in a watermarked content (when H_1 is true), which is usually referred to as the false negative probability. Conversely, the dark shaded region corresponds to the probability of detecting a watermark in non-watermarked content (when H_0 is true), which is referred to as the false positive probability. Note that these probabilities are a function of the threshold value T used in making decisions. Different pairs of false positive and false negative probabilities can be obtained by varying the threshold, as seen in Fig. 19.7.

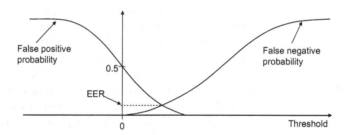

Fig. 19.7. False positive rate and false negative rate as functions of detection threshold.

The value at which the two probability curves cross each other is referred to as the equal error rate (EER), which is the optimum point if both types of errors are equally costly. Generally, EER is used to compare the performance of competing algorithms. In practical copy protection applications, however, the cost of making a false positive decision (declaring that a watermark is present when there is none) is much higher than the cost of false negatives. For instance, in forensic tracking applications, accusing an innocent user (a false positive) undermines the credibility of the whole system, whereas failing to accuse a guilty one (a false negative) only affects one instance with a single piece of content. In both playback control and forensic tracking applications, the thresholds are set to guarantee a fixed small false positive rate while trying to minimize the false negative rates. As the false positive rates are only dependent on host signal characteristics (not on what a malicious attacker may do to remove the watermark), fixing the false positive rate is also more practical.

19.3 Client-Server Architecture with Forensic Watermarking

In this section we will introduce and discuss a general architecture that facilitates the forensic tracking DRM model of Fig. 19.2. The concrete implementation of this architecture highly depends on the content distribution model. For illustrative purposes, we make the following assumptions:

1. Content distribution is performed in a client-server architecture in which the number of distribution servers is much smaller than the number of clients. In particular, we do not consider peer-to-peer networks.
2. The distribution links from the servers to the clients are secure and authenticated.
3. All delivered content is marked with a transaction-dependent watermark, encoding an ID of the transaction.

A sketch of a generalized architecture based on these assumptions is presented in Fig. 19.9. At the server, the multimedia content is available in the desired compressed format (e.g., MP3, MPEG, AAC, DIVX, etc). At the time of a download request, compressed content is watermarked with a transaction ID (tID). This ID may include or may be associated with other information such as a user ID (uID), a content ID (cID) or a time-stamp. The transaction ID as well as all accompanying information are stored in a transaction table, which is used to track down the guilty customer if an infringement occurs. Finally, the watermarked content is sent to the client through a secure and authenticated link. The client receives the encrypted and watermarked content. At this point we do not differentiate between the option of storing the content in encrypted form at the client or having it in the clear. In practical systems that are on the market today we see both variants occurring. In the following sections, we address the complexity and security issues of the proposed architecture.

19.3.1 Secure Distribution

Security is an important issue in any DRM system as it enables trusted exchange of information between the parties involved. Unfortunately state-of-the-art watermarking techniques do not reach a level of security which is

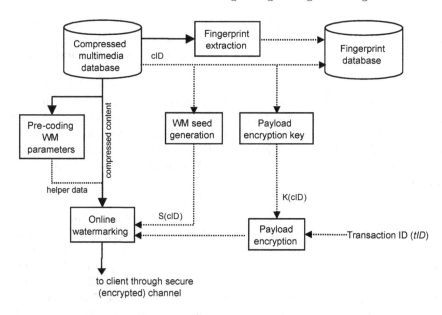

Fig. 19.8. Watermark embedding mechanism. Figure adapted from [33].

comparable to those of cryptographic algorithms. It should be assumed that malicious attackers are able, with major or minor efforts, to attack the watermark. Therefore, in our approach, we do not attempt to make the system provably secure, but concentrate on introducing measures to make malicious attacks as difficult as possible. We address the following two most important attack scenarios:

1. **Copy attacks.** In this attack [16], a watermark is estimated and *transplanted* from one watermarked piece of content to another one. As a result, the watermark payload no longer points to the correct user and transaction ID, thereby compromising the forensic tracking ability.
2. **Watermark payload rendering.** In this attack, the embedded watermark is modified in such a way that the payload points to a different transaction. Again, this compromises forensic tracking.

Figure 19.8 shows a more detailed description of the distribution server, which implements countermeasures against these two attacks. To prevent the copy attack, we make the watermark content dependent. We use spread spectrum watermarks (see Sect. 19.2), whose associated basic watermark patterns w are generated using a pseudo-random number generator from a specific seed S. Specifically, we choose S such that

$$S = G(cID), \tag{19.2}$$

where G is a hash function. In this manner, the watermark is tied to one specific piece of content. Estimating and transplanting the watermark to different content will lead to either a detection failure or to an invalid combination of cID and S.

The watermark payload rendering attack can be prevented by using a sparse representation for the watermark payload (see below) and a further layer of encryption. Suppose that E denotes an encryption function and $K(cID)$ is the encryption key derived from the content identification number (a detailed description of the key derivation process is beyond the scope of this chapter), then we choose the watermark payload pL to have the following structure:

$$pL = E_{K(cID)}(tID, 0000, CRC), \tag{19.3}$$

where CRC represents a cyclic redundancy code of tID. Zero padding and the CRC code are introduced to make the set of valid payloads sparse in the space of all possible bit-sequences: maliciously modifying the encrypted payload will most likely also modify at least one of the zero padding bits or the CRC. Detection of non-zero padding bits or an invalid CRC indicates that the payload was tampered with and is not valid for further use. Note that zero-padding is given here as an optional functionality, since a modification of tID will also result in mismatch with the associated cID and other information with high probability.

In order to compute the payload according to (19.2) and (19.3), it is necessary to know the content identification number cID, which determines both the encryption key $K(cID)$ and the watermark seed S. At the time of embedding, the identification number may be extracted from meta-data stored alongside the compressed multimedia data. However, at the time of watermark detection, the content may have been subjected to various intentional or unintentional attacks. Among others, any meta-data could have been stripped from the media file. Therefore, we need a robust identification mechanism at the detector to identify the received content and reliably reconstruct cID therefrom. This mechanism can be based on the audio fingerprint algorithm proposed in [11]; alternatively content could be identified on the basis of content semantics from a database with human assistance. While building the media database during set-up, a fingerprint, comprised of characteristic audio features, is derived from the content and stored in a separate database; this fingerprint uniquely identifies a song without resorting to meta-data. The forensic watermark detector makes use of this fingerprint database in order to identify incoming media signals and compute associated watermark seeds and encryption keys.

19.3.2 Efficient Watermark Embedding

In the proposed DRM system, the efficiency of the server is of crucial importance; one server should be able to serve as many clients as possible. Considering the architecture of Fig. 19.9, we notice that most of the computational

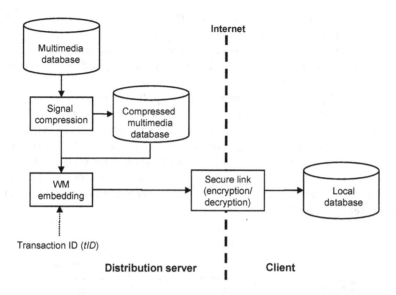

Fig. 19.9. Generalized architecture for distributing multimedia content in a client-server setting. Figure adapted from [33].

effort on the server side is spent on watermark embedding. Thus, the watermark embedder should be constructed in such a way that multiple users can be served at the same time, and that the effective download time is minimized.

Only a few papers are dedicated to the efficiency of the watermark embedding process. In 2000, Crowcroft [6] was the first to file a patent application on efficient watermark embedding for spread-spectrum based algorithms. Two copies of a single song are embedded with different watermarks. At the time of distribution, a switch takes the two watermark signals as inputs and multiplexes them into a single new watermark signal. The switch controls the effective payload (see also [3]). In line with this concept, [27] introduced the digital container scenario, and [1] demonstrated the multiplexing concept for an FFT-based audio watermark algorithm. Another contribution to the efficiency problem originates from [22]. Based on the original ideas from [6], they propose an efficient watermark architecture in a multi-cast distribution scenario.

19.3.3 Forensic Watermark Detector

The *forensic watermark tracker*, shown in Fig. 19.10, can be used to detect watermarks in allegedly illegal content. Since embedded watermarks are content dependent, we first extract the fingerprint of the incoming content in order to reconstruct the content identification number cID. This number is mapped to a watermark seed S, which is then used by a (correlation) detector to extract the watermark. A successful detection will result in a payload, representing the encrypted transaction number tID, see (19.3). Using the encryption key, the transaction number can be reconstructed. In turn, by utilizing the transaction table stored at the servers, this ID can be mapped to a user ID, a content ID and a time-stamp.

A number of postprocessing steps can be applied in order to check the reliability of the recovered data. First, it should be checked whether the content IDs originating from the fingerprint and from the transaction table match. In the case of a mismatch, this indicates a tampered watermark. Furthermore, the zero-padding and the CRC code in (19.3) should be verified. If, in addition to these constraints, the confidence level of the watermark detector is sufficiently high, then the forensic tracker has succeeded in finding the origin of the content in question.

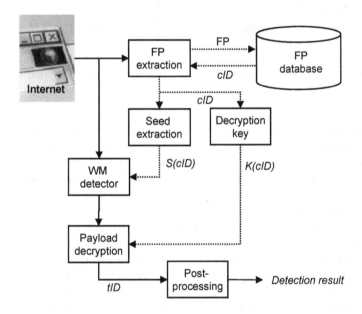

Fig. 19.10. Functional architecture of the forensic watermark tracker. Figure adapted from [33].

19.4 Conclusions

In this chapter, we have shown how digital watermarks can be utilized in DRM systems to enforce usage rules across digital and analog domains. In particular, we discussed the use of watermarks in forensic tracking applications.

We believe that forensic tracking functionality is an opportunity to balance the consumers' desire to enjoy content without restrictions and the content owners' interests in preventing illegal distribution. We anticipate that forensic tracking DRM systems will be instrumental to the further growth of the electronic content distribution market.

References

1. M. Arnold, and Z. Huang, "Fast audio watermarking concepts and realizations", Electronic Imaging 2004, Security and Watermarking of Multimedia Content VI, San Jose, USA, 2004.
2. E. Becker, W. Buhse, D. Gnnewig, N. Rump (editors), Digital rights management: Technological, Economic, Legal and Political Aspects, Springer Verlag, Berlin 2003.
3. J. Benaloh, "Key Compression and its Application to Digital Finger-printing", Technical report, Microsoft Research, 2000.
4. I.J. Cox, J. Kilian, F.T. Leighton and T. Shamoon, "Secure spread spectrum watermarking for multimedia", IEEE Transactions on Image Processing, Volume 6, pp. 1673–1687, 1997.
5. I. Cox, M. Miller, and J. Bloom, "Digital Watermarking." San Francisco, Morgan Kauffman, 2002.
6. J. Crowcroft, C. Perkins, and I. Brown, "A method and apparatus for generating multiple watermarked copies of an information signal," WO patent application 00/56059, 2000.
7. S. Czerwinski, R. Fromm, T. Hodes, "Digital music distribution and audio watermarking", UCB IS 219, technical report, 1999.
8. V. M. Dasilva and E. S. Sousa, "Multicarrier orthogonal CDMA signals for quasisynchronous communication systems", IEEE Journal on Selected Areas in Communications, vol. 12, pp. 842–852, 1994.
9. Digital Cinema Initiatives LLC, "Digital Cinema System Specification, v1.0", July 2005, available at http://www.dcimovies.com/.
10. J. Fridrich and M. Goljan, "Comparing Robustness of Watermarking Techniques", Electronic Imaging'99, The International Society of Optical Engineering, Security and Watermarking of Multimedia Contents, Vol. 3657, San Jose, CA, 1999.
11. J. Haitsma and A.A.C. Kalker, "A highly-robust audio fingerprinting system with efficient search strategy," 3rd international conference on music information retrieval, Paris, France, 2002.
12. F. Hartung and M.Kutter, "Multimedia watermarking techniques", Proc. IEEE, vol. 87, pp. 1079–1107, 1999.
13. W. Jonker and J. Linnartz, Digital Rights Management in Consumer Electronics Products, IEEE Signal Processing Magazine, Special Issue on Digital Rights Management, vol. 21, no. 2, pp. 82-91, 2003.
14. T. Kalker, Considerations on Watermark Security, IEEE Workshop on Multimedia Signal Processing, October, 2002.
15. M. Kutter and F.A.P. Petitcolas, "A Fair Benchmark for Image Watermarking Systems", Electronic Imaging'99, The International Society of Optical Engineering, Security and Watermarking of Multimedia Contents, Vol. 3657, San Jose, CA, 1999.

16. M. Kuter, S. Voloshynovskiy, A. Herrigel, "The watermark copy attack," Electronic Imaging 2000, Security and Watermarking of Multimedia Content II, San Jose, USA, 2000.
17. G. Langelaar, I. Setyawan, and R. Lagendijk, "Watermarking digital image and video data: a state-of-the-art overview", IEEE Signal Processing Magazine, vol. 17, pp. 20–46, 2000.
18. A.N. Lemma, J. Aprea, W. Oomen and L. van de Kerkhof, "A temporal domain audio watermarking technique", IEEE Transactions on Signal Processing, Vol. 51, No. 4, pp. 1088–1097, April, 2003.
19. M. Maes, T. Kalker, J.-P.M.G. Linnartz, J. Talstra, F.G. Depovere and J. Haitsma, "Digital watermarking for DVD video copy protection", IEEE Signal Processing Magazine, Volume 17, Issue 5, pp. 47–57, 2000.
20. B. G. Mobasseri, "Exploring CDMA for watermarking of digital video", Proceedings of the SPIE, vol. 3657, pp. 96–102, 1999.
21. A.W.J. Oomen, M.E. Groenewegen, R.G. van der Waal and R.N.J. Veldhuis, "A Variable-Bit-Rate Buried-Data Channels for Compcact Disc", In the Proceedings of the 96th AES convention, Amsterdam, 1994.
22. R. Parviainen and P. Parnes, "Large scale distributed watermarking of multicast through encryption", in Communications and multimedia security issues of the new century, Kluwer, pp. 149-158, 2001.
23. F. A. P. Petitcolas and R. J. Anderson, Weaknesses of Copyright marking systems, Multimedia and Security Workshop, ACM Multimedia'98, Bristol, UK, September 1998.
24. R. Prasad and S. Hara, "Overview of multicarrier CDMA", IEEE Communications Magazine, pp. 126–133, Dec. 1997.
25. B. Schneier, Applied Cryptography, New York, Wiley, 1997.
26. Secure Digital Music Initiative (SDMI), Call for Proposals for Phase II Screening Technology, Version 1.0, February 24, 2000.
27. M. Steinebach, S. Zmudzinski, F. Chen, "The digital watermarking container: Secure and Efficient Embedding," Proceedings of the Multimedia and Security Workshop, Magdeburg, Germany, 2004.
28. M. Swanson, M. Kobayashi, and A. Tewfik, "Multimedia data-embedding and watermarking technologies", Proc. IEEE, vol. 86, no. 6, pp. 1064–1087, June 1998.
29. L. Vandendorpe, "Multitone spread spectrum multiple access communications system in a multipath Rician fading channel", IEEE Trans. Veh. Technol., vol. 44, pp. 327–337, 1995.
30. H.L. van Trees, "Detection, Estimation, and Modulation Theory", Reprint edition, Wiley-Interscience, New York, USA, 2001.
31. M. van der Veen, F. Bruekers, J. Haitsma, T. Kalker, A.N. Lemma and W. Oomen, "Robust, Multi-Functional and High-Quality Audio Watermarking Technology", 110th AES convention Amsterdam, The Netherlands, May 12-15, 2001.
32. M. van der Veen, A. Lemma, F. Bruekers, T. Kalker and J. Aprea, "Security issues in digital audio watermarking," European Signal Processing Conference (EUSIPCO), Toulouse, France, 2002
33. M. van der Veen, A. Lemma, and A.A.C. Kalker, "Electronic content delivery and forensic tracking," Multimedia Systems, vol. 11, no. 2, pp. 174-184, 2005.

Person-Based and Domain-Based Digital Rights Management

Paul Koster

Philips Research
The Netherlands

Summary. This chapter discusses two important concepts in digital rights management (DRM). The first concept is authorized domains, which bind content to a domain allowing, content to be accessible on a set of devices. The second concept is person-based DRM, which binds content to a person and makes it available after authentication. Special focus is given to the combination of these concepts, which we call the personal entertainment domain (PED). We discuss the advantages and present the architecture of this concept.

20.1 Introduction

This chapter discusses domain- and person-based aspects of digital rights management (DRM), which is introduced in Chap. 17. Early DRM systems for audio/video electronic content delivery bound content to a device. We call this device-based DRM. These systems effectively manage access to content, but people generally consider them too restrictive. They want to use their bought content on all their devices. We discuss two approaches to this problem. The first approach is based on domains, also called authorized domains (AD) [1,2]. For an AD the general idea is that content can flow freely between the devices that belong to the domain. Examples among domain-based DRM systems include OMA DRM 2.0 [3,4] and Apple Fairplay [5,6]. Other proposals are xCP [7] and SmartRight [8].

The second approach is person- or identity-based DRM. This concept binds content to a person's identity and enables this user to render his content at any time and place after authentication. Person-based DRM is not commonly found in mainstream DRM systems although the concept has existed for some time. For example, Rosenblatt discusses the Musicrypt technology, which makes content accessible using biometric authentication [9]. Other examples include the OPERA project, which uses mobile phones for authentication [10] and enterprise DRM, where content is bound to corporate user accounts [9].

Both domain- and person-based DRM have their disadvantages as the next section clarifies. The personal entertainment domain (PED) concept combines the two approaches. Thereby, it realizes the advantages while avoiding the disadvantages. The next section evaluates alternative DRM concepts. This is followed by the architecture of PED.

20.2 DRM Concepts Compared

We present a number of DRM concepts and evaluate them against criteria: (1) content proliferation, i.e., the control and scope of content distribution. This criterion represents the main security requirement for content providers; (2) content availability and social flexibility, i.e., the ease of content access anywhere and sharing with authorized persons; (3) user experience and transparency, i.e., the perceived complexity for users. These three criteria are not an exhaustive list of criteria for DRM. However, these criteria relate to the identity component of DRM licensing. Furthermore, these are the criteria on which the DRM concepts that follow can be differentiated. The following sections discuss alternative approaches. Table 20.1 depicts a summary of the results.

Table 20.1. Summary DRM concepts evaluation. +/o/- indicates good/average/poor score on the criterion.

	Device-based DRM (with tethered devices)	Device-based AD	Person-based DRM	PED
Content proliferation	+	+	+	+
User experience and transparency	-	+	o	+
Content availability and social flexibility	-	o	+	+

20.2.1 Device-Based DRM with Tethered Devices

Device-based DRM with support for tethered devices belongs to the early attempts to make DRM content available on more devices. Key characteristics of this concept (see Fig. 20.1) are: (1) content is bound to one device on which it can be rendered, (2) content can be transferred from the first device to up to a maximum number of tethered devices under some conditions and rendered on those devices, (3) content is bound to the tethered devices and cannot be distributed further. SDMI [11] was an early initiative that attempted to deal with portable devices using the concept of tethered devices. A more recent example is Windows Media DRM (WM DRM) [12]. WM DRM distinguishes between two types of tethered devices, namely storage and rendering devices such as portable media players, and streaming network rendering devices without storage such as media extenders [13,14]. The concept of tethered devices is often justified by the argument that such tethered devices are resource constrained and cannot support the full DRM functionality.

The device-based DRM concept with tethered devices meets the content proliferation criterion, because the transfer to tethered devices is subject to conditions and limitations. The concept scores less well on user experience since there is no true flexibility since content is bound to one device where all DRM features are available, and the separate rules and conditions for tethered devices limit transparency. The same reasons also contribute to a low score on availability and social flexibility, e.g., enjoying some content at another place distributing the content using a network instead of carrying devices is not supported.

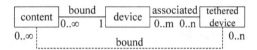

Fig. 20.1. Device-based DRM with tethered devices.

20.2.2 Device-Based Authorized Domain

The concept of (authorized) domains (AD) has been introduced in response to device-based DRM [1]. It introduces a domain identity that groups devices. This replaces the direct binding between content and devices. This allows users to purchase, render and manage their content on more than one device. Key characteristics of the device-based domain concept (see Fig. 20.2) are: (1) content is bound to the domain when it is acquired, (2) content can be exchanged between and rendered on domain devices, (3) a domain consists of a maximum number of devices, (4) a device may be member of a number of domains. Solutions implementing this concept are OMA DRM 2.0 [3,4], Fairplay [5,6], xCP [7] and SmartRight [8].

Device-based AD scores better on the criteria than device-based DRM with tethered devices. The proliferation of content is strictly controlled by the entity or component that manages which devices belong to the domain. The user experience criterion is met by the simplicity of the concept. Of course, a user needs to manage his domain, but in practice this is limited to a one-time installation procedure. The availability and social flexibility criterion is met to some extent. For example, a limitation on a reasonable number of domain devices is good, while further restrictions would decrease its attractiveness. Rendering content just once at another device requires a registration followed by a deregistration to the domain. This is not flexible and degrades availability. Social flexibility is hindered when multiple users bind content to the same shared domain. Some systems force this behaviour, allowing only one domain in an environment, e.g., SmartRight. Divorce scenarios are difficult to support in that case, because users cannot take their content because it is bound to a single shared domain. Solutions that promote separate domains per user score better with respect to this. Examples include typical server-based systems like OMA DRM 2.0 and Fairplay. Fairplay also includes the concept of tethered devices (iPods), but this does not affect its score against the criteria.

Fig. 20.2. Device-based AD structure.

20.2.3 Person-Based DRM

In parallel to device-based DRM the idea of person-based DRM developed. Its key characteristics (see Fig. 20.3) are (1) content is bound to a user, and (2) content is accessible after user authentication for the duration of the authentication session. The person-based DRM concept has been known for some time. For example rights expression languages such as ODRL have means to express the binding of content to a person identity [15] and solutions exist in which biometric user authentication enables access to DRM content [9]. Corporate enterprise DRM binds content to user accounts present in the corporate IT infrastructure. The OPERA project put person-based DRM in practice using the mobile-phone infrastructure and the user's SIM card for authentication [10]. Fairplay has some person-based characteristics with its notion of a user account on a server and registration/authorization of PCs, but the persistent nature of this authorization makes it more like a device-based AD.

Person-based DRM meets the criteria of controlled content proliferation if secure and convenient user authentication mechanisms and policies are used. Availability of the content is also very good and content sharing is possible when people come together. Transparency is good since there is one major rule, but user convenience is not that positive due to the expiration of authentication sessions. This requires regular reauthenticating for devices at home.

The person-based DRM concept is currently not widely used for multimedia content given its prerequisites for an authentication infrastructure, which is not sufficiently or cost-effectively available. An authentication infrastructure consists of the hardware, software and services to authenticate users.

A person-based DRM system puts the user at the centre of the content experience. Special attention must therefore be paid to privacy. For this purpose anonymous buying, hiding of identities in licenses and pseudonimity techniques may be used [16]. Chapter 23 addresses privacy for DRM in more detail.

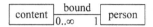

Fig. 20.3. Person-based DRM.

20.2.4 Personal Entertainment Domain

In search of a DRM concept that best matches the criteria we propose to combine the concepts of device-based AD and person-based DRM. This results in the personal entertainment domain (PED) concept [17]. PED is characterized by (see Fig. 20.4): (1) a single user is the member/owner of the domain, (2) content is bound to that user representing the right to use the content, (3) a number of devices is bound to the user forming the domain (AD), (4) domain content can be accessed on the set of domain devices, (5) domain content can be accessed on other devices after user authentication for the duration of the authentication session, (6) devices may exchange content directly, and (7) devices may be a member of multiple domains. This allows PED to offer convenient content usage at home on domain devices, including the sharing of content among family members. Furthermore, it enables people to access their content anywhere and at any time after user authentication.

PED meets the criteria. It meets the content proliferation criterion due to the policy that governs domain management and user authentication. It also supports availability and social flexibility with content well since content can be rendered anywhere, and the clear ownership of content makes it easy to handle changes in social relations. Social flexibility is further increased by the ease of sharing content by sharing devices, as is typically done in families. All family members register the shared device in their personal domain. User experience and transparency is good, because the concept is simple with only two general rules to access content on devices. Furthermore, the binding of bought content to the users leads to an intuitive form of content ownership. The prerequisite of an authentication infrastructure applies to PED as it does for person-based DRM in general. However, PED offers an alternative to access content, which relaxes this need.

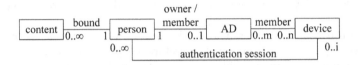

Fig. 20.4. Personal entertainment domain.

Current DRM systems do not provide all the characteristics of PED. OMA DRM 2.0 supports the binding of devices to a domain. It also supports the binding of content to a user's SIM identity in the rights expression, but only to restrict the access to content further, in addition to the domain mechanism. This means that content is restricted to a set of devices where the user is also authenticated, while in PED content is restricted to a set of devices or to a device where the user is authenticated. Fairplay also shares characteristics with PED since it is based on a user account and the persistent authorization of devices. However, Fairplay lacks user authentication sessions of limited duration.

PED anticipates future support for domains with multiple persons by separating person identity from domain identity. This would allow people to use their family's content also at remote locations. Content would still be bound to the user owning rights to it, and the domain would still belong to one person, but the other users would have a membership relation with the domain.

20.3 Personal Entertainment Domain Architecture

The PED architecture builds further on the architecture of person- and domain-based DRM systems. This section presents architectural options to realize PED.

20.3.1 Data Overview

PED structures data objects as depicted by Fig. 20.5. It is a refinement of the PED concept depicted in Fig. 20.4 extended with typical DRM elements such as licenses [18]. We consider the case where each content item has exactly one license. The person identity is linked to the license during the license issuing process. Rights expression languages such as ODRL [11] and XrML allow expression of this binding in the rights expression. Alternatively, the binding is a reference in the license structure itself, e.g., as a reference identifying the user key protecting the content key. The license is also bound to a domain. The next sections discuss in more detail the representations and management of keys, persons, domains and devices.

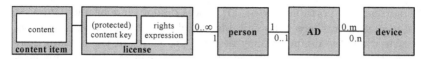

Fig. 20.5. PED data overview.

20.3.2 Component Overview

Figure 20.6 depicts the components that realize the PED functionality. Common components found in domain-based DRM systems are the DRM client, license server and domain manager. For example in OMA DRM 2.0, DRM agents and rights issuers realize these functionalities. The user token component is optional. It is responsible for user authentication when authentication involves hardware such as smartcards. The inclusion of a DRM terminal in the architecture eases support of devices with limited user interfaces and illustrates that both the domain manager and the DRM client need interaction with the user in his role as domain and device owner. All components except the DRM terminal must be trustworthy, i.e., meet the compliance and robustness rules of the DRM system, because they have access to content or cryptographic keys.

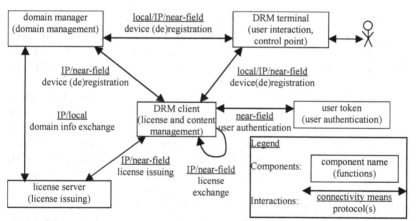

Fig. 20.6. PED component and interaction overview. Connectivity means: combined on the same device (local), connected through a network (IP), wired/wireless connection with a limitation on the distance (near-field).

20.3.3 Deployment

The component architecture allows many deployment scenarios. For example, the domain manager can be in the network as in OMA DRM 2.0 or Fairplay, it can be local to a device as in SmartRight, or it can be portable on a smartcard or portable device [17]. Local domain management may be advantageous when there is no suitable stakeholder to run it as a network service, or when the domain policy requires proximity of the domain manager and the DRM clients. On the other hand, central domain management in the network may offer features like centralized control and easy and direct audit facilities.

Another aspect is the difference between centralized and distributed domain management, i.e., one or more domain managers. More domain managers only have use in combination with local domain management. An example system is xCP where different managers can manage separated clusters, which can be joined. Transparent communication of the domain composition to users is an issue in this case. Currently deployed DRM systems such as OMA DRM 2.0 and Fairplay use a more practical centralized domain manager.

Ideally, each DRM client is deployed on a device together with a DRM terminal, allowing straightforward domain management operations using the user interface of the device. Online services and components may be controlled for example from a Web browser or dedicated application running on a device.

20.3.4 Key and License Management

Key and license management for PED is concerned with the secure management of content keys. Only compliant components have access to these keys. Also the number of potential receivers is kept as small as possible. In the PED architecture this means that the license server and the DRM client have access.

Two alternative approaches to protect the content keys have been identified. First, device keys can protect them. However, this has the drawback that licenses must be distributed to other devices using a dedicated secure license exchange protocol. This approach further excludes storage of content keys on non-secure storage independent from a device, e.g., on a CD. This is also referred to as the bit-bucket architecture [7]. Advantages of this approach are the potential to include compliance verification in the protocol and better tracking of the location of licenses.

Second, user or domain keys can protect content keys, which are different terms but technically equivalent. For convenience, we continue to use the term domain key. The domain key is used to encrypt the content key. The domain key is only made available to compliant components such as the DRM client, domain manager, license server and optionally the user token. Furthermore, the domain key in PED is only distributed to a DRM client after a successful registration to the domain or user authentication.

Devices that are no longer entitled to have the domain key should delete it to maintain this constraint. Since deletion cannot be guaranteed, a mechanism to update the domain key is required. Practical and user experience considerations for such updates dictate that it only applies to new content. The effect is that newly issued content does not play on excluded devices.

Compliance of components is verified as part of the delivery of the domain key and license issuing. Compliance verification is typically done using compliance certificates of devices. Alternatively, broadcast encryption is used [7]. Revocation is more complex, especially the distribution of fresh revocation information to devices that are not always online requires a solution tailored to the system deployment [19]. Specifically for PED, revocation is difficult to take into account when distributing the domain key from the user token to DRM clients after offline user authentication.

Domain-based DRM in general does not combine well with statefull licenses, e.g., licenses that allow content to be rendered twice. User experience is bad, because it is hard to divide such plays over DRM clients. PED is not an exception to this although it makes clear to whom the state belongs. Models such as OMA DRM 2.0 where state holds per device instead of per domain are especially hard to understand both in terms of consumer experience and content proliferation. Liu addresses this by proposing both state per domain and a count manager as central component in a domain to manage state [20].

Import from other content protection systems is a special operation on licenses. PED behaves similar to other domain-based DRM systems except that the content is bound to a user identity instead of domain.

20.3.5 User Identity and Authentication

User identities in PED enable a person to obtain and access content. User identities may also be used to control access to a user's domain and devices. A user's identity includes a unique user identifier. A typical representation is an online account at a service provider consisting of a username, password and other information. A user identity has associated authentication mechanisms and credentials, e.g., an identity certificate with an associated key pair. The user identity must be trusted, because it is used for DRM purposes. Therefore, trusted parties manage the user identity and associated authentication mechanisms.

An important property of the authentication mechanism is that the user cannot share his credentials. Authentication tokens or biometrics can accommodate this. Username/password authentication provides less assurance since they are easily shared. However, online verification can prevent simultaneous large-scale sharing. Alternatively, sharing is not prevented but discouraged, e.g., because sharing would imply sharing some privacy-sensitive information or giving access to other valuable resources [21].

Hardware token authentication such as smartcards or SIM cards can be used for authentication. The benefit of using hardware tokens is that they are robust against cloning, can hold user keys without the user having access to them, and can enforce close proximity between the token and device to which it authenticates. Another advantage is that the user token can hold the information for autonomous authentication to a DRM client. This could also include the domain key, but this has disadvantages as explained in the section on key management. Management of the link between users and tokens typically means that the token stores the user credentials, e.g., certificate and related keys. Tokens may also have a token (device) identity. The separation between user and token identity is advantageous since they serve different purposes and also their lifecycle differs. Revocation in this context can be supported on three levels. The user identity should be revoked when the private key of the user is compromised or when the user is banned from using the system. Tokens should be revoked when they are not compliant anymore, e.g., when it is hacked or cloned. The link between a user and user token should be revoked when the token may not be used anymore to authenticate the user, e.g., in the case of breakage, loss or theft. Revocation status may be verified as part of the authentication process.

Biometrics may be used for identification and authentication in DRM. Biometrics cannot be used to encrypt the content since they are not secret. The advantage of biometrics, when applied correctly, is that it proves that a user is at a certain device, which PED needs. The initial enrolment is done in conjunction with an online service that couples the biometrics profile to a user's identity. Upon a biometric authentication this profile must be available. In PED this can be done efficiently because the user identity is known for the cases where authentication is triggered by the attempt to use a user-bound license.

These authentication mechanisms are technically sound, but are often difficult or costly to deploy. Therefore, it is advantageous for PED to build on existing infrastructures that provides these mechanisms already. Furthermore, this better supports heterogeneous environments. Identity federation makes this possible, e.g., by applying ID-FF or SAML [22]. Identity federation links the user's DRM identity to another identity. Attention must be paid to content proliferation when identities are federated, because multiple authentication mechanisms allow for the sharing of authentication credentials and have the risk that identities that belong to different users are federated. A first defense for PED is to limit the number of identities that may be federated for this purpose together with verification that identities belong to the same user when federating them.

20.3.6 Domain Management

Domain Representation. A domain is typically represented by at least an identifier and references to its member devices. PED also specifies the member/owner user. In addition a domain typically has related information such as cryptographic keys. Optionally, the domain representation also includes the identity and address of its domain manager. An indication of the domain policy is useful in cases where the domain policy is flexible and the domain manager is independent of the license server.

The distribution and management of the domain information differs per system. In certain cases, e.g., OMA DRM 2.0 and Fairplay, most information is kept by the domain manager and only an identifier and domain key is shared with the DRM clients. Distributing more information such as the list of domain devices can have its advantages such as signaling the domain members to all devices or optimizing domain membership revocation [17,19].

Domain Policy. The domain policy specifies under which conditions entities are entitled to be part of the domain and thereby largely defines the scale of content proliferation in PED.

The domain policy may be fixed for the system or not. For a non-fixed policy it is furthermore an important difference if the license issuer and domain issuer belong to the same organization. Most domain-based DRM systems have a domain policy that is fixed for the system. OMA DRM 2.0 is an exception where the domain policy is determined by the individual rights issuers. On one hand this is convenient since rights issuers control the domains to which they deliver content. On the other hand, a fixed policy contributes to transparency of the solution to the users. A flexible architecture allows domains defined by a domain manager with an arbitrary domain policy to be shared with multiple license servers.

The domain policy must be comprehensive and transparent. The PED policy is typically characterized by a maximum number of devices per domain. This is similar to other systems like Apple Fairplay with its limit of five authorized PCs, xCP, SmartRight or OMA DRM 2.0. Devices may be a member of multiple domains to support sharing of content between people sharing devices. Although it provides good user experience, it is not common to all domain-based systems, e.g., SmartRight does not allow this.

The domain policy is enforced by the domain manager, but may also be enforced partially by other components such as the DRM client. An example is the duration of the authentication session. In case that the domain policy is not fixed then the policy must be parameterized and communicated, e.g., together with distribution of the domain key to the DRM client.

Further policy rules may be required to counter specific threats against limited content proliferation. However, it is important to select a balanced set of policy rules such that in normal circumstances a user does not encounter the additional rules. Some examples follow. Limiting the number of (de)registrations to a maximum per time unit for either the domain manager or the DRM client prevents the attack where users share premium content by (de)registering devices one after another in a short time frame. Similarly, a maximum number of authentications per DRM client or user token per time frame discourages a similar attack on user authentication.

Local domain managers can require direct proximity by requiring a near-field communication interface for registering DRM clients, which limits content proliferation to places where the domain manager goes. Limiting the exchange of licenses between domain devices to near-field channels is sometimes proposed, but is against the philosophy of networked DRM.

Table 20.2. PED (de)registration overview

	Situation	Domain policy	User consent
Domain manager –DRM client registration	Normal registration	Integrally enforced	Domain and device owner
Domain manager –DRM client deregistration	Normal deregistration	Integrally enforced	Domain or device owner
Standalone DRM client deregistration (without domain manager)	Offline device ownership transfer or device reset	Reclaim procedure to enable new device registration	Device owner
Standalone domain manager deregistration (without DRM client)	Device lost, broken or stolen	Procedure to deregister DRM client and reclaim position	Domain owner

Device Registration and Deregistration. The device registration and deregistration protocols have the form of a request and response interaction between DRM client and domain manager. The result typically is a domain key in the case of registration and removal of domain credentials in the case of deregistration. Table 20.2 presents an overview including the exceptional (de)registration cases. These cases require a procedure to reclaim the position of the removed device and free it for future device registrations. These procedures are defined by the domain policy and must have drawbacks or limitations to provide a disincentive to users to abuse this mechanism to effectively obtain more domain devices. For example, Fairplay addresses both cases by allowing somebody to deregister all domain devices at once at the domain manager, but only once a year.

(De)registration protocols must address the interests of the user in his role as domain and device owner, e.g., unwanted (de)registrations via the network may not be possible.-Typically, the domain owner is the identity to which the domain is bound, or who has physical access to the domain manager in the case that it is deployed on a token. The device owner is typically the person that has physical access to the device, unless access control is defined based on user identities. When user identities are involved the identities and authentication mechanism of PED can be reused. In other cases user confirmation may consist of pressing a button, putting a device in registration mode, or assuming implicit domain owner consent when a domain manager token is in physical proximity to a DRM client.

20.4 Conclusions

This chapter presented an evaluation of DRM concepts and the PED architecture. PED combines the strengths of both person-based and domain-based DRM. PED is characterized by: (1) content is bound to persons, (2) a person has a number of domain devices on which his content can be rendered, and (3) it can be rendered on devices after user authentication for the duration of the authentication session. PED allows a user to enjoy his content any time, anywhere and on any device. PED further allows sharing of content with relatives or friends by sharing devices that can belong to multiple domains. By means of the domain policy, content proliferation is strictly controlled. The domain policy defines the maximum number of devices in a domain and the duration of an authentication session. PED is practical to implement, potentially as an extension to current domain-based DRM systems. The required identity and authentication infrastructure can be provided with modern authentication mechanisms and identity management technology.

References

1. R. Vevers, C. Hibbert: Copy Protection and Content Management in the DVB. In: IBC Conference Publication, Amsterdam, IBC2002, 15-9-2002. pp. 458-466
2. S.A.F.A. van den Heuvel, W. Jonker, F.L.A.J. Kamperman, P.J. Lenoir: Secure Content Management in Authorised Domains. In: IBC Conference Publication, Amsterdam, IBC2002, 15-9-2002. pp. 467-474
3. Open Mobile Alliance: *DRM Architecture: Approved Version 2.0*, 3-3-2006.
4. Open Mobile Alliance: *DRM Specification: Approved Version 2.0*, 3-3-2006.
5. Apple: iTunes Music Store: Authorizing your computer. http://www.apple.com/support/itunes/musicstore/authorization. Cited 2005.
6. Wikipedia: FairPlay. http://en.wikipedia.org/wiki/FairPlay. Cited: 21-3-2006
7. F. Pestoni, J.B. Lotspiech, S. Nusser: xCP: peer-to-peer content protection. IEEE Signal Processing Magazine. 21(2): 71-81 (Mar 2004)
8. Thomson: *SmartRight: Technical white paper*, version 1.7, January 2003.
9. B. Rosenblatt, B. Trippe, S. Mooney: *Digital Rights Management*: Business and Technology (M&T Books, New York 2002)

10. S. Wegner (ed.): *OPERA - Interoperability of Digital Rights Management (DRM) Technologies: An Open DRM Architecture*, Eurescom, 2003.
11. Secure Digital Music Initiative: SDMI Portable Device Specification: Part 1, Version 1.0, 8-7-1999
12. Microsoft: Windows Media Digital Rights Management. http://www.microsoft.com/windows/windowsmedia/drm/default.aspx. Cited 2005.
13. Microsoft: Next Generation Windows Media DRM for Consumer Electronics Devices. In: WinHEC2004, 2004.
14. Microsoft: Windows Media Connect - Connectivity Solution for Networked Media Players. In: WinHEC2004, 2004.
15. Iannella, R.: *Open Digital Rights Language (ODRL) Version 1.1*, 2003.
16. C. Conrado, M. Petkovic, W. Jonker: Privacy-Preserving DRM, In: *Secure Data Management*, 2004. Lecture Notes in Computer Science, vol 3178 (Springer, Berlin Heidelberg New York 2004)
17. R.P. Koster, F.L.A.J. Kamperman, P.J. Lenoir, K.H.J. Vrielink: Identity based DRM: Personal Entertainment Domain. In: *Communications and Multimedia Security*, Salzburg, Austria, September 19-21 2005. Lecture Notes in Computer Science, vol. 3677 (Springer, Berlin Heidelberg New York, 2005) pp. 42-54
18. S. Guth: A Sample DRM System. In: *Digital Rights Management: Technological, Economic, Legal and Political Aspects*. Lecture Notes in Computer Science, vol. 2770 (Springer, Berlin Heidelberg New York 2003)
19. B.C. Popescu, B. Crispo, F.L.A.J. Kamperman, A.S. Tanenbaum: A DRM Security Architecture for Home Networks. In: *ACM Workshop on Digital Rights Management*, 2004.
20. Q. Liu, R. Safavi-Naini, N.P. Sheppard: Maintaining Count Constraints in a Household Domain in DRM. In: *IEEE International Workshop on Software Support for Portable Storage*, 2005.
21. S. Brands: Rethinking Public Key Infrastructures and Digital Certificates; Building in Privacy (MIT Press, August 2000)
22. Liberty Alliance Project: Liberty ID-FF Architecture Overview, version 1.2, 2005.

Digital Rights Management Interoperability

Frank Kamperman

Philips Research
The Netherlands

Summary. Digital rights management (DRM) interoperability is becoming a necessity due to the wide variety of content protection systems. DRM interoperability problems occur on three system layers: protected content, licenses, and trust and key management. Solutions for DRM interoperability can be based on format and platform interoperability. Furthermore, three interoperability case studies are discussed: DVB, Coral, and MPEG-IPMP(X), highlighting three typical DRM interoperability solutions.

21.1 Introduction

DRM is the collection of technologies for electronically enforcing business rules on digital information [1]. Information may be music or movies, but can also be text, pictures, or other types of data. In general, technologies used in DRM include cryptography, secure content packaging, license management and the digital representation of rights, key and trust management, and signal-processing techniques such as content watermarking and fingerprinting. Watermarking and fingerprinting are, however, not further considered in this chapter on DRM interoperability.

The DRM definition above includes protection systems for content delivery over IP networks [2], i.e., the Internet, but also conditional access (CA) systems for pay-TV [3-5]. The term DRM is used in relation to Internet delivery systems in the remainder of this chapter. CA is commonly used for pay-TV systems. DRM systems control the *usage* of data. DRM systems are different from and much more extensive than copy control systems, which only control or prevent the (illegal) *copying* of data.

Interoperability is the ability of two or more systems or components to exchange information and to use the information that has been exchanged [6]. DRM interoperability is interoperability in the case that the systems or components are DRM systems or components, or systems or components using DRM information, e.g., a device playing a DRM-protected movie. DRM interoperability enables the use of content protected by a certain DRM system on devices implementing another DRM system.

This chapter is organized as follows. It starts with discussing the need for DRM interoperability. It then introduces a model to help explain a DRM system and identify the (technical) problems for DRM interoperability. Subsequently, two types of solutions, called format interoperability and platform interoperability, are discussed. The chapter then gives some use cases as illustrations of interoperability solutions. This is followed by a discussion on business and user aspects of to DRM interoperability. The chapter ends with a conclusion and literature list.

21.2 The Need for DRM Interoperability

Various types of security solutions exist for protecting content delivery to the consumer and his/her devices in the home. CA systems with various proprietary solutions protect pay-TV services. Examples of CA systems are VideoGuard [7] and Mediaguard [8]. DRM systems protect content delivery via the Internet. Examples of such systems are Fairplay [9], used in Apple's iTunes, Windows Media DRM [10] or Marlin DRM [11]. An example of a secure content delivery system to mobile phones is OMA-DRM [12]. The VCPS [13] and AACS [14] systems are meant for the protection of content distribution using optical discs.

The trend is for more devices to become connected to the Internet or to other devices, enabling content transfer with Internet services or between devices. Users increasingly expect to be able to use acquired content on different devices and to access different content delivery services with a single device. As an example, users would expect that a mobile phone, implementing OMA DRM, could buy and play iTunes content.

There would be no (technical) interoperability problems if only one content protection system were used to protect all content. This is, however, not the case, as shown by the many examples above. It is also not expected due to the different protection solutions already deployed in the market today and the fact that there are different types of devices and different content delivery channels with different characteristics, and different business interests. DRM interoperability solutions are therefore required given consumer expectations, the trend for networking, and the many different protection solutions employed today.

21.3 Basic DRM System Model

This section briefly explains the architecture and operation of a DRM system and its implementation in a client device.

21.3.1 Data and System Model

Fig. 21.1 shows a simple DRM data and system model for the client side, i.e., for devices able to playback DRM-protected content. The following basic data objects typically occur in a DRM system: protected content, licenses, keys, and certificates. Protected content and license are the prime data objects, while keys and certificates are merely used in the protection of the content and licenses.

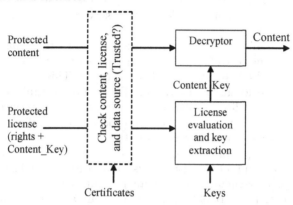

Fig. 21.1. DRM data and system model: client side

Content is a digital, usually compressed form (e.g. MPEG) of audio or video, although other type of data, e.g., text, maybe used. Data encryption with a Content_Key takes care of the content protection. A content identifier (Content_Id) typically identifies content.

A license contains rights data specifically related to a piece of content identified by a Content_Id. Examples of such rights data are that the content may only be used for a limited period, or can only be copied once, etc. Rights are often expressed in a rights description language, like XrML [15] or ODRL [16], but they can also be implicitly known (Fairplay [9]) or in a procedural way (Marlin DRM [11]). Rights data may also contain a user identifier (User_Id) and/or device identifier (Device_Id) to indicate to whom or what the rights apply. Often a license also contains the Content_Key required to decrypt protected content.

Cryptographic techniques like encryption and hashing protect the integrity and confidentiality of content and licenses against hackers. The data object keys indicate the cryptographic keys in the key hierarchy used for license protection. Keys can already be present in a device, but can also distributed later in a secure manner, e.g., in a way similar to licenses.

Licenses should be transferred between trusted sources and trusted sinks (devices). Trusted devices can be considered compliant, i.e., behave according the rights in the license, and robust, i.e., are implemented such that they are difficult to hack. Typically a trust infrastructure, often based on certificate hierarchies, takes care of this. Certificates can already be present in a device, but can also be distributed later, e.g., in a way similar to licenses.

The trust infrastructure is the most important item in relation to DRM interoperability. Two technically identical DRM implementations, linked to a different trust infrastructure and authority, might not be able to communicate, because they do not trust each other. The trust infrastructure can therefore be used to control which services and devices can participate in the system and which not. Furthermore, it enables enforcing of all types of (compliance and robustness) rules on the services and devices that do participate in the system.

Important to note is that the size of protected content is typically in the range of Mbytes (Audio) to Gbytes (Video). The size of licenses is typically in the hBytes (hundreds of bytes) to kBytes range. This difference in size is important for the feasibility of various DRM interoperability solutions. Protected content and licenses can be transferred from a service provider to a user combined or separately. The size of keys and certificates is in the range of that of licenses and interoperability solutions suitable for licenses also work for these types of objects.

The handling of content, licenses, keys, and trust in a DRM system is called content management, license management, key management, and trust management, respectively. Key management and trust management are typically highly interwoven. They are therefore treated together from now on.

Fig. 21.1 shows that a DRM client roughly consists of the following functional blocks: a block to decrypt the protected content, called a decryptor, a block to evaluate licenses and handle keys, called a license evaluator and key extractor, and functionality for trust management. Furthermore a client typically contains a (user-interaction) application for interfacing between a user and the DRM system (not shown in the figure).

21.3.2 DRM System Interoperability

DRM system interoperability relates to content management, license management, and trust and key management, and can technically be achieved in two ways: through format interoperability (the format of certain data objects is standardized) or platform interoperability (functional blocks in an implementation can be addressed in a standardized way), or a combination of both methods. The coming sections elaborate the two methods. For further reading, [17-19] give more-detailed DRM system models for analyzing interoperability.

21.4 DRM Format Interoperability

Fig. 21.2 presents an interface model for two DRM systems, A and B, trying to interoperate. The figure shows the two main data objects, protected content and licenses in two rectangular boxes for the DRM systems A and B. The fact that the data objects may be different for the different DRM systems is denoted by the prime. The black bars represent the trust and key management, and they are also drawn vertically to show that trust and key management also contributes to content and license protection. The arrows show that, on three main interfaces, a mismatch between the systems may exist. These interfaces include the two types of basic data objects protected content, and licenses, and also trust and key management messaging.

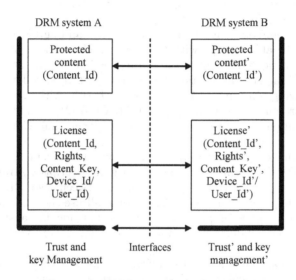

Fig. 21.2. DRM system interface model.

One of the solutions to transfer content from DRM system A to DRM system B is to translate the format of the protected content, the license, and trust and key management data from system A to system B. Translations, however, are not that easy, as explained later.

Another approach, preventing translations, is to deliver content and licenses in all formats required simultaneously. Although this approach prevents translations, it uses the number of DRM systems times as much bandwidth.

Yet another approach is to implement all DRM systems required inside the same device. Although this approach saves bandwidth, it uses in principle the number of DRM systems times as much device resources, and may give additional licensing cost for the DRM system implementations.

We may use translations (processing required), parallel delivery (bandwidth required), or parallel implementation for DRM interoperability (storage required) to achieve DRM interoperability, as shown in the previous paragraphs. These are the extremes of the spectrum of solutions. In the following subsections we focus on optimizations for DRM interoperability, which from a technical point of view is a trade-off between processing, bandwidth, and storage/implementation requirements. Such trade-offs, however, are not based purely on technical grounds, as business reasons may be even more important.

21.4.1 DRM Object Standardization

This subsection addresses the different objects from the model in Fig. 21.2 one by one. Note that, for true interoperability, solutions for all layers are required otherwise we only have partial interoperability.

The way to eliminate the content protection interoperability problem is to agree on a common content protection format and agree that all DRM systems must be able to cope with this format. The advantages of this approach are that no re-encryption or retransmission of content is required. Protected content standardization has in the past been followed in DVB by standardizing on an MPEG-transport stream with DVB common scrambling for content encryption [20]. ISMACryp [21] is another example of standardization on the content protection layer that can be used in DRM systems.

Rights language standardization is the answer to prevent translations of rights. If all DRM systems used the same rights description, translation of rights in licenses when transferring content between two DRM systems would not be required anymore, as they would all use the same format and expressions. A number of proposals have been made for a standardized rights expression language. The most well known are XrML [15] and ODRL [16].

The key management and trust infrastructure are typically considered proprietary to a particular DRM system as they to a large extend determine the security of the system and control over the system. The author is not aware of any specific standardization in this field. Note, that this statement does not cover examples of standardization of key management and trust as part of standardization of a complete DRM system. An example of such a system is OMA DRM [12], which standardizes key management and trust management. For intra-OMA interoperability, however, OMA relies on an external trust authority.

Content identification (Content_Id) is independent of DRM, i.e., it would also exist if DRM were not an issue. Examples of content identification standardization are the international standard recording code (ISRC) [22] used on compact disc digital audio and MPEG-21 work on digital item identification (DII) [23]. Device and user identification (Device_Id and User_Id) are typically DRM system dependent.

21.4.2 DRM Object Translations

Next to object standardization, it is possible to perform translations of rights expressions, content identifiers, device/user identifiers, key management data, etc. Exact rights expression translation is, however, difficult and mathematically hard to solve [24]. The reason is that rights expression languages can be very extensive and that different schemes of expressions for rights do not map nicely onto one another. This is just like natural languages, which e.g., might have words that cannot directly be expressed in another language. Therefore, direct mathematical translations between such objects are often not possible. The next tactic that may be followed is to limit the number of possibilities in the rights expressions and only allow for a limited set of translations. In this case a translation table can be used to translate objects from system A to system B. The disadvantage is that this approach limits the flexibility of rights expression languages and makes them to some extent redundant. Yet another approach would be to translate an expression in a system A to the closest expression used in a system B. With continuous translations, however, this results in a deviation from the original expression. The magnitude of this deviation may make it unacceptable. In an approach that, for the content provider is safe, rights in system A are translated to the closest subset in system B, but this always results in a further limitation of rights for the user. A content provider may not like the approach of using the nearest equivalent.

The most generic solution for object translation is the introduction of a service to aid in the transfer process. This service is, in principle, able to counter any situation. This solution works for licenses, but also for key and trust management related data objects. It may also provide for issuing data objects under the control of a different trust infrastructure and thereby give the possibility of circumvent trust-related interoperability problems. The Coral consortium for DRM interoperability follows this service-based approach [25]. The Coral case study later in this chapter elaborates on this system. The papers [26-28] describe translations of DRM objects and the use (translation) services in more detail.

21.4.3 DRM Object Transport and Use Standardization

A lighter form of object format standardization is to standardize on how objects are transferred and in what type of containers, without directly specifying the contents of such objects. This approach is often employed together with platform standardization and is highlighted in the DVB interoperability case study later in this chapter. Note that this approach only provides for limited interoperability, as the contents of the objects are not dealt with.

21.5 DRM Platform Interoperability

DRM systems are for the most part implemented in software, but may also have specific hardware components. Fig. 21.3 shows a model of a platform suitable for DRM system implementation and useful to study DRM platform interoperability.

The lower layer of the platform model contains the system resources provided by the hardware and system software. Examples of such resources are a hardware content decryptor, a cryptographic coprocessor, or e.g., hardware-based watermark detector.

A virtual machine allows for a hardware/software abstraction layer. It would allow for the use and downloading of interoperable DRM functionality, e.g., in the form of Java software, on different hardware and software platforms. An example of such a plug-in would be an encryption algorithm. Of course, downloading native software, indicated by the native software plug-in in the figure, could also do this. Such downloadable software is indicated in the middle layer of the platform model.

The highest layer of the model represents the application(s). An example of an application is the content management part of a DRM system, or even a complete DRM system.

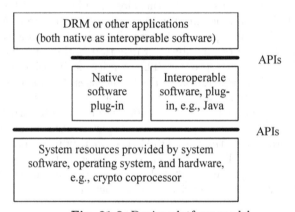

Fig. 21.3. Device platform model.

The lower layers of the platform implementation stack provide services to the upper layers of the platform using Application Programming Interfaces (APIs). Fig. 21.3 shows two type of APIs: APIs for the system resources on the platform itself and APIs that can be instantiated by software that implement them to, e.g., provide for specific required DRM functionality.

This model shows that we may use platform generalization, e.g., by using plug-ins with interoperable or native code, and API-type interoperability solutions to access platform functionality. These solutions are further elaborated on below.

21.5.1 Hardware and Operating System Standardization Level

The easiest thing to do would be to standardize on the platform hardware and operating system (OS) basics. Anyone can then make a DRM system to run on that platform. If a certain piece of content is protected with DRM system X, then just download DRM system X on to your platform, which enables you to use the content. In practice this happens on the PC platform using x86-compliant hardware and the Windows OS.

Although standardizing on hardware and OS looks straightforward it has a number of disadvantages. It is expensive, as it has to be prepared for all types of DRM systems and applications, and cannot be optimized for a specific purpose. We also have different type of devices on the market (e.g., besides PCs, mobile phones, and portable music players.) for which a generic hardware and OS solution might not be suitable. Furthermore, for various business reasons it is very hard to agree on one platform for all types of devices and, last but not least, it would be bad for innovation.

21.5.2 Functional Component and Interface/API Standardization

To cope with the disadvantages of the approach described above it is possible to standardize on certain functionality and the way of accessing it on the platform. An example is to standardize on the cryptographic algorithms used in DRM systems like AES, RSA or elliptic curve. Typically cryptographic operations are expensive compared to other tasks of a DRM system and do not really determine the security, provided that a strong enough cipher is chosen. They also do not determine the functionality of the DRM system, as the latter is mainly determined by the rights expressions. It therefore makes a lot of sense to do this for implementation efficiency reasons.

For flexibility reasons we may also choose a plug-in infrastructure to build a DRM system on a client. One approach is to standardize a signaling mechanism with the protected content on how it is protected and what types of plug-ins are required. Instead of downloading a whole new DRM system, only specific parts need to be downloaded (or might already be resident), resulting in a more efficient, but still flexible way of implementing DRM systems compared to just hardware and OS standardization. The best know example of this approach is MPEG-IPMP(X) [29] described as a case study later in this chapter.

A flexible plug-in approach may also be attractive to be able to renew parts of the DRM system in the case of a system hack. Plug-ins could be software plug-ins or even hardware plug-ins, e.g., the common interface in the DVB Multicrypt solution [20].

21.5.3 Platform Generalization

A problem with different devices is that they are often based on different platforms, so that downloading a piece of (native) software code works on one device, but not on another. This requires the generation of native software suitable for all platforms available, which is undesirable from a cost and software management point of view.

A solution to this problem is to define a virtual machine to achieve platform interoperability. In this case software can be built for use on many platforms. Such a solution for conditional access systems has been proposed in [30] and by OPIMA [31].

Note that we can define virtual machine functionality for any functional part of the DRM system. We might define, e.g., a Java VM suitable to buildup the complete DRM system, but we might also choose to define a VM for a specific functional part of the DRM system, e.g., for the processing of licenses as is done in Marlin DRM [11].

21.5.4 Interoperability Case Studies

DVB

Fig. 21.4 shows a schematic example of a DVB CA system [20]. The left side of the figure shows the transmission side, while the right side shows the CA-related functionality in a set-top box.

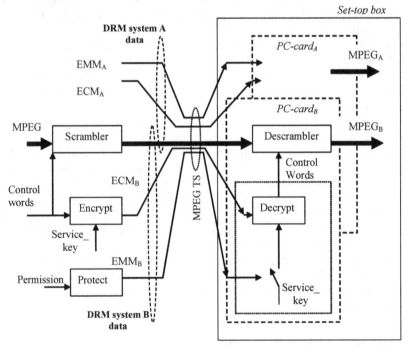

Fig. 21.4. DVB conditional access with SimulCrypt and MultiCrypt.

In a CA system protected content is the encrypted (scrambled) MPEG-TS (transport stream), a license is a combination of an entitlement management messege (EMM) with entitlement control messages (ECMs) containing the Content_Keys which are called control words. In this example a Service_Key encrypts these control words.

DVB achieves interoperability in two ways, called SimulCrypt and MultiCrypt. SimulCrypt requires an MPEG-TS encrypted with the DVB common scrambling algorithm (common protection format) and standardizes ECM and EMM containers (common container format). Note that it does not standardize the content of the ECM and EMM containers, as these are CA system specific. With SimulCrypt multiple CA systems (e.g., A and B) can simultaneously transmit their own ECMs and EMMs, while they share the transmission of protected content. The DRM client then selects the ECMs and EMMs compliant with the implemented CA system. SimulCrypt is a format type of interoperability. The MultiCrypt solution standardizes upon an interface to a PC-card, which can contain a specific CA system implementation. Depending on the CA system desired (A or B), another PC card is plugged into the DRM client. MultiCrypt is a platform type of interoperability.

Coral Consortium

Coral interoperability is a format interoperability solution based on Web services [25]. Coral enables conversion of protected content, licenses, and identifiers (Content_Id, License_Id, Device_Id) between different DRM systems, and handing over trust from one DRM system to another by dedicated services on the Internet.

DRM (independent) tokens aid in license translation. DRM tokens represent rights, but are *not* in a specific DRM format. The idea is that the service provider knows the rights that are represented by the token, and is able to encode that in the different expressions required by the various DRM systems. The tokens therefore act as a source for deriving DRM specific licenses and prove the purchase and agreed use of content. So, if required, a license for DRM system A can be derived from the token, and likewise for a DRM system B. Therefore, a direct translation between licenses for different DRM systems does not occur. A new license is simply derived from the DRM-independent token, avoiding translation problems between system A and B. Coral requires Internet connectivity to operate, but only at the time of license acquisition.

Fig. 21.5 shows how Coral may achieve interoperability. In the figure rectangles indicate data, services or devices, ellipses indicate roles (of a service) note: the service implementing a role is not always shown in the figure for clarity reasons, i.e., an ellipse is not always connected with a rectangle. Suppose a license issuer issues DRM-A content and a license, together with a DRM token. It subsequently transfers the content and license to a DRM-A device (1a), and the DRM token to a DRM-token service (1b). If a user desires to use the content on a device with DRM system B the following happens: device B contacts device A for the content and DRM token (2). Device B (with its Coral client role) then contacts the

Rights Mediator role including information on the requesting entity (device B), the requested outcome, and the location of the DRM token service (3). The rights mediator contacts an identity manager to synchronize the different identities in the system (Content_Id, User_Id, Device_Id) (4) and the DRM-token service for the corresponding DRM token (5). The rights mediator next contacts a DRM system B based distribution service using the DRM token to request for a DRM system B license (6), which subsequently generates, if allowed, and transfers a license to the DRM-B device (7), possibly with help of the rights mediator.

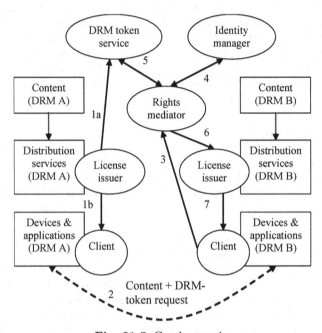

Fig. 21.5. Coral scenario.

Content translation can take two forms. The first option is to decrypt it and send it over a standardized secure authenticated channel, where on the other side it is encrypted again in the correct format. The second option is re-downloading from a content service in the desired format.

MPEG-IPMP(X)

MPEG intellectual property management & protection (IPMP) extension (X) [29] uses a combination of a DRM format and platform interoperability. So-called IPMP information notifies clients how data is protected in an MPEG-IPMP system, which is a type of format interoperability. It, for example, describes how encryption is performed. With this information a client knows what type of tools to use to access the content. If any required tool is not present in the client the IPMP information indicates a download location using a URL. Additionally, the required tools might be delivered together with the content.

The client needs to be able to download and handle the tools. APIs and messaging between the tools have been specified to enable use of the tools on the client, which is a type of platform interoperability. The tools might be dedicated executable modules or modules running on a VM.

A DRM system partly is a real-time system and the problem with downloading tools etc. in this case is that it is often unclear how many resources a downloaded tool requires and if the platform can handle it real time. For a powerful PC this might not be a problem, but for a resource-constrained consumer device it is. This is one of the problems for the use of MPEG-IPMP(X) in the CE domain.

21.6 Business and Trust Issues around DRM Interoperability

DRM systems and DRM interoperability are very much business related, as DRM may be seen as a technical aid to enable certain business models. Typically, a service provider needs to make considerable investments to set up a service delivery chain and therefore also wants the sole right to get the fruits from that investment. A DRM system controls service delivery, enforces payment for the service, and ensures that only authorized parties (both services as devices) can participate (and therefore that unauthorized parties cannot) based on a trust infrastructure.

Such service-provider-operated systems are called vertically built systems. Interoperability with other systems is not always in the interest of the party running the system. The authorization policies within the trust infrastructure determine if interoperability is supported even if good technical interoperability solutions exist.

Horizontal systems would allow a user to access services from different providers. If such services use different DRM technology, commonly agreed interoperability solutions are required.

21.7 Conclusion

DRM interoperability problems occur on three main layers: content protection, license management, and trust and key management. A full DRM interoperability solution must cover all three layers.

We distinguish two types of DRM interoperability: format interoperability and platform interoperability. In practice DRM interoperability solutions are often a combination of interface and platform interoperability and their design is dependent on business requirements. A generic format interoperability solution is Coral. Coral, however, requires Internet connectivity during license acquisition. A generic platform interoperability solution is

MPEG-IPMP(X). This solution is, however, less suitable for specific CE devices.

DRM interoperability has technical elements, as well as business elements, which can be exercised through the trust and key management layer. So, even if technical solutions for DRM interoperability are in place, business reasons may prevent the authorization (i.e., by not adding them in the trust infrastructure) of other alien entities to participate in the system.

Acknowledgement

I would like to thank the many people who gave useful comments and suggestion when writing this chapter, but specifically I would like to mention Rob Koenen, Joost Reuzel, and Paul Koster.

References

1. InterTrust. About DRM. 2006.
   http://www.intertrust.com/main/overview/drm.html
2. B. Rosenblatt, B. Trippe, and Stephen Mooney, *Digital Rights Management: Business and Technology*. M&T Books, 2002.
3. B.M. Macq and J.-J.Quisquater. Cryptology for digital TV broadcasting. In *Proceedings of the IEEE*, vol. 83, no. 6, pp. 944-957, 1995.
4. EBU (European Broadcast Union). Functional model of a conditional access system. In *EBU Technical Review*, winter 1995, pp. 64-77, 1995.
5. L.C. Guillou and J.-L. Giachetti. Encipherment and conditional access. In *SMPTE Journal*, June 1994, pp. 398-406, 1994.
6. IEEE, *IEEE Standard Computer Dictionary: A Compilation of IEEE Standard Computer Glossaries*. IEEE Press, 1990.
7. Videoguard. 2006. http://www.nds.com
8. Mediaguard. 2006. http://www.nagra.fr
9. Fairplay DRM. 2006. http://en.wikipedia.org/wiki/FairPlay
10. Microsoft. Windows Media Digital Rights Management. 2005.
    http://www.microsoft.com/windows/windowsmedia/drm/default.aspx
11. Marlin DRM. 2006. http://www.marlin-community.com/
12. Open Mobile Alliance. 2004. http://www.openmobilealliance.org/
13. Video Content Protection System (VCPS). 2006.
    http://www.licensing.philips.com/vcps
14. Advanced Access Content System (AACS). 2006. www.aacsla.com/home
15. ContentGuard. XrML. 2003. http://www.xrml.org/
16. R. Iannella. Open Digital Rights Language (ODRL) Version 1.1. 2003.
    http://www.w3.org/TR/odrl/
17. P.A. Jamkhedkar and G.L. Heileman. DRM as a layered system. In *ACM workshop on digital rights management DRM '05*, pp. 11-21, 2005. ACM Press.

18. G.L. Heileman and P.A. Jamkhedkar. DRM interoperability analysis from the perspective of a layered framework. In *Proceedings of the 5th ACM workshop on digital rights management DRM '05*, pp. 17-26, 2005.
19. S. Guth, *Interoperability of Digital Rights Management Systems via the Exchange of XML-based Rights Expressions.* Vienna University of Economics and Business Administration, 2004.
20. D.J. Cutts. DVB conditional access. In *Intl. Broadcast Convention Conf. Proceedings*, vol. 428, pp. 129-135, 1996.
21. ISMA. Internet Streaming Media Alliance implementation specification version 1. 28-8-2001.
22. ISRC (International Standard Recording Code). 2006. www.ifpi.org/isrc/
23. Information Technology — Multimedia Framework — Part 3: Digital Item Identification. ISO/IEC FDIS 21000-3, 2002. MPEG.
24. N. Chong, S. Etalle, and P.H. Hartel. Comparing Logic-based and XML-based Rights Expression Languages. In *Proc. on the Move to Meaningful Internet Systems* vol. 2889 of LNCS, pp. 779-792, 2003.
25. Coral Consortium. Coral Consortium Whitepaper. 2006. Coral Consortium Corporation. www.coral-interop.org
26. R.H. Koenen, J. Lacy, M. Mackay, and S. Mitchell. The long march to interoperable digital rights management. In *Proceeding of the IEEE*, 92(6), pp. 883-897, 2004.
27. R. Safavi-Naini, N.P. Sheppard and T. Uehara. Import/Export in Digital Rights Management. In *ACM Workshop on Digital Rights Management*, pp. 99-110, 2004.
28. A.U. Schmidt, O. Tafreschi and R. Wolf. Interoperability challenges for DRM systems. In *Intl. Workshop for Technology, Economy, Social, and Legal Aspects of Virtual Goods*, 2004.
29. T. Senoh, T. Ueno, T. Kogure, S. Shen, N. Ji, J. Liu, Z. Huang, and C.A. Schultz. DRM renewability & interoperability. In Consumer Communications and Networking Conference, CCNC, pp. 424-429, 2004.
30. F. Kamperman and B.J. van Rijnsoever. Conditional Access System Interoperability Through Software Downloading. IEEE Transactions on Consumer Electronics, [47] pp. 47-54, 2001.
31. B.J.van Rijnsoever, P. Lenoir, and J.P.M.G. Linnartz. Interoperable Protection for Digital Content. Kluwer Academic Publishers. Journal of VLSI Signal Processing, [34], pp. 167-179, 2003.

DRM for Protecting Personal Content

Hong Li and Milan Petković

Philips Research
The Netherlands

Summary. Privacy is becoming a serious concern in the connected world. This chapter presents privacy issues, requirements and privacy protection concepts related to consumers' private content. First, privacy issues and requirements are described by means of several scenarios. Then, a DRM approach for protecting ownership and controlled sharing of private content is presented. A system is introduced for realizing such a privacy-enhancing approach for home media centers. Particular solutions for protecting and sharing personal content, ownership management, and content deletion in a privacy-preserving way are described.

22.1 Introduction

In the emerging connected world, consumers are beginning to have their own digital history, which includes photos, home videos, messages, medical records, etc. As with his history and content from others, a consumer prefers his own style, in which he enjoys and manages the content and shares personal digital experiences with others anywhere at anytime. A multi-personalized infotainment environment is expected to provide such personal infotainment for multiple users, e.g., family members and friends.

Such a connected multi-personalized environment brings a number of issues, however. Among these are serious privacy issues regarding online private content and the behavior of individuals and families, as well as the threat of being observed or attacked by other users and hackers [1,2]. This is because the informational home borders are blurred by digital technologies. The dissemination of personal information is far greater than people imagine. On the other hand, consumers are becoming increasingly aware of privacy issues and are taking them more seriously. Electronic privacy protection against organizations that collect personal data is being promoted and legislated [3,4,5]. There are also requirements for protecting privacy between users within the home [6]. Another issue concerns owner-controlled content sharing. Very often, people would like to share personal content with their family or friends, but they would like to keep control of the shared content. In this case, it is desired that sharing users, with whom content is shared, cannot further share the content with others.

This chapter presents the privacy issues, requirements and concepts of privacy protection for consumer electronic products in a connected home. First, privacy issues and requirements are described by means of several scenarios. Then, a DRM approach for protecting ownership and controlled sharing of personal content is presented. A system is introduced for realizing such a privacy-enhancing approach for home media centers. Particular solutions for protecting and sharing personal content, ownership management, and content deletion in a privacy-preserving way are described.

22.2 Scenarios and Requirements

In this section, we present a scenario that describes several different usages of a home media center. After describing the motivating scenario, we identify the security issues involved. Focus is set on confidentiality, i.e., the protection of user data, activities, and behavior with respect to outsiders, but also with respect to the other users of the same system. In addition, authentication, data integrity, and system availability issues are also discussed.

22.2.1 Scenario

Alice, Bob, their daughter Carol and son Dave have bought a home multimedia server. They use it to play movies and music, to watch TV and photos, and to share their digital memories with friends and relatives. The server is also connected to the Internet, allowing them to use it remotely but also to share their home videos with the outside world. Moreover, they are capable of specifying what and with whom they share. So Alice, who has just come back from a tennis tournament, can share the photos she made there with her friends from the tennis club. She also selects the most interesting photos to share with her colleagues from work. When distributing the photos to her colleagues, Alice specifies the rights in such a way that they can only watch but not edit and copy them, because last time her office mate edited her photo in a funny way and published it on the Web. Although he is not in her sharing list anymore, she would appreciate it very much if she had been able to revoke all the photos she previously gave him.

Bob, who works as a freelance consultant, often uses the multimedia server not only for entertainment but also for his business needs. When far away on a business trip, he connects to the server, authenticates, and downloads his confidential documents and presentations. Sometimes, during his long business trips he also works remotely on the server. He also maintains the server.

Carol, who is on vacation in Greece, is using the server to upload video from her camera and immediately distribute it to family members and her best friends. Some parts of the video she finds very nice and wants to share with a larger group of her friends. However, while reviewing the video she has found some embarrassing pieces, which she does not want to show to anyone. Nevertheless, she stores even those parts securely on the home server and attaches them to her top-secret workspace, which she can open only in the privacy of her own room, later when she is back. She also uses the server to give a very nice photo she took in Greece to her best friend as a gift.

Sometimes Dave also uses the server privately to stream a comic strip in the form of an e-book to the display in his room. That helps him to read it without having his mum complaining about his learning behavior. Now, Dave is using the server with one of his friends from school. They are editing the videos they recorded yesterday while skating. As they are doing that together and they are also together in the video, they consider the result as co-work and would like to co-own it. They want to share it with others, but as Dave does not like his skate bravura so much, he wants to personally approve each sharing.

Finally, Alice and Bob's friends and family can use the server when they stay over, for instance. Then they are able to watch and store their favorite content on the server in a private way, so that even Alice and Bob do not have access to the content. However, if Bob notices that disk space is reduced, he can clean such invisible content.

22.2.2 Privacy Issues and Requirements

A basic privacy issue in the scenario is that Alice and her family would like to *control who* (themselves or others) *can access what* (which content). As the server is connected to the Internet, without good protection their data could be revealed to unwanted parties. This is especially vital for Bob, who manages his highly confidential documents on the server. Furthermore, the family members would also like to have *privacy inside their home* and manage personal data confidentially with respect to outsiders as well as the rest of the family. For example, Carol does not want the other family members to see the embarrassing parts of her holiday video. She does not even want them to know that they exist. However, she wants to keep them, as they are memories.

However, the family members *share some of their data with others* outside the family, e.g., friends, colleagues, relatives, etc. Alice wants to share a number of photos with her friends from the tennis club, but only a subset with her colleagues. She is not happy if her office mate is able to edit the photos she gave him and distribute them to other people. Obviously, users would like to be able to specify what and to whom they share and to keep the sharing under their control. Additional privacy issues arise when people with whom they share data do not conduct themselves as they are expected to (as Alice's office mate).

Another important requirement arises from the scenario with Dave, where he and his friends create a co-owned home video. So, the system *must support co-ownership*. Furthermore, it might support management and sharing of this content in various ways (as Dave wanted to approve each sharing requested by his friend).

In addition to providing co-ownership management, the server should also support *transfer of ownership*, as Carol wants to give her photo as a gift to her best friend. This has to be done securely (which means that Carol's ownership is revoked) and privately, possibly in an *offer-accept way*.

The server preserves the privacy of family members and even of *guests*, who can store personal content on the server privately. In that case no one can see the existence of that content. However, this could result in a considerable reduction of storage space. Therefore, one of the important requirements is that a family member can *clean the storage*.

Obviously, the aforementioned scenarios impose a number of privacy and security requirements in addition to the ones described above. As they are out of the scope of this chapter, we only list them:

- The server should also support behavior (e.g., usage habits) privacy of users
- Remote use of the server should be secure
- Simultaneous services for multiple users should be privacy preserving.

22.3 DRM Approach for Protecting Ownership and Controlling Sharing

Digital rights management (DRM) is a collection of technologies that provide content protection by enforcing the use of digital content according to granted rights. It enables content owners and providers to protect their copyrights and maintain control over distribution of and access to content. However, in contrast to the significant effort that has been put into the protection of copyrighted commercial content in current DRM systems, controlled sharing of personal content is often ignored.

In this chapter, we discuss using a DRM system to satisfy the privacy requirements identified in the previous section. The idea is to reuse the concepts defined in DRM systems for commercial content owners. As these systems are not meant for personal content they are not directly applicable and have to be extended to provide controlled sharing of personal content. This effectively means that the user who is the owner of the content takes over the role of content and license provider and therefore becomes involved in content and license creation as well as content protection tasks. Considering personal content, it is most likely that owners will share content with other users. Therefore the model of *person-based* DRM (see Chap. 20 for details), where rights to access content are granted to persons rather than devices, is used as a basis for the presently described DRM system for private content.

In this private content protection model, a hybrid cryptographic approach is used to protect content. A personal content item is encrypted with a symmetrical content key (also called an asset key). The content key is protected using the public keys of persons who have access rights to the content item.

In contrast to DRM approaches for commercial content, ownership plays an important role in a DRM system for personal content. Firstly, each piece of content in the system must have an owner. This is achieved by an ownership license, shown in Fig. 22.1. The content owned by User1 is protected by the content key, which is stored in a so-called ownership license (OL) of User1. This OL is encrypted with the user public key. Using his private key, User1 can decrypt his license to get the content key, so that he can decrypt and see the content.

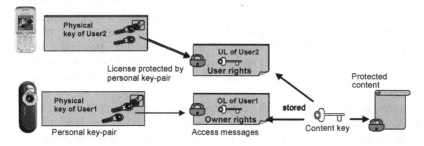

Fig. 22.1. Private content protection model

Secondly, the content owner User1 can also grant access rights to User2 for this protected content, he can create a usage license (UL) with certain usage rights and the content key, and encrypt the UL with the public key of User2. Then User2 is able to get the content key using his private key.

Finally, in addition to proof of ownership and controlled sharing, a DRM system for personal content must provide functionality for ownership management. This includes transfer of ownership (in the case of selling or giving away) as well as management of content owned by multiple persons. Solutions to these problems will be addressed later in this chapter.

22.4 System Architecture

In Philips Research, a trusted multi-personalized entertainment server (TeMPES) has been developed to realize the person-based content protection model. This section describes the architecture of the TeMPES platform, which has an embedded secure subsystem and uses portable physical keys to enforce content protection cryptographically.

22.4.1 Physical Key and Secure Subsystem

The physical key is a tamperproof user identity device that contains a crypto processor for license management functionality. Furthermore, it has secure memory that stores the private/public key pairs of a person and his family. So, without exposing the private keys to other components or devices, the physical key is capable of performing the processes necessary to realize private content protection using the private keys. The necessary processes include authentication, secure communication, making a digital signature, and creating and using digital licenses. The physical key can establish a secure channel interface to the secure subsystem to communicate content keys and other confidential information. The physical key can be a portable device like a smart card. It can be used for authenticating the user when it is inserted into the secure subsystem. The secure subsystem has a secure module, which contains a device key-pair and a cryptographic processor. The secure module can establish trust and secure communication with physical keys and other compliant devices. The processor has high performance for content encryption and decryption. The secure module has interfaces to its host device to access, e.g., content storage and content players.

The secure module and the physical key work together to achieve the protection of private content: the secure module encrypts or decrypts a content file using a content key, which is stored in personal messages that can only be handled by the physical key. The secure module and the physical key form a basic secure platform to protect and manage private content and data. In this way, neither private keys nor content keys are revealed to any person or any untrusted component or device.

22.4.2 Usage License (UL)

The UL, as shown in Fig. 22.2, is a message that consists of a message identifier, a user ID block, an owner ID block, two asset blocks and a signature block. Each block is 256 bytes, which is large enough for 2048 bit encryption. A UL is created for each user of an asset.

Message identifier	User ID block	Owner ID block	Asset block				Asset block (copy)	Signature block	
	User's public key	Owner's public key	Asset ID	Asset rights	Asset key	Spare	Copy of the asset block	Hash of MC	Spare
	Plaintext	Plaintext	Encrypted by user's public key				Encrypted by user's public key	Encrypted by owner's private key	
	←			Message content (MC)			→		

Fig. 22.2. The usage license.

The user and owner ID blocks contain the user's public key and the owner's public key. The two asset blocks contain identical information about an asset: the asset ID pointing to the content file, the asset key used for asset encryption, and the asset rights granted to the user. One block is encrypted with the user's public key, whereas the other block is encrypted with the owner's public key. The signature block contains a hash of the other four blocks in the UL to ensure the integrity of every bit in the blocks. The signature block is then encrypted by the owner's private key: this ensures that only the owner's physical key can create this signature. Any physical key can check the integrity of the message by decrypting the signature block using the owner's public key and verifying the hash.

The owner uses the same UL mechanism to access his own content. In this case, he has an ownership license (OL) with an identical user ID and owner ID, and full access rights in the asset blocks.

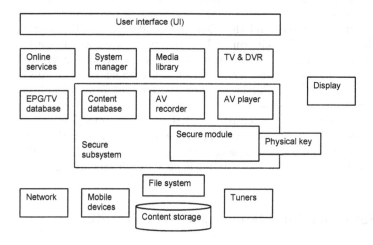

Fig. 22.3. Introducing content protection in a PVR server or a media center PC

22.4.3 The TeMPES Architecture

Fig. 22.3 shows how a secure subsystem is integrated in a personal video recorder (PVR) server or a media center PC, to deploy the private content protection cryptographically.

In Fig. 22.3, a user can see typical PVR functions via the user interface (UI), such as the system manager for managing device settings, the online services for access online shops and stations, the media library for accessing local photos and AV content, and the TV&DVR for time-shifting or recording TV programs. These applications use several components. For instance, the media library uses a content database to manage thousands of photos and songs stored via the file system on the n-gigabyte content storage, so that a user can quickly search or play interesting content with the AV player. The TV&DVR uses the tuners or the network to receive programs, which can be immediately shown on the display, or recorded or time-shifted with the content storage. The TV&DVR uses the EPG/TV database to manage the information of TV channels and electronic program guide (EPG), and to help the user to record programs. The EPG/TV Database updates the latest broadcasting schedules (e.g., for the coming two weeks) and also stores metadata of programs, e.g., the abstract, the genre, the actors and so on. The TV&DVR may use a profile or keywords to find and record programs for the user automatically. The PVR server can be connected to mobile devices, such as an MP3 player, a digital camera or other PVR servers.

The secure subsystem introduces two new components: a secure module and a physical key. It includes three other PVR components extended with content protection functions and interfaces: content database, AV recorder and AV player.

The secure subsystem and the physical key determines if a user has access to his private UI mode, and which list the content database provides for the protected content. A user can only see the content for which he has access rights. When a user wants to play protected content, the secure subsystem calls the AV Player to open the content from the file system, and sends the license to the secure module and the physical key to create a content decryptor. The decryptor is added to the content playback process chain for decrypting the content. Then the chain can play the plain text content stream. Similarly, the secure subsystem can use the AV Recorder and the secure module to create an encrypted private recording.

22.5 Solutions for Managing Private Content

In this section we present solutions for sharing private content and ownership management, such as ownership transfer and co-ownership.

22.5.1 Protecting and Sharing Private Content

A user can protect his plain text content file using his physical key. The secure subsystem asks the physical key to create a private asset, i.e., an asset key and an OL as in (1). The OL is signed using the private key PP_{owner}, and the public key PK_{owner} appears in both the user ID and the owner ID fields. The subsystem receives the asset key and encrypts the content. After the encrypted content and the OL are stored, the plain text file is removed and only the owner can access and manage the protected content.

$$\{PK_{owner}, PK_{owner}, E_{PKowner}[AssetID, Rights=Ownership, Assetkey], E_{PKowner}[AssetID,$$
$$Rights=Ownership, Assetkey]\}sign_{PPowner} \qquad (1)$$

An owner can grant sharing rights of his content file to another user, by asking his physical key to create a sharing UL as shown in (2) using necessary information, such as his OL, the public key of the selected user and selected access rights. The selected user can then access the content with the sharing UL and his physical key. Note that before the physical key creates a sharing UL, it verifies if the received OL and the physical key have the same private key. In this way only the owner can create sharing ULs.

$$\{PK_{user}, PK_{owner}, E_{PKuser}[AssetID, Rights=View, Assetkey], E_{PKowner}[AssetID, Rights=View,$$
$$Assetkey]\} sign_{PPowner}. \tag{2}$$

An owner can revoke sharing rights by checking and deleting the sharing ULs. Note that it could be difficult for the owner to completely remove the copies of the revoked UL, especially when the user uses a remote device. In this case, one possible solution is to have the user's physical key to check an online trusted server that stores up-to-date ULs safely. Another solution is to set an expiration date in the asset block of the UL. This requires regular updates of the ULs by the owner's physical key, which could be troublesome in terms of performance and the availability of the owner's physical key.

22.5.2 Ownership Transfer

Transfer of the ownership of a piece of personal content could be done simply by copying the content in the clear between users. In addition, they could sign a contract of the transfer to make it legal. We propose a solution using DRM technologies in a much more sophisticated, secure and efficient way.

In the proposed solution an owner (owner 1) is able to transfer the ownership of his content in an offer-accept way. The whole protocol is shown in Fig. 22.4 and described below.

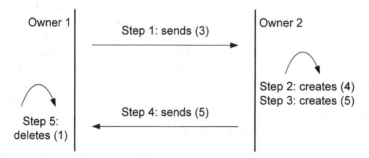

Fig. 22.4. Protocol of ownership transfer

Owner 1 uses his physical key and his OL to create a special UL as in (3) with a 'TakeOwnership' right to a selected user (owner 2). After the physical key of owner 2 receives and checks the offer in (3), owner 2 can choose to refuse or accept the offer. If he accepts, the system starts to complete the transfer. First, his physical key creates a new OL using the special UL (3). Owner 2 can re-encrypt the content (which is recommended) to ensure a full ownership takeover. If he decides to do so, the subsystem will generate a new asset key (AssetkeyNew) and re-encrypt this content, therefore the new OL is as in (4). After taking over the content, the new owner's physical key creates a clean-up UL (5) for the old owner with a clean-up right.

$$\{PK_{owner2}, PK_{owner1}, E_{PKowner2}[AssetID, Rights=TakeOwnership, Assetkey],$$
$$E_{PKowner1}[AssetID, Rights=TakeOwnership, Assetkey]\}sign_{PPowner1}. \tag{3}$$

$$\{PK_{owner2}, PK_{owner2}, E_{PKowner2}[AssetID, Rights=Ownership, AssetkeyNew],$$
$$E_{PKowner2}[AssetID, Rights=Ownership, AssetkeyNew]\}sign_{PPowner2}. \tag{4}$$

$$\{PK_{owner1}, PK_{owner2}, E_{PKowner1}[AssetID, Rights=Clean-upOwnership, Assetkey],$$
$$E_{PKowner2}[AssetID, Rights=Clean-upOwnership, Assetkey]\}sign_{PPowner2}. \tag{5}$$

When the old owner's private environment sees the clean-up UL (5), the system removes the old OL and all the old ULs of the content. If the old licenses are together with the content copies distributed to other devices or sharing users, the system needs to revoke them (using, e.g., a black revocation list). Optionally, the old owner's system can send to the new owner a signed confirmation that the old ownership is cleaned-up. This will be necessary if the new owner would like to be assured that the old owner could not claim the ownership anymore.

Let us describe the possible attack. It is obvious that the OL given in (1) can be easily copied. So, a dishonest old owner can copy his OL before the protocol and then, after the protocol, try to introduce to the system the OL copy, so that he can keep ownership. To prevent that, the system (physical key of the old owner that is compliant) can permanently store the ULs (3) and (5) as proof of the revocation of the OL (1). In this way, if the old owner tries later to reintroduce the OL copy, his physical key will refuse that message. The old owner might also try to cheat by claiming that he never received the clean-up UL. However, this is solved by the previously proposed extra step, which involves confirmation that the old ownership is cleaned up. Similarly, the physical key of the new owner can permanently store UL (3) and the confirmation of the cleaning-up of the old ownership as legal proofs of the ownership transfer. Using these messages, the new owner can legally prove ownership.

Note that all old sharing relations are removed after an ownership transfer. The new owner may restore old sharing rights, but it is a privacy concern of all involved people: the new owner, the old owner and the old sharing users.

22.5.3 Multiple Owners and Co-ownership

Very often it is difficult to determine who in the family is the owner of a piece of homemade content. By nature, some content may have multiple owners, and this makes ownership management more difficult.

One simple solution to co-ownership is to allow each owner to have one copy of the content, so that they can do what they want with the copy. In other words, independent multiple ownership. Another straightforward solution is to allow an owner to grant co-ownership of the same piece of content to other users. Both solutions could be done similarly using the procedure of ownership transfer in the previous section. For the latter, however, the old ownership and perhaps (depending on the agreement between co-owners) old sharing relations with other users are not removed. The new owner obtains co-ownership, while the old owner keeps it, so that each owner has an OL. However, these simple solutions leave unresolved problems and have disadvantages with respect to privacy and content management. First, it is a privacy problem that an operation of one of the owners of a co-owned piece of content, e.g., sharing the content with a user, may not be acceptable to the other owners. Second, the system needs extra management to maintain the information of all owners and copies. Another issue for the second solution is that it needs mechanisms to align the operations of each owner, such as re-encryption or deletion.

In order to solve the aforementioned problems, we propose new types of OLs for multiple-owned content as follows.

$$\{\text{AMS, PK}_{\text{owner1}}, \text{PK}_{\text{owner1}}, \text{E}_{\text{PKowner1}}[\text{AssetID1, Rights=Ownership, Assetkey1}],$$
$$\text{E}_{\text{PKowner1}}[\text{AssetID1, Rights=Ownership, Assetkey1}]\}\text{sign}_{\text{PPowner1}} \tag{6}$$

$$\{\text{AMM, LinkToAMMS, PK}_{\text{owner2}}, \text{PK}_{\text{owner2}}, \text{E}_{\text{PKowner2}}[\text{AssetID2, Rights=Ownership,}$$
$$\text{Assetkey2}], \text{E}_{\text{PKowner2}}[\text{AssetID2, Rights=Ownership, Assetkey2}]\}\text{sign}_{\text{PPowner2}} \tag{7}$$

$$\{\text{AMMS, CoRights, PK}_{\text{owner1}}, \text{PK}_{\text{owner2}}, \text{PK}_{\text{owner3}}, \text{E}_{\text{PKowner1}}[\text{AssetID2, Rights=Ownership,}$$
$$\text{Assetkey2}], \text{E}_{\text{PKowner2}}[\text{AssetID2, Rights=Ownership, Assetkey2}], \text{E}_{\text{PKowner3}}[\text{AssetID2,}$$
$$\text{Rights=Ownership, Assetkey2}]\}\text{sign}_{\text{PPowner1}} \text{sign}_{\text{PPowner2}} \text{sign}_{\text{PPowner3}} \tag{8}$$

First, a tag is added to the OL to indicate if multiple persons own the content: an AMS tag in (6) indicates single ownership of content by $\text{PK}_{\text{owner1}}$; an AMM tag in (7) indicates a piece of multiple-owned content. Following the AMM tag, a LinkToAMMS tag links the OL to the related multiple-ownership license (8). The multiple-ownership license or the AMMS message has an AMMS tag, a CoRights block, and public keys of all co-owners. The CoRights block specifies the rights of co-owners with respect to managing the content. For example, the CoRights can enforce that physical keys of other owners and their explicit confirmation are needed if one of the owners wants to create a sharing UL for a third person. It can also state that confirmation of n from m owners is needed for sharing. In that case n owners must explicitly approve the sharing. The AMMS message has multiple signatures (each owner has their own signature). In the process of defining co-ownership, each owner signs the AMMS message and his AMM message as proof of his co-ownership.

The multiple-owned content can be created from initially single-owned content using a protocol similar to the transfer of ownership, but with a co-ownership offer and a CoRights policy. Having agreed on this, the protocol uses the physical keys of the old and the new owner(s) to create and sign the AMMS and AMM messages, while the old AMS message of the first owner is revoked. The AMMS and AMM message can also be created immediately when the co-owners introduce the content into the system. The co-owners present their physical keys to the system and perform the protocol in which the AMM and AMMS message will be created with an agreed CoRights policy. After that, they sign sequentially the AMMS so that signatures of all owners are present. Finally each owner signs his AMM message, independent of the other owners.

If a co-owner wants to change the policy for sharing, he can propose new CoRights. The system will inform other co-owners about the proposal and ask them for confirmation. Only when all owners confirm the proposal by signing the new AMMS will the system revoke the old messages, create new AMM messages (with a link to the new AMMS message), and in practice apply the new policy.

One of the owners can share multiple-owned content with a third party if the CoRights policy allows it. Using the AMMS and his AMM message, his physical key can generate a UL (9) for the third party.

$$\{\text{AMM, LinkToAMMS, PK}_{\text{user1}}, \text{PK}_{\text{owner1}}, E_{\text{PKuser1}}[\text{AssetID2, Rights=View, Assetkey2}],$$
$$E_{\text{PKowner1}}[\text{AssetID2, Rights=View, Assetkey2}]\}\text{sign}_{\text{PPowner1}} \qquad (9)$$

$$\{\text{AMM, LinkToAMMS, PK}_{\text{user1}}, \text{PK}_{\text{owner1}}, E_{\text{PKuser1}}[\text{AssetID2, Rights=View, Assetkey2}],$$
$$E_{\text{PKowner1}}[\text{AssetID2,Rights=View,Assetkey2}]\}\text{sign}_{\text{PPowner1}}\text{sign}_{\text{PPowner2}}\text{sign}_{\text{PPowner3}} \qquad (10)$$

If the CoRights in the AMMS message require confirmation of multiple owners, this UL is not valid until the necessary number of owners have signed the UL, as, e.g., in (10), or they have each created such a UL as in (9) for the user. The physical key of the user enforces the CoRights in the AMMS message, when it is used to access the content. Group signatures [7,8,9] can also be used here instead of signatures or ULs from individual co-owners. This preserves the anonymity of individual owners.

By introducing the AMM and AMS tags and AMMS message, a TeM-PES device always knows if multiple owners own an asset. Furthermore, as the UL for a user is linked with the AMMS message, the device will immediately know who the other owners are. So, information about all co-owners is maintained and no on-line synchronization between owners is needed. This solution considerably simplifies the content management and ownership management of multiple-owned content, and has no side effects on content access operation.

22.5.4. Deletion

Deletion is a tricky operation if the content is used or owned by multiple users. In different contexts, the traditional deletion operation can have different implications: deleting content (the asset file) and getting free space back, deleting access rights and deleting ownership.

In the TeMPES system, a sharing user is able to delete the access rights (UL) to content shared with him, but not the content file owned by others unless it is his personal copy or the owner has granted such rights. It is dangerous for privacy and for unintended data loss to give a sharing user rights to delete the asset, although this is convenient for the system user.

An owner has full rights to his content. When the owner wants to delete his single-owned content, the system will delete the stored content file and return free space. If the content is protected, all ULs and the OL of this content will also be removed. Sharing users lose access to the content at the same moment. For content owned by multiple owners, if one owner deletes the content, the system just deletes his ownership of the content and the sharing rights he has granted, i.e., the OL and ULs he has created. The system will usually not delete the content until the last owner deletes the content or unless all owners have agreed that a single owner can remove the content file.

There should also be a clean-up command that allows for the deletion of content that is invisible to all authorized users of a system. Invisible content could be created, e.g., by a guest or by damage of data due to malfunction. The privileged users may have a clean-up function that can remove all ULs and OLs of non-privileged users, and eventually delete the invisible content. In general, one can say that the content asset is only deleted if there are no remaining licenses for that content.

Note that deleting a co-ownership OL (7) obliges the system to notify other owners by making a new AMMS message (8) that excludes all fields related to this old co-owner. Alternatively, a homomorphic signature scheme [7] can be used in the AMMS message, so that the system could create such a new AMMS message and valid signatures without asking the co-owners to sign again. Here we still need to prevent a co-owner from deleting other co-owners and confiscating the content. This can be done by storing such a message in a secure storage or letting the system sign such a message with its key using a normal signature scheme.

22.6 Conclusions

Privacy is becoming a serious concern in the connected world. Therefore, advanced privacy solutions will be required in the connected home entertainment environment, especially when the entertainment is personalized. As different people have different privacy needs, it is important to provide a range of privacy protection options to consumers.

In this chapter, a home media center that supports consumer privacy in various ways has been described. As privacy protection influences all management operations on the data, operations such as importing, sharing, publishing and deleting have been investigated and solutions have been presented. Special focus has been put on ownership management, which forms the foundation of privacy protection. Furthermore, a solution for transferring ownership in an easy and secure way has been developed. Next to that, solutions have been worked out to manage co-ownership, which allows multiple owners to properly manage the content and grant rights (e.g., for sharing) in an agreed way.

References

1. US House Committee on Energy and Commerce, Subcommittee on Commerce, Trade and Consumer Protection Prepared Witness Testimony of Dr. Alan Westin May 8, 2001. In book: Ann Cavoukian / Tyler J. Hamliton, *The Privacy Payoff*, ISBN: 0070905606, McGraw-Hill Ryerson, 2002.
2. S. Gutwirth, *Privacy and the Information Age*, ISBN 0-7425-1746-2, Rowman & Littlefield Publishers, Inc. 2002.
3. EPIC & Privacy International, *Privacy & Human Rights, an international survey of privacy laws and developments*, ISBN 1-893044-18-1, Electronic Privacy Information Center (EPIC), 2003.
4. OECD, "Guidelines on the Protection of Privacy and Transborder Data Flows of Personal Data", 1980. Available from: www.oecd.org/document/18/0,2340,en_2649_34255_1815186_1_1_1_1,00.html
5. Directive 95/46/EC of the European Parliament and of the Council of 24 October 1995 on the Protection of Individuals with Regard to the Processing of Personal Data and on the Free Movement of such Data. http://europa.eu.int/comm/internal_market/privacy/law_en.htm
6. M. Takagi, "Multimedia Security - Guideline for privacy protection of equipment and systems in use and disused", proposal to IEC TC100, IEC TC100/808NP, April 2004.
7. R. Johnson, D. Molnar, D. Xiaodong Song, D. Wagner, "Homomorphic signature schemes", In RSA Conference on Topics in Cryptology, Springer-Verlag, 2002, pp. 244-262.
8. G. Ateniese, J. Camenisch, M. Joye, and G. Tsudik, "A practical and provably secure coalition-resistant group signature scheme", In M. Bellare, editor, Proceedings of Crypto 2000, volume 1880 of LNCS, pp. 255–70. Springer-Verlag, Aug. 2000.
9. G. Ateniese, G. Tsudik, and D. Song, "Quasi-efficient revocation of group signatures", In M. Blaze, editor, Proceedings of Financial Cryptography 2002, March 2002.

23

Enhancing Privacy for Digital Rights Management

Milan Petković, Claudine Conrado, Geert-Jan Schrijen and Willem Jonker

Philips Research
The Netherlands

Summary. This chapter addresses privacy issues in DRM systems. These systems provide a means of protecting digital content, but may violate the privacy of users in that the content they purchase and their actions in the system can be linked to specific users. The chapter proposes a privacy-preserving DRM system in which users interact with the system in a pseudonymous way, while preserving all the security requirements of usual DRM systems. To achieve this goal, a set of protocols and methods is proposed for managing user identities and interactions with the basic system during the acquisition and consumption of digital content. Privacy-enhancing extensions are also proposed. Unlinkable purchase of content, which prevents content providers from linking all content purchased by a given user, is discussed. Moreover, a method that allows a user to transfer content rights to another user without the two users being linked by the content provider is provided.

23.1 Introduction

Thanks to the Internet, which provides an excellent trading infrastructure, nowadays digital content distribution has become one of the most quickly emerging activities. As a consequence of this trend and the success of one of the first online music shops, Apple's iTunes, which has recently sold its 500 millionth song [1], a number of shops have been opened [2-6] and both consumers and content providers have clearly shown great interest in electronic distribution of audio and video content.

Digital content can, however, be easily copied, exchanged and distributed illegally, which is obviously a threat for the content industry. This has triggered active research on technologies that can protect digital content from illegal use. One of the most important of these technologies is digital rights management (DRM) technology that provides content protection by enforcing the use of digital content according to granted rights. It enables content providers to protect their copyrights and maintain control over the distribution of and access to content. The most widely used DRM systems nowadays in the mainstream entertainment arena are Microsoft Windows Media DRM 10 [7] and Apple's FairPlay [8], which are the two big players for PC-centric music services. Other DRM systems are Sony's Open MagicGate [9], Helix from RealNetworks [10] and Thomson's SmartRight [11].

Early DRM systems were device based, which means that rights were bound to devices and content was only accessible on a specific device. However, in order to allow a consumer to access his content anytime, anywhere, on any device, the idea of person-based DRM has emerged, as discussed in Chap. 20. Furthermore, some companies are investigating new concepts such as authorized domains [12-14] and personal entertainment domains (PEDs) [15], which take into account (along with the requirements of content owners) the requirements of content consumers. In PEDs, for instance, content can freely flow inside a domain (typically a household), so that it can be freely copied inside that domain and exchanged among the domain devices. However, the system controls transactions between different domains.

To protect the content and enforce the rights given in a license, a DRM system normally identifies a user and monitors the usage of content. Therefore, DRM systems are very privacy-invasive, violating the users' privacy in many ways. For example, they do not support anonymous and un-linkable buying or transfer of content as in the traditional (physical) business model where a user anonymously buys a CD using cash. Furthermore, they generally involve tracking of the usage of content in order to enforce the rights [16,17]. In person-based DRM systems, e.g., a user has to authenticate himself each time he accesses a piece of content. Therefore, information such as user identification, content identification, time and place of access, etc., can be collected. The same holds for device-based DRM systems, except that user identification may not be straightforward, but through other data that can be linked to the user.

As privacy is becoming increasingly important in the connected digital world, the possibility of creating user profiles or tracking users creates numerous privacy concerns. In order to overcome the aforementioned privacy problems in DRM systems, this paper proposes several methods to enhance privacy. The main idea is to allow a user to interact with the system in an pseudonymous way during the whole process of buying and consuming digital content. This has to be done in a way that all the security requirements of the usual DRM systems are satisfied. This means that content providers must be assured that content is used according to issued licenses and cannot be illegally copied. Furthermore, we discuss a solution that prevents the linkability of purchase actions by anonymous users. Finally, an approach is presented to anonymously transfer licenses, so that a piece of content can be sold or gifted to another user without the content provider being able to link the two users.

The remainder of the chapter is organized as follows. In Sect. 23.2, the basic privacy-preserving DRM (PPDRM) system is introduced. Section 23.3 discusses a solution that extends the basic system to support unlinkable purchase of content. In Sect. 23.4, the system is extended to support anonymous transfer of licenses. Finally, Sect. 23.5 draws conclusions.

23.2 Basic System

In the basic PPDRM system, a user is represented by means of pseudonyms, which are decoupled from the user's real identity. Based on these pseudonyms, the system tackles a number of threats to the privacy of the users of this system, and also related threats to the security of the system. These threats are mentioned below and are handled by the PPDRM system by means of protocols discussed in the next sections.

The association between a user's real identity and content owned by the user is the main privacy threat circumvented by PPDRM. This association may happen if personal licenses are used for content access, and it allows the tracking of users while they access content. To avoid that, the system exploits persistent (i.e., long-term) user pseudonyms.

A common security threat in DRM systems is the hacking of devices, e.g., personal smart cards and devices on which content is accessed. The PPDRM system avoids this threat by means of compulsory mutual compliance checks between smart cards and devices. Such checks, however, may violate users' privacy. To avoid that, the system exploits temporary (i.e., short-term) user pseudonyms.

Although users do not disclose their real identity in the system, there is still a threat to their privacy, which is the linkability of a user's content purchase actions via his persistent pseudonym. The PPDRM system deals with this problem by means of a mechanism which allows users to renew their persistent pseudonyms. The system also prevents the user from misusing the system by transferring their licenses to others.

Finally, the transfer of licenses between users causes important security and privacy threats. For example, a user may be able to continue using his licenses after he has transferred them to another user. Concerning privacy threats, the association between the user who transfers and the user who receives a given license is typically disclosed. To avoid these threats, the PPDRM system makes use of invalidation lists and anonymous licenses issued by the CP.

Entities in the basic PPDRM system include the *user*, the *content provider* (CP) and the *compliant device* (CoD), a device that behaves according to the DRM rules. Related to the CoD, there is the *compliance certificate issuer for compliant devices* (CA-CoD). Moreover, there is the *smart card* (SC), which is the user ID device. In the following sections, where no confusion may be caused (e.g., in the description of protocols), the user and his smart card are referred to interchangeably. Related to the smart card there are the *smart card issuer* (SCI) and the *compliance certificate issuer for smart cards* (CA-SC).

Figure 23.1 depicts the different transactions performed involving the entities mentioned above. These transactions and different aspects of the system are described in the sections below, where references to the numbered links in Fig. 23.1 are made at the appropriate points.

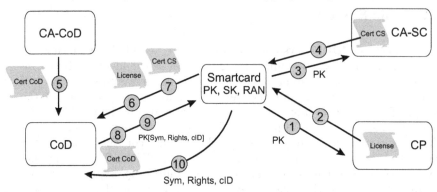

Fig. 23.1. Interactions among different entities of the PPDRM system.

23.2.1 Acquisition of a Smart Card by the User

The acquisition of a smart card by the user is done in an anonymous way. The user buys a smart card from a retailer, taken from a pool of identically looking smart cards pre-issued by the SCI. Each smart card contains a different public-private key pair (PK, SK) and an unset personal identification number (PIN), e.g., all PINs are set initially to 0000. The SCI guarantees that, as long as the PIN is unset, the public key of that specific card is not revealed to any party. So, when the user interacts for the first time with the card, he is asked to set a PIN, after which the card becomes active and reveals its public key PK. The PIN can never be reset back to the null value, so the user is sure that he is the first one to learn that PK. Once set, the PIN can be used to activate the card to allow its engagement in transactions with other entities. The PIN should be kept secret by the user, which guarantees that the card can only be used by *that* user. This activation procedure is assumed and will not be explicitly mentioned in the smart card's transactions in the remainder of this chapter.

With the setup above, no one should be able to make an association between the user's real identity and the PK. Note that the private key SK is securely stored on the smart card and is not accessible to the user nor to any other party (except of course the SCI). This is a crucial security aspect of the system. As can be seen in the next section, the leakage of the SK would allow the user to, e.g., freely distribute all (unencrypted) content for which he bought a license.

Security assumptions in this context are (i) the public key PK of a SC is revealed and the PIN number is set only after the first transaction, and (ii) the private key SK corresponding to the public key PK is stored secretly and only known to the SC.

23.2.2 Acquisition of the Content and the Rights by the User

The acquisition of content and licenses is performed as follows. The user's SC contacts the CP with the request via an Internet connection using an anonymous channel. This can be implemented, e.g., via a mix network [18] or a simpler proxy service [19]. The anonymous channel hides the user's IP address and prevents the user identity from being derived from the IP address. After an anonymous payment scheme is conducted (such as the pre-payment scheme described in [20]), the user's SC sends the public key PK to the CP (link 1 in Fig. 23.1). It is assumed that the SCI keeps track of all smart cards it has issued and of their behavior by means of a revocation list with the PKs of hacked SCs. With this setting, the CP can check with the SCI whether PK is legitimate and whether it belongs to the revocation list or not. If it does not, the CP can create the right or license for that content. The content itself is encrypted by the CP with a symmetric key, Sym, randomly chosen by the CP, and sent to the user (link 2 in Fig. 23.1) together with the license, whose format is given in (1). Both, content and license, can then be stored by the user, e.g., on an optical disk or personal device.

$$\{ \text{PK}[\text{Sym}//\text{Rights}//\text{contentID}] , \text{H}(\text{Rights}//\text{contentID}) \}_{\text{signCP}} \qquad (1)$$

In the license above, PK encrypts the concatenated value [Sym//Rights//contentID], where Rights describe the rights bought by the user, contentID identifies the content and signCP is the CP's signature on the certificate. The hash of (Rights//contentID) is also added to the license to allow a compliant device to check these values upon a content access request (as discussed in Sect. 2.4). The CP's signature on both terms in the license guarantees that these terms have indeed been created by the CP. Moreover, given that the PK encrypts the value [Sym//Rights//contentID], the SC is the only entity that can obtain the key Sym from the license by using the private key SK. Furthermore, a compliant SC (as attested by the compliance certificate discussed in the next section) will reveal the key Sym only to a compliant device during the content access action.

The license in (1), if seen by any party, e.g., on the user's optical disk, does not reveal the public key PK nor the rights, nor the content identifier, so it preserves the user's privacy with respect to content and rights ownership. Therefore, if found in the user's possession, it does not compromise the user's privacy. Note, however, that an eavesdropper may have been able to associate the public key PK sent to the CP with the license sent back by the CP during a buying transaction, if these values were sent on the clear. Therefore, the anonymous channel used should also be secret, i.e., the exchanged data should be encrypted.

The CP learns the association (PK↔(contentID, Rights, Sym)) during purchase, but not the user's real identity due to the anonymous channel.

Security assumptions in this context are (i) there is a mechanism in place to allow the user to pay anonymously for the license he requests, (ii) the user contacts the CP via an anonymous channel, (iii) the channel is also secret, and (iv) the SCI is responsible for keeping track of hacked SCs (i.e., those whose secret key SK has been revealed or whose functionality has been changed in any way).

23.2.3 Acquisition of SC Compliance Certificate by the User

To ensure security of the protocol between the user's SC and the CoD, a mutual compliance check is performed. That means that the SC checks the CoD's compliance but must also show an SC's compliance certificate to the CoD. The acquisition of this certificate is described below.

The SC's compliance certificate does not contain the user public key PK, but is issued by the CA-SC with a frequently renewed SC's pseudonym, for reasons given below. To obtain this certificate, the user's SC contacts the CA-SC via an Internet connection using an anonymous channel, as in the interaction with the CP above. Again, the anonymous channel used must be secret to prevent eavesdropping on the channel. The user's SC sends its public key PK (link 3 in Fig. 23.1) with a request for the certificate, and the CA-SC checks with the SCI whether PK belongs to the revocation list or not. If it does not, the CA-SC generates a pseudonym for the SC, say a random number RAN, and issues the following compliance certificate, which is sent to the SC (link 4 in Fig. 23.1):

$$\{H(RAN), PK[RAN]\}_{signCA\text{-}SC}, \qquad (2)$$

where H is a one-way hash function, PK encrypts RAN and signCA-SC is the signature of the CA-SC on the certificate.

The compliance certificate above does not reveal the public key PK nor the SC's pseudonym RAN. Furthermore, the only entity which can obtain RAN from the certificate is the SC (by decryption with the private key SK). The value RAN may then be checked by the device via the hash value in the certificate. The use of a pseudonym RAN allows the device (verifier) to check the compliance of the SC without learning its public key PK from the certificate. Moreover, the linkability of different shows of a given SC's compliance certificate can be minimized since a frequent renewal of the compliance certificates (and, as a consequence, of the pseudonyms RAN) is a requirement of the DRM system. This can be achieved by including an expiration date in the compliance certificate.

On the other hand, there are different methods to prevent the linkability of pseudonyms. For example, the convertible credentials described in [21] allow a user to obtain a credential from a given organization under a given pseudonym, and show that credential to another organization under another pseudonym. This type of approach involves protocols which are significantly more complex than the simple protocols described in this paper, which involve only simple hash operations.

During the acquisition process of the compliance certificate, the CA-SC learns the association (PK↔RAN), but not the user's real identity due to the anonymous channel.

Security assumptions in this context are (i) the user contacts the CA-SC via an anonymous channel, (ii) the channel is also secret, and (iii) the SCI is responsible for keeping track of hacked SCs.

23.2.4 Access to Content by the User

Finally, the user can access the content for which he bought the license. This can be performed on any CoD, which may be trusted or untrusted by the user (note that the discussion below on possible compromises to the user's privacy is only relevant in the case of *untrusted* CoDs). The encrypted content and the license may both be stored, e.g., on a user's portable device. Alternatively, the license (but likely not the encrypted content) may be stored in the user's SC. Whichever the case, license and content are both transferred to the CoD (link 6 in Figure 23.1). This allows this device to check the license (as described below), and further decrypt and render the content to the user if allowed. But before that happens, a mutual compliance check must be performed as described next.

The CoD proves its compliance by means of a CoD compliance certificate. This certificate is issued by the CA-CoD (which certifies the CoD's public key) and sent to the CoD beforehand (link 5 in Figure 23.1). Upon the compliance check, the certificate is shown to the SC (link 8 in Fig. 23.1). The SC must therefore store the public key of the CA-CoD. This key may be changed periodically, which obliges the CoD to periodically renew its compliance certificate, thus allowing revocation of CoDs. This solution is preferred to that of including an expiration date in the CoD compliance certificate, as the SC may not have a clock. Moreover, periodic change of the CA-CoD's public key also implies that the SC must renew that key periodically. This could be done, e.g., when the SC obtains its own compliance certificates from the CA-SC, as this authority could also safely provide the SC with the CA-CoD's public key. Once the CoD has been checked, the SC proves its compliance by showing the pseudonymous compliance certificate in (2) to the CoD (link 7 in Fig. 23.1). As mentioned above, the SC can obtain the value RAN and send it to the CoD which checks the value via the term H(RAN). Since the CoD can have a clock, the SC compliance certificate may contain a time of issuance and a validity period added to it, which obliges the SC to periodically renew the certificate when it gets too old. Note that it is also in the interest of the SC to renew its compliance certificate often enough so as to minimize the linkability mentioned above.

If the mutual compliance check is positive, the CoD sends the term PK[Sym//Rights//contentID] from the license to the SC (link 9 in Fig. 23.1), which then decrypts the term and sends the values Sym, Rights and contentID back to the CoD (link 10 in Fig. 23.1). Note that, although the compliance of the SC is checked by the CoD, it is always possible that a dishonest SC has not yet been detected. Therefore, to ensure that the SC sends the correct values of Rights (and contentID), the CoD checks the hash value in the license which has been previously transferred to it. Only if it is correct, the CoD uses Sym to decrypt the content and gives the user access to it, according to Rights.

During access to content by the user, the CoD learns the association (RAN↔(contentID, Rights, Sym)). The CoD may also learn the user's real identity, as the user is now physically present in front of the CoD (e.g., the CoD may have a camera). However, the public key PK of the user is never revealed to the CoD at the time of content access. Therefore, this compromises the user's privacy only concerning the specific content and rights involved in the access transaction. The threat is of course higher if the user accesses many different pieces of content on the same CoD. This type of attack cannot really be avoided. Considering this is not the case, what the proposed mechanism prevents is that a content access action by a user on a CoD, possibly under the control of an attacker, may easily allow the attacker to learn all other content bought by the user. Moreover, if the attacker does not learn the user's real identity, the mechanism limits the number of transactions for which the user may be tracked by a given CoD, as RAN changes often.

Security assumptions in this context are (i) the CA-CoD is responsible for keeping track of the CoD's behaviour as well as for issuing compliance certificates for those devices, (ii) a compliant SC will send the right values and only reveal the decryption key Sym to a compliant device (CoD), and (iii) the CoD will not reveal the key Sym to any party, except for perhaps another (proven) compliant device.

23.3 Non-linkable Purchase of Content

In this section, the basic PPDRM is extended to prevent linkability by the CP of content purchased by a given user with public key PK. Linkability may compromise a user's privacy if the association between PK and his real identity is disclosed to the CP for at least one piece of content. This means that the association is disclosed for all content bought by that user. The solution is based on user pseudonyms, which can be used to buy different pieces of content, and includes the steps of pseudonym certification and anonymous purchase.

23.3.1 System Assumptions

It is assumed that users have a Diffie-Hellman key pair and that from the original public key new public keys are derived, which can be certified by a trusted certification authority (referred to as CA). The system parameters g, p and q are chosen as in general Diffie-Hellman key agreement [22], with g referred to as the group generator. The user's private key is SK $\in$ [1,q-1] and the corresponding public key is generated as PK $= g^{SK}$ mod p. For brevity, the modulo operation will be omitted in the remainder of this section.

With the assumptions above, public key encryptions can be implemented as El-Gamal encryptions [23]. For signing messages, the digital signature standard (DSS) [24] with the digital signature algorithm (DSA) can be used since it uses Diffie-Hellman keys. The reader may also refer to [25] for more details on the cryptographic tools and protocols mentioned in this section.

23.3.2 Pseudonym Acquisition and Certification

The user must have his pseudonyms (in the form of new public keys) certified at the CA before he can use them to buy content rights from the CP. The communication steps between the user and the CA are explained below and depicted in Fig. 23.2.

The user sends his original public key PK to the CA, which allows the CA to check with the SCI whether PK is legitimate and whether it belongs to the revocation list or not. If all checks are successful, the two parties proceed to establish a secure authenticated channel (SAC). Next, the user creates a random value α and sends it securely to the CA (alternatively, the CA may generate α and send it to the user). With α and PK, the CA creates the pseudonym PK* by raising PK to the power α, i.e., PK$^* =$ PK$^{\alpha}$ $= g^{\alpha SK}$. The new public key PK* is created in this way for reasons discussed below. Next, the CA creates and signs a digital certificate containing the pseudonym PK* and securely sends it back to the user's SC. This certificate proves that the pseudonym PK* belongs to a user with a legitimate PK. It is assumed that the CA keeps track of all pseudonyms generated from (i.e., associated with) a given public key, but that it keeps this information confidential. This is only disclosed to the SCI if this authority discovers that the SC with PK^* has been hacked. This allows the SCI to add that SC to the revocation list, by entering not the pseudonym PK^* but its original public key PK to the list.

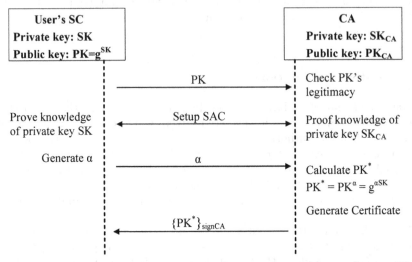

Fig. 23.2. Protocol for acquisition and certification of a pseudonym (new public key) by a user with the CA.

The new public key PK^* corresponds to a new private key SK^* which can be easily computed by the SC as $SK^* = \alpha SK$. Moreover, only the SC (and no other party, including the CA) can calculate this key, so SK^* can be kept secret by the SC in the same way as the original private key SK. With this crucial security aspect of the system taken into account for pseudonyms as well, the CP can issue pseudonymous licenses for content access with the format shown in (1), as it will be seen in the next section. Therefore, once calculated by the SC, the new key SK^* must be securely stored (i.e., no party should be able to access that key in the SC).

23.3.3 Content Rights Purchase

The purchasing procedure is similar to the procedure described in Sect. 2.2. It is explained below and illustrated in Fig. 23.3.

After the user contacts the CP via an anonymous channel requesting the rights to given content under a given pseudonym, an anonymous payment scheme is conducted. The pseudonym certificate is then sent to the CP, which checks the signature on the certificate. If it is correct, the CP can issue a license as shown in (3) with the pseudonym PK^* as subject, which can then be sent to the user. Note that this license has the same format as the license given in (1).

$$\{ PK^*[Sym//Rights//contentID] , H(Rights//contentID) \}_{signCP} \qquad (3)$$

As noted before, to prevent an eavesdropper from being able to associate the public key PK^* sent to the CP with the license sent back by the CP during the buying transaction, the communication channel must be secret.

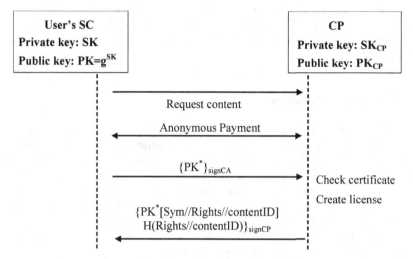

Fig. 23.3. License purchase by a user under a pseudonym PK^* certified by the CA.

23.3.4 Content Access

Once in possession of the license as given in (3), the user can access the content on any CoD. The encrypted content and the license are transferred to the CoD, which then performs a mutual compliance check with the SC. The CoD compliance certificate and the SC pseudonymous compliance certificate are described in Sect. 2.4. The latter is issued with a dynamic value RAN and is obtained from the CA-SC under public key PK (i.e., PK, and not PK^*, encrypts the value RAN in the certificate).

As before, after the mutual compliance check, the CoD sends $PK^*[Sym//Rights//contentID]$ to the SC, which decrypts it using SK^*. The values Sym, Rights and contentID are then sent back to the CoD. If the value H(Rights//contentID) checks with the received values, the CoD decrypts the content and gives the user access to it in accordance to Rights.

23.4 Anonymous Transfer of Licenses

A user should be able to transfer his license to another user. This transfer must be done in a way that prevents the original owner from still being able to access the content after the transfer by using the license. It is further required here that the transfer be anonymous, i.e., no party learns the association between the two users. Therefore, a solution is discussed below which extends the basic PPDRM to tackle license invalidation and license anonymization. The same procedure applies if the user bought his license under a pseudonym, which simply replaces PK in all interactions with the CP.

23.4.1 License Invalidation

To allow a user (referred to as the first user) to transfer his license, he contacts the CP via an anonymous channel, authenticates with his public key PK, presents the license to be transferred to the other user (referred to as the second user) and provides the second user's public key PK'. Note that here the CP learns the connection between the two users. The CP marks that license with PK as "to be invalidated", so before the CP creates a new license with PK', invalidation of the old license must be dealt with.

The invalidation problem can be solved by including in the compliance certificate of the first user's SC a list with all the licenses that are to be invalidated. This can be done when the SC obtains its compliance certificate. The CA-SC contacts the CP and asks for that list for PK. The CP uses the symmetric key Sym_i to identify a given invalidated license i, and creates a list with the values H(Sym_i // Time). H( ) is a one-way hash function used to conceal the values of Sym_i and to reduce the size of the terms in the invalidation list, and the current time (Time) is concatenated with each Sym_i to prevent the linkability of compliance certificates issued for PK in different occasions. Once the list with H(Sym_i // Time) values and the value Time are sent to the CA-SC, the CP considers as resolved the invalidation of the licenses of PK and can create the new license for the second user, which includes public key PK'. The SC's compliance certificate now has the format as in (4).

$$\{ \text{H(RAN), PK[RAN], Time, H(Sym\_1//Time), H(Sym\_2//Time),..., H(Sym\_n // Time) }\}_{\text{signCA-SC}} \quad (4)$$

At the present time, a typical SC [26] may store such a compliance certificate with an invalidation list with up to about 500 invalidated licenses. If the invalidation list becomes too big to be stored on the SC, then the certificate with the invalidation list can be stored, for instance, on a server in the network or on an optical storage medium.

As before, upon a user request for content access on a CoD, the SC must present its compliance certificate. After a mutual compliance check, the CoD sends PK[Sym//Rights//contentID] to the SC, which decrypts it and sends back the values Sym, Rights and contentID. But before the CoD uses Sym to decrypt the content to give access to the user, it calculates H(Sym//Time) and checks whether this value is in the invalidation list of the SC's compliance certificate or not. Only if it is not, the CoD proceeds with the handling of the access request.

23.4.2 Anonymous Licenses

In the previous section, the CP learns the association between the first and second user (i.e., between their public keys) when the license transfer is requested. If this is unwanted by the users, generic licenses in which a user identity is not specified can be used, as described below.

The generic license above (from now on referred to as *anonymous license*) is a license for a specified content with specified rights, but which is not associated with an identity (i.e., with a public key). Such a license can be issued by the CP for an anonymous user who pays for a given content with given rights as well as for the first user who requested the invalidation of his license, as described in the previous section. Since the license is not associated with any identity, it can be transferred (given, sold, etc.) to any other person. This person can later present the anonymous license to that CP and exchange it for a personalized license as given in (1). The latter can then be used for content access.

A security threat in this procedure is that users may copy the anonymous license and redeem multiple copies at different times. To prevent that, before the CP issues the anonymous license, a unique identifier is assigned to it. If this identifier is chosen by the CP, however, it will be able to link the public keys of the first and second user via that identifier. In order to prevent that, blind signatures [27] can be used, as described below.

A secret random identifier ID is created by the first user, who blinds this value (e.g., by multiplying ID by another randomly chosen value) and sends it to the CP. The user may also send a specification for new rights, NewRights, which are to be associated with the anonymous license, provided that NewRights allow less than the original rights. This possibility allows a user to give to another user a license with more restrictive rights than the original rights he had, if he so wishes.

For each combination of rights and content {Rights, contentID}, the CP has a unique pair of public-private keys. It is assumed here that the set of all rights is pre-specified consisting of, say, R rights and the set of all content has C items. So the CP must have $R \times C$ different public-private key pairs. Therefore, when the CP receives the data {Blind[ID], NewRights} from the first user, it signs Blind[ID] with the private key of the combination {NewRights, contentID} and sends back the value {Blind[ID]}$_{\text{signed-NewRights-contentID}}$. The user then un-blinds the signed identifier to obtain {ID}$_{\text{signed-NewRights-contentID}}$. This protocol is depicted in Fig. 23.4 for content CD_1, and old and new rights as $Rights_1$ and $Rights_2$, respectively.

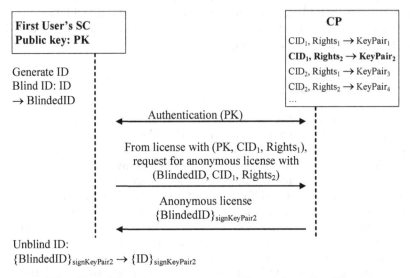

Fig. 23.4. Obtaining an anonymous license from the CP.

Next, the un-blinded value is sent to the second user together with the license specification {NewRights, contentID}. The second user can now contact the CP anonymously to obtain a personalized license. He authenticates himself and sends {ID}$_{\text{signed-NewRights-contentID}}$ and {NewRights, contentID} to the CP. The CP finds the correct key pair and checks its own signature in the value ID. If correct, the CP issues a personalized license to the second user, as given in (5), and sends it to the user.

$$\{ \text{PK'}[\text{ Sym'}//\text{NewRights}//\text{contentID }], \text{H}(\text{NewRights}//\text{contentID}) \}_{\text{signCP}} \qquad (5)$$

The protocol carried out between the second user and the CP is depicted in Fig. 23.5 for the example given in Fig. 23.4.

After the issuance of the license above, the value ID is entered by the CP into a list of used IDs. This prevents the personalized license request for an already redeemed anonymous license.

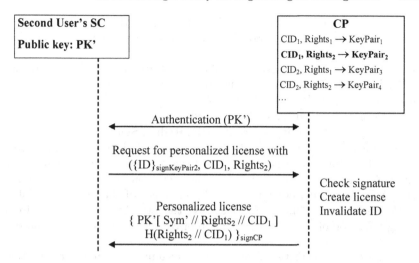

Fig. 23.5. Redeeming the anonymous license for a personalized one.

Note that the invalidation of the old license of the first user must be dealt with before the CP issues an anonymous license for that user. This allows an unlinkable transfer of licenses between users which is also secure. Another application relates to the business model of motivating users to buy a certain content, for instance, buy one, get a second one for free. The second license can be issued as an anonymous license which can be transferred to any person.

23.5 Discussion

A privacy-preserving DRM system is described, which protects users' privacy while preserving the system's security. Below, the privacy and security aspects of the system (basic as well as with extensions) are discussed.

User privacy is achieved in the DRM system by decoupling the user's real identity from his identifiers in the DRM system (i.e., PK and RAN). Concerning the relevant entities in the system, the following holds for a user with public key PK:

- The SCI learns the association (PK ↔ PK*), but only if the SC is hacked.
- The CP learns the association (PK ↔ (contentID, Rights, Sym)).
- The CA-SC learns the association (PK ↔ RAN).
- The CoD learns the association (RAN ↔ (contentID, Rights, Sym)).

It is therefore the case that, even by collusions of the parties above, the real identity of the user cannot be revealed since no parties know that identity.

The above statement regarding collusions is untrue only if an attacker can obtain user-related information from the CoD after a content access transaction happens. In this case, the associations

- (user's real identity ↔ RAN), and
- (user's real identity ↔ (contentID, Rights, Sym))

become known to him (if that information can be linked to the user's real identity). If collusion is not possible, however, the privacy damage is minimized: the attacker cannot learn the user's public key PK from the CoD, RAN changes periodically and only one piece of content is associated with the user's real identity. In this way, the attacker is prevented from creating a full log of the user's ownership of content and pattern of content usage.

To ensure the security of the DRM system, a compulsory mutual compliance check between SC and CoD must be carried out upon a content access transaction. The SC checks whether the CoD is compliant by means of a compliance certificate issued by the CA-CoD, and the CoD, in its turn, checks the SC for compliance, also by means of a compliance certificate. These certificates must be renewed often in order to ensure that the checks are up-to-date. The privacy of the user is preserved with the use of temporary pseudonyms (the RAN values) for the SC.

A privacy-enhancing extension of the system allows a user to further protect his privacy by purchasing content under different pseudonyms. In this case, the CP is unable to link all content bought by the same user, thus protecting his privacy. The various pseudonyms of the user must however be certified at a trusted authority (the CA) to guarantee the system security. Pseudonym certification guarantees that the pseudonyms

- are calculated from the original user's public key PK by the CA,
- are stored by the CA, connected with PK, and only revealed under certain conditions.

An additional privacy-enhancing extension of the system concerns the transfer of licenses between users. The solution proposed also guarantees the security of the DRM system, as explained below.

Security can be ensured with the invalidation of transferred licenses by means of the compliance certificate in (4). It includes the invalidation list with all invalidated licenses of a given SC. The frequent renewal of this certificate is important and done in the interest of both, the user and the DRM system, for the following reasons:

- for the user, it is done to minimize linkability, via the pseudonym RAN, of the user's content access requests to different content, and

- for the DRM system, it is done as a requirement of the CoD to check if the certificate (and therefore the license invalidation list) is too old via the value Time.

The user might not mind the linkability above, which would cause infrequent or no renewal actions on the part of the user. The renewal can be, however, forced as a requirement of the CoD, in order for that device to frequently get renewed values of invalidated licenses of PK.

The use of anonymous licenses in the license transfer process ensures user privacy. These licenses are anonymous (as they do not include any user identifier) and can be redeemed at the CP for real usable licenses. They must, however, include a unique identifier to be checked by the CP to prevent an anonymous license from being copied and redeemed multiple times. While guaranteeing system security, this unique identifier allows the CP to link the two users involved in the transfer. The use of blind signatures, however, ensures that this is not possible.

References

1. iTunes Music Store Downloads Top Half a Billion Songs, http://www.apple.com/pr/library/2005/jul/18itms.html
2. MSN Music Entertainment, http://music.msn.com/
3. RealPlayer Music Store, http://www.real.com/musicstore/
4. Sony Connect www.connect.com/
5. Rhapsody, http://www.rhapsody.com/
6. Napster, http://www.napster.com/
7. Windows Media 10 Series: Digital Rights Management (DRM), Internet Document, http://www.microsoft.com/windows/windowsmedia/drm/default.aspx
8. Apple's website, http://www.apple.com; see also http://en.wikipedia.org/wiki/FairPlay
9. Sony's Open MagicGate, Internet Document, http://www.sony.net/Products/OpenMG
10. Helix DRM from Real, Internet Document, http://www.realnetworks.com/products/drm
11. SmartRight, Internet Document, http://www.smartright.org
12. W. Jonker, J.-P. Linnartz, "Digital rights management in consumer electronics products", IEEE Signal Processing Magazine, Volume: 21, Issue: 2, 2004, pp. 82–91.
13. S.A.F.A. van den Heuvel, W. Jonker, F.L.A.J. Kamperman, P.J. Lenoir, "Secure Content Management in Authorised Domains", In Proceedings of the International Broadcasting Convention (IBC), 2002.
14. DVB-CPT, DVB-CPT Authorized Domain: Definition / Requirements, cpt-018r5, 2002
15. P. Koster, F. Kamperman, P. Lenoir and K. Vrielink, "Private Entertainment Domain: Concept and Design", Conf. on Communications

and Multimedia Security (CMS2005), September 19-21 2005, Salzburg, Austria.

16. J. Feigenbaum, M. J. Freedman, T. Sander and A. Shostack, "Privacy Engineering for Digital Rights Management Systems", In Proceedings of the ACM Workshop on Security and Privacy in Digital Rights Management, 2001.

17. Electronic Privacy Information Center (EPIC) – digital Rights Management and Privacy, Internet Document, http://www.epic.org/privacy/drm /default.html

18. D. Chaum, "Untraceable Electronic Mail, Return Addresses and Digital Pseudonyms", Communications of the ACM, vol. 24, no. 2, February 1981.

19. Anonymizer, http://www.anonymizer.com/

20. C. Conrado, F. Kamperman, G.J. Schrijen and W. Jonker, "Privacy in an Identity-based DRM System", Proceedings of the 14th International Workshop on Databases and Expert Systems Applications, Prague, Czech Republic, 2003.

21. A. Lysyanskaya, *Pseudonymous Systems*, Master's Thesis at the Massachusetts Institute of Technology, June 1999.

22. W. Diffie and M. Hellman, "New directions in cryptography", IEEE Transactions on Information Theory, 22, pp. 644–654, 1976.

23. T. Elgamal, "A Public-Key Cryptosystem and a Signature Scheme Based on Discrete Logarithms", IEEE Transactions on Information Theory, v. IT-31, n. 4, 1985, pp. 469–472 or CRYPTO 84, pp. 10–18, Springer-Verlag.

24. Digital Signature Standard (DSS), Internet Document, http://www.itl.nist.gov/fipspubs/fip186.htm

25. A. J. Menezes, P. C. van Oorschot, S. A. Vanstone, *Handbook of Applied Cryptography*, CRC Press, 1997.

26. Smart Card Basics, Internet Document, http://www.smartcardbasics.com

27. D. Chaum, "Blind signatures for untraceable payments", Advances in Cryptology: Proceedings of Crypto'82, Springer-Verlag, 1982.

Part V

Selected Topics on Privacy and Security in
Ambient Intelligence

The Persuasiveness of Ambient Intelligence

Emile Aarts[1], Panos Markopoulos[2], and Boris de Ruyter[1]

[1] Philips Research, The Netherlands
[2] TU Eindhoven, The Nethertlands

Summary. Ambient intelligence (AmI) is a novel concept for embedded computing that builds on the large-scale integration of electronic devices into peoples' surroundings and the ubiquitous availability of digital information to the users of such environments. The concept however is not only concerned with the integration of computing in the background but, as a direct result of the disappearing computer and the corresponding interaction technologies, it calls for novel means of control that support the natural and intelligent use of such smart environments, emphasizing predominantly social aspects. As the familiar box-like devices are replaced by hidden functions embedded in the surroundings, the classical meaning and implication of security and trust needs to be revisited in the context of ambient intelligence. In this chapter, we briefly revisit the foundations of the AmI vision by addressing the role of AmIware, which refers to the basic and enabling AmI technologies, and by presenting some basic definitions of ambient intelligence. Next we discuss the meaning and role of persuasion on the basis of models and theories for motivation originating from cognitive science. Notions such as *compliance* and *ambient journaling* are used to develop an understanding of the concept of ambient persuasion. We also address the ethics of ambient intelligence from the point of view of a number of critical factors such as trust and faith, crossing boundaries, and changing realities. The chapter concludes with a summary of findings and some final remarks.

24.1. Introduction

Recent technological advances have enabled the miniaturization of embedded hardware thus facilitating the large-scale integration of electronic devices into peoples' backgrounds. In addition, novel interaction concepts have been developed that support the natural and intelligent use of such systems, emphasizing the social aspects of the technology embedding. The resulting computing paradigm, which is called ambient intelligence (AmI), provides users with new means to increase their productivity, increase their well-being, or enhance their expressiveness [1].

In addition to the physical benefits provided by hardware embedding, AmI environments exhibit a number of features that rely on adequate social embedding such as context awareness, personalization, adaptation, and anticipatory behavior. However, as the familiar box-like form factors of devices will disappear to be replaced by pointers to their functional properties embedded in the environment, new interaction concepts will be developed that differ substantially from the traditional box-related user interfaces. The classical concepts and definitions of trust and security will be challenged by the resulting AmI applications, and they need to be readdressed to meet the needs and requirements imposed by the use of hidden technologies. Although many technologies in the area of copyright protection, firewalls, data encryption and digital signatures can increase the security of AmI environments, there is a need to convince the end user to trust such secured AmI environments. This raises the question of persuasiveness in relation to ambient intelligence. To discuss this issue we introduce the concept of ambient persuasion as the extent to which AmI technology supports convincingly natural interaction with smart environments. In this chapter we elaborate on this concept and derive a framework for the discussion of the resulting challenges and issues

The chapter is organized as follows. First we introduce the foundations of the AmI vision based on the notion of AmIware, which refers to the enabling AmI technologies in the areas of processing, storage, displays, and connectivity. Next we briefly review the concept of ambient intelligence and the paradigm shift its realization will introduce with respect to ethical issues in general and trust and security specifically. The body of the chapter is devoted to the concept of persuasiveness in smart environments. We elaborate on issues such as motivation and learning as a theoretical framework for the development of user requirements for persuasiveness in ambient intelligence. The chapter concludes with a summary of findings and recommendations.

24.2. AmIware

It is generally known that the integration density of systems on silicon doubles every 18 months. This regularity, which is known as Moore's law [2], seems to hold a self-fulfilling prophecy because the semiconductor industry has followed it already for more than three decades. Also, other characteristic quantities of information processing systems, such as communication bandwidth, storage capacity, and cost per bit of input-output communication seem to follow similar rules. These developments have given rise to a new kind of miniaturization technology called AmIware, which enables the integration of electronics into peoples' environments. We mention the following examples. The introduction of the blue laser in digital recording made it possible to construct miniaturized consumer devices that can record tens of hours of video material. Consequently, small personal digital assistants and storage devices can be constructed that support video functionalities. Poly-LED technology made it possible to construct matrix-addressable displays on foils of a few microns thickness, thus enabling the development of flexible ultra-thin displays of arbitrary size. Similar technologies have been used to produce light-emitting foils that can not only replace lighting armatures but also turn any smooth surface into a lighting device. Developments in materials science have enabled the construction of electronic foils that exhibit paper-like properties. These so-called electronic-paper devices introduce a new dimension in the use of electronic books or calendars. Advanced LCD projection technologies allow very large high-definition images to be displayed on white walls from a small invisible built-in unit. Novel semiconductor process technologies make it possible to separate the active silicon area from its substrate, and to put it onto other carriers such as glass, polymer foils and cloth, thus enabling the integration of active circuitry into tangible objects and clothing. Advanced LED technologies enable the integration of light-emitting structures into fabric. The resulting photonic textiles can be used in carpets, drapes, furniture, and clothes. Advances in digital signal processing have made it possible to apply audio and video watermarks that enable conditional access, retrieval, and copy protection of audio and video material. Compression schemes such as MPEG4 and MPEG7 enable the effective transmission and composition of video material. Recent developments in speech processing and vision introduce interaction technology for the development of conversational user interfaces, which are a first step towards the development of natural interfaces. These are just a few examples. For a more detailed treatment we refer to [3].

AmIware makes it feasible to integrate electronics into any conceivable physical object, i.e., into clothes, furniture, carpets, walls, floors, ceilings, buildings, objects, etc. This opens up new opportunities for electronic devices, because it implies that we can close the age of the box and enter a new age in which functionalities such as audio, video, communication, and gaming, which were confined to boxes up to now, may become freely available from the environment, supporting people to have free access to their functionality and enabling natural interaction with them.

24.3. Ambient Intelligence

Ambient intelligence aims to take the integration onset of embedded devices one step further by realizing environments that are sensitive and responsive to the presence of people [4]. The focus of ambient intelligence is on the user and his experience from a consumer electronics perspective, which introduces several new basic problems related to natural user interaction and context-aware architectures supporting human-centered information, communication, service, and entertainment. For a detailed treatment of ambient intelligence we refer the reader to Aarts and Marzano [5] who cover in their book many different related aspects ranging from materials science to business models and issues in interaction design.

24.3.1. A Definition of Ambient Intelligence

In their book, Aarts and Marzano [5] formulate the following five key elements of ambient intelligence:
1. *Embedded*: many networked devices that are integrated into the environment
2. *Contextaware*: that can recognize persons and their situational context
3. *Personalized*: that can be tailored towards their needs
4. *Adaptive*: that can change in response to actions, and
5. *Anticipatory*: that anticipate peoples' desires without conscious mediation.

As already mentioned, ambient intelligence is a new paradigm that is based on the belief that future electronic devices will disappear into the background of people's environment, thus introducing the challenging need to enhance user environments with virtual devices that support natural interaction of the user with the integrated electronics. The new paradigm is aimed at improving the quality of life of people by creating the desired atmosphere and functionality via intelligent, personalized, interconnected systems and services. The notion *ambient* in ambient intelligence refers to the environment and reflects the need for typical requirements such as distribution, ubiquity, and transparency. Here, distribution refers to non-central systems control and computation; Ubiquity means that the embedding is overly present, and transparency indicates that the surrounding systems are invisible and non-obtrusive. The notion *intelligence* in ambient intelligence reflects that the digital surroundings exhibit specific forms of social interaction, i.e., the environments should be able to recognize the people that live in it, adapt themselves to them, learn from their behavior, and possibly show emotion. In an AmI world people will be surrounded by electronic systems that consist of networked intelligent devices that are integrated into their surrounding and that provide them with information, communication, services, and entertainment wherever they are and whenever they want. Furthermore, the devices will adapt and even anticipate peoples' needs. AmI environments will present themselves in a very different way than our contemporary handheld or stationary electronic boxes, as they will merge in a natural way into the environment surrounding us, hence allowing for more-natural and human interaction styles.

24.3.2. What is New?

The major new thing in ambient intelligence is the involvement of the user. Most of the earlier computing paradigms such as personal, mobile, and ubiquitous computing were aimed in the first place at facilitating and improving productivity in business environments, but it goes without saying that these developments have played a major role in the development of ambient intelligence. The next step, however, is to bring connectivity, interaction, interoperability, and personalization to people and into people's homes. This is not simply a matter of introducing productivity concepts to consumer environments. It is far more than that, because a totally new interaction paradigm is needed to make ambient intelligence work. Contemporary concepts of productivity are to a large extent still based on the graphical user interface known as the *desktop metaphor* that was developed by Tesler [6] in the 1970s, and which has become a world standard in the mean time. What we need is a new metaphor with the same impact as the desktop metaphor but which enables natural and social interaction within AmI environments, and this is a tremendous challenge. Philips' HomeLab [7] is an example of an experience prototyping environment in which this challenge is addressed. It is a laboratory consisting of a house with a living room, a kitchen, a hall, a den, two bedrooms, and a bathroom that supports rapid prototyping with integrated speech control, wireless audio-video streaming, and context-awareness technology. It enables the realization of new applications within short development times. HomeLab is also equipped with sophisticated observation systems that allows behavioral scientists to observe users in an unobtrusive way for possibly long periods of times. In this way it has been shown that it is possible to investigate the true merits of novel AmI applications through extensive user studies [8]. Over the years it has become obvious from the studies conducted in HomeLab that the impact of novel AmIware is not determined by its functionality only but also to a large extent by its persuasiveness. Therefore, we have started to investigate this issue in more detail and below we report on some of our findings.

24.4. Persuasion

In their discussion on security in AmI environment, Verbauwhede et al. [9] argue that traditional solutions for providing security will fail in AmI environments since these techniques traditionally focus on the communication channel and assume that the environments connected by this channel is secure. Similarly, for trust there needs to be more emphasis on the environment than on the communication channel. Since it is fundamentally different to create trust in an environment than in a communication channel, there is a need to involve different strategies for creating end-user trust in

AmI environments. These strategies bring forward a paradigm shift in user–system interaction concepts characterized by the following two changes:

1. The role of applications and services will change from traditional access and control means towards lifestyle assistants.
2. The emphasis on perceived user value will change from usability towards creating user experiences such as presence, connectness, and immersion.

This paradigm shift in user-system interaction implies that it becomes increasingly important to obtain insight into the human factors that influence human behavior. When considering behavioral change, three concepts appear: *persuasion, motivation,* and *learning*; see Fig. 24.1.

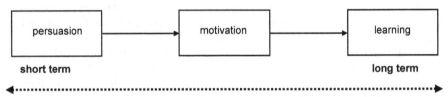

Fig. 24.1. The relation between persuasion, motivation and learning.

Persuasion is an attempt to change attitudes and/or the behavior of persons without using force or deception. A *motive* is a need or desire that causes a person to act. Learning is the modification of a behavioral tendency by experience that is not simply attributed to the process of growth. While persuasion reflects a momentary effect, learning implies a more long-term change of behavior.

How human behavior is driven or motivated and how it can be modified has been one of the most important research topics in psychology for many decades. In fact, motivation as a cause for behavior plays an important role in learning. Although motivation does not always imply learning, learning relies on motivation to happen. Learning is defined as the modification of a behavioral tendency by experience that is not simply attributed to the process of growth.

24.4.1. Models and Theories of Persuasion

Influencing people to change their behavior is not a new area of research. In fact, human sciences have been investigating for a long time how an individual's behavior can be changed by external factors. Whereas sociology studies the human as a member of a social structure, psychology studies the human as an individual. From a sociological point of view, Durkheim [10] has argued that an individual's behavior is determined by the societal structures of which this individual is a part. In psychology much attention has been attributed to processes of learning and behavioral change. Theories on learning and human motivation have put forward numerous models for influencing and changing human behavior.

Several theories on human motivation have been developed that approach the issue from the human as an individual. Below we mention a few important ones.

- **Behavioral approaches** position behavioral change as a consequence of conditioning. Pavlov [11] founded one of the first models of motivation. With his theory of classical conditioning, an unconditioned stimulus that has an unconditioned response, is associated with a conditioned stimulus. A more sophisticated approach to behavioral changes is the operant conditioning approach. Thorndike [12] was the first to use the concept of instrumental learning. Following this early work many studies used the mechanism of associating certain responses with stimuli. Later, Skinner [13] described operant conditioning as an approach for learning voluntary responses. By (i) using positive and negative reinforcement, (ii) varying the amount of time between stimulus and response, and (iii) varying between a fixed and variable ratio for giving a reinforcer, different learning effects are obtained.

- **Cognitive approaches** rely on reasoning to explain behavioral changes. The drive for changing behavior is found in the effect of knowledge (presence or absence) and reasoning upon this knowledge. The cognitive dissonance theory states that the realization of a person that there is a discrepancy between present knowledge serves as a drive for behavior to remove or reduce this disequilibrium [14]. Variants of the cognitive approaches are found in the attribution and expectancy theory. The attribution theory states that a person tries to attribute success and failure to themself or others. Additional, the person can have control or not over these attributions.

- **Expectancy theory** views motivation as the product of perceived probability of success (expectancy), connection of success, and reward (instrumentality) in relation to the value of obtaining the goal (valance). All three aspects must have a high score in order to achieve motivation. The expectancy theory of motivation was first introduced by Vroom [15] and has been applied since to many empirical studies that were aimed at revealing the mechanisms underlying certain specific deferring human behavior such as alcoholism and violence.

- **Dual process models** explain behavioral change by means of a combination of both reflective (i.e., more rational or cognitive) and impulsive (i.e., more emotional or reactive) mechanisms [16]. The underlying hypotheses for these models can be formulated as follows.
    - Behavior is the effect of two distinct systems of information processing: a reflective and an impulsive system
    - Both systems work in parallel but the impulsive system is always used

- The reflective system requires more cognitive capacity than the impulsive system. As a consequence the reflective system is easier to disturb.
- The elements of information used in the reflective system are related through semantic relations while the elements in the impulsive system are related on the basis of contiguity and similarity

- **Captology** refers to a series of principles for technological solutions to influence human behavior [17]. In captology the human is studied as interacting with technology. More specific, this research area has investigated how technology can persuade people to change their behavior and attitudes. Persuasion is defined as an attempt to change attitudes or behaviors (or both) without using force or deception [17]. This persuasion should be intended by the designer of a system and is built into a product or service. Following the theory of captology, technology can be persuasive due to the following actions.
  - Making things easier, reducing complexity
  - Guiding users through a step-by-step process
  - Personalizing to the user and context
  - Suggesting things to the user at the right time
  - Monitoring the user so that the user can learn from himself
  - Monitoring others so that the user can learn from others
  - Conditioning the user

In the next section, we combine the concept of ambient intelligence and the notion of behavioral change into an approach we call ambient persuasion.

24.5. Ambient Persuasion

We use the term ambient persuasion to refer to the use of AmIware in a context-aware and networked infrastructure to enable context-sensitive system behavior and deliver persuasive content that is tailored to the user at the right time and at the right place. Potentially, ambient persuasion combines all the key elements of ambient intelligence, presented in the previous sections, in order to apply persuasive strategies. Fogg [17] has identified the following persuasive strategies as relevant.

1. *Reduction* replaces a complex task by a simpler one by virtue of the introduction of automation and computation, but also by virtue of anticipation of a defining characteristic of ambient intelligence.
2. *Customization and tailoring* adjusts messages and content to the beliefs and needs of the person. Personalization is an essential aspect of ambient intelligence; in this case it covers not the superficial aspects of the

system behavior but addressing the specific needs, problem and situation of the individual. This requires very rich, privacy-sensitive models of users that go beyond simple habits and preferences, and include aspects of their personality, their health status, the social network and context, etc. It requires embedding ambient intelligence in the social context of a person, a notion that extends the definition of ambient intelligence to cover also aspects of social intelligence [18].

3. *Suggestion* reminds people to perform certain behaviors at opportune moments. Prompting of behaviors then needs to be sensitive to context, a central aspect of ambient intelligence.

4. *Self-monitoring* allows people to monitor themselves and to inform themselves about how they could modify their behaviors. Self-monitoring can be very tedious; it will be argued below that ambient intelligence opens up the opportunity to facilitate this process and thus achieve persuasion.

24.5.1. Compliance

A particularly promising domain for studying persuasion concerns health care and especially how people can be motivated to adopt healthier lifestyles. In the domain of medicine the general problem of persuasion has been called compliance. Winnick [19] defines *compliance* as *the extent to which a person's behavior coincides with medical or health advice.* Compliance is recognized as a major challenge in medical research, especially when treatment protocols are individualized or situation-dependent or where the patient is unsupervised and so reporting on compliance is not reliable [20]. AmI technology offers new possibilities supporting the monitoring of compliance behaviors and triggering persuasive interventions.

To give the reader some idea regarding the intricacies of achieving compliance, we shall examine the case of asthma treatment in pediatrics. Asthma treatment attracted the interest of captologists early on and remains a challenge for medical research after decades of relevant research. There are some persuasive technologies that have been designed for asthmatic children, though they have not always been described under this label. We mention two examples. *Quest for the code* is an educational video game for adolescents; the game simulates social encounters with pop idols for teenagers. Children are presented with facts about asthma and are quizzed about it. *Bronkie the bronchiasaurus*, is a Nintendo-based system in which players (children aged 7-12) help a cartoon character manage its asthma [21]. Lieberman reports a longitudinal study that showed that children could cope better with their asthma as a result of playing with Bronkie.

These two examples are software applications for game platforms or PCs, that achieve persuasion through drilling behaviors and knowledge while playing a computer game. An alternative approach that has more potential for embedding in the targeted context is to embed persuasion in interactive artifacts. A recent example for the case of asthmatic children is the *Funhaler* a novel asthma spacer device for pre-school children where inhalation produces whistling sounds and moves a toy fitted in the device. It looks very much like a standard inhaler into which a transparent compartment is inserted containing a toy and producing the sounds when the child inhales. An evaluation relying on reports by the parents claimed that the Funhaler achieved a 38% improvement in compliance [22].

The Funhaler relies on fun as an extrinsic motivator for compliance. The enjoyment of the sound and movement is unrelated to the illness or the treatment and provides a short-lived reward that loses its value after a few repetitions. In general, it is known that motivating user behavior using only external rewards will not have lasting effects on behavioral change, with compliance gradually declining when the external motivation is removed [23]. We can expect that the lasting effects of the Funhaler will be limited. It seems like a promising solution to solve the problem of children refusing to use an inhaler device. In order to achieve persistent effects regarding compliance there should be more effort paid to educating children through technology and providing them with persuasive advice regarding their asthma treatment at appropriate moments and places.

A major research challenge for the medical field is the need for better data on compliance, e.g., in some cases mothers report 60% compliance where pharmacy records show only 12% (see [19]). There are numerous research results pointing in the same direction. Self-report on compliance or, more generally, obtaining compliance data through surveys is not reliable. The need to monitor and facilitate self-monitoring emerges as a very useful and attainable target for the health care technologies of tomorrow.

24.5.2. Ambient Journaling

Returning for a moment to the strategies of persuasion mentioned above, we saw the need to facilitate self-monitoring. We need to get away from relying on memory or paper/journals regarding compliance to a regime and to move towards systems and services that will serve this purpose reliably. In the domain of healthcare it is clear that the technological challenges lying ahead to support compliance are exactly those needed to support the development of persuasive technologies. We shall call these technologies *ambient journaling*. They require the combination of observable data regarding the behavior studied with self-report data, obtained by the user either through direct prompting at the moment or by retrospective prompting shortly after the event.

In the medical field, a specialized survey method that is quite well established for studying compliance, also used in the survey of mothers mentioned above, is the *24-hour behavioral recall interview,* where the interviewer inquires into compliance behaviors over the last 24 hours. This method is limited by the reliability of self-reporting in retrospective interviews and cannot capture compliance data accurately, e.g., in the case of asthma the time separating an inhalation and an asthmatic crisis, the frequency of the inhalations, etc.

The need to develop technology and methodology to support user research in the field is a current issue in psychology and human–computer interaction research. Kahneman et al. [24], for example, have proposed the day reconstruction method, a direct analogue to the 24-hour behavioral recall interview, which is aimed at characterizing daily life experiences in terms of affective state over the day. Methodological studies have examined how audio and photographic capture impacts diary studies (see [25]), but diary methods are still prone to recollection and compliance problems when the initiative for recording all data is left to the informant. In order to study daily-life activities a sensor-based variant of experience sampling has been proposed, called the event sampling method [26]. According to Larson and Csikszentmihalyi [27] experience sampling involves prompting users to self-report at random, or at scheduled moments in the day, thereby forcing through the protocol the timing of the inquiry. In cases where a very specific type of activity of short duration may happen at different moments in time, such as taking prescribed medication, experience sampling can be very inefficient. It is preferable that reporting is tied to relevant events rather than be randomly/arbitrarily invoked upon the informant.

The challenges for the future are clear: ambient journaling is an essential constituent for ambient persuasion but will also itself be the most appropriate tool for assessing its success. It calls for developments in technology that will allow problem-specific detection of events and situations, and that will prompt context-specific requests from users.

Reflecting on our definition of ambient journaling as our research target, we have come full circle to the defining characteristics of ambient intelligence. Where some of the earliest visions of ambient intelligence shared the idea of creating some model of the context and of user activities in order to automate some daily chores or facilitate information access, we have demonstrated the need to create technological infrastructure and to design appliances to support users to create their own model themselves. This should not surprise the reader. As ambient intelligence puts the user as a human and as an individual person in a pivotal position, it should not surprise us that, when we move towards delivering applications where the stakes are high (health, well-being), then the central issue is to let the user easily and reliably construct and maintain the model of themselves, their activities and context. Predictably, the need to control what information is captured about oneself, and its disclosure and usage emerge as necessary user needs to protect the privacy of individuals in this emerging technological landscape.

24.6. The Ethics of Ambient Intelligence

The opportunities of ambient persuasion also comes with threats. Can AmI environments become persuasive in such a way that people put faith and trust into them? Do people want to cross the boundaries of their private and safe worlds, and can they change seamlessly between real and virtual worlds? Below we treat some of these issues in more detail.

24.6.1. Trust and Faith

One of the central questions in the social acceptance of ambient intelligence is whether people will be able to adapt to the feeling that their environments are monitoring their every move, waiting for the right moment to take care of them. Much of this acceptance will depend on the functional benefit of such environments and on their ability to interact with people in a natural way. People also frequently express concerns about the lack of safety and security in such systems because they could be extremely vulnerable to intrusion and damage caused by outsiders. The fact that large amounts of possibly personal information could be freely floating around without appropriate protection is threatening. Also the concern that an environment in which electronics makes autonomous decisions on a large scale could get out of control needs to be taken seriously.

Of a different scale are the concerns that are raised by the fact that personalization requires registration and recording of user behavior. The explicit knowledge about a so-called digital soul of human beings requires the development of different standards for social behavior, and it might even be desired to protect people against their own attitude. Finally, people raise their concerns against the absolutistic technological nature of ambient intelligence. Pushing ambient intelligence to the extreme might lead to a world full of digital surrogates for about everything that is conceivable. Ten years ago Rheingold [28] already listed several threats that may result from the omnipresence of technology, giving rise to virtual worlds, and most of them still hold true after more than a decade of discussion.

24.6.2. Crossing the Boundary

Another issue we will need to consider at some point will be the desirability of ambient intelligence being incorporated into an even more intimate ambience – our own bodies. We are already incorporating intelligence into our clothing, and we are quite happy to have a pacemaker built into our bodies. Warwick took things a step further by having a chip implanted into his wrist linked to the median nerve, which operates the muscles of the hand. It was part of a larger project called Cyborg [29], partly funded by spinal injury organizations. Evidently, this has a medical justification.

But how long will it be before we accept the implantation of chips for nonmedical reasons? Attitudes towards the body are already changing. Body piercing, tattoos and cosmetic surgery are much more common than a generation ago. More recently, the company Applied Digital Solutions received the go-ahead from the food and drug administration (FDA) to market a chip that can be injected into children or Alzheimer's patients, so that they can be traced by GPS. If this sort of product finds widespread public acceptance, will we have crossed an important boundary? Where will people draw the line between the organic and the inorganic, the real and the artificial? And how will that affect how we view and treat our AmI environments, and each other?

24.6.3. Different Realities

A less obvious, but equally fundamental issue that awaits us is an ontological one – about the nature of existence itself, or at least how we perceive it. McLuhan [30] argued that the medium was the message – that we were becoming more interested in television, for instance, than reality. Baudrillard [31] thinks this is only the beginning. He argues that the traditional relationship between media and reality is being reversed. Increasingly, the media is no longer seen as just reflecting or representing reality. They constitute a new, hyper-reality that's felt to be even more real than real reality. The fact that we call semi-staged programs like *Big Brother* reality TV probably says more about what people think of as real than we suspect.

Will we get so used to interacting with our ambient intelligence that it will affect the way we interact with real people? If we come to experience more of the real world through technology rather than directly through our senses, are these indirect experiences less valid? Is hyper-reality less valid than physical reality? Where can we draw the boundary between physical reality and imagination? We may not want to get into deep philosophical discussions like this, but at some point and in some form, these are issues we will need to confront.

24.7 Conclusion

Ambient intelligence should be viewed as a new paradigm for consumer and professional electronics that can claim to be a revolution in the design, appearance, and use of electronics in ordinary life. It may support and facilitate simple and recurrent tasks, but it may also lead to a culture very much different from today's, resulting from the expansion of the use of media into a world in which physical and virtual experiences are merged, supporting personal expression, business productivity, and lifestyles of people. Specifically the concept of ambient persuasion offers great opportunities for AmIware to influence human behavior in AmI environments.

It goes without saying that we have great expectations for ambient intelligence. Technology, however, will not be the limiting factor in its realization: trust and faith in AmI environments are most important for end-user acceptance. In this chapter a number of concerns that should be taken into account when developing AmI environments have been discussed.

References

1. E. Aarts and J. Encarnaçao (eds.) (2006), *True Visions: The Emergence of Ambient Intelligence*, Springer, Berlin.
2. R.N. Noyce (1977), Microelectronics, Scientific American 237(3), pp. 63-69.
3. S. Muhkerjee, E.H.L. Aarts, M. Ouwerkerk, R. Rovers, and F. Widdershoven (eds.) (2005), AmIware: Hardware Drivers for Ambient Intelligence, Springer, Berlin.
4. E. Aarts, H. Harwig, and M. Schuurmans (2001), Ambient Intelligence, in: J. Denning (ed.) The Invisible Future, McGraw Hill, New York, pp. 235-250.
5. E. Aarts and S. Marzano (eds.) (2003), The New Everyday: Visions of Ambient Intelligence, 010 Publishing, Rotterdam.
6. L.G. Tesler (1991), Networked computing in the 1990s, Scientific American 265(3), pp. 54-61.
7. E. Aarts and B. Eggen (eds.) (2002), *Ambient Intelligence Research in HomeLab,* Neroc Publishers, Eindhoven.
8. B. de Ruyter, E. Aarts, P. Markopoulos, and W. IJselsteijn (2005), Ambient Intelligence Research in HomeLab, Engineering the User Experience, in: W. Weber, J. Rabaey, and E. Aarts, Ambient Intelligence, Springer, Berlin, pp. 49-61.
9. I. Verbauwhede, A. Hodjat, D. Hwang, and B.C. Lai (2005), Security for Ambient Intelligent Systems, in: W. Weber, J.M. Rabaey, and E. Aarts (eds.), Ambient Intelligence, Springer, Berlin, pp. 199-121.
10. E. Durkheim (2002), *Moral Education,* Dover Publications, New York.
11. I.P. Pavlov (2003), *Conditional Reflexes,* Dover Publications, New York.
12. E. Thorndike (1999), *The Elements of Psychology*, Routledge, Milton Park.
13. B.F. Skinner (1965), The Technology of Teaching, Proceedings of the Royal Society of London, Biological Sciences 162, pp. 427-470.
14. L. Festinger (1957). *A Theory of Cognitive Dissonance*, Stanford University Press, Stanford.
15. V. Vroom (1964), *Work and Motivation*, Wiley, New York.
16. F. Strack and R. Deutsch (2004). Reflective and Impulsive Determinants of Social Behavior, Personality and Social Psychology Review 8(3), pp. 220-247.
17. B.J. Fogg (2002), *Persuasive Technology*, Morgan-Kaufmann, San Fransico.
18. B. de Ruyter, P. Saini, P. Markopoulos, and A. van Breemen (2005b), Assessing the Effects of Building Social Intelligence in a Robotic Interface for the Home, Interacting with Computers 17(5), pp. 522-541.

19. S. Winnick, D.O. Lucas, A. Hartman, and D. Toll (2005), How do you improve Compliance? Pediatrics 115(6), pp. 718-724.
20. D. Fielding and A. Duff (1999), Compliance with treatment protocols: Interventions for children with chronic illness, Archives of Disease in Childhood 80, pp. 196-200.
21. D. Lieberman (1997), Interactive video games for health promotion: effects on knowledge, self-efficacy, social support and health, in: R.S. Street, W.R. Gold, and T. Manning, Health Promotion and Interactive Technology: Theoretical Applications and Future Directions, Lawrence Erlbaum, pp. 103-120.
22. P.M. Watt, B. Clements, S.G. Devadasan, and G.M. Chaney (2003), Funhaler Spacer: improving adherence without compromising delivery, Archives of Disease in Childhood 88, pp. 579-581.
23. L. Festinger and J.M. Carlsmith (1959), Cognitive consequences of forced compliance, Journal of Abnormal Social Psychology 58, pp. 203-210.
24. D. Kahneman, A.B. Krueger, D. Schkade, N. Schwarz, and A.A. Stone (2004), A survey method for characterizing daily life experience: The Day Reconstruction Method (DRM), Science 306, pp. 1776-1780.
25. S. Carter, J. Mankoff (2005), When Participants Do the Capturing: The Role of Media in Diary Studies, Proceedings CHI 2005.
26. S. Intille, E. Munguia Tapia, J. Rondoni, J. Beaudin, C. Kukla, S. Agarwal, and L. Bao (2003), Tools for studying behavior and technology in natural settings, Proceedings UBICOMP 2003, LNCS 2864, Springer, Berlin, pp. 157-174.
27. R. Larson and M. Csikszentmihalyi (1983), The Experience Sampling Method, New Directions for the Methodology of Social Behavioral Science 15, pp. 41-56.
28. H. Rheingold [1993], The Virtual Community, Addison-Wesley, Reading.
29. Cyborg (2002), www.kevinwarwick.com
30. M. McLuhan (1964), Understanding Media: The Extensions of Man, MIT Press, Cambridge.
31. J. Baudrillard (1968), "Le Système des objets", Gallimard, Paris, reprintend in M. Poster (ed.) (1988), Jean Baudrillard: Selected Writings, Stanford, pp. 10-29.

Privacy Policies

Marnix Dekker[1], Sandro Etalle[2], and Jerry den Hartog[2]

[1] TNO ICT, The Netherlands
[2] University of Twente, The Netherlands

Summary. Privacy is a prime concern in today's information society. To protect the privacy of individuals, enterprises must follow certain privacy practices while collecting or processing personal data. In this chapter we look at the setting where an enterprise collects private data on its website, processes it inside the enterprise and shares it with partner enterprises. In particular, we analyse three different privacy systems that can be used in the different stages of this lifecycle. One of them is the audit logic, recently introduced, which can be used to keep data private while travelling across enterprise boundaries. We conclude with an analysis of the features and shortcomings of these systems.

25.1 Introduction

In the last decade people have started to use network services for many tasks in their everyday lives. For example, there is now widespread use of Internet services such as online stores. Often, to be able to use such services, users have to reveal privacy-sensitive data, e.g., about their home address, to the enterprise operating the services. Usually these data are collected for a particular purpose, for instance to provide a (better) service to the users. However, once these privacy-sensitive data have been disclosed, the enterprise could also misuse them, e.g., by trading them to marketing agencies. Nowadays there exist laws to prevent this, demanding that enterprises comply with precise privacy practices [1, 2]. For instance, the European Union (EU) in 1995 issued a directive to its member states that regulates the collection, storage and processing of personal data [1]. In 2002 this directive was extended to adapt to the ongoing changes in the electronic communications sector [2], affirming the importance of privacy and the importance of aligning the privacy laws of the different EU member states. Among other things, the directives demand that enterprises only collect private data for specified, explicit and legitimate purposes and that the data may not be processed in ways incompatible with those purposes [1]. To see an example of how the EU directives translate to requirements for computer systems, consider the setting of an online store. On the checkout page, the store requests the credit card number and the home address of users making a purchase. In addition, it asks users if their address can be given to partners for the purpose of promotional mailings. For instance, the store sells airplane tickets, while the partners offer hotel rooms and cars for rental. The first requirement that follows from the directive is that the checkout page must contain explicit statements about the purposes for which the credit card data and the home address data are collected. The second requirement is that the enterprise's Web server, other systems in the backend and systems at the partner sites, must not process the data for purposes other than those stated on the checkout page.

In this setting, the lifecycle of the private data consists of three stages. The first stage is the moment of collection by the enterprise. The second stage is the processing inside the enterprise, while the third stage is the processing outside the enterprise, at the partner sites. In this chapter we illustrate three (complementary) privacy systems, each of which can be used in one of the these stages: Surveys [3] show that, for websites, P3P [4] is the most widely used system for the expression of the purposes for which private data are collected. Therefore, in Sect. 25.2, we analyze P3P and we give an example of how it is used in practice. Secondly, in Sect. 25.3, we analyze E-P3P [5], which was designed precisely to address the problem of ensuring that, inside the enterprise, private data are used for the right purposes (for related work see Sect. 25.5). Finally, in Sect. 25.4 we analyze the audit logic, a system introduced recently [6], that can be used for the protection of private data across enterprise boundaries. Although we focus on Internet services in this chapter, we should mention that these issues also occur in other scenarios such as the processing of (privacy-sensitive) location data of mobile phones [7].

25.2 Privacy Statements

Web sites often ask users to disclose their private data, like name, address, email address etc.; this information may be needed by the Web service to provide a better service, though it could also be used for other unwanted purposes. This raises the need to inform the user about how his personal data are being treated, e.g., who will see it, for how long it will be stored, and for which purposes it is going to be used. Actually, in many countries, websites *have* to provide a *privacy statement* explaining how personal data are used [1, 8].

However, privacy statements are often too long and detailed to be understood by the ordinary internet user. P3P, which was introduced in 1997 by the W3C but only became an official recommendation in 2002, was devised to solve this problem by supporting automatic analysis of privacy statements. P3P is now used by many popular websites [3].

P3P allows enterprises to translate their privacy statements into a standardized XML-based format, using a common vocabulary, to be placed on their websites [4]. When a website supports P3P, a visitor can employ an automatic tool to analyze the website's privacy statement and quickly decide if they are satisfactory. To illustrate how it works, let us see an example.

Example 1. Claudia visits an online store and after choosing a product she goes to the checkout page. Here she fills out a form with some private data: i.e., her name and credit card number. The store states in a privacy statement that it will use these data only to complete the transaction. In addition, the checkout form has a nonobligatory field for the customer's email address. The store states (in a second privacy statement) that this information will be used for promotional mailings. Both privacy statements can be translated into P3P. The resulting policy is shown in Fig. 25.1.

```
<POLICIES xmlns="http://www.w3.org/2000/P3Pv1">
 <POLICY name="checkout"
          entity="Store, 5th Avenue, Manhattan, PO 10001, USA">
 <DISPUTES>service="PrivacySeal.orG/DisputeResolution"</DISPUTES>
 <ACCESS><none/></ACCESS>
  <STATEMENT>
   <PURPOSE><current/></PURPOSE>
   <RECIPIENT><ours/></RECIPIENT>
   <RETENTION><stated-purpose/></RETENTION>
   <DATA-GROUP>
    <DATA ref="#user.name"/>
    <DATA ref="#dynamic.miscdata"/></DATA-GROUP>
  </STATEMENT>
  <STATEMENT>
   <PURPOSE><contact required="opt-in"/></PURPOSE>
   <RECIPIENT><ours/></RECIPIENT>
   <RETENTION><stated-purpose/></RETENTION>
   <DATA-GROUP>
    <DATA ref="#online.email"/></DATA></DATA-GROUP>
  </STATEMENT></POLICY></POLICIES>
```

Fig. 25.1. A sample P3P policy

This allows us to see the elements of a P3P policy. In the first place, the *entity* indicates the issuer of the policy. Secondly, the *disputes* element describes how possible conflicts over the privacy policy may be resolved (e.g., by which court, or other entity). This is not binding, in the sense that the enterprise is still subject to legal ways to resolving a privacy dispute. The *access* element indicates whether the submitted data may be accessed by the subject after it has been collected. This can be used for instance to verify the accuracy of the collected data. This policy states that access is not possible. Finally, the key elements of the P3P policy are the *statements*, which describe, per data item, for which *purpose* it is collected, who is allowed to access it (in the *recipient* element) and for how long it will be stored (in the *retention* element). In the figure the purposes are respectively *current*, which refers to the online purchase and *contact*, which indicates that the information can be used to contact the user for marketing of services or products. The purpose element may also contain an attribute indicating how a user can express his consent to the purpose. In this case, explicit *opt-in* is required for the purpose of contact. The recipient value *ours* means that the data can only be accessed by the store (i.e., it will not be given to third parties), while the retention value *stated-purpose* means that the data will only be retained for a period needed for the stated purpose. The *data* element is specified by a reference to an element in a so-called P3P data schema, e.g., `#online.email`. The data schema defines the format and the meaning of the data elements that may occur in a P3P policy. In the example, by not specifying a data schema, we use P3P's default data schema.

Going back to our example, if Claudia's browser supports P3P, it can compare the above policy with Claudia's privacy preferences. One of these preferences states that she wants to be warned when sites request information for purposes other than *current*. In this case the browser, can notify her that she *may or may not supply her email address for marketing of services or products*. Her advantage is that she does not have to read the site's privacy statement to find out what they mean and which fields are optional.

Since its introduction in 1997, P3P has received considerable attention [8]. Its deployment was particularly stimulated by the introduction in 2001 of a privacy slider in Microsoft's Internet Explorer 6. This privacy slider allows the user to determine which websites may set and retrieve *cookies*, according to their P3P policies. Cookies from websites with no P3P policies (or with an unsatisfactory one) are blocked by the browser.

A drawback of P3P is that, despite its simplicity, P3P policies can be ambiguous [9]. For instance, one could refer to the same data element twice with different retention periods, within the same policy. Ambiguities may result in legal risks for the issuers as their policies may be interpreted in unexpected ways [10]. This also makes the development of P3P-compliant browsers more difficult. As a matter of fact, despite the fact that P3P was designed to be interpreted by browsers, there is no definition of how a browser should interpret policies, and there are no guidelines for writing browser-friendly policies [10].

Finally, we should mention that, while P3P addresses the problem of representing a website's privacy policy, it does not address the problem of enforcing them. The use of P3P alone does not give assurance about the *actual* privacy practices in the backend of the website. Critics have even suggested that the online industry, by adopting P3P, is only giving an appearance of protecting privacy, to avoid stricter legislation [11].

25.3 Enterprise Privacy

As mentioned earlier, in many countries, legislation regulates the collection and use of private data. This requires enterprises to enforce privacy policies that prescribe, for example, when certain data should be deleted, by whom it may be accessed, and for which purposes. As we saw in the previous section, P3P can be used to represent such privacy policies on websites, but it does not address the problem of enforcing them inside the enterprise. The platform for enterprise privacy practices (E-P3P) — introduced in 2002 by Karjoth et al. — addresses exactly this problem [5]. E-P3P provides an XML-based language to express privacy policies as well as a framework with specific privacy functionality to enforce these policies.

In the E-P3P architecture an enterprise collects private data at so-called *collection points*. Here individuals, e.g., customers, submit private data to the enterprise, after agreeing with the enterprise's privacy statements. Each collection point has a *form* which associates the private data with its subject, declares its *type*, e.g., medical record or postal address, and the subject's *consent choices*. This association remains intact in the enterprise's backend and it may even travel to another enterprise. In E-P3P this is called the *sticky policy paradigm* [5]. The sticky policy does not refer to enterprise policies but refers to the privacy statements and the filled-in consent choices on the data collection form that stick to the private data.

The privacy officer of the enterprise declares, by using E-P3P's policy language, the privacy policies by specifying who can access which type of data for which purposes. The privacy policy can also refer to the subject's consent choices and to certain privacy obligations, e.g., *delete the data in 30 days*. Operations in the enterprise's legacy applications are then mapped to terminology used in the privacy policies, and, in the reverse direction, privacy obligations used in the privacy policies are mapped to operations in the legacy applications. For example, the send operation of a mass-mailer system, used in the marketing department, is mapped to the term *read for the purpose of marketing* in the privacy policy. Conversely, the term *delete the subject's email* in the privacy policy is implemented as an unsubscribe operation of a mailing-list system.

Finally, access to the private data of a subject is granted in two steps. The access to the legacy enterprise application is evaluated by an access control system, for instance taking into account employee roles, which is independent of the E-P3P system. Then, the legacy application makes an access request to a *privacy enforcement system* for the subject's private data. The privacy enforcement system decides whether access should be granted by evaluating the enterprise policy and by matching against the subject's consent choices. If access is granted, then the privacy enforcement system also executes possible privacy obligations specified in the enterprise policy.

Example 2. Consider the previous example of an online store collecting private data on its checkout page. The enterprise that owns the online store wants customers to trust its privacy practices. To this end, it has published privacy statements on the checkout page and uses E-P3P to ensure that enterprise systems behave according to them. These privacy statements specify that Claudia's name and credit card number may be accessed by the employees from the billing department provided that the purpose is billing and that the data are subsequently deleted. In addition, employees may use Claudia's email address for marketing purposes, if Claudia opted in to this purpose. The corresponding E-P3P policy is shown in Fig. 25.2.

```
<ep3pPolicy
  version = '1.2'
  issuer = 'Store'
  vocabulary-ref = 'http://www.Store.com/Voc'
  default-ruling='deny'>
   <rule>
    <dataCategory>allData.creditCardData</dataCategory>
    <purpose>business.billing</purpose>
    <userCategory>employees.billing</userCategory>
    <ruling>ALLOW</ruling>
    <action>read</action>
    <obligation action=deleteWithIn(30)></obligation>
    <condition/></rule>
   <rule>
    <dataCategory>allData.contactData</dataCategory>
    <purpose>business.marketing</purpose>
    <userCategory>employees</userCategory>
    <ruling>ALLOW</ruling>
    <action>read</action>
    <obligation\>
    <condition>OptInToMarketing=True</condition></rule>
</ep3pPolicy>
```

Fig. 25.2. A sample E-P3P policy

Now suppose that an employee of the marketing department wants to send an email with promotions to a number of customers (including Claudia), by using a mass-mailing system. The mass-mailing system, after checking that the employee is authorized to use the system, sends a request to the E-P3P privacy enforcement system to see whether access should be allowed on the basis of the enterprise's privacy policy. The request is shown in Figure 25.3. This request is *matched* against the E-P3P policy by the policy enforcement engine. The policy prescribes to check whether Claudia gave consent to receiving promotional mailings, in which case the privacy enforcement system grants the request, allow, otherwise, it will reject the request, deny, which is also the default value. This example shows the key elements of an E-P3P policy: a reference to the vocabulary used, the policy's default-ruling and the policy's ruleset. The

```
<ep3pQuery>
<userCategory>employees</userCategory>
<dataCategory>allData.contactData</dataCategory>
<purpose>business.marketing</purpose>
<action>Read</action>
</ep3pQuery>
```

Fig. 25.3. A sample E-P3P request

ruleset is a list of E-P3P rules that declares which user categories can perform which actions on which data categories and for which purposes. The vocabulary allows one to define *hierarchies* of data categories, purposes, and data users, which are convenient to refine a privacy policy in a hierarchical sense. For example, the allow ruling inherits downwards in the hierarchies: when a rule allows a request for allData, then a request for allData.creditCardData is also allowed. Denials, on the other hand, are inherited both downward and upward, for example if a rule denies access to allData.creditCardData, then the requests for allData or allData.creditCardData.cardType are also denied.

E-P3P was introduced by Karjoth et al. [5], while the full XML-based language and semantics for E-P3P policies was defined by Ashley et al. [12]. EPAL [13], a language very similar to (and derived from) E-P3P[3], was submitted by IBM to the W3C for standardization, but at the time of writing it has not been endorsed. IBM has also implemented EPAL in the *IBM Tivoli privacy manager*, a system providing automatic management of private data to bring down the enterprise's costs of privacy management and to decrease the risks of unauthorized disclosures. As we mentioned, E-P3P also allows data to be moved from one enterprise to another, together with the form that was used to collect it: the sticky policy paradigm. In this way, the destination enterprise receives private data with a privacy policy, the enforcement of which might require the composition of policies or checking that one policy is a *refinement* of the other. The precise definition of the composition and refinement operations for E-P3P policies is given by Backes et al. [14]. It is worth remarking that, although the names E-P3P and P3P are very similar, they are used in different settings. One is used to manage privacy rules internal to an enterprise, the other is used to communicate, in a standardized way, privacy policies to Internet users. To link these two aspects, Karjoth et al. [15] propose to generate and publish P3P policies directly from internal enterprise privacy policies and to update them regularly to reflect the enterprise's current practices. Yu et al. [9] on the other hand argue that P3P policies should be more long-term promises, which should not change each time an internal business rule is updated.

---

[3] EPAL does not have some of the advanced features of E-P3P such as hierarchies for obligations and conditions, or procedures for the composition of policies.

25.4 Audit Logic

Where P3P and E-P3P offer methods for specifying privacy policies and enforcing these policies within an organization, the issue of how to protect privacy when data can be modified and/or travels across different companies remains open. For example, the next chapter of this book addresses the issues of negotiating policies and making privacy policies consistent across organizations. In this section we describe the audit logic [6], which provides an alternative approach to privacy protection. The audit logic addresses the issue of compliance to policies for data that move across different security domains.

Example 3. Company A and B are members of a federation that shares customer contact information for the purpose of marketing. The federation rules require that the companies build audit trails for their commercial mailings, which may be checked by an independent authority.

When company A collects information from clients it also asks for permission to provide this information to its partners, e.g., through a *Do you want to receive offers from our partners?* checkbox on a webform. When this box is selected the email address is shared with company B, which is given permission to send one email a month regarding its offers.

After the contact information is provided to company B, company A can no longer control the use of these data; even if both company A and B are using P3P and/or E-P3P, company A cannot ensure that the data are used according to its privacy policy. A method is needed which will allow company A to place a privacy policy on the data and a system that gives A confidence that this policy will be adhered to.

When data leaves the security domain, access control [16, 17, 18] is not sufficient for protecting the data; as the control over the access moves with the data. Digital rights management (DRM) techniques [19, 20] on the other hand are designed to ensure policy compliance for data that move across security domains. Licenses and keys are needed to access the data and describe the policies for these data. While the data-centric approach of licenses is useable for providing the privacy policies, DRM techniques are often not flexible enough or have requirements, such as the need for special (trusted) hardware, which are not realistic in our corporate collaboration scenario. For a privacy protection mechanism to be viable it should not unduly increase the costs or required effort for the companies involved.

In the audit logic, compliance to policies is not enforced a priori but instead users may have to justify their actions a posteriori, i.e., users may be audited. By holding the users accountable for their actions afterwards, policy violations are prevented by deterrence rather than by prevention. In order to do this, auditors only use audit trails, which are already present in most enterprises, although it may be necessary to protect these audit trails more strongly, for instance by using techniques from tamper-proof logging [21].

The audit logic framework

The audit logic framework consists of agents executing actions, optionally logging these actions and being audited to check if their actions adhered to the relevant (privacy) policies. Actions can be, e.g., sending an email to an address, reading and updating information in a medical file, but also providing a new policy to another agent. Figure 25.4 shows an example execution in the framework. In the first step (I), agent a provides a policy ϕ to agent b which b records in his log (II). Next (III) agent b reads document d, which is stored in the company database. At a later point the auditing authority, which is checking access to privacy-sensitive files, finds the access of b (IV) and requests b to justify this access (V). In response, b shows that the access was allowed according to the policy ϕ, which was provided by a. The auditor, initially unaware of a's involvement, can now (VI) audit a for having provided the policy ϕ to b.

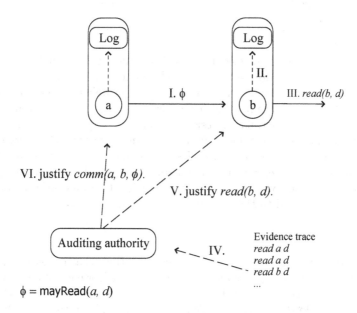

Fig. 25.4. Sample deployment depicting actions, the logging and interaction with an auditor.

The policy language

As illustrated by the example, policies express permissions to execute actions. For example a policy may be mayRead(b, d) expressing the permission to execute the action read(b, d). Besides expressing basic facts and permissions, the policy language of the audit logic allows combination of permissions and adding requirements or obligations, e.g., $\mathtt{mayRead}(b,d) \wedge \mathtt{mayWrite}(b,d)$ expresses that b may both access and update document d and $\mathtt{isSysAdmin}(b) \rightarrow \mathtt{mayWrite}(b,d)$ expresses that b may update document d provided he is a system administrator. The constructions mentioned provide an expressive language for writing privacy policies for a given agent. To enable agents to provide permissions to other agents, an additional construct *says to* is provided: This construct is used to describe delegation rights, e.g., a $\mathtt{says}$ $\mathtt{mayRead}(b,d)$ to b expresses that a is allowed to give the policy $\mathtt{mayRead}(b,d)$ to b.

Logged actions

When b receives the policy from a, b decides to store this policy in his log. The log is assumed to be secure and only able to store actions that actually happened and only when they happen. For the sending of policies this reflects the assumption that communications are nonrefutable; b will be able to prove that a sent the policy.

Deriving permissions

When an agent wants to execute an action, the decision has to be made whether the policies allow this action. The policy framework uses a logical derivation system to decide whether a given set of policies, facts and obligations is sufficient to obtain a given permission, e.g., if b is a system administrator and got the permission $\mathtt{isSysAdmin}(b) \rightarrow \mathtt{mayRead}(b,d)$ then b has the permission to read document d: $\mathtt{isSysAdmin}(b), a$ $\mathtt{says}$ $\mathtt{isSysAdmin}(b) \rightarrow \mathtt{mayRead}(b,d)$ to $b \vdash_b \mathtt{mayRead}(b,d)$. Using the derivation system, agents can build a *compliance proof*, i.e., a formal deduction in the derivation system that shows that an action was allowed by the policies. Compliance proofs can be stored, communicated to the auditing authority and automatically checked.

Auditing

The auditing authority can ask users to justify actions that it observed. When audited the user needs to provide a compliance proof for each of these actions. The auditing process can be done effectively; the user should already have built a proof before executing the action and the audit authority only needs to check the correctness of the proof, which is relatively straightforward.

Note that the auditing authority may actually consist of different entities for the different companies; in this case an entity auditing one company relies on the other entities to audit actions outside of its authority.

Implications

In the audit logic misuse is not prevented but deterred: *auditing authorities* have a mandate to check whether the data were used in compliance with the policies. Hence users should be *auditable* and sufficient *audit trails* should be available to the auditors. This fits well with, e.g., hospitals or companies, where users can be held accountable for their actions and audit trails are often already part of the (security) requirements. It may be hard to realize these requirements in certain settings, such as large open networks (e.g. P2P), but even in such open settings a kind of audit trail is present (EU law demands that ISPs keep IP traffic records of their users).

25.5 Related Work

An extensive survey of social, legal and technical aspects of P3P was given by Hochheiser [8]. In a more technical approach, Yu et al. [9] investigated the semantics of P3P: they found several inconsistencies and showed how to restrict the language to avoid them. Byers et al. [3] surveyed the use of P3P on a large number of websites. They argue that a large number of websites is not compliant with the P3P specifications, and that this may yield legal problems for these websites. The P3P preference language (APPEL) [22] was developed by Cranor et al. to allow users to express preferences about P3P policies. With APPEL, users can specify which P3P policies they find acceptable and which not. Yu et al. [9] developed another kind of P3P preference language. This approach is based on the semantics of P3P, unlike APPEL, which is based on the syntax of P3P. Related to P3P is the resource description framework (RDF) [23]. RDF was developed to represent information on the Web in a machine-readable format. Although it is not specifically intended to be used for privacy practices, it may be used to express P3P policies. RDF has been proposed as an alternative to APPEL [22].

E-P3P is an extension of Jajodia et al.'s flexible authorization framework (FAF) [24]. Like E-P3P, FAF provides a policy language that can specify both positive and negative authorizations and uses hierarchies for objects and users. However, FAF does not allow the use of obligations, and does not include a special construct to express the purpose of an access request. The notion of privacy obligations in E-P3P is similar to the provisions in Jajodia's provisional authorization specification language (pASL) [25]. Here a principal is granted access to an object if it causes certain conditions to be satisfied. In E-P3P, obligations are treated opaquely, as methods that are called and return a value, while in pASL obligations are treated more in detail by using a temporal logic. E-P3P shares some similarities with XACML [26], an OASIS standard for access control systems. XACML is XML-based and uses object and data hierarchies, as well as conditions and obligations. XACML is also inspired by FAF [24], and, although it is not specifically intended for enterprise privacy policies, it can be used for protecting private data inside an enterprise. As an example of this a policy for the protection of medical records is shown [26]. Although XACML does not have a special *purpose* construct, like the one in E-P3P, it has been added in XACML's so-called privacy profile.

Anderson [27] compares EPAL [13] and XACML and concludes that EPAL corresponds mostly to a subset of XACML and that it lacks certain features required for access control and privacy. Stufflebeam et al. [28] present a practical case study of E-P3P and P3P. Here the authors implement a number of health care policies in both EPAL and P3P. Among other things, they conclude that many promises expressed in natural-language privacy policies are neither expressible in P3P nor enforceable with EPAL. More closely related to the audit logic, originator control (ORCON) policies [29] were introduced as an alternative for discretionary and mandatory policies. In mandatory access control, the receiver of a document cannot change the access rights on the document, while in discretionary access control, the receiver of the document can always change the rights on it. In ORCON policies, the original owner of the data can always change the access rights on the data, while the current owner of the data cannot do so. This fits well with the privacy regulations, in which the subject should retain control over its personal data [1]. Also in the audit logic, the owner of the data can always change the rights on the data, however in the audit logic those rights are not stored centrally but can be moved between systems in a completely distributed setting. The policy language of the audit logic is based on a formal logic. Abadi [30] surveys a number of different distributed access control models that are based on formal logics. In these models an authorization request or an authentication credential corresponds to a logical formula and its proof corresponds to the authorization or authentication decision. For example, PCA [31] is a system for the authorization of clients to webservers, by using distributed policies. The audit logic, like PCA, uses the fact that checking proofs is easy and places the burden of finding the proofs, which is typically harder, on the clients requesting access. PCA however uses a higher-order (classical) logic, while the audit logic is restricted to first-order logic, rendering a more tractable proof search. A more common example of systems where clients compile part or all of the authorization proof is SDSI [32], which allows clients to chain together certificates to prove their authenticity. The audit logic language is closely related to delegation logic [33] and binder [30]. They also use the *says* predicate introduced by Abadi et al. [30], which however cannot be nested inside another says, for instance to express K *says* (M *says* P). This restriction is absent in the audit logic. Also in the audit logic we use a refined form of the *says* predicate, by specifying also the target agent. Conrado et al. [20] propose to use DRM to enable privacy distributed systems and vice versa to use privacy as a driver for a wider use of DRM. Licensescript is a novel DRM language using Prolog code to encode more content licenses [19]. DRM however, unlike the audit logic, requires the use of special hardware, which may make it hard to implement in the enterprise's legacy systems.

25.6 Conclusions

In the P3P system, privacy statements are formatted using XML and a common vocabulary, to allow for automatic analysis of the statements. P3P is well established in the sense that there are many popular websites that use P3P [3]. Also there are a number of tools that generate natural-language statements from P3P statements [8]. A drawback of P3P is that it does not distinguish between different types of access. For example, it is impossible to specify that certain employees may update personal data, while others may not. This makes it cumbersome to use for certain enterprise privacy policies.

The E-P3P system addresses this. E-P3P distinguishes between different types of access and enables the use of obligations and conditions. Although E-P3P itself is not an endorsed standard, it corresponds to a subset of an OASIS standard, i.e., the XACML access control language [26]. In a way they are complementary because E-P3P assumes the existence of access control policies, independent of the privacy policies. E-P3P policies can contain prohibitions, i.e., rules that deny access, which makes the language more expressive than the language used in the audit logic. However it seems complicated to move E-P3P policies from one enterprise to another. The new policy may cause conflicts and it may even be bypassed altogether due to other policies that are incompatible [14]. Moving policies may be needed in enterprise collaborations where private data are exchanged, guarded by policies. Furthermore, the use of E-P3P can only give assurances to other enterprises when they assume that the enterprise is trusted to implement E-P3P correctly [5]. This may be a too strong assumption in the setting where enterprises dynamically form coalitions to exchange private data.

In the audit logic this assumption is relaxed. Here it is assumed that the enterprise can misbehave, while compliance to privacy policies can be verified by (external) auditors, through a formal auditing procedure. The audit logic is designed for a distributed setting, and it is easy to move policies across enterprise domains, for instance accompanying private data. However, when policies are sent from one enterprise to another, the question is raised whether one can trust the sender of the policy. For example, a rogue enterprise could be set up for the purpose of distributing false privacy policies to other enterprises. To solve this problem one could extend the audit logic with a trust management system to facilitate trust decisions about the sources of policies. Furthermore, it may be interesting to couple the reputation of enterprises to the outcome of past audits, like in reputation-based systems [34]. Finally, the audit logic uses formal (first-order) logic to express policies and lacks a tool that translates policies to natural language, like those for for P3P. Such a translation to natural language is important to improve the useability of policies based on formal logic [35].

References

1. EU Parliament and Council: The data protection directive (95/46/EC) (1995)
2. EU Parliament and Council: Directive on privacy and electronic communications (2002/58/EC) (2002)
3. S. Byers, L.F. Cranor, D. Kormann: Automated analysis of P3P-enabled web sites. In: Proc. Int. Conf. on Electronic Commerce (ICEC). (2003) pp. 326–338
4. L. Cranor, M. Langheinrich, M. Marchiori, M. Presler-Marshall, J. Reagle: The Platform for Privacy Preferences 1.0 (P3P 1.0) specification – W3C recommendation 16 april 2002. http://w3.org/TR/P3P (2002)
5. G. Karjoth, M. Schunter, M. Waidner: Platform for enterprise privacy practices: Privacy-enabled management of customer data. In R. Dingledine, P.F. Syverson eds.: Proc. Int. Workshop on Privacy Enhancing Technologies (PET). Lectures in Computer Science, Springer (2002) pp. 69–84
6. J.G. Cederquist, R. Corin, M.A.C. Dekker, S. Etalle, J.I. den Hartog: An audit logic for accountability. In Winsborough, W., Sahai, A., eds.: Proc. Int. Workshop on Policies for Distributed Systems and Networks (POLICY), IEEE Computer Society Press (2005) pp. 34–43
7. A.R. Beresford, F. Stajano: Location Privacy in Pervasive Computing. IEEE Pervasive Computing **2**(1) (2003) pp. 46–55
8. H. Hochheiser: The platform for privacy preference as a social protocol: An examination within the U.S. policy context. ACM Transactions on Internet Technology (TOIT) **2**(4) (2002) pp. 276–306
9. T. Yu, N. Li, A.I. Antón: A formal semantics for P3P. In: Proc. Workshop On Secure Web Service (SWS), ACM Press (2004) pp. 1–8
10. M. Schunter, E.V. Herreweghen, M. Waidner: Expressive Privacy promises - how to improve P3P. W3C Workshop on the Future of P3P (2002)
11. J. Cattlet: Open letter to P3P developers. `http://junkbusters.com/standards.html` (1999)
12. P. Ashley, S. Hada, G. Karjoth, M. Schunter: E-P3P privacy policies and privacy authorization. In Samarati, P., ed.: Proc. Workshop on Privacy in the Electronic Society (WPES), ACM Press (2002) pp. 103–109
13. P. Ashley, S. Hada, G. Karjoth, M. Schunter: (Enterprise privacy authorization language (EPAL 1.2) - W3C member submission 10 november 2003)
14. M. Backes, B. Pfitzmann, M. Schunter: A toolkit for managing enterprise privacy policies. In Gollmann, D., Snekkenes, E., eds.: Proc. European Symp. on Research in Computer Security (ESORICS), Springer (2003) pp. 162–180
15. G. Karjoth, M. Schunter, E.V. Herreweghen: Translating privacy practices into privacy promises -how to promise what you can keep. In: Proc. Int. Workshop on Policies for Distributed Systems and Networks (POLICY), IEEE Computer Society Press (2003) pp. 135–146
16. S. Jajodia, P. Samarati, V.S. Subrahmanian, E. Bertino: A unified framework for enforcing multiple access control policies. In Peckham, J., ed.: Proc. Int. Conf. on Management of Data (SIGMOD), ACM Press (1997) pp. 474–485
17. J. Park, R. Sandhu: Towards usage control models: Beyond traditional access control. In E. Bertino ed.: Proc. Symp. on Access Control Models and Technologies (SACMAT), ACM Press (2002) pp. 57–64
18. R. Sandhu, P. Samarati: Access control: Principles and practice. IEEE Communications Magazine **32**(9) (1994) pp. 40–48

19. C.N. Chong, R. Corin, S. Etalle, P.H. Hartel, W. Jonker, Y.W. Law: Licens-eScript: A novel digital rights language and its semantics. In K. Ng, C. Busch, P. Nesi eds.: Proc. Int. Conf. on Web Delivering of Music (WEDELMUSIC), IEEE Computer Society Press (2003) pp. 122–129

20. C. Conrado, M. Petkovic, M. van der Veen, W. van der Velde: Controlled sharing of personal content using digital rights management. In E. Fernández-Medina, J.C. Hernández, L.J. García eds.: Proc. Int. Workshop On Security in Information Systems (WOSIS) (2005) pp. 173–185

21. C.N. Chong, Z. Peng, P.H. Hartel: Secure audit logging with tamper-resistant hardware. In Gritzalis, D., di Vimercati, S.D.C., Samarati, P., Katsikas, S.K., eds.: IFIP Int. Conf. on Information Security and Privacy in the Age of Uncertainty (SEC), Springer (2003) pp. 73–84

22. L. Cranor, M. Langheinric, M. Marchiori: A P3P preference exchange language 1.0 (APPEL 1.0) (2002)

23. O. Lassila, R.P. Swick: Resource Description Framework (RDF) Model and Syntax Specification – W3C Recommendation 22 February 1999 (2002)

24. S. Jajodia, P. Samarati, M.L. Sapino, V.S. Subrahmanian: Flexible support for multiple access control policies. ACM Transactions on Database Systems 26(2) (2001) pp. 214–260

25. S. Jajodia, M. Kudo, S. Subrahmanian: Provisional authorization. (In: Proc. 1st Int. Workshop on Security and Privacy in E-Commerce (WSPEC))

26. OASIS Access Control TC: eXtensible Access Control Markup Language (XACML) Version 2.0 – Oasis Standard, 1 Feb 2005 (2005)

27. A. Anderson: Comparison of two privacy languages: EPAL and XACML. Sun Technical Report TR-2005-147 (2005)

28. W.H. Stufflebeam, A.I. Antón, Q. He, N. Jain: Specifying privacy policies with P3P and EPAL: lessons learned. In: Proc. Workshop on Privacy in the Electronic Society (WPES). (2004) p. 35

29. J. Park, R. Sandhu: Originator control in usage control. In: Proc. Int. Workshop on Policies for Distributed Systems and Networks (POLICY), Washington, DC, USA, IEEE Computer Society (2002) p. 60

30. M. Abadi: Logic in access control. In Kolaitis, P.G., ed.: Proc. Symp. on Logic in Computer Science (LICS), IEEE Computer Society Press (2003) pp. 228–233

31. A.W. Appel, E.W. Felten: Proof-carrying authentication. In Tsudik, G., ed.: Proc. Conf. on Comp. and Comm. Sec. (CCS), ACM Press (1999) pp. 52–62

32. R.L. Rivest, B. Lampson: SDSI – A simple distributed security infrastructure. Presented at CRYPTO'96 Rumpsession (1996)

33. N. Li, B.N. Grosof, J. Feigenbaum: Delegation logic: A logic-based approach to distributed authorization. ACM Transactions on Information and System Security (TISSEC) 6(1) (2003) pp. 128–171

34. V. Shmatikov, C.L. Talcott: Reputation-based trust management. Journal of Computer Security 13(1) (2005) pp. 167–190

35. J.Y. Halpern, V. Weissman: Using first-order logic to reason about policies. In Focardi, R., ed.: Proc. Computer Security Foundations Workshop (CSFW), IEEE Computer Society Press (2003) pp. 187–201

Security and Privacy on the Semantic Web

Daniel Olmedilla

L3S Research Center and University of Hannover
Germany

Summary. The semantic Web aims to enable sophisticated and autonomic machine-to-machine interactions without human intervention, by providing machines not only with data but also with its meaning (semantics). In this setting, traditional security mechanisms are not suitable anymore. For example, identity-based access control assumes that parties are known in advance. Then, a machine first determines the identity of the requester in order to either grant or deny access, depending on its associated information (e.g., by looking up its set of permissions). In the semantic Web, any two strangers can interact with each other automatically and therefore this assumption does not hold. Hence, a semantically enriched process is required in order to regulate automatic access to sensitive information. Policy-based access control provides sophisticated means to support the protection of sensitive resources and information disclosure. This chapter provides an introduction to policy-based security and privacy protection by analyzing several existing policy languages. Furthermore, it shows how these languages can be used in a number of semantic Web scenarios.

26.1 Introduction

Information provided in the current Web is mainly human oriented. For example, HTML pages are human understandable but a computer is not able to understand the content and extract the concepts represented there, that is, the meaning of the data. The semantic Web [1] is a distributed environment in which information is self-describable by means of well-defined semantics, that is, machine understandable, thus providing interoperability (e.g., in e-commerce) and automation (e.g., in searching). In such an environment, entities which have not had any previous interaction may now be able to automatically interact with each other. For example, imagine an agent planning a trip for a user. It needs to search for and book a plane and a hotel taking into account the user's schedule. When the user's agent contacts a hotel's website, the latter needs to inform the former that it requires a credit card in order to confirm a reservation. However, the user may probably want to restrict the conditions under which her agent automatically discloses her personal information. Due to such exchange of conditions and personal information, as well as its automation, security and privacy become yet more relevant and traditional approaches are not suitable anymore. On the one hand, unilateral access control is now replaced by bilateral protection (e.g., not only does the website state the conditions to be satisfied in order to reserve a room but the user agent may also communicate conditions under which a credit card can be disclosed). On the other hand, identity-based access control cannot be applied anymore since users are not known in advance. Instead, entities' properties (e.g., the user's credit card or whether a user is a student) play a central role. Both these properties and conditions stating the requirements to be fulfilled by the other party, must be described in a machine-understandable language with well-defined semantics allowing other entities to process them. Systems semantically annotated with policies enhance their authorization process allowing, among others, to regulate information disclosure (privacy policies), to control access to resources (security policies), and to estimate trust based on parties' properties (trust management policies) [2].

Distributed access control has addressed some of these issues, though not solved them yet. Examples like KeyNote [3] or PolicyMaker [4], which are described in Chap. 8, provide a separation between enforcement and decision mechanisms by means of policies. However, policies are bound to public keys (identities) and are not expressive enough to deal with semantic Web scenarios. Role-based access control (see Chap. 5) also does not meet semantic Web requirements since it is difficult to assign roles to users which are not known in advance. Regarding user's privacy protection, the platform for privacy preferences (P3P), which is described in Chap. 25, provides a standard vocabulary to describe webserver policies. However, it is not expressive enough (it is a schema, not a language, and only describes the purpose for the gathered data) and it does not allow for enforcement mechanisms. On the other hand, a wide variety of policy languages have been developed to date [5, 6, 7, 8, 9], addressing the general requirements for a semantic Web policy language: expressiveness, simplicity, enforceability, scalability, and analyzability [10]. These policies can be exchanged between entities on the semantic Web and therefore they are described using languages with well-founded semantics.

The policy languages listed above differ in expressivity, the kind of reasoning required, features and implementations provided, etc. For the sake of simplicity, they are divided according to their protocol for policy exchange between parties, depending on the sensitivity of policies. On the one hand, assuming that all policies are public and accessible (typical situation in many multi-agent systems), the process of evaluating whether two policies from two different entities are compatible or not consists of gathering the relevant policies (and possibly relevant credentials) from the entities involved and checking whether they *match* (e.g., [11]). On the other hand, if policies may be private (the typical situation for business rules [12]), it implies that not all policies are known in advance but they may be disclosed at a later stage. Therefore, a *negotiation* protocol in which security and trust is iteratively established is required [13].

However, specifying policies is as difficult as writing imperative code, getting a policy right is as hard as getting a piece of software correct, and maintaining a large number of them is even harder. Fortunately, ontologies and policy reasoning may help users and administrators with the specification, conflict detection and resolution of such policies [5, 14].

This chapter first describes how policies are exchanged and how they interact among parties on the semantic Web, with a brief description of the main semantic Web policy languages and how ontologies may be used in policy specification, conflict detection and validation. Then, some examples of application scenarios are presented, where policy-based security and privacy are used, followed by some important open research issues. This chapter focuses only on policy-based security, privacy and trust on the semantic Web and does not deal with approaches based on individual trust ratings and propagation through a web of trust providing a means to rate unknown sources [15, 16, 17].

26.2 Policy-Based Interaction and Evaluation

Policies allow for security and privacy descriptions in a machine-understandable way. More specifically, service or information providers may use security policies to control access to resources by describing the conditions a requester must fulfil (e.g., a requester to resource A must belong to institution B and prove it by means of a credential). At the same time, service or information consumers may regulate the information they are willing to disclose by protecting it with privacy policies (e.g., an entity is willing to disclose its employee card credential only to the webserver of its employer). Given two sets of policies, an engine may check whether they are compatible, that is, whether they match. The complexity of this process varies depending on the sensitivity of policies (and the expressivity of the policies). If all policies are public at both sides (the typical situation in many multi-agent systems), provider and requester, the requester may initially already provide the relevant policies together with the request and the evaluation process can be performed in a one-step evaluation by the provider policy engine (or an external trusted matchmaker) and return a final decision. Otherwise, if policies may be private, as it is, for example, typically the case for sensitive business rules, this process may consist of several steps of negotiation in which new policies and credentials are disclosed at each step, advancing after each iteration towards a common agreement. In this section we give an overview of both types of languages. The main features of these languages are shown in Table 26.1. Additionally, we use the running policy "only employees of institution XYZ may retrieve a file" to illustrate an example of each language.

26.2.1 One-Step Policy Evaluation

Assuming that policies are publicly disclosable, there is no reason why a requester should not disclose its relevant applicable policies together with its request. This way, the provider's policy engine (or a trusted external matchmaker if the provider does not have one) has all the information needed to make an authorisation decision. The KAOS and REI frameworks, specially designed using semantic Web features and constructs, fall within this category of policy languages, those which do not allow policies themselves to be protected.

Table 26.1. Comparison of KAOS, REI, PeerTrust and Protune[1]

Policy language	Authorization protocol	Reasoning paradigm	Conflict detection	Meta-policies	Loop detection
KAOS	One-step	DL	Static detection and resolution		
REI	One-step	DL + variables	Dinamyc detection and resolution	Used for conflict resolution	
PeerTrust	Negotiation	LP + ontologies			Distributed tabling
Protune	Negotiation	LP + ontologies		Used for driving decisions	

KAOS Policy and Domain Services

KAOS services [5, 18] provide a framework for the specification, management, conflict resolution and enforcement of policies, allowing for distributed policy interaction and support for dynamic policy changes. It uses OWL [19] ontologies (defining, e.g., actors, groups and actions) to describe the policies and the application context, and provides administration tools (KAOS administration tool - KPAT) to help administrators to write down their policies and hide the complexity of using OWL directly. A policy in KAOS may be a positive (respectively negative) authorization, i.e., constraints that permit (respectively forbid) the execution of an action, or a positive (respectively negative) obligation, i.e., constraints that require an action to be executed (respectively waive the actor from having to execute it). A policy is then represented as an instance of the appropriate policy type, associating values to its properties, and giving restrictions on such properties (Fig. 26.1 sketches part of a KAOS policy).

---

[1] DL refers to description logic while LP stands for logic programming

KAOS benefits from the OWL representation and description-logic-based subsumption mechanisms [20]. Thus, it allows one to, for example, obtain all known subclasses or instances of a class within a given range (used during policy specification to help users choosing only valid classes or instances) or detect policy conflicts (by checking the disjointness of subclasses of the action class controlled by policies). KAOS is able to detect three types of conflicts, based on the types of policies that are allowed in the framework: positive vs. negative authorization (a policy allows access and but another denies it), positive versus negative obligation (a policy obliges to execute an action while another dispensates from such obligation) and positive obligation versus negative authorization (a policy obliges to execute an action but another denies authorization for such execution). KAOS resolves such conflicts (also called harmonization) based on assigning preferences to policies and resolving in favor of the policies with higher priority (Sect. 26.2.3 will extend on this).

Finally, KAOS assumes a default authorization mechanism in case no policy applies to a request. It can be either "permit all actions not explicitly forbidden" or "forbid all actions not explicitly authorized".

```
<owl:Class rdf:ID="RetrieveFileAction">
  <owl:intersectionOf>
    <owl:Class rdf:about="#AccessAction"/>
    <owl:Class>
      <owl:Restriction>
        <owl:onProperty rdf:resource="#performedBy"/>
        <owl:someValuesFrom>
          <owl:Class>
            <owl:oneOf rdf:parseType="Collection">
              <owl:Thing rdf:about="#EmployeeInstitutionXYZ"/>
            </owl:oneOf>
          </owl:Class>
        </owl:someValuesFrom>
      </owl:Restriction>
    </owl:Class>
  </owl:Restriction>
  </owl:intersectionOf>
</owl:Class>

<policy:PosAuthorizationPolicy rdf:ID="PolicyRetrieveFileAction">
  <policy:controls rdf:resource="#RetrieveFileAction"/>
  <policy:hasPriority>1</policy:hasPriority>
</policy:PosAuthorizationPolicy>
```

```
<policy:Policy rdf:ID="RetrieveFilePolicy">
  <policy:grants rdf:resource="#Perm_Employee_XYZ">
</policy:Policy>

<policy:Granting rdf:ID=#Perm_Employee_XYZ">
  <policy:to rdf:resource="#PersonVar">
  <policy:deontic rdf:resource="Perm_Retrieve_File">
</policy:Granting>

<deontic:Permission rdf:ID="Perm_Retrieve_File">
  <deontic:actor rdf:resource="#PersonVar">
  <deontic:action rdf:resource="&action;RetrieveFile">
  <deontic:constraint rdf:resource="#IsEmployeeXYZ">
</deontic:Permission>

<constraint:SimpleConstraint rdf:ID="IsEmployeeXYZ">
  <constraint:subject rdf:resource="#PersonVar">
  <constraint:predicate rdf:resource="&emp;affiliation">
  <constraint:object rdf:resource="&emp;XYZ">
</constraint:SimpleConstraint>
```

Fig. 26.1. Example of KAOS (left) and REI (right) policies

REI

REI 2.0 [21, 11] expresses policies according to what entities can or cannot do and what they should or should not do. They define an independent ontology which includes the concepts for permissions, obligations, actions, etc. Additionally, as in KAOS, they allow the import of domain-dependent ontologies (including domain-dependent classes and properties). REI 2.0 is represented in OWL-Lite and includes logic-like variables in order to specify a range of relations.

REI policies (see Fig. 26.1 for an example) are described in terms of deontic concepts: permissions, prohibitions, obligations and dispensations, equivalently to the positive/negative authorizations and positive/negative obligations of KAOS. In addition, REI provides a specification of speech acts for the dynamic exchange of rights and obligations between entities: delegation (of a right), revocation (of a previously delegated right), request (for action execution or delegation) and cancel (of a previous request).

As in the KAOS framework, REI policies may conflict with each other (right versus prohibition or obligation versus dispensation). REI provides mechanisms for conflict detection and constructs to resolve them, namely, overriding policies (similar to the prioritization in KAOS) and definition at the meta-level of the global modality (positive or negative) that holds (see Sect. 26.2.3 for more details).

26.2.2 Policy-Driven Negotiations

In the approaches presented previously, policies are assumed to be publicly disclosable. This is true for many scenarios but there exist other scenarios where it may not hold. For example, imagine a hospital revealing to everyone that, in order to receive Alice's medical report, the requester needs an authorization from Alice's psychiatrist. Another example: imagine Tom wants to share his holiday pictures online only with his friends. If he states publicly that policy and Jessica is denied access, she may get angry because of Tom not considering her as a friend. Moreover, policy protection becomes even more important when policies protects sensitive business rules.

These scenarios require the possibility to protect policies (policies protecting policies) and the process of finding a match between requester and provider becomes more complex, since not all relevant policies may be available at the time. Therefore, this process may consist of several steps of negotiation, by disclosing new policies and credentials at each step, and therefore advancing after each iteration towards a common agreement [13]. For example, suppose Alice requests access to a resource at e-shop. Alice is told that she must provide her credit card to be granted access. However, Alice does not want to disclose her credit card just to anyone and she communicates to the e-shop that, before it gets her credit card, it should provide its Better Business Bureau certification. Once e-shop discloses it, Alice's policy is fulfilled and she provides the credit card, thus fulfilling e-shop's policy and receiving access to the requested resource (see Fig. 26.2).

Below, the two most recent languages for policy-driven negotiation are presented. They are also specially designed for the semantic Web. However, we refer the interested reader to other languages for policy-based negotiations [22, 23, 24], which may be applied to the semantic Web.

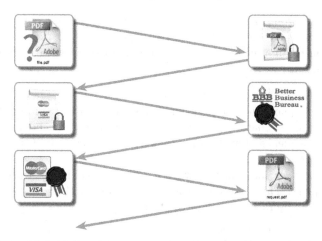

Fig. 26.2. Policy-driven negotiation between Alice and e-shop

PeerTrust

PeerTrust [7] builds upon previous work on policy-based access control and release for the Web and implements automated trust negotiation for such a dynamic environment.

PeerTrust's language is based on first-order Horn rules (definite Horn clauses), i.e., rules of the form "$lit_0 \leftarrow lit_1, \ldots, lit_n$" where each lit_i is a positive literal $P_j(t_1, \ldots, t_n)$, P_j is a predicate symbol, and the t_i are the arguments of this predicate. Each t_i is a term, i.e., a function symbol and its arguments, which are themselves terms. The head of a rule is lit_0, and its body is the set of lit_i. The body of a rule can be empty.

Definite Horn clauses can be easily extended to include negation as failure, restricted versions of classical negation, and additional constraint-handling capabilities such as those used in constraint logic programming. Although all of these features can be useful in trust negotiation, here we only describe other, more unusual, required language extensions. Additionally, PeerTrust allows the import of RDF-based meta-data, therefore allowing the use of ontologies within policy descriptions.

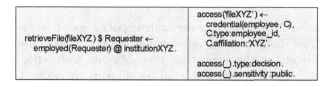

Fig. 26.3. Example of PeerTrust (left) and Protune (right) policies

References to Other Peers PeerTrust's ability to reason about statements made by other peers is central to trust negotiation. To express delegation of evaluation to another peer, each literal lit_i is extended with an additional *Authority* argument, that is

$$lit_i @ \text{Authority}$$

where *Authority* specifies the peer who is responsible for evaluating lit_i or has the authority to evaluate lit_i. The *Authority* argument can be a nested term containing a sequence of authorities, which are then evaluated starting at the outermost layer.

A specific peer may need a way of referring to the peer who asked a particular query. This is accomplished by including a *Requester* argument in literals, so that literals are now of the form

$$lit_i @ \text{Issuer} \$ \text{Requester}$$

The *Requester* argument can also be nested, in which case it expresses a chain of requesters, with the most recent requester in the outermost layer of the nested term.

Using the *Issuer* and *Requester* arguments, it is possible to delegate evaluation of literals to other parties and also express interactions and the corresponding negotiation process between parties (see Fig. 26.3 for an example).

Signed Rules Each peer defines a policy for each of its resources in the form of a set of definite Horn clause rules. These and any other rules that the peer defines on its own are its *local* rules. A peer may also have copies of rules defined by other peers, and it may use these rules to generate proofs, which can be sent to other entities in order to give evidence of the result of a negotiation.

A signed rule has an additional argument that says who signed the rule. The cryptographic signature itself is not included in the policy, because signatures are very large and are not needed by this part of the negotiation software. The signature is used to verify that the issuer really did issue the rule. It is assumed that, when a peer receives a signed rule from another peer, the signature is verified before the rule is passed to the DLP evaluation engine. Similarly, when one peer sends a signed rule to another peer, the actual signed rule must be sent, and not just the logic programmatic representation of the signed rule. More-complex signed rules often represent delegations of authority.

Loop Detection Mechanisms In declarative policy specification, loops may easily occur and should not be considered as errors. For example, declarative policies may state at the same time that "anyone with write permissions can read a file" and "anyone with read permissions can write a file". If not handled accordingly, such loops may end up in nonterminating evaluation [25]. In practice, policies, including for instance business rules, are complex and large in number (and typically not under the control of a single person), which increases the risk of loops and nontermination during dynamic policy evaluation. A distributed tabling algorithm can safely handle mutual recursive dependencies (loops) in distributed environments. Due to the security context, other aspects like private and public policies and proof generation must be taken into account [25].

Protune

The Provisional trust negotiation framework (Protune) [9] aims at combining distributed trust management policies with provisional-style business rules and access-control-related actions. Protune's rule language extends two previous languages: PAPL [22], which until 2002 was one of the most complete policy languages for trust negotiation, and PeerTrust [7], which supports distributed credentials and a more flexible policy protection mechanism. In addition, the framework features a powerful declarative meta-language for driving some critical negotiation decisions, and integrity constraints for monitoring negotiations and credential disclosure.

Protune provides a framework with:

- A trust management language supporting general provisional-style[2] actions (possibly user-defined).
- An extendible declarative meta-language for driving decisions about request formulation, information disclosure, and distributed credential collection.
- A parameterized negotiation procedure, that gives a semantics to the meta-language and provably satisfies some desirable properties for all possible meta-policies.
- Integrity constraints for negotiation monitoring and disclosure control.
- General, ontology-based techniques for importing and exporting meta-policies and for smoothly integrating language extensions.

The Protune rule language is based on normal logic program rules $A \leftarrow L_1, \ldots, L_n$ where A is a standard logical atom (called the *head* of the rule) and $L_1, \ldots, L_n$ (the *body* of the rule) are literals, that is, L_i equals either B_i or $\neg B_i$, for some logical atom B_i.

A *policy* is a set of rules (see Fig. 26.3 for an example), such that negation is applied neither to *provisional predicates* (defined below) nor to any predicate occurring in a rule head. This restriction ensures that policies are *monotonic* on credentials and actions, that is, as more credentials are released and more actions executed, the set of permissions does not decrease.

The vocabulary of predicates occurring in the rules is partitioned into the following categories: *decision predicates* (currently supporting allow() which is queried by the negotiation for access control decisions and sign() which is used to issue statements signed by the principal owning the policy, *abbreviation predicates* (as described in [22]), *constraint predicates* (which

---

[2] Authorizations involving actions and side effects are sometimes called provisional.

comprise the usual equality and disequality predicates) and *State Predicates* (which perform decisions according to the state). State predicates are further subdivided in *state query predicates* (which read the state without modifying it) and *provisional predicates* (which may be made true by means of associated actions that may modify the current state like, e.g., $credential(), declaration(), logged(X, logfile\_name))$.

Furthermore, meta-policies consist of rules similar to object-level rules. They allow the inspection of terms, check groundness, call an object-level goal G against the current state (using a predicate $holds(G)$), etc. In addition, a set of reserved attributes associated to predicates, literals and rules (e.g., whether a policy is public or sensitive) is used to drive the negotiator's decisions. For example, if p is a predicate, then p.sensitivity : private means that the extension of the predicate is private and should not be disclosed. An assertion p.type : provisional declares p to be a provisional predicate; then p can be attached to the corresponding action α by asserting p.action :α. If the action is to be executed locally, then we assert p.actor : self, otherwise we assert p.actor : peer.

26.2.3 Policy Specification, Conflict Detection and Resolution

Previous sections described how the semantic Web may benefit from the protection of resources with policies specifying security and privacy constraints. However, specifying policies may be as difficult as writing imperative code, getting a policy right is as hard as getting a piece of software correct, and maintaining a large number of them is only harder. Fortunately, the semantic Web can help administrators with policy specification, and detection and resolution of conflicts.

Policy specification Tools like the KAOS policy administration tool (K-PAT) [5] and the PeerTrust policy editor provide an easy-to-use application to help policy writers. This is important because the policies will be enforced automatically and therefore errors in their specification or implementation will allow outsiders to gain inappropriate access to resources, possibly inflicting huge and costly damage. In general, the use of ontologies on policy specification reduces the burden on administrators, helps them with their maintenance, and decreases the number of errors. For example, ontology-based structuring and abstraction help maintain complex software, as they do with complex sets of policies. In the context of the semantic Web, ontologies provide a formal specification of concepts and their interrelationships, and play an essential role in complex Web service environments, semantics-based search engines and digital libraries. Nejdl et al. [14] suggest using two strategies to compose and override policies, building upon the notions of mandatory and default policies, and formalizing the constraints corresponding to these kinds of policies using F-Logic. A prototype implementation as a Protégé plug-in shows that the proposed policy specification mechanism is implementable and effective.

Conflict detection and resolution. semantic Web policy languages also allow for advanced algorithms for conflict detection and its resolution. For example, in Sect. 26.2.1 it was briefly described how conflicts may arise between policies, either at specification time or runtime. A typical example of a conflict is when several policies apply to a request and one allows access while another denies it (positive versus negative authorization). Description logic based languages may use subsumption reasoning to detect conflicts by checking if two policies are instances of conflicting types and whether the action classes that the policies control are not disjoint. Both KAOS and REI handle such conflicts (like right versus prohibition or obligation versus dispensation) within their frameworks and both provide constructs for specifying priorities between policies, hence the most important ones override the less important ones. In addition, REI provides a construct for specifying a general modality priority: positive (rights override prohibitions and obligations override dispensations) or negative (prohibitions override rights and dispensations override obligations). KAOS also provides a conflict resolution technique called policy harmonization. If a conflict is detected the policy with lower priority is modified by refining it with the minimum degree necessary to remove the conflict. This process may generate zero, one or several policies as a refinement of the previous one (see [5] for more information). This process is performed statically at policy specification time, ensuring that no conflicts arise at runtime.

26.3 Applying Policies on the Semantic Web

The benefits of using semantic policy languages in distributed environments with automated machine–machine interaction have been described extensively in previous sections. This section aims at providing some examples of its use in the context of the Web, (semantic) Web Services and the (semantic) grid. In all cases, different solutions have been described addressing different scenarios from the point of view of one-step authorization or policy-driven negotiations.

26.3.1 Policies on the Web

The current Web infrastructure does not allow the enforcement of user policies while accessing Web resources. Web server authentication is typically based on authentication mechanisms in which users must authenticate themselves (either by means of certificates or typing a user name and password). Semantic Web policies overcome such limitations of the Web.

Kagal et al. [6] describe how the REI language can be applied in order to control access to Web resources. Web pages are marked up with policies specifying which credentials are required to access such pages. A policy engine (bound to the webserver) decides whether the request matches the credentials requested. In case it does not, the webserver could show which credentials are missing. Furthermore, Kolari et al. [26] presents an extension to the platform for privacy preferences (P3P) using the REI language. The authors propose enhancements using REI policies to increase expressiveness and to allow for existing privacy enforcement mechanisms.

PeerTrust can be used to provide advanced policy-driven negotiations on the Web in order to control access to resources [7, 27]. A user receives a signed (by a trusted authority) applet after requesting access to a resource. Such an applet includes reasoning capabilities and is loaded in the Web browser. The applet automatically imports the policies specified by the user and starts a negotiation. If the negotiation succeeds, the applet simply retrieves the resource requested or, if necessary, redirects the user to the appropriate repository.

26.3.2 Semantic Web Services

Semantic Web services aim at the automation of discovery, selection and composition of Web services. Denker et al. [28] and Kagal et al. [11] suggest extending OWL-S with security policies, written in REI, like e.g., whether a service requires or is capable of providing secure communication channels. An agent may then submit a request to the registry together with its privacy policies. The matchmaker at the registry will filter out incompatible service descriptions and select only those whose security requirements of the service match the privacy policies of the requester.

Differently, Olmedilla et al. [29] propose the use of the PeerTrust language to decide if trust can be established between a requester and a service provider during runtime selection of Web services. Modelling elements are added to the Web service modelling ontology (WSMO) in order to include security information in the description of Semantic Web Services. In addition, the authors discuss different registry architectures and their implications for the matchmaking process.

26.3.3 Semantic Grid

Grid environments provide the middleware needed to access distributed computing and data resources. Distinctly administrated domains form virtual organizations and share resources for data retrieval, job execution, monitoring, and data storage. Such an environment provides users with seamless access to all resources they are authorized to access. In current Grid infrastructures, in order to be granted access at each domain, user's jobs have to secure and provide appropriate digital credentials for authentication and authorization. However, while authentication along with single sign-on can be provided based on client delegation of X.509 proxy certificates to the job being submitted, the authorization mechanisms are still mainly identity-based. Due to the large number of potential users and different certification authorities, this leads to scalability problems calling for a complementary solution to the access control mechanisms specified in the current grid security infrastructure (GSI) [30].

Uszok et al. [31] present an integration of the KAOS framework into Globus Tookit 3. Its authors suggest offering a KAOS grid service and providing an interface so grid clients and services may register and check whether a specific action is authorized or not. The KAOS grid service uses the KAOS policy services described in Sect. 26.2.1 and relies on the Globus local enforcement mechanisms.

Alternatively, Constandache et al. [32] describe an integration of policy-driven negotiations for the GSI, using semantic policies and enhancing it by providing automatic credential fetching and disclosure. Policy-based dynamic negotiations allow more-flexible authorization in complex Grid environments, and relieve both users and administrators from up-front negotiations and registrations. Constandache et al. [32] introduce an extension to the GSI and Globus Toolkit 4.0 in which policy-based negotiation mechanisms offer the basis for overcoming these limitations. This extension includes property-based authorization mechanisms, automatic gathering of required certificates, bidirectional and iterative trust negotiation and policy-based authorization, ingredients that provide advanced self-explanatory access control to grid resources.

26.4 Open Research Issues

Although there has been extensive research in recent years, there exist still open issues that must be solved [33]. The following provides a nonexhaustive list of issues which have not yet been given enough attention, or that still remain unsolved and crucial challenges in order to have a semantic policy framework adopted in real-world applications.

- Adoption of a *broad notion of policy*, encompassing not only access control policies, but also privacy policies, business rules, quality of service, agent conversation, mobility policies, etc. All these different kinds of policies should eventually be integrated into a single framework.
- *Strong and lightweight evidence*: Policies make decisions based on the properties of the peers interacting with the system. These properties may be strongly certified by cryptographic techniques, or may be reliable to some intermediate degree with lightweight evidence gathering and validation. A flexible policy framework should try to merge these two forms of evidence to meet the efficiency and usability requirements of Web applications. Independently to prevention techniques, audits can be explored to detect malicious behaviour (see Chaps. 24 and 25 for more details).
- These desiderata imply that trust negotiation, reputation models, business rules, and action specification languages have to be integrated into a single framework at least to some extent. It is crucial to find the right tradeoff between generality and efficiency.
- *Automated policy-driven negotiation* is one of the main ingredients that can be used to make heterogeneous peers effectively interoperate.

- *Lightweight knowledge representation and reasoning* does not only refer to computational complexity; it should also reduce the effort to specialize general frameworks to specific application domains; and the corresponding tools should be easy to learn and use for common users, with no particular training in computers or logic.
- The last issue cannot be tackled simply by adopting a rule language. Solutions like *controlled natural-language syntax for policy rules*, to be translated by a parser into the internal logical format, will definitively ease the adoption of any policy language.
- *Cooperative policy enforcement*: A secure cooperative system should (almost) never say *no*. Web applications need to help new users in obtaining the services that the application provides, so potential customers should not be discouraged. Whenever prerequisites for accessing a service are not met, Web applications should explain what is missing and help the user to obtain the required permissions. As part of cooperative enforcement, advanced *explanation mechanisms* are necessary to help users understand policy decisions and obtaining the permission to access a desired service.

26.5 Conclusions

This chapter provides an introduction to policy-based security and privacy management on the semantic Web. It describes the benefits of using policies and presents four of the most relevant policy languages in the semantic Web context. These four languages are classified according to whether policies are assumed to be public or else may be protected. The former consists of a single evaluation step where a policy engine or a matchmaker decides whether two policies are compatible or not. Examples of this kind of evaluation are the KAOS and REI frameworks. If policies may be protected (by e.g., other policies), the process is no longer a one-step evaluation. In this case, policies guide a negotiation in which policies are disclosed iteratively increasing the level of security at each step towards a final agreement. Examples of these kind of frameworks are PeerTrust and Protune. Furthermore, semantic Web techniques can be used to ease and enhance the process of policy specification and validation. Conflicts between policies can be found and even resolved automatically (either by meta-policies or by harmonization algorithms).

In order to demonstrate the benefits and feasibility of semantic Web policies, several application scenarios are described, namely the Web, (semantic) Web Services and the (semantic) grid. Finally the chapter concludes with a list of open research issues that prevent existing policy languages from being widely adopted. This list is intended to help new researchers in the area to focus on those crucial problems which are still unsolved.

References

1. T. Berners-Lee, J. Hendler, and O. Lassila. The Semantic Web. *Scientific American*, May 2001.
2. G. Antoniou, M. Baldoni, P.A. Bonatti, W. Nejdl, and D. Olmedilla. Rule-based policy specification. In Ting Yu and Sushil Jajodia, editors, *Decentralized Data Management Security*. Springer, 2006.
3. M. Blaze, J. Feigenbaum, and A.D. Keromytis. Keynote: Trust management for public-key infrastructures (position paper). In *Security Protocols, 6th International Workshop*, volume 1550 of *LNCS*, pages 59–63, Cambridge, April, 1998. Springer.
4. M. Blaze, J. Feigenbaum, and M. Strauss. Compliance checking in the policy-maker trust management system. In *Financial Cryptography, Second International Conference*, volume 1465 of *LNCS*, pages 254–274, Anguilla, British West Indies, February 1998. Springer.
5. A. Uszok, J.M. Bradshaw, R. Jeffers, N. Suri, P.J. Hayes, M.R. Breedy, L. Bunch, M. Johnson, S. Kulkarni, and J. Lott. KAoS policy and domain services: Toward a description-logic approach to policy representation, deconfliction, and enforcement. In *POLICY*, page 93, 2003.
6. L. Kagal, T.W. Finin, and A. Joshi. A policy based approach to security for the semantic web. In *The Semantic Web - ISWC 2003, Second International Semantic Web Conference, Sanibel Island, FL, USA, October 20-23, 2003, Proceedings*, LNCS, pages 402–418. Springer, 2003.
7. R. Gavriloaie, W. Nejdl, D. Olmedilla, K.E. Seamons, and M. Winslett. No registration needed: How to use declarative policies and negotiation to access sensitive resources on the semantic web. In *1st European Semantic Web Symposium (ESWS 2004)*, volume 3053 of *LNCS*, pages 342–356, Heraklion, Crete, Greece, May 2004. Springer.
8. M.Y. Becker and P. Sewell. Cassandra: Distributed access control policies with tunable expressiveness. In *5th IEEE International Workshop on Policies for Distributed Systems and Networks (POLICY 2004), 7-9 June 2004, Yorktown Heights, NY, USA*, pages 159–168. IEEE Computer Society, 2004.
9. P. A. Bonatti and D. Olmedilla. Driving and monitoring provisional trust negotiation with metapolicies. In *6th IEEE International Workshop on Policies for Distributed Systems and Networks (POLICY 2005)*, pages 14–23, Stockholm, Sweden, 2005. IEEE Computer Society.
10. G. Tonti, J.M. Bradshaw, R. Jeffers, R.Montanari, N. Suri, and A. Uszok. Semantic web languages for policy representation and reasoning: A comparison of KAoS, Rei, and Ponder. In *International Semantic Web Conference*, pages 419–437, 2003.
11. L. Kagal, M. Paolucci, N. Srinivasan, G. Denker, T. W. Finin, and K.P. Sycara. Authorization and privacy for semantic web services. *IEEE Intelligent Systems*, 19(4):50–56, 2004.
12. K. Taveter and G. Wagner. Agent-oriented enterprise modeling based on business rules. In *ER '01: Proceedings of the 20th International Conference on Conceptual Modeling*, pages 527–540. Springer-Verlag, 2001.
13. W.H. Winsborough, K.E. Seamons, and V.E. Jones. Automated trust negotiation. DARPA Information Survivability Conference and Exposition, IEEE Press, Jan 2000.

14. W. Nejdl, D. Olmedilla, M. Winslett, and C.C. Zhang. Ontology-based policy specification and management. In *2nd European Semantic Web Conference (ESWC)*, volume 3532 of *LNCS*, pages 290–302, Heraklion, Crete, Greece, May 2005. Springer.
15. M. Richardson, R. Agrawal, and P. Domingos. Trust management for the semantic web. In *The Semantic Web - ISWC 2003, Second International Semantic Web Conference, Sanibel Island, FL, USA, October 20-23, 2003, Proceedings*, LNCS, pages 351–368. Springer, 2003.
16. J. Golbeck and J.A. Hendler. Accuracy of metrics for inferring trust and reputation in semantic web-based social networks. In *Engineering Knowledge in the Age of the Semantic Web, 14th International Conference, EKAW 2004, Whittlebury Hall, UK, October 5-8, 2004, Proceedings*, LNCS, pages 116–131. Springer, 2004.
17. J. Golbeck, B. Parsia, and J.A. Hendler. Trust networks on the semantic web. In *Cooperative Information Agents VII, 7th International Workshop, CIA 2003, Helsinki, Finland, August 27-29, 2003, Proceedings*, LNCS, pages 238–249. Springer, 2003.
18. J.M. Bradshaw, A. Uszok, R. Jeffers, N. Suri, P. J. Hayes, M.H. Burstein, A. Acquisti, B. Benyo, M. R. Breedy, M.M. Carvalho, D.J. Diller, M. Johnson, S. Kulkarni, J. Lott, M. Sierhuis, and R. van Hoof. Representation and reasoning for DAML-based policy and domain services in KAoS and nomads. In *The Second International Joint Conference on Autonomous Agents & Multiagent Systems (AAMAS)*, Melbourne, Victoria, Australia, July 2003.
19. M. Dean and G. Schreiber. OWL web ontology language reference, 2004.
20. F. Baader, D. Calvanese, D.L. McGuinness, D. Nardi, and P.F. Patel-Schneider, editors. *The Description Logic Handbook: Theory, Implementation, and Applications*. Cambridge University Press, 2003.
21. L. Kagal. *A Policy-Based Approach to Governing Autonomous Behaviour in Distributed Environments*. PhD thesis, University of Maryland Baltimore County, 2004.
22. P. Bonatti and P. Samarati. Regulating Service Access and Information Release on the Web. In *Conference on Computer and Communications Security (CCS'00)*, Athens, November 2000.
23. N. Li and J.C. Mitchell. RT: A Role-based Trust-management Framework. In *DARPA Information Survivability Conference and Exposition (DISCEX)*, Washington, D.C., April 2003.
24. J. Trevor and D. Suciu. Dynamically distributed query evaluation. In *Proceedings of the twentieth ACM SIGMOD-SIGACT-SIGART Symposium on Principles of Database Systems*, Santa Barbara, CA, USA, May 2001.
25. M. Alves, C. Viegas Damásio, D. Olmedilla, and W. Nejdl. A distributed tabling algorithm for rule based policy systems. In *7th IEEE International Workshop on Policies for Distributed Systems and Networks (POLICY 2006)*, London, Ontario, Canada, 2006. IEEE Computer Society.
26. P. Kolari, L. Ding, S. Ganjugunte, A. Joshi, T.W. Finin, and L. Kagal. Enhancing web privacy protection through declarative policies. In *6th IEEE International Workshop on Policies for Distributed Systems and Networks (POLICY 2005)*, pages 57–66, Stockholm, Sweden, June 2005. IEEE Computer Society.
27. S. Staab, B.K. Bhargava, L. Lilien, A. Rosenthal, M. Winslett, M. Sloman, T.S. Dillon, E. Chang, F.K. Hussain, W. Nejdl, D. Olmedilla, and V. Kashyap. The pudding of trust. *IEEE Intelligent Systems*, 19(5):74–88, 2004.

28. G. Denker, L. Kagal, T. W. Finin, M. Paolucci, and K.P. Sycara. Security for daml web services: Annotation and matchmaking. In *The Semantic Web - ISWC 2003, Second International Semantic Web Conference, Sanibel Island, FL, USA, October 20-23, 2003, Proceedings*, LNCS, pages 335–350. Springer, 2003.
29. D. Olmedilla, R. Lara, A. Polleres, and H. Lausen. Trust negotiation for semantic web services. In *1st International Workshop on Semantic Web Services and Web Process Composition (SWSWPC)*, volume 3387 of *LNCS*, pages 81–95, San Diego, CA, USA, July 2004. Springer.
30. Grid Security Infrastructure. http://www.globus.org/security/overview.html.
31. A. Uszok, J.M. Bradshaw, and R. Jeffers. Kaos: A policy and domain services framework for grid computing and semantic web services. In *Trust Management, Second International Conference, iTrust 2004, Oxford, UK, March 29 - April 1, 2004, Proceedings*, LNCS, pages 16–26. Springer, 2004.
32. I. Constandache, D. Olmedilla, and W. Nejdl. Policy based dynamic negotiation for grid services authorization. In *Semantic Web Policy Workshop in conjunction with 4th International Semantic Web Conference*, Galway, Ireland, November 2005.
33. P.A. Bonatti, C. Duma, N. Fuchs, W. Nejdl, D. Olmedilla, J. Peer, and N. Shahmehri. Semantic Web policies - A discussion of requirements and research issues. In *3rd European Semantic Web Conference (ESWC)*, Lecture Notes in Computer Science, Budva, Montenegro, June 2006.

Private Person Authentication in an Ambient World

Pim Tuyls and Tom Kevenaar

Philips Research
The Netherlands

Summary. Biometrics is a convenient way to identify and authenticate individuals in an ambient world. This can only be done if biometric reference information is stored in the biometric system. Storing biometric reference information without any precautions will lead to privacy and security problems. In this chapter, we present technological means to protect the biometric information stored in biometric systems (biometric template protection). After describing the most important methods that can be used for template protection, the most promising method based on techniques from the field of secure key extraction will be described in more detail and example implementations will be given for every stage of the template protection process.

27.1 Introduction

In an ambient world, systems will anticipate and react to people's behavior in a personalized way. Clearly this requires that these systems have access to reference information linked uniquely to the individuals using the system. Consequently, in an ambient world personal information will be stored in a large number of locations and, if this personal information is not properly protected, a huge privacy problem may arise.

Biometrics (i.e., fingerprints, face, iris, voice,...) are examples of such information that is linked uniquely to an individual and is becoming increasingly popular for person identification. This is mainly due to the fact that they are very convenient to use: they cannot be lost or forgotten and therefore they are much preferred over passwords and tokens.

In order to use biometrics for identification or authentication, reference information has to be measured using an *enrollment device* during the so-called *enrollment* phase. This phase is carried out at a trusted authority who stores the reference information in the biometric system (e.g., a database). During *authentication* a person first claims her identity. Then, the biometric of that person is measured using an *authentication device* and compared with the reference data corresponding to the claimed identity. When the authentication measurement and the reference measurement are sufficiently close, it is concluded that the authentication measurement originates from the person with the claimed identity and authentication is successful. In the other case, it is concluded that this person does not have the claimed identity.

There is no doubt that, when the system described above is implemented without any additional precautions, privacy problems arise. Since biometrics are unique characteristics of human beings, they contain privacy-sensitive information. Moreover, a compromised biometric identifier is compromised forever and can not be reissued (people have only ten fingers, two eyes,...). This stands in sharp contrast with passwords and tokens, that can easily be reissued. Also, when the biometric reference information is not stored with adequate protection in a database, it can be used to perform cross-matching between databases and track people's behaviour. A malicious employee of a bank can for instance find out that some biometric identifiers in his database also appear in the database of a night club. It is further well known that, based on the reference information in a database, fake biometric identifiers can be made that pass the identification test. Finally, in many countries legislation obliges institutions to properly protect the stored personal information.

The threats mentioned above become less severe if we assume that the database owner (or verifier) can be trusted. The problem is, however, that this is an unrealistic assumption also considering *Qui custodiet custodies?* or *Who guards the guardians?* In this chapter we present technological means to protect the biometric templates stored in biometric systems, also referred to as *template protection*.

27.2 Requirements for Template Protection

In this section we first consider two approaches that might be considered to achieve template protection. From the drawbacks of these approaches we then derive the security requirements for template protection.

27.2.1 Naive Approaches

One might think that encryption of biometric templates solves the problem. We show here that a straightforward application of encryption does not solve the privacy problem with respect to the verifier.

Assume that we use a symmetric key encryption scheme (the system works similarly for a public key scheme). All sensors get a secret key K which is equal to the secret key of the verifier. During enrollment a biometric X of a person is measured, X is encrypted with the key K and $E_K(X)$ is stored in the reference database. During authentication the measurement of the same biometric results in the value Y (close to X due to noise). The sensor encrypts the value Y with the key K and sends $E_K(Y)$ to the verifier. The verifier is faced with the problem of comparing $E_K(X)$ with $E_K(Y)$. However, encryption functions have the property that $E_K(X)$ and $E_K(Y)$ are very different even when

X and Y are very close (but not equal). Hence, given only the values $E_K(X)$ and $E_K(Y)$ the verifier cannot decide whether X and Y originate from the same person. This implies that the verifier must decrypt $E_K(X)$ and $E_K(Y)$ to obtain X and Y and find out whether they are sufficiently similar. But in that case the verifier knows X and hence the system does not provide privacy with respect to the verifier. It only prevents an eavesdropper from obtaining X or Y.

The problem of storing reference information also exists with password authentication. In order to protect passwords against the owner of the database and eavesdropping, the following measures are taken. During *enrollment* a cryptographic hash function H is applied to a chosen password *pwd* and the hash of the password $H(pwd)$ together with the username or identity *ID* is stored in the (public) database for authentication. For example, in the UNIX system this database can be found in the directory: /etc/passwd. During authentication the identity *ID* and the password *pwd'* are entered and $(ID, H(pwd'))$ is sent to the verifier. The verifier then compares $H(pwd')$ with $H(pwd)$ and when $H(pwd) = H(pwd')$ access is granted to the computer, otherwise access is denied. The security of this system follows from the fact that H is a one-way function: given $H(pwd)$ it is *very hard* to compute *pwd*. Hence, for the owner of the database as well as for the eavesdropper it is infeasible to retrieve *pwd* from $H(pwd)$.

Ideally, one would like to mimic the password authentication scheme in the case of biometrics. The problem is, however, that biometrics are inherently noisy and that H is a one-way function. These functions are very good for security purposes but have no continuity properties. Applying the password authentication scheme implies that $H(X)$ is stored in the reference database. During authentication the value Y is obtained, which is typically close to X when X and Y originate from the same person, but in general they are *not* equal due to noise. Therefore, due to the one-way property of H, even when X and Y are very close, $H(X)$ and $H(Y)$ will be very different.

This means that other approaches for template protection must be considered and we will give an overview of the most important existing approaches in Sect. 27.3. Before that we give some security assumptions and requirements for template protection systems.

27.2.2 Requirements

Security Assumptions

The scenarios in the previous section illustrate that an encryption approach to template protection does not work because the verifier must be trusted. Hashing biometric templates is not feasible because biometric measurements are inherently noisy. In order to come up with a template protection system, the following security assumptions are made.

- Enrollment is performed at a trusted authority (TA). The TA enrolls all users by capturing their biometrics, performing additional processing and adding a protected form of the user data to a database.
- The storage is vulnerable to attacks both from the outside and from the inside (malicious verifier).
- During the authentication phase an attacker is able to present artificial biometrics at the sensor.
- All capturing and processing during authentication is tamper resistant, e.g., no information about biometrics can be obtained from the sensor. The sensor is assumed to be trusted; it does not distribute measured information.
- The communication channel between the sensor and the authentication authority is public, i.e., the line can be eavesdropped by an attacker.

Requirements

The requirements for an architecture that does not suffer from the threats mentioned in the introduction are:

- The information that is stored in the database does not give sufficient information to make successful impersonation possible.
- The information in the database provides the least possible information about the original biometrics, in particular it reveals no sensitive information about the persons whose biometrics are stored.
- When a biometric measurement of the same person is contaminated with noise, authentication (or identification) should still be successful if the noise is not too large.

Note that an architecture that meets those requirements, guarantees that the biometric cannot be compromised and can handle noisy biometric measurements.

27.3 Approaches to Template Protection

Recently the template protection problem was recognized by several authors and techniques were proposed that can be used to solve the problem. In this section we give an overview of the most important techniques.

27.3.1 Cancelable Biometrics

In [1] the authors introduce an approach known as cancelable biometrics. During enrollment, the image of a biometric is obtained, for example, the image of a fingerprint, a face, iris. In order to protect its privacy, the biometric image is distorted using a parametrized one-way geometric distortion function before storing it in a biometric system. The function is made such that from the distorted image it is difficult to retrieve the original image and matching can be done using the distorted images. Furthermore, using a different parameter for the distortion function, it is possible to derive several distorted images from a single biometric image (template). This allows for storing different (distorted) biometric reference information in different biometric applications (versatility) and to reissue biometric templates (renewability). Although cancelable biometrics satisfies most requirements of a biometric template protection system mentioned in Sect. 27.2.2, its major drawback is that it is difficult to build a mathematical foundation for this approach that allows an assessment of the security properties of the system.

27.3.2 The Fuzzy Vault Scheme

The fuzzy vault method as introduced in [2] is a general cryptographic construction allowing the storage of a secret S in a vault that can be locked using an unordered set $\mathcal{X}$. The secret S can only be retrieved from the vault using a set $\mathcal{Y}$ if the sets $\mathcal{X}$ and $\mathcal{Y}$ have sufficient overlap. The authors mention biometric template protection as a possible application where $\mathcal{X}$ is the biometric template obtained during enrollment. During authentication, the rightful owner of the secret can unlock the vault using a measurement of his biometric $\mathcal{Y}$ that is sufficiently similar but not necessarily identical to the measurement $\mathcal{X}$ used to lock the vault (see also Sect. 27.2). Like the method in Sect. 27.3.1 this method also has the required properties of versatility and renewability.

The special property of the fuzzy vault scheme is that it can be (un)locked using *unordered* fuzzy sets. This makes this method well suited for biometric templates that are represented by such sets. In most cases, however, biometric templates are best represented as ordered data structures such as feature vectors. The most important exception is where fingerprints are characterized using the locations of minutiae. These locations are most naturally represented as unordered fuzzy sets and an initial attempt to use the fuzzy vault scheme in the setting of fingerprints is given in [3]. Little work is reported yet in using the fuzzy vault scheme for other modalities than minutiae-based fingerprints.

27.3.3 Extracting Keys from Noisy Data

The approach for extracting cryptographic keys from noisy data refers to a collection of methods developed by several authors [4, 5, 6, 7, 8, 9, 10, 11, 12] that refer to the situation where two parties communicate over a public channel and want to derive a secret cryptographic key. The underlying mathematical principles for these methods are well understood and security proofs are available.

It was recognized that the above methods for key extraction also apply in a biometric template protection setting and work most naturally with biometric modalities that can be represented as feature vectors in a high-dimensional space. Since most biometric modalities can be represented as feature vectors, the methods for key extraction can be used to protect the templates of a wide range of modalities. In the rest of this chapter we will therefore concentrate on this approach to template protection.

27.4 Robust Key Extraction from Noisy Data

In the past years there has been much interest in the secure extraction of robust strings from noisy data. In this section we first give a general setting of the problem and the steps required to achieve secure extractions. Then, the general setting will be mapped onto template protection for biometrics.

27.4.1 General Setting

A general setting (e.g. [11]) is given in Fig. 27.1 containing three parties traditionally called Alice, Bob and Eve. Alice and Bob communicate over a public communication channel and the adversary Eve eavesdrops on this channel. The purpose of Alice and Bob is to derive, by communicating over their public channel, a common string about which Eve has only a negligible amount of information.

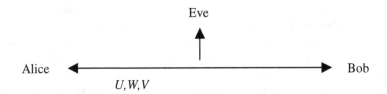

Fig. 27.1. General setting for secure extraction of robust strings from noisy data. U, W and V are the messages communicated between Alice and Bob.

Typically, Alice and Bob start with two correlated strings which they obtained from some source. Alice and Bob then go through the following steps.

- Advantage distillation (e.g. [10]): by communicating U, Alice and Bob create a string X (possibly with errors) about which Bob has more information than the attacker Eve and thus Alice and Bob have created an advantage over Eve.
- Information reconciliation (e.g. [9]): Alice and Bob exchange error information W to correct errors in X and arrive at a common string K.
- Privacy amplification (e.g. [13]): by communicating the information V over their public channel, Alice and Bob compress the string K to a string S about which Eve has only a negligible amount of information.

In the following section we will explain how this general setting is used in the context of biometrics.

27.4.2 Application to Biometrics

Interpretation of Roles

In order to use the general setting explained in Sect. 27.4.1 in the context of template protection for biometrics, the roles of Eve, Alice, Bob and their public communication channel are interpreted as follows: Alice is interpreted as the enrollment device, Bob is interpreted as the authentication device, the communication channel is interpreted as (public) storage in the biometric system, and Eve is an attacker who has access to this storage. In this setting, it is reasonable to assume that the enrollment device (Alice) and the authentication device (Bob), which both have access to a biometric measurement of an individual, already have an advantage over the adversary Eve, who does not have access to the biometric measurements because biometrics are considered to be private. Consequently, an advantage distillation step is not required such that the biometric setting of robust key extraction can be depicted as in Fig. 27.2.

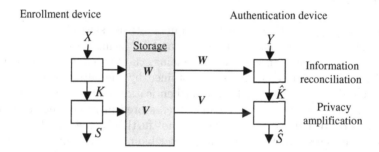

Fig. 27.2. General biometric setting for secure extraction of robust strings from noisy biometrics.

Thus, in order to extract secure and robust strings from biometrics, only two steps are required: information reconciliation and privacy amplification. These two steps will be discussed in detail in Sect. 27.5 and Section 27.6, respectively. But first the representation of biometric templates is discussed.

Representation of Biometric Templates

Biometric templates are processed measurement data and usually represented as so-called feature vectors $\mathbf{F}$ in a high-dimensional space $\mathbb{R}^l$. In the context of template protection we assume that these feature vectors can be described in the discrete domain $\mathcal{F} = \{0,1\}^n$ of binary strings of length n without too much loss of information. The resulting random variable describing an enrollment measurement is denoted by X^n while the authentication measurements are denoted by Y^n. We assume that the authentication measurement Y^n corresponding to an enrollment measurement X^n can be seen as an observation of X^n over a noisy channel such that Y^n might contain a number of bit errors compared to X^n.

Deriving binary strings that can be protected by template protection methods is a research area in itself because of the wide range of biometrics modalities and representations . In Sect. 27.7, a method is described that transforms biometric feature vectors in $\mathbb{R}^l$ to binary strings of length n which can be protected.

27.5 Information Reconciliation

As explained in the previous sections, the first step in deriving a robust string from a biometric is to correct errors. This information reconciliation step is explained in the following sections.

27.5.1 Theory

Information reconciliation extracts a common string, say $K^m \in \mathcal{K}$ with $\mathcal{K} = \{0,1\}^m$, from two correlated strings X^n and Y^n using only communication over a public channel. In a biometric setting, the two correlated strings are the biometric measurement $X^n \in \mathcal{F}$ obtained by the enrollment device and the string $Y^n \in \mathcal{F}$ obtained by the authentication device. The information communicated over the public channel (i.e., stored in the biometric system) is denoted by W belonging to a space $\mathcal{W}$ not further defined at this time. An attacker has access to W and possibly other biometric measurements Z^n.

An information reconciliation method consists of a pair of functions $G : \mathcal{F} \times \mathcal{W} \rightarrow \mathcal{K}$ and $J : \mathcal{F} \times \mathcal{K} \rightarrow \mathcal{W}$. In order to work properly the following properties are required. First, for all $x, y, z \in \mathcal{F}$ and for all $k \in \mathcal{K}$, we have that

$$\text{If } d(x,y) < \delta \quad \text{then } G(y, w = J(x,k)) = k, \qquad (27.1)$$

$$\text{If } d(x,z) > \delta \quad \text{then } G(z, w = J(x,k)) = \perp, \qquad (27.2)$$

where $d(\cdot, \cdot)$ is some distance measure. This means that if the distance between X^n and Y^n is small enough (smaller than some δ), the enrollment device and the authentication device both can obtain the common string K^m using the function G. In contrast, if the distance between X^n and some Z^n is too large, the string K^m will not be obtained. The information W (publicly) stored in the biometric system by the enrollment device is generated using the function J. This property (27.1)-(27.2) is called δ-contracting, as introduced in [5].

Because we assume that the information W is publicly stored in the biometric system and the string K^m should be secret, clearly, a second property for the function for the function J is required. Given $W = J(X^n, K^m)$ and possibly an other biometric template Z^n, an attacker should not learn too much about K^m.

In the following section, a practical implementation of the functions J and G will be given.

27.5.2 An Example of an Information Reconciliation Scheme

In this section we give a practical implementation of information reconciliation based on error correcting codes (ECCs), which is in fact a reformulation of the fuzzy commitment scheme introduced in [4]. Another implementation can be found in, for example, [5].

Consider a binary error correcting code $\mathcal{C}$ with parameters $[n, m, 2d + 1]$ such that the code words have length n, there are m information symbols per code word and a maximum of d errors per code word can be corrected. During the enrollment phase, X^n is measured and a code word $C_K^n \in_R \mathcal{C}$ is chosen randomly by encoding a random value K^m. The public information W is computed as $W = X^n \oplus C_K^n$. In this context, the information W is usually called *helper data*, which is stored in the biometric system.

During the authentication phase, the biometric identifier Y^n is obtained. Then, one computes $\hat{C}_K^n = Y^n \oplus W = (Y^n \oplus X^n) \oplus C_K^n$ and finally the decoding algorithm of the error correcting code is used to decode $\hat{C}_K^n$, resulting in $\hat{K}^m$. It can be seen that when the Hamming distance $d(X^n, Y^n)$ between X^n and Y^n is less than or equal to d, decoding $(Y^n \oplus X^n) \oplus C_K^n$ will result in $\hat{K}^m = K^m$. Otherwise a decoding error or a random code word is obtained.

A schematic representation of this approach is given in Fig. 27.3.

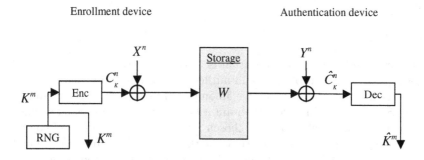

Fig. 27.3. A practical information reconciliation system.

The following theorem regarding the properties of this scheme was proven in [6] and assumes that X^n is a uniformly random iid sequence such that the bits in the string X^n are generated uniformly at random and independently.

Theorem 1 *The information reconciliation scheme described above has the following properties,*

$$\mathbf{I}(K^m; W) = 0, \tag{27.3}$$

$$\mathbf{I}(X^n; W) \approx nh(p), \tag{27.4}$$

where h is the binary entropy function defined by $h(p) = -p \log p - (1 - p) \log(1 - p)$.

$\mathbf{I}$ indicates mutual information and p is the probability that two corresponding bits in X^n and Y^n are different. It follows from the second property that the helper data reveals some information about the original biometric input X^n and it is shown in [5, 8] that this information leakage cannot be made negligibly small and consequently, full privacy in an information-theoretic setting cannot be achieved in this way. In contrast, it follows from the first property, that given the helper data W, an adversary does not learn anything (from an information-theoretic point of view) about the derived key K^m. The string K^m derived from this scheme is a secure key and no privacy amplification step is needed. This is due to the fact that we assumed the data X^n to be a uniformly random iid sequence. In case this assumption does not hold, we have $\mathbf{I}(K^m; W) \neq 0$ and privacy amplification is required, which will be explained in the following section.

27.6 Privacy Amplification

It follows from the previous section, that if the input biometric X^n is not uniformly random distributed, an additional privacy amplification step is needed. In this section it is explained how this can be achieved (see also [13] for more details).

27.6.1 Theory

The purpose of privacy amplification is to compress the common string K^m known both to the enrollment and authentication device in such a way that an attacker is left with a negligible amount of information on the compressed string $S^s \in \{0, 1\}^s$. In order to obtain a highly secure compressed string S^s, the compression function $H_{(2)}$ is chosen randomly from a family of compression functions. The actual choice V of the compression function from the family is made during enrollment and stored (publicly) in the biometric system. Not just any family of compression functions can be used for privacy amplification but a special group of functions that can be used are so-called *2-universal* which is defined as follows.

Definition 1 *A class $\mathcal{H}$ of functions $\mathcal{A} \to \mathcal{B}$ is 2-universal if for all distinct $a_1, a_2 \in \mathcal{A}$, the probability that $H_{(2)}(a_1) = H_{(2)}(a_2)$ is at most $1/|\mathcal{B}|$ when $H_{(2)}$ is chosen randomly from $\mathcal{H}$ according to the uniform distribution.*

This definition says that the functions $H_{(2)}$ do not favor any particular values in $\mathcal{B}$. Intuitively, when this would not be the case, this would give an attacker some knowledge on the compressed string S. More formally, the security of the privacy amplification step follows from the left-over hash lemma. This lemma appears in many forms but the formulation below is taken from [14].

Theorem 2 *If $\mathcal{H}$ is a family of 2-universal functions from m bits to s bits $(\mathcal{A} = \{0,1\}^m$ and $\mathcal{B} = \{0,1\}^s)$ and K^m is a random variable with values in $\{0,1\}^m$ with collision entropy $\mathbf{H}_2(K^m) \geq s + 2\log\frac{1}{\epsilon} + 1$, then,*

$$\delta((H_{(2)}, H_{(2)}(K^m)), (H_{(2)}, U_s)) \leq \epsilon$$

where $H_{(2)}$ is drawn uniformly at random from $\mathcal{H}$ and U_s is a uniform random variable on $\{0,1\}^s$ and δ denotes the statistical distance between the probability distributions of $(H_{(2)}, H_{(2)}(K^m))$ and $(H_{(2)}, U_s)$.

This technical result says that, if strings of length m are compressed to strings of length $s < m$ using a randomly chosen 2-universal function, that the distribution of the resulting strings S^s is, in some sense, close to a uniform distribution.

In the following section we give an example implementation of a 2-universal function.

27.6.2 An Example of a Privacy Amplification Scheme

Although the definitions and proofs regarding 2-universal functions are rather involved, an implementation can be made quite efficiently. The goal of privacy amplification in the context of biometrics is to compress the string K^m obtained after information reconciliation to a string S^s of length s. A possible implementation uses binary Galois fields $GF(2^m)$ [12].

For privacy amplification on a string K^m, the binary string K^m is interpreted as an element in the field $GF(2^m)$. The family of compression functions $\mathcal{H}$ is defined as $H_{(2)}(x^m; V) = [V \cdot x^m]_s$ where $\cdot$ denotes multiplication in the Galois field $GF(2^m)$, $[\cdot]_s$ denotes taking the first s bits of an element in this field (truncation), and V indicates the actual choice of the compression function. In order to choose one compression function from this family, a value V is chosen uniformly random from the same field $GF(2^m)$. Because a multiplication in a binary Galois field can be done with at least the same efficiency as a normal multiplication, the implementation of the compression function can also be done efficiently.

Thus, in the biometric system the enrollment device chooses a uniformly random a value V from the Galois field $GF(2^m)$ and stores this value in the biometric system. During privacy amplification, this value is multiplied with K^m and the result is truncated to s bits, leading to a secret string S^s.

The whole scheme, containing information reconciliation and privacy amplification, is depicted in Fig. 27.4. An additional piece of information not present in Figs. 27.1 and 27.2 is $H(S^s)$, which is the cryptographically hashed version of the S^s. This is due to the fact that many biometric applications perform authentication (or identification) against stored reference information. Since storing only V, W as reference information does not suffice and S^s can reveal information on X^n, the hash of S^s together with V and W is stored. Storing the hash of S^s is similar to the password scenario in Sect. 27.2.1.

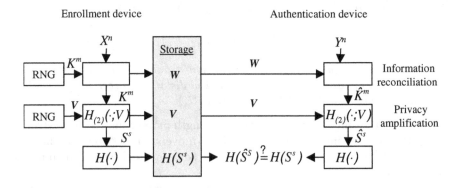

Fig. 27.4. The complete architecture based on information reconciliation and privacy amplification.

Summarizing, we have the following steps in a biometric system used for authentication.

Enrollment device

- Obtain a biometric measurement X^n.
- Derive information reconciliation parameters K^m and W using X^n as input (for example, using the the architecture in Fig. 27.3). Store W in the biometric system.
- Derive privacy amplification parameters S^s and V using K^m. For example, choose V randomly in a Galois field and compute S^s as the truncated value of $V \cdot K^m$ in this Galois field. Store V in the biometric system.
- Calculate the cryptographic hash $H(S^s)$ of S^s and store the result in the biometric system.

Authentication device

- Obtain a biometric measurement Y^n.
- Perform information reconciliation on Y^n using W (for example, using the the architecture in Fig. 27.3 resulting in $\hat{K}^m$).

- Perform privacy amplification on $\hat{K}^m$ using V resulting in $\hat{S}^s$.
- Calculate the cryptographic hash $H(\hat{S}^s)$. If $H(S^s) = H(\hat{S}^s)$, authentication is successful.

This concludes the explanation of template protection. In the following section a method is given for deriving binary strings from biometric templates.

27.7 Binary Sequence Extraction

In the previous sections, we assumed that biometric measurements are represented as binary strings X^n and Y^n. It was also implicitly assumed that, when two measurements are only slightly different, this will result in binary strings that have a small (Hamming) distance. In this section we give a method that derives such binary strings.

In order to derive the binary sequences X^n we assume that biometric templates are available in the form of feature vectors $\mathbf{F} \in \mathbb{R}^l$. By discussing the individual blocks in Fig. 27.5, it will be explained how the feature vectors $\mathbf{F}$ are transformed into the binary sequences X^n.

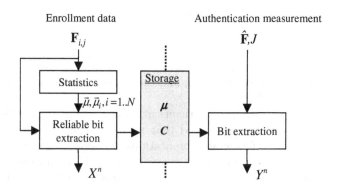

Fig. 27.5. Binary sequence extraction with N enrolled users.

We assume that, during an enrollment phase, we collected a set of feature vectors $\{\mathbf{F}_{i,j}\}_{i=1...N, j=1...M}$, where $\mathbf{F}_{i,j}$ denotes the j-th feature vector of the i-th user such that we have N users and M feature vectors per user and we have in total NM feature vectors. The feature vector $\mathbf{F}_{i,j} \in \mathbb{R}^l$ has components $(\mathbf{F}_{i,j})_r$, $r = 1 \ldots l$.

Statistics This block estimates the mean feature vector $\boldsymbol{\mu}_i$ of user i and the mean $\boldsymbol{\mu}$ over all enrollment feature vectors.

Reliable Bit Extraction For every user i a binary string $Z_i \in \{0,1\}^l$ is derived by quantising $\boldsymbol{\mu}_i$ around $\boldsymbol{\mu}$ such that for $r = 1 \ldots l$

$$(Z_i)_r = \begin{cases} 0 & \text{if } (\mu_i)_r \leq (\mu)_r, \\ 1 & \text{if } (\mu_i)_r > (\mu)_r . \end{cases} \qquad (27.5)$$

Next, the *reliability* or *robustness* of a bit $(Z_i)_r$ is determined. In a general setting, the probability $P_{i,r}$ is estimated that $(Z_i)_r$ is different in the enrollment and authentication phase. A smaller value for $P_{i,r}$ results in a more reliable bit. One possibility to estimate $P_{i,r}$ is to assume that individual features $(\mathbf{F})_r$ have a Gaussian distribution. From $(\mathbf{F}_{i,j})_r, j = 1 \ldots M$ it is then possible to estimate the standard deviation $s_{i,r}$ for the r-th feature of user i and from this, using $(\mu_i)_r$, estimate $P_{i,r}$. This process is depicted in Fig. 27.6.

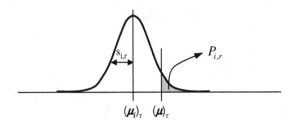

Fig. 27.6. An illustration of estimating $P_{i,r}$ assuming a Gaussian distribution of individual features.

Finally the binary string $X^n \in \{0,1\}^n$ is generated for user i by selecting the n most reliable components of Z_i and the vector $\mathbf{C}_i$ containing the indices of the reliable bits in Z_i.

Bit Extraction During the authentication phase of a claimed identity J, a noisy feature vector $\hat{\mathbf{F}}$ is obtained that must be transformed in a binary sequence Y^n. On $\hat{\mathbf{F}}$ the following computations are performed: (i) A bit string $\hat{Z} \in \{0,1\}^l$ is derived by comparing the value of each component $(\hat{\mathbf{F}})_r$ with the mean value $(\mu)_r$ according to Eq. 27.5 (where μ_i is replaced by $\hat{\mathbf{F}}$ and Z_i is replaced by $\hat{Z}$), (ii) Using the indices in $\mathbf{C}_J$, n components from $\hat{Z}$ are selected yielding a bit string Y^n.

Some initial results of this approach are given in [15, 16].

27.8 Conclusions

Biometrics are a convenient way to identify and authenticate individuals in an ambient world. In this chapter, technological means where discussed to protect the biometric reference information that has to be stored in biometric systems. The most promising approach to protecting biometric information is based on methods developed for secure key extraction from noisy data. An overview of these methods was given and it was explained how they can be used in the context of protecting biometric information.

References

1. N.K. Ratha, J.H. Connell, R. Bolle (2002) Enhancing Security and Privacy of Biometric-based Authentication Systems IBM Systems Journal, Vol. 40, No. 3, 2002.
2. A. Juels, M. Sudan (2002) A Fuzzy Vault Scheme Proc. Intl Symp. Inf. Theory, A Lapidoth, E.Teletar, Eds., pp.408, 2002.
3. U. Uludag, S. Pankanti, A.K. Jain (2005) Fuzzy Vault for Fingerprints, Proc. 5th Int. Conf. on Audio- and Video-Based Biometric Person Authentication (AVBPA 2005), Springer LNCS 3546, pp.310-319, 2005.
4. A. Juels, M. Wattenberg (1999) A Fuzzy Commitment Scheme In G. Tsudik, Ed., 6th ACM Conf. Computer and Communication Security, pp.28-36, 1999.
5. J.P. Linnartz, P. Tuyls (2003) New shielding functions to enhance privacy and prevent misuse of biometric templates, Proc. 3rd Conf. on Audio and Video Based Person Authentication, LNCS 2688,pp.238-250, Springer-Verlag, 2003.
6. P. Tuyls, J. Goseling (2004) Capacity and Examples of Template Protecting Biometric Authentication Systems, Biometric Authentication Workshop (BioAW, Prague, 2004), LNCS 3087, pp.158-170, 2004.
7. P. Tuyls, M. van Dijk (2005) Robustness Reliability and Security of Biometric Key Distillation in the Information Theoretic Setting, Proc. 26th Benelux Symposium on Information Theory, 2005.
8. Y. Dodis, L. Reyzin, A. Smith (2004) Fuzzy extractors: How to generate strong keys from biometrics and other noisy data, Proceedings of Eurocrypt 2004, LNCS 3027, pp.523-540, Springer-Verlag, 2004.
9. G. Brassard, L. Salvail (1994) Secret-key reconciliation by Public Discussion, Advances in Cryptology, EUROCRYPT'93, Springer Verlag, LNCS 765, pp.410-423, 1994.
10. M.J. Gander, U.M. Maurer (1994) On the secret-key rate of binary random variables Proc.1994 IEEE International Symposium on Information Theory, p.351, 1994.
11. U.M. Maurer, S. Wolf, (1999) Unconditional Secure Key Agreement and the Intrinsic Conditional Information, IEEE Trans. on Information Theory, Vol. 45, no. 2, 1999, pp.499-514.
12. C.H. Bennett, G. Brassard, C. Crepeau, U.M. Maurer (1995) Generalized privacy amplification IEEE Transactions on Information Theory, Vol. 41, no. 6, pp.1915-1923, November 1995
13. V. Shoup (2005) A Computational Introduction to Number Theory and Algebra, Cambridge University Press, 2005
14. A.D. Smith (2004) Maintaining Secrecy When Information Leakage is Unavoidable, Ph.D. Thesis, MIT, August 2004.
15. P. Tuyls, A. Akkermans, T. Kevenaar, G.J. Schrijen, A. Bazen, R. Veldhuis (2005) Practical biometric template protection system based on reliable components, Proc. 5th Int. Conf. on Audio- and Video-Based Biometric Person Authentication (AVBPA 2005), LNCS 3546,Springer Verlag pp.436-446, 2005.
16. T.A.M. Kevenaar, G.J. Schrijen, M. van der Veen, A.H.M. Akkermans, F. Zuo (2005) Face Recognition with Renewable and Privacy Preserving Binary Templates, 4th IEEE Workshop on automatic identification advanced technology (AutoID 2005), LNCS 3546, pp.21-25, Springer Verlag, 2005.

RFID and Privacy

Marc Langheinrich

Institute for Pervasive Computing, ETH Zurich
Switzerland

Summary. Radio-frequency identification (RFID) technology has become one of the most hotly debated ubiquitous computing technologies, and public fears of its alleged capability for comprehensive surveillance have prompted a flurry of research trying to alleviate such concerns. The following chapter aims at introducing and briefly evaluating the range of proposed technical RFID privacy solutions. It also attempts to put the problem of RFID privacy into the larger perspective of both applications and policy, in order to properly assess the feasibility of the discussed solutions.

28.1 Introduction

What is it that makes RFID technology such a controversial issue these days? Seasoned newsreaders might be reminded of the heated discussions surrounding the introduction of the printed bar code in the 1970s,[1] where the comprehensive numbering of supermarket items fueled fears of a dawning apocalypse [1]. But what used to be the domain of conspiracy theorists and Christian fundamentalists has since spread to average consumers who increasingly see their privacy threatend by hidden spychips that would potentially allow retailers, governments, and crooks to secretly monitor an individual's habits, behavior, and movements.

Most obvious is the rise of general concern on the Web: between November 2003 and March 2006, the same set of Google queries for "RFID" and "RFID and privacy" not only saw a 14-fold increase in RFID-related pages (from roughly half a million to over 80 million), but also an increasing share of those mentioning privacy concerns, rising from 42% up to 68% in November

---

[1] On June 26, 1974, the first product with a bar code was scanned at a check-out counter. It was a 10-pack of Wrigley's Juicy Fruit chewing gum, which is now on display at the Smithsonian Institution's National Museum of American History.

2005.[2] Internet campaigns such as CASPIAN's 2003 "Boycott Benetton"[3] and the German 2003 Big Brother Award for the Metro group,[4] a large retailer, repeatedly warn that RFID would "create an Orwellian world where law enforcement officials and nosey retailers could read the contents of a handbag – simply by installing RFID readers nearby" [3].

At the same time, consumer surveys seem to paint a different picture. A recent European study [4] finds that only 18% of consumers have even heard of RFID technology, and that only 8% of those view its use unfavorably. Advocates point out that RFID technology already enjoys widespread acceptance across a wide variety of applications, such as car immobilizers, contactless ski passes, automated toll gates, and RFID-based payment systems. None of these systems, it seems, have so far induced consumer concern or privacy issues.

This chapter primarily attempts to disentangle the intricacies surrounding today's public debate on the widespread deployment and use of RFID systems. In doing so, it will briefly survey the currently proposed technical solutions to RFID privacy and try to assess their feasibility. However, it will also attempt to clearly state both the capabilities and the limits of the technology behind RFID, as well as evaluate the practicality of commonly cited privacy invasions from RFID, especially in light of alternative (and maybe much more effective) methods of data solicitation.

28.2 RFID Primer

With all the potential doomsday scenarios that critics like to associate with the use of RFID systems, why would anybody even consider doing this? This is because RFID systems offer three distinct advantages over traditional identification systems:

1. *Automation.* While optical bar codes require a line of sight for readout, i.e., either careful orientation of tagged goods with respect to the reader, or manual intervention, RFID tags promise unsupervised readouts. This increases the level of automation possible, as tagged items do not need precise orientation during the readout process.[5]
2. *Identification.* RFID tags also offer a much higher information density (and thus ultimately capacity) than bar codes, allowing manufacturers and vendors not only to store a generic product identifier on an item (e.g., "This is a bar of lavender soap"), but an individual serial number (e.g., "This is lavender soap, bar 293813"), which in turn can point to a

---

[2] Measurements by the author. The general idea, as well as the November 2003 numbers, go back to Ravi Pappu [2].
[3] See www.nocards.org and boycottbenetton.org
[4] See www.bigbrotherawards.de/en/2003/.cop/
[5] See Sect. 28.2.1 in this chapter for practical limitations.

database entry with detailed item information (e.g., "produced on May 14, 2005, in plant 5, unit 67").

3. *Integration.* The wireless coupling between reader and tag also allows manufacturers to integrate tags unobtrusively into products, thus freeing product design as well as making identifiers more robust (e.g., protection from dirt, but also against removal).

The primary use of an RFID tag is for the purpose of *automated identification,* or *AutoID* for short. This is exactly what its predecessor – the bar code – was created for. In 1948, a local food-chain store owner had asked researchers at the Drexel Institute in Philadelphia for a way to automatically read the product information during checkout [5]. Similarly, RFID technology is now being hailed as the next step in checkout-automation, completely eliminating checkout lines as shoppers can simply walk through a supermarket gate and have all their items automatically billed to their credit card within seconds.

However, another set of applications additionally requires not only identification, but also authentication. The idea of *token-based authentication* is that both items and users can be reliably identified, based on an unforgeable token that they carry.[6] Users can thus prove their entitlement to a specific service (e.g., to enter a building) while items can prove their authenticity (e.g., an expensive watch, organic food, or medical drugs). One of today's most ubiquitous RFID applications, the car immobilizer, is a good example. Here, a transponder embedded into the car key is able to reply with a proper identification when read (i.e., when put into the ignition), thus identifying itself as the proper key.[7] A fourth reason for using RFID is therefore its support for secure authentication:

4. *Authentication.* RFID tags can provide for a much stronger authentication than bar codes, as they can prevent unauthorized duplication (either through cryptographic means[8] or by database lookups for detecting duplicates).

Similar applications are wireless ticketing systems (e.g., ski-passes), wireless payment systems (like the ExxonMobil SpeedPass[9]), and of course the recently developed biometric Passport (ePass) standard.[10] All of these require nontrivial cryptographic support in the RFID tag, as those need to be

---

[6] Other ways of authenticating people would be based on what you know (e.g., a password), what you are (i.e., biometric identification), where you are (i.e., your location), and what you do (personal traits).

[7] Note that this is separate from being able to open the car doors remotely. For this, a battery-powered infrared or radio transmitter typically sends an encrypted pulse to the car. Those two might share the same key casing, however.

[8] This is similar to a smart card, which proves its authenticity by properly encoding a (random) challenge sent by the reader. Simply reading out the chip for duplication is impossible, as the secret encoding key is never given out.

[9] See www.speedpass.com.

[10] See www.icao.int/mrtd/publications/doc.cfm.

safe from cloning and counterfeiting. Otherwise, attackers could simply make up their own tags (counterfeiting) or copy a valid original (copying) and thus gain free skiing, free gasoline, or free entry. Besides the general convenience of RFID with its automated reading, the resistance to cloning attacks is thus another big advantage over the traditional bar code. While authentication applications can in principle also be implemented using bar codes, these cannot be protected from duplication attacks, thus requiring online verification to identify duplicated tokens.

28.2.1 Technology Overview

RFID systems are composed of RFID tags and at least one RFID reader. RFID tags are attached to the objects to be identified, while the RFID reader reads from and possibly also writes to the tags. RFID tags consist of a so-called coupling element for communication (and potentially also for supplying the tag with energy) and a microchip that stores, among other things, data including a tag identification number. The reader forms the radio interface to the tags and typically features some internal storage and processing power in order to provide a high level interface to a host computer system to transmit the captured tag data.

While all RFID systems are made up of these two components – a reader and a number of tags – a wide variety of different RFID systems exist to address the requirements of individual application scenarios. Finkenzeller [6] provides a comprehensive classification of the various commercially available RFID systems, while Want [7] offers a succinct introduction to the general principles.

RFID tags can be categorized into two classes: *passive* RFID tags do not possess their own power supply – the reader supplies the tags with power through the coupling unit along with data and clock pulses. *Active* RFID tags, on the other hand, feature a battery in order to extend their transmission range and reliability.[11] Most of today's privacy concerns focus on applications utilizing passive RFID tags: smart checkouts in supermarkets through tagged merchandise; human identification through tag injections under the skin; RFID-tagged banknotes, medical drugs, or luxury goods for preventing counterfeiting; or passports with embedded tags for the secure storage of biometric data. Popular articles, however, often like to quote the capabilities of *active* tags when discussing the implications of RFID deployment, thus arriving at powerful surveillance scenarios based on the significantly higher read ranges of the battery-powered models. Obviously, both prices and battery sizes will prevent the use of active RFID tags in most consumer scenarios (e.g., on cans, chewing-gum packs, banknotes, or in passports).

---

[11] There are also *semi-active* tags that have an internal battery for powering their microchip, yet use the reader's energy field for actually transmitting their data, allowing them to use much smaller batteries.

Passive RFID systems typically operate in one of five frequency bands: between 100-135 kHz (LF, or low frequency), at 13.56 MHz (HF, or high frequency), at 868/915 MHz (UHF, ultra-high frequency),[12] and at 2.45 and 5.8 GHz (MW, or microwave). The actual frequency band used in a particular application is relevant to the privacy discussion as the laws of physics – and in particular the propagation characteristics of electromagnetic waves – set different boundaries in each of those areas, which ultimately determine much of the capabilities of an RFID system.

This is mainly due to a process known as *coupling* – the process of energy transfer between two different media. As tags in passive RFID systems do not come with their own power supply, the reader must supply the tag with sufficient energy to both process its commands and transmit back the reply. It can do so wirelessly – through its radio signal – with the help of the tag's coupling element, either through *electromagnetic* or *inductive* (magnetic) coupling.[13] The reader's signal thus not only communicates commands to the tag, but also powers the tag's microprocessor and allows the tag to send back its reply.

Inductive coupling, used in both HF and LF systems, works very much like a transformer, though with much lower efficiency.[14] For this to work, the tag must be within the reader's magnetic field (called the *near-field region*), as further away all of the field's energy breaks away from the antenna and becomes an electromagnetic wave commonly known as a radio signal (called the *far-field region*). The range of this boundary is inversely proportional to the employed frequency [8] – in HF system, for example, it lies around 3.5 m. Since beyond this range all field waves detach themselves from their originating antenna, it is impossible to use inductive coupling in the far field [6]. Consequently, inductively coupled LF and HF tags cannot be powered (and thus read) from further away than the range of the near field. In practice, read ranges are typically much smaller, as the magnetic field strength in the near field also diminishes with the cube of the distance between the reader coil and tag, resulting in read ranges of typically less then 1.5 m for LF and around 1 m for HF systems [9]. Even though larger antenna coils in both readers and tags can mitigate this effect, physical size constraints in many applications limit antenna sizes and thus read ranges.

Systems operating in UHF and MW instead employ *electromagnetic* coupling in the *far field*, similar in principle to crystal-set radios.[15] Instead of coils

---

[12] The 868 MHz band is only licensed in Europe, while it is at 915 MHz in the U.S.

[13] It is also possible to use *capacitive coupling*, i.e., having capacitors in both the tag and the reader. However, this only works for very small distances, and is only used to *communicate* with the tag, not to power it (energy is typically supplied using inductive coupling in such systems) [6].

[14] The reader creates an alternating current in a coil that generates an alternating magnetic field, which in turn interacts wirelessly with the tag's coil (i.e., its coupling element) to induce a corresponding current inside the tag.

[15] Crystal-set radios are able to operate without batteries as they capture enough energy from the received radio signal.

and magnetic fields, electromagnetic coupling uses dipole antennas and radio signals on both readers and tags. However, the energy in far-field communication follows an inverse square law for both sending energy to the tag and receiving a return signal, thus yielding a $1/d^4$ law for the overall communication channel [8].[16] Highly sensitive electronics inside UHF and MW readers allow them to decode the backscattered signal from the tags, typically yielding higher read ranges than their LF or HF counterparts (up to 5-7 m). Future tags are expected to require less energy from the reader, thus increasing the potential read range of such systems even further. However, the overall signal attenuation will still continue to limit nominal read ranges to some reasonable distance (i.e., dozens, not hundreds, of meters).

The choice of coupling technology also influences the *anti-collision* protocol employed to regulate the communication between a reader and multiple tags. Regulation is necessary as tags do not have the means to detect other tags nearby. This would result in multiple tags answering concurrently to the same reader request, thus potentially interfering with each other's modulated or backscattered replies. As the anti-collision protocol governs the lower-level communication between tags and readers, which potentially includes tag IDs and thus might allow eavesdropping, its choice also influences privacy risks.

UHF and MW systems typically use a *deterministic* anti-collision protocol based on binary trees, in which the reader systematically queries each possible ID prefix. As long as the reader detects a collision (i.e., if two or more tags with the same prefix as indicated by the reader are within range), the reader increases the length of the prefix (e.g., by adding a 1 to it) until a single tag ID can be singularized. It then replaces the bit it added last with its inverse and continues – should more collisions occur – to increase the length of the prefix [10]. The advantage of this scheme is that the reader will eventually read every tag within range, though it requires high data rates in order to be practically feasible.

Slower LF and HF systems use *probabilistic* methods instead, based on the so-called slotted ALOHA algorithm: The reader first sends out the number of timeslots it is willing to wait for an answer to all tags within range. Tags then randomly pick one of these slots and send their reply only when their time has come. Setting this initial number of timeslots is difficult. If the reader picks too many slots, most timeslots will be empty and thus time gets wasted. If it decides on too few, many tags will attempt to reply at the same time, resulting in signal interference and thus requiring another query round. In such instances, readers typically instruct tags that they have already identified to remain silent in subsequent rounds, in order to speed up the identification process of the remaining tags. While probabilistic methods can operate more

---

[16] Note that, in contrast, inductive coupling does not need a separate return signal to communicate from reader to tag – information is transmitted by changing the amount of energy the tag draws from the field.

efficiently than deterministic ones, they cannot guarantee that all tags within range can be identified within a given time.

28.2.2 RFID Limitations

While the possibilities of RFID are certainly impressive, both the laws of physics and (even more so) practical concerns often limit what is possible. For example, when it comes to RFID read ranges, *higher* may not always be *better*. Many RFID applications require the identification of a *particular* item (or set of items) in a particular location, e.g., the contents of *your* grocery bag at the checkout, not the items of the person behind you in line; the validity of *your* skipass, and not the one of the person behind you in line; the authenticity of *your* passport, and not the one behind you at border control. As such, the fact that one might be able to construct a system with much higher read ranges *in principle* does not mean that the application would work better – in most instances, this would only increase the rate of false readouts. This is especially important to keep in mind when arguing about the capabilities of future systems, as a common reply to today's technical limitations is the spectre of future progress: "While this [range limitation] may be true today, industry experts say plans for building far more sensitive RFID signal receivers are in the works" [3]. Even if one could construct a system with such an improved readout capability (again, within the physical limits), most applications might not work at all with such increased ranges.

However, as [11] points out, the envisioned (so-called *nominal*) read range of a system is actually only partly relevant. While a system might be *built* to support only a few centimeters read range, a determined attacker might still achieve larger distances (the *rogue read range*) by using larger antennas and/or higher signal transmission power. For example, [12] claims that a HF tag with a nominal read range of about 10 cm can be read from up to 50 cm, while [13] reports some 30 meters for reading a single UHF tag (nominal read range less than 10 meters).

The *tag-to-reader eavesdropping range* can even be larger than the rogue read range, as a second reader might simply overhear the signals being sent back from a tag to a legitimate reader, without itself having to be close (or powerful) enough to actually power the tag. Last not least, the *reader-to-tag eavesdropping range* is typically much larger than any of the above ranges, as even legitimate readers must operate at power levels that not only transmit information (i.e., commands) to the tags, but also supply enough energy to the tag to process and reply to these commands. Consequently, their signals can potentially be received hundreds of meters away [11].

Of course, reports on record-setting RFID read-ranges must be taken with a grain of salt. This is because read records are often achieved under idealized conditions, such as simulators or lab environments. For example, the UHF read range record as reported in [13] used two very large directional antennas with a laser viewfinder in order to optimally focus its field on a specific tag

– hardly equipment that would be easy to hide, let alone predictably use on moving targets (e.g., shoppers). Finke and Kelter [14] report eavesdropping on an HF tag interchange from as far as three meters, though their snooping antenna had to be aligned perfectly with the legitimate reader's antenna, and they concede that they would need a large number of repeated (identical) readouts to actually decode the received signal.

This is due to the nature of electromagnetic coupling, where the orientation between tags and the reader antenna does affect the potential energy transfer to the tag. Ideally, tags are orientated parallel to the reader's antenna. In the worst case, however, a tag that is oriented completely perpendicular to an antenna might not receive any energy in the process, and would thus not be detected at all. This is why many industrial solutions actually use multiple readers with different antenna or coil orientations, e.g., placed sequentially along a conveyor belt, to pick up a tag no matter its orientation.[17]

Another problem for the practical use of RFID tags is the sensitivity of electromagnetic fields to the materials in close proximity to the tags, especially water[18] for UHF and MW tags, and ferrous metals for just about any RFID tag. The carefully tuned RF circuits of an RFID system will often only operate under the planned circumstances and will become detuned when placed next to or near to a non-envisioned material, or even another tag (this effect is called *tag detuning*).

Last but not least, size does matter. While a number of manufacturers already offer sub-millimeter-sized RFID tags (e.g., Hitachi's current generation of mu-chips has a size of less that 0.2 mm^2; its next generation will have only about 0.02 mm^2), these numbers usually do not include the antenna size. Without any antenna, or an equally small one, the effective read range of such tags is only a few millimeters, again limited by the laws of physics. Conversely, tags with a larger read range would need larger antennas as well, making it difficult to hide them maliciously.

28.3 RFID Privacy Challenges

If the previous section provided one fact about RFID systems, it would be that their effective use requires careful planning and controlled deployment. While specific applications (car immobilizer, factory supply-chain management, etc.) can be designed in such a way that these factors are minimized, the list of potential problems – tag detuning, orientation problems, radio interferences – will most likely render RFID systems impractical for the use

---

[17] Note that due to signal interference, two or more readers cannot operate in parallel, so a more space-constrained solution would require switching multiple readers and/or antennas on and off in order to achieve the same effect.

[18] Humans are an excellent source of water, with more than half of the body mass being water. Similarly, groceries like tomatoes, or of course juices and soda, seriously affect RF fields.

as a general surveillance infrastructure. However, even when discarding the often exaggerated capabilities of RFID tags, these still represent a significant privacy problem – at least in principle – due to their enhanced means for identification. The above mentioned advantages of RFID are in this respect its biggest drawbacks:

1. *Automation.* Reading an RFID tag does not require the help of the person carrying the tag, nor any manual intervention on behalf of the reader. Thus, simple reader gates can easily scan large numbers of tags, making data acquisition much easier.
2. *Identification.* The ability to identify individual items instead of only whole classes of items significantly improves the ability to identify an individual. This would facilitate, e.g., the creation of detailed consumer or citizen profiles.
3. *Integration.* Not only that the act of reading a tag can be completely hidden from the tag carrier (especially when operating at larger distances), also the fact that a tag is present in a particular product will be hard to ascertain for an individual without special detection equipment.
4. *Authentication.* The above points become especially critical given the increasing amount of sensitive information, e.g., health information, payment details, or biometric data, that are stored on or linked to tags used in authentication systems.

These four attributes of RFID applications threaten two classes of individual privacy: *data privacy* and *location privacy*. The location privacy of a person is threatened if a tag ID that is associated with that person is spotted at a particular reader location. These IDs do not need to be unique – Weiss [15] points out that certain combinations of nonunique tags might still form unique *constellations* of items that can be used to identify an individual. Knowing that a person's car has been detected passing a certain toll station, or that a person's shoes have entered a particular building allows others to infer (though not prove) the location and ultimately the activity of that person.

Once tags carry more than just an identifier, but also a person's name or account number, data privacy may be violated. This happens if unauthorized readers eavesdrop on a legitimate transaction, or if rogue readers trick a tag into disclosing its personal data. A special case of data privacy are product IDs that disclose the (otherwise not visible) belongings of a person, e.g., the types and brands of clothing one is wearing, the items in one's shopping bag, or even the furniture in a house. Note that in the latter case, the actual *identity* of the victim might very well remain unknown – it might be enough to know that *this* person carries a certain item.

28.3.1 Consumer Fears

There are three principal ways of violating an individual's data and/or location privacy: clandestine scanning, eavesdropping, and data leakage:

- *Clandestine scanning.* The tag data is scanned without the tag-carrier's consent. This might disclose personal information (data privacy) either indirectly, e.g., by revealing the contents of bags that one cannot see through otherwise, or directly, e.g., by revealing personal data such as the name of a user or the date that a particular item has been bought. If several clandestine scans are pooled, *clandestine tracking* can reveal a data subject's movements along a tag-reading infrastructure (location privacy).
- *Eavesdropping.* Instead of reading out a tag directly, one can also eavesdrop on the reader-to-tag channel (or even the tag-to-reader channel) and receive the IDs of the tags being read due to the employed anti-collision protocol.
- *Data leakage.* Independent of the actual RFID technology is the threat of having applications read out more information from a tag than is necessary, or storing more information than needed. This is of course a threat common to all data-gathering applications, though the envisaged ubiquity of RFID-based transactions renders it highly relevant in this context. Fabian et al. [16] also point out the vulnerability of the underlying commercial product information network to data disclosure attacks.

So how would an RFID privacy violation look in practice? Andrew Kantor, a columnist for USA Today, envisions the following: "A department store's RFID system recognizes that you're carrying an item you bought there last week. Now it knows who you are. And if there are readers scattered about, it knows where you're going. Come home to a phone call, 'Mr. Kantor – we noticed you were shopping for a television...' " [17]. Forbes Magazine predicts: "As the shopper enters the store, scanners identify her clothing by the tags embedded in her pants, shirt and shoes. The store knows where she bought everything she is wearing." [18] These *shopping scenarios* and the associated *profiling* are probably the most widespread RFID privacy fears.

Criminal scenarios are almost as prevalent: "Sophisticated thieves walk by homes with RFID readers to get an idea of what's inside. Slightly less sophisticated thieves do the same thing in a parking lot, scanning car trunks" [17] and "Using mobile readers, future pickpockets could find out how much cash someone would carry"[19] [19]. Potential criminal activities are not only confined to burglary: "In the future, there will be this very tiny microchip embedded in the envelope or stamp. You won't be able to shred it because it's so small... Someone will come along and read my garbage and know every piece of mail I received" [20].

Also high on the list are comprehensive *surveillance scenarios*, where critics foresee "the development of a seamless network of millions of RFID receivers strategically placed around the globe in airports, seaports, highways, distribution centers, warehouses, retail stores, and consumers' homes, all of which are constantly reading, processing, and evaluating consumer behaviors and purchases" [3]. This seems especially likely with the use of RFID tags in

---

[19] Translation from the German original by the author.

passports: "Would you mind if your passport would hide an RFID chip with all kinds of private data in it? Government agencies and corporations could find out where you are, what car you drive at the moment, which ailments you have, or if you receive unemployment benefits"[20] [19]. This fear is also kindled by recent reports of RFID implants for both leisure [21] and work [22].

Interviewing 30 consumers about their concerns with respect to RFID, Berthold et al. [23] additionally identified the fear of being held responsible for RFID-tagged objects (e.g., by tracking down perpetrators of minor offenses such as soft-drink bottles being discarded in public parks), and fears pertaining to the use of RFID to control the behavior of consumers (e.g., smart fridges that limit the number of soft drinks being dispensed).

28.3.2 Privacy Threats

Obviously, some of the above scenarios are more likely than others. It is surprising, however, that the most prominent examples are also often the least plausible ones.

Take for example the threat of covert profile building by unscrulpous marketers and retailers, banding together to observe your every moves and then surprising you with deep insights into your current (commercial) needs and wishes. Not only would such behavior be illegal in most countries that feature data protection laws, retailers would also risk alienating potential customers with such overt spying, should this fact ever be disclosed. But why spy on your customers if they would give you the information voluntarily? The example of consumer loyalty cards show that many consumers are willing to have their personal data recorded in commercial databases – in return for tangible benefits (e.g., miniscule discounts). The real threat to shopper's privacy would thus lie much more with their own desire to peruse future RFID-based loyalty programs, than in sinister plots to secretly monitor them against their will.

Criminal scenarios seem equally implausible. A thief looking for wealthy shoppers might simply wait in front of a high-street jewelry shop, or look out for shoppers carrying huge oversized boxes out of electronics stores with the words "plasma TV" written across. The discussion on tag detuning in Sect. 28.2.2 above should have made clear that scanning a car's trunk would be as impossible as scanning the content's of a house (the latter example would also fail based on reading range alone, unless thieves resorted to parking a car with a huge antenna dish mounted on top – hardly unobtrusive). Again, the real threat lies much more with the proliferation of insufficiently secured token-based access control systems, such as electronic payment cards or biometric passports. Several researchers have demonstrated that the security of these systems can often be easily broken, resulting in more or less severe forms of identity theft [24, 25].

---

[20] Translation from the German original by the author.

Having governments use RFID to build a comprehensive surveillance infrastructure is probably the least likely development. Industry groups estimate costs of well over a trillion dollars to create a national spy network in the US, covering all airports, rail and bus terminals, public offices, libraries, schools, parks, stores, etc. [26].[21] Additionally, given the trivial means of disabling for example the RFID tag in a passport through shielding, such an infrastructure would hardly be difficult to circumvent. Implants could equally be shielded with a corresponding metallic mesh fabric, though the small size of implantable chips as well as human tissue anyway typically imply a maximum reading distance of a few centimeters only – hardly suitable for readout without the subject's consent. Instead, the increased amount of RFID-based data traces might, similarly to today's mobile phone and ISP connection records, create a desire by law enforcement to access logs of commercial providers in the case of a particular crime or threat. As such, the fears reported by Berthold et al. [23] of an increase of direct control through traceable items strike much closer to home.

This is, then, the true danger of RFID technology to our privacy: its means of automated data collection, and with it the increased amounts of data traces available on all levels of our lives. More data means more ways of accidentally disclosing such information, e.g., on a public Web page through a system malfunction, and more needs of others of getting access to this data; data that is increasingly given out voluntarily in order to use novel, RFID-enabled services.

28.4 Technical RFID Privacy Mechanisms

The previous sections served to show two things. Firstly, that much of today's discussion on RFID is based on invalid assumptions regarding technical capabilities and societal realities. And secondly, that at the core of the debate, a number of issues are nevertheless threatening substantial privacy values. This section, then, tries to enumerate and analyze the number of proposed technical solutions to those problems. It is important to note that these should not be viewed in isolation, but rather as complementing each other, as well as corresponding social norms, laws, and regulations.

28.4.1 Securing Media Access Protocols

As mentioned above, the power asymmetry between reader and tag makes it possible that information sent from reader devices (and to some extent also

---

[21] Obviously, governments could focus on neuralgic points only, e.g., border stations and airports (the introduction of RFID-enabled passports implies just that). However, in contrast to a comprehensive "spy network", such a deployment will not significantly change today's governmental data-collection methods, which already make use of machine-readable documents in such locations.

the tag's reply) can potentially be subject to *eavesdropping* through malicious readers, even at distances larger than the nominal or rogue read range. This is especially critical since it also applies to perfectly legitimate interactions, i.e., when tags only talk to authenticated readers. As pointed out in Sect. 28.3 above, both the means of RFID for *identification* and *authentication* might threaten an individual's privacy under such circumstances.

Obviously, sending sensitive information from the tag back to the reader might threaten data privacy if overheard. The obvious solution is to encrypt the communication channel between readers and tags. However, this might still allow attackers to learn the ID of the tag (thus threatening location privacy, and possibly data privacy), since many anti-collision protocols send it in the clear on the lower communication levels (see Sect. 28.2.1). Even an otherwise anonymous tag ID might in this way threaten location privacy due to the potential for identifying constellations (see Sect. 28.3 above).

To prevent the transmission of tag IDs in probabilistic protocols (where it is used for silencing already identified tags, cf. Sect. 28.2.1), tags can instead use temporary session IDs that they choose at random whenever a reader starts a query. While the ID is then constant over the course of the session (and thus facilitates addressing the tag, e.g., for requesting the real ID's value), it is lost as soon as the reader cuts the field's energy [27].

For deterministic protocols, Weis et al. [28] propose that, instead of sending a whole prefix, readers would only send the command "transmit next bit" to the tags. As long as their corresponding bit positions are identical, no collision would occur[22] and the reader would be able to note the common bit prefix incrementally. Once two tags differ at position i, the reader would just as before use a select command to pick a subtree, but instead of sending the complete prefix to the tags, it would send a single bit indicating which part of the subtree should reply next. In order to hide this information from any eavesdropper, the reader XORs it with the previous, error-free bit. As the value of this bit was only sent from the tags to the reader, a malicious reader outside this communication range (but inside the reader's forward channel) will not be able to know the true value of the next selected bit. The tags, on the other hand, know their own ID, and accordingly the bit value at the previously queried position, thus sharing a common secret with the reader that can be exploited for every conflicting bit position.

28.4.2 Tag Deactivation and the Kill Command

The most effective privacy protection for RIFD-tagged items is the deactivation of the tag, as it reliably prevents *clandestine scanning* of a tag's *identification* data. In its simplest and most reliable form, this would imply that vendors and manufacturers embed tags only into detachable labels and outer product packaging that can be discarded before use. For tags embedded into

---

[22] A collision only occurs if two tags send different bit values.

the actual product itself (e.g., into the garment of a sweater, or a can of soda), removal of the tag would not be an option – tags would need to be deactivated in situ. In standards for item-level tagging of consumer products, compliant tags must implement a kill command [29]. The basic idea is simple: After selling a tagged item to the consumer, the embedded tag is permanently deactivated at checkout. This renders the tag inaccessible to subsequent reader commands and thus prevents any tracking beyond the point of sale.

As simple as the idea sounds, it is hard to implement in practice. In order to prevent malicious silencing of tags (e.g., for shoplifting), each tag features an individual unlock code that must be sent by the reader, together with the kill-command, thus significantly increasing data management costs. Also, in situ deactivation itself is difficult for the consumer to verify, as no visible cues would be present. Karjoth and Moskowitz [30] alternatively propose to use scratch-off or peel-off antennas in order to make the silencing process both more visible to consumers and less prone to unnoticed deactivation attacks. Additionally, their solution only removes the wireless communication capabilities but leaves the tag (and its data) intact, thus allowing for continued use of the information in the tag – simply not in the (privacy-violating) automated and unnoticed fashion of regular RFID tags. On the other hand, such a manual approach would increase the burden on the consumer, as one would need to manually disable each tag, while an automated kill command could be implemented as part of the checkout process. At the same time, however, [31] points out that small businesses such as kiosks might not be able to afford the corresponding equipment, even though they would inevitably sell tagged merchandise (e.g., soda cans or razor blades).

28.4.3 Access Control

Preserving the benefits of *automated identification* after checkout while at the same time preventing *clandestine scanning* of the tagged data seems to be a contradiction. Yet with proper access control, one could envision that only authorized parties could read out personal RFID tags (i.e., tags containing personal information, or tags affixed to personal items that thus disclose the carrier's location), while queries from rogue readers would simply be ignored.

A simple solution to access control is to obstruct the reader signal by means of a metal mesh or foil that encloses the tag. With the inclusion of RFID tags into passports, a number of vendors begun offering coated sleeves for protecting the passport while not in use. Obviously, this will not be a solution for groceries or clothing. Juels et al. [32] propose a so-called blocker-tag that jams tree-based anti-collision protocols, thus making it impossible to read out tags nearby when present. It does so by simply responding to all possible prefixes, thus creating the impression of trillions[23] of tags being

---

[23] Fully simulating all possibilities of a, say, 64-bit ID would actually be more than just a few trillions. An (implausibly) fast reader able to read 100,000 tags per second would be busy for over four billion years reading all 2^{64} tags.

present that both hide the real tags present, as well as stalling the reader due to the (apparently) large number of tags to be read out. As it is cheap to manufacture (about the price of a regular tag), it could even be integrated into paper bags, masking any shopping items within. In order to prevent jamming of legitimate read-outs, the authors propose the use of a *privacy-bit* [33] on each regular RFID tag that would be set in the same fashion as the proposed tag deactivation – during checkout. Blocker tags would then only jam readers that attempt to read tags with this privacy bit.

A number of authors have proposed cryptographic hashes that hide the real ID of a tag behind a so-called meta ID, requiring readers to know a certain password (typically the tag's original ID) in order to unlock it again [11]. However, as a single fixed meta ID would not solve the problem of location privacy, i.e., unwanted tracking and profiling, these meta IDs would need to change periodically, e.g., upon each read request. But with an ever-changing ID, even legitimate readers might have a hard time figuring out the correct password of a tag in order to unlock it. This implies the need for significant data management structures to keep track of one's items and their current meta IDs – a requirement that questions the practicability of such a scheme. Even if one assumes a single password for all of one's personal items (e.g., a smart phone furnishes a key to the supermarket's point-of-sale device during checkout), the associated *key management problem* would still be significant (imagine buying things for other people, or forgetting your phone at home).

28.4.4 Proxys

The previous paragraph already alluded to a powerful mobile device that could aid consumers with their everyday RFID management, specifically in order to prevent both *clandestine scanning*, as well as *data leakage* during authorized tag readouts. For example, Juel et al.'s blocker tag could equally well be implemented on a mobile phone, allowing more-sophisticated blocking strategies, e.g., based on location (do not block readout at home, allow scanning of clothing at your favorite clothing store, etc.) [34]. This could allow RFID systems to still operate *automatically* and use *integrated* and unobtrusive tags.

Flörkemeier et al. [35] additionally propose to incorporate explicit privacy policies into RFID protocols, thus requiring readers to both identify themselves and their operators, as well as explicitly stating the purpose of each tag readout. While every consumer might not be willing or able to afford such an RFID-compliant mobile device, this solution would nevertheless allow independent agencies to audit reader signals and verify that they comply with their stated privacy policies (or, for that matter, that they actually send one).

Proxy approaches are especially interesting in conjunction with public policy proposals that aim at making the tagging and data collection process more transparent. While many legal experts point out that the principles of data protection laws such as collection minimization, transparency, purpose limitation and choice apply equally to RFID [36], US scholars have long since called for voluntary notice and choice requirements for RFID-tagged merchandise [37]. Having legitimate readers transmit detailed privacy policies could significantly improve privacy awareness.[24]

28.5 Conclusions

RFID technology offers a powerful new way of automating the identification of everyday items. It also opens up new ways of conveniently authenticating ourselves and our devices, facilitating improved services and better security.

However, while RFID technology has come a long way since its inception, it is hard to use it as an all-seeing surveillance infrastructure that many critics fear. Reliability will certainly continue to improve, yet even if one were able to minimize the rate of false readouts, most envisioned big brother scenarios would still be prohibitively expensive to realize, yet poor in performance. Further advancements in read ranges might actually be unhelpful, as most item-level applications actually require limited read ranges. And once a service has been implemented using a particular coupling technology, frequency, and antenna design, even rogue readers will not be able to arbitrarily raise the possible read ranges due to the fickle laws of physics governing RFID communication.

Still, behind many of the often contrived examples cited in today's press do lie a number of substantial threats to privacy: the improved means of subtly exerting influence and control through the large amounts of personal data that might be collected – not covertly, but as part of freely chosen services such as loyalty programs, recommender systems, or payment schemes; the increased risk for identity theft and credit fraud through poorly implemented RFID authentication systems; and the ever-looming desire of society to reuse existing data for secondary purposes, especially when it comes to security (e.g., the war on terror) and safety (e.g., road safety).

Technology can play an important role when it comes to minimizing the risks from malicious attackers, yet it can hardly prevent voluntary data disclosures and self-inflicted surveillance systems. Proper guidelines and laws must complement technical notice and choice solutions in order to protect the rights of consumers to their data. Initiating the public debate on the needs and limits of personal privacy in future smart environments is certainly a welcome side-effect of today's sometimes sensational RFID coverage.

---

[24] Note that illegal readers can always send out fake privacy policies (or send none at all), so this approach does not *prevent* illegal readouts, but instead regulates what constitutes *legal* and *illegal*, thus providing the basis for legal enforcement (e.g., suing individuals or companies using such fake policies on the grounds of deceptive business practices).

References

1. M.F. Relfe. *When Your Money Fails.* League of Prayer, Montgomery, AL, USA, January 1981.
2. S. Garfinkel and B. Rosenberg, editors. *RFID: Applications, Security, and Privacy.* Addison-Wesley, July 2005.
3. EPIC – Electronic Privacy Information Center. Radio frequency identification (RFID) systems. The A to Z's of Privacy Website, 2006.
4. Capgemini. RFID and consumers – what European consumers think about radio frequency identification and the implications for business, February 2005.
5. S.A. Brown. *Revolution at the Checkout Counter: The Explosion of the Bar Code.* Wertheim Publications in Industrial Relations. Harvard University Press, Cambridge, MA, USA, 1997.
6. K. Finkenzeller. *RFID Handbook: Fundamentals and Applications in Contactless Smart Cards and Identification.* Wiley, 2003.
7. R. Want. RFID – a key to automating everything. *Scientific American,* 290(1):46–55, January 2004.
8. R. Want. The magic of RFID. *ACM Queue,* 2(7):41–48, October 2004.
9. M. Lampe, C. Flörkemeier, and S. Haller. Einführung in die RFID-Technologie. In E. Fleisch and F.n Mattern, editors, *Das Internet der Dinge – Ubiquitous Computing und RFID in der Praxis,* pages 69–86. Springer, 2005.
10. C. Law, K. Lee, and K.Y. Siu. Efficient memoryless protocol for tag identification (extended abstract). In *Proceedings of the Fourth International Workshop on Discrete Algorithms and Methods for Mobile Computing and Communications,* pages 75–84. ACM Press, 2000.
11. A. Juels. RFID security and privacy: A research survey. *IEEE Journal on Selected Areas in Communication,* 24(2):381–394, February 2006.
12. Z. Kfir and A. Wool. Picking virtual pockets using relay attacks on contactless smartcard systems. In *Conference on Security and Privacy for Emerging Areas in Communication Networks – SecureComm 2005.* IEEE, September 2005.
13. B. Krebs. Leaving Las Vegas: So long DefCon and Blackhat. washingtonpost.com Weblog, August 2005.
14. T. Finke and H. Kelter. Abhörmöglichkeiten der Kommunikation zwischen Lesegerät und Transponder am Beispiel eines ISO14443-Systems. BSI White Paper, 2004.
15. S.A. Weis. *Security and Privacy in Radio-Frequency Identification Devices.* Master's thesis, Massachusetts Institute of Technology, Cambridge, MA, USA, May 2003.
16. B. Fabian, O. Günther, and S. Spiekermann. Security analysis of the object name service for RFID. In *Proceedings of the 1st International Workshop on Security, Privacy and Trust in Pervasive and Ubiquitous Computing,* July 2005.
17. A. Kantor. Tiny transmitters give retailers, privacy advocates goosebumps. USAToday.com – CyberSpeak, December 19, 2003.
18. C.R. Schoenberger. The internet of things. *Forbes Magazine,* 2002(6).
19. M. Zeidler. RFID: Der Schnüffelchip im Joghurtbecher. Monitor-Magazin, January 8, 2003.
20. M. Roberti. Big brother's enemy. RFID Journal, July 2003.
21. R. Curnow. The privacy to pay for VIP status. *CNN.com,* October 6, 2004.
22. Spychips.org. Two U.S. employees injected with RFID microchips at company request. Press Release, February 2006.

23. O. Berthold, O. Günther, and S. Spiekermann. Verbraucherängste und Verbraucherschutz. *Wirtschaftsinformatik*, 47(6):1–9, 2005.

24. A. Juels. Attack on a cryptographic RFID device. Guest Column in RFID Journal, February 28, 2005.

25. J. Lettice. Face and fingerprints swiped in Dutch biometric passport crack. *The Register*, January 30, 2006.

26. Association for Automatic Identification and Mobility. The ROI of privacy invasion. RFID Connections Webzine, January 2004.

27. Auto-ID Center/EPCglobal, Cambridge, MA, USA. *900 MHz Class 0 Radio Frequency (RF) Identification Tag Specification*, 2003.

28. S.A. Weis, S.E. Sarma, R.L. Rivest, and D.W. Engels. Security and privacy aspects of low-cost radio frequency identification systems. In D. Hutter et al., editor, *Security in Pervasive Computing – First International Conference, Boppard, Germany, March 12–14, 2003, Revised Papers*, volume 2802 of *Lecture Notes in Computer Science*, pages 201–212. Springer, 2003.

29. Auto-ID Center/EPCglobal, Cambridge, MA, USA. *860 MHz-930 MHz Class 1 Radio Frequency (RF) Identification Tag Radio Frequency & Logical Communication Interface Specification*, 2002.

30. G. Karjoth and P.A. Moskowitz. Disabling RFID tags with visible confirmation: clipped tags are silenced. In V. Atluri et al., editor, *Proceedings of the 2005 ACM Workshop on Privacy in the Electronic Society (WPES 2005)*, pages 27–30, Alexandria, VA, USA, 2005. ACM Press.

31. R. Stapleton-Gray. Scanning the horizon: A skeptical view of RFIDs on the shelves, July 2005.

32. A. Juels, R.L. Rivest, and M. Szydlo. The blocker tag: Selective blocking of RFID tags for consumer privacy. In S. Jajodia et al., editor, *Proceedings of the 10th ACM Conference on Computer and Communication Security*, pages 103–111, Washington, D.C., USA, 2003. ACM Press.

33. A. Juels. RFID privacy: A tecnical primer for the non-technical reader. In K. Strandburg and D. Stan Raicu, editors, *Privacy and Technologies of Identity: A Cross-Disciplinary Conversation*. Springer, 2005.

34. A. Juels, P. Syverson, and D. Bailey. High-power proxies for enhancing RFID privacy and utility. In G. Danezis and D. Martin, editors, *Privacy Enhancing Technologies (PET)*, May 2005.

35. C. Flörkemeier, R. Schneider, and M. Langheinrich. Scanning with a purpose – supporting the fair information principles in RFID protocols. In H. Murakami et al., editor, *Ubiquitous Computing Systems – Second International Symposium, UCS Tokyo, Japan, November 8–9, 2004, Revised Selected Papers*, volume 3598 of *Lecture Notes in Computer Science*, pages 214–231. Springer, June 2005.

36. Data Protection Commissioners. Resolution on radio frequency identification. 25th International Conference of Data Protection and Privacy Commissioners, November 2003.

37. S. Garfinkel. An RFID bill of rights. *Technology Review*, 105(8):35, October 2002.

Malicious Software in Ubiquitous Computing

Morton Swimmer

IBM Zürich Research Laboratory GmbH
Switzerland

Summary. Malware (malicious software) is rampant in our information technology infrastructures and is likely to be so for the foreseeable future. We will look at various types of malware and their characteristics and see what defenses currently exist to combat them. Various aspects of ubiquitous computing will likely prove game-changers for malware and we will look into how the problem will evolve as ubiquitous computing (UbiComp) is deployed.

29.1 Introduction

When in August 2005, thousands of spectators at an athletics event in Finland received an unsolicited application via Bluetooth, many were too distracted and perhaps trusting to avoid accepting it for installation. The problem was that, even though the recipient could always decline the installation, a nearby mobile phone that was infected with the Cabir worm would continuously try to reinfect all phones in its ad-hoc personal area network. The only defense was to turn off Bluetooth or move out of range. In a stadium environment, the latter was not realistic as the more users accepted and installed the worm, the harder it was to find a 'quiet' spot. If the worm had been able to circumvent the user, the worm would surely have taken over all the stadium's compatible phones in a very short time.[1] As it was, only a few dozen phones were reported infected, but this example shows how worms may affect an environment where networking is ubiquitous and ad-hoc.

Malicious software, malware for short, has the tendency to circumvent security mechanisms that may be in place. Even when the security is well designed and implemented, malware will either coerce the user to circumvent it, or exploit a vulnerability somewhere in the system to spread itself or act. In this chapter, we will first look at what malware is, then we will look at how current systems can be defended against malware and how effective these

---

[1] http://www.theregister.co.uk/2005/08/12/cabir_stadium_outbreak/

measures are. Lastly we will look into the ubiquitous computing future and see how this development will change the landscape for malware.

29.2 Types of Malware

Malicious software (malware) can be viewed as intentionally dysfunction software [1]. Ordinary software always contains a number of bugs which may manifest themselves in negative ways, perhaps causing data loss or leakage. The bugs may be caused by honest mistakes or sloppiness, but not malicious intent. In the case of malware, data loss or leakage, or other negative aspects of the software are entirely intended by the malware writer. In many borderline cases, it may be hard to determine the intent of the programmer, leaving the final classification difficult for those who must do this.

29.2.1 Trojan Horses

A *trojan* (short for *Trojan horse*) is a program that is presumed by the user to be bona fide, but in which a malicious and undocumented payload has been intentionally placed.

The standard definition of a trojan is:

Definition 1 (trojan). *A Trojan horse is defined as a piece of malicious software that, in addition to its primary effect, has a second, nonobvious malicious payload.*

The definition hinges on the payload as there are no other measurable characteristics.

Definition 2 (payload). *The payload of a malware is the effect it has on other system objects.*

We can further refine the payload's capabilities to violations of *integrity*, *confidentiality* and/or *availability* as well as *malware dropping*.

Trojan authors can release their prodigy in a completely untargeted manner, for instance using Usenet news or spamming to coax enough users to run it. This method is used to create a large pool of "bots" (compromised machines) that can be used for spamming or other purposes, often rented or sold on a for-fee basis by criminal hackers. On the other hand, the perpetrator may have a specific target and may hack into the target systems to install the trojan.

So, on the whole, the common definition of a trojan is a weak one because it is not specific enough to help an anti-malware analyst determine whether it is a trojan or an ordinary piece of software. For some subtypes of trojan we may be able to define more-specific characteristics that we can use to identify a subclass of the entire Trojan horse set. There are currently products on the market or in research labs that attempt to do just that but with only moderate success so far.

Backdoor trojan

A particularly interesting variant of trojan is the *backdoor trojan*, which is confidentiality violating by allowing access to the target system by the hacker. It is one thing to hold the credentials to access a system, but as these can be revoked, it is far better for the malicious hacker to create a backdoor circumventing the security to begin with.

As with many trojans, the line between legitimate programs and backdoors is very thin. Witness various remote access programs, such as VNC[2] that are viewed as legitimate, and BackOrifice 2000[3], which usually is not. However, both programs have similar functionalities.

Spyware

Spyware is a name for a specific kind of confidentiality-violating trojan that spies on the user's activity or account contents and relays this data to the attacker. It is different from the backdoor trojan in that the attacker does not access the machine themselves. Spyware is also different from typical trojans in that they try to gain some legitimacy by surreptitiously stating their intentions in the EULA[4]. However, they are still considered trojans as the spyware functionality is usual quite unrelated to the primary functionality of the software.

Droppers

A further type of trojan is purely of the type malware dropping. This can be useful for various reasons. For one, some malware cannot exist naturally as a file and must be inserted into memory by the dropper so that they can run, as was the case with the CodeRed worm. Another reason to use a dropper is to heavily obfuscate the contained malware payload to avoid detection. Droppers are always local-acting.

Definition 3 (local-acting). *Malware is* local-acting *if its target is on the same machine as itself.*

Exploits

We use the term *exploit* to mean those programs that inject code into a running program. The job of the exploit is to establish communication with the target program and bring it to the point where the code can be inserted, usually via a buffer-overflow vulnerability. The insertion requires padding the code

---

[2] see http://www.realvnc.com

[3] see http://www.bo2k.com

[4] End-user license agreement

appropriately before and after, or packaging the code in any other appropriate means that causes it to be executed.

An exploit is unlike ordinary droppers in that it injects code into a running program. Although this is not necessary, it is usually *remote-acting*. The injection process is called *parasitic*.

Definition 4 (remote-acting). *Malware is* remote-acting *if the target of the malware resides on a different machine.*

Definition 5 (parasitic). *The* parasitic *property is one that requires a target host to be physically modified. We use the terms* prefix, infix, *and* postfix *to describe where the bulk of the malware is placed, before, inside and appended, respectively. The parasitic property is one of the* insituacy *properties of malware.*

We call the injected code *shellcode* and it usually behaves like a backdoor trojan giving the user shell access to the target environment. This environment can be a remote system or a different user ID on the local system.

29.2.2 Viruses

Viruses are not the oldest malware threat, but they have lived up to the fears of the pioneers of antivirus research in the mid 1980s. They have become a major security issue for all who must maintain computer systems and networks (which includes a surprising number of ordinary users). Furthermore, while well-thought-through attacks used to be rare, malware has become more sophisticated and sinister recently, leading one to suspect that virus writing is no longer the realm of amateurish kids with no real agenda. Instead, it has become a money-making endeavor, by compromising machines to be used as spam-bots, for collecting private and confidential information or other uses.

Right from the genesis of the virus problem, there was already a robust formal definition of the *virus property* that had been established by Cohen [2]. However, an acceptable human-readable definition of a computer virus took a while to establish. Cohen informally defined viruses as:

Definition 6 (computer virus). *A computer virus is a program that can infect other programs by modifying them to include, a possibly evolved, copy of itself.*

Cohen also defines the *infection property* as:

Definition 7 (infection property). *With the* infection property, *a virus can spread throughout a computer system or network using the authorizations of every user using it to infect their programs. Every program that gets infected may also act as a virus and thus the infection spreads.*

However, over the course of years and experience with actual viruses from the wild, a newer (informal) definition was developed:

Definition 8 (computer virus). *A computer virus is a routine or program that can infect other programs or routines by modifying it or its environment so that running the program or routine will result in the execution of a possibly modified copy of the virus.*

This definition deemphasizes the manipulation of actual code by allowing the environment to be modified as well.

Viruses in particular can benefit from plurality of operational environments so that they can spread more widely, and there have been many cases of this in the past.

Definition 9 (multi-environment). *Malware has the* multi-environment *property if it is capable of running on multiple environments. These are defined as a real or virtual execution platform and an associated object model.*

For example, a PC may run object models Microsoft Windows or Linux that are both distinct environments despite using the same CPU.

The essence of a virus is its self-propagation and the transitivity characteristic of multi-hop spread is the core to any virus definition.

Definition 10 (multi-transitive). *A malware is* multi-transitive *if it affects a target in a way that includes a fully functional version of itself that can, in turn, affect other targets.*

The insituacy of a virus is also core to the definition and refers to how the target of a virus is affected and this concept can also be applied to other malware.[5] A virus may be parasitic, exositic (Def. 5 and 12), as well as non-parasitic (Def. 11).

Definition 11 (nonparasitic). *Malware is* non-parasitic *if it does not modify its target.*

Definition 12 (exositic). *Malware is* exositic *if it affects the target only indirectly by modifying the target's environment to induce the malware to be run when the target is executed.*

The core characteristics of a virus are therefore transitive and either parasitic or exositic. Of course, we are talking about a stereotypical virus and there have been some borderline cases not included in this. Other properties that viruses have exhibited in the past are polymorphism and stealth (Def. 13 and 14).

Definition 13 (polymorphism). *Malware exhibits the* polymorphism *property if it obfuscates its persistent manifestation. This can occur through encrypting regions of its code, or through code permutations, amongst other methods.*

---

[5] insituacy comes from in situ (Latin) which means in place.

Definition 14 (stealth). *We refer to the* stealth *property as the ability of malware to hide itself from an external observer.*

These properties refer to a number of ways in which a virus or potentially any malware may hide from the user or system administrator. Polymorphism aims at make detection hard for an antivirus and reverse-engineering difficult for the virus analyst. Stealth hides tell-tale characteristics that might have otherwise given the malware away from the user, system administrator or some monitoring program.

Worms

Viruses and worms are very similar in certain ways. The similarity to viruses comes from a worm's transitivity. The core and secondary characteristics of worms are essentially the same as for viruses. The main differences are in locality and insituacy. Worms are always remote-acting and can also be non-parasitic, i.e., the worm can create an entire new object that has no dependence on an existing object, whereas parasitic infection is extremely rare with worms unless it operates as a virus within the local machine.

29.3 Malware and Security in Current Systems

Ideally, we should be able to prevent malware activity on our system or prevent it from getting on our system in the first place. At least we should be able to hope that we can prevent the malware from doing any damage. In the latter case we must prevent the malware from violating the *confidentiality*, *integrity* and *availability* of the data and the system. In the following sections, we will see how various relevant prevention practices can be applied.

29.3.1 Memory protection

Historically, the platform on which malware proliferated the best, PCs running MS-DOS, at first had the worst memory protection possible: none. The pioneering work done by the malware writers on the MS-DOS platform cannot easily be replicated on current platforms, but there are certainly holes in current designs that are being exploited as they become known.

Enforcing Memory Access Classes

At the very least, we need to protect the operating system processes from the user space, but protecting user spaces from each other is also important. Usually, these protections are built into the CPU and the operating system uses them.

However, even with properly enforced memory protection, malware has been able to install itself in protected memory by arranging for it to be run on the next machine startup, whereupon it will install itself as a driver or otherwise affect the protected kernel. All this is done using normal privileges and standard procedures for installing programs.

CPU-assisted memory protection is not always available. Many low-cost embedded devices lack such protections for hardware cost reasons. One workaround for this problem is to set a non-interruptible timer before executing user code that reloads the operating system from scratch after running the program for a reasonable time. Though not a great idea, at least the user program cannot take over the CPU permanently. This problem is likely to be an issue with many UbiComp devices, which must be as cheap as possible, but this solution is well adapted to applications where the device only runs for a very short time anyway.

Buffer Overflow Protection

Buffer overflows (BoF) occur when the size of input data exceeds the size of the buffer the program has reserved for it (see Fig. 29.1). If the buffer has been allocated on the stack, the buffer is overrun and other data on the stack will be overwritten. Used maliciously, as in the case of an exploit, the buffer is filled until the data overruns the return address of the function. When the function returns, it incorrectly jumps to the location that has been overwritten in place of the original return address. By carefully crafting the insertion buffer, the exploiter can cause arbitrary code to be executed.

An important approach is to prevent code execution on the stack, where normally we should only assume transient data to reside. Recently, the AMD and Intel processors for PCs have acquired execution protection but require operating system support, which is not universal yet. Prior to that, projects such as PaX[6] and OpenWall[7] implemented the same functionality in software.

The problems with the approach revolves around the fact that code is legitimately (and surprisingly) being executed on the stack in some applications. GNU's C compiler generates so-called *trampoline code* on the stack for implementing nested functions. This is not actually a frequently used feature but it does occur often enough to make stack protection problematic. The next problem is with *codecs*[8] code, which are often implemented by generating an optimized piece of code in a buffer and then executing it. However, if this sort of coding can be avoided, execution restrictions can help, even if not all types of BoF attacks[9] can be prevented.

An alternative approach to stack execution protection is to only protect the call return address that must be overwritten for a BoF attack to work.

---

[6] http://pageexec.virtualave.net/

[7] http://www.openwall.com/

[8] *Coding/Decoding* of multimedia bitstreams.

[9] The class of return-into-libc attacks is one prominent example.

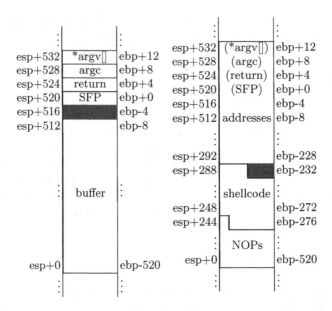

Fig. 29.1. Stack contents before and after a stack buffer is overflowed by the attack string comprising of no-ops, the shellcode and finally candidate addresses to facilitate the jump to the NOP section. In this diagram that refers to an Intel x86 CPU, *esp* and *ebp* are the stack and base pointers, respectively, and *ebp+4* will always point to the return in typical use.

The most common approach is to encrypt the return address in a way that is difficult to anticipate by the attacker, but not overly computationally intensive for the operating system. Before the function returns, the return address is decrypted. If the memory where the return address is stored has been overridden by a BoF attack and the perpetrator has not correctly anticipated the encryption scheme, the decrypted return address will not contain a valid address and an illegal instruction or memory access control exception occurs when the CPU jumps there (e.g., see [3, 4]).

Potentially, bounds-checking all allocated buffer could be used to prevent the buffer overflow in the first place, but without fast hardware support, a software-only solution will be too slow to be useful.

29.3.2 Perimeter Defense

In dealing with malware that acts from remote our preference is to prevent it it from entering the system in the first place. One very common method is to place a firewall, an email filter or some other defense on the edge of an intranet or at the network interface of a machine.

Firewalls and IPSs

Firewalls are filters that act as a conduit for all traffic in and out of the organization. They are very good at directionally limiting traffic of certain types of services or from ranges of IP addresses. A very common setup is, in broad terms, to block all external traffic into the intranet except to a few services to certain machines in the so-called DMZ.[10] A firewall will be able to block worms coming in from the outside if set up like this and the DMZ machines are not vulnerable.

So-called, intrusion prevention systems (IPS) are conceptually similar to firewalls except that they can also filter based on content. They can be used to strip out code in requests coming in from the outside to prevent malware-based attacks. Blocking worms using an IPS is increasingly done even at boundaries inside an intranet for performance reasons: the added worm traffic had been using too much network bandwidth and hinders the clean-up process.

Scanning Email/News Gateways

Much malware infiltrates an organization via news and email. It is still a threat that will probably never completely go away and the opportunities to prevent malware spread are evident. Email worms usually spread via executable attachments, as the email body is by default text-only. It should be noted that some email systems use a rich-text format that may allow code in the text as well. In more standard systems, the email or news is already in MIME or RFC 822 formats, and the malware resides as an attachment that is either automatically executed where this is possible or is clicked upon by the user. Note that nothing in the Internet standards require executable attachments to be executed automatically—this is done at the discretion of the vendors and it is a practice that needs to be discouraged.

TCP Wrappers and Personal Firewalls

TCP wrappers are a form of *personal firewall*, which in turn is a firewall implemented on the client machine [5]. TCP wrappers allow the system administrator to prefilter requests to TCP services and allow or disallow accesses based on a set of rules he or she defines.

Whereas TCP wrappers are normally used for incoming traffic, personal firewalls are used for both incoming and outgoing traffic. Certain forms of outgoing traffic can be indicative of spyware in action and so the personal firewall is usually configured to allow only certain programs access to external resources and only very few external connections to certain programs.

---

[10] DMZ=demilitarized zone, a term that conjures up the border between North and South Korea that acts as a buffer between the highly militarized border zone. In a corporate network, it usually houses the external Web and mail servers.

As with ordinary firewalls, these can be difficult to set up properly. Furthermore, the firewall may be susceptible to discretionary tampering from the malware if the access controls on the machine allow this.

There is the potential for doing more-intensive packet analysis at a personal firewall or TCP wrapper than with ordinary firewalls, as the packets must be assembled at this point anyway. The scanning overhead for malware code is also more reasonable as the applications the malware relies on are on the machine, and if they are not, the malware should not pose a threat to that machine. However, we are left with the problem of identifying what constitutes illegal code: we need a very detailed policy as to what is permissible and what not.

29.3.3 Organizational Measures

Organizational means can be more effective at preventing some aspects of malware, or at least their effects, than traditional prevention mechanisms. These could be simply a set of *best practices* and user education that, when followed, should prevent at least common malware-related problems. For instance, email viruses can be prevented by using or avoiding certain email client software, configuring the client to avoid certain dangerous features and educating users not to run executable attachments. Other more-specific methods are discussed below.

Configuration Control

Malware that contain the stealth and/or malware-dropping properties, i.e., of the type that may modify the system to hide from sight, or install other malware deep in the system, can be prevented through strict configuration management. A system that provides accountability and configuration rollback features was proposed by Povey in the *Tudo* [6] project. Like sudo, Tudo grants elevated rights to a user, but also takes a snapshot of the configuration before the privileged command is executed. This way, the configuration change can be rolled back if the change turned out to be a bad one. As malware must modify the configuration of a system to implement stealth or install certain types of malware, forcing it to go through such a change-control system allows the modifications to be undone once discovered. In such a system, the change control must be tamper resistant.

Hardware-Assisted Tamper Resistance

To create a form of mandatory control that cannot be circumvented, there have been efforts to implement hardware-assisted security into PC systems.[11] By creating a trusted keystore and some protected cryptographic hardware

---

[11] see https://www.trustedcomputinggroup.org/ and http://www.opentc.net

with boot control, it is hoped that the operating system can be booted into a known secure state and verified remotely. The effect on malware is to prevent successful stealth efforts if the important parts of the system configuration are tightly controlled. Currently it is not self-evident that hardware-assisted security will provide the protection against malware that is hoped.

29.3.4 Access Control

We have already discussed memory access control in Sect. 29.3.1. However, access control typically operates on files in the file system, but often other system objects are also put under its control. One aspect of access control (AC) systems is the decision mechanisms. These range from the per object attributes of Unix, where access right are set for the user, a group of users, and the rest, to a full access matrix defining accesses for each subject/object combination in the matrix model. Even more-complex AC systems have been explored and implemented (see Chap. 4 of this book).

Discretionary versus Mandatory Access Control

The most common form of AC mechanism is discretionary. This form of access control leaves security at the discretion of the object's owner. Discretionary access control (DAC), is only weakly effective against malware in general as the malware will act with the user's privileges and can effect the whole of the user's sphere of influence. The rest of the system is also endangered when the malware has the mono- or multi-transitivity properties. This is because, when a user with other privileges executes an instance of malware, the malware will spread within this new user's sphere of influence and so on. Stealth and tunneling can be prevented if system hooks are protected. Ultimately DAC can be effective at containing the virus as long as a privileged user does not execute the malware, but this should not be relied on.

Using DAC remains a weak choice for malware prevention and what is necessary is *mandatory access control* (MAC), where data carries a security label that cannot be manipulated except with special authority. Once a piece of data is labeled confidential, it cannot be declassified [7, 8] at a user's discretion. Of course, some types of malware, in particular viruses, may be able to elevate privilege levels if a user of a higher level executes an infected object to allow such a declassification [2], so even MAC is not an absolute protection. If the information flow policy limits both executing up and down a level malware will be restricted to this level, but the resulting system may not be useable for practical purposes.

Code Signing Schemes

Another form of access control are the code signing schemes that exist in a few variations for Java and Windows ActiveX applets. In such a scheme, compiled programs, or a package of programs and data files are signed by some trusted authority. Provided the user is in possession of the signer's public key, he can verify the authenticity of the program or bundle, leaving him or her to decide if the signer can be trusted. The user is faced with decisions like (1) whether the third party can be trusted and (2) what to do if the code is not signed at all. The latter problem is troubling as such a scheme must mandate only using signed code to be effective. Any exception may undermine the entire scheme. Once malware has been able to subvert such a mechanism, the scheme is useless. For this reason, it is most frequently used to verify the validity of code that is being imported into a system, but not for installed code.

The problem of trust in the third party is probably the most troubling as it is precisely what such a scheme should counter. We want to establish trust in the code, however, there has been at least one case where a malicious party registered its public key with a trusted third party under a very similar name to a more well-known company. As the nuances in the company name are lost on most users and the trusted third party does not check for such misrepresentations, many users were being duped.[12]

Finally, code signing is only effective in an uncompromised system. Once malware has gained control of the system, it may compromise the code verification process.

29.3.5 Reactive Measures Against Malware

Proactive technology is ultimately not enough as these will be circumvented if the opportunity arises. We therefore require technologies that are able to identify the malware after it becomes known, and therefore we call these knowledge-based systems reactive. There are two such technologies in wide use and we will look at them in the next two sections.

Antivirus

From the very first antiviruses to the present ones, all vendors must do the same thing: after receiving a virus sample, they must verify it and then integrate detection for it into their product. While the detection methods are no longer simple pattern matching, the paradigms are still the same. Recently, antiviruses have also expanded their scope to include other malware, leading to problems of verifying that a sample is malware in some borderline cases.

Antiviruses can take various forms depending on how they are deployed. The classical scanner is called an *on-demand* scanner, as it is needed to scan partial or complete file systems. Another common form is the *on-access* scanner, which scans objects as they are used. Scanners can also be deployed at

---

[12] Verisign wrote about this problem on: http://www.verisign.com/developer/ notice/authenticode/

gateways or to monitor network traffic, although the methods modern scanners use usually require full packet reassembly before scanning and may be a network bottleneck in practice.

Intrusion Detection Systems

Network intrusion detection systems are related to antiviruses in that the vendors too generate their signatures only after an attack becomes known. Although not all attacks are malware-based, a good many signatures can be found for worms, exploits and other remote-acting malware.

Alternatively, the IDS can be in the target system monitoring for virus-like resource usage patterns [9]. Although this method still requires prior knowledge of virus activity, it does not need to be updated as frequently, as it uses more-generic patterns.

Behavior-based intrusion detection systems can also be useful. As an experiment at IBM Research, such an IDS was used to first capture the expected behaviour or a program and then at run-time match against this model of expected behaviour.

29.4 Malware and Security in UbiComp Systems

One significant change in the IT landscape that UbiComp brings is the sheer number of addressable devices in the world. The number could easily be a factor of 100 larger than currently in use, and there is a good chance that it will be much more than that. That malware can exist for these small devices despite their limited capacity and intermittent connectivity was shown in [10]. This experiment involved setting up an infrastructure that was susceptible to an SQL injection attack if the contents of the RFID tags were not sanitized before use and no vulnerabilities in the tags were abused. However, in future such RFID-based devices will be far more complex and exhibit similar vulnerabilities as current larger systems. In the following sections we will look at various aspects of what is currently projected for the UbiComp world in light of the inevitable malware problem.

29.4.1 The Diversity Factor

Apart from the explosion in the number of devices, the nature of devices will be much more diverse than current systems, which are very much dominated by Intel CPU hardware and the Microsoft Windows operating system. There is no denying that malware thrives on a mono-culture. Greer et al. make the argument that the dominance of a single operating system is a significant security risk and therefore a threat to a society that relies on computer services [11]. Certainly, the economics of scale offered by the current mono-culture benefit the malware writers by increasing the value of each vulnerability they find on that platform. Surely, the UbiComp future can only be better?

Unfortunately, there is no simple solution to the mono-culture problem. Trivially, we need more variety in systems. Realistically, we need a variety much larger than we can possibly achieve to come close to the rich diversity of nature where every instance of a species is truly an individual. Certainly, UbiComp will introduce greater variety, but in is unrealistic to believe that the devices will not share a common operating system over a great diversity of devices. Economics alone will dictate this.

In conclusion, UbiComp will introduce a richer diversity of devices, but this is unlikely to be enough to serve as a protection mechanism alone.

29.4.2 Topographical Changes to the Malware Landscape

Current computer systems vary from being connected for minutes to continually. Many of the UbiComp devices will only be able to connect when they are activated for a short period of time and by some event. Either a hub polls such devices on a regular basis by providing them with power and the opportunity to respond, making the devices dependent on this hub, or they are activated by some external or internal event (e.g., a floor tile is stepped on, generating power with a piezo-electric device) and broadcast their status.

Therefore, the topology in UbiComp will be rich in ad-hoc hierarchies of dependent systems and most nodes in the network will not be directly reachable. This, and the huge address space, will change how malware (self-)deployment occurs. Currently, the strategy for many worms is to target random addresses in the entire address space (e.g., the CodeRed II worm). It is highly unlikely that this strategy will create the critical mass to create an epidemic this way [12], so more context-aware strategies will be needed.

Manual deployment of trojans will probably not be feasible at all because the devices may be hard to reach. However, there is no reason to believe that the malware writers will not adapt and write specialized installation programs.

What a less homogeneous topology will give us are better opportunities to detect malware by their spread patterns. Topological detection, e.g., as proposed by Cheung et al. [13], will become more relevant in this environment. The need for hubs also give us logical points of defense where antiviruses and IDS software can be deployed in the network, although conversely they will be popular attack targets.

The Affects of Node Mobility

Many UbiComp devices are mobile by virtue of a user having physical possession of it and moving from location to location. Apart from being a nightmare for routing purposes, if this becomes necessary for the devices to communicate, it poses a great opportunity for malware to spread.

UbiComp expects (and even encourages) ad-hoc networking, so our expectation on an UbiComp environment is to allow our mobile devices to communicate with it without restriction. This may be to allow a personal preferences device to tell the various elements of the room how to reconfigure themselves. However, by the same token, malware on one of the mobile devices will have the opportunity to spread to this new environment. The malware can then spread from this environment to the next user who comes along. If you think back to our opening example of the Cabir worm spreading within a stadium, this scenario is already upon us in a limited way.

Lack of Formal Management

It will be impossible to manage every detail of UbiComp networks and this is not even anticipated. At best, the system administrators can merely set the parameters and deploy trusted agents to do some maintenance and manage the bridge nodes to the managed local-area network (LAN). The actual connectivity between UbiComp devices will largely be ad-hoc.

To make such a system workable, a lot will rely on service discovery protocols such as ZeroConf[13] or IPv6 SLP [14]. These protocols allow devices to find or offer services on the local LAN or ad-hoc network. For more-persistent services, various DNS extensions exist for storing information about these. Advertising services thus make it easier for malware to find vulnerable machines that are also local and thereby quicker to target. It also gives malware the opportunity to offer bogus services locally, which may lead to information leakage, denial of service or other compromises of the network. Successfully avoiding these types of attacks will be difficult if the systems are to be self-configuring.

29.5 Conclusions

The malware problem looms large for system administrators that must maintain security in our current systems, but a mélange of tools has kept the problem at bay. UbiComp is a game-changer though, and could disrupt this fragile balance. On one hand, there are opportunities for better defenses in UbiComp, but at the same time, the problem will be many magnitudes larger and more complex. Since the UbiComp world will not be upon us overnight, but will be a long process with many long-lived components, it is vital that security is designed into every part of the standards and the devices right from the start.

---

[13] http://www.zeroconf.org/

References

1. K. Brunnstein. From antivirus to antimalware software and beyond: Another approach to the protection of customers from dysfunctional system behaviour. In *22nd National Information Systems Security Conference*, 1999.
2. F. Cohen. *Computer Viruses.* PhD thesis, University of Southern California, 1985.
3. M. Frantzen and M. Shuey. StackGhost: Hardware facilitated stack protection. In *Proceedings of the 2001 USENIX Security Symposium*, August 2001.
4. T. Chiueh and F.H. Hsu. RAD: A compile-time solution to buffer overflow attacks. In *Proceedings of the 21st International Conference on Distributed Computing Systems (ICDCS-01)*, pages 409–420, Los Alamitos, CA, USA, April 2001. IEEE Computer Society.
5. W. Venema. TCP WRAPPER: Network monitoring, access control and booby traps. In *Proceedings of the 3rd UNIX Security Symposium*, pages 85–92, Berkeley, CA, USA, September 1992. USENIX Association.
6. D. Povey. Enforcing well-formed and partially-formed transactions for UNIX. In *Proceedings of the 8th USENIX Security Symposium*. USENIX Association, August 1999.
7. P.A. Karger. Limiting the damage potential of discretionary Trojan horses. In *Proceedings of the 1987 IEEE Symposium on Security and Privacy*, pages 32–37, April 1987.
8. D. Bell and L. LaPadula. The Bell-LaPadula model. *Journal of Computer Security*, 4:239–263, 1996.
9. B. Le Charlier, A. Mounji, and M. Swimmer. Dynamic detection and classification of computer viruses using general behaviour patterns. In *Proceedings of the Fifth International Virus Bulletin Conference*, Boston, MA, USA, 1995. Virus Bulletin, Ltd.
10. M.R. Rieback, B. Crispo, and A.S. Tanenbaum. Is your cat infected with a computer virus? In *Fourth Annual IEEE International Conference on Pervasive Computing and Communications*, 2006.
11. D. Geer, R. Bace, P. Gutmann, P. Metzger, C.P. Pfleeger, J.S. Quaterman, and B. Schneier. Cyberinsecurity: The cost of monopoly. Technical report, CCIA, September 2003.
12. J.O. Kephart and S.R. White. Directed-graph epidemiological models of computer viruses. In *Proceedings of the 1991 IEEE Computer Society Symposium on Research in Security and Privacy*, pages 343–359, Oakland, CA, USA, May 1991.
13. S. Cheung, R. Crawford, M. Dilger, J. Frank, J. Hoagland, K. Levitt, J. Rowe, S. Staniford-Chen, R. Yip, and D. Zerkle. The design of GrIDS: A graph-based intrusion detection system. Technical report CSE-99-2, Department of Computer Science, University of California at Davis, Davis, CA, January 1999.
14. E. Guttman. Service location protocol modifications for ipv6. Internet Request for Comment RFC 3111, Internet Society, May 2001.

Index

Gustavo Alonso, ETH Zentrum,
Zürich, Switzerland;
Fabio Casati, Harumi Kuno, Vijay Machiraju
Hewlett-Packard, Palo Alto, CA, USA

Web Services

Concepts, Architectures and Applications

XX, 354 p. Hardcover
ISBN 3-540-44008-9

Like many other incipient technologies, Web services are still surrounded by a tremendous level of noise. This noise results from the always dangerous combination of wishful thinking on the part of research and industry and of a lack of clear understanding of how Web services came to be. On the one hand, multiple contradictory interpretations are created by the many attempts to realign existing technology and strategies with Web services. On the other hand, the emphasis on what could be done with Web services in the future often makes us lose track of what can be really done with Web services today and in the short term. These factors make it extremely difficult to get a coherent picture of what Web services are, what they contribute, and where they will be applied. Alonso and his co-authors deliberately take a step back. Based on their academic and industrial experience with middleware and enterprise application integration systems, they describe the fundamental concepts behind the notion of Web services and present them as the natural evolution of conventional middleware, necessary to meet the challenges of the Web and of B2B application integration.

Rather than providing a reference guide or a "how to write your first Web service" kind of book, they discuss the main objectives of Web services, the challenges that must be faced to achieve them, and the opportunities that this novel technology provides. Established, as well as recently proposed, standards and techniques (e.g., WSDL, UDDI, SOAP, WS-Coordination, WS-Transactions, and BPEL), are then examined in the context of this discussion in order to emphasize their scope, benefits, and shortcomings. Thus, the book is ideally suited both for professionals considering the development of application integration solutions and for research and students interesting in understanding and contributing to the evolution of enterprise application technologies.

Contents: Part I: Conventional Middleware 1) Distributed Information Systems 2) Middleware 3) Enterprise Application Integration 4) Web Technologies Part II: Web Services 5) Web Services 6) Basic Web Services Technologies 7) Service Coordination Protocols 8) Service Composition 9) Outlook Bibliography; Index

Carlo Batini, Università di Milano Bicocca, Italy;
Monica Scannapieco, Università di Roma La Sapienza, Italy

Data Quality

2006 XIX, 262 p. 134 illus.
ISBN 3-540-33172-7

Poor data quality can seriously hinder or damage the efficiency and effectiveness of organizations and businesses. The growing awareness of such repercussions has led to major public initiatives like the "Data Quality Act" in the USA and the "European 2003/98" directive of the European Parliament.

Batini and Scannapieco present a comprehensive and systematic introduction to the wide set of issues related to data quality. They start with a detailed description of different data quality dimensions, like accuracy, completeness, and consistency, and their importance in different types of data, like federated data, web data, or time-dependent data, and in different data categories classified according to frequency of change, like stable, long-term, and frequently changing data. The book's extensive description of techniques and methodologies from core data quality research as well as from related fields like data mining, probability theory, statistical data analysis, and machine learning gives an excellent overview of the current state of the art. The presentation is completed by a short description and critical comparison of tools and practical methodologies, which will help readers to resolve their own quality problems.

This book is an ideal combination of the soundness of theoretical foundations and the applicability of practical approaches. It is ideally suited for everyone – researchers, students, or professionals – interested in a comprehensive overview of data quality issues. In addition, it will serve as the basis for an introductory course or for self-study on this topic.

Contents: 1. Introduction to Data Quality.- 2. Data Quality Dimensions.- 3. Models for Data Quality.- 4. Activities and Techniques for Data Quality- 5. The Object Identification Process.- 6. Data Quality Issues in Data Intregration Systems.- 7. Methodologies for Data Quality Measurement and Improvement.- 8. Tools for Data Quality.- References.- Index.

Bing Liu, University of Illinois at Chicago, IL, USA

Web Data Mining

2007 XIX, 532 p. 177 illus.
ISBN 978-3-540-37881-5

Web mining aims to discover useful information and knowledge from the Web hyperlink structure, page contents, and usage data. Although Web mining uses many conventional data mining techniques, it is not purely an application of traditional data mining due to the semistructured and unstructured nature of the Web data and its heterogeneity. It has also developed many of its own algorithms and techniques.

Liu has written a comprehensive text on Web data mining. Key topics of structure mining, content mining, and usage mining are covered both in breadth and in depth. His book brings together all the essential concepts and algorithms from related areas such as data mining, machine learning, and text processing to form an authoritative and coherent text.

The book offers a rich blend of theory and practice, addressing seminal research ideas, as well as examining the technology from a practical point of view. It is suitable for students, researchers and practitioners interested in Web mining both as a learning text and a reference book. Lecturers can readily use it for classes on data mining, Web mining, and Web search. Additional teaching materials such as lecture slides, datasets, and implemented algorithms are available online.

Contents: 1) Introduction - 2) Association Rules and Sequential Patterns - 3) Supervised Learning - 4) Unsupervised Learning - 5) Partially Supervised Learning - 6) Information Retrieval and Web Search - 7) Link Analysis - 8) Web Crawling - 9) Structured Data Extraction: Wrapper Generation - 10) Information Integration - 11) Opinion Mining - 12) Web Usage Mining - References, Index

the language of science

springer.com

Josef Pieprzyk, Macquarie University, Sydney, NSW, Australia;
Thomas Hardjono, VeriSign Inc., Wakefield, MA, USA;
Jennifer Seberry, University of Wollongong, NSW, Australia

Fundamentals of Computer Security

2003 X, 604 p. 40 illus.
ISBN 978-3-540-43101-5

This book presents modern concepts of computer security. It introduces the basic mathematical background necessary to follow computer security concepts. Modern developments in cryptography are examined, starting from private-key and public-key encryption, going through hashing, digital signatures, authentication, secret sharing, group-oriented cryptography, pseudorandomness, key establishment protocols, zero-knowledge protocols, and identification, and finishing with an introduction to modern e-business systems based on digital cash. Intrusion detection and access control provide examples of security systems implemented as a part of operating system. Database and network security is also discussed.

This textbook is developed out of classes given by the authors at several universities in Australia over a period of a decade, and will serve as a reference book for professionals in computer security. The presentation is selfcontained. Numerous illustrations, examples, exercises, and a comprehensive subject index support the reader in accessing the material.

Contents: Introduction - Background Theory - Private-Key Cryptosystems - Public-Key Cryptosystems - Pseudorandomness - Hashing - Digital Signatures - Authentication - Secret Sharing - Group-Oriented Cryptography - Key Establishment Protocols - Zero-Knowledge Proof Systems - Identification - Intrusion Detection - Electronic Elections and Digital Money - Database Protection and Security - Access Control - Network Security - References - Index